EARTH & SPACE SCIENCE

Exploring the Universe

Dr. Gustavo Loret de Mola

The McGraw-Hill Companies

Author

Gustavo Loret de Mola, EdD

Dr. Gustavo Loret de Mola is a science educator with more than 35 years teaching and administrative experience at the middle school, high school, and college level. He holds a BS degree in education from the University of Miami, a MS degree in science from Nova University, and an EdD in Educational Leadership from Nova University. Dr. Loret de Mola taught high school science for 11 years before serving as a Project Science Manager for Dade County Public Schools and a middle school Assistant Principal. Dr. Loret de Mola then served 20 years as District Science Supervisor for Dade County Public Schools. As a committee member, Dr. Loret de Mola helped develop the Teacher Certification Tests in Science for the State of Florida. He also served as the State Chairperson for the State of Florida Life Sciences Instructional Materials Council. Currently, Dr. Loret de Mola continues to work in the sciences as adjunct professor at the University of Miami where he teaches science and science methodology courses for graduate students in education.

Series Consultants

Richard Audet, EdD
  Roger Williams University

Matthew Marino, PhD
  Washington State University

Barbara Scott, MD
  Los Angeles Unified School District

Lisa Soll, BS
  San Antonio Independent School District

Content Reviewers

Amy Bates, MED, Plano, TX
Carly Merrill, Long Beach, CA
Sandra Nichols, MS, MS, Andover, CT
Surey Rios, BS, Miami, FL

ELL Consultant

Mary Smith, MA, Merced, California
Brian Silva, Long Beach, California

Laboratory Reviewer

Garrett Hall, Pleasant Hill, Iowa

Laboratory Safety Consultant

Jeff Vogt, MED, West Virginia University at Parkersburg

About the Cover

Photo credits are on pages 497–498.

---

www.WrightGroup.com

Send all inquiries to:
Wright Group/McGraw-Hill
P.O. Box 812960
Chicago, IL 60681

ISBN 978-0-07-704148-9
MHID 0-07-704148-8

1 2 3 4 5 6 7 8 9 YAK 13 12 11 10 09 08 07

The McGraw·Hill Companies

Contents

Unit 1   **Exploring Earth**   **2**
Chapter 1 **Studying Earth Science**   **3**
              1.1   What Is Earth Science?   4
              1.2   Methods and Measurements in
                    Earth Science   8
              Chapter 1 Summary   14
Chapter 2 **Mapping Earth**   **16**
              2.1   Understanding Maps   17
              2.2   Using Topographic Maps   22
              2.3   Mapmaking and Technology   26
              Chapter 2 Summary   30
              Science Journal   32

Unit 2   **Composition of the Earth**   **34**
Chapter 3 **Matter and Atoms**   **35**
              3.1   Earth's Elements   36
              3.2   How Atoms Combine   41
              3.3   Changes in Matter   47
              Chapter 3 Summary   52
Chapter 4 **Minerals**   **54**
              4.1   What is a Mineral?   55
              4.2   Mineral Identification   59
              Chapter 4 Summary   64
Chapter 5 **Rocks**   **66**
              5.1   Earth's Rock Types   67
              5.2   Igneous Rocks   70
              5.3   Sedimentary Rocks   74
              5.4   Metamorphic Rocks and
                    the Rock Cycle   78
              Chapter 5 Summary   82
              Science Journal   84

Unit 3   **Forces in the Earth**   **86**
Chapter 6 **Plate Tectonics**   **87**
              6.1   Inside Earth   88
              6.2   Continents in Motion   92
              6.3   The Theory of Plate Tectonics   99
              6.4   Plate Tectonics & Mountain
                    Building   105
              Chapter 6 Summary   110
Chapter 7 **Earthquakes**   **112**
              7.1   What are Earthquakes?   113
              7.2   Measuring and Locating
                    Earthquakes   118
              7.3   Earthquakes and Society   123
              Chapter 7 Summary   128
Chapter 8 **Volcanoes**   **130**
              8.1   What are Volcanoes?   131
              8.2   Volcanic Eruptions   136
              8.3   Volcanoes, People, and Earth   140
              Chapter 8 Summary   144
              Science Journal   146

Unit 4   **Earth's Changing Surface**   **148**
Chapter 9 **Weathering and Soil Formation**   **149**
              9.1   Weathering   150
              9.2   Rate of Weathering   154
              9.3   From Rocks to Soil   158
              Chapter 9 Summary   164
Chapter 10 **Erosion and Deposition**   **166**
              10.1 Water Erosion and Deposition   167
              10.2 Erosion Caused by Glaciers   173
              10.3 Wind Erosion and Deposition   178
              10.4 Gravity's Role in Erosion and
                    Deposition   182
              Chapter 10 Summary   186
              Science Journal   188

Unit 5   **Earth's History**   **190**
Chapter 11 **Studying the Past**   **191**
              11.1 What are Fossils?   192
              11.2 Relative Dating   196
              11.3 Absolute Dating   200
              Chapter 11 Summary   204
Chapter 12 **Geologic Time**   **206**
              12.1 The Geologic Time Scale   207
              12.2 Precambrian Time and
                    the Paleozoic Era   212
              12.3 The Mesozoic Era   216
              12.4 The Cenozoic Era   220
              Chapter 12 Summary   224
              Science Journal   226

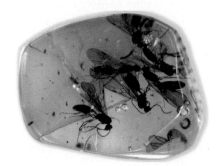

Unit 6	**Earth's Atmosphere and Weather**	**228**
Chapter 13	**The Atmosphere**	**229**
	13.1 Characteristics of the Atmosphere	230
	13.2 Heat and Earth's Atmosphere	236
	13.3 Air Pressure and Winds	241
	Chapter 13 Summary	246
Chapter 14	**Weather**	**248**
	14.1 Water in the Atmosphere	249
	14.2 Weather Patterns	254
	14.3 Severe Weather	259
	14.4 Predicting the Weather	265
	Chapter 14 Summary	270
Chapter 15	**Climate**	**272**
	15.1 What is Climate?	273
	15.2 Classifying Earth's Climates	278
	15.3 Climate Change	282
	15.4 Human Impacts on Climate	287
	Chapter 15 Summary	292
	Science Journal	294
Unit 7	**Earth's Waters**	**296**
Chapter 16	**Freshwater**	**297**
	16.1 Stream and River Development	298
	16.2 Stream and River Deposits	304
	16.3 Lakes and Wetlands	307
	16.4 Groundwater	312
	Chapter 16 Summary	316
Chapter 17	**Oceans**	**318**
	17.1 The World's Oceans	319
	17.2 Properties of Ocean Water	324
	17.3 Motions of the Oceans	328
	Chapter 17 Summary	336
Chapter 18	**The Marine Environment**	**338**
	18.1 The Ocean's Edge and Floor	339
	18.2 Life Zones in the Ocean	345
	18.3 The Changing Ocean	350
	Chapter 18 Summary	354
	Science Journal	356
Unit 8	**Earth's Resources and Environment**	**358**
Chapter 19	**Earth's Natural Resources**	**359**
	19.1 Earth's Natural Resources	360
	19.2 Conventional Energy Resources	364
	19.3 Alternative Energy Resources	368
	Chapter 19 Summary	372
Chapter 20	**Human Impact on Earth's Resources**	**374**
	20.1 Human Impact on Land	375
	20.2 Human Impact on Air	381
	20.3 Human Impact on Water	386
	Chapter 20 Summary	390
	Science Journal	392
Unit 9	**Exploring Space**	**394**
Chapter 21	**Earth and Its Moon**	**395**
	21.1 Planet Earth	396
	21.2 Earth's Moon	400
	21.3 Astronomy	404
	Chapter 21 Summary	410
Chapter 22	**The Solar System**	**412**
	22.1 The Formation of the Solar System	413
	22.2 Planetary Motion	416
	22.3 The Inner Planets	420
	22.4 The Outer Planets	426
	Chapter 22 Summary	432
Chapter 23	**Stars**	**434**
	23.1 Earth's Sun	435
	23.2 Classifying Stars	439
	23.3 The Life Cycle of Stars	443
	Chapter 23 Summary	446
Chapter 24	**Galaxies and the Universe**	**448**
	24.1 Galaxies	449
	24.2 The Universe	452
	Chapter 24 Summary	456
	Science Journal	458
	Appendix A—Laboratory Safety	460
	Appendix B—The Metric System	461
	Appendix C—Star Chart	462
	Appendix D—Periodic Table	463
	Glossary/Index	464
	Credits	507

How to Use the Book

This book contains many features to help you learn science. Becoming familiar with these features will help you get more from this book.

Before You Read

Units: Units start with a list of the chapters and major science questions.

Chapters: Chapters start with a **Key Concept** that introduces the big scientific idea of the chapter. Introductions and **Think About** link the science concepts of the chapter to everyday life.

Lessons: Lessons start with **Learning Goals** and **Vocabulary** to give you an idea of the key points of the lesson.

As You Read

SciLinks: Codes let you use the Internet to learn more about the chapter topic.

Reading Activities: **Before You Read** asks you to answer questions, fill out charts, and make predictions about the lesson. **As You Read** keeps you on the right track while you are in the middle of the lesson. **After You Read** brings together what you learned throughout the lesson and asks questions about the lesson.

Science Activities: **Explore It!** activities offer small, quick, and fun experiments to do at your desk or at home. **Explain It!** activities give you an opportunity to explain scientific ideas in writing. **Extend It!** activities offer science topics that you can research to learn more about.

Special Features: **Did You Know?** boxes are full of interesting facts relating to the lesson. **People in Science** tells the stories of some key figures in science. **Science Connection** tells how the lesson topics relate to other subjects or other branches of science. **Figure It Out** questions will help you understand the pictures and their captions.

After You Read

Chapter Summaries: Each chapter ends with a summary of key points, vocabulary, and a set of questions that will help you prepare for the chapter test.

Beyond the Book: The **Student Workbook** reviews the key science concepts and vocabulary terms related to each chapter. The **Laboratory Manual** is designed to give you a hands-on science experience. The **Student CD-ROM** lets you explore the text and the science concepts in greater detail.

Flip through the book and examine all of its features. Get a good feel for how the features work, and have fun learning science!

Unit 1

Exploring Earth

Chapter 1

Earth Science

How do Earth scientists study the parts of Earth and the processes that shape and change our planet?

Chapter 2

Mapping Earth

How can maps be used to locate exact places and describe features on Earth?

Studying Earth Science

KEY CONCEPT Earth science is the study of Earth and its parts and the processes that shape and change our planet.

Think about how your body works as you walk down the street. Bones and muscles provide a structure for your body and help you move. Blood carries energy to your muscles and carries waste away from them. Your skin helps control your body temperature. Every step you take involves the coordination of different systems in your body.

Like the systems in your body, Earth's systems interact with one another. The living things on Earth depend on water and air to live. Earth's inner layers interact with Earth's surface to create volcanoes and mountains. Water on Earth's surface interacts with the air above Earth to produce weather. A mixture of gases surrounds Earth and protects the life below from harmful radiation from space.

Think About How Things Work Together

- In your Science Notebook, write one or two sentences summarizing how the parts of your body work together to blow air into a balloon.
- Identify one or more natural processes on Earth that work together to move water from one place to another.

www.sclinks.org

Branches of Earth Science
Code: WGES01

Before You Read

Create a K-W-L-S-H chart in your Science Notebook. Title the chart *Earth Science*. In the column labeled *K*, write what you already know about Earth science. In the column labeled *W*, write what you want to learn about Earth science.

Earth science is the study of Earth and its surroundings. It includes Earth's parts and the processes that shape and change our planet. Earth science also includes the study of Earth's place in the solar system and the rest of the universe. It even includes the study of how stars and planets form and how they have changed over time. Some changes happen quickly while others might take millions or even billions of years to occur.

Many different parts of Earth interact, or work together, to cause these changes. For example, in 1872, an English scientist named Robert A. Smith discovered and described acid rain. Acid rain forms when certain chemicals are released into the air and combine with water droplets to form acid. The acid then falls to Earth as acid rain. Acid rain can harm plants and animals. This is one example of a process that results from the interaction between Earth's air and water.

Earth's Systems

Scientists who study Earth have identified four major Earth systems: the hydrosphere, the atmosphere, the lithosphere, and the biosphere. These systems are interconnected. This means that changes in one system often cause changes in the other systems. All of these systems work together to shape and change our planet.

The Hydrosphere Earth's **hydrosphere** is made up of all the water on Earth. The most obvious form of water is its liquid state. The hydrosphere also includes water in its vapor form in the atmosphere and in its frozen, solid form in glaciers. The water in Earth's oceans, seas, rivers, lakes, glaciers, and atmosphere is all part of the hydrosphere. Groundwater, or water beneath Earth's surface, is also part of the hydrosphere. About 97 percent of the water on Earth is salt water, and only about three percent of the water on Earth is freshwater. You will learn more about Earth's hydrosphere in Unit 7.

a

b Freshwater = 3%
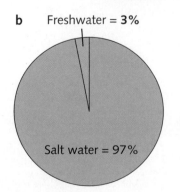
Salt water = 97%

Figure 1.1 Scientists have been studying Earth's systems for hundreds of years. **a)** It wasn't until satellites were sent into space during the 1960s that humans were able to see a photo of the entire Earth. Which forms of water are visible in this photo? **b)** The pie chart shows the percentages of freshwater and salt water on Earth.

The Atmosphere   Earth's **atmosphere** is the layer of mixed gases that surrounds Earth. All weather events, such as the one shown in **Figure 1.2**, take place in the atmosphere. Other planets have atmospheres, but Earth's atmosphere contains the right mixture of chemicals to support life. It keeps Earth from becoming too hot or too cold, and protects all life-forms from the Sun's harmful rays. You will learn more about how Earth's atmosphere works with other Earth systems to produce weather in Unit 6.

Figure It Out

1. Which of Earth's systems can you see evidence of in this photo?
2. Explain how different Earth systems might interact during a tornado.

Figure 1.2 Tornadoes are one of the many severe weather events that can be observed while studying Earth's atmosphere.

The Lithosphere   The **lithosphere** is the hard, outer shell of Earth. You walk on Earth's lithosphere every day. Earth is made up of three major layers: the core, the mantle, and the crust. The lithosphere is made up of the crust and the solid, upper part of the mantle.

Beneath the upper mantle is a partially melted layer. This layer and the core work with the lithosphere to shape Earth's surface. For example, these interactions might cause spectacular volcanic eruptions or the formation of mountains. The positions of mountains, which are made of lithosphere, sometimes determine where water will flow. The tallest mountains on Earth even affect our weather. You will learn more about Earth's lithosphere in Units 2, 3, and 4.

 Explain It!

In your Science Notebook, write a paragraph explaining what the hydrosphere is and how it interacts with other Earth systems.

As You Read

In the column labeled *L* in your K-W-L-S-H chart, write several things you have learned about Earth science and the four major Earth systems. Work with a partner to add or correct the information in your chart.

Underline the systems of which human beings are a part.

The Biosphere   The **biosphere** is made up of all the living things on Earth and their environments. From ants and amoebas to zebras and zooplankton, everything that is alive is part of the biosphere. Humans are a part of the biosphere. The interactions of Earth's systems produce the conditions needed for life on our planet. Without the minerals in soils and water, plants would not be able to grow. With no atmosphere containing oxygen, humans and other mammals would not be able to breathe. You will learn more about Earth's biosphere in Units 5, 7, and 8.

Branches of Earth Science

All scientists who study some part of Earth are Earth scientists. The main branches of Earth science are atmospheric science, oceanography, geology, and astronomy.

Atmospheric Science   The branch of science that includes any study of the atmosphere is called **atmospheric science**. One important branch of science within atmospheric science is meteorology. **Meteorology** is the study of weather patterns in the atmosphere. Atmospheric scientists, however, study many things besides weather. For example, some atmospheric scientists study carbon, a chemical element that is present in the atmosphere. Changes in the amount of carbon in the atmosphere have been linked to global warming.

Oceanography   The study of Earth's oceans is **oceanography**. Oceanographers study a broad range of topics. They often use information from other sciences such as physics, chemistry, and biology in their research. Some oceanographers study ocean currents that help shape weather patterns on Earth. Others focus on studying carbon in the oceans. Oceans absorb carbon, in the form of carbon dioxide, from the atmosphere. Scientists need to know if this added carbon affects the plants and animals that live in the ocean. Many oceanographers examine the fantastic life-forms that live in the deepest parts of the oceans, such as those shown in **Figure 1.3**.

Figure 1.3 Brightly colored corals were among some of the life-forms discovered on Retriever Seamount in the Atlantic Ocean. Living at about 2,100 meters below the ocean surface, these corals provide a home for many living things.

Geology   The study of anything having to do with the solid Earth is **geology**. Geologists may discover clues to Earth's history, study earthquakes, or study the quality of soils for growing food. Some geologists become experts in one area. For example, a geologist who studies volcanoes is called a volcanologist (vohl kan AH luh jist). Some volcanologists risk their lives in order to observe volcanoes just before they erupt.

Astronomy   The study of objects and events beyond Earth's atmosphere is **astronomy**. Astronomers study amazing things, including stars, planets, and galaxies. Some astronomers try to find out if there is life anywhere else in the universe. Recently, astronomers discovered evidence that water was once present on the planet Mars. This discovery is important because water is one of the key ingredients for life as we know it. This evidence will be discussed further in Chapter 22.

Other Earth Sciences   In addition to the four main branches, there are many other branches of Earth science. **Hydrology** is the study of water and how it moves on Earth. To understand hydrology, scientists must learn about geology and how water flows beneath the ground. Hydrologists also have to understand atmospheric science and how water moves through the atmosphere. **Geography** includes the study of Earth's features, such as mountains, rivers, and oceans, and the distribution of life on Earth. Geographers must understand geology and how Earth's features form. They must understand how water and Earth's atmosphere shape those features. Geographers also study the biosphere and how people affect other living things.

CONNECTION: History

The leading thinkers in the world once thought that Earth was at the center of the universe. The idea that Earth was not the center of the universe caused great debate.

Figure 1.4 The Whirlpool Galaxy, shown in this image from the Hubble Space Telescope, was discovered by astronomers studying other objects in the universe.

After You Read

1. List the four main branches of Earth science.

2. Compare and contrast the atmosphere to the hydrosphere. How are they similar? How are they different?

3. Look at your completed K-W-L columns. Write a well-developed paragraph explaining what Earth science is and why it is important to understand Earth's systems. Complete your K-W-L-S-H chart by writing what you would still like to learn about Earth science in the *S* column. Write how you can learn the information in the *H* column. Provide specific information about how you will locate the information you need. For example, you might use the resources in your school library to get started.

Before You Read

Use the lesson title, headings, and subheadings to create a lesson outline. Use the lesson title as the outline title. Label the headings with the Roman numerals *I* through *III.* Use the letters *A*, *B*, *C*, etc., for the subheadings. Use the numerals 1, 2, 3, etc., to record information you want to remember.

Have you ever noticed interesting rocks and wondered about their shapes or colors? Maybe you have counted the number of seconds between a bolt of lightning and the thunder that follows. If you have done these things, you have acted like a scientist. Scientists look for patterns to help explain and predict events. Observing, questioning, and measuring are all parts of the scientific method.

The Scientific Method

The scientific method is a series of steps that scientists use to answer questions or solve problems. Within each step are a variety of ways to apply the step. Scientists may choose to use all of the options, or just some of them. The most important thing is for scientists to use the steps of the scientific method to learn more about the questions they are investigating.

Ask a Question The first step in the scientific method is to ask a scientific question. A scientific question is based on observations a scientist has made. After making observations, a scientist researches the subject to learn what other people have learned about it. Based on observations and research, the scientist forms a question. For example, a scientist may ask the question, "Can all samples of quartz scratch glass?"

Figure 1.5 Making observations of patterns around you is an important part of the scientific method. What might you say about the rocks in this photo?

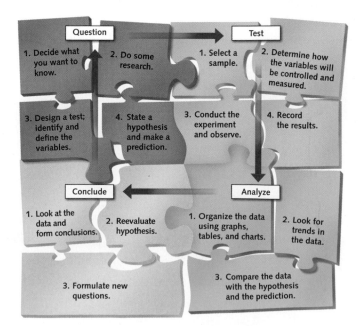

Figure 1.6 The scientific method is like a puzzle. Once each piece is placed, a bigger and more complete picture or result is obtained.

Question
1. Decide what you want to know.
2. Do some research.

Test
1. Select a sample.
2. Determine how the variables will be controlled and measured.

3. Design a test; identify and define the variables.
4. State a hypothesis and make a prediction.

3. Conduct the experiment and observe.
4. Record the results.

Conclude
1. Look at the data and form conclusions.
2. Reevaluate hypothesis.
3. Formulate new questions.

Analyze
1. Organize the data using graphs, tables, and charts.
2. Look for trends in the data.
3. Compare the data with the hypothesis and the prediction.

Form a Hypothesis The next step is to form a hypothesis (hi PAH thuh sus; plural: hypotheses). A **hypothesis** is a possible answer to a scientific question. A hypothesis is based on everything the scientist has observed and learned about the topic. A hypothesis must also be testable. In other words, the scientist must be able to plan an experiment to either support the hypothesis or to show that it is not correct. Hypotheses are stated as a prediction in an if-then format. For example, based on experience, a scientist might form the hypothesis that if the sample is quartz, then it can scratch glass.

Test the Hypothesis Next, a scientist tests the hypothesis. This is done by gathering data, or information, to help determine whether the hypothesis is supported or not. Often, scientists will run a controlled experiment to test a hypothesis. A **controlled experiment** tests only one factor at a time. It compares what happens in two situations where only one thing has been changed. A factor that can change in an experiment is called a **variable**. Think about the scientist who wants to conduct an experiment to determine if all samples of quartz can scratch glass. The variables include the types of quartz, the conditions of the samples, the amount of pressure applied to the quartz on the glass, and the glass itself. If the variables are changed throughout the experiment, it will not be possible to figure out which variables determine if quartz can scratch glass.

Figure 1.7 Every variable must remain constant except for the independent variable. In this experiment, the type of quartz is the independent variable.

PEOPLE IN SCIENCE Antoine-Laurent Lavoisier 1743–1794

Antoine-Laurent Lavoisier was a French scientist who lived from 1743 to 1794. Much of Lavoisier's early work was in geology. He is best known today, however, as a chemist. Lavoisier showed that water is made up of the gases hydrogen and oxygen. He did this by making water from the two gases and then separating it back into those gases. Lavoisier also demonstrated the relationship between the presence of oxygen and combustion, or burning.

Lavoisier was a member of the French Academy of Sciences. The Academy was working on the development of a common system of measurement called the metric system. Lavoisier was a strong supporter of the metric system, and he used it in his work. Lavoisier worked indirectly for the government as a tax collector. In this role, he encouraged the French bank to use a decimal system of money. This system was similar to the metric system of measurement.

Figure 1.8 Volcanic events involve a great number of variables. For this reason, it is easier for scientists to collect data about them by making observations, rather than by carrying out controlled experiments.

The variable that is changed in an experiment is called the **independent variable**. It is called independent because it does not rely on anything else in order to be changed. The scientist changes it. By changing only one variable at a time, scientists can learn how one thing affects other things that are part of the experiment. In the quartz experiment, the different types of quartz are the independent variable.

A variable that might change during an experiment is called a **dependent variable**. Something that is dependent relies on another variable. Whether the glass is scratched or not is the dependent variable. All other variables must remain unchanged.

Some experiments have two groups. In the **control group**, all the variables are kept the same. This control group is used for comparison. The control group shows what would have happened if nothing had been changed. In the **experimental group**, the independent variable is changed.

It is not easy to run a controlled experiment outside of a laboratory because there are too many changing variables. Consider a volcanic eruption. Studying the events that lead up to and after the eruption can only be done in the field. In cases such as these, scientists collect data and record observations to test their hypotheses.

Analyze Data   After recording the data and observations from their tests, scientists must analyze the results. To do this, they carefully look for patterns, changes, or unexpected results in their data. Often, scientists will create tables, graphs, or charts to help them organize and recognize patterns in their data.

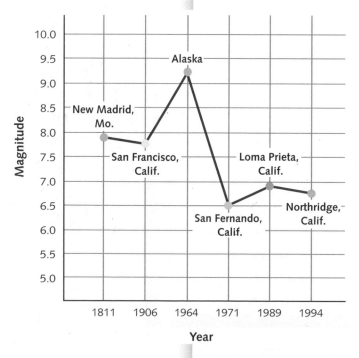

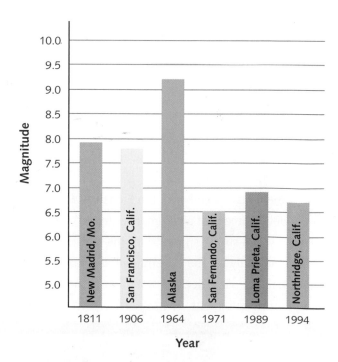

Figure 1.9 The same data can be shown in different ways. Here, U.S. earthquake data has been plotted on both a line graph and a bar graph.

Draw Conclusions Based on a careful study of the data, scientists compare the patterns he or she observes to the original hypothesis. The first question the scientist usually asks is whether the data supports the hypothesis or not. Think about the scientist testing the hypothesis that all quartz scratches glass. She would record the results of each scratch test and compare the data. If every piece of quartz that was tested scratched the glass, then the hypothesis was supported by the data. In many experiments, however, the data does not support the hypothesis. When this happens, it is up to the scientist to find out what part of the hypothesis was wrong. Often, a scientist will use the results to come up with a new hypothesis. This new hypothesis must also be tested, and the process begins again.

Communicate Results When the scientific investigation is complete, scientists share what they have learned by publishing their results in research journals or by giving presentations at scientific meetings. This is the last step of the scientific method. Because of this, it is important for scientists to be good writers. Research journals only accept papers that have been peer reviewed—that is, read and evaluated by other scientists. A scientific paper must contain enough information to allow other scientists to repeat the experiment. By repeating the work, they can also test the hypothesis. If the hypothesis holds true after being tested by many scientists, it might be called a theory. A **theory** explains scientific results that are supported by many trials, or runs, of the experiments.

As You Read

Read the information in your outline. Work with a partner to add or clarify your facts.

List the steps of the scientific method in your Science Notebook.

Important Safety Rules for Science Experiments

1. Read the directions carefully before beginning any experiment.
2. Always follow your teacher's instructions.
3. Pay special attention to safety symbols listed in the investigation.
4. Wear safety goggles and protective clothing during any experiment using chemicals or sharp objects or if they are listed in the laboratory instructions.
5. Securely fasten long hair or loose clothing before starting an experiment.
6. Never eat or drink during an experiment. Do not use science equipment for eating or drinking.
7. Do not taste or breathe in any of the chemicals or other substances used for an experiment.
8. Never touch live animals while doing research outdoors.
9. Know what to do in case of an emergency. Always know the location of emergency exits and safety equipment.
10. Immediately report any accident or injury to your teacher.
11. When cleaning up, make sure to follow your teacher's directions about how to get rid of chemicals safely.
12. Wash your hands with soap and water after working in the lab or in the field.

Figure It Out

1. Which do you think is the most important rule for science experiment safety?

2. Explain what you should do if a glass beaker falls and breaks while you are working in the lab.

Figure 1.10 Follow these rules to stay safe in the lab or while collecting data outdoors.

CONNECTION: Language Arts

Some common words can have different meanings when they are used in science. *Volume* is one of those words. In your Science Notebook, draw or write what you think the word *volume* means in science.

A System of Measurement

During the 1700s, people used many different units to describe measurements. To prevent confusion, scientists developed a way of measuring that is used in all sciences. This system is called the **International System of Units**, or the **SI system**. It is a modern version of the metric system. They are both based on the number 10. This makes it very simple to convert from one unit to another by dividing or multiplying by 10. The SI system is now used in most countries and by scientists everywhere.

Length The meter (m) is the SI unit used to measure length. There are 100 centimeters (cm) in a meter, so a centimeter is $\frac{1}{100}$ of a meter. There are 1,000 millimeters (mm) in a meter, so a millimeter is $\frac{1}{1,000}$ of a meter. Measuring tapes and meter sticks are used to measure lengths that are up to several meters long. In Earth science, many distances are much longer than one meter. In such cases, distances are measured in kilometers (km). A kilometer is equal to 1,000 meters.

Volume The **volume** of an object is the amount of space that it takes up or contains. The volume of standard objects can be determined by using formulas. For example, the formula used to determine the volume of a cube or a rectangular prism is:

> **volume = length × width × height**

The standard SI unit for volume is the cubic meter (m³).

Unlike solids, the volumes of liquids or gases are often measured in liters (L). A liter is not an SI unit, but because it is important and widely used, it is accepted for use within the scientific community. Smaller volumes can be measured in milliliters (mL). There are 1,000 milliliters in a liter. One way to measure the volume of a liquid is by pouring the liquid into a container that has measured markings on it, such as a graduated cylinder.

Mass The amount of matter, or stuff, in an object is called **mass**. It is measured in units of kilograms (kg). A kilogram contains 1,000 smaller units called grams (g). Grams are used to describe the mass of smaller objects. Very small masses are measured in milligrams. There are 1,000 milligrams (mg) in one gram. Mass is measured using a balance.

Figure 1.11 Electronic balances and triple beam balances are both used to measure mass.

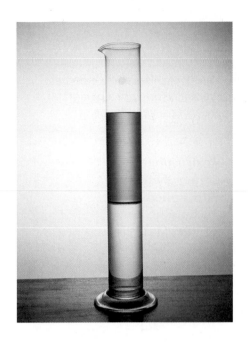

Figure 1.12 One of these liquids has a higher density than the other. Which liquid has the higher density?

Density Density describes the amount of mass that fills up a given space, or volume. The density of an object is calculated by dividing its mass by its volume. The formula for calculating density is:

$$density = \frac{mass}{volume}$$

The units of density are made up of a unit of mass and a unit of volume. Common units for density are kilograms per meter cubed (kg/m^3) and grams per centimeter cubed (g/cm^3). Note that by rearranging the formula, the volume of objects with unusual shapes, such as rocks, can be determined. The densities of two liquids are compared in **Figure 1.12**.

Time The period during which something takes place is time. The SI unit of time is the second (s). Scientists often measure time using seconds or minutes. There are 60 seconds in one minute and 60 minutes in one hour. Short periods of time are measured in parts of one second, such as milliseconds (ms). There are 1,000 milliseconds in a second. Time is usually measured using a watch or a clock.

Temperature Temperature is the measure of how hot or cold an object is. Temperature is measured using a thermometer. Many scientists use the Celsius (C) temperature scale. On this scale, temperatures are measured in degrees Celsius (°C). Water freezes at 0°C and boils at 100°C. In the SI system, temperature is measured using the Kelvin (K) scale. Zero on this scale is the absolute coldest anything can be. Zero Kelvin (0K) is equal to −273°C.

The scale you are probably most familiar with is the Fahrenheit scale. On this scale, water freezes at 32°F and boils at 212°F. Fahrenheit measurements are generally not used in science.

Explore It!

Taking measurements is an important science skill. Using a ruler, measure the length, width, and height of your science book. Multiply these measurements together to calculate the volume of the book. Use a balance to determine the mass. Then calculate the density of your science book. If you have time, calculate the density of your pencil and your paper.

Did You Know?

Across the solar system, not every day contains the same amount of time. A day is the amount of time it takes for a planet to rotate once on its axis. A day on Mercury is shorter than a day on Earth.

After You Read

1. Explain the term *hypothesis*.
2. Compare an independent variable with a dependent variable.
3. Do you know what causes rocks to naturally break apart? Use the information in your outline to explain how you could use the scientific method to examine this question. Write your answer in your Science Notebook.

KEY CONCEPTS

1.1 What Is Earth Science?

- Earth science is the study of Earth and its parts and the processes that shape and change our planet.

- Scientists have identified four major Earth systems: the hydrosphere, the atmosphere, the lithosphere, and the biosphere.

- The main branches of Earth science are atmospheric science, oceanography, geology, and astronomy.

- There are many other branches of Earth science. They include hydrology and geography.

1.2 Methods and Measurements in Earth Science

- The scientific method is a series of steps that scientists use to answer questions or solve problems.

- Scientists ask questions, form hypotheses, make observations, conduct experiments, analyze data, and draw conclusions.

- A hypothesis is a possible answer to a scientific question.

- A scientific theory is an explanation of scientific results that has been supported by repeated experiments.

- Standard SI units include the meter for length, the kilogram for mass, the Kelvin for temperature, and the second for time. Celsius is commonly used for temperature. The standard SI unit for volume is the cubic meter. Liquid volume is typically recorded in liters.

- Data should always be collected carefully. Safety procedures must always be followed when carrying out experiments.

VOCABULARY REVIEW

Write each term in a complete sentence or write a paragraph relating several terms.

1.1
hydrosphere, p. 4
atmosphere, p. 5
lithosphere, p. 5
biosphere, p. 6
atmospheric science, p. 6
meteorology, p. 6
oceanography, p. 6
geology, p. 7
astronomy, p. 7
hydrology, p. 7
geography, p. 7

1.2
hypothesis, p. 9
controlled experiment, p. 9
variable, p. 9
independent variable, p. 10
dependent variable, p. 10
control group, p. 10
experimental group, p. 10
theory, p. 11
International System of Units (SI system), p. 12
volume, p. 12
mass, p. 12
density, p. 13

PREPARE FOR CHAPTER TEST

To prepare for the chapter test, create a question from each Learning Goal. Use the information in your Science Notebook to answer each question. Then use these answers to write a well-developed essay about the chapter. Use the Key Concept on the first page of this chapter as your topic sentence.

True or False

If the statement is true, write "true." If it is false, change the underlined word or words to make the statement true.

1. The <u>biosphere</u> is the layer of mixed gases that surrounds Earth.

2. The study of Earth's oceans is <u>oceanography</u>.

3. A <u>hypothesis</u> explains important scientific results and has been supported by many experiments.

4. Four of Earth's systems are the biosphere, the atmosphere, the lithosphere, and the <u>coronosphere</u>.

5. An object's density can be determined by dividing its <u>weight</u> by its volume.

6. The SI unit of time is the <u>second</u>.

Short Answer

Answer each of the following in a sentence or brief paragraph.

7. Explain one way that Earth's hydrosphere interacts with Earth's atmosphere.

8. List and describe four of Earth's systems.

9. Describe what a geologist does and give some examples of what a geologist might study.

10. Explain the parts of a controlled experiment.

11. Briefly explain how you could determine the density of an unknown solid.

12. Name one measurement tool. Tell what quantity it is used to measure. Then give an example of how you might use it in a scientific experiment.

Critical Thinking

Use what you have learned in this chapter to answer each of the following.

13. **Compare and Contrast** How is hydrology like oceanography? How are they different?

14. **Apply** If your height measures 150 cm, how tall are you in meters? How tall are you in millimeters?

15. **Apply Concepts** Use the scientific method to describe the steps you would take to study ocean waves.

Standardized Test Question

Choose the letter of the response that correctly answers the question.

16. According to the table below, one kilometer is also equal to which quantity?

    A. 1,000 meters

    B. 1,000 centimeters

    C. 10,000 millimeters

    D. 10,000,000 micrometers

Prefix	Abbreviation	Relative Size
mega	M	1,000,000 times
kilo	k	1,000 times
centi	c	$\frac{1}{100}$
milli	m	$\frac{1}{1,000}$
micro	μ	$\frac{1}{1,000,000}$

Test-Taking Tip

If you don't know an answer and you won't be penalized for guessing, make an educated guess. Use context clues if you don't understand the question.

Mapping Earth

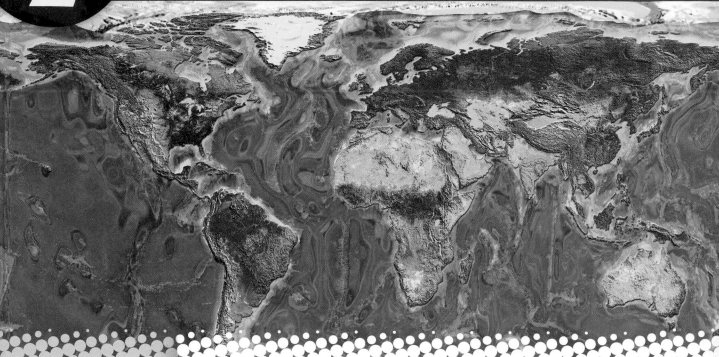

KEY CONCEPT Maps are important tools for locating exact places and describing features on Earth.

Imagine that you have moved to a new city. You have some free time and want to learn your way around. Where is the park? Is there a library?

In this situation, it would be useful to have a diagram that showed the location of places near your new home. It might show streets, parks, hospitals, stores, and other features. This kind of diagram is called a map. Maps can show areas of different sizes. While a map of the United States might include your new town, it would not be useful for finding a park. Instead, you would want a map that shows a close-up of the area near your home.

Think About Maps

Make a list of places near your home that are important to you and your friends. Draw a diagram that shows where these places are located in relation to each other. Be sure to label each location.

- Would the diagram, or map, that you drew be useful for taking a trip to a location 100 miles away? Why or why not? What would the map be useful for?

- In your Science Notebook, explain why your map is useful.

www.scilinks.org

Mapping **Code: WGES02**

Before You Read

In your Science Notebook, make a concept map showing the relationships between the vocabulary terms in the lesson. Start by writing and circling the term *Map projection*. Draw three smaller circles next to this circle and write *Mercator projection*, *Conic projection*, and *Azimuthal projection*. Fill in any additional information you know about each type of map.

Think about what it would be like to start your first day at a new school. How would you find your way around school? It might be helpful to have a map that shows the locations of your classrooms and other important places such as the gym, music room, and lunchroom. Maps are useful tools for understanding the locations of objects and places.

What is a map?

A **map** is a representation of a certain area or part of an area. Maps have many uses. They can show where restaurants and movie theaters are located. Maps can show the fastest route for an ambulance to take to a hospital. Maps are especially useful for Earth science. For example, they can show the courses of major rivers or small streams. They can even be used to show rainfall patterns in different regions of a country, as shown in **Figure 2.1**.

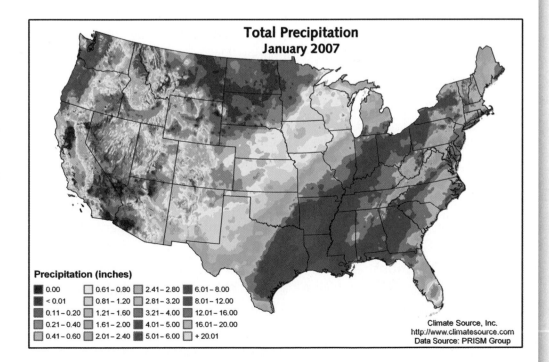

Total Precipitation
January 2007

Climate Source, Inc.
http://www.climatesource.com
Data Source: PRISM Group

Precipitation (inches)

0.00	0.61–0.80	2.41–2.80	6.01–8.00
< 0.01	0.81–1.20	2.81–3.20	8.01–12.00
0.11–0.20	1.21–1.60	3.21–4.00	12.01–16.00
0.21–0.40	1.61–2.00	4.01–5.00	16.01–20.00
0.41–0.60	2.01–2.40	5.01–6.00	+ 20.01

Figure 2.1 Scientists can use maps such as this one to analyze rainfall patterns and climate changes across the United States.

Map Projections

Most maps are two-dimensional, which means they are flat. They can be drawn on a piece of paper. The surfaces of planets, however, are not flat. Earth is almost spherical, or shaped like a ball. A map **projection** is a way to draw a view of a round object on a flat surface. Because a map projection is a flat drawing of a round object, it will never be a perfect drawing. It will be distorted, or pulled or twisted out of shape. Projections used to make maps are separated into groups according to how they are made. These groups include Mercator projections, conic projections, and azimuthal projections.

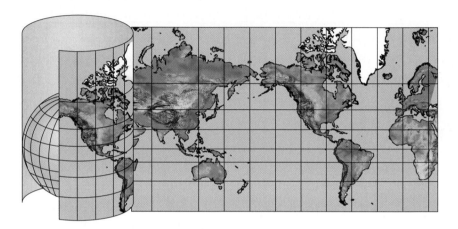

Figure 2.2 In a Mercator projection, the positions of surface features are transferred onto a cylinder-shaped paper.

Mercator Projections A **Mercator projection** is made when the points and lines of a globe are transferred onto a cylinder of paper, as shown in **Figure 2.2**. Mercator projections are able to show almost all of Earth on one continuous piece of paper. The only areas that are not shown are the very top and bottom of Earth, also known as the far polar regions.

Mercator projections show the cardinal directions—north, south, east, and west—as straight lines. This makes a Mercator projection useful for traveling on Earth's surface, especially on the ocean. A Mercator projection, however, distorts the size of land near Earth's poles. This projection causes Greenland, which is near the north pole, to appear larger than Australia. Australia is actually much bigger than Greenland.

Conic Projections A **conic projection** is made by transferring the points and lines from a globe onto a cone. The cone is then unrolled to form a flat map. **Figure 2.3** shows that the cone touches Earth along one line that circles the globe. The shapes of land that fall along this line are shown accurately. As you move north and south from this line, however,

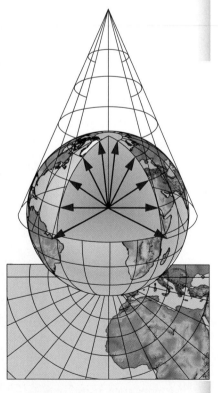

Figure 2.3 In a conic projection, landforms are transferred onto a cone-shaped piece of paper.

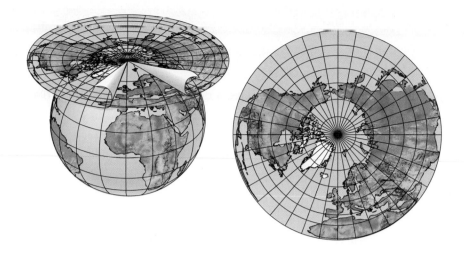

shapes of features become less accurate. For this reason, conic projections are excellent for mapping small areas. They are often used to make road and weather maps.

Azimuthal Projections   An **azimuthal** (a zuh MUH thul) **projection** is made by transferring the points and lines on a globe onto a flat piece of paper that touches the globe at only one point, as shown in **Figure 2.4**. The point where the paper touches the globe is often the north pole or the south pole. The areas near this point are represented accurately. The shapes of land masses become more distorted farther away from this point. A useful feature of azimuthal projections is that they accurately show the shortest path between two points. This makes azimuthal projections especially helpful for planning air-travel routes.

How to Locate Places on Earth

Even with a map, it can be hard to communicate the exact location of a place on Earth. It would be hard to find Washington, D.C., if the only information available was that it is in the middle of the right-hand side of North America. Mapmakers and ship's navigators came up with a common system to locate places on Earth. They created a set of imaginary lines called lines of latitude and longitude. These lines form a grid pattern over the entire planet. By knowing where a location is on this grid, people can find and describe the exact locations of places on Earth.

Latitude   Lines of latitude are circles that run east and west over the surface of Earth. The line of latitude that is used as a base for measurement is called the equator. The equator runs around the middle of Earth, halfway between the north and south poles. The equator divides Earth into two equal halves, the northern and southern hemispheres. Lines of latitude are used to measure distance north or south of the equator. **Latitude** is measured in degrees (°). The equator is 0° latitude. The north pole is 90° north latitude and the south pole is 90° south latitude.

As You Read

Review the concept map you started in your Science Notebook. Add important information you have learned. Write notes along the arrows that connect the concepts in order to help you remember how the words are related. Then add the rest of the vocabulary terms in the lesson to your concept map and show their relationships.

What is another name for the line of latitude that is located halfway between the north and south poles?

The equator, which runs halfway between the north and south poles, is a logical place for a reference line of latitude. There is no similar place for a reference line for longitude. Before 1884, different mapmakers used different lines of longitude as 0° longitude. In 1884, a panel of 25 countries chose a line that runs through Greenwich, England, as the universal reference line. It is called the prime meridian.

CONNECTION: Social Studies

Maps often show the names of countries and their borders, which are sometimes called political boundaries. Over time, however, names and even borders of countries can change. In Asia, the country that was once known as Burma is now known as Myanmar. The country of Siam is now called Thailand. In Africa, the Belgian Congo is now called Congo, and Rhodesia is now called Zimbabwe. In the United States, the territory once called Dakota Territory is now known as North Dakota and South Dakota. The Utah Territory once contained all of Utah and Nevada as well as parts of Arizona, New Mexico, and Colorado.

Figure It Out

1. What is the name of the line of longitude that is the reference for all longitude measurements?
2. Would a location in Europe have a north or south latitude? Explain.

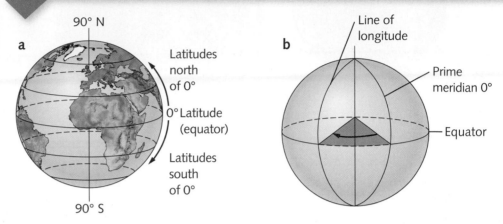

Figure 2.5 a) Lines of latitude are circles that run east and west parallel to the equator. **b)** Lines of longitude are semicircles that run from the north pole to the south pole.

Distances that are less than one degree of latitude apart can be broken down into minutes (') of latitude. Each degree of latitude is made up of 60 minutes. Each minute of latitude is made up of 60 seconds (") of latitude. The latitude of Washington, D.C., is thirty-eight degrees, fifty-three minutes north, or 38° 53' N.

Longitude

Lines of longitude are semicircles that run from the north pole to the south pole. The reference line of longitude, which serves as the base for longitude measurements, is called the **prime meridian**. It passes through Greenwich, England. Lines of longitude are used to measure distances east and west of the prime meridian. **Longitude** is measured in degrees (°). Points to the east of the prime meridian are labeled from 0° to 180° east longitude. Points to the west of the prime meridian are labeled from 0° to 180° west longitude. The line representing 180° east longitude is the same as the line representing 180° west longitude. This line of longitude runs from the north pole to the south pole on the opposite side of Earth from the prime meridian. Together, the prime meridian and the 180° meridian divide Earth into two equal halves—the eastern and western hemispheres. Like degrees of latitude, degrees of longitude can be divided into minutes and seconds. There are 60' of longitude in one degree and 60" of longitude in one minute. The longitude of Washington, D.C., is seventy-seven degrees, two minutes west, or 77° 02' W.

Naming Locations   The exact location of a place on Earth can be described by giving the latitude and longitude of that place. For example, with a map showing latitude and longitude and the information that Washington, D.C., is located at 38° 53' N, 77° 02' W, you could easily locate the city on the map.

Map Directions

A compass rose shows how the map is positioned in relation to north. For some maps, though, there are two directions called north. This is because there are two north poles: the magnetic north pole and the geographic north pole. The magnetic north pole is the pole toward which compasses point. The geographic north pole, also called **true north**, is the pole around which Earth rotates. As shown in **Figure 2.7**, these poles are not in exactly the same location. When using a compass to explore Earth's surface, one needs to make a correction for the difference between geographic north and magnetic north. This angle of correction is called **magnetic declination** (de kluh NAY shun). Magnetic declination is different depending where on Earth you are located.

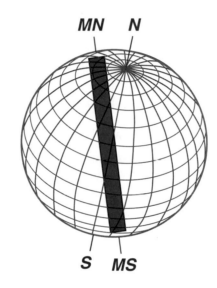

Map Scales

One feature that should appear on all maps is a map scale. A **map scale** tells how big or small the map is in comparison to the area that it represents. A map's scale is given as a ratio. The ratio tells how many units in real space correspond to one unit on the map. For example, some maps have a ratio of 1:24,000. This means that one unit on the map is equal to 24,000 units on the surface the map represents. A map unit can be anything, but generally it is a centimeter or an inch.

Figure 2.6 A compass rose indicates a map's position in relation to north.

Figure 2.7 The magnetic north pole and geographic north pole are not located in exactly the same place on Earth. Because compasses point to magnetic north, compass readings often need to be corrected to account for this difference.

Extend It!

Look at a map of your state that shows longitude and latitude. Try to locate your city or a larger city near you. Determine the latitude and longitude of your town and of the state capital. Determine the direction you would have to travel from your town to the state capital.

After You Read

1. Explain how latitude and longitude are used to locate a point on Earth.

2. Two maps are drawn on pages of the same size. The first map has a 1:24,000 scale, while the second has a 1:240,000 scale. Which map shows a larger area of Earth? How do you know?

3. Look at your completed concept map. Write a well-developed paragraph that explains how the vocabulary words are related.

Learning Goals

- Explain how contour lines are used to represent elevation.
- Read elevations and features from a topographic map.
- Explain how a map legend is a useful feature of a map.

New Vocabulary

topographic map
contour line
elevation
contour interval
index contour
map legend

Did You Know?

Contour lines that represent elevation can also be used to show the depth of features below the surface of a body of water. Underwater contour lines are called bathymetric contour lines.

Before You Read

Read the lesson title, headings, and Learning Goals, and look at the figures. Predict what you think you will learn in this lesson. Write your predictions in two or three sentences in your Science Notebook.

Imagine that you have been hiking all day and are looking for a place to set up camp. You see a set of trail signs. The signs say that there are two campgrounds located in opposite directions. Each is about a mile away. You are tired and would rather follow a flat trail than a steep trail. How would you know which campground was located along the flatter trail? A topographic map of the area would tell you.

Topographic Maps

A **topographic** (tah puh GRA fihk) **map** shows the topography, or surface features, of Earth. It is a two-dimensional representation of Earth's surface. Many topographic maps show natural features, such as rivers, forests, and hills. Topographic maps may also show human-made features such as roads, bridges, and buildings.

Contour Lines   A **contour line** is a line on a topographic map that connects points that all have the same elevation. **Elevation** is the height of an object above sea level. The elevation at sea level is 0. By examining contour lines on a topographic map, you can determine the elevation of a point or area on the map. If two points lie on the same contour line, they have the same elevation. The points are at the same height above sea level. Hikers use the contour lines on a topographic map to find out which trails stay level and which ones change in elevation.

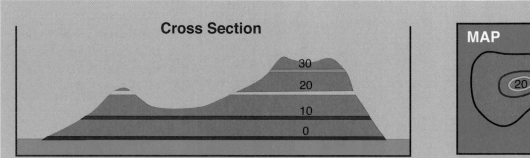
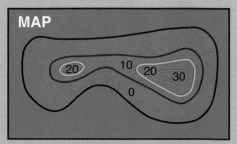

Figure 2.8 These maps show a side view, or cross section, and a map view of the same island. In both views, every point on the island that has an elevation of 10 m is represented by a red contour line.

Contour Intervals Topographic maps use contour lines to show differences in elevation. The topographic map in **Figure 2.9** shows a portion of Yosemite National Park in California. Two contour lines that run next to each other have different elevations. The difference in elevation between one contour line and the next is called the **contour interval**. Different maps may have different contour intervals. For example, a map of a mountainous area with large changes in elevation will likely have a large contour interval such as 40 ft. Maps of very flat areas often have contour intervals of 5 ft.

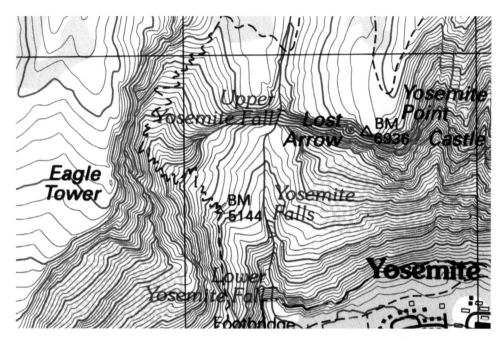

Figure 2.9 This map shows the area around Yosemite Falls in Yosemite National Park. Because the area has large changes in elevation, the contour interval for this map is 40 ft.

The spacing of contour lines also indicates the steepness, or slope, of the land. If contour lines on a map are very close together, the slope of the land represented is steep. If contour lines are spaced far apart, the slope of the land represented is not steep.

The United States Geological Survey, or USGS, has created a set of topographic maps for the entire United States. Contour intervals on USGS topographic maps do not use the SI system. The contour intervals on USGS topographic maps are measured in feet rather than meters. A common contour interval for these maps is 20 ft.

As You Read

Read the predictions you made about this lesson in your Science Notebook. Were your predictions accurate? Revise your sentences if necessary. Then think of a question you have about something related to the chapter. Predict the answer to your question.

What do contour lines on topographic maps show?

Index Contours On USGS topographic maps, every fifth contour line is an index contour line. **Index contours** are drawn darker and thicker and are often the only contour lines labeled with elevation. Index contours make it easier to read topographic maps. For example, suppose you are using a map with a 40-foot contour interval. How is the elevation of a mountain peak that is two contour intervals above an index contour determined? First, determine the elevation of the index contour; then add two contour intervals to that value.

Figure It Out

1. An index contour is drawn every fifth contour interval. What is the elevation difference between two index contours that are next to each other on this map?

2. The steepest slope on a topographic map is shown where the contour lines are closest together. Where is the steepest slope on this map?

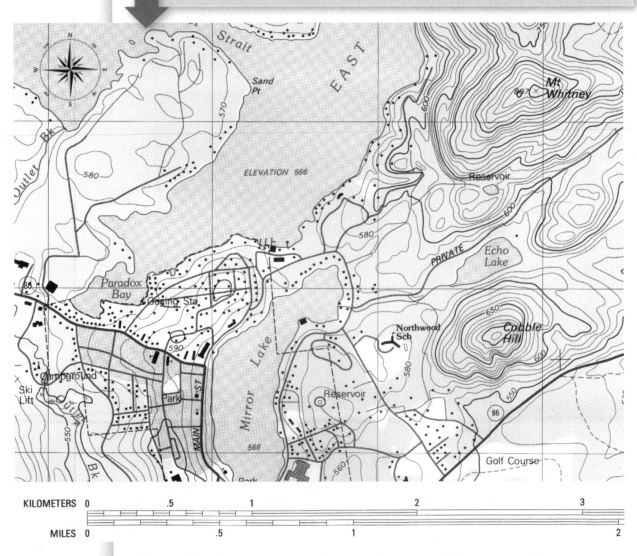

Figure 2.10 This USGS topographic map shows part of the area around Lake Placid, New York.

Peaks and Depressions When contour lines form a closed loop on a map, they represent either the top of a hill or the bottom of a depression. It would be difficult to tell the difference between a hilltop and the bottom of a depression on a map without extra marks. The contour lines of depressions are marked with short, straight lines inside each contour circle. These short lines point toward the bottom, or center of the depression, as shown in **Figure 2.11**.

Explore It!

Using the topographic map provided by your teacher, determine where the highest point on the map is and the elevation of that point. Then, noting where the slope is the steepest around this point, suggest a route up to the point that follows the gentlest slope.

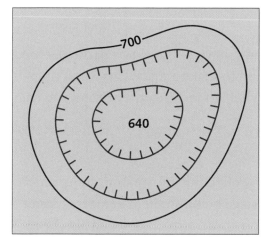

Figure 2.11 These depression contour lines, have short line segments pointing toward the center of the depression. They show that the center of the area has a lower elevation than the outer part of the area.

Map Legends

Topographic maps often represent both human-made and natural features on Earth's surface. Symbols are used to represent the different features on a map. A **map legend** is a part of a map that explains what the symbols used on the map represent. Common map symbols include black squares for buildings, red lines for highways, and black dotted lines for trails. Contour lines are usually brown. Wooded areas are usually shown in green. Bodies of water, such as lakes, ponds, rivers, and oceans, are usually shown in blue. A sample map legend is shown in **Figure 2.12**.

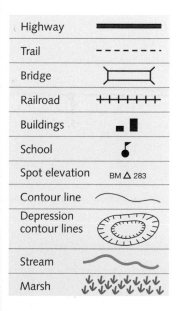

Figure 2.12 Map legends explain what the symbols on maps represent.

After You Read

1. Reread your prediction from As You Read. Did your prediction accurately answer your question? Revise your answer if necessary. Share your question with a partner. After sharing, find the specific section in the chapter that supports your response to your partner's question.

2. Explain the relationship between a contour interval and an index contour.

3. Describe two instances in which a topographic map would be useful. Describe two other instances in which you would need a different kind of map.

Mapmaking and Technology

Learning Goals

- Explain how remote sensing images are created.
- Identify the parts of the Global Positioning System.
- Explain how a GIS is useful for answering geographic questions.

New Vocabulary

remote sensing
pixel
sonar
Global Positioning System (GPS)
geographic information system (GIS)

Before You Read

In your Science Notebook, begin a concept map with the term *Mapmaking technology* in the center. Add the words *Remote Sensing, pixel, Sonar, Global Positioning System (GPS),* and *geographic information system (GIS)* in smaller circles. Leave space around each term.

Not too long ago, mapmakers would have to travel to a particular area to collect the information they needed to make a map. This was a time-consuming practice. Today, with the help of technology, mapmaking has changed a great deal.

Remote Sensing

Remote sensing is the process of collecting information about an object or area from far above the surface being studied. Remote sensing can be as simple as taking photographs from airplanes. It can also be as advanced as using satellites with sensors to record what humans cannot see. Maps of Earth's surface, its ocean depths, and even its atmosphere can be made using remote sensing and sensors mounted on satellites.

The human eye can detect only a small part of the Sun's energy. The energy we can see is called visible light. Most modern remote sensing systems detect the energy from the Sun that we cannot see. This energy is either absorbed by Earth or reflected back into space. Remote sensors also collect information about the waves of energy coming from Earth's surface. The sensors measure and record the energy of those waves.

Figure 2.13 a) Scientists and engineers worked together to create the *Landsat 7* satellite, which was launched in April 1999. **b)** This remote sensing image of Washington, D.C., was taken by the *Landsat 7* satellite.

a

b

A sensor is usually divided into many smaller parts. Each part of the sensor records an energy reading for a small square of the area of Earth's surface being observed. This small square, or basic unit, of the area being observed is called a **pixel**. The more parts the sensor is divided into, the more pixels there are, and the more information the sensor collects. This results in a picture with more detail.

When the sensor has recorded readings for each pixel, this information is sent back to a computer on Earth. This computer processes the information to create an image of Earth's surface that humans can see.

Figure 2.14 shows aerial photographs of Nantucket, Massachusetts. The photo in **a** was taken using more pixels. Image **b** shows what an image would look like if the sensor created an image using fewer pixels.

Remote sensing satellites can record information about large areas of Earth because they are high above its surface. Quickly moving satellites can record images of many areas of Earth's surface in a single day!

Explain It!

In your Science Notebook, write a few sentences explaining how remote sensors can be improved to show more detail.

Figure It Out

1. If each pixel were smaller, would it take more pixels or fewer pixels to cover the island? Explain your answer.

2. Would a satellite image of Nantucket be more accurate if it had smaller pixels or larger pixels? Why?

a

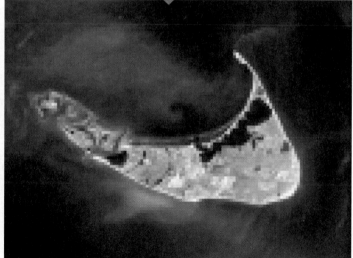

b

Figure 2.14 These photos of Nantucket Island show how the use of more pixels results in an image with more detail.

As You Read

Look at the term *Remote sensing* in your concept map. Below the term, write its definition. To the upper left of the term, draw a picture that helps you remember the definition. To the upper right of the term, write a sentence that uses the word correctly.

As you read, complete the vocabulary map for each term.

Did You Know?

The GPS was built by the United States Department of Defense. During the 1980s, the U.S. government made the technology available to everyone. Handheld GPS receivers have an accuracy of about ten meters. More advanced receivers, such as those used by surveyors and the military, are much more accurate. They can give locations with an accuracy of one centimeter or less.

Figure 2.16 Handheld GPS receivers are small and easily carried.

Sonar

Sonar is a system that uses sound waves to detect and measure objects underwater and on the ocean floor. Sound waves are sent out from a sonar device toward the area to be observed. The sound waves reflect off objects in the area. Some of the sound waves travel back through the water to the sonar device. There, the device collects and records the energy carried by these waves. This information is used to make a picture of the features and objects on the ocean floor.

Figure 2.15 This shipwreck on the ocean floor was located using sonar.

The Global Positioning System

The **Global Positioning System**, or **GPS**, is made up of at least 24 satellites in orbit around Earth. It allows people to find their exact locations on Earth. Each of these satellites constantly sends out a signal that contains the time and the satellite's location in space. A GPS receiver on Earth uses the information sent by the satellites to calculate its own location. A receiver must get signals from at least four satellites to be able to pinpoint its location exactly. It is usually possible for a receiver to pick up signals from seven or more satellites at one time.

Because GPS receivers operate continuously, they can record changes in position over time. They can show the path the receiver has taken and how fast the receiver has been moving. This makes the GPS useful for navigation. Planes and ships use the GPS to plot their course. Handheld GPS receivers have become popular for runners, bicyclists, car drivers, and hikers. The GPS is also used by scientists to identify the exact locations of things such as active volcanoes or wildlife. For example, scientists tracking the movement of wolves in a mountain range can use GPS receivers attached to the animals to record exactly where the wolves have traveled.

Geographic Information Systems

A **geographic information system**, or **GIS**, is a computer-based tool for representing information on maps. A GIS allows its users to combine different layers of information, known as data layers, to make new maps. For a particular area, individual data layers might include the locations of roads, how much rain falls across the area, the elevation of the area, and the quality of the soil.

Figure 2.17 shows how a GIS combines data layers to help scientists look for answers to questions. For example, a scientist might wonder if the occurrence of earthquakes in an area depends on the location of volcanoes. A GIS can be used to layer earthquake data on top of volcano location data. This would create a map that compares where earthquakes have occurred to the locations of volcanoes.

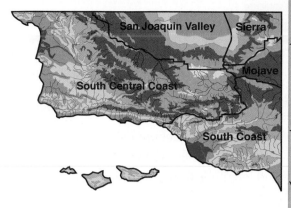
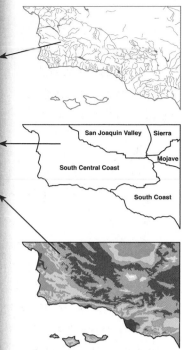

Figure 2.17 Using a GIS, different data layers are placed on top of one another to create a specialized map.

◉ CONNECTION: Ecology

In the Gap Analysis Program, biologists and mapmakers work together to preserve the habitats of plants and animals across the United States. Scientists want to prevent plant and animal populations from becoming cut off or isolated as a result of land development and construction. This program relies on the creation of special maps of different regions of the country. The maps indentify different ecosystems, or areas of land with a specific climate and plant and animal life. To create these maps, biologists use remote sensing to identify the different ecosystems of a region. Once biologists have gathered data for an entire region, mapmakers use a GIS to create maps. These maps show where the different ecosystems are located. Biologists use these specialized maps to determine whether different species of plants and animals have enough habitat. The information gathered through the Gap Analysis Program is used to help policy-makers plan the locations of new conservation lands.

After You Read

1. Look at the concept map in your Science Notebook. Revise any definitions, sentences, or pictures if necessary. Then use your concept map to answer the questions below.

2. Explain how most modern remote sensing is done.

3. Compare and contrast a GIS and the GPS.

Summary

KEY CONCEPTS

2.1 Understanding Maps

- A map is a representation of a certain area or part of an area.

- Because a planet is not flat, map projections are used to draw planets' surfaces in two dimensions.

- The three main types of map projections are Mercator projections, conic projections, and azimuthal projections.

- Lines of latitude and longitude form a grid of imaginary lines that cover Earth and give the exact location of a point on Earth.

2.2 Using Topographic Maps

- Topographic maps use contour lines to represent the elevation of features on the maps.

- An index contour is a thicker and darker contour line that is usually drawn every fifth contour interval.

- Tops of hills and depressions are both represented by closed loops on a topographic map, but depressions have short line segments that point toward the bottom of the depression.

- A map legend shows the symbols used on the map and what the symbols represent.

2.3 Mapmaking and Technology

- Remote sensing is a way of collecting information about something at a distance without touching what is being studied.

- Most modern remote sensing is done by measuring the energy carried by waves that reflect off the area being studied.

- The Global Positioning System (GPS) is a system that includes an Earth-based control center and at least 24 satellites that can be used to determine precise locations.

- A geographic information system (GIS) is a computer system that can combine different data layers to create maps.

VOCABULARY REVIEW

Write each term in a complete sentence or write a paragraph relating several terms.

2.1
map, p. 17
projection, p. 18
Mercator projection, p. 18
conic projection, p. 18
azimuthal projection, p. 19
latitude, p. 19
prime meridian, p. 20
longitude, p. 20
true north, p. 21
magnetic declination, p. 21
map scale, p. 21

2.2
topographic map, p. 22
contour line, p. 22
elevation, p. 22
contour interval, p. 23
index contour, p. 24
map legend, p. 25

2.3
remote sensing, p. 26
pixel, p. 27
sonar, p. 28
Global Positioning System (GPS), p. 28
geographic information system (GIS), p. 29

PREPARE FOR CHAPTER TEST

To prepare for the chapter test, create a question from each Learning Goal. Use the information in your Science Notebook to answer each question. Then use these answers to write a well-developed essay about the chapter. Use the Key Concept on the first page of this chapter as your topic sentence.

True or False

If the statement is true, write "true." If it is false, change the underlined word or words to make the statement true.

1. Every two-dimensional map uses a <u>representation</u> to draw a view of a round object on a flat surface.

2. An azimuthal projection is drawn as if a piece of paper were touching Earth at <u>one point</u>.

3. Latitude and <u>longitude</u> are measurements that allow one to give an exact location for a point on Earth.

4. A <u>bathymetric</u> map can be used to tell the height of a hill.

5. The <u>Geographic Information System</u> includes a system of satellites that broadcast time and location information.

6. <u>Distortion</u> occurs when an image of a round object is projected onto a flat surface.

Short Answer

Answer each of the following in a sentence or brief paragraph.

7. Explain the difference between an azimuthal projection and a conic projection.

8. Describe how latitude and longitude are used to give the location of a point on Earth.

9. Compare and contrast a contour line and an index contour.

10. Explain why a map would be hard to read without a legend.

11. Describe how sonar is used to create an image of an underwater area.

12. Explain why a geographic information system can be useful for scientists.

Critical Thinking

Use what you have learned in this chapter to answer each of the following.

13. **Compare and Contrast** How are a map and a globe similar? How are they different?

14. **Infer** Look at the map below. Explain the likely reasoning for building the road along Burr Run.

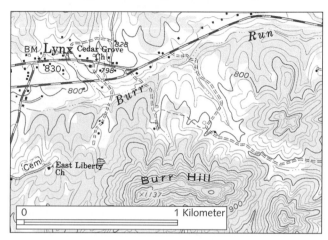

15. **Apply Concepts** Describe how you could use a GIS to confirm the statement that human population distribution is determined by the amount of rainfall an area gets.

Standardized Test Question

Choose the letter of the response that correctly answers the question.

16. On a topographic map, what type of feature is represented by a circle with short lines pointing toward the center?

    A. a hill

    B. a steep slope

    C. a depression

    D. a body of water

Robots on the Ocean Floor

MOST OF EARTH'S land features have been mapped. But the floor of the Arctic remains as mysterious as the surface of Venus. It lies hidden under a thick ice sheet, in a place that is too cold and dark to study. As a result, most of it remains unexplored and unmapped.

That situation will change within the next few years when a pair of small robots dives into the Arctic from a ship above the ice cap. Their destination will be the Gakkel Ridge. It is the deepest and most isolated of the volcanic ridges that snake through Earth's ocean bottom. The robots' task is to collect specimens of the strange organisms that might live there—and make the first maps of this area of the undersea mountain chain.

Scientists are eager to study the ridge because no one has studied this unique area in detail before. Like all mid-ocean ridges, the Gakkel Ridge is a place where two of the plates that make up Earth's crust meet. In other oceans, scientists have discovered hydrothermal vents at these cracks. The vents spew out very hot water and chemicals from deep inside Earth. The chemicals support unusual communities of organisms.

In 2001, scientists did the first organized sampling at the ridge. Small robotic submarines tested the water, looking for the chemicals that usually come from vents. They found the chemicals, proving the vents were down there—somewhere. But that expedition could not locate the vents or map them.

In 2007 or 2008, scientists will return to the Arctic Ocean on a ship that can cut through the thick ice. They will bring along two remote-controlled autonomous underwater vehicles, or AUVs, named *Puma* and *Jaguar*. The AUVs will dive beneath the ice cap and look around. *Puma* will carry sensors that can detect the hot plumes of water and chemicals hydrothermal vents release.

Once *Puma* finds a vent, *Jaguar* will dive closer to the sea bottom. It will use sonar to map the area around the vent. *Jaguar* will send out sound waves that will bounce off the features on the sea bottom and back to a receiver. With this data, a computer will make a map showing the features of the seafloor. Samples of organisms around the vent will also be collected.

Scientists are excited about the unusual life-forms they may find at the vent. This chance to make the first detailed maps of this remote area of the ocean floor will make this mysterious part of our world a little less so.

CAREER CONNECTION: GIS TECHNICIAN

GIS TECHNICIANS love a puzzle—and they get lots of them. They often start with a mapping problem. Then they set out to gather the data they need to find a solution. Their tool is a GIS, or Geographic Information System. GIS is a computer database that can store, link, and display many kinds of data about a location.

Although GIS is not a map, it is often used to make maps. But GIS can give information in a way most maps cannot. GIS can layer many types of data on a single map. A GIS technician can quickly produce maps that mix data to answer many questions about a location.

What kinds of questions do GIS technicians answer? For example, what is the best place for a new shopping center? Is there a nonpolluted area of a county where a company can dig a new well? Or, where does a city need traffic lights or stop signs installed?

In the last case, a technician would work with a GIS that contains a map of the city's streets and borders. She would have already entered data for many of the city's features, such as the locations of parks, hospitals, schools, fire stations, street lights, and stop signs. The GIS might also contain digital data on population or

Answering the Question: Where Am I?

THIS IS A SIMPLE QUESTION, but it's also an important one. Knowing exact location allows an ambulance driver to speed straight to the site of an accident. It lets a rescue crew locate a ship lost at sea. It lets airplane pilots find their way thousands of miles around the globe, even in cloudy weather.

The Problem: Finding Exact Location

Finding exact locations on Earth's surface was a problem for centuries, especially at sea. By the 1700s, sailors had several tools to find latitude. But longitude was trickier. The key to longitude is time. For each 15 degrees you move west or east, you gain or lose an hour. So knowing the time where you are at sea and the time at some known location on land tells you the distance between the two points—and your east-west position. John Harrison solved the longitude problem in 1764. He invented a clock that kept accurate time at sea. But this system could only determine position within a few kilometers.

A High-Flying Solution

Today, satellites are used to determine location. People all over the world rely on the Global Positioning System, or GPS, to find where they are. Its 24 satellites

constantly broadcast their position and the time. With signals from three satellites, receivers can find their position within about 18 meters. That helps planes, boats, cars, and even some hikers find their way.

Some people think the sky is the limit on what a new and improved GPS might do. So in 2008, Galileo will come online. Galileo will have 30 satellites. It will also locate objects more exactly than GPS. There are plans to put small receiver chips for Galileo in cell phones, cars, and even on people. You would be able to use your cell phone to find your way around. People with medical problems might wear both body sensors and a receiver chip. If a person had a heart attack, an ambulance crew could locate and treat him or her fast. Scientists could also use signals from Galileo to measure the height of ocean waves. The new satellite net might then become part of a tsunami early warning system. Scientists are constantly thinking of new ways to use this technology. The sky really is the limit.

the locations of car accidents and fires. To answer the traffic light question, the GIS technician might pull up data on intersections where there have been at least ten accidents in the last two years. Then she might add intersections without traffic lights or signs. The new map would show city planners all the dangerous intersections that do not have traffic lights or stop signs. This would help them decide where to put new ones.

GIS technicians work in many places, from city governments to NASA. GIS technicians need to know computer programming and GIS software. The job also requires some background in Earth science, geography, and mapping. GIS technicians often have an associate or bachelor's degree. Experience also means a lot in this field.

Investigative Reporting

Review the above article on GPS, and do additional research to find other uses for the system. Then identify a possible new use for the present system or Galileo. Write a proposal to present to someone who might use your idea. Make a drawing that shows how it works. Then present your idea to the class.

Composition of the Earth

Chapter 3

Matter and Atoms

What are atoms and matter, and where are they found?

Chapter 4

Minerals

What characteristics do all minerals share with one another, and what makes each unique?

Chapter 5

Rocks

How do rocks change in structure and composition over time?

Matter and Atoms

KEY CONCEPT Everything on Earth is made up of matter, and all matter is made up of atoms.

What is in a blueberry muffin? If you use a magnifying lens to look at a muffin, you can see blueberries and muffin crumbs. But if you have ever baked muffins, you know that they have more than two ingredients. The ingredients include flour, butter, sugar, eggs, and salt.

Even if you look at all of these ingredients, you cannot see every part of a muffin. Each ingredient is made of components, or smaller parts. These components are so small that you cannot see them with a magnifying lens or a microscope. Did you know that everything throughout the universe is made of components that small?

Think About Components

Describe the parts of a wooden pencil. What materials are used to make each part? What is the smallest part of each material that you can see?

- Use a magnifying lens to examine each part of the pencil. Describe what you see.

- In your Science Notebook, describe what the smallest component of the pencil might look like.

www.scilinks.org

Matter **Code: WGES03A**
Structure of Atoms **Code: WGES03B**

Learning Goals

- Define *matter* and *element.*
- Describe the parts and structure of an atom.
- Explain how elements are organized in the periodic table.

New Vocabulary

matter
element
atom
proton
neutron
electron
nucleus
atomic number
atomic mass
ion
isotope

Recall Vocabulary

mass, p. 12

3.1 Earth's Elements

Before You Read

In your Science Notebook, start a concept map about the word *matter.* Write *Matter* in the middle of a blank page. Then write anything you already know about matter in the space around the word. Draw a line from each of your thoughts to the center of the concept map.

What do pencils, water, and oxygen all have in common? They are all made of matter. **Matter** is anything that has mass and takes up space. On Earth, there are three common kinds of matter: solids, liquids, and gases. A pencil is a solid. It has its own shape. Water is a liquid. When water is poured into a container, it becomes the shape of the container. Oxygen is a gas. When oxygen is poured into a container, it expands to fill the entire container. All three kinds of matter have different properties, but they are all made of the same basic substances.

Elements

All matter is made of elements. An **element** is a substance that cannot be broken down into simpler substances by normal physical or chemical means. Silver is an example of an element. People can melt silver, bend silver, and make silver into different shapes. But none of these actions can break down silver into a simpler substance.

Scientists have identified more than 110 elements. Ninety-two of these elements occur naturally on Earth. The rest of the elements have been made in laboratories. Each element has a one-, two-, or three-letter chemical symbol. Scientists use these symbols as abbreviations for the elements. The names and symbols of some of the elements are listed in **Figure 3.1**. The names and symbols of all of the elements are listed in the Appendix on p. 464.

Figure 3.1

Elements and Chemical Symbols

Element	Symbol	Element	Symbol	Element	Symbol
hydrogen	H	aluminum	Al	copper	Cu
helium	He	silicon	Si	silver	Ag
carbon	C	sulfur	S	iodine	I
nitrogen	N	chlorine	Cl	gold	Au
oxygen	O	calcium	Ca	mercury	Hg
sodium	Na	iron	Fe	lead	Pb

Figure It Out

1. What is the symbol for carbon? What is the symbol for copper?
2. Choose one of the elements in **Figure 3.1**. Describe at least two objects that contain the element.

Atoms

Elements cannot be broken into simpler substances, but a large chunk of an element can be broken into smaller chunks of that same element. What would happen if you took a chunk of silver and kept breaking it into smaller and smaller pieces? Eventually, you would end up with one silver atom. An **atom** is the smallest unit of an element that has all of the characteristics of that element. Atoms are very small. About 100 million atoms can fit along the diameter of a penny.

The word *atom* comes from a Greek word that means "indivisible." People used to think that atoms could not be divided into smaller parts. Then scientists discovered particles that are smaller than atoms. It turns out that all atoms are made of the same kinds of particles. The number and arrangement of these particles determine the properties of the atoms.

There are three basic particles that make up atoms: protons (PROH tahnz), neutrons (NEW trahnz), and electrons (ih LEK trahnz). A **proton** is a tiny particle with a positive electric charge. A **neutron** has about the same mass as a proton, but it does not have any electric charge. It is neutral.

An **electron** is a tiny particle that has a negative electric charge. An electron's charge is the exact opposite of a proton's charge. Thus, when an electron and a proton are together, the two charges cancel each other out. The mass of an electron is about 2,000 times less than the mass of a proton or neutron. If the mass of an electron were one pound, the mass of the protons and neutrons together would be 4,000 pounds.

Extend It!

A subatomic particle is any particle that is smaller than an atom. Research which subatomic particle was identified first. Who identified it? How was it identified? Has anyone identified a particle that is smaller than a proton, a neutron, or an electron? Based on your research, predict whether scientists might identify more subatomic particles in the future.

Figure 3.2 A large diamond can be broken into smaller diamonds. All diamonds are made out of carbon atoms. Each carbon atom contains protons, neutrons, and electrons. The great hardness of diamonds is related to how the carbon atoms are arranged.

Atomic Structure

At the center of every atom is a **nucleus** (NEW klee us, plural: *nuclei*). The nucleus contains all of an atom's protons and neutrons. Nearly all of an atom's mass is in its nucleus. Yet, the nucleus is a very small part of an atom. If an atom were the size of a baseball stadium, its nucleus would be about the size of a marble on the pitcher's mound. Much of an atom is empty space. The drawings in this chapter, such as the ones in **Figure 3.3**, are one way that atomic structure is represented.

Racing around the nucleus of an atom are the atom's electrons. The electrons move quickly and do not stay in one place. However, they are more likely to be found in some places than in others. The areas where electrons are most likely to be found are called energy levels. You can think of energy levels as the rings of seats that circle a baseball stadium. Each ring of seats contains a certain number of seats. Similarly, each energy level can hold a greater number of electrons than the previous level. Atoms with more electrons have more energy levels.

The outermost energy level of an atom is important. The number of electrons in this energy level has a big influence on the properties of the atom. Some atoms have enough electrons to completely fill all of their energy levels. These atoms are very stable and do not combine easily with other atoms. Some atoms do not have enough electrons to completely fill their outermost energy level. These atoms are less stable and they are more likely to combine with other atoms. In the next lesson, you will learn more about how atoms combine.

As You Read

Work with a partner to add information about elements, atoms, protons, neutrons, and electrons to the concept map in your Science Notebook.

Explain how each new word is related to matter.

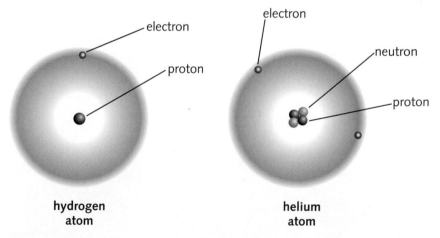

hydrogen
atom

helium
atom

Figure 3.3 Two common elements are hydrogen and helium. Atoms of both elements have a single energy level. This energy level can hold up to two electrons. Which element do you think is more stable? Why?

Atomic Numbers

All elements are made out of atoms, and all atoms are made out of protons, neutrons, and electrons. What makes the atoms of one element different from the atoms of another element? Each kind of atom has a unique number of protons. The number of protons in an atom is called the **atomic number** of the atom. Every element has its own atomic number. The **atomic mass** of an element is equal to the total mass of the protons and neutrons. Elements with higher atomic numbers have higher atomic masses.

The atomic number of an atom is sometimes equal to the number of electrons in the atom. An atom that has equal numbers of electrons and protons does not have an electric charge. The positive charges of the protons cancel out the negative charges of the electrons. An atom that has no electric charge is called a neutral atom.

Ions

Atoms of the same element can have different numbers of electrons. This happens when an atom gains or loses electrons. This gives the atom a negative or positive electric charge. An atom with an electric charge is called an **ion** (I ahn). A negatively charged ion is an atom that has more electrons than protons. A positively charged ion is an atom that has fewer electrons than protons. The number of electrons in an atom does not change what kind of atom it is. However, as discussed earlier in the chapter, the number of electrons does affect the properties of the atom.

Isotopes

Atoms can also have different numbers of neutrons. Atoms of the same element that have different numbers of neutrons are called **isotopes** (I suh tohps). The number of neutrons in an atom affects the mass of the atom. Isotopes with more neutrons are more massive than isotopes with fewer neutrons.

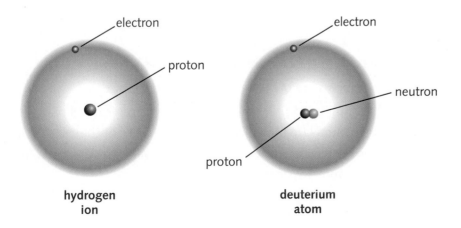

hydrogen ion

deuterium atom

Figure 3.4 Both of these drawings show hydrogen atoms. Which atom has more mass?

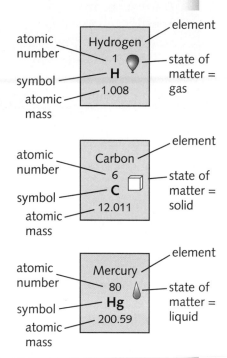

Figure 3.5 The periodic table includes the name, atomic number, chemical symbol, and atomic mass of each element. The atomic mass of an element is a measure of the amount of matter in one atom of the element. The table also shows the state of matter in which each element usually occurs.

Organizing the Elements

Scientists often organize large groups of things into smaller groups that have common properties. This can make it easier to describe and study the things in the group. Dmitri Mendeleev (1834–1907) was one of the first scientists who tried to organize the elements. He noticed a few patterns in the chemical properties of the elements. In 1869, he made a table that grouped the elements based on these properties. Since then, scientists have made improvements to the table. They have added more information about the elements. They have also added newly discovered elements. The modern version of the table is called the periodic table of the elements. A copy of it is in the Appendix on p. 464.

The periodic table has rows and columns of boxes. Each box has information about one element. This information includes the element's name, its chemical symbol, and its atomic number. Each box also shows whether the element usually occurs as a solid, a liquid, or a gas.

Elements in the rows of the periodic table are arranged by atomic number. Recall that the atomic number of an atom tells how many protons are in the atom. The atomic numbers in a row increase from left to right. An element on the left side of a row has fewer protons than an element on the right side of the same row.

Elements in the columns of the periodic table are also grouped in a logical way. All of the atoms in a given column have the same number of electrons in their outermost energy level. For example, all of the atoms in the first column of the table have one electron in their outermost energy level. This causes the atoms to have similar chemical properties. All of the elements in this column, except hydrogen, are metals and all react easily with other chemicals.

After You Read

1. Name and describe the three basic particles that make up atoms.
2. Explain how elements are organized in the periodic table.
3. Make sure that your concept map includes information from all of the sections in this lesson. Use the information to think about the concept of matter. In your Science Notebook, write a well-developed paragraph that synthesizes what you have learned about matter.

3.2 How Atoms Combine

Before You Read

Look at the figures and read the headings and boldfaced words in this lesson. Use what you read to predict what you will learn about how atoms combine. Write your predictions in your Science Notebook.

Only 92 elements occur in nature, but there are many more than 92 different substances on Earth. This is because atoms of different elements can combine to form new substances. Most things on Earth—including plants, animals, rocks, and water—are made of the atoms of more than one kind of element. Some things are made of only a few kinds of atoms. For example, water is made of just two kinds of atoms: hydrogen and oxygen. Other things are made of many kinds of atoms. Your body is made of about 40 kinds of atoms. Different combinations of the atoms form the skin, bones, muscles, and other parts of your body.

Chemical Bonds

Atoms combine with one another to become more stable. They do this by forming chemical bonds. A **chemical bond** is a force that holds two atoms together. A few kinds of atoms, such as helium and neon, are naturally stable. They have the right number of electrons to fill their outermost energy level. These atoms usually do not combine with other atoms.

Most atoms do not have enough electrons to completely fill their outermost energy levels. They are not stable. These atoms must lose electrons, gain electrons, or share electrons to become more stable. One of the main ways for atoms to do this is to form chemical bonds with one another. There are three main kinds of chemical bonds: covalent, ionic, and metallic.

Figure 3.6 Just four elements make up over 90 percent of the mass of all of these living things. Which elements do you think they are? Nearly every living thing on Earth contains different combinations of these four elements.

Covalent Bonds   Two unstable atoms can become more stable by sharing electrons. The bond that forms between two atoms that share electrons is called a **covalent** (koh VAY lunt) **bond**. For two atoms to share electrons, the outermost energy level of each atom must overlap. Electrons in the overlapping area can then move around both atoms. Each atom fills its outermost energy level with the shared electrons. A covalent bond is formed, and both atoms become more stable. Hydrogen atoms often form covalent bonds with one another. A single hydrogen atom has only one electron. But the atom's one energy level needs two electrons to be full. If two hydrogen atoms share electrons, both atoms can have a full energy level. The proton in the nucleus of each atom is attracted to the shared pair of electrons. This attractive force is the bond that holds the two atoms together.

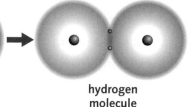

hydrogen atom   hydrogen atom   hydrogen molecule

Figure 3.7 Two hydrogen atoms form a hydrogen molecule.

Two or more atoms that are held together by covalent bonds are called **molecules** (MAH lih kyewlz). Some molecules are made up of a single kind of atom. For example, a molecule of hydrogen is made up of two hydrogen atoms. Other molecules are made up of more than one kind of atom. For example, a molecule of water is made up of two hydrogen atoms and one oxygen atom.

The formation of a water molecule is shown in **Figure 3.8**. An atom of oxygen has six electrons in its outermost energy level. This energy level needs a total of eight electrons to be full. Each hydrogen atom has one electron in a single energy level. Recall that this energy level needs a total of two electrons to be full. To form a water molecule, the oxygen atom shares one electron with each hydrogen atom. Each hydrogen atom shares its one electron with the oxygen atom. The shared electrons fill the energy levels of all three atoms. With filled energy levels, the atoms are much more stable than they were before they combined.

Ionic Bonds   Not all atoms share electrons to become more stable. Sometimes one atom transfers one or more of its electrons to another atom. The atom that loses electrons becomes a positively charged ion.

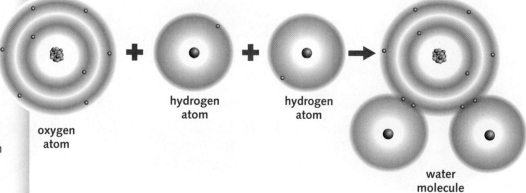

hydrogen atom   hydrogen atom   oxygen atom   water molecule

Figure 3.8 Two hydrogen atoms and one oxygen atom form a water molecule.

The atom that gains electrons becomes a negatively charged ion. The two ions can combine by forming an ionic (i AH nihk) bond. An **ionic bond** holds together two ions that have equal and opposite charges.

Sodium and chlorine are two kinds of atoms that form ionic bonds with one another. A sodium atom has only one electron in its outermost energy level. A chlorine atom needs one electron to fill its outermost energy level. When a sodium atom transfers its electron to a chlorine atom, both atoms become more stable. The sodium atom becomes a positively charged ion. The chlorine atom becomes a negatively charged ion. The two ions are attracted to one another. An ionic bond holds them together. The combined ions form a new substance called sodium chloride. Sodium chloride is the scientific name for table salt.

As You Read

Look back at your predictions about how atoms combine.

Add any new information that you have learned to your Science Notebook. Be sure to include descriptions of the three main kinds of chemical bonds.

How do ions form?

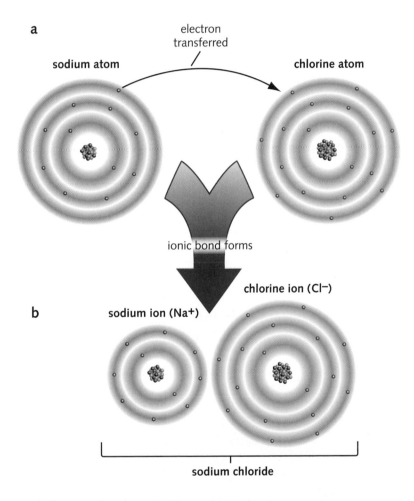

Figure 3.9 a) At room temperature, sodium is a soft, silvery metal. Chlorine is a poisonous green gas. **b)** Atoms from the two elements combine to form harmless table salt. Sodium and chlorine form an ionic bond.

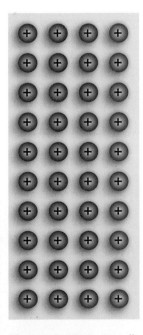

Figure 3.10 In metallic bonds, every electron is shared with every proton. The protons are often described as floating in a "sea" of electrons.

Metallic Bonds The third kind of chemical bond is called a metallic bond. Metallic bonds hold metals together. Examples of metals are gold, copper, and iron. In a **metallic bond**, all of the electrons are shared by all of the atoms. Metals lose electrons easily to form positive ions. A solid metal is made up of a grid of positive ions surrounded by electrons. The electrons move freely throughout the metal. The metals in gold rings, copper pipes, and iron fences are all held together with metallic bonds.

All paints are mixtures. They contain pigments and a material that holds the pigments together. Pigments are colored materials that have been crushed and ground up into small particles. Long ago, painters ground up seeds, plants, and rocks to make pigments. They used fat, blood, spit, and other materials to hold the pigments together. Modern paints contain pigments from nature as well as pigments made in laboratories. Some of the materials used to hold the pigments together include oil, egg yolk, plaster, and plastic.

Classifying Matter

Matter can be classified into three groups. The groups are based on the number of different elements in the matter and the way that the atoms of the elements are combined. The three groups of matter are elemental matter, compounds, and mixtures.

Elemental Matter   A material that is made up of a single kind of element is called **elemental matter**. A single atom that has not combined with any other atoms is the simplest form of elemental matter. Only a few elements exist in nature in this form. One example is argon, one of the gases in air. Diamonds are another example of elemental matter. They are made of carbon. There are no other kinds of atoms in diamonds.

Compounds   Most materials on Earth are made up of more than one kind of element. **Compounds** are materials that contain two or more chemically combined elements. All living things contain compounds. Most nonliving things on Earth are also made of compounds. The atoms in compounds can be held together by covalent bonds or ionic bonds. Water is a compound that is held together by covalent bonds. Table salt is a compound that is held together by ionic bonds.

Mixtures   Many materials on Earth are not simply elemental matter or compounds. They are combinations of these forms of matter. Two or more materials that are combined in a nonchemical way are called a **mixture**. There are two kinds of mixtures: heterogeneous mixtures and homogeneous mixtures.

Heterogeneous Mixtures   A heterogeneous (he tuh rah JEE nee us) mixture is a mixture with visible parts. An example is soil. Soil is a mixture of rock pieces, plant pieces, insect parts, water, and air. When you look at soil, you can see and identify individual pieces.

Figure 3.11 a) A diamond is elemental matter. **b)** Salt is a compound. **c)** Soil is a mixture.

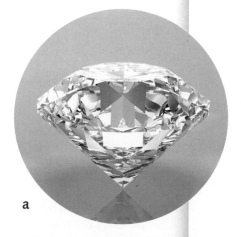

a

b

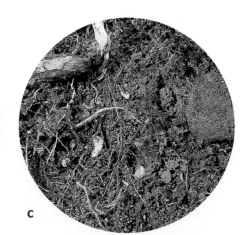

c

Homogeneous Mixtures   A homogeneous (hoh muh JEE nee us) mixture is a mixture whose individual parts are impossible to see. Another name for a homogeneous mixture is a solution. Solutions can be solid, liquid, or gaseous. A nickel coin is an example of a solid solution. A nickel looks like it is made of just one kind of metal, but it is actually a mixture of the metals nickel and copper. Salt water is an example of a liquid solution. It contains water, salt, and other substances. The air you breathe is an example of a gaseous solution. It is made up of nitrogen, oxygen, and other gases.

Chemical Formulas

Some elements, such as einsteinium, have long names. Many compounds have even longer names. Examine **Figure 3.12** for some examples. Scientists use chemical formulas to make it faster and easier to describe elements and compounds. Chemical formulas list the numbers and kinds of atoms in elements and compounds.

The chemical formula for a single atom of an element is the same as the chemical symbol for the element. The chemical formula for a molecule lists the symbols of all of the atoms in the molecule. The number of each kind of atom is written as a subscript next to the atom's symbol. If there is no subscript, there is only one atom of that kind in the molecule. The chemical formula for water is H_2O. The H_2 means that a water molecule contains two atoms of hydrogen, and the O with no subscript means that it contains one atom of oxygen.

Chemical formulas are also used to describe ionic compounds. Though these compounds are not made of molecules, subscripts can be used in the same way. A common ionic compound is table salt. It consists of ionically bonded sodium and chlorine ions. There is one sodium ion for every chlorine ion. The chemical formula for table salt is NaCl.

Chemical Formulas of Some Common Substances

Common Name	Scientific Name	Chemical Formula
aspirin	acetylsalicylic acid	$C_9H_8O_4$
baking soda	sodium bicarbonate	$NaHCO_3$
chalk	calcium carbonate	$CaCO_3$
plaster of paris	calcium sulfate	$CaSO_4$
table salt	sodium chloride	NaCl
table sugar	sucrose	$C_{12}H_{22}O_{11}$
water	dihydrogen monoxide	H_2O

Figure 3.12 This table lists the chemical formulas of some common substances.

Figure It Out

1. What kinds of elements are in aspirin? How many of each kind of atom are in one molecule of aspirin?

2. Describe a mixture that you could make using two or more substances from the table.

Chemists often group solutions into one of two groups based on how they react with water. The two groups are called acids and bases. Lemon juice, vinegar, ammonia, and drain cleaner are all common solutions. Lemon juice and vinegar are acids. When mixed with water, acids break down and release hydrogen ions (H^+). Ammonia and drain cleaner are bases. When mixed with water, bases break down and release hydroxide ions (OH^-).

Acids and bases are used every day. Stomach acids help to digest food. Liquid soap is a base. The only solution that is not an acid or a base is water that has been purified. This water is called distilled water and is a neutral solution.

The pH Scale

Scientists use a scale called a pH scale to describe the strengths of acids and bases. The pH scale goes from 0 to 14. Distilled water is in the middle of the scale. It has a pH of 7. Anything with a pH of less than 7 is an acid. Stronger acids have lower pH values. Anything with a pH of more than 7 is a base. Stronger bases have higher pH values.

Many scientists need to measure the pH values of materials to perform their jobs. A food chemist might measure the pH of a new kind of juice drink to make sure it is not too acidic. A botanist might measure the pH of soil to determine what kinds of plants would grow best in it. A biologist might measure the pH of a lake to figure out whether a certain kind of fish could live there. Scientists often use pH paper or a pH probe to measure pH. These tools can also be used to measure the pH values of solutions in science class.

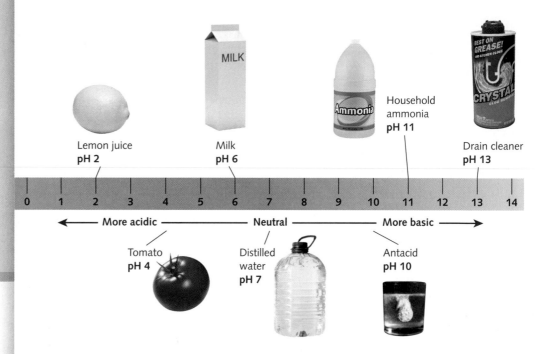

Figure 3.13 The pH values of some common materials are shown on this scale.

After You Read

1. Using the predictions and notes you wrote in your Science Notebook, compare and contrast the three main kinds of chemical bonds.

2. Describe the difference between a compound and a mixture.

3. The chemical formula for a molecule of table sugar is $C_{12}H_{22}O_{11}$. Explain what information this formula tells you about the atoms in the molecule.

3.3 Changes in Matter

Learning Goals

- Compare and contrast physical changes and chemical changes.
- Describe how matter changes state.
- Explain how chemical reactions change matter.
- State the law of conservation of mass.

New Vocabulary

chemical reaction
reactant
product
law of conservation of mass

Before You Read

Make a T-chart in your Science Notebook. Write *Physical Changes* on one side. Write *Chemical Changes* on the other side. Write anything you already know about these kinds of changes on the T-chart.

Suppose that someone gave you a piece of paper and asked you to change it in some way. What would you do? You could rip it into pieces, fold it into a paper airplane, or burn it in a fire. All of these things would make the paper look different. Only one, however, would actually change the molecules that make up the paper.

Changes in Matter

Matter occurs on Earth in three states—solid, liquid, or gas. There are two basic kinds of changes that can happen to matter. The first is a physical change. When matter goes through a physical change, the matter changes in some way, but the molecules of the matter do not change. Ripping and folding paper are examples of physical changes. The paper gets smaller after it is ripped. It looks different after it is folded, but it is still paper. None of the molecules have changed. There are many other examples of physical changes in everyday life. Breaking glass, melting ice, and grinding chalk into powder are all examples of physical changes.

The second kind of change that can happen to matter is a chemical change. When matter goes through a chemical change, new molecules are formed. Burning paper is an example of a chemical change. After the paper is burned, it is no longer paper. The molecules in the paper combine with molecules in the air to form different compounds. Many chemical changes take place in everyday life. Examples include rusting iron, baking bread, and digesting food.

Figure 3.14 The wood is changing in both photos. Which photo shows a physical change? Which photo shows a chemical change? How can you tell?

Changes in State

A common and important kind of physical change to matter on Earth is a change in state. A change in state occurs when matter goes from one state to another. Lake water freezing, ice cubes melting, and a rain puddle evaporating are all examples of changes in state. In order to understand how changes in state occur, you should first understand how the atoms and molecules of matter are arranged in each state.

Solids   Rubber bands, plastic wrap, and wood are all solid at room temperature. The atoms or molecules that make up solids are packed together very tightly. They are fixed in place and cannot move freely. All solids have a definite shape and a definite volume.

Liquids   Water, orange juice, and olive oil are all liquid at room temperature. The atoms or molecules in a liquid are not packed together as tightly as they are in a solid. The atoms or molecules move freely among themselves in the liquid state. For this reason, liquids do not have a definite shape. They do, however, have a definite volume. This is because the atoms or molecules in a liquid do not have enough energy to move far apart from one another.

Figure 3.15 Gases do not have a definite shape or volume. The helium in these balloons takes the shape of the balloon. These helium balloons rise because the helium inside them is lighter than the surrounding air.

Gases Hydrogen, helium, and oxygen are all gases at room temperature. The atoms and molecules in gases are not packed together tightly at all. They can move freely throughout the entire space that is available to them. For this reason, gases do not have a definite shape or a definite volume.

When matter is warmer than absolute zero (−273 K), its atoms are in a constant state of vibration. How fast they are vibrating determines the state they are in. For matter to change state, the movement of its atoms or molecules must change. This can happen if energy is added to or removed from the matter. It can also happen if the pressure around the matter changes.

Adding Energy One way to add energy to matter is to heat it. Adding heat energy to matter makes the atoms or molecules in the matter move faster. If enough heat energy is added to a solid, its atoms or molecules will break out of their fixed positions and will start to move around one another. Most solids will turn into liquids. If more heat energy is added, the atoms or molecules in the liquid will move even faster. Eventually, they will have enough energy to break free from one another and move around in whatever space is available to them. This is what happens when a liquid turns into a gas.

Removing Energy Removing heat energy from matter makes its atoms or molecules move more slowly. If enough heat energy is removed from a gas, it will turn into a liquid. If enough heat energy is removed from a liquid, it will turn into a solid.

As You Read

Add information about changes in state to the *Physical Changes* column of your T-chart. Write one or two sentences below the chart to explain why a change in state is a physical change. Share your chart with a partner. Add or correct any necessary information.

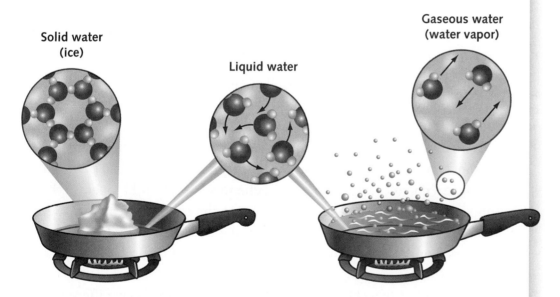

Solid water (ice)

Liquid water

Gaseous water (water vapor)

Figure 3.16 Adding heat to ice causes it to melt. When water boils, it changes into water vapor.

Changing Pressure   Pressure is a force that pushes on something. Changes in pressure can also cause matter to change state. An increase in pressure forces the atoms or molecules in the matter to move closer together. This can cause a gas to change into a liquid or a liquid to change into a solid. A decrease in pressure allows the atoms or molecules in the matter to spread farther apart. This can cause a solid to change into a liquid or a liquid to change into a gas.

It is important to remember that any change in the state of matter is a physical change. The atoms or molecules that make up the matter do not change. They might be closer together and move more slowly, or they might be farther apart and move more quickly, but they do not become new substances.

Figure 3.17 Some fire extinguishers contain liquid carbon dioxide. Carbon dioxide is normally a gas at room temperature. But high pressure inside the fire extinguisher forces the carbon dioxide molecules to move close together. This keeps the carbon dioxide in liquid form while it is inside the extinguisher. As soon as the carbon dioxide is released into the air, it turns back into a gas.

Chemical Changes

Unlike physical changes, chemical changes do turn matter into something new. Another name for a chemical change is a chemical reaction. A **chemical reaction** is a process during which one or more substances are turned into one or more new substances. The original substances are called **reactants**. The new substances are called **products**.

Before a chemical reaction begins, chemical bonds hold together the atoms or molecules of the reactants. During the chemical reaction, these bonds are rearranged. The atoms are combined in new ways to make the products. For example, hydrogen (H) plus oxygen (O) combine to make water (H_2O).

The products of a chemical reaction can have completely different properties than the reactants. For example, hydrogen and oxygen are usually gases at room temperature. Both catch fire easily. But a chemical reaction between the two gases can form water—a liquid that is used to put out fires.

Chemical Equations

A chemical equation is a quick, easy way to show the reactants and products that are involved in a chemical reaction. The reactants are listed on one side of the equation. The products are listed on the other side. An arrow points from the reactants to the products.

The chemical equation for the reaction between hydrogen and oxygen is $2H_2 + O_2 \rightarrow 2H_2O$. The two in front of the H_2 means that two molecules of hydrogen are involved in the reaction. Since there is no number in front of the O_2, only one molecule of oxygen is involved.

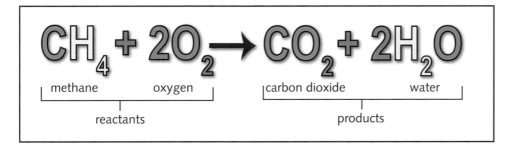

methane   oxygen   carbon dioxide   water

reactants   products

Figure 3.18 This chemical equation shows what happens when methane combines with oxygen. How many molecules of water are formed in the reaction?

Conservation of Mass

Notice that the same kinds of atoms are listed on both sides of a chemical equation. The number of each kind of atom is also the same on both sides. No atoms are destroyed, and no new atoms are created. The **law of conservation of mass** states that mass cannot be created or destroyed during a chemical reaction. One of the first scientists to investigate the idea behind this law was Antoine Lavoisier (1743–1794), who is discussed in Chapter 1. He did many experiments with chemical reactions, during which he compared the total mass of the reactants to the total mass of the products. He found that the two masses were always the same. The law of conservation of mass is sometimes called Lavoisier's law.

Figure It Out

1. How many atoms are on the reactants side of the equation? How many atoms are on the products side of the equation?

2. How can you tell that this equation represents a chemical change?

After You Read

1. Review the information in your T-chart. In your Science Notebook, write a well-developed paragraph that compares and contrasts physical changes and chemical changes. Include at least one example of each kind of change.

2. Describe how chemical reactions change matter.

3. State the law of conservation of mass and explain what it means.

KEY CONCEPTS

3.1 Earth's Elements

- Matter is anything that has mass and takes up space.
- All matter is made up of elements. An element is a substance that cannot be broken down into simpler substances by normal physical or chemical means.
- An atom is the smallest unit of an element that has all of the characteristics of that element.
- The three basic particles that make up atoms are protons, neutrons, and electrons.
- All of the elements are organized in the periodic table of the elements.

3.2 How Atoms Combine

- When atoms form chemical bonds with other atoms, they become more stable. The three main kinds of chemical bonds are covalent bonds, ionic bonds, and metallic bonds.
- Two or more atoms that are held together by covalent bonds are called molecules.
- Matter can be classified into three groups: elemental matter, compounds, and mixtures.
- Chemical formulas list the number and kind of atoms in elements and compounds.

3.3 Changes in Matter

- Physical changes and chemical changes are the two basic kinds of changes that can happen to matter.
- The atoms and molecules of matter do not turn into new substances during a physical change.
- New substances are formed during a chemical change. Another name for a chemical change is a chemical reaction.
- Chemical equations describe the reactants and products involved in chemical reactions.
- The law of conservation of mass states that mass cannot be created or destroyed during a normal chemical reaction.

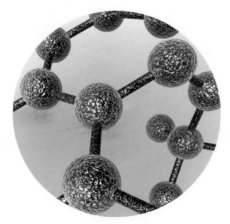

VOCABULARY REVIEW

Write each term in a complete sentence or write a paragraph relating several terms.

3.1
matter, p. 36
element, p.36
atom, p. 37
proton, p. 37
neutron, p. 37
electron, p. 37
nucleus, p. 38
atomic number, p. 39
atomic mass, p. 39
ion, p. 39
isotope, p. 39

3.2
chemical bond, p. 41
covalent bond, p. 42
molecule, p. 42
ionic bond, p. 43
metallic bond, p. 43
elemental matter, p. 44
compound, p. 44
mixture, p. 44

3.3
chemical reaction, p. 50
reactant, p. 50
product, p. 50
law of conservation of mass,
  p. 51

PREPARE FOR CHAPTER TEST

To prepare for the chapter test, create a question from each Learning Goal. Use the information in your Science Notebook to answer each question. Then use these answers to write a well-developed essay about the chapter. Use the Key Concept on the first page of this chapter as your topic sentence.

True or False

If the statement is true, write "true." If it is false, change the underlined word or words to make the statement true.

1. The <u>nucleus</u> is the smallest unit of an element that has all of the characteristics of that element.

2. Elements in the rows of the periodic table are arranged by <u>atomic number</u>.

3. The two kinds of chemical bonds in which atoms share electrons are covalent bonds and <u>ionic bonds</u>.

4. Materials that contain two or more different elements that are chemically combined are called <u>mixtures</u>.

5. An ice cube melting and turning into liquid water is an example of a <u>physical change</u>.

6. The number of atoms on one side of a chemical equation is always <u>equal to</u> the number of atoms on the other side.

Short Answer

Answer each of the following in a sentence or brief paragraph.

7. How does a change in the number of electrons or neutrons change an atom?

8. List the kinds of basic information that is provided in the periodic table.

9. Describe the three main kinds of chemical bonds.

10. Why is oxygen gas—which is made up of two oxygen molecules—considered elemental matter rather than a compound?

11. Explain two different ways to make matter change from one state to another.

12. How did Antoine Lavoisier investigate the idea behind the law of conservation of mass?

Critical Thinking

Use what you have learned in this chapter to answer each of the following.

13. **Analyze** Do you think the way that the periodic table is organized makes sense? What aspect(s) of the organization do you find useful? What aspect(s) do you find confusing?

14. **Infer** One atom has an extra electron in its outermost energy level. Another atom needs one more electron to fill its outermost energy level. What kind of chemical bond do you think might form between the two atoms? Explain your answer.

15. **Design** A friend of yours thinks that turning liquid water into ice is a chemical change rather than a physical change. Design a one-page flyer that explains why your friend is mistaken. The flyer should include a written description and illustrations.

Standardized Test Question

Choose the letter of the response that correctly answers the question.

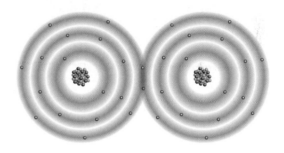

16. What type of chemical bond is illustrated in this diagram?

   A. electron bond

   B. covalent bond

   C. ionic bond

   D. metallic bond

Test-Taking Tip

Circle key words in difficult questions to help you focus on what the question is asking. If you do not understand a key word and you are allowed, ask the teacher what it means.

Chapter 4

Minerals

KEY CONCEPT All minerals share some characteristics; however, each mineral has its own set of unique properties.

Have you ever played the game 20 Questions? A person thinks of an object and says whether it is an animal, a vegetable, or a mineral. Another person can ask up to 20 questions about the object to try to figure out what it is. In the game, a mineral is anything that is not alive. It is true that no mineral is alive, but in science the word *mineral* has a much more specific meaning. Think about what you already know about minerals. Use what you know to answer the questions below.

Think About Minerals

Take a look at the following list of materials: coal, topaz, peanut, steel, bone, silver, diamond, sugar, quartz, salt. Five of these materials are minerals, and five are not. Can you tell which are which?

- Work with a partner. Make a 5-row table with two columns, one labeled *Mineral* and one labeled *Not Mineral*. Each column should contain five materials from the list.

- In your Science Notebook, explain how you sorted the materials into groups. Try this activity again after you read the chapter to check your answers.

www.scilinks.org
Minerals **Code: WGES04**

54

4.1 What Is a Mineral?

Learning Goals

- Describe the five characteristics of minerals.
- Explain three ways that minerals form.
- Name the eight most common elements in Earth's crust.

New Vocabulary

mineral
inorganic
crystal
magma

Recall Vocabulary

matter, p. 36
element, p. 36
atom, p. 37
compound, p. 44

Before You Read

In your Science Notebook, write the word *Mineral* in the center of a blank page and circle it. Draw a large circle above the word. Draw two large circles below the word. Connect each of the large circles to the center circle.

You know that minerals are not alive. However, just because something is not alive does not mean that it is a mineral. Rubber, cotton, and aluminum are not alive, but they are not minerals either. So what is a mineral? A **mineral** is a naturally formed, inorganic, solid substance that has a definite chemical composition and a crystal structure. Some examples of minerals are gold, pyrite, and graphite.

Characteristics of Minerals

A few billion years ago, it would have been easy to tell whether something was a mineral. Nearly every solid thing on Earth was a mineral or was made up of minerals. Things became more complicated after life-forms evolved. Wood, bones, shells, and other plant and animal matter are now common on Earth. These materials are not minerals. Neither are any of the materials that people make and add to Earth. These days, it can be hard to tell whether something is a mineral. So how can it be done?

Look back at the definition of a mineral. It names five characteristics of minerals. A material with all five of these characteristics is a mineral. A material that is missing one or more of these characteristics is not a mineral. Each characteristic of minerals will now be described in greater detail.

Figure 4.1 You are probably familiar with the mineral graphite. Among other things, it is used to make pencil fillings.

Extend It!

Research why the elements aluminum and silicon are not minerals. Find out whether any minerals contain these elements. Based on your research, explain why you think most minerals are made up of compounds rather than single elements.

Naturally Formed   There are about 3,800 different types of minerals on Earth. All of them are formed in nature. Minerals can form in the ocean, on the ground, or underground. Minerals are not made in laboratories or factories. Steel, concrete, and window glass all have some characteristics of minerals. These materials, however, are not minerals because people make them. There is no place on Earth where steel, concrete, or window glass is formed in nature.

Inorganic   All minerals are **inorganic** (ihn or GA nihk). Substances that are inorganic are not made of plant or animal matter. Minerals are not alive, and have never been part of living things. Coal is not a mineral because it is made from the remains of plants. Bones and teeth are not minerals, because they are formed by living things.

Solid   If something is a liquid or a gas, it is not a mineral. All minerals are solids. Liquids and gases such as oil, water, and oxygen are not minerals. Ice that forms in nature, however, is a mineral.

Definite Chemical Composition   Each type of mineral has a definite chemical composition. This composition is written as a chemical formula. The chemical formula tells what types of elements are in the mineral. About 20 minerals are made up of a single element. Examples are gold (Au), copper (Cu), and diamond (C). The rest of the minerals are made up of compounds. Their chemical formulas give the ratios of the elements that they contain. For example, the mineral hematite contains two iron atoms for every three oxygen atoms. Its chemical formula is Fe_2O_3. You could break hematite into many pieces, but each piece would still have the same ratio of iron atoms to oxygen atoms.

Figure It Out

1. Based on cinnabar's chemical symbol, name the two elements that are present in cinnabar. What is the ratio of these elements within the mineral?

2. What are the two elements that make up the mineral halite? Another name for this mineral is salt. Describe an everyday use for halite.

Cinnabar (HgS)   Halite (NaCl)   Hematite (Fe_2O_3)

Figure 4.2 The chemical formula of a mineral provides information about the elements within it.

Some minerals vary a little in their chemical makeup. Their chemical formulas can reflect this fact. For example, the mineral olivine has the formula $(Mg, Fe)_2SiO_4$. This means that there are two atoms of magnesium *or* two atoms of iron for every group of silicon and oxygen atoms in the mineral. The ratio of magnesium to iron in two samples of olivine might be different. However, this ratio is always within a certain narrow range. The result of this variation is a difference in color. Olivine that contains more magnesium (Mg) is pale yellow-green to olive green in color. Olivine that is richer in iron (Fe) is brownish-green in color.

Crystal Structure A **crystal** (KRIHS tul) is a solid substance whose atoms are arranged in a specific repeating pattern. All minerals have a crystal structure. Sometimes, the crystal structure can be observed by looking at the mineral itself. This is true when a mineral forms in an open space and grows into one large crystal. This single crystal may take the shape of one of the six major crystal systems shown in **Figure 4.3**. Other times, the individual crystals are so small that they can only be seen with magnification. In either case, the atoms that make up the mineral are still arranged in an orderly and repeating pattern.

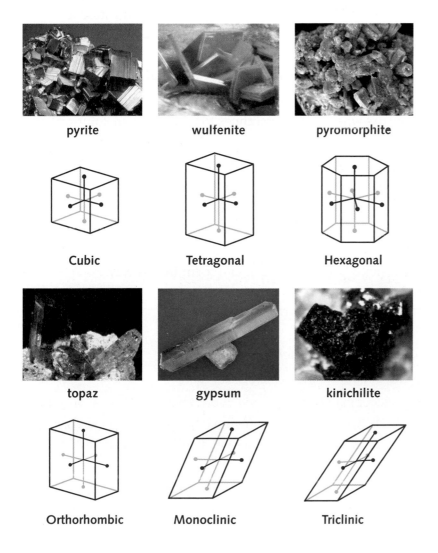

pyrite   wulfenite   pyromorphite

Cubic   Tetragonal   Hexagonal

topaz   gypsum   kinichilite

Orthorhombic   Monoclinic   Triclinic

As You Read

Use what you have learned so far to fill in your concept map about the word *Mineral*.

In one of the large circles, write a definition of the word. In another circle, write a sentence about the word. In the last circle, draw a picture to illustrate the word.

Did You Know?

Some materials, such as opal, have all but one of the characteristics of minerals. They do not, however, have a crystal structure. These materials are known as mineraloids.

Figure 4.3 The shape of a mineral's crystals depends on the way that the atoms are arranged within the mineral.

The Formation of Minerals

There are three main ways that minerals form. They can form through the cooling of magma, through evaporation, or through precipitation.

Cooling of Magma   Minerals can form when magma (MAG muh) cools. **Magma** is melted rock beneath Earth's surface. Magma is a very hot liquid, but it can cool and harden under the right temperature and pressure conditions. This can happen above or below Earth's surface. As magma cools, its atoms begin to move more slowly. Sometimes, they react chemically with one another to form new compounds. The atoms and compounds form mineral crystals as the magma hardens. This is how different minerals form from the same magma. **Figure 4.4** shows the eight most common elements in Earth's outer-most layer, the crust. Most of the minerals in the crust are made up of these elements.

Evaporation   Sometimes minerals are dissolved in liquid water. They are mixed so thoroughly with the water that they are impossible to see. When the water changes state from a liquid to a gas, mineral crystals are left behind. This change in the liquid's state is called evaporation (ih va puh RAY shun). Gypsum is a mineral that can form in this way.

Precipitation   Minerals can also form through a process called precipitation (prih sih puh TAY shun). Precipitation occurs when solid substances form in a liquid solution. How can a solid form in a liquid? The process often starts with a solution of hot water that contains large amounts of dissolved substances. Sometimes, so many substances are dissolved in the water that the liquid cannot hold any more. If more substances are added to the water, crystals can form in the solution. Also, cold water cannot hold as many dissolved substances as hot water. Sometimes crystals form as a hot solution cools. Calcite is a mineral that can form in this way.

Figure It Out

1. Which element makes up almost half the mass of Earth's crust?
2. Make up a mnemonic device to help you remember the eight most common elements in Earth's crust.

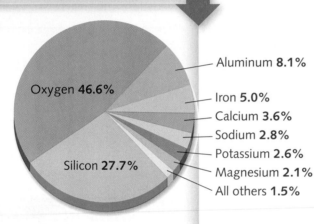

Aluminum **8.1%**

Iron **5.0%**

Calcium **3.6%**

Sodium **2.8%**

Potassium **2.6%**

Magnesium **2.1%**

All others **1.5%**

Oxygen **46.6%**

Silicon **27.7%**

Figure 4.4 Oxygen, silicon, and aluminum are the most abundant elements in Earth's crust.

Figure 4.5 The formations in this cave were made by the precipitation of calcite from water.

After You Read

1. Name and describe five characteristics of minerals.
2. Summarize the three ways that minerals can form.
3. Look at the concept map that you made about the word *Mineral*. In your Science Notebook, write a well-developed paragraph about minerals. Include your own definition of the word and at least three examples of minerals.

4.2 Mineral Identification

Learning Goals

- Name several physical properties of minerals.

- Explain how physical properties can be used to identify minerals.

- Describe how minerals are used.

New Vocabulary

streak
luster
cleavage
fracture
density
specific gravity
hardness
ore
gemstone

Recall Vocabulary

mass, p. 12

Before You Read

Create a K-W-L-S-H chart in your Science Notebook. Write *How to Identify Minerals* at the top of the chart. In the *K* column, write what you already know about how to identify minerals. In the *W* column, write what you want to learn about how to identify minerals.

Look at the two minerals below. One of the minerals is pyrite, and the other is gold. It is difficult to tell which is which. Pyrite is often called "fool's gold" because it looks like gold. Pyrite is common, while gold is rare. This makes pyrite worth much less than gold. During the Gold Rush of 1849, many people went to California to look for gold. Newcomers often confused pyrite with gold. Those with experience could easily tell the difference, even though the minerals look so similar. How could they do this? They knew the properties of pyrite and gold.

Figure 4.6 Two different minerals are shown here. Although their colors are similar, their other properties are very different.

Properties of Minerals

Each mineral has a unique set of physical properties. Examining a single property, however, is not usually enough to identify a mineral. Both pyrite and gold have a brassy yellow color, so additional properties must be studied in order to tell them apart. It turns out that color is one of the only things that the two minerals have in common. Gold is softer and denser than pyrite. The two minerals break in different ways. Their powder is different colors. These differences can be used to tell a sample of pyrite from a sample of gold. This lesson discusses how to use some common physical properties to identify pyrite, gold, and many other minerals.

Color   The easiest property to identify is a mineral's color. Color alone, however, is not enough to identify a mineral. Many minerals, such as pyrite and gold, have similar colors. Also, different samples of the same mineral can be different colors. For example, quartz can be many colors, including white, pink, and gray. There are a few minerals that have unique colors. In most cases, however, color alone is not enough to identify a mineral.

Streak   The outside color of a mineral might not help much with identification, but sometimes another kind of color can be useful. **Streak** is the color of a mineral when it is ground into a fine powder. Every mineral has a characteristic streak. If a mineral is rubbed across a hard white surface, the mark that it leaves behind is its streak. A mineral's streak is not related to the outside color of the mineral. Pyrite's streak is always greenish black, and gold's streak is always yellowish. Comparing the streaks of these two minerals is a good way to tell them apart. If two minerals have the same color and the same streak, other properties must be used to tell them apart.

Luster   Another useful visual property of minerals is **luster**. Luster is the shininess of a mineral. It is a description of how well the mineral reflects light. Scientists use words such as *metallic, glassy,* and *dull* to describe luster. A mineral with a metallic luster is very shiny. Both gold and pyrite have metallic lusters. A mineral with a glassy luster has the shininess of broken glass. Clear quartz crystals have a glassy luster. A mineral with a dull luster does not reflect light very well at all. Calcite and some hematite have dull lusters. **Figure 4.8** shows more examples of minerals and their lusters.

Figure 4.7 An unglazed, white porcelain tile is often used as a streak plate. Streaks of pyrite and gold are shown on the streak plate above. Which streak belongs to pyrite? Which belongs to gold?

 Explain It!

In your Science Notebook, explain why only looking at the color of a mineral is not the best way to identify it. What else should be done to properly identify a mineral?

Diamond

Turquoise

Talc

Figure 4.8 Diamond has a brilliant luster. Turquoise has a greasy or waxy luster. Talc has a pearly luster.

Cleavage and Fracture   Examining the broken sides and edges of a mineral can sometimes help to identify it. The way that atoms are arranged in a mineral can affect how the mineral breaks. Some of the bonds that hold the atoms together are weaker than other bonds. Minerals tend to break where the bonds are weakest. A mineral has **cleavage** (KLEE vihj) if it breaks smoothly and evenly along one or more planes of weakly bonded atoms. Mica is a mineral that has cleavage along one plane. It breaks easily into smooth sheets. A mineral has **fracture** (FRAK chur) if it breaks in random places. Some minerals have smooth, curved fractures. Other minerals, such as quartz, have sharp, splintery fractures.

Density   The arrangement of the atoms in a mineral can also affect the mineral's **density** (DEN suh tee). Density is a measure of the mass per unit volume of a material. The density of a mineral is related to the mass of its atoms and how tightly the atoms are packed together. Think about diamond and graphite. Both are made of carbon, but the atoms in diamond are packed together more closely than the atoms in graphite. Diamond is therefore denser than graphite.

Specific Gravity   Sometimes it is helpful to compare the density of a material to the density of a common substance. **Specific gravity** is the ratio of a material's density to the density of water. The specific gravity of gold is 19.3. The specific gravity of water is 1. This means that a bucket of gold would be almost 20 times heavier than the same size bucket of water. The specific gravity of pyrite is 6.5. A bucket of pyrite would also be heavier than a bucket of water. It would not, however, be as heavy as a bucket of gold.

As You Read

In the column labeled *L* in your K-W-L-S-H chart, write three or four important things that you have learned about how to identify minerals.

Explain why it might be useful to look at more than one physical property when trying to identify a mineral.

Explore It!

Your teacher will give you several mineral samples. First, determine the hardness of each sample. Next, describe the color and luster of each sample. Then, use a streak plate to determine the streak of each sample. Also, observe whether each sample appears to have cleavage or fracture. Use a mineral identification chart to try to identify each of the samples.

a

b

Figure 4.9 a) Mica cleaves into thin, flexible sheets. All of the sheets are parallel to one another, as in a stack of paper. **b)** Sulfur breaks with a conchoidal (kahn KOY dul) fracture that makes smooth, curved surfaces shaped like the inside of a shell.

The Iron Age was an important period in history that began more than 2,500 years ago. During this period, people started to use iron to make most of their tools and weapons. They got the iron from heating iron ores such as hematite. Iron tools helped make farming easier. Iron weapons changed the way wars were fought. Iron is still very important today. It is used to build cars, bridges, and many other objects.

Hardness   The **hardness** of a mineral is a measure of how well it resists being scratched. Soft minerals, such as talc, are easy to scratch. Hard minerals, such as quartz, are difficult to scratch. In 1812, a German scientist, Friedrich Mohs (1773–1839), devised a scale to compare the hardness of various minerals. The Mohs hardness scale ranks the hardness of ten minerals from 1 to 10. Talc has a hardness of 1. It can be scratched by all of the other minerals on the scale. Diamond has a hardness of 10. It can scratch all of the other minerals on the scale. None of the other minerals can scratch diamond. **Figure 4.10** shows the hardness of all ten minerals. It also shows the hardness of some common objects. You can use these objects to estimate the hardness of any mineral.

Uses of Minerals

A good field guide to minerals describes the physical properties of many minerals. Sometimes it also gives examples of how people use each mineral. You use products made from minerals every day. Pencils, cars, coins, glass, and computers are only a few of the many objects that contain minerals.

Ores   The minerals in most everyday objects come from ores. An **ore** is a material that can be removed from the ground for a profit. All ores contain at least one valuable mineral. After an ore is removed from the ground, it is often crushed. The valuable minerals in the ore are then removed using heat, electricity, or chemicals. Many of the metals that you use every day come from ores. For example, aluminum is present in an ore called bauxite. Aluminum is used in many objects, including soda cans, the metal rings on pencils, and aluminum foil.

Figure It Out

1. What is the hardness of a mineral that can scratch an iron nail but cannot scratch a glass plate?

2. Explain the advantages and disadvantages of using only your fingernail, a copper penny, an iron nail, a glass plate, and a steel file to estimate the hardness of a mineral.

Mohs Hardness Scale

Reference Mineral	Hardness
diamond	10
corundum	9
topaz	8
quartz	7
feldspar	6
apatite	5
fluorite	4
calcite	3
gypsum	2
talc	1

Figure 4.10 The approximate hardness of some common materials are compared with those of the minerals on the Mohs hardness scale.

steel file (6.5)
glass plate (5.5)
iron nail (4.5)
copper penny (3.5)
fingernail (2.5)

PEOPLE IN SCIENCE Kinichi Sakurai   1912–1993

Kinichi Sakurai was born in Tokyo, Japan, in 1912. He began collecting minerals as a child, and his interest in minerals remained strong as he got older. In 1950, Sakurai earned a PhD in mineralogy—the study of minerals.

Over the years, Sakurai discovered and wrote about several new minerals. He helped to write a book called *Minerals of Japan,* and he never stopped collecting minerals. By the time he died, Sakurai had collected more than 15,000 mineral samples.

One of the most amazing things about Sakurai is that he did not make his living as a mineralogist. His main job was to manage his family's chicken restaurant. He collected minerals as a hobby. All the same, Sakurai was well respected. There are only a few people, including Sakurai, who have minerals named after both their first and last names. In 1965, the mineral sakuraiite was named after his last name. In 1981, the mineral kinichilite was named after his first name. Sakurai died in 1993. His collection of minerals is now located at the National Science Museum in Tokyo.

Gemstones   Most minerals are valued for their usefulness, but some are valued for other reasons. Minerals that are valued for their beauty, durability, and rarity are called **gemstones**. Examples of gemstones include beryl, diamond, and topaz. These minerals are often cut and polished for use in jewelry. Some gemstones are also used for other purposes. For example, diamonds that are not of gem quality are commonly used to coat saws, drills, and other cutting tools. These tools can cut through almost anything.

Did You Know?

Diamond is the hardest natural substance on Earth. It is much harder than corundum, the next hardest mineral on the Mohs hardness scale. The Mohs scale is not linear. If it were, the hardness of diamond would be about 42.

Figure 4.11 Gemstones come in a wide variety of colors.

After You Read

1. Name several physical properties of minerals.

2. Look at the K-W-L-S-H chart in your Science Notebook. Use the information in the *K, W,* and *L* columns to write a paragraph about how to identify minerals. Complete the chart by filling in the *S* and *H* columns. In the *S* column, write what you would still like to know about mineral identification. In the *H* column, write how you can find this information. Be specific.

3. Describe at least three uses for minerals.

Summary

KEY CONCEPTS

4.1 What Is a Mineral?

- A mineral is a naturally formed, inorganic, solid substance that has a definite chemical composition and a crystal structure.
- Minerals form when magma cools and crystallizes. Different minerals can form from the same magma.
- Minerals form from the evaporation of liquids. They also form when solids precipitate from solutions.
- The eight most common elements in Earth's crust are oxygen, silicon, aluminum, iron, calcium, sodium, potassium, and magnesium. Most of the minerals in Earth's crust are made up of these elements.

4.2 Mineral Identification

- Some of the physical properties of minerals include color, streak, luster, cleavage, fracture, density, specific gravity, and hardness.
- Physical properties are useful for identifying minerals.
- Many of the minerals that you use every day come from ores.
- Gemstones are minerals that are valued for their beauty, durability, and rarity.

VOCABULARY REVIEW

Write each term in a complete sentence, or write a paragraph relating several terms.

4.1
mineral, p. 55
inorganic, p. 56
crystal, p. 57
magma, p. 58

4.2
streak, p. 60
luster, p. 60
cleavage, p. 61
fracture, p. 61
density, p. 61
specific gravity, p. 61
hardness, p. 62
ore, p. 62
gemstone, p. 63

PREPARE FOR CHAPTER TEST

To prepare for the chapter test, create a question from each Learning Goal. Use the information in your Science Notebook to answer each question. Then use these answers to write a well-developed essay about the chapter. Use the Key Concept on the first page of this chapter as your topic sentence.

True or False
If the statement is true, write "true." If it is false, change the underlined word or words to make the statement true.

1. All minerals are formed in <u>factories</u>.

2. The chemical composition of a mineral is written as a chemical <u>equation</u>.

3. Mineral crystals can form when water <u>evaporates</u> from a solution that contains dissolved minerals.

4. <u>Luster</u> is the color of a mineral when it is ground into a fine powder.

5. You can use a fingernail to scratch any mineral that has a hardness of <u>less than</u> 2.5.

6. An ore is a material that is made up of one or more valuable <u>gemstones</u>.

Short Answer
Answer each of the following in a sentence or brief paragraph.

7. Name the five characteristics of minerals.

8. Explain why coal is not a mineral.

9. Compare and contrast the formation of minerals through evaporation with the formation of minerals through precipitation.

10. Explain why color is often not the best physical property to use when trying to identify a mineral.

11. Describe at least three ways that you could tell the difference between a sample of pyrite and a sample of gold.

12. How is a mineral's density different from its specific gravity?

Critical Thinking
Use what you have learned in this chapter to answer each of the following.

13. **Evaluate** Salt and sugar look similar. Explain why one is a mineral and the other is not.

14. **Infer** A typical streak plate has a hardness of about 7. A diamond has a hardness of 10. What do you think would happen if you tried to use a streak plate to find the streak of diamond? Explain your answer.

15. **Analyze** Why do you think a mineral must be beautiful, durable, and rare to be considered a gemstone?

Standardized Test Question
Choose the letter of the response that correctly answers the question.

Mohs Hardness Scale	
Reference Mineral	**Hardness**
diamond	10
corundum	9
topaz	8
quartz	7
feldspar	6
apatite	5
fluorite	4
calcite	3
gypsum	2
talc	1

16. An unknown mineral can scratch quartz. Diamond can scratch the unknown mineral. According to the Mohs hardness scale, which of the following could be the hardness of the unknown mineral?

   A. 2

   B. 4

   C. 6

   D. 8

Test-Taking Tip

After you read a multiple-choice question, answer it in your head before reading the choices provided. This way the choices will not confuse or trick you.

Chapter 5

Rocks

KEY CONCEPT Rocks are mixtures of minerals that change in structure and composition over time.

Imagine your family is driving across the wheat fields of South Dakota. The land is flat as far as you can see. After a nap, you wake up to see the landscape pictured above. The Badlands of western South Dakota were shaped by wind, water, and gravity.

Many of Earth's resources go through cycles. Water moves from the ocean to the air to the land and back to the ocean again. Nitrogen in the air is removed by bacteria, used by plants, and released back into the air. Rocks go through their own cycle of changes over thousands of years.

Think About Cycles

Think of something in your home that goes through a cycle. Laundry and dishes are two possible examples.

- What are the steps in the cycle you have chosen? What would happen in your home if the cycle you have chosen were to stop?

- Write a paragraph in your Science Notebook explaining what you think would happen if the natural cycles of Earth's resources were to stop.

www.scilinks.org

Rocks **Code: WGES05**

5.1 Earth's Rock Types

Learning Goals

- Explain the processes by which rocks are formed and shaped.

- Explain how scientists classify rocks.

Before You Read

Reword the Learning Goals in this lesson to form questions. Write the questions in your Science Notebook. Leave several blank lines below each question to take notes as you read the lesson.

New Vocabulary

rock
igneous rock
sediment
sedimentary rock
metamorphic rock
composition
texture

Recall Vocabulary

mineral, p. 55
crystal, p. 57
ore, p. 62

Earth's crust is made of rock, from the highest mountains to the deepest parts of the ocean floor. A **rock** is a naturally occurring solid mixture of one or more minerals. Some rocks contain fossils, which are the remains of animals and plants. In other words, rocks may contain minerals and the remains of animal or plant life. Thousands of different types of rocks exist. Most of these rocks are millions of years old. Others have formed more recently. The structure and composition of rocks provide clues to the processes that formed them.

Humans have used rocks for many thousands of years. Early humans relied on rock caves for shelter. They later learned to construct tools and homes from rocks. Today, people continue to use rocks for construction, art, fuel, and jewelry. Scientists use clues in rocks to learn about Earth's history and the history of the solar system. The fossils in some rocks also provide clues about life on Earth millions of years ago.

Did You Know?

Like humans, some animals make tools from rocks. They use these tools to help them get food. For example, sea otters carry rocks that they use to crack open sea urchin shells. Egyptian vultures drop stones onto ostrich eggs to break them open.

Figure 5.1 People have used rocks for tools, art, and building materials for thousands of years. Look at the photographs. What other uses for rocks can you think of?

Types of Rocks

Rocks are classified based on how they form. The three main types of rocks are igneous, sedimentary, and metamorphic. An example of each rock type is shown in **Figure 5.2**. Rocks beneath Earth's surface are squeezed by the weight of the rocks above them. The temperature deep inside Earth can be high enough to cause rocks to melt and become magma. Rocks that form when magma cools and crystallizes are called **igneous** (IHG nee us) **rocks**. They might form below Earth's surface or on Earth's surface. Where they form depends on the location of the melted rock.

Most sedimentary rocks are formed from rock particles that have been transported away from their source and deposited by wind and water. These particles are called **sediment**. Sediment might also include bits of dead organisms and the shells of sea animals. Over time, as layers of sediment build up, they are cemented together to form **sedimentary rocks**. These layers are called strata (singular: stratum).

Metamorphic rocks are formed when extreme heat, pressure, or chemical reactions change existing rocks into new rocks. The new rocks usually differ from the original rocks in their physical and chemical properties.

As You Read

As you read, take notes that will help you answer the questions you wrote in your Science Notebook. Include the vocabulary terms in your notes. As you are able, answer each question. Compare your answers to a partner's and make any corrections or additions that are needed.

What is one difference between rocks and minerals?

a

Figure 5.2

a) Granite is an igneous rock that forms when magma crystallizes below Earth's surface.

b

b) Sandstone is a sedimentary rock that forms wherever sand-sized sediment is laid down, buried, and cemented together.

c

c) Gneiss is a metamorphic rock that forms when granite is exposed to high pressure and temperature.

Composition and Texture

Rocks are classified into the three main types—igneous, sedimentary, and metamorphic—based on how they form. Each of these main types of rock is divided into even smaller groups based on differences in composition and texture. The **composition** of a rock refers to the minerals in it. For example, granite is composed of the minerals quartz, feldspar, and biotite mica. The rocks in **Figure 5.3** show how mineral composition affects the appearance of individual rocks.

The **texture** refers to the sizes, shapes, and positions of the grains that make up a rock. Texture provides clues about how and where a rock formed. Within each major rock type, texture refers to a slightly different physical property. The rock samples in **Figure 5.4** each show a different texture. A trained geologist can often tell how a rock was formed by looking at its texture.

Figure 5.3 Mineral composition is what makes individual rocks distinct. **a)** Gabbro is composed of the dark minerals pyroxene, amphibole, and plagioclase feldspar. **b)** Marble is composed of calcite. **c)** This sandstone is composed mainly of quartz.

Figure 5.4 a) Conglomerate (kun GLAHM rut) has a coarse texture. **b)** Schist (SHIHST) has a layered texture. **c)** Some basalt has holes that give it a vesicular texture.

Figure It Out

1. Which rock looks like it is made of pieces of sediment that have been cemented together?

2. Describe how you think the holes in the basalt came to be there.

After You Read

1. Review the questions and answers you wrote in your Science Notebook. Use the information from the lesson and your Science Notebook to describe how you think materials that make up rocks below Earth's surface eventually appear at Earth's surface.

2. What is the difference between a rock's composition and its texture?

3. Explain how a rock made of one mineral might be different from a rock made of more than one mineral.

Learning Goals

- Describe how igneous rock forms.
- Explain how texture and mineral composition are used to classify igneous rocks.
- Compare and contrast extrusive and intrusive igneous rocks.

New Vocabulary

extrusive igneous rock
intrusive igneous rock

Recall Vocabulary

magma, p. 58
density, p. 61

5.2 Igneous Rocks

Before You Read

Create a concept map for the lesson in your Science Notebook. Begin by writing *Igneous rocks* in a large circle. Draw several smaller circles around this circle and connect each small circle to the center circle with a line. Then look at the pictures and subheadings in this lesson. Predict what you will write in the smaller circles of your concept map.

Magma

Most rocks melt when they are heated to temperatures of 800°C to 1,200°C. The heat in Earth's upper mantle and lower crust reaches these temperatures. Scientists think that the heat below Earth's surface is left over from the time of Earth's formation and from the decay of radioactive elements within Earth. Magma, or melted rock, may remain underground or it might rise to Earth's surface through volcanoes. Magma that cools and crystallizes becomes igneous rock. The type of igneous rock formed depends on the composition of the magma and the time it takes for the magma to cool and become solid.

Magma Composition   Rocks contain a mixture of minerals. Each mineral, made up of different elements, has a specific melting point. As the temperature of rock increases, more and more minerals melt into magma. However, the temperature of the magma may never get high enough to melt all of the minerals. **Figure 5.6** shows what happens when an igneous rock does not completely melt into magma. The magma will have a chemical composition different from that of the original rock. When this magma cools and crystallizes, the new igneous rock will have a mineral composition that is different from the original rock. This is one way that different types of igneous rocks form.

Figure 5.5 Lava is magma that flows out of Earth's surface. When lava cools, it solidifies and forms igneous rock. This lava is cooling and crystallizing into basalt.

Figure 5.6 a) When rock melts into magma, minerals with high melting points may remain solid. **b)** Magma is often a mixture of crystals and liquid.

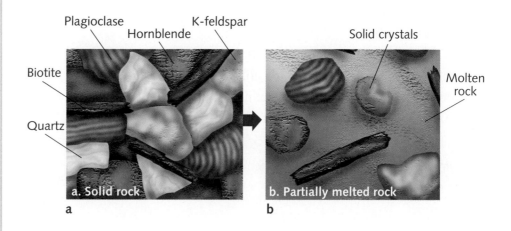

Plagioclase   Hornblende   K-feldspar

Biotite

Quartz

a. Solid rock

a

Solid crystals

Molten rock

b. Partially melted rock

b

Classifying Igneous Rock

Geologists classify igneous rocks based on two physical properties: texture and mineral composition. Both of these physical properties are combined to assign names to the various types of igneous rocks.

Texture In igneous rocks, the size of individual crystals and the rocks' physical appearance describe their texture. Igneous rocks are broadly classified as either extrusive or intrusive. **Extrusive igneous rocks** form from molten material that has cooled and crystallized close to or on Earth's surface. Contact with air or water causes molten material to cool rapidly. This rapid cooling does not allow time for large crystals to form. As a result, the texture of extrusive igneous rocks is fine-grained, meaning they contain small crystals.

Magma that pushes into surrounding rocks and crystallizes underground forms **intrusive igneous rock**. Because the surrounding underground rock insulates the magma, it cools slowly. This slow cooling provides time for large, visible crystals to form. As a result, intrusive rocks have coarse-grained textures. This means they contain large mineral crystals. Intrusive rock formations may be large and contain valuable minerals and gemstones. **Figure 5.8** shows how intrusive and extrusive igneous rocks can be formed during a volcanic eruption.

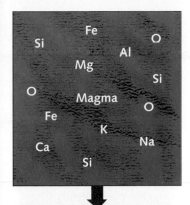
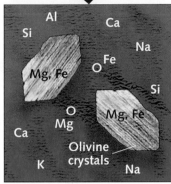

Figure 5.7 When magma begins to cool, minerals with high melting points crystallize first. This causes a change in the chemical composition of the magma. This is another way that different igneous rocks form.

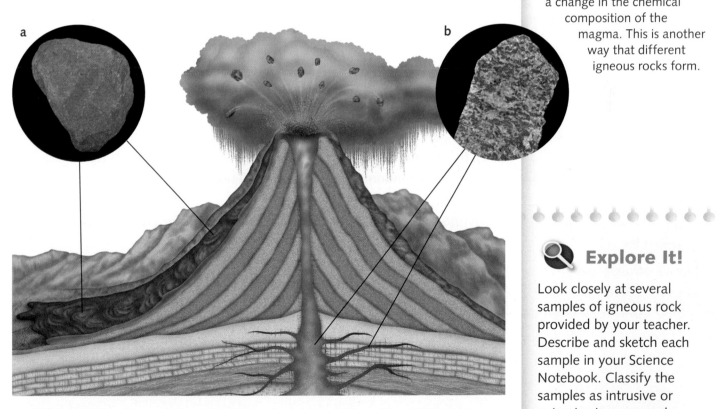

Figure 5.8 a) Extrusive rocks on Earth's surface cool quickly and form fine-grained igneous rocks such as rhyolite. **b)** Intrusive rocks beneath Earth's surface cool slowly and form coarse-grained rocks such as granite.

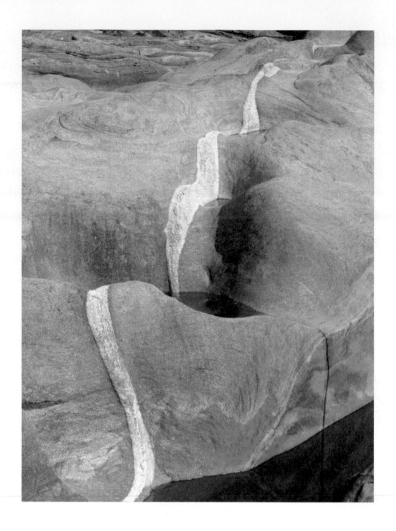

Figure 5.9 Intrusive igneous rocks often cut across rock layers. Because the magma cooled slowly as this rock formed, the crystals in this intrusion are large enough to see with unaided eyes. Weathering and erosion exposed this light-colored intrusive rock.

Rocks such as pumice (PUH mus) and some types of basalt contain holes left by expanding gases. This is called vesicular texture. Pumice can be so full of holes that it floats on water. Rocks made of tiny fragments of volcanic glass and rock, called tuff, are produced when lava is blown out into the atmosphere during violent volcanic eruptions. Lava that cools very quickly contains no crystals at all. This rock has a glassy texture and is called obsidian.

Mineral Composition Geologists describe the color of igneous rocks as ranging from light to dark. Once the minerals in a rock are identified, it is easy to determine the type of igneous rock being examined. **Figure 5.10** shows how this is done. The left-hand side of the chart lists rocks that are light in color—granite, rhyolite, and pegmatite. They contain light-colored minerals such as potassium feldspar, quartz, and white plagioclase feldspar. They also contain smaller amounts of darker minerals. These rocks are referred to as granitic. These rocks make excellent building materials because they are strong and resistant to weathering.

Figure 5.10
Igneous rocks are
classified by their
mineral composition
and crystal size.

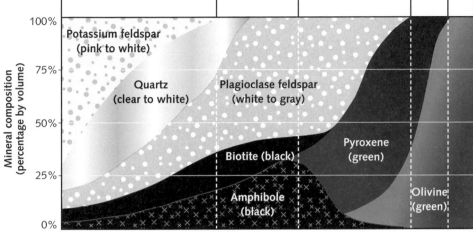

Classification of Igneous Rocks						
	Granitic	Intermediate	Basaltic	Ultrabasic		Texture
Extrusive	obsidian		basaltic glass			glassy (noncrystalline)
	rhyolite	andesite	basalt			fine-grained
Intrusive	granite	diorite	gabbro	peri-dotite	dun-ite	coarse-grained
	pegmatite					very coarse-grained

Mineral composition (percentage by volume)

100%
75%
50%
25%
0%

Potassium feldspar (pink to white)

Quartz (clear to white)

Plagioclase feldspar (white to gray)

Biotite (black)

Pyroxene (green)

Amphibole (black)

Olivine (green)

Figure It Out

1. Which of the rocks cooled slowly? How do you know?

2. What easily distinguishes basaltic rocks from granitic rocks?

The right-hand side of the chart lists dark-colored rocks such as basalt, gabbro, and peridotite. They contain dark minerals such as pyroxene and grey-to-black plagioclase feldspar plus smaller amounts of other dark minerals. They are referred to as basaltic and ultrabasic. Rocks that contain mineral compositions that are in the middle of the chart are called intermediate igneous rocks. Andesite and diorite are intermediate igneous rocks.

CONNECTION: History

The discovery of gold, diamonds, and other precious minerals in rocks is a big part of American history. Gold in California and Alaska brought thousands of miners to these unsettled areas during the 1800s. During the 1970s, a huge deposit of diamonds drew miners to northwestern Canada.

After You Read

1. What determines the type of igneous rock that will form from cooling magma?

2. Review the concept map you created in your Science Notebook. In a group of four students, explain your concept map. Then work with a partner to make additions or corrections to your concept map. Use the information on your updated concept map to describe the major ways that igneous rocks are classified.

3. Would you expect to find large crystals in an extrusive rock? Explain.

Before You Read

Many processes occur in a specific sequence. In your Science Notebook, describe something you do every day that takes place in a series of ordered steps. Create a sequence map in your Science Notebook. Now, imagine doing one of the steps out of order. As you read, pay close attention to the order of events leading to the formation of sedimentary rocks.

Sedimentary Rock Formation

Much of Earth's surface is covered by sediment that has been deposited by wind and water. Sedimentary rocks are formed when sediment becomes compacted and cemented together.

Weathering, Erosion, and Deposition   The formation of sedimentary rocks begins with weathering. Weathering occurs when rocks get broken into pieces by the effects of wind, water, ice, changing temperatures, and gravity. There are two types of weathering: chemical weathering and physical weathering. Physical weathering causes rock to break into smaller pieces, without changing the chemical makeup of the minerals it contains. In contrast, chemical weathering causes the minerals in a rock to dissolve or chemically change in other ways. These two processes are discussed in more detail in Chapters 9 and 10.

Weathered rock particles are transported to new locations by wind, moving water, gravity, and glaciers through the process of erosion. **Deposition** occurs when sediment eventually comes to rest on the ground or sinks to the bottom of bodies of water. Over time, layers of deposited sediment build up on top of one another.

Compaction and Cementation   New layers of sediment may be loosely packed with many air and water pockets. Sediment in lower layers becomes compacted, or squeezed together, due to the increasing weight and pressure of the layers above it. Over time, water seeps through this sediment. **Cementation** occurs when the dissolved minerals in the water form crystals between the grains. This cements the sediment together into solid rock. The minerals in the water determine the type of cement produced. Silica forms silica cement, calcite forms calcite cement, and iron oxide forms hematite cement.

Sedimentary Rock Formation

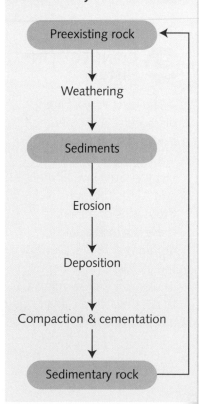

Figure 5.11 This diagram shows how some sedimentary rocks form.

Types of Sedimentary Rocks

Sedimentary rocks are classified based on how they were formed. The three main types of sedimentary rocks are clastic, chemical, and organic.

Clastic Rocks   **Clastic sedimentary rocks** are made of fragments of previously existing rocks. Rock and mineral fragments are called clasts. When clasts become cemented together, they form clastic rocks. Clastic sediment can range in size from tiny particles to huge rocks. **Figure 5.12** shows how clastic rocks are classified by the size of their particles.

Figure 5.12

Classification of Clastic Sediment

Particle Size	Sediment	Rock
>256 mm 256–64 mm 64–2 mm	boulder cobble } gravel pebble	conglomerate
2–0.062 mm	sand	sandstone
0.062–0.0039 mm	silt	siltstone
<0.0039 mm	clay	mudstone or shale

Figure It Out

1. Which type of sediment has the smallest particles? Explain how you know.

2. Which types of clastic rocks are made up of particles smaller than sand?

Chemical Rock   **Chemical sedimentary rocks** are formed when water evaporates from oceans and lakes, leaving behind dissolved minerals. For this reason, chemical sedimentary rocks are also called evaporites. A glass of salt water left on a windowsill can illustrate this process. When the water evaporates, salt crystals are left behind.

Figure 5.13 These spectacular limestone formations built up slowly as water dripped into a cave, evaporated, and deposited minerals.

As You Read

As you read the lesson, record the steps of sedimentary rock formation in the sequence map in your Science Notebook.

Compare and contrast how clastic and chemical rocks form.

Bedding

Fossils

Ripple marks

Mud cracks

Figure 5.14 Geologists use features of sedimentary rock to learn about conditions on Earth long ago.

Organic Rock   **Organic sedimentary rocks** form from the remains of once-living organisms. Limestone is the most common organic sedimentary rock. It forms in the ocean. Limestone is often a mixture of clay-sized calcite particles and the shells of organisms that lived in the sea. When the organisms die, their shells settle to the seafloor, where they become buried by sediment and more shells. Over time, this sediment becomes cemented and forms limestone. **Figure 5.14** shows limestone containing the preserved remains, or fossils, of sea life. Coal is another type of rock that is formed from the remains of living things. It is made from plants that lived millions of years ago.

Features of Sedimentary Rock

The distinct horizontal layers often contained in sedimentary rocks are called **bedding**. These layers can differ from one another depending on the kind, size, and color of their sediment. The rate at which sediment was deposited can also affect the thickness of the layers.

Geologists often look at the individual grains of minerals in sedimentary rock for clues about its formation. For example, a sedimentary rock may contain minerals that commonly occur in granite. This suggests that the pieces that make up the sedimentary rock came from granite that was broken down and weathered. The shape of the grains provides additional information about their history before deposition. Clasts that have traveled a long distance tend to be smaller and rounder.

The effects of wind, water, the Sun, and even raindrops can be preserved in sedimentary rocks. Ripple marks record the motion of wind and water on newly deposited sediment. Cracks in mudstone show that a shallow body of water dried out in the Sun. Raindrops can create small pits in fine-grained sediment. Every detail of a sedimentary rock reveals information about the conditions at the time the sediment was deposited.

Fossils   The preserved remains or traces of organisms that once lived are called **fossils**. Sometimes, when a plant or animal dies, it is buried before it decomposes. Over time, parts of the buried organism may be replaced by minerals and turned into rock. Fossils in sedimentary rock provide scientists with information about plants, animals, and environments of the past. For example, a fossil of coral is evidence of a saltwater environment. Fossils range from bones, teeth, shells, and other hard body parts to footprints, tunnels, and root marks. The ages of fossils tell scientists how long ago the layer of sediment they occur in was deposited.

CONNECTION: Paleontology

During the 1920s, a sheepherder in Utah discovered a large black bone. The bone was clearly not from a sheep. Scientists came to investigate the site, and thousands of dinosaur bones were discovered. This wonderful find raised many questions. What caused the deaths of the dinosaurs? Why were there so many more predators than plant eaters present at the site?

Scientists who study fossils are called paleontologists (pay lee ahn TAH luh justs). They use geologic evidence to help them answer questions about early life. The sedimentary rocks at the Utah site show that it was once a shallow marsh. Ancient floods deposited layers of mud, which eventually became mudstone. Cracks in the mudstone indicate that the area experienced droughts that dried up the water.

One theory suggests that the dinosaurs in this area died during the drought, as indicated by the clues in the mudstone. As the marsh dried up, dinosaurs came to drink in the remaining pools. Predators gathered to eat the easy prey. After the last water disappeared, the predators died, too. Rains returned and flooding covered the dinosaur bones with mud. Preserved in the mud, the bones gradually turned into fossils. Millions of years later, these sedimentary rock features provided a window into the dramas of the past.

Explain It!

In your Science Notebook, write a compelling letter to the governor of your state. Explain why it is important to protect an open area where you and your friends discovered what appears to be a huge fossilized turtle shell. Describe what types of information scientists and the public might learn from the fossil and the rocks surrounding it.

After You Read

1. Use the notes in your Science Notebook to help you list the steps in the formation of sedimentary rock.

2. In which type of sedimentary rock would you expect to find a fossilized plant?

3. How might you explain the presence of rock containing coral fossils in what is now the middle of the United States?

5.4 Metamorphic Rocks and the Rock Cycle

Before You Read

Look at the photographs and diagrams in this lesson. Discuss them with a partner. In your Science Notebook, write two questions that this lesson might answer. Your questions should relate to something you would like to learn about metamorphic rocks.

Formation of Metamorphic Rock

The process of change from one form to another is called **metamorphism**. Metamorphic rocks are formed when high temperature and pressure combine to change the texture, mineral makeup, or chemical makeup of rock *without* melting it. Rocks can undergo metamorphism by a combination of heat and pressure or by heat or pressure acting alone. Metamorphic rocks can also form when hot fluids come in contact with rocks. Metamorphic rock can form from all three types of rock—igneous, sedimentary, and even metamorphic.

Pressure Most metamorphic change is caused by increased pressure. The force of gravity pulls everything on Earth toward its center. On Earth's surface, we feel only the mild pressure of the layers of the atmosphere pressing down on us. Under layers of rock, however, the pressure is much greater. The pressure at a depth of 16 km can be 4,000 times as great as the pressure on Earth's surface. Metamorphic rock generally forms at depths greater than two kilometers. The high pressures that form metamorphic rocks can be generated in two ways. These include vertical pressure caused by the weight of rocks above or forces generated as rock masses are squeezed during mountain building.

Temperature The temperature at which metamorphic rock forms is typically between 50°C and 1,000°C. Metamorphism does not melt rock. This is because pressure from layers of rock above raises the melting point of the rock. The high temperatures needed for metamorphism to occur come from both Earth's internal heat and from magma that comes in contact with the rock.

sandstone (sedimentary) → quartzite (metamorphic)

granite (igneous) → gneiss (metamorphic)

Figure 5.15 Sedimentary and igneous rocks can be transformed into metamorphic rock by the heat and pressure inside Earth.

Types of Metamorphism

Regional metamorphism occurs when large areas of Earth's crust are affected by high pressure and temperature. This is usually caused by pieces of Earth's crust, called tectonic plates, colliding with one another. Pressure that squeezes results in the crumpling or folding of the crust. This forms mountain ranges or belts. **Figure 5.16** shows the type of regional metamorphism that occurred during the formation of the Rocky Mountains in Canada. The processes that cause this to happen are discussed in Chapter 6.

Figure 5.16 The rock layers that make up this mountain were metamorphosed as the mountain was formed. The intense heat and pressure inside Earth allowed the rock layers to fold and bend without breaking.

Another way rock can undergo metamorphism is by coming into contact with magma. **Contact metamorphism** occurs when magma comes in contact with solid rock and causes the texture and mineral composition of the rock to change. This can happen when magma intrudes, or is injected, into rock layers. Because temperature decreases with increasing distance from the intrusion, the metamorphic effects also decrease with distance from the intrusion. For this reason, minerals that crystallize at high temperatures are located closest to the intrusion, where it is hottest.

Different combinations of pressure and temperature produce different groups of metamorphic minerals. Geologists can make maps of the positions of these different minerals. They can then use the maps to interpret how hot the intrusion was and where the intrusion occurred.

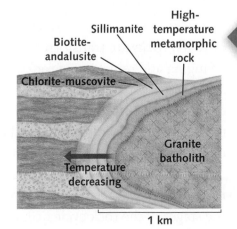

Figure 5.17 Contact metamorphism occurs when molten rock comes in contact with solid rock. The types of minerals formed change with distance from the igneous intrusion.

Extremely hot water can also cause changes in minerals. **Hydrothermal metamorphism** occurs when water heated by volcanic activity dissolves minerals, breaks them down, and deposits new minerals. The hot water might introduce new elements, change the chemical composition of the minerals, and form a new rock.

Textures of Metamorphic Rock

All metamorphic rock has one of two textures: foliated or nonfoliated. **Foliated metamorphic rock** contains wavy layers and sometimes bands of minerals. These layers form under high pressure. Foliated rocks resemble the pages, or folios, of a book. Gneiss and schist are common foliated rocks. **Nonfoliated metamorphic rock** does not appear to have any regular pattern. It is made up of minerals that form with blocky crystal shapes. Quartzite and marble are two common types of nonfoliated rocks.

Texture		Composition	Rock Name
Foliated	nonlayered — fine grained	chlorite / mica / quartz	slate
	nonlayered — coarse grained	feldspar / amphibole / pyroxene	phyllite
			schist
	Layered — coarse grained		gneiss

Texture		Composition	Rock Name
Nonfoliated	coarse grained	deformed grains of any rock type	metaconglomerate
	fine to coarse grained	quartz	quartzite
		calcite or dolomite	marble

Figure 5.19 Metamorphic rocks are classified by degree of foliation and mineral content.

The Rock Cycle

Rocks may not appear to change. However, over thousands or millions of years, rocks are transformed by natural forces. The continuous changing and remaking of rocks over time is called the **rock cycle**. There are many possible ways rocks can change from one type to another. For example, metamorphic rock may change into other kinds of metamorphic rock. It could also melt again and become igneous rock. Igneous rock could wear away and become part of sedimentary rock. Unlike other cycles in nature, the rock cycle has no definite sequence. Rocks can follow many different pathways through the rock cycle. As **Figure 5.20** shows, the stages of the rock cycle occur both beneath and above Earth's surface.

a

b

Figure 5.18 a) High heat and pressure caused the minerals in this rock to separate into light- and dark-colored bands forming gneiss. **b)** No layering is present in these marble columns and floor.

Extend It!

Visit a local outcropping of rock. Take along a rock field guide to help you identify the rocks you see. Make a sketch of the rock formation in your Science Notebook. Get closer to a small area of rock and make a close-up sketch of its surface. Describe the texture or features you can see. Based on your observations, can you identify the rock as igneous, sedimentary, or metamorphic?

Journey Through the Rock Cycle A possible journey of a rock through the rock cycle might occur as follows. An igneous rock, such as granite, may become exposed to wind, rain, and ice at Earth's surface. Over time, it slowly erodes and breaks apart. These pieces are washed into streams and are eventually broken down into sand-sized pieces of sediment. This sediment is carried by streams to a river, where it is deposited on the riverbed. Over many years, layers of this sediment build up. The weight of the upper layers of sediment increases the pressure on the lower layers. Then minerals that are dissolved in water precipitate between the individual grains. This cements them together. Particles that were once part of granite, an igneous rock, have now become part of sandstone, a sedimentary rock. Continued increase in temperature and pressure eventually causes the sandstone to change to quartzite, a metamorphic rock.

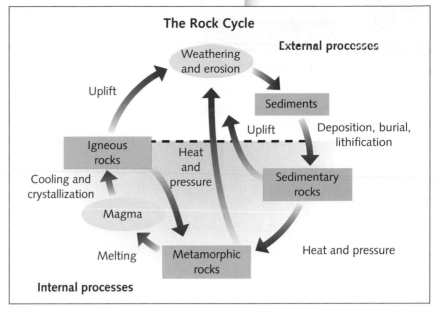

The Rock Cycle

Figure 5.20 The rocks of Earth's crust are constantly changing from one type to another, as shown in this diagram of the rock cycle.

a   b

Figure 5.21 Through the rock cycle, the materials that make up **a)** granite, an igneous rock, may change and eventually become **b)** quartzite, a metamorphic rock.

CONNECTION: Art

The metamorphic rock marble is valued by artists for making sculptures and detailing buildings. The interlocking grains in marble give it a smooth texture when carved. The statue *David* by Michelangelo in Florence, Italy, is a stunning example of what can be done with marble.

After You Read

1. Explain why metamorphism typically occurs deep inside Earth.

2. Were you able to answer the questions in your Science Notebook? Think of another question you could ask about the types of metamorphic rock. Answer your question using information from the lesson.

3. What causes hydrothermal metamorphism?

Summary

KEY CONCEPTS

5.1 Earth's Rock Types

- Rocks are classified into three main types: igneous, sedimentary, and metamorphic. They are classified further based on differences in composition and texture.

- Igneous rocks form as magma cools and crystallizes.

- Metamorphic rocks form when rocks are exposed to increased heat and pressure or exposed to hot fluids.

- Sedimentary rocks form over time as layers of sediment build up and become cemented together.

- Metamorphic rocks are formed when chemical reactions and extreme heat or pressure change existing rocks into new rocks.

5.2 Igneous Rocks

- Extrusive igneous rock forms from quickly cooling magma, near or on Earth's surface, forming small crystals. Intrusive igneous rock forms as magma cools slowly inside Earth, forming larger crystals.

- Igneous rocks are classified by their texture, which includes grain size, and by their mineral compositions.

5.3 Sedimentary Rocks

- The steps of sedimentary rock formation include weathering, erosion, deposition, compaction, and cementation.

- Clastic sedimentary rocks are made of the fragments of previously existing rocks.

- Chemical sedimentary rocks are formed when water evaporates from oceans and lakes, leaving behind dissolved minerals.

- Organic sedimentary rocks form from the remains of once-living organisms.

- Features of sedimentary rock include bedding, fossils, ripple marks, and mud cracks.

5.4 Metamorphic Rocks

- Metamorphic rocks are formed when high temperature and pressure combine to change the texture, mineral makeup, or chemical makeup of rock *without* melting it.

- Regional metamorphism occurs when belts of Earth's crust are affected by high pressure and temperature.

- Contact metamorphism occurs when molten rocks come in contact with solid rock.

- Hydrothermal metamorphism occurs when hot fluids dissolve minerals, break them down, and deposit new minerals.

- Metamorphic rocks may be foliated or nonfoliated.

- The rock cycle is the continuous changing and remaking of rocks over time.

VOCABULARY REVIEW

Write each term in a complete sentence or write a paragraph relating several terms.

5.1
rock, p. 67
igneous rock, p. 68
sediment, p. 68
sedimentary rock, p. 68
metamorphic rock, p. 68
composition, p. 69
texture, p. 69

5.2
extrusive igneous rock, p. 71
intrusive igneous rock, p. 71

5.3
deposition, p. 74
cementation, p. 74
clastic sedimentary rock, p. 75
chemical sedimentary rock, p. 75
organic sedimentary rock, p. 76
bedding, p. 76
fossil, p. 76

5.4
metamorphism, p. 78
regional metamorphism, p. 79
contact metamorphism, p. 79
hydrothermal metamorphism, p. 80
foliated metamorphic rock, p. 80
nonfoliated metamorphic rock, p. 80
rock cycle, p. 80

True or False

If the statement is true, write "true." If it is false, change the underlined word or words to make the statement true.

1. All metamorphic rock has one of two <u>textures</u>: foliated or nonfoliated.

2. A characteristic feature of sedimentary rock is bedding, or <u>vertical</u> layering.

3. Rock formed from cooling magma is called <u>metamorphic</u> rock.

4. The remains of organisms form <u>chemical</u> sedimentary rock.

5. <u>Unlike</u> other cycles in nature, the rock cycle has no definite sequence.

6. <u>Extrusive</u> igneous rock forms underground.

Short Answer

Answer each of the following in a sentence or brief paragraph.

7. What determines the composition of a rock?

8. How can intrusive igneous rocks become exposed at Earth's surface?

9. Why is it important for geologists to work gently and slowly while digging up fossils?

10. Explain why fossils only occur in sedimentary rocks.

11. Why do extrusive igneous rocks have smaller crystals than intrusive igneous rocks?

12. What role does cementation play in the formation of sedimentary rocks?

PREPARE FOR CHAPTER TEST

To prepare for the chapter test, create a question from each Learning Goal. Use the information in your Science Notebook to answer each question. Then use these answers to write a well-developed essay about the chapter. Use the Key Concept on the first page of this chapter as your topic sentence.

Critical Thinking

Use what you have learned in this chapter to answer each of the following.

13. **Classify** Classify the following two rocks: (a) a dark rock with large, visible crystals, (b) a dark rock containing old plant remains. Use as many adjectives as you can for each rock.

14. **Compare and Contrast** How is the formation of icicles similar to the formation of chemical sedimentary rock in caves? How are the two processes different?

15. **Predict** Would rock formed by contact metamorphism be foliated or nonfoliated? Explain your reasoning.

Standardized Test Question

Choose the letter of the response that correctly answers the question.

16. What could a geologist deduce about this igneous rock?

    A. It cooled very rapidly under the ground.

    B. It cooled slowly under the ground.

    C. It cooled very rapidly on Earth's surface.

    D. It cooled slowly on Earth's surface.

Test-Taking Tip

When writing an essay, make an outline first. This will help you organize ideas, important vocabulary, and key concepts.

Mountains of Coal

HOW OFTEN EACH DAY do you turn on a light, surf the Internet, or use the microwave? Americans use more energy each day than any other group of people on Earth.

The Problem: Satisfying the Huge Need for Electricity

To keep all that electricity flowing, thousands of power plants in the United States burn fuels such as coal, oil, and natural gas. It takes 20 million barrels of oil and more than 2 million tons of coal each day just to keep lights and air conditioners on.

The United States is increasingly looking to coal to meet these huge electricity needs. In fact, half of the electricity produced in the United States comes from burning coal. Why coal? The cost of coal is rising more slowly than the cost of fuels such as oil and natural gas. The United States also has huge supplies of coal that could last for 200 years or longer.

Much of that coal is in the Appalachian Mountains—or rather *under* them. Beneath the forests and mountains of states such as West Virginia and Kentucky lies low-sulfur bituminous coal. This coal burns hotter and cleaner than some other types of coal.

For years, coal companies dug shafts deep into the mountains to reach the coal. However, a newer type of coal mining called mountaintop removal has become more common. Instead of tunneling into the mountains, dynamite is used to blow the mountains to bits. The rubble that was once the mountain is pushed into nearby valleys. Then huge, cranelike machines called draglines scoop out the coal. These machines are as tall as a 20-story building and remove the coal in chunks as big as a football field!

Good Idea or Bad Idea?

Mountaintop removal has its advantages. First, it's efficient. The process can dig a lot of coal faster than any other method. It also requires fewer people, so costs are lower. Laws require coal companies to restore the land after each area is mined. They fill in the deep holes, cover the area with soil, and plant grasses and some trees.

Unfortunately, mountaintop removal causes environmental problems. More than 1,000 miles of streams are now buried by the rubble that has been pushed into valleys. The aquatic life of these streams is gone. During heavy rains, water that was once absorbed by forest plants now runs off the cleared land, causing more frequent flooding. What's more, hundreds of thousands of acres of forest have been lost. The forest ecosystem that covers these mountains is part of the largest area of temperate forest left on Earth. It is rich in plant and animal species. Trees and grasses can be planted after mining, but there is no way to restore this ecosystem in all of its complexity.

People, too, have felt the impact of mountaintop removal. For some, it has been positive because the mining has provided jobs. For others, the effects have not been good. The explosions that blow off the mountaintops send debris down mountainsides and fill the air with choking dust. The mining disturbs underground water supplies, drying up or contaminating wells. Slurry ponds, full of liquid wastes left after washing the coal, sometimes break, causing black, toxic goo to pour down hillsides into communities and water supplies. Unable to live under such conditions, many families that had lived near these mountains for generations have moved away.

Is there a solution?

Our energy needs are increasing. As a result, so is our need to mine resources such as coal. Are there other energy resources that would meet our needs with less environmental damage? What if we continue to mine large amounts of coal? Is mountaintop removal the best way to mine it? Or would other methods—even those that are more costly—be better because they have less of an impact on people and the land? These are all tough questions.

Diamonds

WHAT'S THE BIGGEST diamond ever found on Earth? It is a gem discovered in South Africa in 1905 that weighed more than a pound. Recently, scientists discovered an even larger diamond—just not on Earth. Nicknamed Lucy, it's about the size of a small moon—about 2,500 miles across. Lucy is a white dwarf. White dwarfs are the hot, dead centers of stars that have used up their fuel. The diamond star is about 50 light-years away. Heat and chemical changes have compressed its center into what may be the biggest diamond in the galaxy.

Diamond is a beautiful, sparkly mineral. In the case of Lucy, it is also an amazing mineral. The most important property of diamond is its hardness. In fact, diamond is Earth's hardest naturally occurring substance. As a result, most diamonds aren't used for rings and bracelets. About 80 percent of the world's diamonds are used in industry to cut and grind stone, metals, concrete, eyeglasses, computer chips, and other gems.

What makes diamond so hard? It is made of almost pure carbon, but so is graphite, which is much softer. The key to diamond's hardness is its crystal structure. Diamonds form deep within Earth. There, intense pressure and heat rearrange the atoms in carbon. In graphite, just three of carbon's four outermost electrons bond with other carbon atoms. In diamond, all four form covalent bonds with neighboring carbon atoms. This forms a strong, rigid crystal structure—carbon in its most condensed form.

Today, it is possible to make diamonds in a lab. The process involves applying high pressure and heat to graphite, just as in nature. Small diamonds can be made this way in minutes. Making very large diamonds, however, is still a job for nature.

Research and Report

You've just learned about diamond. Now choose another mineral or rock. Research your choice at the library or on the Internet. Then create a chart that shows its properties and common uses. Present your chart in class. Include a sample or picture of your rock or mineral. If possible, show your class a product, structure, or process that uses your rock or mineral.

CAREER CONNECTION: PLANETARY GEOLOGIST

BEING A PLANETARY geologist can be interesting and fun, but it can be frustrating, too. You get to study what it's like on other planets. You help plan missions that leave Earth to study objects in space. You never actually *go* to these worlds yourself, however, unless you become an astronaut. Despite these facts, most planetary geologists wouldn't want to do anything else.

Planetary geologists study the surface features and rocks of the other planets and moons in our solar system. They base their studies on their knowledge of Earth's geology. Instead of exploring in person, however, they use data transmitted to Earth by space probes. The work of planetary geologists has taught us what we know about the surfaces of the Moon, Mars, and other planets. When NASA plans a mission to another world, planetary geologists are part of the team.

They help choose the best place to land. When astronauts are on the Moon, or a rover is rolling around on Mars, planetary geologists help interpret images and data.

Planetary geologists usually have a doctorate in geology or planetary sciences. The government employs many of these scientists at agencies such as NASA or the U.S. Geological Survey. They also teach at universities and do research that helps us better understand the planets of our solar system.

Forces in the Earth

Chapter 6

Plate Tectonics

How do the interactions between Earth's moving tectonic plates result in the formation of many of our planet's features, including mountains and volcanoes?

Chapter 7

Earthquakes

What causes earthquakes, how do they affect people, and how can people prepare for them?

Chapter 8

Volcanoes

How has volcanic activity shaped Earth's surface, and what effect does it have on landforms, people, and climates?

Plate Tectonics

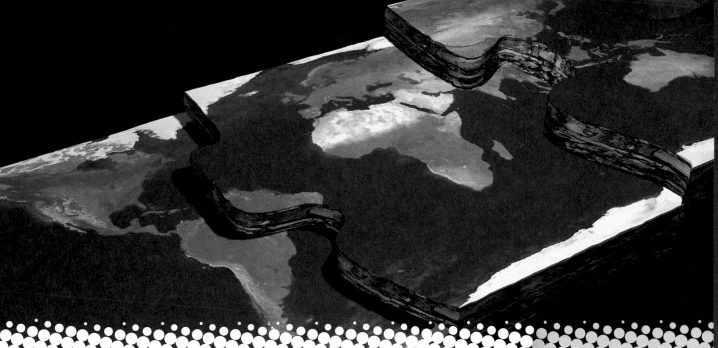

KEY CONCEPT Interactions between Earth's moving tectonic plates result in the formation of many of our planet's features, including mountains and volcanoes.

Have you ever put together a jigsaw puzzle? If you have, you know that each piece fits together with several other pieces. Together, they form a larger image. Think about what would happen to the picture if two pieces slowly began to move apart. The puzzle's picture might stretch or tear. If pushed together, one piece might slide under another piece or the pieces might rise up at the seam.

Earth's crust is made of huge puzzlelike pieces that fit closely together. The movement of each piece affects all of the pieces around it. These movements create changes on Earth's surface.

Think About Pushes and Pulls

Think about three train cars attached together on a track. If the front car is pulled forward, the other two cars will also be pulled forward.

- In your Science Notebook, draw a picture of two train cars attached together. Then draw a second picture showing what might happen if the two cars were pushed slowly toward each other with great force.

www.scilinks.org

Plate Techtonics **Code: WGES06**

Learning Goals

- Explain two ways scientists define Earth's layers.
- Identify the three compositional layers of Earth.
- Identify the five physical layers of Earth.

New Vocabulary

crust
mantle
core
lithosphere
asthenosphere
lower mantle
outer core
inner core

Before You Read

In your Science Notebook, make a concept map showing the relationships between the vocabulary words. Start the concept map with the word *Earth*. Around *Earth*, write the words *Crust, Mantle,* and *Core*.

It is easy to make observations about what is on Earth's surface. Soil, rocks, mountains, valleys, and other features cover Earth's surface. However, Earth scientists have always wondered what is inside Earth. Because no one has ever been to the center of Earth, scientists use indirect observations to increase their knowledge about Earth's interior.

Scientists now know that Earth is made up of a number of different layers. These layers can be defined in two ways. One way is to differentiate the layers by their compositions, or what they are made of. The other way to differentiate the layers is by their physical properties such as density, ability to flow, and temperature.

Composition of Earth

Earth can be divided into three layers based on their different compositions. These layers are called the crust, the mantle, and the core.

The Crust The outer layer of Earth is called the **crust**. The crust contains large amounts of silicon and aluminum. Its thickness ranges from 5 to 100 km. There are two types of crust: continental crust and oceanic crust. Continental crust is thicker than oceanic crust. The usual range of thickness for continental crust is 20 to 70 km. Oceanic crust usually ranges from 4 to 9 km thick. Continental crust is made up of materials that are similar to granite.

Figure 6.1 The crust is the outermost layer of Earth's surface. There are two types of crust: the thinner, denser oceanic crust and the thicker, less dense continental crust.

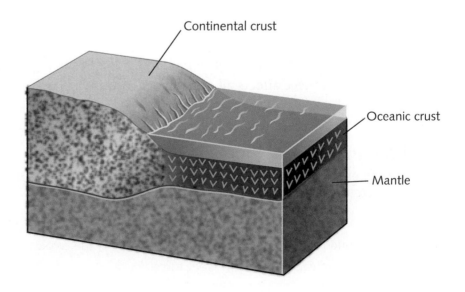

Continental crust

Oceanic crust

Mantle

Oceanic crust, on the other hand, is basaltic. It is made up of basalt-like rocks. The minerals that make up basalt have higher densities than the minerals that make up granite. For this reason, oceanic crust is denser than continental crust.

The Mantle The layer of Earth between the core and the crust is the **mantle**. It is about 2,900 km thick. The mantle contains a high concentration of olivine-rich rocks. These rocks contain large amounts of iron and magnesium. No one has ever observed the mantle directly. In 2005, scientists with the Integrated Ocean Drilling Program (IODP) drilled through a very thin part of ocean crust to a depth of 1,416 m, only about 305 m from the crust-mantle boundary. A miscalculation in the position of the drill hole may be what stopped them from reaching the mantle.

What is known about the mantle comes mostly from indirect observations. For example, there are places where the movement of rock in Earth's crust sometimes brings rock from the mantle to Earth's surface. When this happens, scientists can observe the rock directly. Magma from the mantle also flows out of active volcanoes on the ocean floor. These volcanoes have helped scientists learn about the composition of the mantle.

The Core Earth's **core** is the layer of Earth that extends from the mantle to the center of Earth. This layer is actually ball-shaped and has a diameter of about 7,000 km. Because it is farthest from Earth's surface, the core is the layer that is the most difficult to study. Scientists think that the core contains large amounts of the elements iron and nickel.

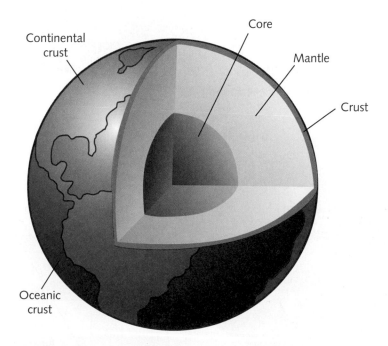

Figure 6.2 Earth is composed of three layers. Starting from the outside, these layers are the crust, the mantle, and the core.

Explain It!

In your Science Notebook, explain which compositional layer is the most difficult for scientists to study. Support your answer with facts from this lesson.

CONNECTION: Literature

During the 1800s, scientists were not the only people interested in Earth science. Authors, politicians, and many others were curious about what was inside Earth. In 1864, the French author Jules Verne published his famous book *Journey to the Center of the Earth*. In this book, the main characters hiked and used a raft to reach the center of Earth. Today, scientists use technology to study Earth's center. Imagine there was a way to dig a hole all the way to Earth's center. What might the machine used to dig this hole look like? Draw a picture of this imaginary machine in your Science Notebook, label its parts, and explain how it would work.

As You Read

Review your concept map. Along the lines connecting the large center circle to the smaller outer circles, write facts to help you remember how the words are related. Then add the rest of the vocabulary words and any other important words from the lesson to your concept map.

Which of Earth's layers is located beneath the lithosphere?

Structure of Earth

Scientists recognize five layers of Earth based on their physical properties. A liquid such as water has different physical properties from a solid such as ice. Earth's layers also have different physical properties. The five layers are the lithosphere, the asthenosphere, the lower mantle, the outer core, and the inner core.

Lithosphere The rigid, relatively cool outer layer of Earth is called the lithosphere. The **lithosphere** is made up of the crust and the solid portion of the upper mantle. The lithosphere is brittle, meaning that it can crack and break. When it does crack, large amounts of force are released. These forces can cause earthquakes. Cracks in the lithosphere can also allow hot material from deeper inside Earth to rise to the surface. Because the lithosphere is the outer layer of Earth, it is the layer that we know the most about.

Asthenosphere The hot layer underneath the lithosphere is the **asthenosphere** (as THE nuh sfihr). The asthenosphere is the part of the upper mantle that can slowly flow. Even though it can flow, the asthenosphere is actually a solid. It responds to heat like a piece of plastic left outside on a hot, sunny day. Even though the hot plastic is still solid, it can be easily bent.

Figure It Out

1. What is the thickest layer of Earth as defined by its physical properties?

2. Identify which compositional layer or layers correspond to the asthenosphere.

Figure 6.3 This image compares the layers of Earth as defined by their physical properties with the layers of Earth as defined by their composition.

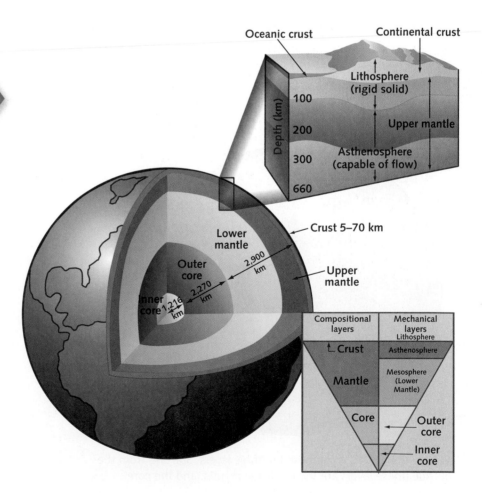

CONNECTION: Acoustics

Acoustics is the branch of physics that studies sound and the behavior of sound waves. Sound waves behave differently depending on the matter through which they travel. In general, sound waves will travel more quickly through denser material and more slowly through less dense material.

Scientists have applied this knowledge of sound waves in many ways. Sonar is a technology that uses the properties of sound waves to study underwater objects and the ocean floor.

Seismologists are scientists who use technology that is similar to sonar to study special waves that travel through Earth. These waves are called seismic waves. Seismic waves can carry a large amount of energy. Naturally occurring seismic waves are produced by earthquakes. Seismic waves and earthquakes are discussed in more detail in Chapter 7.

Scientists sometimes use human-made seismic waves to study Earth's interior. On land, these waves can be created with explosives or with large trucks that shake the ground below them.

Scientists also use machines to monitor waves that travel through Earth. These wave monitors have been used to piece together information about the interior of Earth.

Lower Mantle   The very hot, solid part of the mantle that lies between the asthenosphere and the outer core is the **lower mantle**. Even though the temperature in the lower mantle is very high, this layer of Earth is solid. It cannot flow because very high pressure keeps its molecules from moving.

Outer Core   Earth's core is divided into two parts. The outer, liquid layer of the core is the **outer core**. This section of the core is made up mostly of iron and nickel in liquid form. Iron is a magnetic material and is a strong conductor of electricity. Scientists think that the continuous flow of molten iron in the liquid outer core is the source of Earth's magnetic field.

Inner Core   The solid center of Earth is the **inner core**. The inner core is ball-shaped, and is made up almost entirely of iron. The inner core has an extremely high temperature that would normally melt metal. High pressure, however, causes the inner core to remain solid.

After You Read

1. What are the compositional layers of Earth?

2. Compare the layers of Earth as defined by their composition to the layers of Earth as defined by their physical properties.

3. Examine your completed concept map. Write a well-developed paragraph that explains the relationships between Earth's layers.

6.2 Continents in Motion

Before You Read

Read the lesson title, the headings and subheadings, and the Learning Goals. Then look at the figures. Predict what you think you will learn in this lesson. Write your predictions in two or three sentences in your Science Notebook.

As we look around, we might think that Earth's surface never changes. Mountains seem to stay in the same place from day to day. Hills, valleys, and plains never seem to change. However, all of Earth's land is moving. Different parts move at different rates. Believe it or not, each year a thin strip of California moves about 5 cm northwest relative to the rest of North America, which is moving southeast. South America is moving away from Africa at a rate of about 2.5 cm each year. This movement can be explained using the hypothesis of continental drift and the theory of plate tectonics.

Early Observations

In 1596, a Dutch mapmaker named Abraham Ortelius noticed something on a map. He observed that the continents on either side of the Atlantic Ocean seemed to fit together like puzzle pieces. He proposed an incorrect theory to explain this. He thought that earthquakes and floods had pushed North and South America away from Europe and Africa. Other people at that time had also noticed how the shapes of the continents seemed to fit together.

Figure 6.4 The shapes of the continents on either side of the Atlantic Ocean seem to fit together like the pieces of a puzzle.

Continental Drift

In 1912, Alfred Wegener proposed a hypothesis he called continental drift. The hypothesis of **continental drift** proposed that all of Earth's continents were once joined together as a single landmass. Wegener called this landmass, or supercontinent, *Pangaea* (pan JEE uh), meaning "all Earth." Wegener's hypothesis also proposed that Pangaea started to break into separate pieces around 200 million years ago. Between then and now, the continents slowly drifted to their present positions.

Wegener's hypothesis was new and unique. He had not only proposed that continents could drift apart from one another, he had collected evidence to support his hypothesis. This evidence included fossils, rock formation patterns, and climatic data.

Fossil Evidence *Mesosaurus* was a freshwater reptile that lived 260 million years ago. Fossils of *Mesosaurus* had been discovered on opposite sides of the Atlantic Ocean. Fossils of land animals had also been discovered in the same areas. Because these animals could not have crossed the Atlantic Ocean as it is today, they provided evidence for the hypothesis of continental drift. Fossils of similar animals had also been discovered in different places around the world. This added even more support to the hypothesis. Wegener believed that Pangaea broke apart about 200 million years ago. Because the matching fossils on opposite sides of the ocean were also about 200 million years old, their existence supported his hypothesis.

Another important piece of fossil evidence came from the plant *Glossopteris* (glahs AHP tur us). Fossils of this plant had been collected on a number of continents including Africa, South America, Australia, and Antarctica. Today, these continents all have very different climates. This plant could not have survived in such different climates. Wegener used this evidence to conclude that the *Glossopteris* fossils had once been located much closer to one another. The land they were located on must have broken apart and its pieces must have drifted to their present locations.

200 million years ago

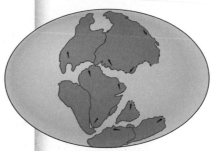

180 million years ago

135 million years ago

66 million years ago

Present

Figure 6.5 According to the hypothesis of continental drift, Pangaea was an ancient supercontinent that contained all of today's continents. This supercontinent began to break up about 200 million years ago. Eventually it broke into the landmasses and continents that are present on Earth today. The red arrows indicate the direction of movement.

Figure It Out

1. Based on the evidence provided by fossils of *Glossopteris*, which continents must have once been connected?

2. Explain why Wegener thought that Antarctica was once closer to the equator than it is today.

Some Evidence of Continental Drift

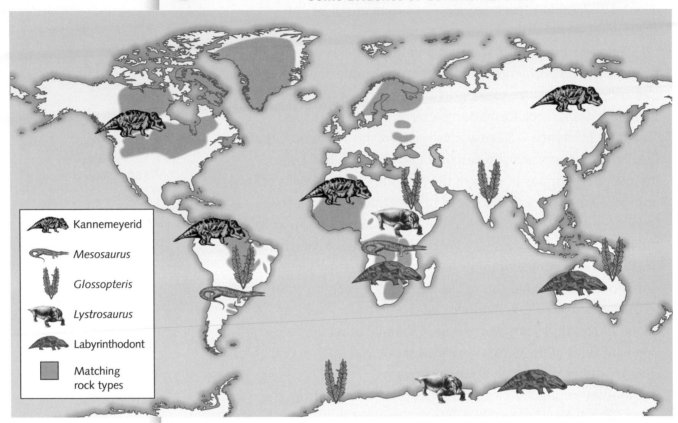

Figure 6.6 Alfred Wegener used fossils and similarities between rock formations on opposite sides of the Atlantic Ocean as evidence that Earth's continents once formed a single landmass.

Evidence from Rock Formations   Wegener thought that as Pangaea had split apart, mountain ranges and other rock formations would have split apart at the same time. He looked for similar mountain ranges on either side of the Atlantic Ocean. He observed that rocks from the Appalachian Mountains in the eastern United States shared similar traits with rocks in Greenland. He also observed similarities between rocks in Africa and South America. All of these rock formations are over 200 million years old. These facts provided more evidence for the hypothesis of continental drift.

Climatic Evidence Wegener also used clues about ancient climates to support the hypothesis of continental drift. Climate is the average weather of an area over an extended period of time. One piece of climatic evidence for continental drift was the existence of coal deposits in Antarctica. Coal forms from dead swamp plants. Swamp plants need a climate much warmer than that of Antarctica to grow. The existence of coal formed from dead swamp plants in Antarctica was evidence of a much warmer climate. Antarctica's climate could only have been warmer if it had once been closer to Earth's equator.

Wegener also used climatic evidence left by glaciers. Glaciers are large, slowly flowing masses of ice that carry dirt and rocks with them. The materials carried by glaciers are deposited when the glacier melts. 290-million-year-old glacial deposits had been discovered in Africa, India, South America, and Australia. These glacial deposits provided evidence that these areas had once been covered by thick ice. Today, none of these continents have climates cold enough for glaciers. Because of this, Wegener believed that these continents must all have been located near the cold south pole. Wegener thought the deposits were carried to their present locations once Pangaea split apart.

As You Read

Reread the predictions you made about this lesson in your Science Notebook. Were your predictions accurate? Revise your sentences if necessary. Then think of a question you have about something related to the chapter. Write your question in your Science Notebook. Then write your predicted answer.

What did Wegener's hypothesis of continental drift propose?

Figure 6.7 Fossil *Glossopteris* leaves occur in such great number that scientists think the plant may have lost its leaves in the fall and grown new leaves in the spring much like maple and oak trees do today. Their widespread occurrence indicates that the land areas where they are found must have once been closer together and had similar climates.

Seafloor Spreading

When Wegener first proposed his ideas, most scientists rejected them. Even though his hypothesis of continental drift was correct, he could not identify a force that could move entire continents. Wegener incorrectly proposed that the continents were pushing through an ocean floor that was not moving. Other scientists argued that if this were true, the rock on the ocean floor would break apart. Alfred Wegener died in 1930. Unfortunately, it wasn't until the 1960s that researchers found evidence that the seafloors were moving along with the continents. Wegener's hypothesis of continental drift was finally complete.

The Theory of Seafloor Spreading   The theory of **seafloor spreading** states that new ocean crust is formed at mid-ocean ridges and destroyed at deep-sea trenches. A mid-ocean ridge is a long, mountainlike feature that runs mostly along the center of Earth's ocean floors. A trench is a long, deep indentation in the ocean floor. Cracks in a mid-ocean ridge allow lighter, less dense magma to rise up and fill them. This forms new ocean crust and pushes the ridge slightly apart. As the ridge spreads, more magma is forced up through the crack. As new ocean crust is formed, it slowly moves away from the ridge toward a deep-sea trench. **Figure 6.8** shows how the ongoing process of seafloor spreading adds new ocean floor to Earth's surface. The theory of seafloor spreading suggests that continents are carried on pieces of oceanic crust that are moving away from each other. This explains the continued widening of the Atlantic Ocean over the past 180 million years.

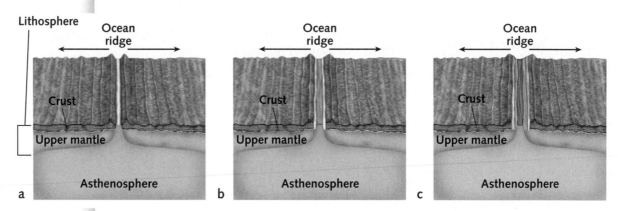

Figure 6.8 a) Magma that forms in the asthenosphere is forced up onto the ocean floor along a ridge and fills the gap that is created. **b)** When the magma cools and hardens, new ocean crust is formed. **c)** The ongoing process of new magma being forced upward, cooling, and hardening adds more crust to the ocean floor.

Collecting Evidence of Seafloor Spreading   Two technologies helped researchers collect evidence of seafloor spreading. The first was sonar and the second was a device called a magnetometer. Sonar is a remote sensing tool that can be used to map the ocean floor. It sends sound waves toward the ocean floor and records how long it takes them to travel back to a receiver. This data provide scientists with the information they need to create an image of the ocean floor.

Earth has a magnetic field. Magnetometers detect small changes in the magnetic field strength of rocks that make up the ocean floor. These measurements are then used to make magnetic maps of the ocean floor. Maps of the ocean floor created by sonar show that there are long underwater mountain ridges in the oceans. Scientists have discovered that earthquakes and volcanoes are common along these ridges. The maps of the ocean floors also show that there are long deep-sea trenches.

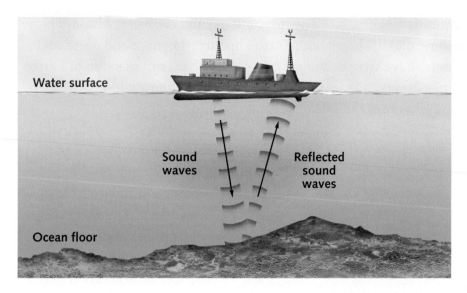

Figure 6.9 Sonar uses reflected sound waves to calculate the distance to the ocean floor. Data collected using sonar have been used to map ocean-floor topography.

Ocean Rock Samples   Scientists collecting rock samples from ocean floors observed a surprising pattern. Rocks from areas close to ocean ridges are younger than rocks near ocean trenches. The farther away from the ridges, the older the rocks. This pattern continues all the way to the deep-sea trenches. The oldest rocks on the ocean floors are present at the ocean trenches. Another surprising discovery was that the oldest rocks in the oceans are younger than those on land. Rocks from the oldest parts of the seafloor are only 180 million years old. This is young compared to continental rocks. Some rocks on dry land are over 3.9 billion years old!

 Extend It!

Hydrothermal vents are holes in the ocean's floor that appear around mid-ocean ridges. The vents shoot out water that is rich in minerals. Formations called black and white smokers are mineral deposits that can form around hydrothermal vents. Research black and white smokers. Draw and label a diagram of a black or white smoker in your Science Notebook. Include information from your research.

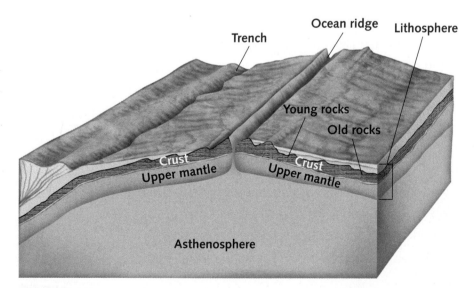

Figure 6.10 The oldest rocks in the ocean crust are present near deep-sea trenches, while the youngest rocks are present near ocean ridges.

Magnetic Reversals The magnetic north pole has not always been in the same place. Throughout Earth's history, the magnetic north and south poles have switched many times. The change in position of Earth's magnetic poles is called a **magnetic reversal**. When a magnetic reversal occurs, Earth's magnetic field reverses direction.

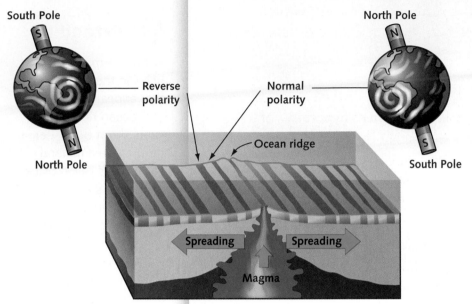

Figure 6.11 Magnetic reversals in the ocean's crust are shown as bands of light and dark colors.

Important evidence of seafloor spreading comes from magnetic reversals recorded in the rocks of the ocean floor. The magma at ocean ridges is rich in iron (Fe). As the magma at the mid-ocean ridge cools and crystallizes, iron-rich minerals form. The crystals within the minerals act like the needle in a compass and line up in the direction of Earth's magnetic field. These minerals record the direction of Earth's magnetic field at the time they were formed. **Figure 6.11** illustrates that as the seafloor spreads, the minerals and rocks are carried slowly away from the mid-ocean ridge. New ocean floor continues to form at the mid-ocean ridge, and the process begins again. Each new band of rock that forms along the mid-ocean ridge records the direction of Earth's magnetic field at the time it formed. When a magnetic reversal occurs, it is recorded in the newly formed rocks. Eventually, parallel bands of rock form on each side of the mid-ocean ridge. Scientists studying the ocean floor were surprised to discover these bands of magnetic minerals pointing in opposite directions. These bands provided proof that the seafloor is spreading.

After You Read

1. Reread your prediction from As You Read. Did your prediction accurately answer your question? Revise your answer if necessary. What new questions do you now have about the chapter? Write them in your Science Notebook. Then work with a partner to answer your questions.

2. Describe two pieces of evidence that support the hypothesis of continental drift.

3. Explain the process of seafloor spreading.

6.3 The Theory of Plate Tectonics

Learning Goals

- Identify three possible causes for tectonic plate movement.
- Identify the three main types of plate boundaries.
- Explain the differences among the three types of convergent plate boundaries.

New Vocabulary

theory of plate tectonics
convection
ridge push
slab pull
divergent boundary
rift valley
convergent boundary
subduction
transform boundary

Before You Read

Use the lesson title and subheadings to create a lesson outline. Use the lesson title as the outline title. Label the lesson subheadings with the Roman numerals *I* through *III*. Use the letters *A, B, C*, etc., under each subheading to record information you want to remember.

Seafloor spreading provided proof for Wegener's hypothesis of continental drift. Seafloor spreading shows that the ocean floor is in motion. Oceanic crust moves and carries the continents with it. A new theory, called plate tectonics, was named to combine the hypothesis of continental drift with the theory of seafloor spreading.

The **theory of plate tectonics** states that Earth's lithosphere is divided into enormous slabs called tectonic plates. There are about twelve major tectonic plates and several smaller ones. Tectonic plates interact with each other at plate boundaries. Plate boundaries are the areas where tectonic plates come together. **Figure 6.12** illustrates the plates that make up Earth's lithosphere and their boundaries. These plates are in constant motion relative to one another.

Earth's Tectonic Plates

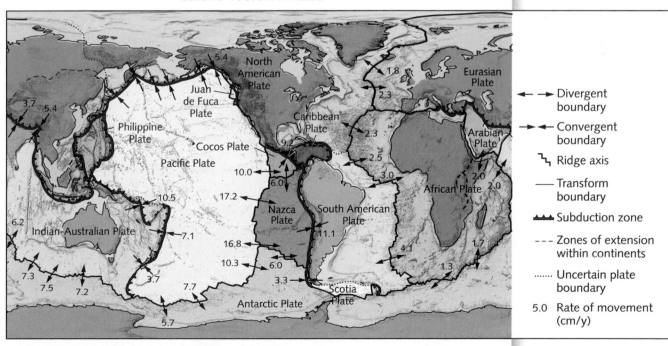

Figure 6.12 Earth's crust is broken into enormous slabs called tectonic plates that interact at plate boundaries.

Possible Causes of Plate Movement

Because the continents and oceans are moving, scientists know tectonic plates are moving. What, though, could cause forces strong enough to move entire tectonic plates? Scientists have identified three possible causes: mantle convection, ridge push, and slab pull.

Mantle Convection The transfer of heat by the movement of heated material is called **convection**. When matter is heated, it expands and becomes less dense. When matter becomes less dense, it also becomes lighter than similar matter around it. For this reason, the heated matter floats, while the unheated matter sinks. This causes a pattern of movement called a convection current. Cooler matter sinks to the bottom, while warmer matter rises to the top.

Scientists think that convection currents in the mantle cause tectonic plates to move. Even though the mantle is solid, part of it—the asthenosphere—can flow. Convection currents in this part of the mantle transfer energy from the hot inner part of Earth to the cooler outer part of Earth. The hot material from the inner part of the mantle is less dense than the cooler material in the outer part of the mantle. This hot material slowly floats toward Earth's crust. At the same time, cooler material in the mantle sinks back toward Earth's center. Together, these movements create convection currents that can be thousands of kilometers wide. The movement in the mantle drags tectonic plates sideways. Convection currents in Earth move very slowly. Scientists think they move at speeds of only a few centimeters per year.

Explain It!

In your Science Notebook, explain why hotter material from the asthenosphere may rise toward the lithosphere.

Figure It Out

1. In what layer of Earth do convection currents occur?

2. Relative to an ocean ridge, in which direction does ridge push cause Earth's crust to move?

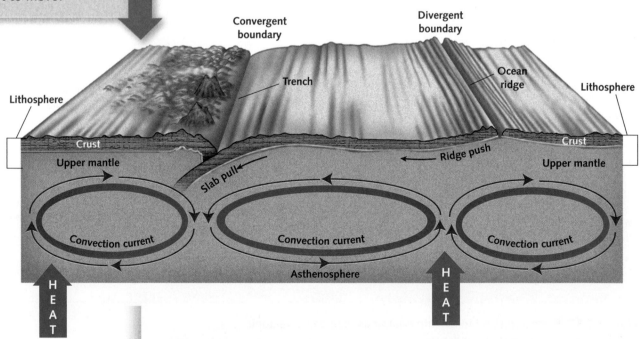

Figure 6.13 Ridge push and slab pull are tectonic processes related to convection currents in the mantle.

Ridge Push   When an ocean ridge is formed on Earth's lithosphere, part of the asthenosphere beneath it rises. This uplifted ridge adds weight to the lithosphere. Scientists believe that the heavy weight of ocean ridges pushes oceanic crust away from them and toward ocean trenches. **Ridge push** is the process by which an ocean plate is pushed away from the mid-ocean ridge and toward a trench. **Figure 6.13** shows ridge push.

Slab Pull   When oceanic crust at the edge of a tectonic plate is pushed out toward a deep-ocean trench, it is eventually pulled down into the asthenosphere. **Slab pull** is the process by which an ocean plate being pulled into the asthenosphere pulls the rest of the plate with it. This happens because oceanic crust is denser than material in the asthenosphere. When the oceanic crust comes into contact with the less dense material in the asthenosphere (at ocean trenches), it is sucked into the asthenosphere. The weight of the plate being sucked into the asthenosphere can pull attached pieces of oceanic crust along with it. Slab pull is shown in **Figure 6.13**.

Tectonic Plate Boundaries

Tectonic plates all have boundaries with other tectonic plates. At some boundaries, plates collide. At others, plates separate or slide past each other. Plate interactions at boundaries can cause earthquakes and volcanic activity. Scientists classify tectonic plate boundaries into three main types. These types are based on how the plates move relative to one another. The three types of tectonic plate boundaries are convergent boundaries, divergent boundaries, and transform boundaries.

As You Read

Look at the information in your outline. Add or correct information as necessary.

Use the information in your outline to write a well-developed paragraph in your Science Notebook explaining possible causes of tectonic plate movement.

Figure 6.14 This map shows the position of some of Earth's major tectonic plate boundaries. The direction of movement determines the type of boundary present. The boundary that runs down the center of the Atlantic Ocean is a divergent boundary. The boundary that runs along the west coast of North America is both a convergent boundary and a transform boundary.

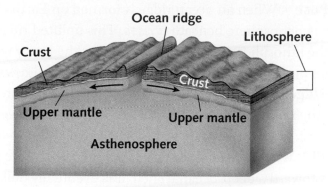

Figure 6.15 Divergent boundaries are places where tectonic plates are separating. Ocean ridges are divergent boundaries on the ocean floor.

Divergent Boundaries   Boundaries between two tectonic plates that are moving away from each other are called **divergent boundaries**. Most of Earth's divergent boundaries are on the ocean floor. When a divergent boundary occurs in an ocean, an ocean ridge is formed. It is along divergent boundaries at mid-ocean ridges that seafloor spreading occurs. The formation of new ocean crust at divergent boundaries often leads to volcanic activity and earthquakes.

Although most divergent boundaries form ridges on the ocean floor, there are some divergent boundaries on continents. When continental crust starts to separate, it stretches and forms a long narrow valley called a **rift valley**. It is likely that the Atlantic Ocean was once a narrow ridge on the supercontinent Pangaea. Over many millions of years, that ridge became a rift valley and expanded due to seafloor spreading. As the ridge expanded, the Atlantic Ocean was slowly formed. There is currently a rift valley being formed in East Africa called the Great Rift Valley. Scientists have predicted that this rift valley will eventually become the world's next ocean.

Convergent Boundaries   When two tectonic plates push into one another, the boundary where they meet is called a **convergent boundary**. There are three types of convergent boundaries depending on the type of crust involved when two plates collide. Remember that there are two types of crust: oceanic crust and continental crust. The three types of convergent boundaries are oceanic-oceanic, oceanic-continental, and continental-continental convergent boundaries. They are shown in **Figure 6.16**.

Oceanic-oceanic convergent boundaries occur when oceanic crust collides with oceanic crust. When two plates with oceanic crust push into one another, the cooler and denser of the two plates slides under the other plate. The process by which one tectonic plate slips beneath another tectonic plate is called **subduction**. The process of subduction creates a subduction zone where a deep-sea trench is formed. The plate that is subducted sinks into the mantle where it melts. Most of the material from the plate that sinks is recycled back into the mantle. However, some of the magma that is formed is forced back to Earth's surface and causes volcanic eruptions. These eruptions form chains of volcanic islands that run alongside the ocean trench. These chains are called island arcs. The Philippine Islands in the Pacific Ocean are an example of such a chain.

When a continental plate converges with an oceanic plate, subduction also occurs. In this case, the oceanic plate is always denser than the continental plate. This means that the oceanic plate is always subducted, or sinks, under the continental plate. This type of convergent boundary also creates an ocean trench and a chain of volcanoes. However, the volcanoes do not form under the oceanic plate. Instead, they form under the continental plate. The result is a mountain range that has many volcanoes. One example of this is the Cascade Range in the western United States.

The third type of convergent boundary is formed when two continental plates collide. When this happens, neither plate is subducted, because both plates have nearly the same density. Instead, the two edges of the continental plates are pushed together and lifted up, creating a high mountain range. The Himalayas in Asia and the Transantarctic Mountains in Antarctica were formed in this way. There is no volcanic activity at this type of boundary and earthquakes are common.

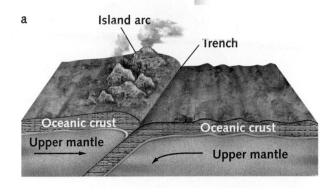

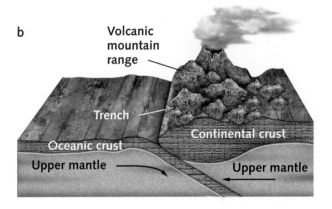

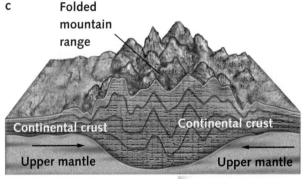

Figure 6.16 Convergent boundaries are classified according to the type of crust involved when two plates collide. There are three types of convergent boundaries: **a)** oceanic-oceanic, **b)** oceanic-continental, and **c)** continental-continental.

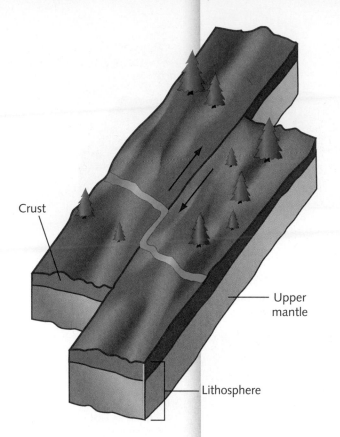

Crust

Upper mantle

Lithosphere

Figure 6.17 Plates slide horizontally past each other along a transform boundary. Transform boundaries are often the locations of shallow earthquakes.

Transform Boundaries   A **transform boundary** occurs when two tectonic plates slide horizontally past each other. Transform boundaries are different from divergent and convergent boundaries. At divergent boundaries, new crust is formed along ridges. At convergent boundaries, old crust is destroyed by subduction. At transform boundaries, however, crust is not created or destroyed. Instead, it changes shape, or is broken. Transform boundaries have long cracks that run along them, sometimes for hundreds of kilometers. These cracks are called faults. Earthquakes often take place along these faults. Though most transform boundaries are in the ocean, some are on continents. One example of a continental transform boundary is the San Andreas Fault in California. Movements along the San Andreas and other faults cause most of California's earthquakes.

Tracking Plate Movement

How are scientists able to tell that tectonic plates are moving? The movement of a tectonic plate is so slow it is difficult to observe. In recent years, scientists have been using the Global Positioning System (GPS) to monitor plate movement. With a network of GPS ground stations and satellites, scientists record the latitude and longitude of a number of locations on Earth. Over time, the latitudes and longitudes of these locations change slightly. By recording these changes over time, scientists have been able to track the rate of movement of the plates around the world.

After You Read

1. Read the lesson outline in your Science Notebook. What are the three types of convergent plate boundaries? Draw and label a diagram of each type.

2. Identify three types of plate boundaries.

3. Explain how the GPS can be used to monitor tectonic plate movement.

Before You Read

Create a K-W-L-S-H chart in your Science Notebook. Think about the term *stress*. In the column labeled *K*, write what you already know about stress. In the column labeled *W*, write what you want to learn about stress.

Rocks tend to be hard. It is unlikely that you could pick up one and break it with your hands. It takes a large amount of force to break most rocks. Yet, forces inside Earth break rocks all the time.

Rock Deformation

In science, **stress** is the amount of force per unit area that is applied to a given material. When rocks change shape due to stress, they undergo **deformation**. Deformation can occur when rocks break or bend. The three main types of stress that can cause rocks to deform are compression, tension, and shear.

Compression is the stress that occurs when something is squeezed. Compression of rocks usually occurs when two tectonic plates collide at a convergent boundary. The Andes mountain range along the west coast of South America is a result of compression at a convergent plate boundary. The second form of stress is tension. **Tension** is the stress that stretches an object. Tension occurs most often at divergent plate boundaries when two plates pull away from each other. **Shear stress** causes a material to stretch and become distorted. Shear stress occurs most often at transform plate boundaries.

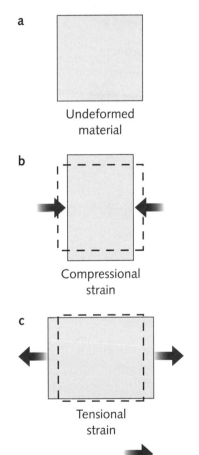

a — Undeformed material

b — Compressional strain

c — Tensional strain

d — Shear strain

Figure 6.18 The effects of the three main types of stress on undeformed material (**a**) are shown in figures **b**, **c**, and **d**. The arrows show the direction of the forces causing the stress. **b)** Compression squeezes the material. **c)** Tension stretches the material. **d)** Shear stress twists and stretches the material.

As You Read

In the column labeled *L* in your K-W-L-S-H chart, write several things you have learned about stress and how it changes rocks.

Which kind of stress causes monoclines to form?

Folding Tectonic forces put stress on rock layers, sometimes causing them to bend. This is called **folding**. There are three main kinds of rock folds: anticlines, synclines, and monoclines. Each of these is shown in **Figure 6.19**. Anticlines and synclines form when rock layers are compressed from the sides. Monoclines form when layers of rock are compressed from above or below. The arrows in the diagram show the direction of stress on the rock layers.

Figure 6.19 Stress on **a)** unfolded rock layers can form **b)** monoclines, **c)** synclines, and **d)** anticlines. Anticlines and synclines form as a result of horizontal compression on rock layers. Monoclines form as a result of vertical compression on rock layers.

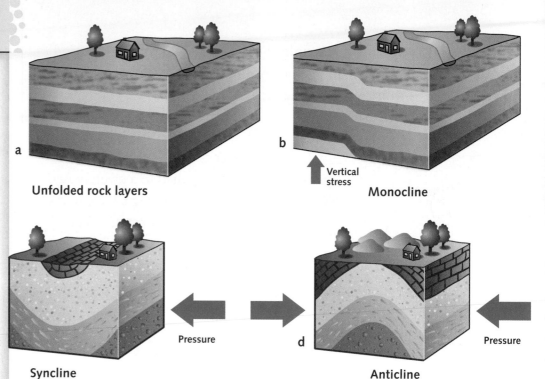

a Unfolded rock layers

b Vertical stress Monocline

c Pressure Syncline

d Pressure Anticline

Faulting

While rocks sometimes bend due to stress, they also sometimes break. When rocks break due to stress, a fault is created. A **fault** is the surface along which rocks break and slide past each other. This surface is called the fault plane. The blocks of Earth's crust on either side of a fault are called fault blocks. Usually, the rock does not break in a line that is perfectly vertical to the ground. When a fault occurs at an angle, the blocks on either side of the fault are called the hanging wall and the footwall. These two types of fault blocks are shown in **Figure 6.20**.

Scientists classify faults into different categories. The type of fault depends on how the footwall and hanging wall move relative to one another. The three main types of faults are normal faults, reverse faults, and strike-slip faults.

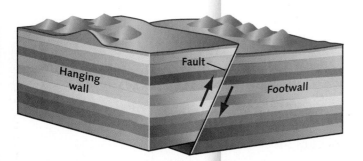

Hanging wall Fault Footwall

Figure 6.20 Whether a fault block is a hanging wall or a footwall depends on its position. The top of a hanging wall is always "hanging" above the fault plane.

Figure It Out

1. In which type of fault is there only horizontal movement of the hanging wall?
2. Which type of fault would be most likely to occur at a divergent boundary?

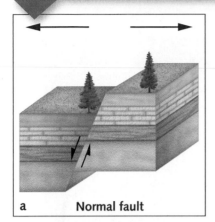

a   Normal fault

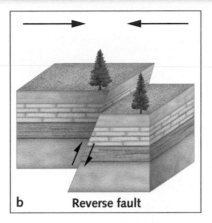

b   Reverse fault

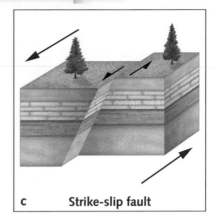

c   Strike-slip fault

Figure 6.21 In these images, the large arrows show the direction of stress on the rocks. The small arrows show the directions of the fault block movements. **a)** Normal faults form when rocks are pulled apart from opposite sides. **b)** Reverse faults form when rocks are squeezed together from opposite sides. **c)** Strike-slip faults form when horizontal stress is applied to the rock.

Normal Faults   When the hanging wall of a fault moves down relative to the footwall, this is called a **normal fault**. Normal faults usually occur when tectonic forces are pulling the lithosphere apart. They are usually caused by tension, and often occur at divergent boundaries.

Reverse Faults   When the hanging wall moves up relative to the footwall, this is called a **reverse fault**. Reverse faults usually occur when tectonic forces push pieces of the lithosphere together. They occur as a result of compression, and often take place at convergent boundaries.

Strike-slip Faults   In the third kind of fault, the hanging wall does not move up or down relative to the footwall. Instead, the hanging wall moves horizontally relative to the footwall when opposing forces cause rock to break. This is called a **strike-slip fault**. Strike-slip faults often form at right angles to transform boundaries.

Types of Mountains

When tectonic plates move and collide with each other, they create great amounts of stress on rocks. These stresses can cause folding and faulting. Sometimes, events such as earthquakes result. Often, the stress causes the land near the plate boundaries to change. Huge amounts of stress can result in the formation of mountain ranges. The four types of mountains are folded mountains, fault-block mountains, dome mountains, and volcanic mountains.

Explore It!

Place a stack of sheets of paper on the table in front of you. Put your hands on either side of the stack and push your hands toward each other. By compressing the stack of paper from the sides, you create a pattern of synclines and anticlines. Now place the stack of paper so that it is half on top of a book. Push the top of the stack of paper downward where it overlaps the edge of the book. Compressing the stack of paper from above creates a monocline.

Folded Mountains When rock layers are pushed together and fold upwards, **folded mountains** are formed. The highest mountains on Earth, the Himalayas in Asia, are an example of a folded mountain range. Folded mountains often occur along continental-continental convergent plate boundaries.

Figure 6.22 This photo shows a folded mountain in northern British Columbia.

Fault-Block Mountains Sometimes, when normal faults occur, the land on one side of the fault drops down relative to the land on the other side. When mountains are formed in this way, they are called **fault-block mountains**. Fault-block mountains can occur along normal faults at divergent plate boundaries. They can also form where the land is under tensional stress. The Grand Tetons in Wyoming are an example of fault-block mountains.

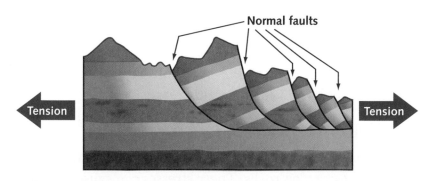

Figure 6.23 With enough tension on Earth's crust, a large number of normal faults can result. Fault-block mountains form when normal faulting causes large blocks of rock to drop relative to other blocks.

Figure 6.24 Mount St. Helens, in Washington State, is one example of a volcanic mountain.

Dome Mountains   **Dome mountains** are formed when Earth's crust heaves upward without folding or faulting occurring. These mountains are the result of massive amounts of magma pushing upward. The Adirondack Mountains of New York State and the Black Hills of South Dakota are examples of dome mountains. Dome mountains do not have to form at plate boundaries.

Volcanic Mountains   When magma erupts onto Earth's surface and forms mountains, they are called **volcanic mountains**. Volcanic mountains tend to form over convergent boundaries at subduction zones. Many of the mountains in the Cascade Range, which runs from Washington State to California, are volcanic mountains.

After You Read

1. Look at your completed K-W-L columns. Complete your K-W-L-S-H chart by writing what you would still like to learn about stress in the *S* column. Write how you can learn the information in the *H* column.

2. Explain the difference between faulting and folding.

3. Describe the three main types of faults and how they form.

Chapter 6

Summary

KEY CONCEPTS

6.1 Inside Earth

- Scientists define Earth's layers by their compositional and physical properties.
- The layers of Earth, as defined by their composition, are the crust, the mantle, and the core.
- The layers of Earth, as defined by their physical properties, are the lithosphere, the asthenosphere, the lower mantle, the outer core, and the inner core.

6.2 Continents in Motion

- According to Wegener's hypothesis of continental drift, all of the continents were once part of a supercontinent called Pangaea. This continent began to break apart about 200 million years ago.
- Wegener used fossils, climatic data, and rock formations to support his hypothesis of continental drift.
- The theory of seafloor spreading states that new ocean crust is formed at ocean ridges and destroyed at deep-sea trenches.
- Sonar and the magnetometer are two technologies that helped researchers collect evidence of seafloor spreading.

6.3 The Theory of Plate Tectonics

- Earth's lithosphere is divided into huge slabs called tectonic plates. These plates are in motion relative to one another.
- Scientists think that mantle convection, ridge push, and slab pull are the main forces that cause tectonic plates to move.
- The three types of tectonic plate boundaries are convergent boundaries, divergent boundaries, and transform boundaries. These boundaries are classified based on how the plates move relative to one another.
- The Global Positioning System (GPS) can be used to measure the motion of tectonic plates.

6.4 Plate Tectonics & Mountain Building

- The three main types of stress that cause rocks to deform are compression, tension, and shear.
- Stress on rocks can cause two types of deformation—folding and faulting. Folding occurs when stress on rock layers causes them to bend. Faulting occurs when stressed rock layers break.
- The three main types of faults are normal faults, reverse faults, and strike-slip faults. The type of fault depends on how the footwall and hanging wall move relative to one another.
- Four types of mountains are folded mountains, fault-block mountains, dome mountains, and volcanic mountains.

VOCABULARY REVIEW

Write each term in a complete sentence or write a paragraph relating several terms.

6.1
crust, p. 88
mantle, p. 89
core, p. 89
lithosphere, p. 90
asthenosphere, p. 90
lower mantle, p. 91
outer core, p. 91
inner core, p. 91

6.2
continental drift, p. 93
seafloor spreading, p. 96
magnetic reversal, p. 98

6.3
theory of plate tectonics, p. 99
convection, p. 100
ridge push, p. 101
slab pull, p. 101
divergent boundary, p. 102
rift valley, p. 102
convergent boundary, p. 102
subduction, p. 103
transform boundary, p. 104

6.4
stress, p. 105
deformation, p. 105
compression, p. 105
tension, p. 105
shear stress, p. 105
folding, p. 106
fault, p. 106
normal fault, p. 107
reverse fault, p. 107
strike-slip fault, p. 107
folded mountain, p. 108
fault-block mountain, p. 108
dome mountain, p. 109
volcanic mountain, p. 109

True or False

If the statement is true, write "true." If it is false, change the underlined word or words to make the statement true.

1. There are <u>four</u> different ways that scientists define Earth's layers.

2. The innermost layer of Earth as defined by its physical properties is the <u>asthenosphere</u>.

3. The hypothesis of <u>continental drift</u> says that all the continents were once part of a giant supercontinent that began to break apart about 200 million years ago.

4. <u>Ridge pull</u> is thought to be one of the causes of tectonic plate movement.

5. Tectonic plate movement can be tracked using the <u>Global Positioning System (GPS)</u>.

6. <u>Faulting</u> occurs when forces act on rocks but they do not break.

Short Answer

Answer each of the following in a sentence or brief paragraph.

7. Explain the difference between a normal and a reverse fault.

8. List and describe the five layers of Earth as defined by their physical properties.

9. Explain the theory of seafloor spreading.

10. Compare and contrast the three types of convergent plate boundaries.

11. Describe three types of faults and at what kind of boundary they are likely to occur.

12. List three types of mountains and explain how each is formed.

PREPARE FOR CHAPTER TEST

To prepare for the chapter test, create a question from each Learning Goal. Use the information in your Science Notebook to answer each question. Then use these answers to write a well-developed essay about the chapter. Use the Key Concept on the first page of this chapter as your topic sentence.

Critical Thinking

Use what you have learned in this chapter to answer each of the following.

13. **Support** Describe evidence that supports the hypothesis of continental drift.

14. **Infer** How might tectonic activity have led people to call the volcanic area around the Pacific Ocean the "Ring of Fire"?

15. **Apply Concepts** Based on the map of Earth's tectonic plates shown below, what kind of mountains might form between the South American Plate and the African Plate?

Standardized Test Question

Choose the letter of the response that correctly answers the question.

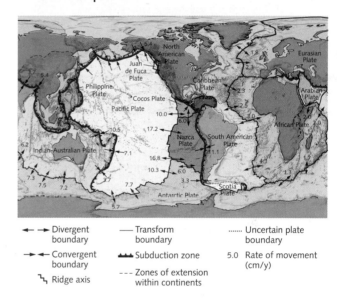

16. What kind of plate boundary exists between the Nazca Plate and the Pacific Plate?

    A. divergent boundary

    B. convergent boundary

    C. transform boundary

    D. compression boundary

Test-Taking Tip

If you finish before time is up, check your answers. Make sure you answered each part of every question and didn't skip any parts.

Earthquakes

KEY CONCEPT Earthquakes are natural events that can cause great damage and loss of human life.

Imagine that the date is October 17, 1989. You are walking down a street in the Marina District of San Francisco, California. Suddenly, the ground under your feet begins to shake violently. Knowing what to do, you move carefully and quickly away from large buildings and power lines. When you reach the middle of a playing field, you lie down and cover your head. The ground shakes up and down, again and again. Finally, the shaking stops. Looking around, you see that a nearby building has collapsed. All of this could have happened to you if you were in San Francisco in 1989 during the Loma Prieta earthquake.

Think About the Ground Shaking

Imagine standing on a trampoline as people are jumping up and down on it.

- How do you think standing on a trampoline while others are jumping might feel like the ground shaking during an earthquake?

- In your Science Notebook, draw two side views of yourself standing on a trampoline. The drawings should show you before and after someone else jumps on the trampoline.

www.scilinks.org

Earthquakes **Code: WGES07**

7.1 What Are Earthquakes?

Before You Read

Create a set of vocabulary cards for this lesson. Use one index card for each vocabulary term. On the front of each card, write one of the vocabulary terms from the lesson. Set the cards aside for use later in this chapter.

Learning Goals

- Identify where most earthquakes take place.
- Explain what causes earthquakes to occur.
- Describe how earthquakes travel through Earth.

New Vocabulary

earthquake
fault zone
focus
epicenter
elastic rebound
seismic wave
primary wave (P-wave)
secondary wave (S-wave)
surface wave
tsunami

Recall Vocabulary

fault, p. 106
mantle, p. 89
deformation, p. 105
stress, p. 105
shear stress, p. 105
theory of plate tectonics, p. 99

If you have felt the ground shake beneath you as a truck drives by, you know what a minor earthquake feels like. Now imagine what it would be like if the shaking was multiplied 100 times! Some earthquakes have caused the ground to move up and down as much as ten meters.

Where do earthquakes happen?

An **earthquake** is the shaking of the ground caused by sudden movement of matter within Earth. Most earthquakes occur at or near the edges of Earth's tectonic plate boundaries, along breaks, or faults, in Earth's crust as shown in **Figure 7.1**. Most earthquakes occur along fault zones. **Fault zones** are areas where complex patterns of faults exist due to tectonic plate movement. One of the largest fault zones in the United States is the San Andreas Fault Zone, along which the Loma Prieta earthquake of 1989 took place. A similar fault zone is the North Anatolian Fault Zone in Turkey. During the 1900s, seven major earthquakes took place along this 900-km-long fault zone.

Earthquakes occur underground in the brittle rock of Earth's lithosphere. The underground location where an earthquake occurs is called the **focus**. The depth of a focus depends on the type of plate boundary at which the earthquake occurs. The point on Earth's surface directly above the focus of an earthquake is the earthquake's **epicenter**.

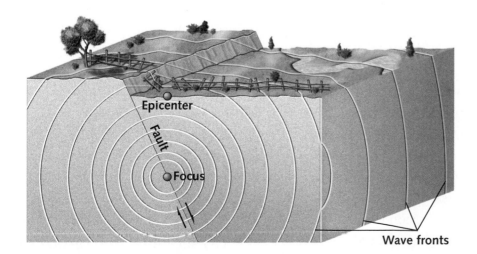

Epicenter

Fault

Focus

Wave fronts

Figure 7.1 The point underground where rock breaks causing an earthquake is the focus. The point on Earth directly above the focus is the earthquake's epicenter.

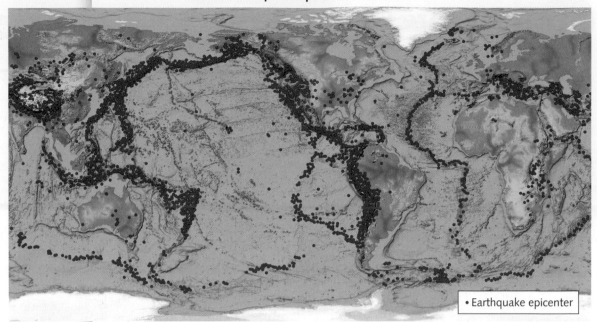

• Earthquake epicenter

Figure 7.2 This map shows the locations of earthquake epicenters that have been plotted by scientists over the years. Most of the world's earthquakes occur in narrow seismic belts that are associated with tectonic plate boundaries.

What causes earthquakes?

The pushing, pulling, and scraping of Earth's tectonic plates against one another causes stress to build up along faults near the plates' edges. When stress builds up in rocks, they begin to change shape. This is called deformation. There are two kinds of deformation: ductile deformation and elastic deformation. Ductile deformation does not lead to earthquakes. Elastic deformation, however, does. This is because there is a limit to how much elastic deformation a rock can withstand before it bends permanently or breaks.

During ductile deformation, rocks change shape slowly over many years due to stress. Rocks changed by ductile deformation permanently keep their new shapes. Ductile deformation does not cause earthquakes because it does not cause sudden motion. However, elastic deformation is more destructive than ductile deformation. During elastic deformation, rocks do not change shape permanently. Instead, they stretch until they reach their limit, or breaking point. The broken pieces of rock then return suddenly to their original shapes, releasing large amounts of energy. **Elastic rebound** is the return of elastically deformed rock to its original shape after the rock has experienced enough stress to cause it to break. The energy released during elastic rebound of rocks is what causes earthquakes. Some earthquakes can release as much energy as the explosion of 6,000,000 tons of dynamite! In comparison, the atomic bomb that was dropped over Nagasaki, Japan, during World War II was equivalent to more than 20,000 tons of TNT.

As You Read

For the vocabulary terms that have already been covered in the lesson, complete your vocabulary cards. On the back of each card, write the definition of the term and the page on which the term is first defined.

What is the difference between ductile deformation and elastic deformation?

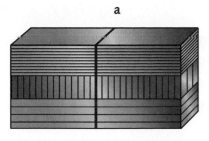
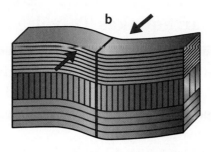
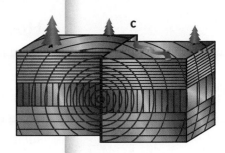

Figure 7.3 a) When too much stress acts on rock layers along a fault, they undergo elastic rebound. In the first view, there is no stress on the rock layers. **b)** In the second view, stress has caused elastic deformation along either side of the fault, and the rock layers are now bent. **c)** In the third view, enough stress has built up to cause the rock layers along the fault to break and return to their original shapes, releasing energy in the form of an earthquake.

Strength and Depth of Earthquakes   The strength of an earthquake and the depth at which it originates depends on the type of tectonic plate motion that causes the earthquake. The first type of motion is transform motion, during which two plates slip past one another. This type of motion causes shear stress, a type of stress that occurs when an object is twisted. It creates strike-slip faults and causes moderate, shallow earthquakes. Convergent motion, during which two plates push together, is the second type of tectonic movement. This type of motion causes compression, a type of stress that occurs when an object is squeezed from opposite sides. It creates reverse faults and leads to strong, deep earthquakes. The third type of motion, divergent motion, occurs when two plates pull away from one another. This type of motion leads to tension, a type of stress that occurs when an object is stretched from opposite sides. It creates normal faults and causes weak, shallow earthquakes. For a diagram showing strike-slip, reverse, and normal faults, refer to **Figure 6.20** in Chapter 6.

Figure It Out

1. Which type of plate motion causes the strongest and deepest earthquakes? Which type of plate motion causes the weakest earthquakes?

2. Which types of faults are associated with the shallowest earthquakes?

3. Describe the characteristics of an earthquake associated with transform plate motion. Use the information in the chart.

Tectonic Plate Motion	Most Common Stress	Most Common Fault Type	Earthquake Strength	Earthquake Depth
transform	shear	strike-slip fault	moderate	0–70 km
convergent	compression	reverse fault	strong	70–700 km
divergent	tension	normal fault	weak	0–70 km

Figure 7.4 This chart shows the characteristics of earthquakes associated with different types of plate motion.

Explore It!

With a partner, stretch a large coiled spring across a table. You should each hold one end of the spring so that it is in contact with the table. First, compress and release some of the coils of the spring to create a wave that travels to your partner. What kind of seismic wave does this resemble? Next, create a wave in the spring that travels like an S-wave. Then create a wave in the spring that travels like a surface wave.

How Earthquakes Travel

When rocks break at the focus of an earthquake, the released energy travels in the form of seismic waves. **Seismic waves** can be felt as the vibrations of the ground during an earthquake. Earthquakes generate three types of seismic waves: primary waves, secondary waves, and surface waves.

The waves that travel fastest from the focus of an earthquake are **primary waves**, or P-waves. P-waves move in a push-pull motion and can travel through solids, liquids, and gases. Because P-waves travel quickly and can pass through all parts of Earth, they are the first seismic waves to be detected during an earthquake. **Secondary waves**, or S-waves, are the second-fastest seismic waves. S-waves move particles from side to side as they move forward. Unlike P-waves, S-waves can only travel through solids. They cannot travel through liquids or gases. The third type of seismic waves, **surface waves**, move in two directions as they pass through rock—side to side and up and down. Surface waves travel along Earth's surface, while P-waves and S-waves travel through Earth's interior. Because they travel through Earth's interior, P-waves and S-waves are also called body waves. **Figure 7.5** shows how each type of seismic wave moves rock particles as it passes through rock.

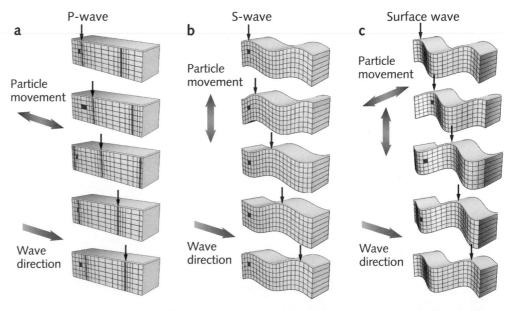

Figure 7.5 Rock particles are shown as small red squares. The red arrows indicate particle movement. The blue arrows indicate wave direction. **a)** P-waves squeeze and stretch rock particles in the same direction the wave is traveling. **b)** S-waves cause rock particles to move at right angles in relation to the direction of the waves. **c)** Surface waves cause rock particles to move from side to side as they pass. At the same time, they cause an up-and-down movement similar to that of an ocean wave.

Tsunamis

The vertical movement of the seafloor during an earthquake can generate a large, powerful, ocean wave called a **tsunami**. During an earthquake, the seafloor may drop down. This creates a dip in the water directly above this spot. Water rushes into this low area and eventually creates an overflow, or high point, at this spot. As the water level evens out, the extra water rushes away from the area in all directions and a large wave is formed. Tsunamis may also be caused by volcanic eruptions or landslides. In these cases, the water is pushed forward as the eruption or landslide occurs, and a large wave is formed.

In deep water, a tsunami wave is barely detectable. As the wave passes over shallower water, it begins to build in height and speed. Tsunami waves can reach heights of more than 30 m and travel at speeds of up to 800 km per hour. Land areas that have shallow, gentle coastlines are in more danger than steep coastlines. This is because the wave has more time to build in height as it approaches the land. When the tsunami reaches land, it can cause great damage and loss of life.

CONNECTION: Physics

There are two general classes of waves: mechanical and electromagnetic waves. Mechanical waves include sound waves, ocean waves, and seismic waves. In order for mechanical waves to travel through space, they need matter, or atoms. Electromagnetic waves include visible light and infrared and ultraviolet radiation. Unlike mechanical waves, electromagnetic waves do not need to move through matter in order to travel through space. This explains why electromagnetic waves from stars can travel through near-empty outer space and appear as visible light to humans on Earth.

Figure 7.6 A powerful earthquake occurred on the floor of the Indian Ocean on December 26, 2004. The resulting tsunami smashed into the west coast of Thailand and other countries bordering the Indian Ocean. More than 225,000 people were killed. This photo was taken in Phuket, Thailand, the day after the tsunami hit. The catastrophe was one of the deadliest disasters in modern history.

After You Read

1. Complete your vocabulary cards and use them to review the meanings of the vocabulary words from the lesson. What is the difference between the focus and the epicenter of an earthquake?

2. Explain the relationship between elastic rebound and the occurrence of earthquakes.

3. In a well-developed paragraph, identify the three types of seismic waves and describe how each travels.

7.2 Measuring and Locating Earthquakes

Before You Read

Create an outline for this lesson. Use the lesson title as the outline title. Label the main headings with the Roman numerals *I* through *III*. Use the letters *A*, *B*, *C*, etc., under each heading to record information you want to remember.

Recording Earthquakes

Seismologists (siz MAH luh jihsts) are Earth scientists who study earthquakes. After an earthquake occurs, they use earthquake-sensing tools to find out when and where it occurred. Seismologists begin their investigation of earthquakes by studying a record of the event. A **seismometer**, or seismograph as it is more commonly called, is a scientific instrument used to record seismic waves. Seismometers record the size and direction of seismic waves as well as the time at which the waves occur. The record created by a seismometer is called a **seismogram**. Most modern seismometers use electronic signals to create digital seismograms. They work, however, in a way that is similar to older mechanical seismometers.

A mechanical seismometer is made up of a metal frame that is firmly attached to Earth's bedrock. Inside the seismometer is a heavy, hanging weight, or mass, suspended from a spring or wire. The mass resists movement, even when the ground shakes the rest of the seismometer. A pen is attached to the mass. This pen draws a line on a piece of paper that covers a rotating drum. The drum is attached to the frame of the seismometer. When the ground shakes, the seismometer frame, the drum, and the paper move. While the paper shakes, the mass and pen stay still. This makes a wavy line on the paper and records the movement of the ground.

Figure 7.7 The seismometer on the left records vertical motion of the ground during an earthquake. The seismometer on the right records horizontal motion.

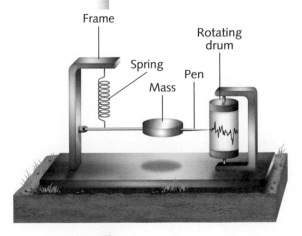

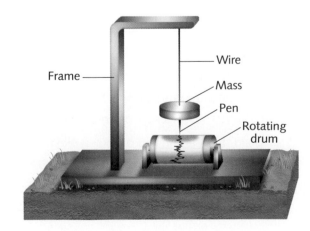

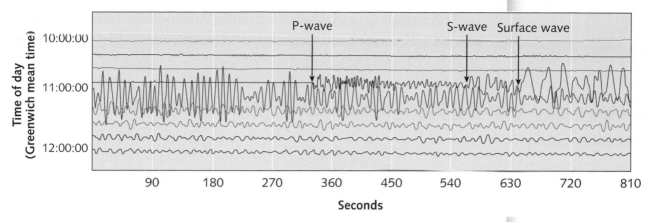

Figure 7.8 This is a section of a seismogram reading taken during an earthquake. Each line represents 15 minutes, and time increases from top to bottom and from left to right. Notice that because P-waves travel most quickly, they arrive first. S-waves arrive second, and surface waves arrive last.

A single seismometer can only record the movement of the ground around it in one dimension. To accurately record the shaking of Earth during an earthquake, scientists usually place three seismometers together. One seismometer records vertical motion, while the other two record two dimensions of horizontal motion.

Locating Earthquakes

Seismologists have collected data from many earthquakes and used the information to construct travel-time curves for P-waves and S-waves as shown in **Figure 7.9**. These curves provide information about the average time it takes seismic waves to travel different distances. These average travel times hold true, no matter where on Earth an earthquake occurs. For example, assume that a particular seismograph recorded that the first S-wave arrived five minutes after the first P-wave arrived. By locating the place on the graph where the two curves are separated by five minutes, one can determine that the epicenter is located 1,500 km from the seismograph station.

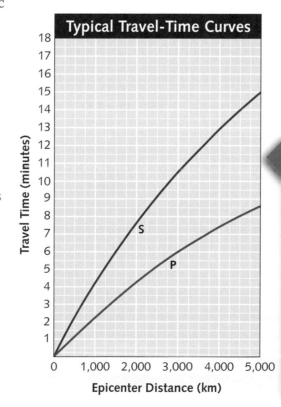

Figure 7.9 Travel-time curves show the time it takes for P-waves and S-waves to travel to seismometers located at different distances from an earthquake's epicenter.

Figure It Out

1. Determine how many minutes it takes for a typical P-wave to travel 3,000 km. How many minutes does it take an S-wave to travel the same distance?

2. Explain what happens to the time separation between the curves for the P-waves and S-waves as the distance they travel increases.

As You Read

Look at your outline. Make sure that you have included additional information. Share your outline with a partner and add any missing information.

What is a seismometer used for?

Explain It!

In your Science Notebook, write a paragraph in your own words explaining why two seismograms from different seismograph stations would not give you enough information to locate the epicenter of an earthquake.

With a reading of the distance from an earthquake's epicenter from just one seismograph, the epicenter of an earthquake could be anywhere on a circle with a radius equal to that distance. As **Figure 7.10** shows, to find the precise location of an earthquake's epicenter, readings from at least three different seismogram locations are needed.

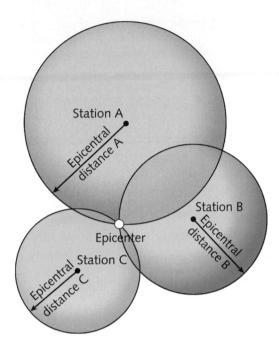

Figure 7.10 To determine the exact location of an earthquake's epicenter, the locations of three seismograph stations are plotted on a map. A circle is drawn around each seismograph station. The radius of each circle equals the distance from each seismograph station to the earthquake's epicenter. (This distance is read from the travel-time graph.) All three circles intersect at only one point. This point is the earthquake's epicenter.

PEOPLE IN SCIENCE Dr. Inge Lehmann   1888–1993

Dr. Inge Lehmann was a Danish seismologist and geophysicist. She was the first woman to have a medal named in her honor by the American Geophysical Union. In 1936, Dr. Lehmann published one of her most notable papers. After carefully studying many seismograms, she observed that the behavior of P-waves seemed odd. The P-waves were deflecting off something in Earth's interior. Based on observations of S-wave behavior, scientists had already determined that Earth's core was liquid. Dr. Lehmann hypothesized that Earth's core had two distinct regions: an inner solid core and an outer liquid core. Her hypothesis, which has been supported by further studies, has become today's accepted theory that Earth has a solid inner core.

Dr. Lehmann had a long and distinguished career, serving as the chief of the Seismological Department at the Royal Danish Geodetic Institute for 25 years. After retiring at the age of 65, she continued her studies and publications. Her later work included research and visits to several universities in the United States. In 1971, Dr. Lehmann was the first woman to receive the William Bowie Medal, the highest honor of the American Geophysical Union.

Measuring Earthquake Strength

Most earthquakes cause little, if any, damage. In fact, of the more than one million earthquakes that occur each year, less than ten percent cause any damage or are even felt by humans. Seismologists have developed several methods to measure the strength of earthquakes. **Magnitude** is a measurement that describes the amount of energy released during an earthquake. The **intensity** of an earthquake is a measurement of how much damage the earthquake causes to structures in a particular location—the higher the magnitude, the greater the intensity. Two scales are commonly used to measure the magnitude of an earthquake: the Richter scale and the moment magnitude scale. The scale most often used to measure the intensity of an earthquake is the modified Mercalli scale.

Richter Scale The **Richter scale** is a magnitude scale developed in 1934 by American seismologist Charles Richter. This scale is the one most commonly referred to in news reports about earthquakes. The Richter scale is based on the size of the largest earthquake waves recorded on a seismogram. The larger the number on the Richter scale, the larger the size of the waves produced by the earthquake. Numbers on the Richter scale are also directly related to the amount of energy released during an earthquake. They measure the size of seismic waves in powers of ten. For example, a magnitude-5 earthquake has waves that are ten times larger than a magnitude-4 earthquake. Similarly, a magnitude-6 earthquake has waves that are 100 times larger than a magnitude-4 earthquake. The amount of energy released between magnitudes on the Richter scale is even larger. Each increase in magnitude represents an increase in the seismic energy released by about 32 times.

Moment Magnitude Scale Today, most seismologists use the moment magnitude scale to measure the strength of earthquakes. The **moment magnitude scale** uses a number of different factors to measure the magnitude of an earthquake. These factors include the size of the fault at which the earthquake started, the stiffness of the rocks that broke at the fault, and the amount of movement along the fault. The moment magnitude scale also uses several types of seismic waves to measure an earthquake's magnitude. In contrast, the Richter scale bases its measurement of magnitude only on the largest seismic waves generated by an earthquake.

Figure 7.11 The damage to this building in the city of Kobe, Japan, was caused by a 1995 earthquake that had a magnitude of 6.9 on the Richter scale. The earthquake destroyed more than 192,000 houses and buildings and more than 5,400 people were killed.

Modified Mercalli Intensity Scale

I.	Not felt except under unusual conditions.
II.	Felt only by a few persons. Suspended objects may swing.
III.	Quite noticeable indoors. Vibrations are like the passing of a truck.
IV.	Felt indoors by many; outdoors by a few. Dishes and windows rattle. Standing cars rock noticeably.
V.	Felt by nearly everyone. Some dishes and windows break, and some plaster cracks.
VI.	Felt by all. Furniture moves. Some plaster falls, and some chimneys are damaged.
VII.	Everybody runs outdoors. Some chimneys break. Damage is slight in well-built structures but considerable in weak structures.
VIII.	Chimneys, smokestacks, and walls fall. Heavy furniture is overturned. Partial collapse of ordinary buildings occurs.
IX.	Great general damage occurs. Buildings shift off foundations. Ground cracks. Underground pipes break.
X.	Most ordinary structures are destroyed. Rails are bent. Landslides are common.
XI.	Few buildings remain standing. Bridges are destroyed. Railroad ties are greatly bent. Broad fissures form in the ground.
XII.	Damage is total. Objects are thrown upward into the air.

Figure 7.12 On the Modified Mercalli Intensity Scale, the higher the Roman numeral, the more damage the earthquake caused.

Modified Mercalli Intensity Scale The **modified Mercalli intensity scale** rates the types of damage and other effects of an earthquake based on the observations of people who experienced it. The scale uses the Roman numerals I through XII to rate the intensity of an earthquake. The higher the Roman numeral, the more damage the earthquake caused.

Depth of Focus Earthquake intensity is also related to the depth of an earthquake's focus. An earthquake with a focus deep below Earth's surface produces smaller vibrations at its epicenter than an earthquake with a shallow focus. The seismic waves from an earthquake with a deep focus also have to travel farther to reach Earth's surface than do the seismic waves from an earthquake with a shallow focus. Because they travel farther, the seismic waves from an earthquake with a deep focus lose some of their energy before reaching Earth's surface. This is why a shallow-focus earthquake with a magnitude of 5 might be more destructive than a deep-focus earthquake with a magnitude of 7. Shallow-focus earthquakes are usually the ones that cause the greatest structural damage and loss of life.

After You Read

1. Review the lesson outline in your Science Notebook. Use the information in your outline to explain how seismograms are related to travel-time curves.

2. Contrast the Richter scale with the modified Mercalli intensity scale.

3. Use the modified Mercalli intensity scale shown above to rate the intensity of the earthquake that caused the damage to Kobe, Japan, shown in **Figure 7.11**.

7.3 Earthquakes and Society

Learning Goals

- Explain what a seismic risk map shows.
- Describe the methods used by seismologists to predict earthquakes.
- List ways to build earthquake-resistant buildings.
- List things you can do to prepare for an earthquake.

New Vocabulary

seismic gap

Before You Read

Preview the lesson by looking at the figures and photos. Read the headings and the Learning Goals. In your Science Notebook, write a paragraph describing what you think the lesson will be about.

Earthquakes are amazing natural events, but they can also be deadly. Seismologists have learned a lot about Earth by studying earthquakes after they have happened. They now know that some areas of Earth are at higher risk for earthquakes than others. Seismologists, however, are still searching for ways to reliably predict exactly when and where an earthquake will occur.

Seismic Risk

From studying seismograms, seismologists know that most earthquakes occur in regions close to tectonic plate boundaries. There are exceptions, however. For example, several disastrous earthquakes have taken place in the central part of the United States, away from any tectonic boundary. Seismic risk is a measure of how likely an area is to experience earthquakes in the future. Seismologists used records of past seismic activity to create the seismic risk map shown in **Figure 7.13**. The areas of the map shown in red have suffered large earthquakes in the past and will probably experience large earthquakes in the future. As you might expect, areas close to the Pacific Ocean, where there is a tectonic plate boundary, have a high risk of seismic damage. There are also areas of high seismic risk in the eastern and central United States.

Seismic Risk Map of the United States

Damage Expected
- None
- Minor
- Moderate
- Major

Figure 7.13 In the United States, areas with the highest seismic risk include Alaska, Hawaii, and some of the western states. Locate your area of the country on the map. What is its level of seismic risk?

There have been many reports over the years of peculiar animal behavior just before an earthquake occurs. This behavior includes dogs howling, fish jumping out of ponds, hibernating snakes leaving their holes, caged birds becoming restless, and nervous cats hiding. Scientists in China have monitored animal behavior related to earthquakes for several decades. They have discovered that, while not all earthquakes lead to unusual animal behavior, some do. More research into the ability of different animals to detect seismic activity could lead to the development of new earthquake prediction methods.

Predicting Earthquakes

Predicting when and where an earthquake will occur is difficult. Monitoring or doing a detailed examination of the history of earthquakes of different magnitudes helps seismologists predict the strengths and locations of future earthquakes. Seismologists also look at the absence of earthquake activity along a fault and the buildup of pressure, or strain, along active faults. These features help seismologists determine the probability that an earthquake will occur along a fault.

Magnitude and Frequency   As discussed in Lesson 7.2, different earthquakes release different amounts of energy. They have different magnitudes, or strengths. Though the occurrence of earthquakes is unpredictable, the magnitude of earthquakes is related to how often they occur. The table in **Figure 7.14** shows that for each step down in earthquake magnitude, the number of earthquakes per year is about ten times greater. This pattern is observed both globally and locally. For example, during the time period that one magnitude-3 earthquake occurred along the San Andreas Fault, about ten magnitude-2 earthquakes occurred in the same area. This information allows scientists to make predictions about the strength, location, and frequency of future earthquakes.

Figure It Out

1. What is the magnitude of an earthquake described as moderate?
2. Calculate approximately how many times more earthquakes with a magnitude of 3–3.9 occur each year than earthquakes with a magnitude of 5–5.9.

Worldwide Frequency of Earthquake Occurrence		
Description of Earthquake	**Moment Magnitude**	**Average Number of Earthquakes per Year**
great	8 and higher	1
major	7–7.9	17
strong	6–6.9	134
moderate	5–5.9	1,319
light	4–4.9	about 13,000
minor	3–3.9	about 130,000
very minor	2–2.9	about 1,300,000

Figure 7.14 This table shows the average annual number of earthquakes at each magnitude level observed since 1990.

Seismic Gaps   Another method that seismologists use to predict earthquakes is the seismic gap hypothesis. A **seismic gap** is a section along an active fault that, when compared to the area around it, has not experienced an earthquake for a long period of time. This hypothesis states that strong earthquakes are more likely to occur at seismic gaps. There is a seismic gap in the fault that runs just south of Tokyo, Japan. While this area of the fault has a history of large earthquakes, it has not experienced an earthquake since 1854. A seismic gap runs through San Francisco along the San Andreas Fault. The last major earthquake in this section of the fault occurred in 1906. Scientists predict a magnitude 7 or higher earthquake will hit San Francisco sometime over the next 30 years.

Strain Accumulation   Seismologists use several measurements to determine the probability of an earthquake striking a particular section of a fault. They measure the strain that has built up in rocks along the fault. They also measure how much strain was released during the last earthquake at that section of the fault. Finally, they factor in the amount of time that has passed since the last earthquake occurred at that section of the fault.

Earthquake Damage

During the strongest earthquakes, the shaking of the ground by surface waves can last as long as several minutes. This prolonged shaking is what causes the majority of earthquake damage. The danger to humans during an earthquake, however, is not from the shaking of the ground itself. It is from the collapse of buildings and other structures that cannot withstand the violent motion.

As You Read
Review the paragraph you wrote based on your preview of the lesson. Was your prediction about the content of the lesson correct? Revise your paragraph based on what you have learned so far.

What causes the most damage during an earthquake?

Figure 7.15 This car was destroyed when a nearby building fell on top of it during a 1999 earthquake in Taiwan.

Earthquake-Resistant Buildings   Engineers have developed a number of ways to construct earthquake-resistant buildings. Reinforced concrete is concrete with steel rods or bars embedded in it. Supporting walls, called shear walls, are made of reinforced concrete. The steel rods in the concrete strengthen the structures of buildings and help resist rocking forces during an earthquake. The walls of buildings may also be strengthened with diagonal steel beams, using a technique called cross-bracing. Devices called base isolators, made of layers of steel and rubber, can also be placed between the building and its foundation. They absorb some of the sideways motion of a building during an earthquake. A moat, or space around the foundation of a building, allows it to sway. In addition to the structural designs described above, very tall skyscrapers must be anchored deeply into the ground. They must be both flexible and structurally strong to withstand a violent earthquake.

Figure 7.16 This photo shows a portion of the Woodrow Wilson bridge that spans the Potomac River. Concrete was poured over these green steel bars to build the foundation and reinforce this concrete bridge.

Earthquake Safety Preparation

In areas likely to experience earthquakes, planning ahead can help people protect themselves and their property from earthquake damage. The first step in preparing for an earthquake is developing a safety plan. This plan should outline what to do before, during, and after an earthquake. Once the plan has been developed, it is important to share it with family members and to follow it closely when an earthquake occurs.

Before an Earthquake   Before an earthquake occurs, it is important to choose a safe meeting place for family members to gather after the earthquake is over. Heavy items located high on shelves in homes should be placed closer to the ground where they will not fall and cause injury. Any known structural weaknesses in the home should be reinforced. Because earthquakes may damage power lines, water pipes, and roads, it is also important to create an earthquake safety kit. This kit should include drinking water, a battery-powered radio and flashlight, a first-aid kit, canned food, a fire extinguisher, and warm clothing.

Figure 7.17 Korean high school students take cover under their desks during an earthquake drill.

During an Earthquake   If you are indoors at the start of an earthquake, the best thing to do is to find a sturdy piece of furniture to hide underneath. If you are outdoors, it is best to find an open location far from buildings, power lines, and other things that could fall to the ground. Lie facedown and cover your head with your arms. If you are in a vehicle, stop the vehicle and stay inside. Remember what you have learned about earthquakes. If you feel one quick burst of shaking, that may just be the P-waves passing. Stay in a safe place for several minutes after the first shaking to allow S-waves and surface waves to pass.

After an Earthquake   After an earthquake passes, remember that there may still be danger. Broken natural gas lines can leak, leading to fires. Weakened buildings can collapse after the shaking caused by the earthquake stops. Fallen power lines can cause fires or electrocution. Stay away from dangerous areas, and go to the location you have planned to meet your family or friends. Use your earthquake safety kit if necessary. There may be aftershocks, or sudden movements of the ground, following an earthquake. You should stay in a secure area until you are sure it is safe to return to your home or school.

Extend It!

Research the kind of natural disaster that is most likely to occur in the area where you live. In your Science Notebook, create a plan indicating what to do before, during, and after such a disaster. Include a list of the items you should have on hand should this disaster strike.

After You Read

1. Explain the seismic gap hypothesis.

2. Explain why it is important to understand the seismic history of an area.

3. Describe the role of shear walls in building earthquake-resistant buildings.

4. Review the paragraph you wrote in your Science Notebook. Use what you have learned in this lesson to list things you should do to protect yourself during and after an earthquake. Include facts and information from the entire lesson.

Summary

KEY CONCEPTS

7.1 What Are Earthquakes?

- Most earthquakes occur at or near Earth's tectonic plate boundaries along breaks, or faults, in Earth's crust.
- The pushing, pulling, and scraping of Earth's tectonic plates against one another causes stress to build up along faults near the plate boundaries. The stress causes the rock to break, sending out waves that shake the ground.
- Energy released by earthquakes travels through Earth in the form of seismic waves.

7.2 Measuring and Locating Earthquakes

- Seismologists use seismographs to detect and record seismic waves.
- By calculating the difference in arrival times between P-waves and S-waves, seismologists can determine the distance from a seismograph to the epicenter of an earthquake. Using readings for the same earthquake from three different seismograph stations, seismologists can plot the exact location of an earthquake's epicenter.
- The strength, or magnitude, of an earthquake is usually measured on the moment magnitude scale. This scale takes into account several factors, including the size of the fault at which the earthquake occurred, the strength of the rocks that broke at the fault, and the amount of movement along the fault.

7.3 Earthquakes and Society

- Seismic risk maps show how likely an area is to experience earthquakes in the future.
- Seismologists monitor seismic gaps, strain along active faults, and the history of earthquakes of different magnitudes to predict the strengths and locations of future earthquakes.
- Buildings can be made earthquake-resistant by using reinforced concrete to build supporting walls, diagonal steel beams to strengthen walls, and base isolators to absorb motion. Tall buildings can be anchored into the ground.
- An earthquake safety plan and kit should be created before an earthquake occurs. During an earthquake, find a safe place far from falling objects and structures and wait until the earthquake is over. After the earthquake, avoid dangerous areas and meet up with friends or family in a safe location.

VOCABULARY REVIEW

Write each term in a complete sentence or write a paragraph relating several terms.

7.1
earthquake, p. 113
fault zone, p. 113
focus, p. 113
epicenter, p. 113
elastic rebound, p. 114
seismic wave, p. 116
primary wave (P-wave), p. 116
secondary wave (S-wave), p. 116
surface wave, p. 116
tsunami, p. 117

7.2
seismologist, p. 118
seismometer, p. 118
seismogram, p. 118
magnitude, p. 121
intensity, p. 121
Richter scale, p. 121
moment magnitude scale, p. 121
modified Mercalli intensity scale, p. 122

7.3
seismic gap, p. 125

PREPARE FOR CHAPTER TEST

To prepare for the chapter test, create a question from each Learning Goal. Use the information in your Science Notebook to answer each question. Then use these answers to write a well-developed essay about the chapter. Use the Key Concept on the first page of this chapter as your topic sentence.

MASTERING CONCEPTS

True or False
If the statement is true, write "true." If it is false, change the underlined word or words to make the statement true.

1. Earthquakes are <u>least</u> likely to occur in fault zones.

2. The fastest seismic waves are <u>surface waves</u>.

3. A <u>seismogram</u> is a record of seismic waves created by a seismograph.

4. Seismologists use the difference in speed between P-waves and <u>surface waves</u> to determine the distance between the seismograph and the epicenter.

5. Most of the damage caused by an earthquake is a result of <u>prolonged shaking</u> of the ground.

6. Areas with the <u>lowest</u> seismic risk are most likely to experience earthquake damage in the future.

Short Answer
Answer each of the following in a sentence or brief paragraph.

7. How do shear walls help buildings withstand earthquakes?

8. Describe how the modified Mercalli intensity scale rates earthquakes.

9. What information do travel-time curves provide?

10. Explain the difference between an earthquake's magnitude and its intensity.

11. Describe what you should do to protect yourself before, during, and after an earthquake.

12. Explain the seismic gap hypothesis.

Critical Thinking
Use what you have learned in this chapter to answer each of the following.

13. **Infer** Two houses are built in an area that experiences frequent earthquakes. One is two stories high and built using unreinforced concrete. The other is three stories high and built using reinforced concrete. Which do you think would better withstand a strong earthquake? Explain your answer.

14. **Diagram** Draw and label a fault along which an earthquake occurs. Be sure to include the epicenter and the focus of the earthquake.

15. **Apply Concepts** Describe an area near your home where you and your family or friends might safely meet following an earthquake.

Standardized Test Question
Choose the letter of the response that correctly answers the question.

16. If an area experiences 300 magnitude-4 earthquakes each year, how many magnitude-3 earthquakes would you expect the same area to have?

   A. 0

   B. 30

   C. 3,000

   D. 30,000

Test-Taking Tip

Quickly look over the entire test so you know how to use your time wisely. Allow more time for sections of the test that look the most difficult.

Chapter 8

Volcanoes

KEY CONCEPT Volcanic activity has shaped much of Earth's surface and continues to affect landforms, people, and climates.

The islands of Hawaii are volcanoes that have built up from the floor of the ocean to the surface. Some of the volcanoes will never erupt again. Others are quiet for now. A few are actively erupting and getting bigger every day. Mount Etna in Sicily, shown above, is an actively erupting volcano on Earth's surface. Volcanoes form when the awesome forces and temperature of inner Earth are released onto its surface.

Think About Making Predictions

One purpose of science is to make useful models of the natural world. A useful model can predict natural events. Scientists who study volcanoes observe and measure volcanic activity of the past and present. They hope to develop scientific models that can predict how volcanoes will behave in the future.

Imagine that you live near a volcano that has not erupted in 100 years. Is it important to know when the volcano will erupt again? What kinds of information do you need in order to predict the volcano's next eruption? Write a paragraph in your Science Notebook explaining how scientific predictions can help people who live near a volcano.

www.scilinks.org

Volcanoes **Code:** WGES08

8.1 What Are Volcanoes?

Learning Goals

- Describe the process by which volcanoes form.
- Explain why volcanoes form at convergent boundaries, divergent boundaries, and hot spots.
- Describe the different types of volcanoes.

New Vocabulary

magma
lava
volcano
hot spot
shield volcano
cinder cone volcano
composite volcano
crater
caldera

Recall Vocabulary

crust, p. 88
mantle, p. 89
divergent boundary, p. 102
convergent boundary, p. 102
subduction, p. 102

Before You Read

Write three facts that you already know about volcanoes in your Science Notebook. Leave six lines of space below each fact. As you read the lesson, add at least two new details to each fact you already know.

Under Earth's crust lies the mantle. The rocks of the mantle are very hot. Because they are also under tremendous pressure, most of the mantle remains solid and cannot melt. Pockets of molten rock, crystals, and gas in the mantle are called **magma**. Magma rises toward the surface because it is hotter and less dense than the surrounding rock. When magma flows out onto Earth's surface, it is called **lava**. Lava and other volcanic material escapes through a vent, or opening, in Earth's crust. The openings are also called **volcanoes**.

Volcanoes can ooze lava, produce gas clouds, or explode violently. Some volcanoes do all three. Volcanoes form in many places around the world, as shown in **Figure 8.1**. Mauna Loa in Hawaii and Mount St. Helens in Washington State are active volcanoes in the United States.

Volcanoes are a major force shaping Earth. Volcanic materials improve some farmland, while leaving other land useless for centuries. Hundreds of thousands of people have been killed in violent volcanic eruptions. Knowledge of volcanoes allows scientists to predict eruptions so that people can move to safety.

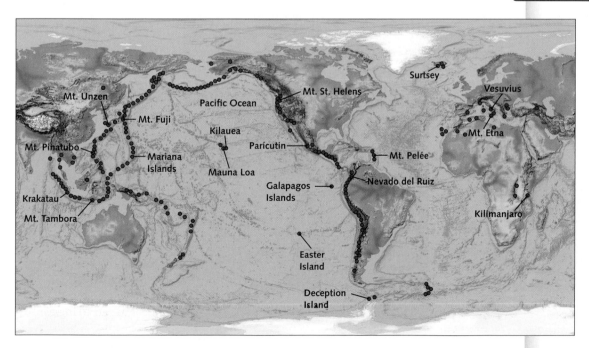

Figure 8.1 Active volcanoes are present in many parts of the world. Compare this map with the map of Earth's tectonic plates in chapter 6.

As You Read

Record the new details that you learned about volcanoes in your Science Notebook. Discuss with a partner the information you added to your Science Notebook. Add or correct information as needed.

Where is the most volcanically active area on Earth?

CONNECTION: Myths & Legends

Volcanoes have long fascinated the people who live near them. Many cultures believed that the trembling ground, lava, and falling ash were caused by the actions of gods. The ancient Romans believed that the god Vulcan produced lava and smoke as he made thunderbolts. Hawaiians believed that the volcano goddess Pele (PAY lay) caused earthquakes by stomping her feet and volcanic eruptions by digging with a magic stick. Mount St. Helens in Washington, Mount Mazama in Oregon, and other volcanoes in the United States also play a part in the myths of some Native Americans.

Where Volcanoes Form

Most volcanoes form along the borders of tectonic plates. Recall from Chapter 6 that tectonic plates float on the asthenosphere and move from place to place. When two plates move away from each other, they form a divergent boundary. Two plates that collide with each other form a convergent boundary. Both types of movement can produce volcanoes.

Volcanoes at Convergent Boundaries Most land volcanoes form at convergent boundaries where an oceanic plate collides with a continental plate. Subduction occurs and the oceanic plate gets pushed under the continental plate into the hot mantle. The part of the oceanic plate in contact with the mantle melts into magma. Heat and pressure force the magma up through the crust at the edge of the continental plate. **Figure 8.1** shows a line of volcanoes circling the Pacific Ocean. These volcanoes make up the Ring of Fire, the most volcanically active area on Earth. The Ring of Fire marks the location of a series of convergent plate boundaries that encircles the Pacific Ocean.

Volcanoes at Divergent Boundaries Many volcanoes form at divergent boundaries, where two oceanic plates are moving apart. The areas where magma oozes up from the mantle to fill in the gap between the plates are called rift zones. Most of the volcanic activity along rift zones happens under water along ocean ridges. As the divergent plates move apart and magma fills in the gaps between them, new ocean floor is formed. Because volcanoes at divergent boundaries often erupt under water, they have little effect on people. Iceland is one of the few places where volcanic activity at rift zones occurs above sea level.

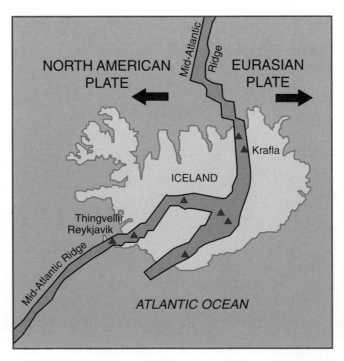

Figure 8.2 Iceland is actually part of a mid-ocean ridge. It is splitting as the North American and Eurasion Plates move apart. The volcanic activity in Iceland offers scientists a unique opportunity to study on land processes that usually happen under water. Active volcanoes appear as red triangles.

Hot Spots   Not all volcanoes form along plate boundaries. Some of Earth's most well-known volcanoes form at hot spots. A **hot spot** is a break in Earth's crust through which magma erupts. These are unusually hot regions of the mantle where columns, or plumes, of magma rise toward Earth's surface. The magma then melts the crust and flows out onto the surface forming a volcano.

Some hot spots are located beneath oceanic crust. After thousands of years, enough lava accumulates on the seafloor to rise above sea level and form a volcanic island. Over time, the oceanic plate a volcano is located on moves. Eventually, the volcano is carried away from the hot spot. At that point, the old volcano stops erupting and a new volcano forms over the hot spot. The Hawaiian Islands are examples of hot spot volcanoes. The island of Hawaii has active volcanoes because it is over a hot spot now. Another volcano, called Loihi, is erupting under water. Thousands of years in the future, Loihi may become the newest Hawaiian island. A hot spot that is positioned below continental crust is under Yellowstone National Park in Wyoming.

CONNECTION: Astronomy

Earth is not the only place in the solar system with volcanic activity. Pictures from space missions have shown volcanoes on most of the planets and on many moons. The volcanoes of Mars look like large Hawaiian volcanoes. At least one of Jupiter's moons has active volcanoes; *Voyager 2* captured images of volcanoes on Io sending plumes of debris 300 kilometers into the atmosphere!

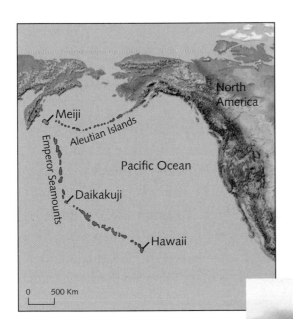

Figure 8.3 The Emperor Seamounts and the Hawaiian Islands have formed above a single hot spot in the Pacific plate. Based on data collected from the oldest volcanoes in this chain, scientists have determined that this hot spot has been active for about 75 million years.

Extend It!

Early Earth had many more active volcanoes than are present today. Research the volcanic history of the area where you live. Did it ever have volcanic activity? If so, how long ago? How deep must you dig to reach volcanic rocks? How far is it to the nearest active volcano? Record your findings in your Science Notebook.

Figure 8.4 As the Pacific Plate moves slowly over a hot spot, the Hawaiian Islands continue to form. Hawaii's Kilauea, the world's most active volcano, is located over a hot spot.

Figure It Out

The diagrams displayed below each type of volcano are drawn to scale and show their relative sizes and shapes.

1. Which type of volcano is the largest? Which type is the smallest?
2. Which type of volcano has the steepest slopes? Which type has the gentlest slopes?

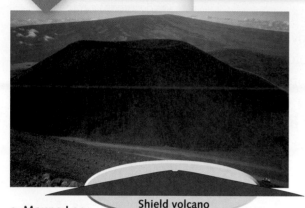

a Mauna Loa, in the background, with cinder cones in the foreground

b The Red Cones in California

c Composite volcano

Figure 8.5 Volcanoes form in very different shapes and sizes.

Types of Volcanoes

The shape of a volcano depends on both the type of material that forms it and the types of eruptions that occur. There are three major types of volcanoes: shield volcanoes, cinder cone volcanoes, and composite volcanoes.

Shield Volcano   As shown in **Figure 8.5a**, a **shield volcano** is a broad, gently sloped mountain with a base in the shape of a circle. One factor that determines the shape of a volcano is the type of lava that erupts from it. Shield volcanoes have basaltic lava, which flows easily and leads to mild explosions. This lava builds up in layers, forming a shield-shaped volcano. Shield volcanoes typically form at hot spots away from the edges of tectonic plates. They are the largest volcanoes on Earth. The volcanoes that make up the Hawaiian Islands are shield volcanoes.

Cinder Cone Volcano   Cinder cone volcanoes have more explosive eruptions than shield volcanoes. A **cinder cone volcano** forms when material ejected high into the air falls back to Earth and piles up around the volcano's vent. As shown in **Figure 8.5b**, cinder cone volcanoes are generally small with steep sides. This type of volcano often forms on the sides of shield and composite volcanoes. The Red Cones on the Long Valley Caldera in California are cinder cones.

Composite Volcano   **Composite volcanoes** form from alternating layers of lava and volcanic rocks and ash. Their thick lava is granitic, which is thicker than basaltic lava and does not flow easily. Eruptions are violent, but the lava does not spread far. Composite volcanoes are much larger than cinder cone volcanoes. As shown in **Figure 8.5c**, composite volcanoes have broad bases and sides that get steeper toward the summit. They typically form near tectonic plate boundaries. Mount Fuji, in Japan, and Mount St. Helens and Mount Rainier (ray NEER), in Washington, are composite volcanoes.

Craters and Calderas   The bowl-shaped depression formed by a volcanic explosion is called a **crater**. Most craters form at the tops or on the sides of volcanic cones. Craters of extinct or active volcanoes may fill with water and form a lake. These craters may continue to bubble with gases from deep below Earth's surface for many years. An empty magma chamber may be left beneath a volcano after an eruption. A **caldera** is a large depression in the ground where the weight of a volcano's slopes causes the roof of the empty magma chamber to collapse inward.

Mid-Ocean Ridges   Much of the volcanic activity on Earth occurs under the oceans where tectonic plates are spreading apart. At these divergent boundaries, magma oozes up to fill the gaps. A chain of underwater volcanoes forms a mid-ocean ridge. Most of the ocean floor is created at mid-ocean ridges. Underwater volcanoes may include hot springs called black smokers. The organisms and ecosystems supported by the chemicals in black smokers are found nowhere else on Earth.

Lava Plateau   Most of the lava on Earth does not come from volcanoes. It erupts from long cracks, or fissures, on Earth's surface. At various times in Earth's history, lava flowed up through fissures and spread evenly over large areas of land, creating a lava plateau. The amount of lava it takes to form a lava plateau is enormous. For example, 170,000 cubic kilometers of lava formed the Columbia Plateau in the northwest United States. Siberia experienced a flood of more than a million cubic kilometers of lava about 250 million years ago. In contrast, the 1980 eruption of Mount St. Helens ejected about 3 cubic kilometers of material.

Figure 8.6 Crater Lake in Oregon is one of the world's best-known calderas. It is about ten kilometers wide. Notice how, because of the collapse of the magma chamber, the traditional volcano shape is no longer present.

Did You Know?

Mauna Kea, a shield volcano on the island of Hawaii, is the world's tallest mountain from base to peak. The volcanic material that makes up Mauna Kea begins below the ocean floor and rises 10,314 meters to the peak of the mountain. Mauna Kea reaches 4,205 meters above sea level. In contrast, Mount Everest, in the Himalayas is 8,800 meters high from base to peak.

After You Read

1. Review the facts you wrote in your Science Notebook. Answer the following question in a well-developed paragraph. How do volcanoes form?

2. Compare and contrast shield volcanoes and composite volcanoes.

3. Explain which type of volcanic feature contains the most lava.

Before You Read

You can often trace back the causes of effects that you observe. In your Science Notebook, describe an example of a cause and its effect from your daily life. Then look for examples of cause and effect as you read about volcanic eruptions.

During a volcanic eruption, magma rises toward Earth's surface. The liquid rock collects beneath the ground in a magma chamber. High pressure forces it up through vents in Earth's surface. Not all volcanic eruptions are explosive. For example, Hawaiian volcanoes often produce quiet lava flows. Nonexplosive eruptions are common at divergent boundaries and hot spots. Other volcanoes explode violently and spew out huge clouds of volcanic material. Volcanoes at convergent boundaries are often explosive.

The scientists who study volcanoes are called **volcanologists**. They have devised a scale to describe the violence of explosive volcanic eruptions. The Volcano Explosivity Index (VEI), shown in **Figure 8.7**, assigns each explosive eruption a number from 1 to 8. The rating is based upon the amount of volcanic material ejected and the height that ash rises into the atmosphere.

Figure 8.7 The Volcano Explosivity Index (VEI) is a scale of the violence of explosive volcanic eruptions.

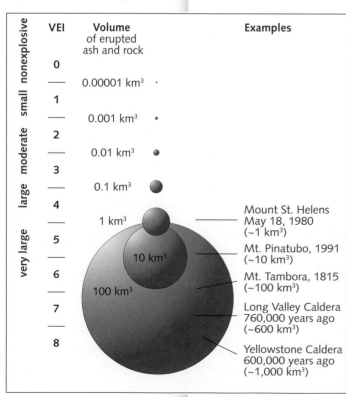

Figure 8.8 Molten rock collects in a magma chamber underground. High pressure forces the magma up through vents, forming a volcano.

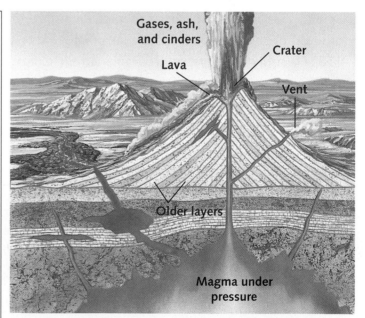

Factors Affecting Eruption Strength

The composition of magma determines the strength of a volcano's eruption. Important factors include the silica content, water content, and gas content of the magma. Lava with a large amount of silica is viscous, or thick and slow flowing. Viscous lava can plug up the vent, allowing pressure to build up inside. When the pressure is high enough, the volcano may erupt in a violent explosion.

Water in magma can also cause explosive eruptions. Water expands as it turns into steam. The expansion of the steam during an eruption can force volcanic material to be spread over a large area. Magma chambers formed by the melting of subducted oceanic plates tend to contain a lot of water.

Gas dissolved in lava also makes it more explosive. Thin, fluid lava allows gas to bubble out without building up a lot of pressure. In contrast, viscous magma traps gases. The pressure in the mantle keeps gas bubbles small. As magma leaves a volcano, the pressure on it drops suddenly. Lower pressure allows the gases to expand quickly, causing rocks, lava, and ash to be thrown high into the air.

Figure 8.9 Mount St. Helens contains magma with high silica and water content. The volcano erupted explosively on May 18, 1980. **a)** Before the eruption, a large bulge formed on the side of the volcano. The bulge was caused by magma under high pressure. Just before the eruption, a magnitude-5.1 earthquake set off a landslide. **b)** Great clouds of ash and steam erupted from the volcano and reached a height of 24.4 km. **c)** The explosion removed 400.5 meters of rock from the mountain and left a large crater in its place. **d)** Volcanic material flowed down the side of the mountain, burning everything in its path.

What erupts from a volcano?

Magma erupts from a volcano either as lava or pyroclastic materials. **Pyroclastic material** is made up of ash, rock fragments, and gases ejected by a volcano. Nonexplosive eruptions produce mostly lava. Explosive eruptions produce mostly pyroclastic material.

Lava   Once magma erupts onto Earth's surface, it is called lava. The name change is important because magma and lava are not the same. Because gases have escaped from lava, its composition is different from that of magma. Its temperature is also cooler because heat has escaped as well. Lava can flow gently from a hole in the ground, or it can be thrown in the air in lava fountains. Magma that contains a lot of gases sends blobs of lava, called bombs, flying through the air. Rivers of lava spread out and may cover many square kilometers before cooling to become solid rock. Lava that cools and hardens under water is called pillow lava because it bulges out like pillows. Lava that flows down into cold water may solidify and immediately shatter into black sand.

Other forms of lava are named after Hawaiian words. Pahoehoe (puh HO ay ho ay) lava has a smooth or ropelike surface. It tends to flow quickly. Pahoehoe lava can form narrow tubes that are cool on the surface while lava continues to ooze out at the ends. Pahoehoe tubes flow around obstacles in their paths, sometimes for ten or more kilometers from the volcano's vent. Aa (AH ah) lava flows slowly and hardens into a rough, rocky surface. Aa lava can form broad flows up to several meters thick that cover everything in their paths. Because pahoehoe and aa lava are chemically similar, pahoehoe may become aa lava as it cools and slows down.

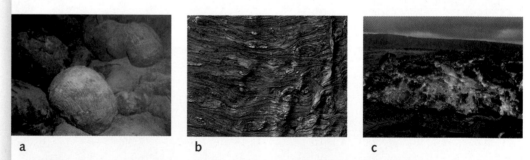

a   b   c

Figure 8.10 Common types of lava include **a)** underwater pillow lava, **b)** ropelike pahoehoe lava, and **c)** rough aa lava.

Volcanic Gases   Volcanoes often release gases into the air. Common gases include water vapor, carbon dioxide, sulfur dioxide, and hydrogen. The gases may be so hot that they glow like a stove burner. This glow can make a volcano appear to be on fire. Volcanic gases are often poisonous. Clouds of volcanic gases can cause smog, acid rain, cool temperatures, and the deaths of local plants, animals, and humans.

Pyroclastic Material As described earlier, the ash and lava fragments ejected by a volcano are called pyroclastic material. Pyroclastic material is produced when magma that explodes from a volcano cools in the air and becomes solid rock. It is also produced when powerful eruptions shatter existing rock. These materials may build up in layers on the slopes of a volcano.

Rock fragments that are thrown into the air and fall to the ground during a volcanic eruption are called **tephra** (TE fruh). As shown in **Figure 8.12**, tephra is classified by size. The largest pieces of tephra are called volcanic blocks. These pieces of solid rock can be as big as houses. Blobs of liquid magma that harden in the air are called volcanic bombs. Lapilli (luh PIH li, singular: lapillus) are pebble-sized pieces of magma that become solid before they hit the ground. Finally, volcanic ash forms when gases in hardening magma expand quickly. As they expand, the walls of the gas bubbles explode into tiny pieces of volcanic glass.

Figure 8.11 Hot pyroclastic material can flow down the slope of a volcano at terrifying speeds.

Figure It Out

1. How would a piece of tephra the size of an apple be classified?
2. Which type of tephra would you expect to find farthest from the volcanic vent?

a

b

c

d

Figure 8.12 Many sizes of rock, or tephra, are ejected from volcanoes. Tephra is named according to its size. **a)** Block, **b)** volcanic bombs, **c)** lapilli, and **d)** volcanic ash are shown.

After You Read

1. Explain what type of eruption would occur at a hot spot with low silica content.
2. Explain the relationship between silica content of magma and magma viscosity.
3. Review the notes in your Science Notebook. Briefly describe the types of pyroclastic material produced by volcanoes.

Learning Goals

- Explain the effects that volcanoes have on Earth and living things.
- Describe the work that scientists are doing to predict volcanic eruptions and prevent the loss of lives and property.

New Vocabulary

dormant
extinct volcano
active volcano

Recall Vocabulary

tsunami, p. 117

Figure It Out

1. What were the causes of death for the three deadliest volcanoes?

2. Is there a clear relationship between the VEI (shown in **Figure 8.7**) and the number of deaths caused by a volcano? Explain your answer.

Before You Read

What does the word *volcano* mean to you? Make a list of your thoughts about volcanoes in your Science Notebook. Then think about what the world would be like if there were no volcanoes. Write a paragraph to describe how the world might be different without volcanoes.

Volcanic Effects on Earth

The effects of volcanic activity can be observed on land, below the ocean, and in the air. Volcanoes shape Earth's crust, both on land and under the sea. Ash and gases from volcanoes can affect global climate patterns. Pyroclastic materials and deep ashfall can cause great damage to human property and life. As shown in **Figure 8.13**, volcanic activity has resulted in about 200,000 human deaths in the last 400 years.

Volcanic Effect on Climate Clouds of fine ash and sulfur-rich gases from a large-scale volcanic eruption may rise many kilometers into the atmosphere. As they circle the globe, the ash and gases can block out enough of the Sun's energy to lower the average temperature on Earth. Earth experienced several very cold years after a series of strong volcanic eruptions in Iceland in 1783. Scientists suspect that major volcanic periods in Earth's history have contributed to global cooling, ice ages, and even mass extinctions.

Ashfall and Pyroclastic Materials While a shallow layer of ash from a volcanic eruption can fertilize soil, deep ashfall can destroy living things and property. Ash that mixes with rain or snow can become heavy and flow like wet cement. As it flows, this heavy mud can carry away roads, bridges, trees, and buildings. Heavy layers of ash can bury crops and cause roofs to collapse. Ash can also dam rivers and cause floods.

Volcano	Year of Eruption	VEI	Estimated Deaths	Main Causes of Death
Vesuvius (Italy)	1631	6	>3,500	lava flows
Mt. Unzen (Japan)	1792	2	14,000	volcano collapse, tsunami
Mt. Tambora (Indonesia)	1815	7	92,000	starvation
Krakatau (Indonesia)	1883	6	36,000	tsunami
Mt. Pelée (West Indies)	1902	4	29,000	pyroclastic flow
Mount St. Helens (United States)	1980	5	62	explosion, pyroclastic flow
Nevado del Ruiz (Colombia)	1985	3	25,000	mudflows

Figure 8.13 Deadly Volcanoes of the Last 400 Years

The most dangerous movement of volcanic material is a pyroclastic flow or surge. Clouds of hot ash, hot rocks, and gas may flow down the sides of a volcano at more than 100 kilometers per hour. Any structure or living thing in the way of the pyroclastic flow is burned and destroyed.

Figure 8.14 The Nevado del Ruiz volcanic eruption in Colombia had a VEI of only 3. However, it caused a mudflow that buried nearby villages and killed 25,000 people. The city of Armero was once located in the center of this photograph.

As You Read

In your Science Notebook, use the facts that you learn to support your ideas about how Earth would be different if there were no volcanoes.

How might a large volcanic eruption affect the world's climate?

Shaping Landscapes and Seascapes Much of Earth's solid surface—both on land and below the sea—is shaped and influenced by volcanic activity. Volcanic eruptions build mountains and plateaus that become lasting additions to Earth's surface. Volcanic eruptions form the seafloor and chains of volcanic islands, such as the Hawaiian Islands. Volcanic ash becomes fertile soil. Volcanic chimney vents at the bottom of the sea provide unique habitats for unusual forms of life.

CONNECTION: Biology

New volcanic material is barren and lifeless, and it appears that nothing can live on the solid rock. Through a process called succession, however, a new living community of plants and animals eventually takes over. The first organisms to return are often pioneer organisms such as algae, lichens, and fungi that are carried in by the wind. These tiny organisms cling to the rocks. Once a food source is established, animals can move in. All of these early colonizers improve conditions for later settlers. Roots break up the solid rock. Dead plants decay and become soil that holds water.

Wet locations facing the wind recover the fastest. Forests can grow on Hawaiian lava within 150 years. Trees can grow on loose pyroclastic material in just five years. In time, it becomes hard to tell that an area was once bare rock. Much of the Pacific Northwest was covered by a tremendous flow of lava that occurred 17 to 12 million years ago. The lush forests of Washington, Oregon, and Idaho prove that life can indeed return to the side of a volcano.

Did You Know?

In southern Japan, volcanic eruptions from nearby volcanoes are a part of everyday life. Children sometimes wear hard hats on their way to school to protect their heads from falling tephra. Japanese schools hold volcano and earthquake drills just as many American schools conduct fire, tornado, or earthquake drills.

Predicting Eruptions

Volcanoes do not erupt on a regular schedule. Only a few volcanoes have been erupting continually for centuries. Most volcanoes remain **dormant**, or inactive, for long periods between eruptions. Volcanoes that have not erupted for tens of thousands of years are called **extinct volcanoes**. On average, there are about 20 volcanoes erupting at any given time on Earth, and 50 to 70 volcanoes erupt each year. Approximately 1,500 land volcanoes have erupted in the last 10,000 years. These volcanoes are considered **active volcanoes**, or volcanoes that are likely to erupt in the future. In addition, there are many thousands of seafloor volcanoes.

Volcanology   One of the main reasons volcanologists study volcanoes is to be able to predict eruptions. The history of past volcanic eruptions can be studied by measuring evidence left in tree rings and in patterns of rock deposits. Many recent eruptions are recorded in the written and spoken history of people who live—or lived—near volcanoes. Volcanologists can learn about volcanoes' eruption patterns from these sources of data.

Volcanologists use several pieces of evidence to predict when a volcano is likely to erupt. Before an eruption, earthquakes and ground movement increase as the magma chamber expands. The side of a volcano may bulge outward as magma moves upward toward the vent. The temperature of the volcano often increases as an eruption grows closer. Finally, gases emitted by the volcano change in amount and type before an eruption. Because it is dangerous to approach an erupting volcano, much of the information used by volcanologists is collected by satellites in space. All of the data are entered into computer programs that issue predictions about the timing and strength of eruptions.

Figure 8.15 Volcanologists can get closer to erupting volcanoes by wearing heat-resistant suits.

Even though satellites can be used to collect most data, volcanologists sometimes need to visit volcanoes. Studying active volcanoes is exciting but dangerous work. Volcanologists wear gas masks to protect them from poisonous gases. Special heat-resistant suits, shown in **Figure 8.15**, allow scientists to collect samples of red-hot lava. Nevertheless, volcanologists are sometimes killed by eruptions while at work. Robotic volcano observers have been developed to collect samples without risking human lives. Someday, these robots may explore volcanoes on other planets and moons in our solar system.

Figure 8.16 The Dante II robotic volcano explorer can take samples of volcanic gases in places that are too dangerous for humans. Scientists will analyze the samples back in the laboratory.

Living with Volcanoes

About 500 million people live near active volcanoes. A volcano may lie dormant for so long that people may not realize that it is still active. People choose to live near volcanoes because old volcanic deposits create good soil for farming. Heat from magma near Earth's surface also provides inexpensive heat and electricity. In addition, valuable gemstones and minerals can be found in volcanic rocks.

Preventing Loss of Life   Volcanologists are improving their ability to predict eruptions. Most of the deaths caused by volcanic eruptions can now be prevented. The 1991 eruption of Mt. Pinatubo in the Philippines and the 1985 eruption of Nevado del Ruiz in Colombia were both correctly predicted by scientists. Unfortunately, predictions are useless if people do not take action. Residents in the path of Mt. Pinatubo were evacuated and tens of thousands of lives were saved. In contrast, officials in Colombia ignored the warnings. As a result, mudflows from Nevado del Ruiz killed 25,000 people.

 Explain It!

With the ability to predict volcanic eruptions, many deaths can be prevented with proper preparation. Write a public service announcement that explains what people should do to stay safe in the event of an impending eruption.

After You Read

1. Describe the evidence used by scientists to predict volcanic eruptions.

2. Explain why so many people live near active volcanoes.

3. Review the notes in your Science Notebook. In what ways can ash from a volcanic eruption be both helpful and harmful?

KEY CONCEPTS

8.1 What Are Volcanoes?

- Volcanoes form when molten rock and other materials in the mantle are forced up through the crust to Earth's surface.

- Volcanoes can form along convergent and divergent boundaries between tectonic plates or at hot spots in the middle of plates.

- The three major types of volcanoes are shield volcanoes, cinder cone volcanoes, and composite volcanoes.

- Mid-ocean ridges, lava plateaus, craters, and calderas are formed by volcanoes.

8.2 Volcanic Eruptions

- Nonexplosive volcanic eruptions are common at divergent boundaries and hot spots, while explosive eruptions are more common at convergent boundaries.

- The violence of a volcanic eruption depends on the silica, water, and gas content of magma.

- Magma from a volcano either erupts as lava or as pyroclastic materials. Common types of lava include pillow, pahoehoe, and aa lava.

- Pyroclastic material is made up of ash, rock fragments, and gases. Volcanic rock fragments that are thrown into the air and then fall to the ground are called tephra.

8.3 Volcanoes, People, and Earth

- Ash and gases from volcanoes can affect global climate patterns. Pyroclastic materials and deep ashfall can destroy human property and life. Volcanoes shape Earth's crust, both on land and under the sea.

- To predict volcanic eruptions, volcanologists use evidence including earthquakes and ground movement, physical changes at a volcanic site, and knowledge of past eruptions and currently active volcanoes.

- Good predictions and timely government action can protect people who live near active volcanoes.

VOCABULARY REVIEW

Write each term in a complete sentence or write a paragraph relating several terms.

8.1
magma, p. 131
lava, p. 131
volcano, p. 131
hot spot, p. 133
shield volcano, p. 134
cinder cone volcano, p. 134
composite volcano, p. 134
crater, p. 135
caldera, p. 135

8.2
volcanologist, p. 136
pyroclastic material, p. 138
tephra, p. 139

8.3
dormant, p. 142
extinct volcano, p. 142
active volcano, p. 142

PREPARE FOR CHAPTER TEST

To prepare for the chapter test, create a question from each Learning Goal. Use the information in your Science Notebook to answer each question. Then use these answers to write a well-developed essay about the chapter. Use the Key Concept on the first page of this chapter as your topic sentence.

True or False

If the statement is true, write "true." If it is false, change the underlined word or words to make the statement true.

1. A <u>caldera</u> is a large depression formed when a volcano's slopes collapse into the empty magma chamber.

2. Pockets of molten rock and other materials in the mantle are called <u>lava</u>.

3. The VEI is a measure of how <u>likely a volcano is to erupt in the near future</u>.

4. <u>Pahoehoe lava</u> flows quickly and has a smooth surface.

5. A volcano that is inactive but may erupt in the future is <u>dormant</u>.

6. Volcanoes at <u>hot spots</u> are likely to erupt explosively.

Short Answer

Answer each of the following in a sentence or brief paragraph.

7. A long-dormant volcano near a large city has begun to release hot gases. What information would a volcanologist collect in order to predict the volcano's future actions?

8. Why does magma rise to Earth's surface?

9. What type of volcanic activity would you expect to find under the sea at a divergent boundary?

10. Explain how silica, water, and gas in magma affect the violence of a volcanic eruption.

11. How can a volcanic eruption in Asia affect the weather in North America?

12. Explain why lava is not usually as dangerous to humans as other volcanic materials.

13. How do volcanologists use modern technology to predict volcanic eruptions?

Critical Thinking

Use what you have learned in this chapter to answer each of the following.

14. **Synthesize** If you could watch a film of the Hawaiian Islands that started several million years ago and moved quickly to the present, what would you see?

15. **Make an Inference** A robot drills a core 900 meters into the surface of another planet. It finds solid volcanic rock 500 meters thick. What type of volcanic activity probably occurred in the planet's past?

16. **Analyze** Discuss the following statement: "Lava and other volcanic materials ruin land forever for living things."

Standardized Test Question

Choose the letter of the response that correctly answers the question.

17. What type of eruption would you expect from a shield volcano?

   A. a nonexplosive flow of lava

   B. a violent explosion with a large ash cloud

   C. thick aa lava flow

   D. alternating explosive and flows of lava and ash

Test-Taking Tip

When writing an essay response, avoid long introductions and conclusions. Be clear and concise in your writing.

Keeping Watch for Tsunamis

ON DECEMBER 26, 2004, a huge wall of water raced in from the sea and slammed ashore in Southeast Asia. It swept away everything in its path—roads, buildings, and hundreds of thousands of people. The wall of water was a tsunami—a huge wave generated by an earthquake on the ocean floor.

Earthquakes occur at plate edges under the sea as well as on land. When an underwater earthquake occurs, downward movement of the seafloor results in the formation of a long, shallow wave. This wave speeds across the ocean surface. In the deep ocean, it is hardly noticeable. It might be 160 kilometers long, but just a few centimeters high. In fact, even a ship passing directly over the wave would hardly be disturbed.

As this harmless wave nears a coast, however, its properties change. The wave slows down in shallower coastal waters. As it does, its water piles up—sometimes to heights of over 30 meters. The high waters sweep inland and wash people and structures out to sea.

The best protection from tsunamis is early warning, but up until the disaster just described, only the Pacific Ocean had a warning system. The United States started it during the 1940s, after a huge tsunami destroyed several villages in Hawaii. For decades, the system used seismometers to detect undersea earthquakes. It also used tide gauges to track sea-surface changes. This type of system, however, could not detect a tsunami moving across the ocean. It could only detect conditions that *might* form a tsunami. There were many false alarms.

Now, a better warning system is being put into place. It uses a network of instruments, called tsunameters, that are placed in the open ocean. The system goes into action when a disturbance occurs on the seafloor. Each tsunameter has a sensor on the seafloor that records changes in water pressure. Pressure changes indicate a passing wave that could become a deadly tsunami. The sensors send the data to a buoy bobbing on the surface. The buoy sends the data up to a satellite. From there, the data is beamed back to receivers at tsunami warning centers. At the warning centers, scientists interpret the data and determine if a shore area is in the path of a tsunami. If it is, they issue a warning. Immediate warnings are crucial, because there may be only a few hours or even a few minutes before the tsunami hits.

People need some time to move from the coast to higher ground.

Hawaii and the west coast of the United States are at risk for tsunamis. The United States has two Pacific warning centers. One in Alaska issues warnings for Alaska, British Columbia, Washington, Oregon, and California. Another center in Hawaii watches the coasts of Hawaii and American territories in the Pacific. It also issues warnings for 25 countries around the Pacific rim.

Most earthquakes do not cause tsunamis, but because tsunamis can be so deadly, warning systems are important. Scientists intend to expand the Pacific network of tsunameters, and they hope to add a few in the Atlantic, too. The Indian Ocean, where the 2004 tsunami did so much damage, is in the process of deploying its first warning system. The people who live along the coasts know that it is long overdue.

Research and Report

Earthquakes and volcanic eruptions are common, but each one has a unique story. With a partner, research an historic earthquake or volcanic eruption. Prepare a report, as if you are a radio reporter on the scene. Tell your audience what is happening around you. Record your report on an audiocassette recorder. Then share it with the class.

Building an **Island**

HAWAII'S NEWEST VOLCANO is active and noisy. It rumbles and shakes. It spews lava over its sides. Each year, it grows just a little bit taller. It is now about 3,000 meters high, taller than Mount St. Helens before its 1980 eruption. Still, you can't actually *see* this towering volcano. Its summit is 1,000 meters below the surface of the sea.

The volcano is Loihi, a growing sea mountain about 27 kilometers off the southeast coast of the Big Island of Hawaii. Like Loihi, all of Hawaii's islands began as undersea volcanoes. They became islands when the volcanoes grew above the sea surface.

Loihi is forming over a hot spot in the Pacific Plate. A hot spot is an area away from a plate edge where magma oozes up through Earth's crust. As tectonic plates move slowly over hot spots, volcanoes form above them. Underwater volcanoes eventually grow into islands with active volcanoes. The volcanoes stay active as long as the island remains over the hot spot. The moving plate eventually carries the island away, and that island's volcanoes become inactive. A new volcano then forms over the part of the plate that has moved over the hot spot. This is how, over millions of years, the long chain of Hawaiian Islands formed.

The island of Hawaii is also over the hot spot now. Kilauea, the world's most active volcano, is on this island. Loihi is forming on the seafloor east of the island of Hawaii. There's a good chance that Loihi will break through the surface of the ocean one day. It will become the newest island in the Hawaiian chain, but don't count on being around when it happens—unless you can wait another 50,000 years!

CAREER CONNECTION: CIVIL ENGINEER

YOU MAY HAVE HEARD of the Golden Gate Bridge, the Sears Tower, and the Hoover Dam. Civil engineers helped design each of these amazing constructions. They design some of the world's biggest, most spectacular structures including dams, bridges, tunnels, highways, and skyscrapers.

Clients come to civil engineers with problems to be solved. For example, a bridge needs to be built across a wide bay to create a faster and more direct way to get from one side to the other. The civil engineer must first answer some questions. Can a bridge be built over the bay at all? What design would make it strong enough to carry a certain amount of traffic? How will the bridge withstand high winds and strong water currents? What will the bridge cost? In places

such as California, where earthquakes are common, there is another question. How can it be designed to resist earthquake damage? The towers, supports, and roadway will need to keep the bridge standing when the ground starts to shake and roll.

Civil engineers enjoy problem solving, planning, and keeping track of details. They usually have at least a bachelor's degree in engineering. They must also know how to use the computer software needed for design. Civil engineers often specialize in a certain type of structure. They might work on buildings or bridges. They might design highways. Some might work on water systems. You will find civil engineers working for private companies as well as government agencies. Civil engineers get great satisfaction from their work. They build things that we depend on every day—and that last for a long time.

Unit 4

Earth's Changing Surface

Chapter 9

Weathering and Soil Formation

Why is the process of weathering important to soil formation?

Chapter 10

Erosion and Deposition

How do the forces of erosion and deposition work together to shape and create landforms?

148

Weathering and Soil Formation

KEY CONCEPT The process of weathering is important to soil formation.

A mountain looks permanent. It stands tall and seems never to change. However, this is not true. There is something more powerful than a mountain. Believe it or not, the work of water, wind, gravity, plants, and animals eventually wear a mountain down. Over time, the solid rock in the mountain is cracked and broken into smaller and smaller pieces. When these tiny rock particles are mixed with organic matter from plants and animals, soil is formed. Soil is important because it provides a place for plants to grow.

Think About Soil

You have seen soil in many different places such as yards, fields, the woods, or even potted plants. Collect a spoonful of soil in a plastic bag. Spill the soil onto a sheet of white paper, and use a magnifying lens to examine what you see.

- What is the soil made up of? Do you see pieces of plants or insects in the soil?

- In your Science Notebook, list what you see in the soil. Then write a well-developed paragraph about where you think the water and nutrients in soil come from. Describe how rocks might change into soil.

www.scilinks.org

Weathering **Code: WGES09**

Learning Goals

- Describe the factors that cause mechanical weathering.
- Describe the factors that cause chemical weathering.

New Vocabulary

weathering
mechanical weathering
frost wedging
abrasion
exfoliation
chemical weathering
acid precipitation
oxidation

Before You Read

In your Science Notebook, create a concept map. Write the term *Weathering* in the center. Draw a circle on each side. Label one circle *Mechanical weathering* and the other *Chemical weathering*.

Figure 9.1 The large flakes that break off granite are called exfoliation sheets. This type of weathering occurs when granite and similar rocks are exposed to changing pressure and temperatures at Earth's surface.

Granite forms deep underground and under very high pressure. When granite is exposed at Earth's surface, there is less pressure on it. The lowered pressure allows the surface of the granite to expand slightly and flake off as shown in **Figure 9.1**. Over time, rain and water cause these large flakes to break apart into smaller and smaller pieces. The pieces continue to break down until they are as fine as sand. The breakdown of rocks into smaller pieces is called **weathering**. There are two major types of weathering—mechanical weathering and chemical weathering.

Mechanical Weathering

Mechanical weathering is the breakdown of rocks into smaller pieces by some physical action. Ice, water, wind, gravity, pressure, plants, or animals may cause the physical actions that break down rocks. When rocks are first broken, they have sharp and angular edges. As the rocks continue to weather, the edges become rounded and smooth.

Ice One of the unique properties of water is that it expands as it freezes. When water fills a crack in a rock and freezes, it widens the crack. As this happens over and over again, the rock is eventually split apart. This physical action, shown in **Figure 9.3**, is called **frost wedging**. It is common in colder climates and in high mountains. Frost wedging occurs more rapidly when the temperature rises above freezing during the day and drops below freezing at night.

Figure 9.2 These piles of rocks were once part of the cliff above.

Freezing is not the only way water causes rocks to break. Rocks are made of minerals. Some minerals absorb water. When the minerals in rocks absorb water, they swell. These swelling minerals can also crack rocks.

Abrasion Wind also causes mechanical weathering. Wind can pick up tiny rock particles and carry them. When the wind carrying these particles hits a rock, the tiny particles scratch the rock's surface. **Abrasion** is the action of rocks and sediment grinding against each other and wearing away exposed surfaces. Abrasion smoothes the sharp edges on both the tiny particles and the rock surfaces they grind against. Abrasion from wind is most common in dry areas, such as deserts.

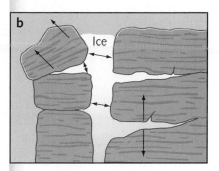

Figure 9.3 a) This granite boulder has been broken by the repeated freezing and thawing of water in its cracks. **b)** When the water freezes, it expands and exerts pressure. The pressure causes the cracks to expand until the rock breaks.

Running water may also cause abrasion. Like wind, running water picks up particles and moves them. Moving water has more energy than wind, so it can pick up larger particles. As they bump into each other and into other rocks, these particles act like sandpaper. They smooth the sharp edges of the rocks of which they come in contact. The smooth, rounded rocks commonly present along streambeds have been worn down by abrasion. Abrasion can also be caused by gravity. Abrasion caused by gravity occurs when rocks grind against one another as they fall or slide down a hill or mountainside.

Pressure Changes in pressure can also cause mechanical weathering. For example, granite flakes apart as it weathers. Granite that is no longer underground is under much less pressure and it slowly expands. As it expands, flakes come off at the surface. The process during which outer rock layers are stripped away is called **exfoliation**. The exfoliated sheets or flakes then begin to weather. This is shown in **Figure 9.1**.

Plants and Animals Plants and animals also cause mechanical weathering. Plant roots may seem fragile, but, over time, they can break rocks. As the roots grow, they get bigger and bigger and exert more pressure on rock. Eventually, the rock begins to break. As the roots continue to grow, they push the pieces of the rock even farther apart.

Animals also cause mechanical weathering. When animals such as rabbits or earthworms burrow into soil, they mix it. This causes new rock particles to be exposed and weathered. Exposing soil particles to air also causes the other kind of weathering—chemical weathering.

Figure 9.4 As this tree trunk grew, it eventually became large enough to break apart the rock.

As You Read

Add the causes of weathering to the proper place on your concept map. Make sure you identify each cause as either mechanical weathering or chemical weathering. Share your map with a partner. Add or correct information as needed.

Did You Know?

The longest cave in the world is Mammoth Cave in Kentucky. This cave has more than 580 km of passages! Mammoth Cave is almost three times longer than the next longest cave.

CONNECTION: Chemistry

The chemical reactions that take place during chemical weathering are often related to acids. The strength of an acid is measured on the pH scale. Water has a neutral pH and is assigned a value of 7. Bases have a pH that is greater than 7, while acids have a pH that is less than 7. Rainwater has a pH value of about 5.6. Vinegar is a mixture of acetic acid and water. It has a pH of about 3 depending on how much acetic acid is present. Other acids are even stronger and have lower pH values.

Chemical Weathering

Chemical weathering is the breakdown of rocks and minerals due to changes in their chemical composition. The most common agents for these chemical reactions are water, carbon dioxide, acids, and oxygen. These chemical reactions result in the formation of new minerals. The new minerals have different properties than the original mineral.

Water Water is an important agent in chemical weathering because it can dissolve many kinds of minerals and rocks. For example, halite is sodium chloride, or table salt. When water flows across the solid mineral halite, the halite dissolves in the water. Water is also important because many chemical reactions take place when water is present.

Figure 9.5 This cave in New Mexico was formed when carbonic acid in rainwater dissolved the limestone rock. Formations that grow up from the floor are called stalagmites. Formations that grow down from the ceiling are called stalactites.

Carbon Dioxide Acids in water can break down rocks and minerals over time. Rainwater naturally contains acids. Carbon dioxide from the atmosphere dissolves in raindrops and forms a weak acid called carbonic acid. Below is the chemical equation that shows how carbonic acid forms:

$$H_2O + CO_2 \rightarrow H_2CO_3$$

water   carbon dioxide   carbonic acid

Carbonic acid reacts with many rocks and minerals. For example, limestone is a type of rock that is made of calcium carbonate. Carbonic acid will dissolve calcium carbonate. Sometimes this process takes place underground and forms caves. Because carbonic acid is a weak acid, it takes a long time to dissolve enough limestone to make a cave.

Acid Precipitation Other chemicals in the atmosphere can also dissolve in rainwater. Air pollution is composed of chemicals from human activity. Two gases from air pollution, sulfur oxide and nitrogen oxide, will also dissolve in rainwater. These form strong acids with a low pH. Rain that contains acids due to air pollution is called **acid precipitation** or, more commonly, acid rain. Because acid precipitation has a low pH, it can dissolve rocks and minerals quickly. Many different types of rocks are used as construction materials. You may have noticed a city building or a stone sculpture in a park that looks worn away or has small pits or holes. This is likely caused over time by acid precipitation.

Figure 9.6 This statue has been placed outside, where it is exposed to rain. Look closely at the "folds" on the statue's shirt. Acid precipitation has caused noticeable chemical weathering on the statue's surface.

Figure It Out

1. What are the effects of acid precipitation on the statue?

2. Describe how you think this statue will look in 100 years.

Acids from Living Things   Living things not only cause mechanical weathering, they can also cause chemical weathering. Lichens are the flat, greenish-yellow organisms often seen growing on trees or rocks. As they grow, lichens produce acids that break down whatever they are growing on. As they break down the surface, they absorb minerals that they need to grow. Decaying plant leaves are another source of acids that cause chemical weathering. These acids break down rocks, which then release important minerals into the soil. Living plants need these minerals to grow. This is an important process in adding minerals to the soil.

Oxygen   Oxygen makes up almost 21 percent of Earth's atmosphere. Oxygen is produced by plants, and is required by both plants and animals. Oxygen chemically combines with many different substances. A common example is rust. Rust forms when oxygen combines with iron to form iron oxide. The chemical reaction of oxygen with other substances is called **oxidation**. Rocks and minerals that contain iron will oxidize. Oxidation weakens rocks and minerals and causes them to break apart.

 Explore It!

Acid precipitation is more acidic than normal rainwater. Any rainwater with a pH less than 5.6 is considered to be acid rain. To see the effects of acid precipitation, pour some vinegar in a bowl and add a piece of chalk. Chalk, like limestone, is made of calcium carbonate. Watch what happens to the chalk in the vinegar. Record your observations in your Science Notebook.

After You Read

1. Review your concept map. Use it to list four causes of mechanical weathering and four causes of chemical weathering.

2. Which type of weathering—mechanical or chemical—is most common where you live? Which is least common? In a well-developed paragraph, answer these questions in your Science Notebook.

3. Where in your area might you look to see examples of mechanical weathering and chemical weathering?

Before You Read

Create a T-chart in your Science Notebook. Label the left column *Causes of Weathering*. Label the right column *Examples*. Skim the lesson and add notes to the left column. Add information to your chart as you read the lesson.

Figure 9.7 Both of these headstones were placed in the same year, but they are in very different conditions. One is still easy to read, while the other is weathered.

Figure 9.8 Granite is made up of many different minerals. The black mineral is mica, the clear crystals are quartz, and the pink-colored mineral is feldspar.

Different kinds of rock weather at different rates. The rate at which a rock weathers depends on many things. These include rock type and composition, climate, gravity, organisms, and surface area.

Sometimes it is easy to see weathering taking place at different rates. As shown in **Figure 9.7**, two headstones in the same cemetery from the same year may look very different. A granite headstone is much more resistant to weathering than a marble headstone. Over time, the lettering on the granite headstone may still be readable, while the lettering on the marble headstone may be worn away.

Rock Type and Composition Affect Weathering

Granite is a much harder rock than marble because the minerals in granite are harder than the minerals in marble. Some of these minerals are also more resistant to weathering than other minerals. Feldspar, for example, weathers faster than quartz. As granite breaks apart, the feldspar erodes away and the quartz is left behind. **Differential weathering** is the process by which some rocks weather faster than others. The headstones are an example of this process.

Climate Affects Weathering

Temperature and moisture are two climate factors that affect weathering. Chemical weathering occurs faster in warmer climates. This is because chemical weathering is caused by chemical reactions, which take place faster at higher temperatures. Climate may also affect the rate of mechanical weathering. Some mechanical weathering is caused by moving water or temperature changes. Climate plays a role in both types of weathering.

Moisture also has a big effect on weathering. For example, Florida is both warm and wet. The state has high humidity because it is close to the ocean. Florida also gets plenty of rain. In contrast, much of New Mexico is a dry desert. Rainfall is scarce. While both Florida and New Mexico have warm temperatures, the levels of humidity and rainfall in the two states differ greatly. Limestone is present in both Florida and New Mexico. In New Mexico, limestone weathers into cliffs. In Florida, however, limestone weathers quickly into low hills. The limestone weathers at different speeds because of the differences in humidity. **Figure 9.9a** shows another area where limestone has weathered quickly.

Unlike the rate of chemical weathering, which is lower in cool areas, the rate of mechanical weathering can be high in cool areas. In mountains, mechanical weathering from ice can take place quickly. In high mountains, especially in summer, the temperature is above freezing during the day and below freezing at night. This causes rapid weathering by frost wedging during the summer. During the winter, when the temperature stays below freezing during the day and night, little mechanical weathering from frost wedging takes place.

a

b

Figure 9.9 a) In eastern West Virginia, chemical weathering has smoothed and rounded the mountains, many of which are made of limestone. **b)** In New Mexico, the dry conditions limit the speed of weathering, and the limestone forms cliffs.

As You Read

In the column labeled *Causes of Weathering*, write three or four important things you have learned about the rate of weathering. As you read, add examples to the right-hand column of your chart.

Identify how the climate where you live affects weathering.

CONNECTION: Chemistry

Chemical reactions take place when atoms either break or make bonds. For a chemical reaction to take place, the atoms need a certain amount of energy. Because atoms are in motion, they have what is called kinetic energy. As temperature increases, the kinetic energy in atoms also increases. The increased kinetic energy means that the atoms are moving faster. Faster-moving atoms are more likely to undergo chemical reactions. This is why chemical reactions, such as chemical weathering, occur faster as temperature increases.

Granite is often used as a building stone. You may have seen granite polished to a smooth, beautiful surface. While this polished surface may appear to be decorative, it actually slows the weathering of the granite. Polishing the granite reduces its surface area. Because less surface area is exposed, weathering is slowed down.

CONNECTION: Art

Humans have been making sculptures from stone for thousands of years. Many early sculptures still survive today. Since the first sculptures were carved, humans have continued to use stones such as marble, limestone, basalt, and granite. A sculpture often starts out as a large block of rock. It is then shaped with special tools. Marble and limestone are both soft rocks that are easy to shape. Basalt and granite are hard rocks that require considerable work to shape. The softer rocks are easier to work with but because of their mineral composition, weather more quickly than the harder rocks.

Figure 9.10 Steep mountain streams have enough energy to move rocks.

Gravity and Weathering

Gravity is what holds objects on Earth. Gravity is also a factor in weathering. In mountains, streams flow quickly and have large amounts of energy because gravity is pulling the water in them downhill. This water carries rocks and sediment with it, causing mechanical weathering. The rocks carried by the streams crash into one another and become more rounded over time. The rocks on the bottom of the stream are scraped and ground against each other. Continuous removal of sediment exposes new rock surfaces to weathering. Because gravity causes water to speed up as it moves down slopes, weathering occurs faster along slopes than it does in flatter areas.

Organisms and Weathering

Organisms also affect the rate of weathering. Decaying plants release carbon dioxide into the soil. This carbon dioxide combines with water to produce carbonic acid. This acid speeds up the weathering of rocks. Living plant roots may also speed up the breaking of rocks. As plant roots that are growing in cracks become larger, the pressure they place on the rock becomes greater too. The increased pressure causes the rock to break apart. For these reasons, forests, which have many plants and are often warm and moist, have high rates of weathering.

Surface Area

Both chemical and mechanical weathering take place on the surface of rocks. **Surface area** refers to the sum of all the areas of the object's surfaces. The more surface area of a rock that is exposed to weathering, the faster the rock will be broken down. For this reason, any weathering process that increases the surface area of a rock will increase its rate of weathering.

Here is another way to think about this concept. You might think that a big rock would weather quickly because it has a large surface area. While a big rock does have a large surface area, it also has a large volume. If you take the rock and break it into smaller rocks, the total volume of all the rocks is the same. The total surface area of all the smaller rocks, however, is greater than the total surface area of the larger rock alone. For this reason, smaller rocks have a higher rate of both chemical and mechanical weathering than do larger rocks.

All the factors discussed in this lesson work together to determine the rate of weathering. The rate of weathering can vary from one place to another, even if both places have identical types of rocks.

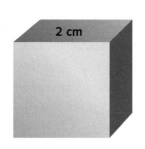

Area = 6 × (2 cm × 2 cm) = 24 cm²
24 cm² × 1 cube = 24 cm²

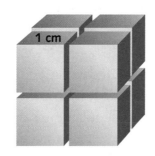

Area = 6 × (1 cm × 1 cm) = 6 cm²
6 cm² × 8 cubes = 48 cm²

Figure 9.11 Mechanical weathering breaks rocks into smaller pieces. Smaller rocks have more surface area relative to their volume than do larger rocks. For this reason, smaller rocks weather more quickly than larger rocks. This diagram shows how the total surface area of a cube increases when it is broken into smaller units.

After You Read

1. Explain gravity's role in weathering.

2. What factors affect the rate of weathering where you live?

3. Review the T-chart in your Science Notebook. Use the information in your chart to write a well-developed paragraph describing how the factors that affect the rate of weathering where you live have shaped the landscape.

 Explore It!

Fill two small containers half full of water. Add 1 teaspoon of table salt to one container. Add 1 teaspoon of rock salt to the other container. Stir each container at the same rate. Keep track of how long it takes each type of salt to completely dissolve in its container. In your Science Notebook, write an explanation of why you think one type of salt dissolved faster than the other.

Figure It Out

1. How does the surface area change as the cube is divided?

2. Explain how changing a rock's surface area might affect its rate of chemical weathering.

 Explain It!

In your Science Notebook, write a paragraph describing how the surface area of a 4-cm × 4-cm cube would change if it were broken into 1-cm × 1-cm cubes.

Learning Goals

- Describe how soils form.
- Describe how climate affects soil formation.
- Explain why soil is a resource.

New Vocabulary

soil
bedrock
parent material
residual soil
transported soil
humus
soil profile
topsoil
subsoil
leaching
erosion

Figure 9.12 Soil is composed of different materials. There are small weathered rock and mineral fragments and bits of plant matter visible in this soil.

9.3 From Rocks to Soil

Before You Read

In your Science Notebook, write each of this lesson's vocabulary words. Leave some space below each word. In your own words, write a definition for each word as you come across it in the lesson.

The small particles that weather from rocks make up a large part of soil. **Soil** is a mixture of rock and mineral particles, organic material, water, and air. Organic matter comes from living things. There are many different types of soil. The type of soil depends on the types of rock and mineral particles as well as the types and amount of organic materials. Some soils are rich in nutrients that plants need to grow, while others have few nutrients.

Soil Composition

The rock and mineral fragments in soil are weathered from the rock layer that lies underneath the soil. The layer of rock underneath the soil is called **bedrock**. The type of bedrock helps determine the type of soil above it. Granite bedrock weathers into minerals that give soil such as that shown in **Figure 9.12** its unique characteristics. Soil that forms from limestone bedrock is different from soil that forms from granite bedrock because it contains different minerals. The type of material that is the source of soil is called **parent material**. A geologist can often identify a soil's parent material just by looking at the soil.

Soil that forms directly above parent bedrock is called **residual soil**. Residual soil is replenished as chemical and mechanical weathering of the bedrock continues to take place under the soil. Soil that forms from material that has been carried in from another location is called **transported soil**. Such material might be transported to new locations by running water, wind, or glaciers.

Humus Another important part of soil is organic matter. In addition to bits of rock and minerals, soil also contains small bits of decayed plant and animal matter called **humus** (HYEW mus). The organic matter in soil may come from decaying leaves and other plant material. Animals also contribute to the organic matter in soil with their decaying bodies and wastes. Humus contains many of the nutrients that plants need to grow. Humus gives soil its dark color. For this reason, soils with a high percentage of humus are dark. Usually, soil with more than 20 percent humus is considered good for growing plants. Soils with little humus are light in color.

Soil Horizons

Soil begins forming at the surface of the bedrock. As the bedrock weathers, more soil forms above it. Because of how soil forms, it ends up in layers called horizons. Each soil horizon has characteristics that separate it from the other soil horizons. **Figure 9.13** shows each soil horizon. These horizons make up a **soil profile**. The A horizon, the layer on the surface, is also called the **topsoil**. The topsoil has more humus than the horizons below it. It is usually the darkest horizon, especially in fertile soil. Fertile soils, which are the best for farming, may take hundreds or even thousands of years to form.

The B horizon, the layer below the topsoil, is called the **subsoil**. The subsoil is usually not as dark in color as the topsoil because it contains less humus. When you look at a soil profile, you will notice that the soil becomes lighter in color closer to the bedrock. When rain falls on soil, it dissolves some of the nutrients and minerals from the topsoil and transports them downward. This downward transport is called **leaching**. The C horizon is composed of partly weathered parent material. This may be bedrock or material that has been transported in from another location.

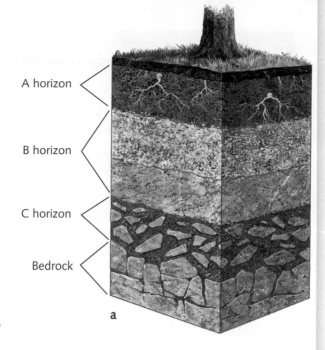

A horizon

B horizon

C horizon

Bedrock

a

b

Figure 9.13 a) This soil profile shows what each soil horizon, or layer, above the bedrock might look like. **b)** Three soil horizons are visible in this soil profile.

PEOPLE IN SCIENCE Justus von Liebig 1803–1873

Justus von Liebig was a German chemist who developed some of the early concepts about soil. Before his work, scientists seldom looked at soil below the A horizon. At that time, scientists felt that only the topmost part of the soil had any effect on plants. Soil scientists in Liebig's time had already worked out a balance sheet that showed how plants took essential nutrients, such as nitrogen, out of the soil and how these nutrients could be replaced with manure. Liebig took this idea further and developed a nitrogen-based fertilizer.

Liebig's work changed the way scientists looked at soil. They began to understand the relationship of parent rocks to soil types. They also began to study how the different soil horizons related to one another. Liebig's use of fertilizer also led to today's modern use of fertilizers in farming.

As You Read

When you come to a vocabulary word in the lesson, use context clues to check your understanding of its definition. If a vocabulary word is used more than once, look back at your list to check your definition of the word. Then write a sentence using the vocabulary word in your Science Notebook.

Figure 9.14
Despite extremely thin topsoil, tropical forests support some of the most abundant vegetation on Earth.

Climate and Soil Formation

Different areas have different types of soils. Recall that different parent rocks result in different types of soils. Climate also affects soil formation. Because climate affects the rate of weathering, it also affects soil development.

Tropical Soils   Tropical areas have high temperatures and heavy rainfall. These conditions usually cause rapid weathering of soils. As water moves through tropical soils, it leaches, or removes, nutrients from the topsoil downward. Heavy rains also wash soils away. As a result, tropical soils are usually thin and have few nutrients.

The roots of tropical plants hold the thin soil in place and keep the rain from washing it away. While the rapid plant growth removes nutrients from the topsoil quickly, it also returns nutrients to the topsoil as plants die and decay. As a result, the plants and soil exist in a delicate balance. Agriculture, logging, and mining in tropical areas can easily upset this balance. Once the vegetation in a tropical area is cut down, the topsoil has nothing to hold it in place, and it is washed away by the rain. Without topsoil, plants can no longer grow in the area.

Arctic Soils   Arctic areas have cold temperatures and little rainfall. These conditions result in a slow rate of weathering. Soil in arctic areas is usually thin and lacking in nutrients. With little rain, it takes a long time for bedrock to weather. As a result, the soil forms very slowly. The plants that grow during the short arctic summer are very small and do not produce large amounts of organic matter as they die and decay. As a result, there is very little humus in the soil. Because they form so slowly and have few nutrients, arctic soils are easily damaged. Once damaged, they take a very long time to recover.

Desert Soils Desert climates receive little rain. This means that the rate of weathering is very slow in deserts just as it is in arctic areas. Because there are few plants in the desert, the soil has little humus. When scarce rain or groundwater seeps into the desert soil, it dissolves the minerals in it. When the water evaporates, the materials that were dissolved by the rain are left behind in the soil. Many of these dissolved materials are mineral salts. These salts can sometimes become so concentrated in desert soils that plants can no longer grow.

Figure 9.15 Very few plants can survive in the harsh desert soils of California's Death Valley.

Temperate Soils Temperate climates include all the nondesert climates between the tropics and the arctic. Temperate areas have some of the most productive soils in the world. This means that temperate soils can support the growth of vegetation in forests, grasslands, and prairies. It also means that temperate soils can support many different food crops. In temperate areas, there is enough rain to cause a high rate of chemical weathering. There is not enough rain, however, to leach all the nutrients from the soil. As a result, the rates of weathering are not as high as they are in the tropics. They are higher, however, than the rates of weathering in desert or arctic areas. Much of the continental United States has a temperate climate.

Temperate soils are usually deep soils meaning that each soil horizon is thick. The topsoil is usually dark and rich with organic matter. Because many plants grow in temperate soils, they add large amounts of humus to the soil.

CONNECTION: Biology

The organic material in soil comes from the decomposition, or breaking down, of plant and animal matter. Without the help of a variety of different organisms, the decomposition of plant and animal matter would not be possible. The organisms that break down organic matter are called decomposers. Without decomposers to recycle nutrients back into soil, plants would not grow. Some common decomposers include earthworms, some insects, millipedes, bacteria, and mushrooms.

Figure 9.16 Areas with a temperate climate can support large-scale farming. So much wheat is grown in the midwestern United States that the region is called the Breadbasket. Much of the agriculture in the United States takes place in this area.

Figure 9.17 Runoff from a rainstorm erodes soil from an Iowa cornfield.

Extend It!

Some deserts have living soil called cryptogamic soil. It is composed of mosses, lichens, fungi, and algae all living together. It is sometimes called "brown sugar soil" because of how it looks. Cryptogamic soils are very delicate. Research cryptogamic soils and write a paragraph about your findings.

Soil as a Resource

People depend on soil to grow many different crops. Soil provides a home to many animals, including those animals that are important to the growth of plants. Soil is also extremely important because it stores water that can later be used by humans, plants, and animals. Most soils take hundreds or thousands of years to develop. Because soil is so important and because it takes so long to develop, it is considered a resource that must be protected.

Rainwater drains away when soil is removed or covered over. For example, if you compare a parking lot to a grassy lawn after a rainstorm, you'll notice that rainwater in the parking lot either flows away or collects in puddles. The water in the puddles quickly evaporates because it has not soaked into the ground. In contrast, the rain that has fallen on the grassy lawn has soaked into the soil. It is stored in the soil for later use by plants and animals.

Soil Conservation

Erosion is the process by which water and wind move soil from one place to another. Plants help protect soil from being eroded by wind

and water. When soil is not protected from erosion, its topsoil is eventually stripped away. One way to protect soil from erosion is by using good agricultural, or farming, practices. With good conservation practices, a farmer can continue to grow crops for many years without harming the soil.

Cover Crops and Strip Cropping Farmers can plant cover crops to prevent soil erosion. A cover crop is planted after the main crop is harvested. Cover crops keep soil from eroding between plantings of the main crops. Depleted nutrients, or nutrients that have been used up by crop growth, are added back into the soil as the cover crops grow and decay. The most common cover crops are soybeans and clover.

Planting alternating strips of different crops in a field is called strip cropping. The plants in alternating strips are selected by their characteristics. For example, crops that grow tightly together and close to the ground might be planted in alternating strips. Between them, a farmer might plant a crop that grows taller and requires more space between plants. The crops that grow closer to the ground help slow the erosion of soil from the less protected crop rows where the plants grow farther from one another.

Figure 9.18 The farmer plowed this field following the contours of the land. Contour plowing reduces erosion of the soil when it rains.

Figure It Out

1. What happens to the water as it flows across a contour plowed field?

2. Predict what would happen if the field were plowed with the rows going down the slope instead of across it.

Did You Know?

The Inca in Peru used agricultural terraces to grow crops on steep slopes high in the Andes. Terraces that were built between the thirteenth and fifteenth centuries are still being used to grow crops today.

Crop Rotation   Crop rotation is a common way to prevent the loss of nutrients in soil. Growing the same crop in a field year after year depletes certain nutrients. Crop rotation is simply growing different types of crops in a field each year. Different crops require different nutrients. When different crops are grown each year, nutrients in the soil are not depleted as quickly. Alfalfa, for example, replaces nutrients used by other crops.

Contour Plowing and Terracing   Contour plowing involves plowing a field in a way that reduces erosion from rain. For example, instead of plowing rows straight up and down a hill, a farmer might plow rows that follow the curves or contours of a slope. This slows down water runoff and helps prevent erosion. Terracing is another way to slow erosion of soil on very steep hills. Farmers use terracing to shape a steep slope into a series of smaller, flatter fields. Terracing has been used by farmers for thousands of years as a way to prevent soil erosion.

Figure 9.19 This hillside was terraced to reduce soil erosion and to make farming easier on the steep slope.

After You Read

1. What are the main components of soil?

2. Explain why humus is important to soil.

3. Read each of the sentences you wrote in your Science Notebook. Check to make sure you used the vocabulary words correctly. Revise sentences in which you used a vocabulary word incorrectly. Use the sentences in your Science Notebook to write a bulleted list of facts about why soil is an important resource and what can be done to protect it.

Summary

KEY CONCEPTS

9.1 Weathering

- Mechanical weathering occurs when ice, water, wind, gravity, pressure, plants, or animals cause rocks to break into smaller pieces.

- Chemical weathering occurs when rocks and minerals are broken down due to changes in their chemical composition. The most common agents of chemical weathering are water, carbon dioxide, acids, and oxygen.

9.2 Rate of Weathering

- The rate at which a rock weathers depends on many factors. These factors include rock type and composition, climate, gravity, organisms, and surface area.

- Mechanical and chemical weathering often work together. Mechanical weathering breaks rocks into smaller pieces, which helps to speed up further mechanical and chemical weathering.

9.3 From Rocks to Soil

- Weathered rock and mineral fragments mix with organic matter called humus to form soil.

- Soils form in layers, or horizons. The uppermost horizon is the topsoil, and it has the most humus. The subsoil contains less humus and larger weathered rock and mineral fragments.

- Soil formation takes place at different rates depending on the composition of the parent rock and the climate.

- Soil is a valuable resource because plants need it to grow. It also stores water for later use by humans, plants, and animals. It also provides homes for animals that help plants to grow. Soil forms very slowly.

- Good agricultural practices, including cover crops, strip cropping, crop rotation, contour plowing, and terracing, can help conserve soil.

VOCABULARY REVIEW

Write each term in a complete sentence, or write a paragraph relating several terms.

9.1
weathering, p. 150
mechanical weathering, p. 150
frost wedging, p. 150
abrasion, p. 151
exfoliation, p. 151
chemical weathering, p. 152
acid precipitation, p. 152
oxidation, p. 153

9.2
differential weathering, p. 154
surface area, p. 157

9.3
soil, p. 158
bedrock, p. 158
parent material, p. 158
residual soil, p. 158
transported soil, p. 158
humus, p. 158
soil profile, p. 159
topsoil, p. 159
subsoil, p. 159
leaching, p. 159
erosion, p. 162

PREPARE FOR CHAPTER TEST

To prepare for the chapter test, create a question from each Learning Goal. Use the information in your Science Notebook to answer each question. Then use these answers to write a well-developed essay about the chapter. Use the Key Concept on the first page of this chapter as your topic sentence.

True or False

If the statement is true, write "true." If it is false, change the underlined word or words to make the statement true.

1. <u>Mechanical weathering</u> changes the chemical composition of rocks.

2. <u>Oxygen</u> takes part in the chemical weathering of some rocks.

3. <u>Low</u> temperature and moisture speed up the rate of weathering.

4. Darker-colored soils usually have a greater amount of <u>humus</u> than lighter-colored soils.

5. <u>Tropical soils</u> are some of the thickest and most fertile soils.

6. Changing the type of crop grown in a field each year is called <u>strip cropping</u>.

Short Answer

Answer each of the following in a sentence or brief paragraph.

7. Explain how trees cause mechanical weathering.

8. Describe how changes in temperature affect frost wedging.

9. What are the sources of acids present in precipitation?

10. Describe how climate affects the rate of weathering.

11. Describe how the parent rock affects soil composition.

12. How does contour plowing reduce erosion?

Critical Thinking

Use what you have learned in this chapter to answer each of the following.

13. **Apply Concepts** Why do caves usually form in areas with limestone bedrock?

14. **Infer** Many of the nutrients in soil will dissolve in water. What might happen to soil in an area with high rainfall?

15. **Compare** Arctic soils are thin because they form from a very slow rate of weathering. What type of soil is most similar to arctic soil?

Standardized Test Question

Choose the letter of the response that correctly answers the question.

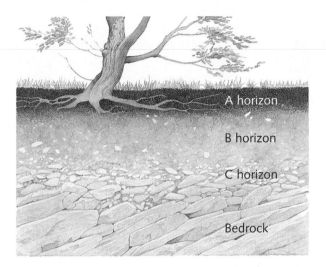

16. Which part of soil contains the most organic matter?

   A. A horizon

   B. B horizon

   C. C horizon

   D. bedrock

Test-Taking Tip

Resist the urge to rush and don't worry if others finish before you. Use all the time you have. If you are able, clear your mind by closing your eyes and counting to five or taking another type of short break. Extra points are not awarded for being the first person to finish.

Erosion and Deposition

KEY CONCEPT The agents of erosion and deposition work together to shape and create landforms.

The Grand Canyon is an immense canyon, cut deep into the Colorado Plateau. It is 446 km long, up to 24 km wide, and up to 1.6 km deep. The Grand Canyon was carved by weathering and erosion. You have learned that erosion removes rock and soil and carries it downstream. Though erosion is usually a gradual process, it can cause significant changes over time. In the case of the Grand Canyon, it took about five to six million years for water, wind, ice, and gravity to carve out the spectacular canyon that exists today. The agents of erosion, water, ice, wind, and gravity, act together to change Earth's landscape. These agents not only shape the land, they also impact human populations.

Think About Forces of Erosion and Deposition

Whether you live in the country or in a city, landforms are all around you. A landform can be anything from a hill to the bank of a river or stream.

• In your Science Notebook, make a list of landforms that you have seen.

• Read over your list and choose a landform that you think was formed by erosion. Write one or two sentences to support your thoughts.

Water Erosion and Deposition

Before You Read

Create a lesson outline. Use the lesson title as the outline title. Label the headings with Roman numerals *I* through *IX*. Use the letters *A, B, C,* etc., under each heading to record information.

Erosion is the transport of weathered materials from one place to another by water, ice, wind, or gravity. There is another process, called deposition, that works along with erosion. **Deposition** is the process by which material is either laid down on the ground or sinks to the bottom of a body of water. Deposition is the final stage of erosion, during which materials that have been transported are dropped in a new location. Erosion and deposition complement each other because all eroded material is deposited somewhere. Together, these two processes are responsible for creating many of the landforms that surround us.

Running Water

Though water is a powerful source of erosion, water erosion usually happens gradually. It begins when a small trickle of water flows in a small channel called a **rill**. Rills commonly form on slopes where gravity causes water to flow downhill. Rill erosion occurs when this running water erodes the side of a slope. When a channel becomes wider and deeper, it is called a **gully**. Gullies can be many meters deep. Erosion often happens more quickly once gullies form because larger amounts of water can flow through them.

a

b

Figure 10.1 a) Rills form as water erodes the softer rock layers in Badlands National Park, South Dakota. **b)** This gully formed on farmland when too much vegetation was removed and rain caused the soil to erode over time.

Flowing Water Has Energy

Water flows downhill because of gravity. Moving water has energy. On a surface with a slight slope, water moves very slowly and has less energy. On a steep slope, water moves quickly and has more energy. This energy enables water to move weathered rock particles. Because fast-moving water has more energy than slow-moving water, fast-moving water can move larger rock particles than slow-moving water can.

Moving water often carries suspended, or floating, sediment such as soil particles. Water in a stream often looks muddy after a rainfall because it contains suspended soil that has been eroded from the land. This soil will either settle to the bottom of the stream or be carried to another location.

As described on the previous page, rills and gullies form on hillsides. When several gullies come together, they form a larger channel called a stream. When streams come together, they form rivers. Streams and rivers erode the land into V-shaped valleys.

Figure 10.3 As the New River flowed through this valley in West Virginia, it formed a V-shaped valley known as the New River Gorge.

When Water Loses Energy

As flowing water slows down, it has less energy. With less energy, water is no longer able to carry as much sediment. The heavier sediment is the first to settle, or be deposited. As the moving water continues to slow down, lighter sediment is deposited. For example, a fast-moving stream may pick up and carry small rocks and bits of soil. As the stream slows down, the small rocks, which are heavier than the soil, will be the first to sink to the bottom. This process continues until the water stops moving and the majority of its sediment is deposited.

Figure 10.2 After heavy rains, it is common to see streams swollen with muddy, brown water. The water appears muddy because it holds suspended particles of soil that were washed off the land surface by rain.

Coastal Deltas

Each year, streams and rivers carry enormous amounts of sediment and weathered materials from the land to coastal areas. When a river or stream enters a large body of water such as the ocean, the water slows down. As it slows, it deposits large amounts of sediment. The buildup of sediment forms deltas, such as the Nile River Delta, shown in **Figure 10.4**. A **delta** is a triangular deposit of silt and clay that forms when a stream enters a large body of water. The name *delta* comes from the triangle-shaped Greek letter *delta* (Δ). Deltas from small rivers and streams may go unnoticed, but big rivers form extremely large deltas. The Nile River delta is so big that it can be seen from space.

Coastal Erosion and Deposition

The ocean is a dynamic place. The water in the ocean is always in motion, and is a strong force for both erosion and deposition. Waves are the most erosive force in the ocean, because they can carry a tremendous amount of energy. During storms, big waves pound the coast and cause much erosion. Even small waves can cause considerable erosion over an extended period of time.

Most erosion occurs at the shoreline. The **shoreline** is where land and a body of water meet. Waves have a strong effect on both erosion and deposition along the shoreline. Waves erode the shoreline and deposit the sand, gravel, or rocks from which beaches are made. A **beach** is any area of the shoreline made up of material deposited by waves. Some beach material is carried to the shoreline by rivers. Other beach material is eroded from land areas located near the shoreline. The type of material on a beach depends on its source. This is why the colors and textures of the materials on shorelines vary from place to place.

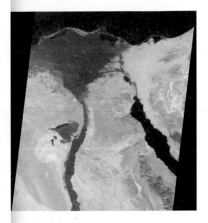

Figure 10.4 The Nile River is the longest river in the world. It flows for more than 6,600 km before it enters the Mediterranean Sea, where it forms a delta. You can see the triangular shape of the delta in this satellite photograph.

As You Read

Review the outline in your Science Notebook. Make sure that you have added any new information. Share your outline with a partner and add any missing information.

Would you expect the smallest particles of sediment to be deposited close to or far from the mouth, or end, of a river? Explain your answer.

a

b

Figure 10.5 Beaches are made of different types of materials that are deposited by waves. **a)** The sand on this Hawaiian beach is black because it is made from eroded basaltic lava. **b)** The sand on this tropical island beach is light in color because it is made from eroded limestone and seashells.

Wave Erosion

The action of waves creates many dramatic coastal features. The power of breaking waves is most obvious at rocky headlands, which are points of land sticking out into the ocean. Over time, as a headland is worn away by waves, a flat surface called a wave-cut platform is formed. This flat area often ends at a steep cliff. Wave-cut cliffs form when waves erode and undercut rock walls.

How quickly cliffs form depends on the strength of the wave action and the hardness of the rock. Sea cliffs made of hard rock, such as granite, erode very slowly. Those made of softer sedimentary rock erode quickly, especially during storms. Other landforms carved by waves include sea arches, sea caves, and isolated rock towers called sea stacks.

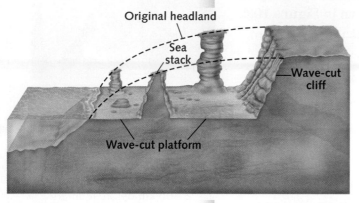

Figure 10.6 The dotted lines show the original shape of this headland, which has been changed by wave erosion.

Figure It Out

1. Do you think more wave erosion occurs when the water is high or low? Explain.

2. If you were walking into the ocean from the beach, how would you know when you had reached the longshore bar?

Longshore Currents

Moving out toward the open ocean, the water becomes deeper for a while, before becoming shallower again. The shallow water just offshore sits above a sandbar, called the **longshore bar**. Longshore bars form in front of most beaches. As the water gets shallower, waves slow down, lose energy, and deposit any sediment that is being carried. The waves then break, and the energy from the breaking waves scour out the area in front of the longshore bar. This deeper water between the shore and the longshore bar is called the longshore trough.

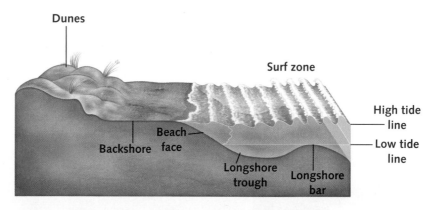

Figure 10.7 Beaches are shaped by daily wave action. The longshore bar is located in the surf zone, beneath the surface of the water. As waves spill over the longshore bar, the longshore current is produced.

As water from incoming waves flows over the longshore bar, a current called the **longshore current** is produced. This current flows parallel to the shoreline. Longshore currents move large amounts of sediment along the shore. In general, this sediment is transported in the direction of the longshore current. In the United States, most longshore currents carry sediment to the south.

Seashore Features Created by Deposition

Most seashores are constantly changing. Sediment is eroded by storm waves and deposited as currents slow down. Longshore currents also move and deposit sediment that builds coastal landforms, including spits and barrier islands. A **spit** is a narrow band of sand that projects into the water from a bend in the coastline. A spit forms where a shoreline changes direction. As a spit grows and crosses a bay, a **baymouth bar** forms.

Figure 10.8 Barrier islands are common along the Gulf and Atlantic coasts. This barrier island along the Outer Banks of North Carolina protects the mainland by stopping the waves before they reach the mainland.

Long ridges of sand that are separated from the mainland and deposited or shaped by the longshore current are called **barrier islands**. Barrier islands can be many kilometers long and several kilometers wide. Salt water coastal lakes called lagoons are shallow, protected bodies of water located behind baymouth bars and barrier islands. Landforms called tombolos are ridges of sand that form between the mainland and an island. **Figure 10.9** illustrates the various coastal landforms described above. All coastal landforms are temporary and unstable. A large storm or changing wave conditions can change the face of an entire shoreline.

Explain It!

Place a handful or two of sediment in a jar. Fill the jar with water and shake it. Set the jar down where it will not be disturbed. After 20 minutes, observe the sediment in the jar. Do you notice anything interesting about the way the sediment settled? In your Science Notebook, explain what has happened.

Figure 10.9 This drawing shows some of the depositional features of coastlines.

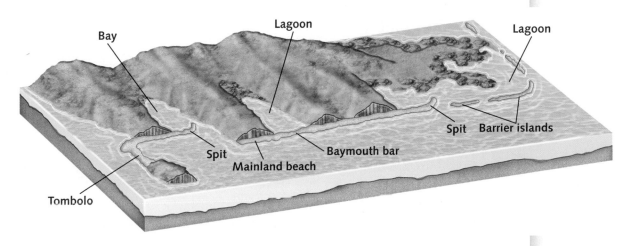

Efforts to Prevent Beach Erosion

As described earlier, shorelines naturally shift and change as longshore currents carry and deposit sand from one area to another. Human efforts to stop sand from naturally moving can have negative effects. For example, the city of Miami Beach built hotels along beach cliffs but soon noticed the cliffs eroding. The city reinforced the cliffs by building sea walls to stop waves from reaching them. The sea walls also prevented sand from moving naturally along the shoreline. As a result, beach sand accumulated along the sea walls on the sides that were hit by waves. The beaches on the other sides of the walls, however, were deprived of sand and eventually disappeared.

Other structures built by humans to prevent beach erosion have caused similar problems. Jetties are walls of concrete built to protect harbor entrances from being clogged by sand. Over time, jetties trap sand upshore from a harbor and prevent it from reaching beaches downshore. Even with jetties, harbor entrances eventually clog with sand that needs to be removed by dredging. This requires the use of large machinery to scoop out and remove the unwanted sediment.

Breakwaters are long piles of rocks dumped parallel to shorelines. They act like coral reefs, causing waves to break before they reach the shore. Breakwaters are often used to create protected areas for boats to anchor. As currents slow down behind a breakwater, they deposit their load of sediment. Eventually, this sand builds up and needs to be removed by dredging. Shoreline engineers are searching for more effective solutions to the ongoing challenge of beach erosion.

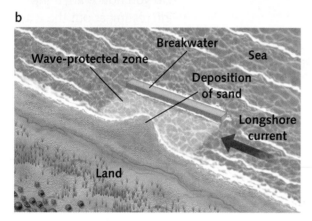

Figure 10.10 a) Jetties prevent sand from reaching downshore beaches. **b)** Breakwaters cause beach sand to accumulate behind them. Eventually, this sand will need to be removed by dredging.

After You Read

1. Describe how erosion and deposition are related.

2. Explain how slope and water flow are related.

3. Review the outline in your Science Notebook. Use the information you wrote to answer this question: How might the sediment at the bottom of a stream indicate the speed of the water that deposited it?

4. Predict how a barrier island might help a coastline during a hurricane.

10.2 Erosion Caused by Glaciers

Learning Goals

- Explain how glaciers form and move.

- Compare and contrast valley glaciers and continental glaciers.

- Describe how glaciers change landscapes.

- Identify landscape features eroded and deposited by glaciers.

New Vocabulary

glacier
valley glacier
continental glacier
cirque
arete
horn
hanging valley
till
moraine
outwash
esker

Before You Read

Preview the lesson by looking at the photos and pictures and by reading the headings and the Learning Goals. In your Science Notebook, write each heading. Leave several blank lines after each one. Then turn each heading into a question. Note what you expect to learn in this lesson.

Moving water causes erosion and deposition. When water freezes, it may seem that it stops moving but that is not always true. Large masses of ice are called **glaciers**. Glaciers have the ability to move across Earth's surface. They shape the landscape by eroding, moving, and depositing huge amounts of rock and sediment. These enormous masses of ice are responsible for creating many of Earth's landforms.

How Glaciers Form

Glaciers form near Earth's poles and in mountainous areas at high elevations. They exist where it is cold enough for snow and ice to last year-round. Layers of snow that have not melted build up year after year in an area called a snowfield. Over many years, the total thickness of this snow layer increases and a glacier begins to form. Eventually, the weight of the top layers of snow creates great pressure on the bottom layers of snow. This pressure forces the bottom layers of snow to partially melt and become ice. Glaciers slowly begin to move as gravity pulls on their huge mass. Because they move, glaciers are sometimes called rivers of ice. Glaciers are divided into two different types—valley glaciers and continental glaciers.

Figure 10.11 This map shows the locations of glaciers throughout the world. Glacial areas appear in white.

Figure It Out

1. In what regions of the world are glaciers located?

2. Do glaciers exist in areas other than the polar regions? If so, how do you think ice stays frozen year-round in these regions?

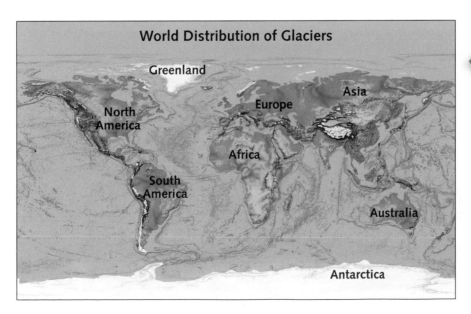

World Distribution of Glaciers

Greenland

Asia

Europe

North America

Africa

South America

Australia

Antarctica

How Glaciers Move

Glaciers begin to move downhill when enough ice builds up on a slope. Glaciers move in two ways. The great weight of the ice causes the base of the glacier to melt and allows the entire glacier to slide forward. This is similar to the way a melting ice cube slides across a smooth surface. Glaciers also move when ice crystals within the glacier slide over one another. When this happens, the upper part, or surface, of the glacier will move faster than its base.

Figure 10.12 Valley glaciers form high in mountains and flow down valleys. They scour the land surface as they move, widening and straightening the valleys into broad U-shapes.

Valley Glaciers

Valley glaciers form in valleys in high mountainous areas. This type of glacier forms all over the world, even in cold, mountainous, tropical areas along the equator. Most valley glaciers begin to flow when the layers of accumulated snow and ice reach more than 20 m in thickness. Sometimes, valley glaciers traveling in two separate valleys that intersect can flow together and form an even larger glacier.

Continental Glaciers

Continental glaciers, also called ice sheets, cover broad continent-sized areas. Glaciers of this kind covered much of Earth's surface during past ice ages when the planet experienced much colder average temperatures. Today, continental glaciers exist only in Greenland, northern Canada, and Antarctica. The Antarctic ice sheet covers almost the entire continent of Antarctica.

Figure 10.13 These research facilities are located on the Antarctic ice sheet at the south pole.

How Glaciers Shape Landscapes

Glaciers are powerful agents of erosion. As a glacier moves, rocks and sediment embedded in the ice act like sandpaper. They grind out scratches called striations and grooves on rock surfaces. These striations and grooves run parallel to the direction of the glacier's movement.

Glaciers also erode the landscape through a process called plucking. Plucking occurs when water at the base of a glacier freezes in cracks in a rock surface. As the body of the glacier ice moves, the material around the ice in the cracks is pulled, or plucked, out. Valley glaciers and continental glaciers create landscapes that are very different from one another. Valley glaciers carve out rugged, more dramatic features from the mountain areas through which they flow. Continental glaciers usually smooth and flatten the landscape.

Figure 10.14 These glacial grooves are located on Kelly's Island, Ohio. They were formed by large rock fragments that were frozen to the bottom of a moving glacier.

Figure 10.15 A valley glacier carved out this spectacular U-shaped valley in the Canadian Rockies.

As You Read

Answer the questions you wrote in Before You Read. Use the answers to write a well-developed paragraph in your Science Notebook explaining what this lesson is about. Describe how this lesson relates to the first lesson in the chapter. Was your prediction correct? Explain.

How do striations and grooves indicate the direction of movement of a glacier that existed in the past?

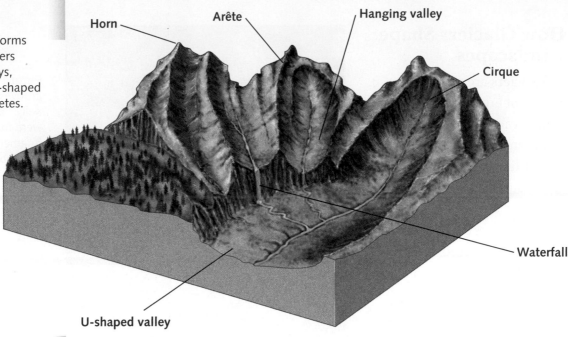

Figure 10.16 Landforms carved by valley glaciers include hanging valleys, cirques, waterfalls, U-shaped valleys, horns, and aretes.

Horn

Arête

Hanging valley

Cirque

Waterfall

U-shaped valley

Extend It!

At various times in Earth's past, much of our planet was covered by vast sheets of ice. These periods are known as ice ages. Earth is currently in an interglacial interval, or a warmer period between ice ages. The most recent ice age ended about 10,000 years ago. Use the library or Internet to learn more about Earth's most recent ice age and some of the landforms that were left behind as the glaciers retreated. Record your findings in your Science Notebook.

Landscape Features Carved by Glaciers

Valley glaciers can create the many landscape features shown in **Figure 10.16**. Bowl-shaped depressions called **cirques** are carved out by glaciers as they flow down the side of a mountain. A sharp, steep ridge, called an **arête**, forms where two cirques on opposite sides of a valley meet. A steep peak in the shape of a pyramid, called a **horn**, forms where there are glaciers on three or more sides of a mountaintop. A famous horn is the Matterhorn in the Swiss Alps. When a smaller valley from higher up on a mountainside meets a larger U-shaped valley, a **hanging valley** is formed. Many beautiful waterfalls are located in hanging valleys.

Figure 10.17 Bridalveil Falls is one of several spectacular waterfalls in Yosemite National Park, California. It is located in the hanging valley of Bridalveil Creek, where it meets Yosemite Valley.

Glacial Deposits

A term used to describe material deposited by glacial ice is **till**. When a glacier melts, till is left behind. Till is made up of sediment ranging in size from large boulders to small particles of clay. When till is deposited along the edge of a glacier, it forms ridges called **moraines**.

As a glacier melts and begins to recede, its melted ice, called meltwater, flows into the valley below it. Sand-sized and smaller particles that have been eroded, carried, and deposited by meltwater streams are called **outwash**. Meltwater streams deposit outwash in an area in front of the glacier called an outwash plain. Meltwater streams flowing under a glacier deposit long, winding ridges of sediment called **eskers**. Sometimes, when glaciers are rapidly melting, or retreating, large blocks of ice can break off of them. The heavy weight of this block forms a depression in Earth's surface called a kettle. Kettles that reach below the water table can form kettle ponds and lakes.

Figure 10.18 A terminal, or end, moraine marks the farthest point that a glacier has moved forward. The terminal moraine of Exit Glacier in Kenai Fjords National Park, Alaska, is clearly visible in this photo.

Figure 10.19 As glaciers retreat, they sometimes create long hill-shaped deposits of till called drumlins. Most of the tree-covered hills in this photo, taken near Waterloo, Wisconsin, are drumlins.

CONNECTION: Economics

Deposits from glaciers that covered Earth in the past have great economic importance today. Many lakes and ponds in New England and the upper Midwest were created by continental ice sheets that once covered the land. Today, these glacial deposits serve as major groundwater reservoirs. Glacial deposits also have great economic value as sand and gravel for building materials.

After You Read

1. What causes glaciers to move?

2. How do rocks embedded in the ice of a glacier erode the landscape?

3. What is a cirque and how is it formed?

4. Review the notes in your Science Notebook. According to your preview and summary, how might a landscape eroded by a valley glacier compare to a landscape eroded by a continental glacier?

Learning Goals

- Describe the conditions that contribute to wind erosion.
- Explain how wind moves sediment and causes erosion.
- Describe the effects of wind erosion.
- Explain the difference between dunes and loess deposits.

New Vocabulary

saltation
suspension
deflation
dune
loess

Before You Read

Create a K-W-L-S-H chart in your Science Notebook. In the column under *K*, write a few notes describing what you already know about wind erosion. Then add what you want to know in the column under *W*. As you read the lesson, add to your chart.

Wind can pick up and carry sediment just as moving water and moving ice can. Unless wind is very strong, however, its ability to erode and carry large particles is not as great as that of water or ice. Even so, wind can shape landscapes through erosion and deposition. Wind erosion is common in dry locations, where there is loose, sandy soil. It is also common in coastal areas, which are likely to experience strong winds.

Wind Erosion

When the wind blows, it picks up and moves small particles by skipping or bouncing them along. This skipping or bouncing motion is called **saltation**. Most sand that is carried by wind is transported by saltation. Wind can also move particles in a rolling motion along the ground. When winds are strong enough, the particles they transport may be carried in the air for long distances. This method of wind transport is called **suspension**.

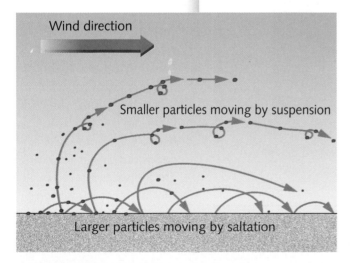

Figure 10.20 Sediment blown by strong winds can be transported by suspension and saltation.

Figure 10.21 The suspended sediment in this photo of a tornado is clearly visible.

Deflation is the lowering of the land surface resulting from the wind's removal of surface particles. During deflation, the wind removes lighter layers of sediment first. Rock fragments that are too heavy to be blown by the wind are left behind. The hard, rocky surface of the land that results from deflation is called desert pavement. In many areas around the world that are intensely farmed, deflation is a problem.

During the 1930s, there was a period with little rain in the Great Plains region of the United States. The natural vegetation that held the soil in place had been removed for farming. Strong winds picked up the loose soil and created destructive dust storms that darkened the skies from Montana to Texas.

As You Read

As you read, begin filling in the *L* column of your K-W-L chart with answers to the questions you wrote in the *W* column. Work with a partner to add to the *L* column of your chart.

How does desert pavement form?

Figure 10.22 This desert pavement is located in the hot, dry desert of Death Valley, California.

Wind can also erode rock surfaces by abrasion. Abrasion occurs when particles rub against the surface of rocks or other materials. Wind abrasion is often caused by sand being blown against rocks or other objects. The blowing of millions of sharp sand grains acts like sandblasting to smooth, polish, or wear away rock. Over millions of years, wind erosion can smooth and erode rocks into interesting shapes.

Figure 10.23 Rocks like this one in Antarctica, shaped by wind-blown sediment, are called ventifacts.

Wind Erosion in the United States

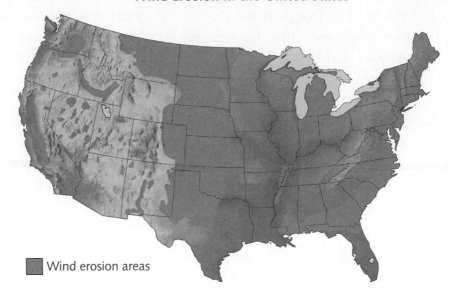

Wind erosion areas

Figure It Out

1. Which areas of the United States do not experience great wind erosion?

2. Why might wind erosion be a problem in the areas on the map that do experience it?

Figure 10.24 Areas, such as deserts and seashores, with little vegetation are subject to wind erosion.

Wind Deposition

All of the material that is carried by wind is eventually dropped, or deposited. Fast-blowing wind can carry more materials and heavier particles than slow-blowing wind. As the wind slows down, some of the materials it is carrying are deposited on the ground.

Dune Formation

When wind hits an obstacle, such as a rock or a plant, it slows down. As it slows, it deposits the heavier material it is carrying. As these materials collect, they create an obstacle that further slows the wind. Over time, wind blowing in the same general direction deposits piles of sand called **dunes**.

Sand dunes vary in size and shape depending on the conditions under which they form. These conditions include the direction and strength of the wind, the amount of sand available, and the amount of vegetation on the landscape. All dunes have a gentle slope located on the side facing the wind, or the windward side. Dunes have a steeper slope on the side that is protected from the wind, or the leeward side.

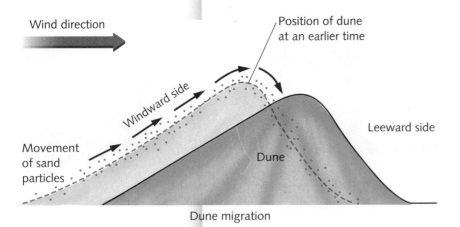

Wind direction

Position of dune at an earlier time

Windward side

Movement of sand particles

Dune

Leeward side

Dune migration

Figure 10.25 As winds blow against dunes, they move sand from the windward side to the leeward side. This causes dunes to move slowly over time in the general direction of the wind.

Loess

Wind also carries and deposits silt-sized particles. These are very light in weight and can travel far distances. Many parts of Earth are covered by thick layers of fine, wind-blown silt deposits called **loess** (luss). It is formed as high winds that blow off of glaciers sweep across open areas of outwash and pick up the silt-sized material within it. Glaciers from the last ice age may have exposed the sediment that makes up loess. Loess is present in much of the midwestern United States. It is also present in Mississippi, Oregon, and Washington. Because they are rich in nutrients and minerals, loess soils are some of the most fertile soils for growing crops.

Figure 10.26 The Loess Hills in western Iowa are made of windblown loess. The silt-sized sediment forms unlayered deposits that are easily eroded.

⊙ CONNECTION: Biology

Sand Dune Lizards in Danger

The sand dune habitat of the small, brown sand dune lizard is a narrow region of southeastern New Mexico and western Texas. The sand dune lizard lives in low, open spaces between sand dunes. It buries itself in sand to regulate its body temperature and to avoid predators. The lizard prefers areas with plenty of short, scrubby trees called shinnery oaks. The rolling dunes in New Mexico where the sand dune lizard lives are being threatened by gas and oil development. They are also threatened by the spraying of poisons to kill the shinnery oaks, which competes with grasses that feed cattle. Because the sand dune lizard's habitat is so rare, this species is threatened with extinction. The U.S. Fish and Wildlife Service recently made the lizard a candidate for listing as an endangered species under the Endangered Species Act.

After You Read

1. How does wind abrasion smooth rocks?

2. What might reduce wind erosion caused by deflation?

3. What causes dunes to move over time?

4. Complete the last two columns of your K-W-L-S-H chart. As wind that is carrying sand and loess slows down, which would it deposit first—the sand or the loess? Use the information in your chart to explain your answer.

Learning Goals

- Identify the four main factors affecting mass movement.
- Describe the different types of mass movement.

New Vocabulary

mass movement
rockfall
landslide
slump
avalanche
flow
mudflow
lahar
creep

10.4 Gravity's Role in Erosion and Deposition

Before You Read

Create a concept map in your Science Notebook. In the center of the page, write and circle the term *Mass movement.* Draw four circles around the center circle. Draw lines connecting each of these four circles to the center circle. Predict some of the words you will use to fill in the circles.

Mass Movement

This chapter has explained how gravity influences the movement of water and ice on Earth's surface. The force of gravity also causes rocks and soil to move downslope. The movement of rock and soil down a slope can occur either very slowly or very quickly.

Mass movement is the downslope movement of loose sediment and weathered rock resulting from the force of gravity. Erosion through mass movement usually occurs after weathering processes weaken rock and break it into smaller pieces. All mass movements occur on land that is sloped. Because there are very few areas on Earth that are completely flat, mass movement occurs almost everywhere.

There are four main factors that affect mass movement. The first is the weight of a material. Heavier material will be pulled more strongly by gravity down a slope. The second factor is how easily a material slides or flows down a slope. For example, mud would tend to flow down a slope more easily and quickly than slightly wet soil. A third factor that might affect mass movement is a sudden event, such as an earthquake, that shakes materials loose from a slope. The fourth factor, water, is discussed on the next page. Some common types of mass movement are shown in **Figure 10.27**.

Figure 10.27 Three common types of mass movement are shown below.

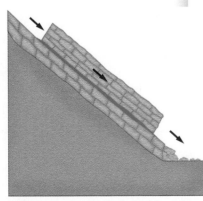

Slide
Moves as block of Earth material

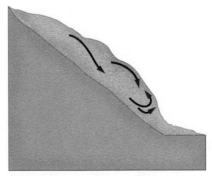

Flow
Movement involves mixing of particles within moving mass

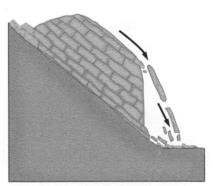

Fall
Free fall of Earth material

1. Which sand holds its shape the best?
2. Why does sand that is saturated, or completely filled with water, tend to slide easily?

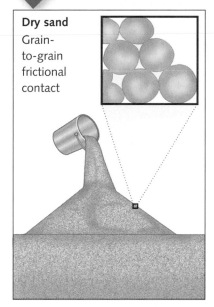

Dry sand
Grain-to-grain frictional contact

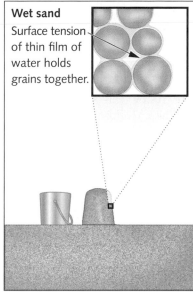

Wet sand
Surface tension of thin film of water holds grains together.

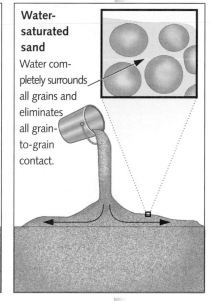

Water-saturated sand
Water completely surrounds all grains and eliminates all grain-to-grain contact.

Figure 10.28 Mass movement is affected by the amount of water in a material. Very dry sand and very wet sand are more likely to slide down a slope than soil containing only a small amount of water.

Water

Water is the fourth factor affecting mass movement. Small amounts of water help to stabilize a slope. Sand or soil that is too dry is more likely to slide than damp sand or soil. The thin film of water between particles of sand or soil helps hold them together. Too much water, however, can make a slope unstable. Soil or sand that is full of water is heavier and more likely to be pulled downslope by gravity. In addition, particles of sand or soil surrounded by water cannot hold tightly to one another and are more likely to slide. In mass movement, water moves along as part of the materials that are being transported. It does not transport materials directly, as it would in a stream or river.

Types of Mass Movement

There are four main types of mass movements: rockfalls, landslides, flows, and creep. Mass movement that happens quickly and suddenly can cause great damage. **Rockfalls** occur when loose rock falls down a steep slope. The rocks that fall may range in size from small fragments to large boulders. Rockfalls often occur at high elevations along roads built on mountainsides or along steep, rocky shorelines.

As You Read

Write the four main types of mass movement in the circles of your concept map. Share your concept map with a partner and add any important information.

How does gravity relate to each type of mass movement?

Landslides are the sudden and rapid movement downhill of a block of soil, rock, and debris. Landslides can reach speeds of up to 200 km/h. They are common on steep slopes. When the mass of material in a landslide moves downhill and leaves a cup-shaped depression behind, a **slump** results. Landslides called **avalanches** occur in mountainous areas with thick accumulations of snow. Landslides that occur underwater can cause the formation of tsunamis.

Figure 10.29 This landslide occurred in La Conchita, California, in June 2005.

CONNECTION: Geography

In the future, scientists may be able to use a new mapping technology to forecast landslides and possibly save thousands of lives. Landslide experts can identify danger zones if they have detailed three-dimensional maps of the area. A new laser and video system called Light Detection and Ranging, or LIDAR, shoots bursts of laser light at hillsides. The data that bounce back allow computers to quickly create detailed maps of the landscape features of the hillside. These amazing maps allow experts to scan regions from an airplane to see if they are vulnerable to landslides.

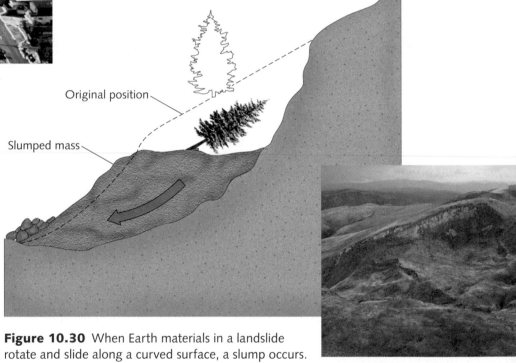

Original position

Slumped mass

Figure 10.30 When Earth materials in a landslide rotate and slide along a curved surface, a slump occurs.

During mass movements called **flows**, Earth materials flow like thick syrup. **Mudflows** are fast-moving mixtures of mud and water. They occur when a large amount of water mixes with soil and rock and then flows downhill. Mudflows often occur in mountainous regions when a long dry season is followed by heavy rains. Rapid mudflows can uproot trees, carry away houses and cars, and destroy objects in their paths. Mudflows called **lahars** occur as a result of volcanic eruptions. The heat from a volcano melts snow on nearby slopes, which mixes with ash and soil. This wet sediment then slides downhill rapidly.

Mass movement does not always happen quickly. **Creep** is the slow, steady, downhill flow of loose, weathered soil. While most slopes seem to be stable, they are actually experiencing creep. The movement is so slow that it is not possible to observe directly. Only the effects are seen. Many factors contribute to creep. Plant roots may break rocks and soils apart over time. Water may loosen rock particles, making it easier for them to move. Burrowing animals, such as groundhogs and gophers, can also loosen the soil.

It is common to see evidence of creep. It often causes fence posts and utility poles that were once straight to tilt. If you look carefully at the trunks of some trees, you might see that they have a bend at the base where they are slipping downhill along with the soil. Creep may also cause walls and underground pipes to crack over time.

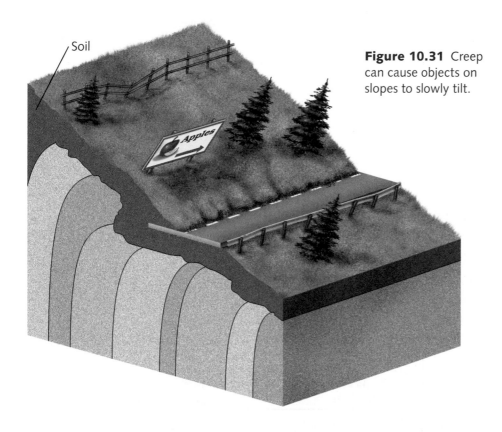

Figure 10.31 Creep can cause objects on slopes to slowly tilt.

Extend It!

On May 18, 1980, Washington State's Mount St. Helens erupted. Hot rocks and gas from the eruption quickly melted snow and ice on top of the volcano. The water from this melting snow mixed with ash and loose rocks to form lahars. Several lahars poured down the volcano into river valleys, destroying roads and bridges and ripping trees from the ground. Find out more about lahars. What can people do to reduce the risk of being caught in these volcanic mudflows? Write a public service announcement in your Science Notebook.

Figure 10.32 These tilted fence posts are evidence of creep.

After You Read

1. Review the concept map you created in your Science Notebook. Write a few sentences summarizing what you know about each type of mass movement.

2. Describe how water influences mass movement.

3. Explain why mass movement is common in mountain areas.

4. How might you know that creep is occurring on a slope?

KEY CONCEPTS

10.1 Water Erosion and Deposition

- Flowing water can move weathered rock particles. Sediment being carried downstream is deposited when water slows down.
- Waves erode the shoreline and deposit the sand, gravel, or rock that forms beaches.
- Spits, baymouth bars, barrier islands, sea cliffs, sea stacks, sea arches, sea caves, and deltas are shoreline features created by erosion and deposition.
- Because shorelines naturally shift and change over time, structures built to prevent shoreline erosion often have negative long-term effects.

10.2 Erosion Caused by Glaciers

- Glaciers form when layers of unmelted snow build up year after year. Glaciers move as gravity pulls on their huge mass.
- Valley glaciers form high in mountains and flow down valleys. They scour the land surface as they move, widening and straightening valleys into broad U-shapes.
- Continental glaciers, also called ice sheets, cover broad continent-sized areas.
- Cirques, aretes, horns, hanging valleys, moraines, outwash plains, and eskers are landscape features created by glaciers.

10.3 Wind Erosion and Deposition

- Wind erosion is common in dry locations where there is loose, sandy soil, and in areas with strong winds.
- Wind picks up particles that erode rocks by abrasion. Wind erosion can lower the land surface through deflation.
- Dunes are wind-deposited piles of sand that form when wind hits an obstacle, slows down, and deposits the heavier materials.
- Loess consists of thick layers of fine, wind-blown silt deposits.

10.4 Gravity's Role in Erosion and Deposition

- Gravity is the force responsible for all mass movement.
- The four main factors affecting mass movement are the weight of the material, the amount of water the material contains, the ability of the material to flow downslope, and sudden events that shake the material loose.
- The four main types of mass movement are falls, landslides, flows, and creep.
- Rockfalls occur when loose rock falls down a steep slope. Landslides are the sudden, rapid movement downslope of a block of soil, rock, and debris. During flows, Earth materials flow like thick syrup. Creep is the slow, steady, downhill flow of loose, weathered soil.

VOCABULARY REVIEW

Write each term in a complete sentence, or write a paragraph relating several terms.

10.1
deposition, p. 167
rill, p. 167
gully, p. 167
delta, p. 169
shoreline, p. 169
beach, p. 169
longshore bar, p. 170
longshore current, p. 170
spit, p. 171
baymouth bar, p. 171
barrier island, p. 171

10.2
glacier, p. 173
valley glacier, p. 174
continental glacier, p. 174
cirque, p. 176
arete, p. 176
horn, p. 176
hanging valley, p. 176
till, p. 177
moraine, p. 177
outwash, p. 177
esker, p. 177

10.3
saltation, p. 178
suspension, p. 178
deflation, p. 179
dune, p. 180
loess, p. 181

10.4
mass movement, p. 182
rockfall, p. 183
landslide, p. 184
slump, p. 184
avalanche, p. 184
flow, p. 184
mudflow, p. 184
lahar, p. 184
creep, p. 185

True or False

If the statement is true, write "true." If it is false, change the underlined word or words to make the statement true.

1. <u>Abrasion</u> is the final stage of erosion in which materials that have been transported are dropped in a new location.
2. <u>Valley glaciers</u> are the largest type of glacier.
3. Valley glaciers carve out <u>V-shaped valleys</u>.
4. Desert pavement forms by <u>deflation</u> from wind erosion.
5. A <u>landslide</u> is a type of rapid mass movement.
6. <u>Lahars</u> may occur during a volcanic eruption.

Short Answer

Answer each of the following in a sentence or brief paragraph.

7. Explain how a gully forms.
8. Explain the effect of the longshore current.
9. Describe the two ways glaciers cause erosion.
10. Explain how a sand dune moves.
11. Describe how loess forms.

Critical Thinking

Use what you have learned in this chapter to answer each of the following.

12. **Apply Concepts** How does the speed of water and its ability to carry sediment change as slope changes?
13. **Compare** How are erosion by a glacier and wind erosion similar?
14. **Apply Concepts** If you lived on a slope with dry, sandy soils, how might you reduce erosion caused by wind and mass movement?

PREPARE FOR CHAPTER TEST

To prepare for the chapter test, create a question from each Learning Goal. Use the information in your Science Notebook to answer each question. Then use these answers to write a well-developed essay about the chapter. Use the Key Concept on the first page of this chapter as your topic sentence.

Standardized Test Question

Choose the letter of the response that correctly answers the question.

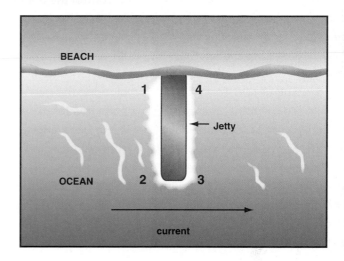

15. A jetty is a human-made structure jutting out into the water from the shore. In this diagram, where is deposition of sand most likely to occur?

    A. 1
    B. 2
    C. 3
    D. 4

Test-Taking Tip

Read each question carefully. Think about what is asked. If you are not sure, read the question again. If you are still not sure, go on to the next question. Sometimes, a later question will help you remember information you need to answer a question you skipped. Remember to check all of your answers before turning in the test.

Taming the Mississippi River

THE MISSISSIPPI River flows through 3,700 km of marshes, meadows, and woodlands as it twists and turns between its source in northern Minnesota and the Gulf of Mexico.

The sediment that the river gathers is carried south toward the sea. Each day, millions of tons of sand and silt are deposited along its course and at its mouth. This deposition created the huge Mississippi River delta and coastal wetlands.

People Change the River

The problem is, these wetlands are disappearing. Each year, 65 to 90 square km of southern Louisiana erodes and sinks under the waters of the Gulf of Mexico. That's a loss equal to the area of one football field each half hour!

In its natural state, the Mississippi floods over its banks regularly. These floods are needed for the deposition of sediment that builds the land. But the floods damage structures built along the river's banks.

Since the first settlers arrived during the 1700s, people have battled the river's floods. Levees and dams have been built to try

to control the flooding and to maintain the river's depth for navigation. Today, the Mississippi River contains thousands of kilometers of levees along its banks, blocking the river from 90 percent of its floodplain. Twenty-nine major dams and several locks control water flow and keep the river deep enough for barges. Shipping canals, such as the Mississippi Gulf Outlet, cause the river to bypass the small passages in the delta. All of this prevents the deposition of sediment along the river and on the delta. Instead, the sediment is deposited into the Gulf of Mexico.

Disappearing Floods and Disappearing Land

The levees, dams, and locks have been successful in controlling much of the flooding along parts of the Mississippi. But they hold back the sediment that the river would otherwise carry to its floodplain, its delta, and the wetlands along Louisiana's coast.

The result is that much of the delta and coastal marshes no longer receive the sediment that built them. Instead, their soft, wet soil sinks a little each year through compression and sea-level rise.

The wetland habitat that is home to many species of fish, shellfish, and waterfowl is also getting smaller. The wetlands also serve as a barrier that protects inland areas from gulf storms. Cities in southern Louisiana are

now more exposed to storms such as hurricanes. Years ago, there were 128 km of marshes and islands between New Orleans and the gulf. Now, there are just 30.

Is there a solution?

In order to save this coastal area, barrier islands must be built and the river must be allowed to overflow its banks and deposit sediment as it did before. Over time, the wetlands can be restored and once again provide protection against storms and erosion.

Of course this would cost billions of dollars and require great changes in the way people live and work along the river. Yearly flooding would mean that some homes and businesses would be lost. Changes in water level could result in dry times when ships could not navigate the river.

Are people willing to give this up in order to save the delta and coastal wetlands? Are they willing to pay the price to do it? These are questions that must be answered.

Niagara Falls **Now**—but **Not Forever**

THE NIAGARA RIVER is an unimportant river. That is, until it tumbles over the 58-meter-high cliff known as Niagara Falls.

Like most falls, Niagara Falls is the product of weathering and erosion. The Niagara River flows over a hard layer of rock called dolomite. Layers of softer rock are underneath. As water plunges over the falls, it pounds the softer rock in the cliff behind it. The water slowly eats away this softer rock. A harder overhang of dolomite is left on top. Eventually, the overhang collapses. Then the falls moves a little farther upstream.

As the cliff erodes, chunks of rock fall and pile up at the base of the falls. Several years ago, scientists decided to "turn off" the falls to clean up the rocks. They built a dam to divert the Niagara River from Niagara Falls and send it over nearby Horseshoe Falls. With Niagara Falls high and dry, scientists cleared away debris and studied the rock. Then they removed the dam. The river rushed back to its old channel—and tumbled down as Niagara Falls once more.

As weathering and erosion continue, Niagara Falls will stop again one day. But this time, the cause will be natural. Erosion has caused the falls to move upstream 11 kilometers during the past 12,500 years. Someday, the cliff may wear away to the point where there will be no falls at all.

CAREER CONNECTION: PARK RANGER

"HOW DID YOU GET such a great job?" Park rangers get this question all the time. Rangers work in some of the country's most beautiful places—from the towering peaks of Alaska's Denali to the rocky coast of Acadia in Maine. Park rangers protect and run our national and state parks. They also help us enjoy them.

A day in the life of a park ranger involves many jobs. Sometimes, rangers are teachers. So they must understand the forces, such as erosion and deposition, which create the beautiful landscapes they work in. When visitors ask questions, rangers can explain how the mountains, canyons, or river valleys in their parks formed. Rangers take visitors on nature hikes. They also help maintain the parks. Over time, storms, floods, and wind can degrade trails. Rangers build new trails and make sure old ones are safe. Some rangers help fight fires in parks. They care for wildlife. Rangers also help people who become ill.

Most rangers have college degrees in subjects such as biology, forestry, parks and recreation, or ecology. They must also be good public speakers and be outgoing and friendly. Some rangers in national parks start as summer interns while they are still in college. If they do well, they have a good chance of being hired as full-time park rangers after they graduate.

If you become a park ranger, don't expect to make a lot of money. Most rangers don't do these jobs to get rich. They love the wild and beautiful places in America. They want to share them with others—and protect them for the future.

Unit 5

Earth's History

Chapter 11 — **Studying the Past**

How does studying fossils, rocks, and rock layers help scientists understand Earth's ancient history?

Chapter 12 — **Geologic Time**

By studying changes in Earth's features and in life over time, scientists are able to understand Earth's long history. How is Earth's geologic time scale divided?

Studying the Past

KEY CONCEPT Scientists study fossils, rocks, and rock layers to understand Earth's ancient history.

Tyrannosaurus rex is a dinosaur that lived more than 66 million years ago. It stood 12 m tall and used its powerful jaws and sharp teeth to capture and eat its prey. No human has ever seen a living dinosaur. So, how have scientists learned so much about them? Dinosaurs, along with many other ancient living things, left behind evidence in the form of fossils, such as preserved footprints and bones. Other evidence has been found in Earth's rocks and rock layers. Through careful study and by applying the scientific method, scientists have been able to explain many facts and events from Earth's ancient history.

Think About Earth's History

Do you know how your neighborhood has changed over the past 100 years? What evidence shows these changes? How has it has changed since the time of the dinosaurs?

- Describe how a place can change over time.

- In your Science Notebook, draw a picture of your neighborhood today. Then draw a picture of your neighborhood at some time before you were born.

www.scilinks.org
Fossils **Code: WGES11**

Learning Goals

- Describe ways that fossils form.
- Explain why scientists study fossils.

New Vocabulary

fossil
mold
cast
permineralization
petrification
carbonaceous film
trace fossil
paleontologist

Before You Read

In your Science Notebook, draw a three-column chart to organize facts about different types of fossils. Label the first column *Fossil Type*. Write *mold*, *cast*, and *permineralization* in that column. Label the second column *How It Forms*. Label the third column *Example*.

Earth is 4.6 billion years old. Throughout these years, how many organisms would you guess have lived on Earth? The number is very, very large, and impossible to count exactly. That's because most organisms lived and died without leaving a trace. Their body parts rotted away or were eaten, or they were broken apart by wind, heat, fire, or water.

However, a small number of organisms left evidence of their existence. A **fossil** is the preserved remains, or trace, of a once-living organism. Fossils range in age from tens of thousands to millions of years old. Fossils provide information that help scientists understand ancient life and important events in Earth's history.

Molds and Casts

Fossils form in sedimentary rocks in a variety of ways. For example, sediment is a mixture of small rock pieces, dirt, and other materials. Over many years, sediment may be pressed together into rock. A dead organism buried in sediment may become preserved as a fossil.

In some cases, the shell of a dead organism decays or is washed away after sedimentary rock hardens around it. The shape of the shell is left behind in the rock, forming a mold. A **mold** is a hollow space in rock that has the shape of the organism or its parts.

Sometimes, sediment fills the mold. The sediment hardens into rock that has the shape of the mold. This type of fossil is called a **cast**. A cast is made by filling a mold.

Figure 11.1 This cast is in the shape of an ancient organism called a bivalve. Sediment filled the hollow space, or mold, that once held the bivalve's remains.

Figure 11.2 During petrification, minerals slowly replaced the wood of this tree, changing it into solid rock.

More Fossil Types

Permineralization is another process that forms fossils. During this process, mineral-rich water slowly seeps into the pore spaces of an organism's bone or shell. When the minerals crystallize, a fossil is formed. It is made up of the organism's original shell or bone plus the newly crystallized minerals. The once-living matter rots away.

Petrification of an organism occurs in a slightly different way. During this process, mineral-rich water seeps into both the organism's soft parts and the pore spaces of the shell or bone. When the new minerals crystallize, the soft parts are completely replaced and the spaces are filled in. Because these processes occur on a microscopic level, fine details of the organism's structures are often preserved.

During another process, heat and pressure force gases and liquids from decaying remains. The gases and liquids leave behind a **carbonaceous** (kar buh NAY shus) **film**. This film is made of carbon or carbon-containing compounds. The film is often in the shape of the original organism.

Can a living organism whose body or shell was not preserved still have left something that became a fossil? The answer is yes. Footprints or the mark of a tail being dragged across mud can become fossils when the mud hardens. Any naturally preserved sign of a living thing's presence is called a **trace fossil**. Fossil footprints are examples of trace fossils. Prints of plant leaves and roots have also become trace fossils.

As shown in **Figure 11.4**, sometimes an entire organism can become a fossil. This happened to insects that were trapped in the sticky sap of certain trees. Over many years, the tree sap hardened into a yellow material called amber. The whole insect is preserved inside.

Freezing can also form a fossil. When glaciers advanced during the last ice age, dead animals sometimes were trapped inside. When the glaciers melted, they left behind fossils that showed little or no decay. For an example, see the fossil of the woolly mammoth on page 195.

Explore It!

To model trace fossils, press and drag some common objects across a flat sheet of modeling clay. Try using coins, pencils, chess pieces, toy animals, feathers, and sticks. Exchange clay sheets with a partner and guess the source of each trace fossil.

Figure It Out

1. Which fossil, the footprints or the insects, is a trace fossil? Explain how this trace fossil was created.

2. Describe the features of the insects shown by their fossils. Explain how the insects were preserved.

Figure 11.3 This rock was once soft mud. The record of a dinosaur that walked across the mud is preserved in the fossil footprints.

Figure 11.4 Tree sap hardened into a clear, yellow material called amber. These insects are perfectly preserved inside.

Lessons from Fossils

Scientists who study fossils are called **paleontologists** (pay lee ahn TAH luh justs). These scientists dig up fossils at sites all over the world. They also spend long hours carefully studying fossils in laboratories.

Fossils are rare and often fragile, so paleontologists must handle them carefully. They observe and record the exact location where each fossil is found. They also take note of the type of rock around the fossil. Every detail about a fossil could be important.

A great deal can be learned from fossils. Conclusions can be drawn about how Earth's living things have changed over time. For example, fossils show how ancient life was different from life today. The fossil leg bones of *Tyrannosaurus rex,* for example, are much larger and are shaped differently than the leg bones of today's animals. Scientists use fossil bones to infer the identity, size, and shape of ancient animals.

Fossils provide other kinds of evidence, too. For example, fossil ferns have been found in Antarctica. Ferns are plants that need warm weather and liquid water to survive. Yet, Antarctica today is cold and icy all year long. The fern fossils are evidence that Antarctica's climate was once much warmer than it is today.

Fossils of fish and other water-dwelling animals are also useful in determining Earth's history. These fossils have been found in rock layers on dry land and even in rock layers that make up mountains. Findings such as these are evidence that an area was once under water. They also suggest that the rocks that make up mountains were lifted up, carrying fossils up with them.

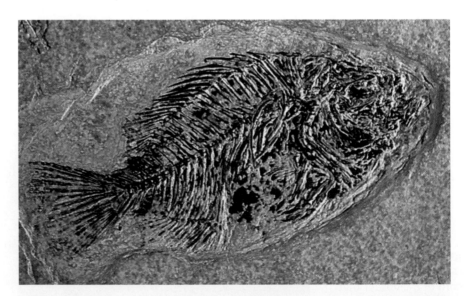

Figure 11.5 Fossils of freshwater fish have been discovered from the 50-million-year-old Green River Formation in Wyoming. The fossils are evidence of a series of deep lakes and semitropical climate that once covered this part of North America.

Earth's Changing Climate

Important information about Earth's climate can be learned from fossils. Climate is the average weather in a place over many years. Fossils, along with other evidence, show that Earth's climate has changed many times.

During the days of the dinosaurs, for example, Earth was much warmer and wetter than it is now. Vast swamps covered much of the planet, providing food for plant-eating dinosaurs and other animals. Scientists suspect that Earth's climate then became colder and drier. Swamps dried up and many plants died. The dinosaurs became extinct, most likely because they lost their food supply and their homes.

Fossils also show that Earth has undergone many ice ages, or spans of very cold weather. During an ice age, huge glaciers and ice caps covered much more of Earth than they do today.

Scientists are concerned that Earth's climate is changing again. Chapter 13 discusses how human actions are contributing to a rise in Earth's average temperature. This change is called global warming. Evidence from the past shows that these changes could have serious consequences now and in the future.

Figure 11.6 A fern fossil indicates that the area where it was found once had a warm, rainy climate.

Figure 11.7 This woolly mammoth has been frozen since the last ice age when it got trapped inside a glacier.

CONNECTION: Economics

People buy and sell fossils of all kinds. The price for rare and unusual fossils can often be thousands of dollars. Once, buying a fossil was only possible in a store. Today, shopping for fossils on the Internet has become common. Research the price of an interesting fossil. In your Science Notebook, explain why you think fossils cost as much as they do.

After You Read

1. Explain how a fossil can form from part of a dead organism, a living organism, or the entire body of an organism.

2. How can fossils reveal changes to Earth's environment and climate? Include two examples in your answer.

3. Review the table you made about different fossil types. In your Science Notebook, write a paragraph describing three things that all fossils have in common.

Learning Goals

- Describe the purpose and methods of relative dating.
- Discuss the principles that scientists use to compare rock layers.

New Vocabulary

original horizontality
superposition
relative dating
cross-cutting relationship
inclusion
unconformity
correlation
index fossil

Before You Read

In your Science Notebook, draw three large boxes to create a sequence chart. You can use this chart to track different sequences of rock formation. Label the first box *Principle,* the second box *First Event,* and the third box *Next Events.*

When a human baby is born, the hospital issues an official document called a birth certificate. It tells the name of the baby, the birth date, and other important facts. When someone dies, a death certificate is issued. It lists facts about the end of that person's life.

For ancient living things, however, the only record of life and death is the fossil record. This record is not written in English or with numerals. You cannot simply look at a fossil and tell how old it is. Nevertheless, scientists are able to state important facts about every fossil they find. They record the location where the fossil was found. They identify the fossil type, body part, and species name. They also use a variety of methods to date, or determine the age of, the fossil.

How do scientists date fossils? They begin by studying the rocks in which the fossils are found.

Figure 11.8 Fossils have been found in many of the rock layers of the Grand Canyon. Why do you think the layer in which a fossil occurs in the canyon provides useful information?

Relative Age

For millions of years, the Colorado River has been flowing over the rocky land of northern Arizona. As the water flows, it breaks down and carries away pieces of rocks. This slow process of weathering and erosion has created the Grand Canyon. In some places, the canyon is more than 1,200 m deep.

The walls of the Grand Canyon are made of distinct rock layers, as shown in **Figure 11.8** and **Figure 11.9**. Most of the layers are made of sedimentary rock. They were deposited long before the Colorado River began flowing. Notice that they are horizontal, or flat. They illustrate the principle of **original horizontality**. This principle states that the sediment that forms sedimentary rocks is deposited in flat or nearly flat layers. Rock layers often become tilted or bent over time. They rarely remain horizontal, as is the case at the Grand Canyon.

It is possible to determine which layer of the Grand Canyon is the oldest. Scientists conclude that in an undisturbed sequence of sedimentary rock, each rock layer lies just above the layer on which it formed. This idea is called the principle of **superposition**. It means that the very bottom layer of the Grand Canyon is the oldest layer. Moving up the wall, the layers become younger.

When ages of rocks are described with words such as *older* and *younger*, the concept of relative dating is being used. **Relative dating** is dating by comparison between two objects. Relative dating does not tell the exact age of a rock layer. It just tells whether it is older or younger than other rock layers around it.

Relative dating applies not only to rocks, but to fossils as well. Remember that most fossils form inside a layer of sedimentary rock. This means that they are about the same age as the rock around them. Scientists have dug out many fossils from the walls of the Grand Canyon. They organize these fossils according to the layers in which they were found. In this way, scientists can understand how the region's communities of living things have changed over time.

Explain It!

In your Science Notebook, write a paragraph that defines relative dating in your own words. Explain its benefits and its limits. Then, give one example of when relative dating would be useful.

Figure It Out

1. Which layer is older: Redwall Limestone or Muav Limestone?

2. Compare the ages of fossils in Coconino Sandstone to those found in higher layers and in lower layers.

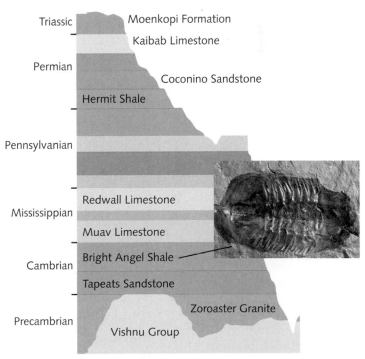

Rock Layers of the Grand Canyon

Triassic — Moenkopi Formation
Kaibab Limestone
Permian — Coconino Sandstone
Hermit Shale
Pennsylvanian
Redwall Limestone
Mississippian
Muav Limestone
Bright Angel Shale
Cambrian
Tapeats Sandstone
Zoroaster Granite
Precambrian — Vishnu Group

Figure 11.9 By applying the principle of superposition, scientists can determine the relative ages of both rock layers and fossils inside the layers. In this way, scientists can determine that this fossil trilobite is from the Cambrian-aged Bright Angel Shale.

Figure 11.10 At Hance Rapids, the diagonal stripe of igneous rock forms a cross-cutting relationship with the horizontal sedimentary rock layers. Which rock layer is youngest?

Figure 11.11 Compare the sections of rock layers shown here. Faulting and other forces from Earth's interior tilted the rocks and broke them apart.

Cross-Cutting Relationships

Not all the rocks of the Grand Canyon fit into flat, simple layers. **Figure 11.10** shows the lower canyon wall at Hance Rapids. Notice the dark brown stripe of rock. It appears to rise at an angle from the floor of the canyon, cutting across the reddish, flatter rock layers. It formed when magma from Earth's interior rose upward and intruded into the sedimentary rocks of the upper crust. The brown stripe is called an intrusion.

The magma intrusion shows another principle of relative dating. According to the principle of **cross-cutting relationships**, a band of rock that intrudes across rock layers must be younger than those layers. At Hance Rapids, the sedimentary rock formed first. Then the magma intruded into it.

Cross-cutting relationships also apply to faults. Faults are cracks in Earth's crust. Mountains form along some faults. Earthquakes occur when there is movement along faults. **Figure 11.11** shows an example of faults that caused the separation of layers of sedimentary rock. The sedimentary rocks formed first, then they were deformed, and then the fault separated the layers.

Inclusions

In geology, an **inclusion** is a piece of one type of rock that is surrounded by another type. According to the principle of inclusions, an inclusion is older than the rock surrounding it. Inclusions may form after a volcano erupts. As lava flows over the land, pieces of the underlying rock may break off. These pieces may then become embedded in the lava. Lava cools and hardens over time. This forms igneous rocks. Such rocks sometimes contain inclusions from the preexisting rock layers.

Unconformity

Remember that Earth's rocks change in many different ways. Together, the changes form a continuous process called the rock cycle. Wind, water, and living things constantly break down rocks. Heat and pressure change existing rock into metamorphic rock. Magma and lava harden into igneous rock.

For these reasons, the rock layers near Earth's surface do not always exist in orderly layers. Instead, rock layers often show unconformity. An **unconformity** is a gap in the rock layer sequence caused by a missing rock layer. A span of time is missing from the rock record. This is usually because a rock layer was weathered and eroded away. The missing span may cover tens of thousands to millions of years.

Correlation

The principles of superposition, cross-cutting relationships, inclusions, and unconformity all apply to rock layers in the same area. For example, all of these principles can be observed in the walls of the Grand Canyon. Scientists also compare rock layers from locations that are far from one another.

Correlation is the matching of rock layers from one geographic region to another. Sometimes, rock layers from different regions match up, or correlate. When this happens, scientists conclude that they formed at the same time and in the same way. The fossils inside them formed at the same time, too. In some cases, fossils in correlated rock layers are nearly identical. This is true even though they may be found thousands of km apart.

Certain fossils may act as index fossils. **Index fossils** indicate a specific period of Earth's history and are used by scientists to date rock layers. They are preserved animals or plants that are typical of a particular span of time or environment. Useful index fossils are abundant and easy to recognize. They are also found over large regions and through relatively short periods of time in the rock record. Correlated rock layers and matching fossils were important evidence for Alfred Wegener's theory of continental drift, discussed in Chapter 6. Such information remains an important part of Earth history studies today.

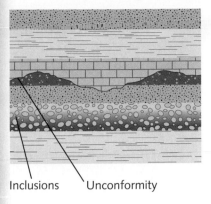

Inclusions   Unconformity

Figure 11.12 An uneven, eroded surface indicates the presence of an unconformity. Most of the layer shown here was eroded before new sediment was laid down.

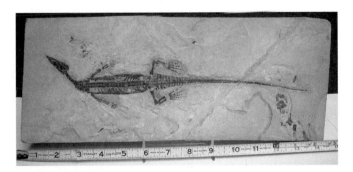

Figure 11.13 Fossils of *Mesosaurus*, a freshwater reptile, have been found in correlated rock layers on both sides of the Atlantic Ocean. Such evidence supports Wegener's theory of continental drift.

After You Read

1. Why do scientists study rock layers to determine the relative age of fossils?

2. Describe the principles of original horizontality, superposition, and cross-cutting relationships.

3. Review the sequence chart you made about rock formation. In your Science Notebook, write a well-developed paragraph explaining three ways that a layer of sedimentary rock could change after it is deposited. Include illustrations.

Learning Goals

- Explain how carbon-14 is used for absolute dating of fossils.
- Identify other methods of absolute dating.

New Vocabulary

absolute dating
isotope
radioisotope
half-life
radiocarbon dating
radiometric dating
dendrochronology
varve
key bed

Before You Read

Draw a five-column table in your Science Notebook. Title the table *Radiocarbon Dating.* Label the columns *Who, When, What, How,* and *Why.* Use the table to organize the facts you learn about radiocarbon dating.

Scientists can determine the relative ages of rocks and fossils by comparing rock layers. To determine the *actual* age of a layer of rock or a fossil, however, scientists must rely on absolute dating. **Absolute dating** is the process of establishing the age of an object by determining the number of years it has existed.

For absolute dating to be accurate, a rock or fossil would need a property that acted like an internal clock. Just like a clock, this property would need to change regularly and predictably over time. It would also have to be possible to observe or measure this property. Do rocks or fossils have a property like this? Remarkably, the answer is yes.

In 1949, American scientist Willard Libby discovered a kind of atomic clock inside the remains of living things. This "clock" begins ticking as soon as an organism dies. He and his colleagues also developed a technique to read this clock. Libby's work earned him the Nobel Prize in chemistry.

Isotopes

All atoms of an element have exactly the same chemical properties. An atom's nucleus (plural: nuclei) is its central core. It is made of tiny particles called protons and neutrons. Sometimes, the properties of the nuclei differ. **Isotopes** are two forms of the same element that contain different numbers of neutrons in their nuclei. A neutron is a particle with no electrical charge. It is in the nucleus of an atom.

Carbon is a very common element in living things. The most common isotope of carbon is named carbon-12. Carbon-12 is extremely stable, which means it does not change over time. But, a much less abundant carbon isotope, called carbon-14, is not as stable. Atoms of carbon-14 slowly decay, or break apart, by radiating particles from their nuclei. For this reason, carbon-14 is an example of a **radioisotope**, or an isotope that decays through radiation.

A snail takes in a small amount of radioactive carbon-14 in its food and from the atmosphere.

The remains of the snail slowly lose carbon-14 through radioactive decay.

To date a fossil from the snail, scientists measure the ratio of radioactive carbon-14 to nonradioactive carbon-12 in a sample of the fossil.

Figure 11.14 Carbon-14 decays at a precise, predictable rate. Scientists use radioactive carbon-14 to date fossils and other carbon-containing objects.

Radiocarbon Dating

Earth's supply of radioactive carbon-14 comes from a reaction in the upper atmosphere between cosmic rays and nitrogen (N). Not much carbon-14 is produced, but the amount is great enough to be taken up by all living organisms on Earth. Every living organism on Earth contains a small but constant percentage of carbon-14 in its body.

Once an organism dies, it no longer takes in radioactive carbon-14 atoms. Instead, its existing supply slowly breaks down, or decays, into other chemical elements. After 5,730 years, an organism's remains contain only half of its original supply of carbon-14. This time span is called the half-life of carbon-14. The **half-life** is the time it takes for one-half of a radioactive sample to decay. After two half-lives, or 11,460 years, the supply of radioactive carbon-14 is halved again. It is one-quarter of the original amount. This process continues in a very predictable way, as shown in **Figure 11.15**.

The decay of carbon-14 is the key to the clock that Libby discovered. Libby measured the ratio of radioactive carbon-14 to nonradioactive carbon-12 inside fossils. Then he used the half-life of carbon-14 to determine the fossils' ages. This method is called **radiocarbon dating**. Radiocarbon dating is one type of radiometric dating. The term **radiometric dating** applies to any method of determining the absolute age of a sample by using radioisotopes. Today, improved technology has made radiometric dating more effective than ever.

As You Read

Enter facts about radiocarbon dating in each column of your table. Tell who developed it, when it was developed, what it is, how it works, and why it is useful.

Figure 11.15

Half-Life of Carbon-14

Age	Half-Lives	Percent of Remaining Carbon-14, Compared to the Original Supply
0	0	100%
5,730 years	1	50%
11,460 years	2	25%
17,190 years	3	12.5%
22,920 years	4	6.25%
28,650 years	5	3.125%

1. A fossil is believed to be about 29,000 years old. Compared to its original supply of carbon-14, how much carbon-14 would remain in the fossil?

2. After how many half-lives will carbon-14 be reduced to $\frac{1}{16}$ (6.25%) of its original amount?

Figure It Out

Limits of Radiocarbon Dating

Although radiocarbon dating is useful, it has some limits. A sample of carbon-14 decays almost entirely in about 60,000 years. Because of this, it is not useful for dating fossils older than 60,000 years. It is also not useful for dating objects that do not contain carbon.

To date Earth's oldest fossils and rocks, scientists must use radioisotopes of elements with longer half-lives. For example, potassium-40 has a half-life of 1.26 billion years. Scientists have used these isotopes to date fossils and rocks that are over three billion years old.

CONNECTION: Chemistry

More than a century ago, Polish chemist Marie Curie was the first person to explain radioactivity. Since then, scientists have used radioactive elements in many ways. They also have learned about their dangers. Large doses of radiation can be toxic or fatal. Marie Curie died from radiation poisoning.

Nuclear power plants run on uranium (U), a radioactive metal. Inside the reactor core, a uranium nucleus is split into pieces. This process, called nuclear fission, releases a great deal of energy.

Physicians use radioactivity to find and treat cancerous tumors.

They inject a patient with very small amounts of certain radioisotopes. Then they monitor where the radioactivity collects in the body. Directing strong radiation at a tumor will slow its growth or destroy it.

Extend It!

Research some of the knowledge learned through dendrochronology. Write your findings as a bulleted list in your Science Notebook. What do you think the trees of today might reveal to scientists of the future?

Figure 11.16
Tree rings are a record of every growing season in the life of the tree.

Tree Rings and Climate Changes

Other dating methods rely on data that is easier to observe. **Dendrochronology** is the science of comparing yearly growth rings in trees to date events and changes in past environments. The age of a tree can be determined by counting the rings in its wood. Rings form because of the yearly cycle of the seasons. Trees grow more during the summer than they do during any other season. Wider rings indicate a good growing season and an agreeable climate. In this way, tree rings serve as records of Earth's climate.

Other records of Earth's climate exist on the floor of some lakes. **Varves** are bands of sediment that have accumulated on lake bottoms. Varves form as melting glaciers drop sediment. Sediment from glaciers is lighter in color and thicker in summer, and darker in color and thinner in winter. By counting and comparing varves, scientists can tell much about temperature changes from thousands of years in the past.

Dramatic Events and Key Beds

In regions around the world, scientists have identified a thin, unusual layer of sedimentary rock. This layer is rich in iridium (Ir), an element that is rare on Earth but common in space. From this and other evidence, scientists have hypothesized that an asteroid struck Earth about 66 million years ago. The crash raised a huge cloud of dust that eventually settled back to Earth's surface, forming the iridium-rich layer. This event also caused climate changes that led, in part, to the extinction of the remaining dinosaurs on Earth.

The iridium-rich layer is an example of a key bed. A **key bed** acts as a time marker to compare rock layers in regions located far from one another. Other key beds may form after major volcanic eruptions. For example, ash from the eruption of Mount St. Helens in 1980 will eventually form a key bed. This key bed will be located in the northwest region of the United States.

CONNECTION: History

How might a historian use carbon-14 dating? In your Science Notebook, describe a question that this dating technique might answer.

Figure 11.17 A thin, iridium-rich rock layer is a key bed found all over the world. In this photo, it is positioned between the light and dark rocks layers above. Most likely, it marks a time millions of years ago when an asteroid struck Earth.

After You Read

1. How can the decay of carbon-14 indicate the age of a fossil?
2. Aside from radiometric dating, identify three methods of absolute dating.
3. Review the table you made about radiocarbon dating. In your Science Notebook, describe the importance of this discovery.

KEY CONCEPTS

11.1 What Are Fossils?

- A fossil is the preserved remains or trace of an ancient living thing. Very few organisms that have lived on Earth became fossils.

- Different types of fossils include molds, casts, petrified remains, fossils that were trapped in ice or sap, and trace fossils.

- Fossils provide evidence of changes to Earth's living things, climate, and landforms.

11.2 Relative Dating

- Scientists study the positions of different rock layers to compare their ages. This process is called relative dating. Scientists assume a fossil is the same age as the rock surrounding it.

- The principles of original horizontality, superposition, cross-cutting relationships, and inclusion all help scientists date rock layers.

- Correlation is the matching of rock layers across distant regions.

11.3 Absolute Dating

- After an organism dies, its remains gradually lose carbon-14, a radioactive isotope of carbon. This forms the basis of radiocarbon dating, a technique used to determine the age of fossils in years.

- In radiometric dating, the half-life of a radioisotope determines the range of ages the radioisotope can be used to date.

- Tree rings and layers of sediment from glaciers and volcanic eruptions also serve as evidence for absolute dating.

VOCABULARY REVIEW

Write each term in a complete sentence, or write a paragraph relating several terms.

11.1
fossil, p. 192
mold, p. 192
cast, p. 192
permineralization, p. 193
petrification, p. 193
carbonaceous film, p. 193
trace fossil, p. 193
paleontologist, p. 194

11.2
original horizontality, p. 197
superposition, p. 197
relative dating, p. 197
cross-cutting relationship,
  p. 198
inclusion, p. 198
unconformity, p. 198
correlation, p. 199
index fossil, p. 199

11.3
absolute dating, p. 200
isotope, p. 200
radioisotope, p. 200
half-life, p. 201
radiocarbon dating, p. 201
radiometric dating, p. 201
dendrochronology, p. 202
varve, p. 203
key bed, p. 203

PREPARE FOR CHAPTER TEST

To prepare for the chapter test, create a question from each Learning Goal. Use the information in your Science Notebook to answer each question. Then use these answers to write a well-developed essay about the chapter. Use the Key Concept on the first page of this chapter as your topic sentence.

True or False

If the statement is true, write "true." If it is false, change the underlined word or words to make the statement true.

1. A <u>botanist</u> is a scientist who studies fossils and ancient living things.

2. The principle of <u>inclusions</u> states that sedimentary rocks form in flat, horizontal layers.

3. Fossilized footprints are examples of <u>trace</u> fossils.

4. A(n) <u>embedded</u> fossil indicates a specific time period in which a rock layer was formed.

5. Radiocarbon dating is possible because dead organisms lose <u>carbon-14</u> at a precise, predictable rate.

6. The method of <u>relative</u> dating determines the age of a fossil in years.

Short Answer

Answer each of the following in a sentence or brief paragraph.

7. What kinds of information about Earth's past can fossils reveal?

8. Earth has been home to a huge number of organisms. Why are fossils rare and unusual finds?

9. At the Grand Canyon, where would you look for the oldest fossils? For the youngest fossils?

10. Describe what happens to a fallen tree trunk as it changes into petrified wood.

11. What are three events that could disturb flat, horizontal layers of sedimentary rock?

12. Which kinds of fossils cannot be dated by radiocarbon dating?

Critical Thinking

Use what you have learned in this chapter to answer each of the following.

13. **Analyze Data** The half-life of carbon-14 is 5,730 years. What can be concluded about the carbon-14 content of an object that is approximately 22,000 years old?

14. **Apply Concepts** A scientist finds several fossils inside the walls of a deep cave. Can she conclude that the deepest fossils are the oldest? Explain why or why not.

Standardized Test Question

Choose the letter of the response that correctly answers the question.

15. In which type of rock do fossils occur?

    A. sedimentary rock

    B. igneous rock

    C. metamorphic rock

    D. eroded rock near the surface

Test-Taking Tip

Use scrap paper to write notes. Sometimes making a sketch, such as a diagram or table, can help you organize your ideas.

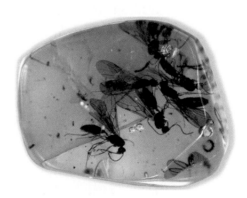

Chapter 12

Geologic Time

KEY CONCEPT By studying changes to Earth and its living things over time, scientists are able to understand Earth's long history.

Do you think that 100 years is a long time? Only a small percentage of the world's population lives that long. New buildings, neighborhoods, and even entire cities can be built in 100 years. Yet, 100 years is as short as the blink of an eye compared to the number of years that Earth has existed.

As you learn about geologic time, remember that it includes both vast spans of years and brief moments. During one such moment, about 65 million years ago, an asteroid struck Earth. Life on the planet was forever changed.

Think About Geologic Time

How do you spend a typical day? Make a time line that begins at midnight and ends at midnight the next day. Label the hours on your time line and record your activities during each hour of the day.

- How does your typical day now compare to your typical day 10 years ago? How do you think it will compare to your typical day 10 years from now?

- In your Science Notebook, explain how a time line for a person's life is similar to and different from a time line for planet Earth.

NSTA

SCI LINKS
THE WORLD'S A CLICK AWAY

www.scilinks.org

Geologic Time **Code: WGES12**

The Geologic Time Scale

Before You Read

In the middle of a page in your Science Notebook, write *Geologic time* and draw a circle around the words. Draw lines from the circle to begin a concept map.

Scientists have determined Earth's age to be about 4.6 billion years. During this time, the planet has undergone huge changes. To make sense of Earth's long history, scientists use a time line called the **geologic time scale**. It is always presented with the oldest time periods at the bottom and younger time periods toward the top.

Eons and Eras of Earth's History

Geologic time is divided into eons, eras, periods, and epochs. **Precambrian Time** is the longest and oldest segment of geologic time. It spans almost 90 percent of our planet's history. Precambrian Time is divided into three eons: the Hadean, the Archean, and the Proterozoic. An **eon**, measured in billions of years, is the longest time unit in the geologic time scale.

As shown in **Figure 12.2** on the next page, the Hadean (hay DEE un) Eon is the oldest division of time. The solar system was forming during this time. The only rocks that exist from this eon are meteorites. The Archean (ar KEE un) Eon is the next oldest division of time and spans between about 3.8 and 2.5 billion years ago. Earth's crust formed during this time. The oldest fossils discovered so far are from the Archean Eon. They are bacterialike fossils 3.5 billion years old. The most recent segment of the Precambrian is the Proterozoic Eon, which began about 2.5 billion years ago.

Phanerozoic Eon The Phanerozoic Eon began about 544 million years ago. It is divided into three **eras**, which are also very long spans of time. Eras are measured in hundreds of millions to billions of years. The three eras, in order from oldest to youngest, are the Paleozoic, the Mesozoic, and the Cenozoic.

The **Paleozoic** (pay lee uh ZOH ihk) **Era** lasted about 345 million years. The first fish evolved during this era, as did land plants and air-breathing, or terrestrial, animals. The **Mesozoic** (mez uh ZOH ihk) **Era** lasted for the next 160 million years. The largest animals to ever inhabit Earth, the dinosaurs, lived during this era.

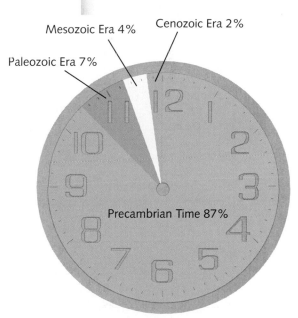

Mesozoic Era 4%   Cenozoic Era 2%

Paleozoic Era 7%

Precambrian Time 87%

Figure 12.1 This circle graph shows what geologic time would look like if it were scaled down to 12 hours. All of human history fits into the last tenth of a second!

1. When did the first reptiles evolve on Earth?

2. Look at the events that occurred during each geologic era. Discuss what might have caused life-forms to change from one era to the next.

Earth's Geologic Time Scale

Eon	Era	Period	Epoch	Years Before Present (mya*)	Distinctive Features
Phanerozoic	Cenozoic	Quaternary	Holocene (Recent)	0.008 to today	• modern humans
			Pleistocene	1.8 to 0.008 mya	• early humans • northern glaciation
		Neogene	Pliocene	5.3 to 1.8 mya	• large carnivores
			Miocene	23.8 to 5.3 mya	• grazing mammals become abundant
		Paleogene	Oligocene	33.7 to 23.8 mya	• large running mammals
			Eocene	55.5 to 33.7 mya	• many modern mammals
			Paleocene	65 to 55.5 mya	• first placental mammals
	Mesozoic	Cretaceous		145 to 65 mya	• first flowering plants • mass extinction event ends the era
		Jurassic		213 to 145 mya	• first birds • first mammals • dinosaurs are dominant life-forms
		Triassic		248 to 213 mya	• first dinosaurs • conifers and cycads become abundant
	Paleozoic	Permian		286 to 248 mya	• mass extinction event ends the era • most marine species including trilobites become extinct • southern glaciation
		Pennsylvanian		325 to 286 mya	• great coal forests • giant insects
		Mississippian		360 to 325 mya	• first reptiles • amphibians and sharks become abundant • seed-bearing ferns
		Devonian		410 to 360 mya	• first amphibians • predatory fish abundant
		Silurian		440 to 410 mya	• terrestrial plants and animals
		Ordovician		505 to 440 mya	• first fishes • invertebrate marine organisms flourish
		Cambrian		544 to 505 mya	• marine organisms flourish and diversify • trilobites dominant
Precambrian Time	Proterozoic			2,500 to 544 mya	• fossils extremely rare • primitive aquatic plants
	Archean			3,800 to 2,500 mya	• evidence of worldwide glaciation • oldest algae dates to 3,800 mya
	Hadean			4,500 to 3,800 mya	• oldest meteorites date to 4,500 mya • no life on Earth

*mya = million years ago

Figure 12.2 The geologic time scale divides Earth's history into specific time periods. Each is defined by the differences in the once-living life-forms present in the rocks from each time period.

The **Cenozoic** (sen uh ZOH ihk) **Era** is the era of the present. It has lasted 65 million years so far. Mammals, including humans, are the largest and most dominant animals of this era. Scientists further divide eras into smaller time spans called **periods**. Like eras, periods differ from one another in terms of plant and animal life. Periods are divided further into **epochs**. The geologic time scale spans Earth's history from its beginning to the present day.

The Living Planet

Scientists learn about Earth's past by studying rocks and fossils. They also apply other knowledge, including studies of weather and climate, earthquakes and volcanoes, plants and animals, and even the atoms that make up matter. All of this knowledge was used to make the time line of Earth's long history shown in **Figure 12.2**.

Alone among the known planets, Earth is home to living things. Why has life thrived on Earth? Why did life begin here? Scientific answers to these questions include the following:

- **Earth's position in the solar system** All life as we know it needs water. Earth is just far enough from the Sun to keep water in a liquid state. In addition, Earth's tilted axis allows for a cycle of seasons and a variety of climates. Changes in weather and climate contributed to the diversity of species.

- **Tectonic plates** Tectonic plates are huge, moving slabs of Earth's crust. Earth's changing landscape and oceans contributed to the change in species over time. In addition, gases from volcanic eruptions helped form Earth's atmosphere.

- **Earth's iron core** Deep inside Earth's interior, a core of iron creates a magnetic field around the planet. This field shields Earth's surface from dangerous ultraviolet rays from space that would otherwise destroy living things.

- **Timing** Life developed as it did due to a long series of events, each setting the stage for the next. Some events, such as asteroid impacts, were quite destructive. However, it was major events that created circumstances that allowed new types of living things to develop.

Look at the land, sky, and community of living things around you. Each has undergone huge changes throughout Earth's long history. Earth will continue to change as long as it exists.

Extend It!

Research one of the groups of plants or animals named in **Figure 12.2**. How has the group changed over time? How has it stayed the same? Create a poster of your findings and present it to the class.

As You Read

Look at the concept map you began in your Science Notebook. In the space around the words *Geologic time*, write at least six terms that describe Earth's long history. Compare your map with a partner's. Make additions or corrections as necessary.

Figure 12.3 The northern lights are always moving across the sky. Their movement is caused by interactions between charged particles from the Sun and Earth's magnetic field.

Evolution

Look back at the photograph of the Grand Canyon on page 196. Most layers of the canyon contain a unique set of fossils. The oldest fossils at the bottom of the canyon differ from fossils in middle layers, which differ from fossils in layers near the top. Elsewhere on Earth, rock layers are not as neatly organized. Nevertheless, a rock layer's age determines the kinds of fossils that it might contain.

The fossil record is evidence that life on Earth has changed over time. The fossil record also shows that species have changed over time in response to changes in their environments. A change in the characteristics that are passed on from one generation to another in a population as a result of environmental change is called **evolution**.

Throughout the 1800s, many scientists proposed that species could change. None, however, stated the case for evolution more strongly than British naturalist Charles Darwin. Darwin defined evolution and its processes, backing his claims with solid evidence. In 1856, Darwin published his theories in a book titled *On the Origin of the Species.* Today, Darwin is recognized as the person who introduced the theory of evolution.

Natural Selection

As Darwin observed, all species have special traits that help them survive and reproduce in their environments. Such traits are called **adaptations**. For example, a fish's fins are an adaptation to help it swim and steer. The thick hair of a bear or moose is an adaptation for surviving cold winters. Beaks, mouths, and jaws are adaptations for eating different types of food.

With his observations as evidence, Darwin argued that species do not change, or evolve, randomly. Rather, environmental factors affect the way adaptations develop. This idea is called **natural selection**. Organisms that thrive in their environment pass their traits on to their offspring. When organisms do not thrive, they do not produce as many offspring and eventually, their unsuccessful traits die with them. This means that in any community, a set of successful and useful adaptations will develop over many generations. When the environment changes, adaptations change too.

Throughout geologic time, Earth's land and climate changed in different ways. When they changed, natural selection resulted in changes to living things as well.

Figure 12.4 As a young man, Charles Darwin (1809–1882) traveled all over Earth on a ship called the HMS *Beagle.* His observations of wildlife provided evidence for his theory of evolution.

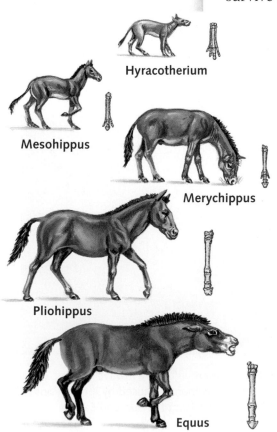

Hyracotherium

Mesohippus

Merychippus

Pliohippus

Equus

Figure 12.5 Over the past few million years, grasses have thrived on the plains of Asia. With more food available, larger species of horses evolved. Fossil bones from these species provide evidence of their evolution.

Extinction

Every organism has a life span. For example, a horse begins life, grows and develops, might reproduce more of its kind, and eventually dies. Species have life spans, too. In some cases, such as that shown in **Figure 12.5**, a species gives rise to, or evolves into, a new species. When all members of a species die, the species is then described as **extinct**.

Species might become extinct for many reasons. The environment might change in a way that affects the species' food or water supply. A new, strong competitor might move into the species' habitat. The climate might change in a way the species cannot tolerate, making it impossible for it to survive. For example, throughout Earth's geologic history, any rapid increase or decrease in temperature has caused extinctions of species.

A **mass extinction** occurs when a severe environmental change quickly kills off a large number of species. Mass extinctions have occurred throughout Earth's history and are documented by the change in fossils contained in the rock layers. Earth's most recent mass extinction occurred 65 million years ago. Many species, including the last of the dinosaurs, became extinct.

Geography of Evolution

What do a kangaroo, a koala, and a spiny echidna all have in common? All are native to the island continent Australia and they exist nowhere else on Earth. How did animals like these evolve? Part of the answer is that their ancestors were isolated, meaning they were separated from animals outside Australia. This allowed them to develop adaptations specially suited to their environment, without competition or influence from animals elsewhere.

As a general rule, populations that are geographically separated from one another will evolve in different ways. This explains the unique animals that are native to islands. For example, the Hawaiian nene (NAY nay), is a gooselike bird shown in **Figure 12.6**. The nene evolved in a small community that lacked skilled predators. As a result, the nene lacks adaptations to defend itself. When mongooses from the mainland reached Hawaii in the 1880s, the nene proved an easy target. After almost becoming extinct, the nene is classified today as endangered.

Figure 12.6 Animals that evolved on small islands, such as the Hawaiian nene, typically do not know how to defend themselves from mainland predators.

Did You Know?

Sugarcane farmers brought mongooses to the Hawaiian Islands beginning in the 1880s. The farmers hoped these predators would hunt rats, which were brought to Hawaii accidentally on ships from the mainland. Today, Hawaiians consider mongooses to be pests because they prey on nenes and other native wildlife.

 **CONNECTION: Math**

Measurements of geologic time include billions of years and millions of years. Write the numerals for one billion, one million, and one thousand. Identify some things that you could measure in billions, millions, and thousands.

After You Read

1. List the three eras of geologic time in your Science Notebook.
2. Identify four reasons why life on Earth evolved and developed as it did.
3. What illustrations or text could be added to **Figure 12.2** to show more about geologic time? Discuss this with a partner.

Before You Read

Draw a T-chart in your Science Notebook. Label one column *Cause* and the other column *Effect*. As you read, pay attention to cause-and-effect relationships.

What if people could travel back to the Precambrian? They would not recognize the planet they now call home. They would also not survive for very long. Before about 1.8 billion years ago, the air lacked oxygen.

As discussed earlier, the Precambrian makes up nearly 90 percent of geologic time. It is divided into three eons: the Hadean, the Archean, and the Proterozoic. As can be imagined, Earth changed in many ways during these very long spans of time.

Earliest Earth

During its very early years, Earth was so hot that most rocks were in a liquid or partly liquid state, even on the planet's surface. Gradually, as Earth cooled, its hard outer layer, or crust, was formed. After about two billion years, there were two distinct types of crust. One type was made of granite and other relatively lightweight rocks. This type of crust would become Earth's continents. The other type of crust was made mostly of denser rocks, such as basalt. This type of crust would become the ocean floor.

Earth's atmosphere was also very different during its early years. Scientists think that Earth's first atmosphere was made up mostly of hydrogen and helium, two very light gases. In fact, these gases are so light that they probably escaped into space. Volcanoes erupted quite frequently during this time and gases from volcanoes replaced these light gases. Nitrogen, carbon dioxide, and water vapor are gases that were added to the atmosphere by volcanoes during this time. These three gases remain part of the atmosphere today.

As the planet continued to cool, most of the water vapor in the air condensed, meaning it changed from a gas to a liquid. This formed the first oceans. Some scientists think that comets, because they are made partly of ice, also may have added water to the oceans.

Figure 12.7 Erupting volcanoes emitted many gases, including carbon dioxide, into Earth's early atmosphere. Carbon dioxide, a greenhouse gas, helped to warm Earth and allowed plants to develop.

The First Living Things

Scientists suspect that life began sometime between 3.9 and 3.5 billion years ago. How did this happen? One theory is that the first organisms were made from carbon-containing compounds in the oceans. These compounds included amino acids, simple sugars, and nucleic acids. The same compounds make up living things today.

The oldest known fossils are dated at 3.8 billion years old. They came from **cyanobacteria**, which are single-celled, ocean-dwelling organisms. Many grew in colonies along rock faces, most likely in shallow water.

Cyanobacteria are still living today. From the photograph in **Figure 12.8**, you might not guess that cyanobacteria have done anything important. But guess again! These organisms performed an early version of photosynthesis. During photosynthesis, light from the Sun is used to combine the raw materials of carbon dioxide and water into food. Oxygen is released as a waste gas.

Throughout the Precambrian, cyanobacteria were performing photosynthesis and releasing oxygen gas. As a result, oxygen levels slowly rose in both ocean waters and the atmosphere. Life could not have continued to evolve as it did without this oxygen supply.

Cyanobacteria also helped plants develop. According to one theory, the cells of the first plants absorbed one or more free-living cyanobacteria. Rather than destroy the cyanobacteria, however, the plant cells kept them alive. They established a relationship in which both organisms benefited. The cyanobacteria helped the plant cells make food by becoming the parts of the plant cell that perform photosynthesis. Today, they are called chloroplasts.

By the end of the Precambrian, the oceans were home to plants that looked like today's seaweed. The first animals, including sponges, corals, jellyfish, and worms, also lived there. Other animals were unlike any that are alive today. All lived in the ocean, where both water and oxygen were available.

As You Read

In each row of your cause-and-effect chart, enter a cause in one column and its effect in the other column. For example, cyanobacteria caused increased oxygen in the atmosphere.

Figure 12.9 Sponges evolved during the Precambrian and have changed very little since then. They filter bits of food from the water through their bodies.

Figure 12.8 Cyanobacteria *(inset)* can grow in huge colonies. Structures called stromatolites form as sediment gets trapped within the cyanobacteria. Layers of sediment and bacteria build up to form these structures. This occurs today much as it did billions of years ago.

Figure 12.10 The Devonian Period is sometimes called "The Age of Fishes."

Figure 12.11 Ferns of the Paleozoic Era grew taller and in greater numbers than they do today. Ferns produce spore cases on the back sides of their leaves that are used in reproduction.

Figure It Out

1. Explain what the figure shows about life during the Devonian Period. What is not shown?
2. Compare the fishes shown here to fishes that live today.

The Paleozoic Era

This era began with an event called the **Cambrian Explosion**. During the span of only a few million years, a huge number of new species evolved in the oceans. Many of these species gave rise to the major types of animals alive today. These include corals, starfishes, worms, and mollusks.

The dominant form of life on Earth during the Paleozoic was a group of animals called trilobites. They were the ancestors of today's arthropods, such as crustaceans, insects, centipedes, and millipedes. Trilobites had large heads, jointed legs, and bodies divided into many segments. Although they were quite successful in diversity and number, a mass extinction resulted in their disappearance by the end of the Paleozoic Era.

Vertebrates are animals with backbones. Fishes, the first vertebrates, became very common and diverse during the Devonian Period. The fishes of the Devonian included many types that have become extinct, such as armor-plated fishes and large, jawless fishes. Other types developed adaptations that allow them to survive today.

Land Plants Life moved onto land during the late Ordovician Period. Organisms resembling lichens evolved onto land first, followed by land plants. The first land plants were small, leafless, and grew close to the ground. They reproduced with spores, simple structures that develop into new organisms without fertilization. They have a hard outer covering that makes them resistant to dry conditions and excess heat.

As time passed, new types of land plants emerged. An important development was vascular tissue, a kind of internal transportation system for plants. **Vascular tissues** carry water and nutrients between plant parts. With this new type of tissue, plants were able to grow larger and to develop stems and leaves. Only the roots of a plant needed to stay in contact with the ground, where they could soak up water.

The first seed plants developed during the late Devonian Period. Unlike a spore, a seed contains its own water and food. A hard covering protects the seed from drying out. This also allows seeds to survive for a long time until conditions are right to begin growing.

By the end of the Paleozoic Era, plants had spread across the land. Ferns grew tall in dense forests. Other successful plants included cycads, which are trees topped with fernlike leaves. Some species of cycads, such as sago palms, are still living today.

Land Animals The first land animals were most likely insects. Yet, vertebrates soon followed. The illustration in **Figure 12.12** shows *Eusthenopteron* [YOO sthen op ter on], a fishlike creature that was able to do a push-up! Scientists learned about it from a fossil bone that dates back to the Devonian Period. They suspect that this animal used its front limbs to push its head out of the water.

Over time, animals such as *Eusthenopteron* gave rise to the first amphibians. The word *amphibian* means "living a double life." Amphibians typically begin their lives in water and then move to land.

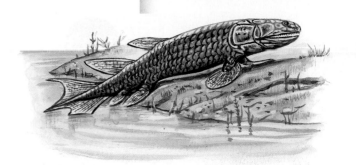

Figure 12.12 When oxygen levels dropped in the sea, *Eusthenopteron* survived by taking in oxygen from the air. This was likely a key step in the development of amphibians.

The Paleozoic Ends

Several mass extinctions occurred during the Paleozoic Era. The mass extinction that occurred during the late Ordovician Period might have been caused by worldwide cooling. Glacial deposits of Ordovician age support this theory. Another mass extinction occurred during the late Devonian Period. Scientists suggest that the increase in land plants led to a decrease in carbon dioxide (CO_2) in the atmosphere. Carbon dioxide is a greenhouse gas that helps warm Earth's atmosphere. Lower levels of CO_2 in the atmosphere may have caused a drop in temperature, leading to the mass extinction.

The Paleozoic Era ended with the largest mass extinction in Earth's history. At least 90 percent of all species living on Earth became extinct. Recently discovered evidence suggests that an asteroid impact might have caused environmental changes around the globe. Scientists also think that the formation of Pangaea, described in Chapter 6, might have contributed to the extinctions.

As Pangaea formed, large areas of marine shorelines and habitats disappeared. Earth's climate became hotter and drier. This change harmed amphibians, but helped a new group of species called reptiles. Tough scale- or plate-covered skins helped keep water inside the reptiles' bodies. Hard shells covered their eggs and kept them from drying out. Reptiles quickly became Earth's dominant animals. These reptiles ruled Earth for 160 million years.

CONNECTION: Language Arts

The word part *cyano-* refers to cyan, a bluish color. Cyanobacteria have a bluish-green color. Research the word parts in the names of some other ancient organisms, such as cephalopod, trilobite, and sphenopsid.

Explore It!

Study photographs of frogs, toads, or other amphibians. If possible, observe live amphibians at a zoo, pet store, or aquarium. Describe their body structures and movements. What body changes were necessary for vertebrates to live on land?

After You Read

1. What are two ways that cyanobacteria changed Earth?
2. Compare how life developed in Earth's oceans with how life developed on land.
3. Review the causes and effects you recorded in the T-chart in your Science Notebook. Did events on land affect life in the ocean? Explain your answer.

Before You Read

In your Science Notebook, draw a chart with three columns. Label the columns *Triassic*, *Jurassic*, and *Cretaceous*. As you preview the lesson, add information about each period to your chart.

The Mesozoic Era began after a tremendous mass extinction. About 180 million years later, it ended in much the same way. During the time in between, reptiles lived all over the planet. Some grew to great heights and sizes. They crawled, walked, ran, swam, and even flew. Other animals also lived during this time. Among these were the first mammals, the group that would succeed and prosper during the next era.

The Triassic Period

The first 42 million years of the Mesozoic Era make up the **Triassic Period**. In many ways it was a period of transition, or gradual change. The period began with the continents joined together as Pangaea. Pangaea was centered over the equator, and much of its climate was especially hot and dry. Slowly, Pangaea broke apart and divided into two large continents separated by a shallow sea. Later, this sea became the North Atlantic Ocean.

Mountains as tall as 10 km (more than 32,000 ft) towered above eastern North America. Weathering and erosion began rounding those mountains and breaking their rocks into soil. Today, these mountains are called the Appalachian Mountains.

Ferns and other Paleozoic plants survived into the Triassic Period. During this time, Earth's largest plants evolved. They are conifers, or cone-bearing trees. Seeds from these cones grow into new trees. Descendants of these large trees, the coast redwoods, *Sequoia sempervirens*, can grow up to 92 m (302 ft) or more.

Of the relatively few animal species that lived at the start of the Triassic Period, many did not survive. Others spread across the land and into the seas. Reptiles grew in number and diversity. Some were small and lizardlike. Other, dolphinlike reptiles grew to more than 15 m (49 ft) long.

Figure 12.13 Predators in the Mesozoic oceans included mosasaurs, ichthyosaurs, and plesiosaurs. Compare these marine animals to the dinosaurs in **Figure 12.15**.

The Jurassic Period

Pangaea continued to break apart during the **Jurassic Period**, which is the middle period of the Mesozoic Era. The oceans that are present today began to form. On land, the global climate was warm and wet. Swamps or shallow inland seas covered much of Earth's surface.

Although the first dinosaurs evolved during the Triassic Period, they became Earth's dominant animals, both in size and number, during the Jurassic Period. **Dinosaurs** were four-legged reptiles, some of which walked upright. Some were small and chickenlike; others were huge grazing animals. Still others were fierce and powerful predators. Dinosaurs lived in nearly every land habitat.

Dinosaurs thrived because of a huge supply of plant matter to support the food chain. Mosses, cycads, ferns, and conifers grew in large forests. So did ginkgos, a type of tree with fleshy seeds. Today, ginkgos are considered to be living fossils because they have not changed since they evolved.

Much smaller animals also thrived during this period. Many new types of insects evolved, including grasshoppers and flies. Among the ocean life were sponges, corals, mollusks, and new species of sharks and other fishes.

Fossils of early birdlike animals date to this period. *Archaeopteryx* (AHR kee AHP tuh rihks) resembled a cross between a dinosaur and a large modern bird. It had teeth, wings, and feathers. *Archaeopteryx* and similar species serve as evidence for a close evolutionary relationship between dinosaurs and birds.

Mammals were another new type of animal. They evolved during either the Jurassic or the late Triassic Period. Early mammals resembled rats or other rodents. They ate insects and stayed out of the dinosaurs' way. Some scientists suggest that they ate dinosaur eggs and helped contribute to the dinosaurs' eventual extinction.

Figure It Out

1. Is *Archaeopteryx* a vertebrate or invertebrate? Explain how you know.

2. Use this illustration to compare dinosaurs to birds and reptiles of today.

Figure 12.14 Are today's birds the descendants of dinosaurs? Paleontologists study fossils from *Archaeopteryx* and other species to help answer this question.

Did You Know?

Years ago, Chinese monks kept the world's only remaining ginkgo trees. Thanks to them, ginkgos are popular shade trees on modern city streets as well as reminders of the Jurassic Period.

Figure 12.15 The Mesozoic Era is often called "The Age of the Dinosaurs." As the era progressed, larger and more powerful dinosaur species appeared.

Discovering Dinosaurs

During the 1800s, scientists noticed that certain fossil bones appeared similar to the bones of today's reptiles. They differed, however, in size, shape, and number. In 1841, British scientist Richard Owen coined the name *dinosauria* for these ancient animals. The name comes from ancient Greek and means "fearfully great lizard."

As time passed, both scientists and the public came to view dinosaurs in much the same way. Dinosaurs were thought to be large, slow, clumsy, and unintelligent. Illustrations showed dinosaurs as gray or brown in color, walking on four legs, and with tails dragging along the ground. **Figure 12.16** shows a typical example.

Yet, these old ideas were wrong. Research from scientists such as Robert Bakker shows that many dinosaurs were fast and nimble. Dinosaurs came in many sizes, shapes, and colors. Dinosaurs that were predators were especially intelligent, as are predators today. Fossil evidence and comparisons with modern animals support all these ideas.

As You Read

In the three-column chart you prepared, enter at least three significant facts for each period of the Mesozoic Era. Share your chart with a partner. Add or correct any necessary information.

PEOPLE IN SCIENCE Dr. Robert Bakker   1945–

When Robert Bakker (BAH ker) was a young boy, he came upon a magazine article about dinosaurs. After reading the article, he knew that dinosaurs were going to be part of his career.

Bakker became a vertebrate paleontologist, and his work helped change people's ideas about dinosaurs. Bakker compares dinosaurs more to birds than to reptiles. With evidence to support each claim, he argues that many dinosaurs were warm-blooded, that they built nests and cared for their young, and that many walked on two legs, not four. All of these characteristics are shared by birds of today.

You can read Bakker's ideas in both scientific journals and in popular books about dinosaurs. Bakker has also worked with animators to present dinosaurs accurately, as he did for the *Jurassic Park* movies.

Megalosaurus, as drawn in the 1800s

Megalosaurus, as drawn today

Figure 12.16 Both pictures show the same species. How have scientists' visions and ideas of dinosaurs changed over time?

The Cretaceous Period

The final period of the Mesozoic Era is called the **Cretaceous Period**. The largest dinosaurs date from this period, including *Tyrannosaurus rex,* shown on page 191. It is important to note that throughout the Mesozoic Era, dinosaur species evolved and became extinct. By the Cretaceous Period, only groups such as the ceratopsians (such as *Triceratops*), pachycephalosaurs (such as *Pachycephalosaurus*), and the tyrannosaurs were living. Earth's warm climate created the conditions necessary to provide food for such huge animals. Warm temperatures also kept Earth's poles free of ice and the sea levels high.

A new type of plant evolved during the Cretaceous Period and proved very successful. This plant was the angiosperm, or flowering plant. Unlike ferns and conifers, flowering plants produce flowers that make seeds. The seeds are embedded in a structure called a fruit. The first flowering plants included magnolias, sassafras, and fig trees. Next to evolve were familiar trees such as oak, maple, and birch.

New types of insects also evolved. Among them were ants, termites, and bees. Bees began spreading pollen among flowers, which helped flowering plants reproduce.

A mass extinction ended the Cretaceous Period. The remaining dinosaurs became extinct, as did most of the sea-living reptiles. What could have caused death on such a large scale? According to one theory, a large asteroid struck Earth. A large asteroid striking Earth would have formed huge dust clouds that blocked sunlight for months, or even years. Without sunlight, plants would not have been able to grow and the food chain would have collapsed. As food supplies ran out, the living creatures depending on them would have ultimately died from starvation.

Over time, Earth's climate became much colder and drier. Reptiles struggle in cold weather because they are cold-blooded and readily lose or gain body heat. Mammals, however, are warm-blooded, meaning their bodies maintain a steady temperature. Their hair and body fat help keep them warm. As Earth's temperature decreased, the "Age of Reptiles" ended and the "Age of Mammals" began.

Explain It!

Geologic evidence supporting the theory that an asteroid hit Earth during the end of the Cretaceous Period has been found on the Yucatán Peninsula of Mexico. How could an event in Mexico kill animals all over the world? In your Science Notebook, write a well-developed paragraph about your hypothesis.

Figure 12.17 Bees and flowering plants evolved on Earth at about the same time. They are an example of coevolution, a situation during which individual species affect one another's development.

After You Read

1. Describe some important changes that took place during each period of the Mesozoic Era.

2. Discuss the dominant presence of dinosaurs during the Mesozoic Era and possible reasons for their extinction.

3. Review the chart you made in your Science Notebook about the events of the Mesozoic Era. How did Earth's climate affect living things during this time?

Learning Goals

- Discuss the causes and effects of Earth's cooling climate during the Cenozoic Era.
- Describe stages of human evolution.

New Vocabulary

Paleogene Period
Neogene Period
Quaternary Period
ice age
primate
hominid
bipedal

Before You Read

Scan this lesson briefly. Create a lesson outline in your Science Notebook using the title and headings of this lesson. Use the outline to think about what you will learn in this lesson.

The Cenozoic Era began 65 million years ago and continues to the present day. The era is sometimes called the "Age of Mammals." Yet many other species thrived during these years and are still thriving today. Insects, birds, fish, flowering plants, and other forms of life all joined with mammals to form diverse communities across Earth.

The **Paleogene Period** is the first period of the Cenozoic Era. It lasted about 41 million years. The second period, the **Neogene Period**, lasted 22 million years. Together, these periods contain five epochs. Each is defined by the percentage of modern animals whose fossils it contains. This is different from the rest of the time periods, which are defined simply by the fossils they contain. The third period, called the **Quaternary Period**, makes up only the last 1.8 million years. We are currently living during the Holocene, or Recent, Epoch.

Ice Ages

Throughout the Cenozoic Era, Earth's tectonic plates continued their slow movements across the globe. North America split completely from Greenland, which in turn split from Europe. This happened as the Atlantic Ocean widened. To the west, a land bridge connecting North America and Asia gradually broke apart. Elsewhere, the continents were moving closer. The Alps rose as the African plate moved north into Europe. The Indian plate pushed north into Asia, lifting and forming the Himalayas.

What changes might such events bring? Scientists propose that these new mountain ranges helped cool Earth's climate. The Cenozoic Era began with a warm, tropical climate, much like that of the previous era. Yet, by the end of the Neogene Period, huge ice sheets covered much of the land. Temperatures had dropped across Earth. Sea levels also dropped because so much water was frozen into ice.

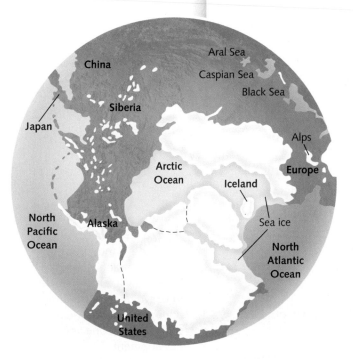

Figure 12.18 In North America, during the last ice age, glaciers spread as far south as what is now Indiana and from the east coast to the west coast. Global temperatures at this time were about 5°C lower than normal.

During the Quaternary Period, Earth's climate changed in a cycle of rising and lowering temperatures that caused the thawing and freezing of glaciers and ice sheets. A span of years that has continuous cold temperatures and ice is called an **ice age**. The last ice age ended about 10,000 years ago. In North America, evidence left by the glaciers, such as till and loess, can be seen across much of the Midwest. When the glaciers melted, they created the Great Lakes and other lakes in the region.

Surviving the Cold

As temperatures cooled, Earth's communities of living things changed. When the Cenozoic Era began, tropical plants covered much of Earth's land. Palm trees and fig trees grew across land that is now the United States and Canada. Gradually, such plants were confined to warmer regions farther south. Another widespread plant, the giant sequoia tree, now only survives in California and Oregon.

In many places, a variety of grasses replaced tropical plants. Grasses could survive the cold weather and did not need large amounts of water. Among the new types of grasses were the wild ancestors of wheat, corn, barley, oats, and rice.

The Rise of Mammals

When dinosaurs became extinct, many new niches opened up to the mammals. A niche is an organism's place in the food web, or its role or function. Over the course of the Cenozoic Era, different mammal groups became fierce predators, effective grazers, and useful scavengers. The new grasslands promoted a diversity of grazing animals as well as predators.

Remember that the first mammals were small and rodentlike. As time passed, their descendants gradually became larger. The development of today's horse is typical of this trend, as shown in **Figure 12.5**. Another example is the whale. The ancestors of whales can be traced to a dog-sized creature that lived on land.

Today, only a few species of very large mammals remain in the wild. These species include whales, giraffes, rhinoceroses, and elephants. Each of these species—along with many others—is threatened or endangered because of human actions. Indeed, over the course of only a few thousand years, humans have dramatically caused a change in conditions on Earth and the life-forms that live on it. Scientists are still trying to understand the extent of human-caused changes to our planet. They are also trying to predict how these changes will affect Earth's future.

As You Read
Look at the outline you created in your Science Notebook. Compare your outline with that of a partner. Make any necessary additions or corrections. For each heading, write one or two sentences to fill in the outline.

Figure 12.19 Woolly mammoths required a large habitat to get the food they needed. Today, loss of habitat threatens the elephant, the mammoth's smaller descendant.

Figure It Out

1. Compare and contrast the sizes and shapes of these skulls.
2. Hypothesize why scientists carefully study the holes and cavities in a hominid skull.

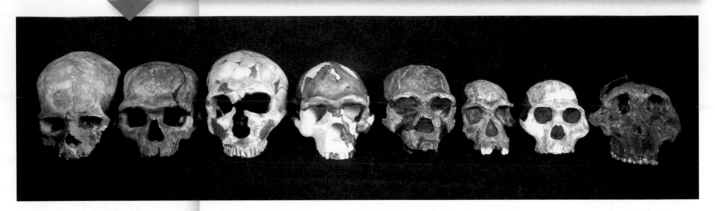

Figure 12.20 Hominid skulls changed in size and shape over time. These skulls help show how the human brain changed and developed.

Human Origins

Thousands of fossils show evidence of early humans and human ancestors. The oldest of these fossils date to the late Neogene Period. This means that humans developed at a time when ice covered Earth.

Scientists classify humans in an order of mammals called **primates**. Other primates include apes, monkeys, and lemurs. Primates evolved from tree-dwelling animals, and many primates live in trees today. Other primates including humans and the largest apes, developed body parts and skills for life on the ground. All primates share many characteristics, including eyes that face forward and hands that can grasp objects.

Hominid is a general term that applies to humans and human ancestors. Unlike apes and other primates, most hominids that lived between 10 and 5 million years ago had relatively large and advanced brains. They also were **bipedal**, meaning they walked upright on two legs.

The oldest accepted hominid is a species called *Australopithecus* (aw stray loh PIH thuh kus). During the 1970s, Donald Johanson and a team of anthropologists from Case Western Reserve University discovered an especially well-preserved fossil of a female *Australopithecus*, which they named Lucy. Above the waist, this early hominid resembles an ape. Below the waist however, it resembles a human. Lucy provides evidence that hominids developed bipedal walking before developing a larger brain capacity.

Other hominids include *Homo habilis*, which means "handy human." These hominids made and used simple tools and lived from about 2 million to 1.5 million years ago. Following them came *Homo erectus*, which means "straight human." This species was likely the first to control the use of fire.

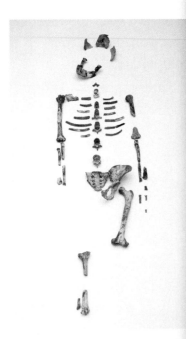

Figure 12.21 Scientists rarely find early hominid skeletons as complete as Lucy, who is at least three million years old. Lucy was ape-like in some ways and humanlike in others.

Modern hominids are classified as *Homo sapiens*, the species to which people today belong. Scientists estimate that the first *Homo sapiens* evolved as early as 400,000 years ago. Early humans included the Neandertals and Cro-Magnons. Both differed somewhat from humans today.

The Success of Hominids

Hominids evolved in eastern Africa. Over thousands of years, humans migrated throughout Africa, Europe, and Asia, and later across the Asia-Alaska land bridge into the Americas.

Today, humans live on all seven continents. Humans have found ways to survive in all sorts of climates and on all sorts of landforms. Some humans have even visited outer space! How did our species come to be so dominant and accomplished? Clearly, the key to the answer is human intelligence. It is the most significant trait that sets humans apart from other species.

Scientists continue to debate explanations for how and why the hominid brain evolved. One theory is that when primates moved from living in trees to living on the ground, developing social groups and language became more important. Such changes depended on the brain. Other scientists point to the evolution of bipedalism as the key step toward intelligence. Walking on two feet frees the hands for advanced tasks, such as using tools.

Human history takes up only a very small fraction of geologic time. A huge number of species came before us, most of which became extinct thousands, or millions, or even billions of years ago. As you continue to study Earth science, remember that Earth experienced many great changes to become the planet it is today. Earth's history is far from over. There are many great changes to come.

Extend It!

Research the structure of the modern human brain. Compare it to the brains of other mammals. Which parts of the brain are unique to humans?

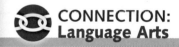

CONNECTION: Language Arts

How did languages begin? Onomatopoeia is the formation or use of words that imitate sounds or actions. A cat's meow is an example. Work in groups to make a list of words that seem like they may have come from sounds or actions. Then compose a poem using your list of words.

After You Read

1. Describe the causes and effects of Earth's cooling climate during the Cenozoic Era.

2. Identify three hominid ancestors of modern humans.

3. Review the outline you wrote in your Science Notebook for this lesson. What else would you like to learn about the Cenozoic Era? Explain why you think this knowledge is important and where you might find the information.

KEY CONCEPTS

12.1 The Geologic Time Scale

- Scientists divide Earth's four-billion-year history into Precambrian Time and the Paleozoic, Mesozoic, and Cenozoic Eras. Each had unique climates and communities of living things.
- Earth's position in space, iron core, and tectonic plates, plus the timing of important events, have all allowed life to develop.
- Evolution is the theory that new life-forms develop, or evolve, from older life-forms.

12.2 Precambrian Time and the Paleozoic Era

- The Precambrian spans about 90 percent of Earth's history. The oldest life-forms evolved during this time.
- Cyanobacteria are the first known ocean-dwelling organisms. These organisms performed an early version of photosynthesis and added oxygen to Earth's early atmosphere.
- The Paleozoic Era began with the Cambrian Explosion.
- Organisms resembling lichens evolved on land first, followed by land plants. The first land animals were most likely insects. Vertebrates soon followed.
- The Paleozoic Era ended with a tremendous mass extinction.

12.3 The Mesozoic Era

- Conifers were Earth's largest plants, and reptiles grew in both number and diversity during the Triassic Period.
- During the Jurassic Period, Earth's modern oceans began to form. The climate on land was warm and wet. Dinosaurs became Earth's dominant animals.
- The largest dinosaurs lived during the Cretaceous Period. The first seed-bearing flowering plants evolved during the Cretaceous as well.
- A mass extinction ended the Cretaceous Period and killed off all of the remaining dinosaurs and many reptiles.

12.4 The Cenozoic Era

- The Cenozoic Era began 65 million years ago and continues to the present.
- The Cenozoic Era began with a warm, tropical climate but later experienced ice ages.
- Mammals became abundant and diverse during this era. Insects, birds, fish, flowering plants, and other forms of life all joined with mammals to form diverse communities across Earth.
- Hominids developed during the ice ages. Modern hominids are classified as *Homo sapiens,* the species to which humans belong.
- Scientists estimate that the first *Homo sapiens* evolved as early as 400,000 years ago.

VOCABULARY REVIEW

Write each term in a complete sentence, or write a paragraph relating several terms.

12.1
geologic time scale, p. 207
Precambrian Time, p. 207
eon, p. 207
era, p. 207
Paleozoic Era, p. 207
Mesozoic Era, p. 207
Cenozoic Era, p. 209
period, p. 209
epoch, p. 209
evolution, p. 210
adaptation, p. 210
natural selection, p. 210
extinct, p. 211
mass extinction, p. 211

12.2
cyanobacteria, p. 213
Cambrian Explosion, p. 214
vertebrate, p. 214
vascular tissue, p. 214

12.3
Triassic Period, p. 216
Jurassic Period, p. 217
dinosaur, p. 217
Cretaceous Period, p. 219

12.4
Paleogene Period, p. 220
Neogene Period, p. 220
Quaternary Period, p. 220
ice age, p. 221
primate, p. 222
hominid, p. 222
bipedal, p. 222

True or False

If the statement is true, write "true." If it is false, change the underlined word or words to make the statement true.

1. The first land plants evolved during the <u>Precambrian</u>.

2. Dinosaurs dominated during the <u>Cenozoic</u> Era.

3. The <u>Cambrian Explosion</u> occurred near the beginning of the Paleozoic Era.

4. Earth's <u>tectonic activity</u> helps to <u>block</u> dangerous radiation from space.

5. <u>Primates</u> include humans, monkeys, apes, and lemurs.

6. Cyanobacteria changed Earth's atmosphere by adding <u>carbon dioxide</u>.

Short Answer

Answer each of the following in a sentence or brief paragraph.

7. How did the mass extinction of dinosaurs help shape life today?

8. What was Charles Darwin's contribution to science?

9. Explain how the development of vascular tissue changed plant life.

10. Describe the first step in the evolution of amphibians.

11. List three living things that shared Earth with the dinosaurs.

12. Compare the time span of human history to that of geologic time.

PREPARE FOR CHAPTER TEST

To prepare for the chapter test, create a question from each Learning Goal. Use the information in your Science Notebook to answer each question. Then use these answers to write a well-developed essay about the chapter. Use the Key Concept on the first page of this chapter as your topic sentence.

Critical Thinking

Use what you have learned in this chapter to answer each of the following.

13. **Apply Concepts** If Earth's climate were to warm significantly, what changes to living things would you predict? Include three examples along with your reasoning.

14. **Compare and Contrast** How is human evolution similar to the evolution of other species? How is it different?

Standardized Test Question

Choose the letter of the response that correctly answers the question.

15. Which span of geologic time has been the shortest?

   A. Precambrian Time

   B. Paleozoic Era

   C. Mesozoic Era

   D. Cenozoic Era

Test-Taking Tip

Avoid changing your answer unless you have read the question incorrectly. Usually, your first choice is the correct choice.

Mass Extinction

EXTINCTIONS AREN'T unusual. Believe it or not, they happen all the time. Extinctions usually happen gradually, over a long period of time. There have been several times throughout Earth's history, however, when more than half the world's life-forms died out over a relatively short period of time. These events are called mass extinctions. You can see when Earth's mass extinctions occurred by looking at the geologic time scale.

Think about the Phanerozoic Eon. This eon is divided into three eras: the Paleozoic, Mesozoic, and Cenozoic. How did scientists decide when one era ended and another began? They looked closely at the fossil record, which showed that life-forms on Earth changed greatly during the time periods corresponding to the divisions between eras. Scientists think each era ended when a catastrophic event caused climate changes that wiped out many species and left a different mix of species behind. The species that survived these catastrophic events adapted to the changed environment, and life on Earth evolved in a different direction. This marked the beginning of a new era.

The biggest mass extinction on Earth happened about 250 million years ago, between the Paleozoic and Mesozoic eras. As a result of this extinction, more than 90 percent of ocean species vanished. Many scientists think a huge meteorite—or maybe several—hit Earth, blasting tons of debris into the atmosphere. The added dust in the air could have decreased the amount of solar radiation reaching Earth. Temperatures would have dropped, creating drastic climate changes. Species that couldn't survive these changes died off fairly quickly.

As a result of this extinction event, a number of different species became dominant during the Mesozoic era. They filled niches that were left empty after the Paleozoic mass extinction. For example, fossils show that the first small dinosaurs evolved at the end of the Triassic period. By the end of the Jurassic, they had become the giant reptiles we know from books and movies. They were Earth's dominant life-form during much of the Mesozoic, but by the end of that era, the dinosaurs were gone, too.

The last of the dinosaurs were wiped out by the most recent mass extinction on Earth. It occurred 65 million years ago, at the end of the Mesozoic Era. This extinction also wiped out 75 percent of plant species and almost all plankton species in the oceans. Some scientists think the cause was a 10-km-wide meteorite that slammed into Earth. Again, the impact sent tons of dust into the air. The blast of hot air from the impact set forests on fire. All of this dust, soot, and other debris circulated in the atmosphere, blocking the sun for months. World temperatures dropped, photosynthesis stopped, and most plants died out. As a result, most large animals, including the dinosaurs, could not survive.

Although giant reptiles died at the end of the Mesozoic, small mammals did not. With the dominant reptiles gone, mammals evolved in the changed conditions. Fossils tell us they were small rodentlike animals, but they became larger and more diverse over time. During the next era, the Cenozoic, mammals became dominant and still are today.

Will there be another mass extinction? No one knows. Scientists can't predict them. If one does occur, life on Earth will probably change greatly again.

Investigative Reporting

Meteorites contributed to the extinction of the dinosaurs. How do scientists know that? What evidence did they find? Do research to find at least one example of this evidence. Write a report in the form of a newspaper article.

A Story in the Ice

WHAT WAS EARTH'S atmosphere like hundreds of thousands of years ago? The answer is frozen in Earth's ice caps. Now, scientists are unlocking those secrets.

Some polar areas are so cold that the ice never melts. New snow and ice piles up year after year, and as particles of snow and ice fall, air is trapped between them. These air bubbles are samples of the atmosphere at the time the ice and snow fell.

Scientists figured out that bubbles in the oldest ice could tell them what Earth's atmosphere was like in the ancient past. Researchers have spent years carefully removing long cores of ice from Antarctica and Greenland. Analysis of air bubbles in these ice cores is telling researchers what Earth's atmosphere was like long before humans inhabited Earth. Scientists have also dropped thermometers deep into the holes from which they removed the ice. They have used these temperature readings to determine what the air temperature was when the snow fell hundreds of thousands of years ago.

One Antarctic ice core is almost three km long! The data collected from this core goes back 800,000 years. Analysis of gases in this ice core showed that levels of carbon dioxide (CO_2) in the air are higher now than they have been in almost half a million years. Data from the ice also shows that global temperatures have risen and fallen with CO_2 levels for thousands of years.

Why is this important? CO_2 is a greenhouse gas—one of the gases that holds heat in Earth's atmosphere and keeps the planet warm. This means that the amount of CO_2 in the atmosphere affects global temperatures. Data shows that Earth's current climate is getting warmer. Many scientists think that this warming is due to human actions that add more CO_2 to the air. The data from the ice cores could help scientists understand how increased CO_2 levels in Earth's atmosphere impacted past climates. This knowledge could help us make decisions about what needs to be done today to protect Earth's environment in the future.

CAREER CONNECTION: PALEONTOLOGIST

ARE YOU INTERESTED in how dinosaurs lived? Are you curious about how meteors that slammed into Earth millions of years ago wiped out most living things? If so, you just might want to become a paleontologist.

Paleontologists use fossils to study the history of life on Earth. They look at fossils to study how life-forms have changed over time. They also study the way fossils are distributed within layers of rock. This tells paleontologists when these past life-forms lived. The rock types that fossils occur in also tell paleontologists about the types of environments the life-forms lived in.

Paleontology is a broad science. Most paleontologists know some geology, biology, chemistry, and even physics. They often work in teams, and must communicate their work to others through reports and lectures.

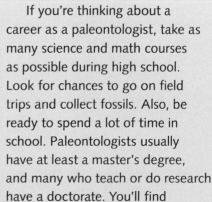

If you're thinking about a career as a paleontologist, take as many science and math courses as possible during high school. Look for chances to go on field trips and collect fossils. Also, be ready to spend a lot of time in school. Paleontologists usually have at least a master's degree, and many who teach or do research have a doctorate. You'll find paleontologists in university classrooms, at government agencies, and in museums. But you'll also find them all over the world, hammer in hand, collecting fossils and studying rocks.

Earth's Atmosphere and Weather

Chapter 13 The Atmosphere

What is the atmosphere, and how does it affect Earth's climate and wind patterns?

Chapter 14 Weather

What factors influence weather, and how can weather be predicted?

Chapter 15 Climate

What is climate, and what factors influence it?

The Atmosphere

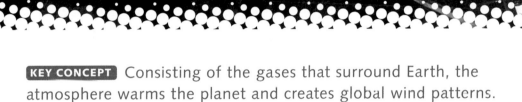

KEY CONCEPT Consisting of the gases that surround Earth, the atmosphere warms the planet and creates global wind patterns.

The atmosphere is made up of gases that we call air. Air contains the oxygen that we need to breathe and a gas called ozone that protects us from harmful radiation from the Sun. Gases in the atmosphere absorb heat energy and prevent some of it from escaping into space. Air keeps the average temperature on Earth at about 15°C—warm enough to keep water in a liquid state. Air moves from the warm equator toward the poles, redistributing heat from the Sun. We call the motion of air *wind*. The interaction between the Sun, the surface of Earth, and the atmosphere creates global wind patterns. Wind is a renewable energy source that today is mainly used to generate electricity.

Think About Wind

How do you know the wind is blowing if you can't see it?

- Write two or three sentences in your Science Notebook about things you have seen that let you know the wind was blowing.

- How powerful can blowing winds be? Describe the effects of strong winds that you might have seen or heard about.

www.scilinks.org

Atmosphere **Code: WGES13**

Learning Goals

- Identify the major components of Earth's atmosphere.
- Explain how air pressure changes with altitude.
- Explain how temperature changes with altitude.
- Describe the layers of the atmosphere.

New Vocabulary

atmosphere
wind
air pressure
barometer
troposphere
lapse rate
tropopause
stratosphere
ozone
mesosphere
thermosphere
ionosphere
exosphere

13.1 Characteristics of the Atmosphere

Before You Read

Create an outline in your Science Notebook using the title and headings from this lesson. Leave space between the headings to note the main concepts as you learn them.

The **atmosphere** is a blanket of gases that surrounds Earth. The gases cannot be seen, but their presence can be felt through wind. **Wind** is the horizontal movement of air. When the motion is slow, a gentle breeze might be felt. If air is moving fast, as during a hurricane, it becomes strong enough to rip trees from the ground and send rooftops flying. Wind reveals the presence of air.

During ancient times, air was considered one of the elements that made up the natural world. The other elements were earth, fire, and water. Today we know that air is not a single element—it is a mixture of gases, each with its own properties. We also now know that the atmosphere, which extends from Earth's surface to outer space, plays a fundamental, or basic, role in supporting life on our planet. It contains the oxygen that we need to breathe. The gases that make up the atmosphere form a blanket that protects Earth's organisms from the dangers of harmful radiation from space. The atmosphere also prevents heat on Earth's surface from escaping into space. Without the atmosphere, Earth would be a very cold planet.

Figure 13.1 This photo shows the atmosphere above Earth as seen by the astronauts aboard the *International Space Station.*

Composition of the Atmosphere

Figure 13.2 shows that the two most abundant gases in the atmosphere are nitrogen and oxygen. Since the formation of the atmosphere hundreds of millions of years ago, the relative amounts of nitrogen and oxygen have changed very little. This is important in terms of supporting the life forms on Earth, because most require oxygen to breathe and many plants require nitrogen to grow.

Water vapor and carbon dioxide are important atmospheric gases as well. Both gases absorb heat, and they both play a critical role in regulating, or controlling, the amount of energy the atmosphere absorbs.

Water is the only component of the atmosphere that exists in three different states of matter: gas, liquid, and solid. Water vapor is the gaseous form of water. It is the source of clouds, rain, and snow. Liquid water is present in clouds as tiny droplets, and falls to the ground as rain. Solid water exists as ice, snow, or sleet. When water changes states, it either absorbs or releases heat. This source of heat plays an important role in the processes that determine weather and climate. This concept is explained in Chapters 14 and 15.

The atmosphere also contains tiny solid particles, such as dust, sea salt from sea spray, and ash from smokestacks and volcanic eruptions. These particles provide a surface on which water vapor can condense into liquid or solid droplets, allowing clouds to form.

Atmospheric Pressure

Although air is invisible, it has mass like any other substance. Air molecules are therefore pulled by gravity toward the center of Earth. The force of gravity is stronger closer to Earth's surface. For this reason, the concentration of air molecules is higher in the lower parts of the atmosphere. The weight exerted on a specific area by the column of air above it is called **air pressure**. Scientists measure air pressure with an instrument called a **barometer**. Air pressure is highest at Earth's surface. Higher in the atmosphere, there are fewer air molecules pushing down from above. As a result, air pressure decreases as the height above Earth's surface increases.

Figure 13.2 Together, nitrogen and oxygen make up about 99 percent of the total gases in Earth's atmosphere. The remaining one percent is a mixture of other gases.

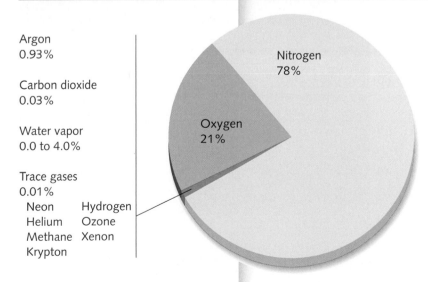

Percentages of Gases that Make Up Earth's Atmosphere

Argon
0.93%

Carbon dioxide
0.03%

Water vapor
0.0 to 4.0%

Trace gases
0.01%
Neon   Hydrogen
Helium   Ozone
Methane   Xenon
Krypton

Nitrogen
78%

Oxygen
21%

Because we live on Earth's surface, the air above our heads constantly pushes down on us. At sea level, the air pushes down on our bodies with a weight of about 1 kg per square cm. Why don't we feel all that pressure? It is because the inward push exerted by the air outside our bodies is balanced by the outward push of the air inside our bodies.

Atmospheric Temperature

Air molecules are in constant motion, bumping into each other and into other surfaces. During these collisions, each molecule transfers some of its energy of motion to other molecules. The energy of motion of an air molecule is related to its temperature. The higher the temperature of a molecule, the more energy it possesses.

Temperature is different from heat. Temperature is a measure of the energy possessed by the molecules or atoms of an object. Heat is a kind of energy that is exchanged when objects at different temperatures come in contact. Heat energy always flows from the warmer to the cooler object. When heat is added to the air, the molecules move faster, and the temperature increases. The opposite happens when air is cooled; the molecules slow down, and the temperature decreases.

Temperature differences in the atmosphere are used to define the layers shown in **Figure 13.3**. The lower levels of the atmosphere receive heat primarily from the surface of Earth. Air temperature decreases with altitude, or height above Earth's surface. This explains why snow can cover the top of a mountain, while a valley below may be covered with grass and flowers. However, as shown in **Figure 13.3**, farther up in the atmosphere, air temperature alternates between warmer and colder conditions. The temperature differences depend on how the atoms and molecules in different parts of the atmosphere absorb and exchange energy from the Sun.

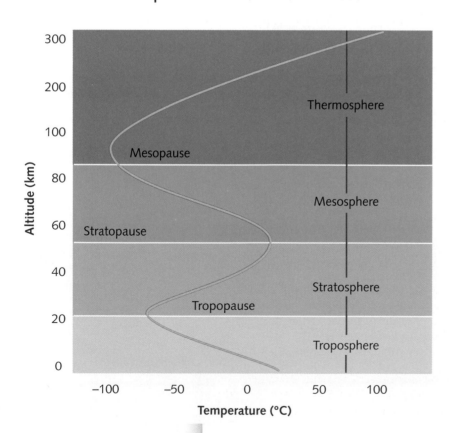

Temperature Variations with Altitude

Figure 13.3 While air pressure in the layers of Earth's atmosphere decreases with altitude, air temperature varies from layer to layer.

Layers of the Atmosphere

The atmosphere is divided into several layers based on the way air temperature changes with altitude. Each layer has a unique composition. **Figure 13.4** shows the layers of the atmosphere.

Troposphere   The layer closest to Earth's surface is called the **troposphere**. It is the densest layer, containing most of the mass of the atmosphere. The troposphere extends about 16 km above Earth's surface at the tropics, and 9 km or less above Earth's surface at the poles. Airplanes fly in this layer of the atmosphere. The temperature within the troposphere generally decreases by about 6.5°C for every kilometer of altitude. This rate of change is called the **lapse rate**. Using the lapse rate, it can be determined that if at sea level the temperature is 26°C, the temperature at the summit of Mount Everest, which is 8.856 km high, drops to a freezing −31°C. The temperature at the upper limit of the troposphere, called the **tropopause**, is about −80°C.

Almost all of Earth's carbon dioxide, water vapor, clouds, air pollution, and life forms are in the troposphere. Most of Earth's weather takes place in the troposphere. The state of the troposphere is constantly changing. In fact, the name *troposphere* means "sphere of change."

1. Which layer of the atmosphere begins at about 50 km above Earth's surface?

2. Which layer of the atmosphere has the highest pressure?

3. Look at both **Figure 13.4** below and **Figure 13.3** on the previous page. In which layer of the atmosphere would you expect to find the highest temperature and lowest pressure?

Figure It Out

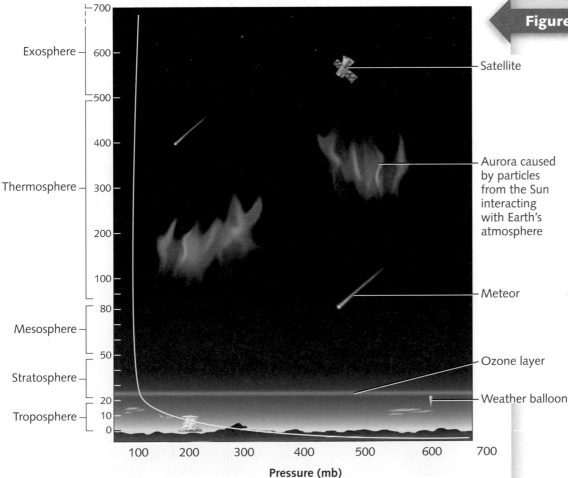

Figure 13.4 Earth's atmosphere is made up of several different layers. Each layer differs in chemical composition and temperature. The yellow line shows how pressure decreases as altitude increases.

As You Read

Your outline of the lesson should now include details about the atmosphere, its composition, its layered structure, and information about how pressure and temperature change with altitude. Compare your outline to a partner's. Make additions or corrections as necessary.

What are the three most common gases in the atmosphere?

Did You Know?

Ozone exists in the troposphere as well as in the stratosphere. Some of this low-lying ozone occurs naturally, but some is the result of human activities. During the sunny summer months, emissions from cars in urban areas combined with intense sunlight result in high levels of ozone in the air. While the stratospheric ozone shields Earth from ultraviolet radiation, ozone in the troposphere is known as "bad" ozone. It causes respiratory problems and damages forests and crops.

Figure 13.5 This diagram shows how ozone forms and absorbs ultraviolet radiation.

Stratosphere   The **stratosphere** is the layer of the atmosphere directly above the troposphere. It starts at the top of the tropopause and extends upward to about 50 km. The stratosphere contains a concentrated layer of ozone that absorbs ultraviolet radiation from incoming sunlight. The upper stratosphere has a higher concentration of ozone than the lower stratosphere. As a result, it absorbs more solar energy than the lower stratosphere. This causes temperatures in the stratosphere to rise with increasing altitude.

The upper part of the stratosphere that contains relatively high amounts of ozone is called the ozone layer. **Ozone** (O_3) is a gas formed by the addition of a third oxygen atom to an oxygen molecule (O_2). The formation of ozone starts when ultraviolet light from the Sun strikes a molecule of O_2 and splits it into two atoms of oxygen (O). Each of these atoms then bonds with other molecules of O_2, creating ozone (O_3). Ozone, in turn, can absorb additional ultraviolet radiation and split back into O_2 and O. The oxygen atom then reacts with O_2 to form O_3 again. **Figure 13.5** shows how this process occurs.

This cycle creates ozone continuously in the stratosphere. It also absorbs 97–99 percent of the ultraviolet radiation from the Sun before it reaches Earth's surface. If ozone did not absorb some of this radiation before it reached Earth's surface, many organisms, including humans, could not tolerate exposure to the Sun for very long. Chemicals produced by human activities destroy the ozone molecules in the stratosphere. Efforts to reduce emissions of these chemicals have been under way since 1989. As a result, the levels of ozone in the stratosphere are slowly recovering. This is discussed in detail in Chapter 20.

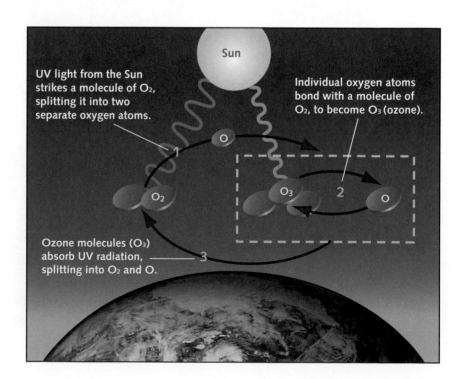

UV light from the Sun strikes a molecule of O_2, splitting it into two separate oxygen atoms.

Individual oxygen atoms bond with a molecule of O_2, to become O_3 (ozone).

Ozone molecules (O_3) absorb UV radiation, splitting into O_2 and O.

Mesosphere   The **mesosphere** is the third, or middle, layer of the atmosphere. It is the coldest part of the atmosphere. The temperature in this layer drops with increasing altitude. At the top of the mesosphere, the temperature is −93°C. The mesosphere is the layer where most meteors burn up and appear as shooting stars to observers on Earth.

Thermosphere   The **thermosphere** is located above the mesosphere. The temperature of the thermosphere increases with altitude and may reach more than 1,000°C at the top. Within the thermosphere is the **ionosphere**. Nitrogen and oxygen atoms in the ionosphere absorb potentially harmful solar energy, including X rays and gamma rays. This absorption contributes to the thermosphere's high temperatures. It also causes the gas particles in the ionosphere to lose electrons and become electrically charged atoms called ions. These charged particles reflect electromagnetic waves, such as radio signals emitted from Earth's surface. In this way, the ionosphere helps transmit radio signals around the world. The electrically charged particles in the ionosphere can also interact with Earth's magnetic field and emit light of different colors. This is the source of the auroras, shown in **Figure 13.6**, that often occur at high latitudes.

Exosphere   The **exosphere** is the outermost layer of Earth's atmosphere. The boundaries of this layer are not clearly defined. It extends from the top of the thermosphere and blends into outer space. The exosphere is composed of very light gases, such as hydrogen and helium. The atmosphere is extremely thin at this elevation, with fewer and fewer molecules. Because of this, satellites can orbit Earth in the exosphere without being slowed by friction.

Extend It!

Auroras are displays of shimmering lights caused by ions in the ionosphere. Go to the library or use the Internet to find out more about this spectacular display and what causes it. Facts might include a list of regions where auroras can be seen and when. In your Science Notebook, write a short report about auroras.

Figure 13.6 At times, the ions in the ionosphere gain enough energy from the Sun to create dazzling light displays called auroras. In the northern hemisphere, they are called the aurora borealis, or northern lights. In the southern hemisphere, they are called the aurora australis, or southern lights. This auroral display was photographed in Michigan.

After You Read

1. List and briefly describe the layers of the atmosphere in order. Begin with the layer closest to Earth's surface. Refer to the outline in your Science Notebook if you need help.

2. Describe how temperature changes in the mesosphere.

3. Explain why the temperature in the stratosphere increases.

Learning Goals

- Describe what happens to radiation that reaches Earth.
- Explain how the processes of radiation, conduction, and convection distribute energy in the atmosphere.
- Explain how the greenhouse effect and global warming are related to Earth's radiation balance.

New Vocabulary

radiation
conduction
convection
greenhouse effect
greenhouse gases
global warming

Figure It Out

1. How much of the incoming radiation from the Sun is reflected back into space by the atmosphere?

2. Predict how an increase in cloud cover might affect the balance between the energy absorbed and the energy reflected back into space by Earth.

Before You Read

Make a concept map of the main idea and important details in this lesson in your Science Notebook. Write the main idea, *Heat and Earth's Atmosphere*, in a circle in the center of the page. As you read, add additional circles to note important supporting details. Connect these circles to the main idea.

The Sun is a powerful energy source. Orbiting the Sun at an average distance of about 150 million km, Earth receives only one-half of one-billionth of the Sun's energy. This might sound like a tiny amount, but it is enough energy to power the circulation of the atmosphere and oceans, and heat the entire surface of the planet!

Solar Energy in the Atmosphere

Energy from the Sun travels through space in the form of radiation. **Radiation** is energy that is transferred as rays called electromagnetic waves. The heat that is felt from a toaster or a campfire is due to radiation. Not all of the energy that reaches Earth's atmosphere makes it to Earth's surface. As **Figure 13.7** shows, about 35 percent of incoming energy from the Sun is reflected back into space by the atmosphere, the clouds, and Earth's surface. Fifty percent of the remaining energy is absorbed by Earth's surface, and 15 percent is absorbed by the atmosphere.

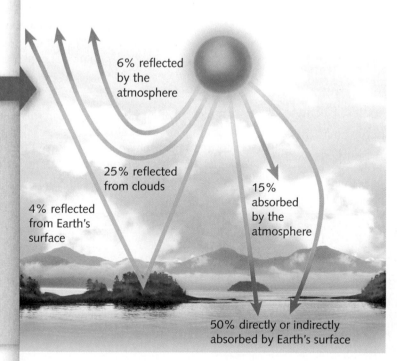

6% reflected by the atmosphere

25% reflected from clouds

4% reflected from Earth's surface

15% absorbed by the atmosphere

50% directly or indirectly absorbed by Earth's surface

Figure 13.7 Different areas of Earth absorb energy and heat up at different rates. Water heats and cools more slowly than land, and darker objects heat up faster than lighter objects.

Heat Transfer by Conduction and Convection

Half of the incoming energy from the Sun is absorbed by Earth's surface, warming the ground. The heat generated is then transferred to, and distributed throughout, the atmosphere through the processes of conduction and convection.

Conduction is the transfer of energy between objects that come into direct contact with one another. It occurs when molecules collide. The warm surface of Earth transfers heat to the layer of atmosphere directly above it through conduction. As the air molecules in the atmosphere gain more energy, they move faster and spread apart. This spreading causes air to rise in the atmosphere, carrying heat upward. As the air rises, it cools until it becomes colder than the surrounding air. Because colder air is denser, it sinks back to the ground, making room for more air to rise and take its place.

Convection, on the other hand, is the transfer of energy by the flow of a heated substance, such as a liquid or gas. For example, a cake bakes in an oven as a result of both convection and conduction. Convection causes the heated air inside the oven to make contact with the cake pan. The cake pan gets hot. Conduction of heat from the cake pan to the cake batter results in a baked cake. **Figure 13.8** shows how the rising and sinking of air sets up a circulation pattern that transfers heat from Earth's surface to higher layers of the atmosphere. This circular movement of air is called a convection current.

Explain It!

In your Science Notebook, write a brief paragraph about how radiation, conduction, and convection distribute heat from an electric heater in a room.

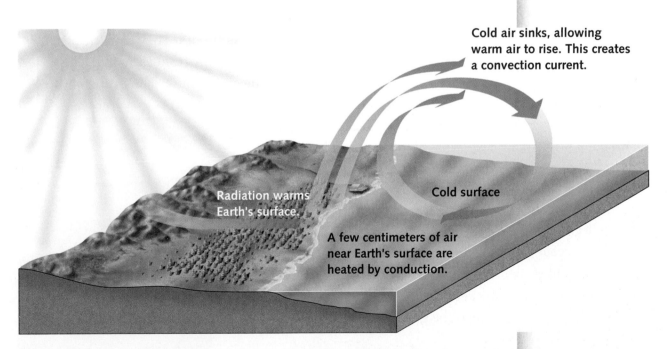

Cold air sinks, allowing warm air to rise. This creates a convection current.

Radiation warms Earth's surface.

Cold surface

A few centimeters of air near Earth's surface are heated by conduction.

Figure 13.8 Energy from the Sun is transferred throughout the atmosphere by radiation, conduction, and convection.

CONNECTION: The Zeroth Law of Thermodynamics

The study of heat transfer is the subject of the field of physical science known as thermodynamics. An object at a higher temperature that is in contact with an object at a lower temperature will transfer heat to the object at the lower temperature. Eventually, as long as they do not lose heat to additional objects, the objects in contact will approach and maintain a constant temperature. They are then said to be in thermal equilibrium.

Thermal equilibrium is the subject of the Zeroth Law of Thermodynamics. This law states: "If two thermodynamic systems are in thermal equilibrium with a third, they are also in thermal equilibrium with each other." This law was the basis for the concept of temperature.

For many years, scientists were not sure exactly what heat was. Some thought it was a form of motion. Other scientists thought it was a type of weightless fluid that could be exchanged between bodies. Today, we know that heat is a form of energy associated with the motion of atoms and molecules, and that temperature is a measure of this energy.

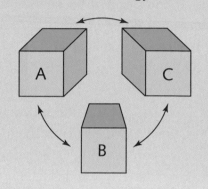

The Greenhouse Effect and Balancing Earth's Temperature

Greenhouses are used to grow plants indoors. They have clear panels that let in light energy but prevent heat energy from escaping. The incoming light warms the inside of the greenhouse. The inside of the greenhouse then radiates the heat into the surroundings. Because the panels trap most of the heat inside, the temperature in a greenhouse increases, helping the plants inside grow. Like panels in a greenhouse, the atmosphere on Earth warms the planet by keeping heat energy close to Earth's surface. The natural heating of Earth's surface caused by certain gases in the atmosphere is called the **greenhouse effect**.

Figure 13.9 The clear panels of a greenhouse let sunlight in but prevent heat energy from escaping.

Solar radiation passes through the atmosphere and is absorbed by Earth's surface. As a result, the surface of Earth warms up and radiates heat back into the atmosphere. Some gases in the atmosphere, called **greenhouse gases**, absorb this heat and prevent it from escaping into space.

Water vapor, carbon dioxide, methane, and nitrous oxide are examples of greenhouse gases. They occur naturally in the atmosphere and moderate, or control, the balance between the energy received and the energy emitted by our planet. Because of the presence of greenhouse gases, Earth receives energy from two sources—the Sun and its own atmosphere. Without the greenhouse effect, the average temperature on Earth would be much colder and the planet would be covered with ice. Chapter 15 discusses the greenhouse effect in more detail.

Because greenhouse gases are involved in warming the planet, most scientists worry that an increase in greenhouse gases is contributing to a rise in global temperatures. This is known as **global warming**. Earth processes are able to continuously recycle the greenhouse gases that occur naturally between the land, ocean, and atmosphere. Data obtained from ice cores collected from many places around the world have shown that up until the Industrial Revolution, during the 1800s, the amount of greenhouse gases in air had remained constant over thousands of years. These ice cores contain a record of the amount of CO_2 in the atmosphere at the time the ice was formed. During the recent past, however, human activities have upset this natural balance. Chapter 15 will discuss human impacts on global warming in more detail.

Extend It!

During the Industrial Revolution, so much coal was being burned to power the increasing number of machines that coal dust was everywhere.

Obtain an eyewitness account of these coal dust days by interviewing someone who may remember these conditions. Share their account with your class. If you can't find a live eyewitness account, use library or Internet resources to obtain one.

Figure 13.10 Scientists have discovered that the overall effect of clouds on Earth's radiation balance varies. It depends on how much of Earth they cover, how thick they are, and how high they are. While thick clouds cool Earth, they also act like greenhouse gases, blocking the escape of heat into space.

The Industrial Revolution began during the mid-1800s with the introduction of the steam engine. Major advances in technology and engineering allowed the manufacturing industry to increase the production of goods using machines instead of manual labor. Steam engines powered by burning coal, a fossil fuel, were used to drive the machinery. Steam engines were also adapted to power ships and locomotives, which started a revolution in transportation. For the first time in history, fossil fuels were burned on a large scale. As a result, the emissions of carbon dioxide into the atmosphere began to increase. Data collected worldwide show that the levels of carbon dioxide in air are still increasing today.

Earth's Radiation Balance   There is a balance between the solar radiation absorbed by Earth and the solar radiation sent back into space. The balance between incoming radiation from the Sun and outgoing heat is called the radiation balance. Over the course of one year, the amount of energy that Earth loses to space is approximately equal to the amount of energy it receives from the Sun. This ensures that our planet has a relatively stable climate. For Earth to remain livable, the amount of energy received from the Sun and the amount of heat energy returned to space must remain equal. As greenhouse gases, such as carbon dioxide, continue to increase in the atmosphere, more of the Sun's energy that was once released back into space could be trapped at Earth's surface. As a result, Earth's temperatures could continue to rise. This, in turn, could eventually affect Earth's radiation balance and negatively impact Earth's communities of living organisms, including humans.

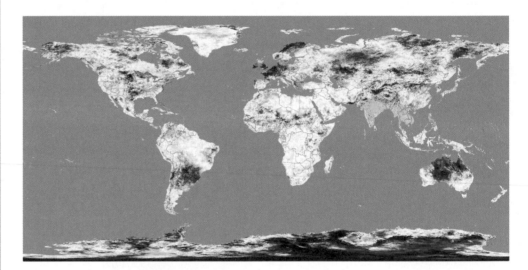

Figure 13.11 This map shows the difference between land surface temperatures from July 2006 compared to the average July land surface temperatures from 2000–2005. The dark red areas show that the 2006 surface temperatures were up to 10°C warmer than during the previous years.

After You Read

1. Explain how energy from the Sun reaches Earth.

2. How is heat transferred to your hands when you touch a bowl filled with warm water?

3. Refer to the completed concept map in your Science Notebook. Summarize how conduction and convection in the atmosphere are related.

4. Write a well-developed paragraph describing how greenhouse gases are related to Earth's radiation balance.

13.3 Air Pressure and Winds

Before You Read

In your Science Notebook, make a two-column chart. Label the first column *Cause* and the second column *Effect*. As you read the lesson, identify causes and effects of the topics you are learning about, and fill in the appropriate columns.

As discussed in Lesson 1, the horizontal motion of air is called wind. All winds are set in motion by differences in air pressure. Winds vary greatly from place to place and from moment to moment. At any given location, the direction from which wind blows, and its intensity, depends on both global climate patterns and local conditions.

What Causes Wind?

Energy from the Sun does not heat Earth evenly. Because of Earth's shape, tropical areas around the equator receive more of the Sun's energy than areas of equal size at the polar regions. As a result, areas near the equator are hotter than areas at higher latitudes. As shown in **Figure 13.12**, this creates an imbalance of energy between Earth's equator and its poles.

As the air over the tropics heats up, it becomes less dense and rises to the top of the troposphere. There, it spreads and moves toward the poles, transferring heat by convection. The rising air creates an area of low pressure at Earth's surface. At the poles, the cold dense air sinks, creating an area of high pressure. Once it reaches Earth's surface, this sinking, cold air spreads away from the poles toward the equator, moving from higher pressure to lower pressure areas. This sets in motion a circulation of air in the atmosphere. As shown in **Figure 13.12**, the circular patterns caused by the rising and sinking of air are called **convection cells**. This motion of air at Earth's surface creates global wind patterns.

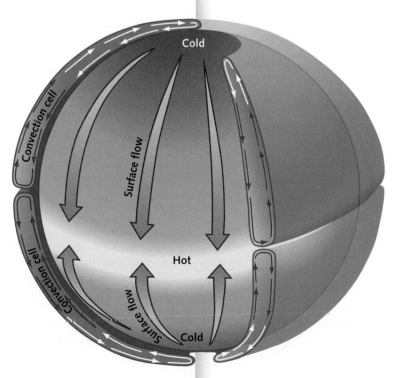

Figure 13.12 The tropics receive more solar radiation and heat up more than the poles. This sets in motion convection cells in each hemisphere that transport air from the equator to the poles and back.

Global Pressure Belts

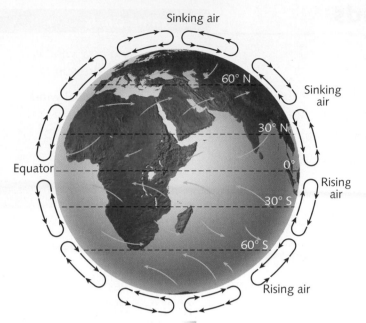

Figure 13.13 Uneven heating and the rotation of Earth create pressure belts that surround the globe. Air sinks and rises between these belts. They occur between the equator and 30° N and 30° S, between 30° N and 60° N and 30° S and 60° S, and between 60° N and the north pole and 60° S and the south pole.

Pressure Belts   Rising air at the tropics moves toward the poles, and transfers heat to higher latitudes. At the poles, cool air sinks and spreads toward the equator. Because of Earth's rotation, there are actually three convection cells in each hemisphere, as shown in **Figure 13.13**. The air moving toward the poles from the equator starts to sink and create belts of high pressure near 30° north latitude and 30° south latitude. From these high-pressure zones, the air splits. Some air returns toward the equator, and some moves toward the next belts of low pressure, located at 60° N and 60° S.

Coriolis Effect   Surface winds moving north or south are deflected by Earth's rotation. To understand how the rotation affects the wind, consider the following. A ball is thrown from the north pole toward the equator. If Earth was not rotating, the ball would travel in a straight line, as shown by the yellow arrow in **Figure 13.14**. Now, assume that from the time the ball is thrown until it reaches the equator, Earth has completed $\frac{1}{4}$ of its rotation. The spot on the equator that should have received the ball is now $\frac{1}{4}$ the way around as well. Thus, the ball lands in the spot that the red arrow is pointing to. This is also shown in **Figure 13.14**. It appears that the ball was thrown in a curved path, even though it was thrown straight.

The same thing happens to wind as it blows north and south. Even though it starts out blowing in a straight line, it ends up blowing along a curved path. Wind that is blowing northward is deflected to the left and wind that is blowing southward is deflected to the right. This deflection of the wind direction due to Earth's rotation is called the **Coriolis effect**.

The Coriolis Effect

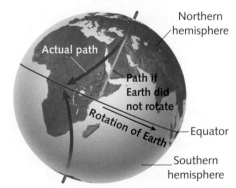

Figure 13.14 The rotation of Earth causes the Coriolis effect. If Earth did not rotate, air would move toward the equator along a relatively straight path, as indicated by the yellow arrow. The rotation of Earth, however, causes the direction of the wind to curve as it moves toward the poles or toward the equator, as indicated by the red arrows.

Global Wind Systems

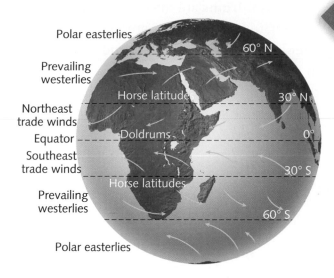

Figure 13.15 The pressure belts and the Coriolis effect act together to create the global wind systems. Each hemisphere has three global wind systems: trade winds, prevailing westerlies, and polar easterlies.

Polar easterlies
Prevailing westerlies
Horse latitude — 30° N
Northeast trade winds
Equator — Doldrums — 0°
Southeast trade winds
Horse latitudes — 30° S
Prevailing westerlies
60° S
Polar easterlies
60° N

Figure It Out

1. Explain how air pressure determines the direction in which winds blow near Earth's surface.

2. Most of the continental United States is located between the pressure belts at 30° and 60° north latitude. In which direction do you expect the prevailing winds to blow across the United States?

Types of Winds

Wind causes air to circulate. There are two main types of winds—global winds and local winds. Global winds move across Earth over long distances in a specific direction. In contrast, local winds can blow from any direction and travel much shorter distances. It is important to note that winds are named for the direction *from which* they blow. For example, a wind blowing from the west to the east is considered a westerly wind.

Trade Winds The **trade winds** are steady global winds that blow from the high pressure belts at 30° north latitude and 30° south latitude toward the low pressure belt located near the equator. As the air moves across Earth's surface, it is deflected by the Coriolis effect. As a result, these winds blow from the northeast to the southwest in the northern hemisphere and from the southeast to the northwest in the southern hemisphere. In the past, sailing vessels traveling from Europe to North America took advantage of the trade winds to cross the Atlantic Ocean.

Westerlies The **prevailing westerlies** are global wind belts that occur between 30° and 60° north latitude and between 30° and 60° south latitude. The westerlies blow toward the poles in a circulation pattern opposite that of the trade winds. In the past, the westerlies brought traders' sailing ships from North America back to Europe.

Polar Easterlies The **polar easterlies** are global wind belts that extend from 60° north latitude to the north pole and from 60° south latitude to the south pole. These winds blow from the high-pressure areas over the poles and are deflected westward by the Coriolis effect. Unlike the westerlies in the midlatitudes, polar easterlies are often weak and irregular.

As You Read

Uneven heating of Earth and the Coriolis effect are the main causes of global wind circulation. As you read this lesson, fill in your cause-and-effect chart with details of how the Coriolis effect influences winds.

How does the Coriolis effect affect wind movement?

The Doldrums and Horse Latitudes

The **doldrums** are the belt of low pressure circling the globe around the equator. Winds in this area are generally weak because air is rising after being heated by the Sun and there is no wind blowing horizontally to fill the sails. The word *doldrums* comes from an Old English word that means "foolish." It is believed that sailors felt foolish when their ships became stranded in this area of weak winds and therefore gave it the name *doldrums*.

The **horse latitudes** are the belt of high pressure located at 30° north latitude and 30° south latitude. The horse latitudes also circle the globe. Winds are weak in the horse latitudes because cool air is sinking and there is no horizontal wind. The lack of wind stranded sailors in these areas, too.

Figure 13.16 Sailing ships need wind to move. Sailors take advantage of the prevailing global winds when sailing long distances.

Jet Streams

In addition to winds at Earth's surface, there are also air circulation patterns higher up in the atmosphere. Narrow bands of fast, high-altitude, westerly winds called **jet streams** blow in the upper troposphere and in the lower stratosphere. Jet streams form at the boundaries between cold and warm air masses. The larger the difference in temperature between the air masses, the stronger the jet stream. The strongest jet stream, the polar jet stream, separates the polar easterlies from the prevailing westerlies. Winds in the jet stream can blow up to 185 km per hour. Unlike other global winds, the jet streams do not follow well-defined paths around Earth. Because jet streams often control the movements of storms, it is helpful for meteorologists to know their locations. Airplane pilots can save time and fuel by flying in the direction of a jet stream.

Local Winds

Local wind patterns are influenced by geography. The presence of large bodies of water, or changes in elevation, can result in uneven heating of Earth's surface. This creates high-pressure and low-pressure areas that produce wind.

Sea and Land Breezes Sea breezes are winds that blow from the ocean toward land during the day. Land breezes are winds that blow from the land to the ocean at night. Sea breezes and land breezes are common in coastal areas and near large lakes. Like other winds, these breezes are the result of uneven heating of Earth's surface. During the day, the Sun heats the land faster than it heats the ocean. The warm air over land rises, creating an area of low pressure. Air moves in from the higher pressure area over the cooler ocean. During the night, the land cools faster than the ocean. The air rises over the warmer ocean creating an area of low pressure, so winds blow from the land toward the ocean.

Mountain and Valley Breezes   Mountain and valley breezes result from uneven heating of Earth's surface due to changes in elevation. During the day, the top of a mountain heats up faster than the valley below. As air rises from the top and slopes of the mountain, it draws in air from the cooler valley. This is called a **valley breeze**. When the valley heats up later in the day, it radiates heat, causing the air above it to rise. The air rising from the valley draws in cooler air from the slopes of the mountain. This is called a **mountain breeze**.

CONNECTION: Geography

Before the magnetic compass existed, the wind rose played an important role in the navigation of sailing ships. Wind roses were diagrams that displayed the direction of prevailing winds at a given location over a period of time. The most common wind rose plot was made up of a circular graphic with eight or 16 lines, one for each compass point, extending from its center. The length of each line was based on the wind frequency from that direction over a period of time. The longest lines corresponded to the most frequent wind directions. These diagrams became known as wind roses because they resembled the petals of a flower.

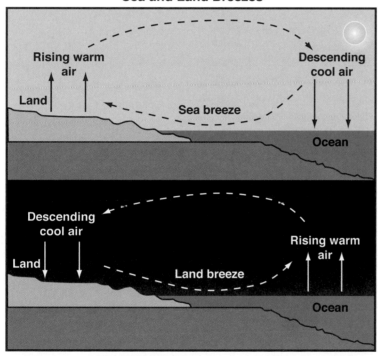

Sea and Land Breezes

Figure 13.17 Sea and land breezes result from uneven heating of land and water. During the day, warm air over the land creates an area of low pressure. Cooler air over the water moves toward the land, producing a sea breeze. At night, air over the water is warmer and creates an area of low pressure. Cooler air from the land moves toward the water, producing a land breeze.

After You Read

1. What causes winds?

2. What causes sea breezes?

3. Review the cause-and-effect chart you completed in your Science Notebook. Explain what causes the doldrums pressure belt at the equator.

Summary

KEY CONCEPTS

13.1 Characteristics of the Atmosphere

- Earth's atmosphere is made up of gases. It is 78 percent nitrogen, 21 percent oxygen, and one percent argon and other gases.

- The atmosphere has mass and is pulled toward Earth by gravity. The number of molecules of gas decreases as altitude increases, resulting in a drop in air pressure.

- The lower levels of the atmosphere receive heat primarily from Earth's surface. This is why air temperature is higher at Earth's surface. It decreases with altitude. Farther up in the atmosphere, air temperature alternates between warmer and colder conditions.

- Earth's atmosphere is made up of five main layers. From Earth's surface to the top layer, they are the troposphere, the stratosphere, the mesosphere, the thermosphere, and the exosphere.

13.2 Heat and Earth's Atmosphere

- Some of the radiation from the Sun that reaches Earth is reflected back into space, some is absorbed by the atmosphere and clouds, and some is absorbed by Earth's surface.

- Earth's surface absorbs radiation and gives off heat as it warms. Air that comes in contact with Earth's surface absorbs heat through conduction. As the air warms, it rises, transferring heat by convection.

- Certain gases in the atmosphere absorb heat and slowly release it back into the atmosphere. The atmospheric warming from these gases is called the greenhouse effect. As these gases increase in the atmosphere, the greenhouse effect intensifies and leads to global warming. For Earth to remain livable, the amount of energy received from the Sun and the amount of heat energy returned to space must remain equal.

13.3 Air Pressure and Winds

- Air on Earth's surface moves from areas of high pressure to areas of low pressure, creating wind.

- The prevailing global winds occur in belts at specific latitudes around the globe. The trade winds are on either side of the equator and blow toward the equator. The prevailing westerlies blow toward the poles. The polar easterlies blow from the poles toward the equator.

- Local winds are caused by the uneven heating and cooling that takes place between land and ocean or between the peaks and valleys of mountains.

VOCABULARY REVIEW

Write each term in a complete sentence or write a paragraph relating several terms.

13.1
atmosphere, p. 230
wind, p. 230
air pressure, p. 231
barometer, p. 231
troposphere, p. 233
lapse rate, p. 233
tropopause, p. 233
stratosphere, p. 234
ozone, p. 234
mesosphere, p. 235
thermosphere, p. 235
ionosphere, p. 235
exosphere, p. 235

13.2
radiation, p. 236
conduction, p. 237
convection, p. 237
greenhouse effect, p. 238
greenhouse gases, p. 239
global warming, p. 239

13.3
convection cell, p. 241
Coriolis effect, p. 242
trade wind, p. 243
prevailing westerlies, p. 243
polar easterlies, p. 243
doldrums, p. 244
horse latitudes, p. 244
jet stream, p. 244
valley breeze, p. 245
mountain breeze, p. 245

PREPARE FOR CHAPTER TEST

To prepare for the chapter test, create a question from each Learning Goal. Use the information in your Science Notebook to answer each question. Then use these answers to write a well-developed essay about the chapter. Use the Key Concept on the first page of this chapter as your topic sentence.

MASTERING CONCEPTS

True or False
If the statement is true, write "true." If it is false, change the underlined word or words to make the statement true.

1. <u>Oxygen</u> is the most abundant gas in air.
2. The ozone layer is in the <u>stratosphere</u>.
3. Rising air currents transfer heat by <u>conduction</u>.
4. <u>Local winds</u> can blow from any direction and travel much shorter distances than <u>global winds</u>.
5. Surface winds flow from areas of <u>low pressure</u> toward areas of <u>high pressure</u>.
6. The <u>trade winds</u> help sailing vessels travel from Europe to North America.

Short Answer
Answer each of the following in a sentence or brief paragraph.

7. Describe why air pressure changes as altitude increases.
8. Explain why temperature increases with elevation in the stratosphere.
9. Describe the greenhouse effect.
10. Explain how wind results from the Sun's uneven heating of Earth's surface.
11. Explain how the Coriolis effect influences the direction of wind.

Critical Thinking
Use what you have learned in this chapter to answer each of the following.

12. **Predict** If there were no ozone, how would temperature change with elevation in the stratosphere?
13. **Infer** Could heat be exchanged by convection in empty space?
14. **Apply Concepts** Why are jet streams able to blow at such high speeds?
15. **Infer** During which part of a round-trip flight across the United States—Connecticut to California and back—would an airplane pilot fly with the jet stream in order to move faster?

Standardized Test Question
Choose the letter of the response that correctly answers the question.

16. Which of the following graphs shows how air pressure changes in the atmosphere?

A.
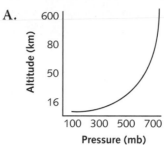

B.
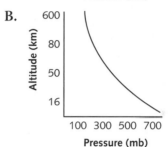

C.
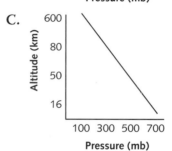

D.
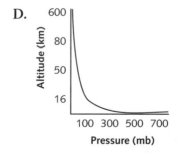

Test-Taking Tip

If more than one choice for a multiple-choice question seems correct, ask yourself if each choice completely answers the question. If a choice is only partially true, it is probably not the correct answer.

Chapter 14

Weather

KEY CONCEPT An understanding of the factors that affect the conditions of the atmosphere helps in predicting weather.

You are ready to go to school, but are surprised when you walk outside. You did not expect it to be raining. Later in the day, it is colder outside than you expected. Snow starts to fall, but you don't have your coat with you. You might have been better prepared if you had looked at a weather forecast. Daily weather forecasts can be found on television, on the radio, in newspapers, and on the Internet.

Sometimes weather forecasts are accurate, and at other times they are not. Weather forecasters make predictions about short-term conditions and changes in the state of the atmosphere. They use this information to predict how these changes might impact our daily lives.

Think About Being Prepared

The weather affects what you wear and what you do outside. Whether it is raining, snowing, sunny, or cloudy, knowing what to expect helps you prepare.

- How do the conditions outside affect what you wear?
- Write a short paragraph in your Science Notebook about a time that you were unprepared for the weather.

www.scilinks.org

Weather **Code: WGES14**

14.1 Water in the Atmosphere

Learning Goals

- Explain the movement of water through the water cycle.
- Compare and contrast humidity and relative humidity.
- Describe the basic cloud types.
- Describe the major types of precipitation.

Before You Read

In your Science Notebook, create a vocabulary map showing the relationships among the lesson title and the vocabulary terms in the lesson. Start by writing the lesson title in the center of the page. While reading the lesson, add each new term to the map and draw arrows to show how it relates to the main topic of the lesson. Also draw arrows between the vocabulary terms to show how they relate to each other.

Water is all around us. We drink water. We see water in lakes, rivers, the ocean, and as rain. Solid water exists as snow and ice. About 97 percent of the water on Earth is in the oceans. The remaining three percent is freshwater. About two-thirds of the freshwater on Earth is frozen in ice caps at the poles. The remaining freshwater is in rivers, lakes, and underground.

Water exists in the air as a solid, liquid, or gas. Solid water exists as snow and sleet. Liquid water exists in clouds as water droplets. Water also exists as a gas in the form of water vapor. At any one time, only a small percentage of Earth's freshwater is present in the atmosphere. This small percentage of water vapor, however, greatly affects Earth's weather. **Weather** is the condition of the atmosphere at a particular place and time. **Meteorology** is the study of atmospheric objects, such as clouds, raindrops, snowflakes, and fog. It also includes the study of events that include thunder and thunderstorms, lightning, and tornadoes.

New Vocabulary

weather
meteorology
water cycle
evaporation
condensation
precipitation
humidity
saturated
relative humidity
dew point
cloud

Recall Vocabulary

wind, p. 230

Figure 14.1 The ability of meteorologists to understand and predict changes in weather helps us plan our days and prepare for dangerous storms.

The Water Cycle

Water is constantly moving between Earth's surface and the atmosphere. This continuous movement of water is called the **water cycle**. **Figure 14.2** shows how water moves through the water cycle.

The energy that drives the water cycle comes from the Sun. Radiation from the Sun heats up the surface of the water and causes evaporation. **Evaporation** is the process of water changing from a liquid to a gas. Because Earth's oceans are so large, they provide the greatest source of evaporating water. Lakes and rivers also add water vapor to the atmosphere through evaporation. As water vapor rises in the atmosphere, it begins to cool and changes back into liquid water. This process is called **condensation**. When water vapor condenses into water droplets in the atmosphere, it forms clouds.

Eventually, these water droplets combine to form larger drops. These larger drops become too heavy to stay in the clouds and eventually fall back to Earth as precipitation. **Precipitation** is any solid or liquid form of water that falls from clouds. It includes rain, snow, sleet, and hail. The water from precipitation soaks into the ground and makes its way into rivers, lakes, and oceans. Some precipitation falls directly into bodies of water. Eventually, the precipitation that has returned to Earth's surface evaporates and the water cycle continues.

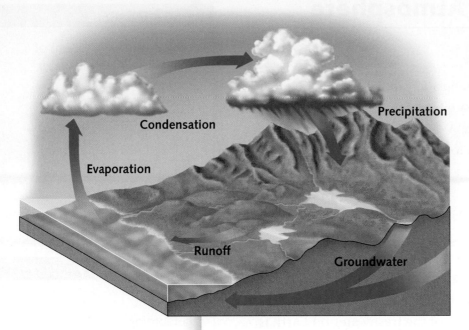

Figure 14.2 Water moves from Earth's surface to the atmosphere and back to Earth's surface in the water cycle.

Humidity

Air in Earth's lower atmosphere always contains some amount of water vapor. Even though water vapor in the atmosphere cannot be seen, it can be measured. **Humidity** refers to the amount of water vapor present in the air.

As water evaporates into the air, the air's humidity increases. The ability of air to hold water vapor is related to its temperature. As shown in **Figure 14.3**, warmer air can hold more water vapor than cooler air.

Relative Humidity When air contains the maximum amount of water vapor it can hold, the air is said to be **saturated**. Usually, the amount of water vapor in the air is less than the maximum amount of water vapor the air can hold. **Relative humidity** is the ratio of the amount of water vapor in a specific amount of air compared to the maximum amount of water vapor that amount of air can hold. Relative humidity is expressed as a percentage. A relative humidity of 100 percent means that the air is saturated with water vapor. A relative humidity of 50 percent means the air contains half the amount of water vapor it can hold. Because warm air can hold more water vapor than cold air, relative humidity changes with temperature.

For example, the temperature in Florida is warm and often hot for much of the year. Sometimes the air in Florida feels humid and sticky. This is because much of Florida is close to the ocean and there is a lot of water vapor in the air. The relative humidity in Florida, therefore, is often high. Inland states, such as Nevada and Arizona, are also hot for much of the year, but the air seldom feels sticky. This is because there are no large bodies of water nearby. As a result, there is little water vapor in the air. The relative humidity in these states is usually low.

As You Read

Continue adding terms to your vocabulary map. Make sure to connect terms to each other when possible. On the lines that connect the terms, explain how the terms are related.

What is the relative humidity of saturated air? Explain your answer.

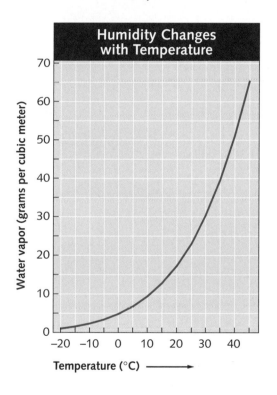

Figure 14.3 The maximum amount of water vapor that air can hold is determined by the air temperature. This graph shows that as air temperature increases, the maximum amount of water vapor in the air increases as well.

Figure It Out

1. Using the graph, determine how much water vapor a cubic meter of air can hold at 30°C.

2. How much water vapor can the same volume of air hold at 40°C?

3. Why do you think the values in questions 1 and 2 differ?

Cloud Formation

Clouds form when warm, moist air rises into the atmosphere and cools. Eventually, the air cools to a temperature at which it is completely saturated. This temperature is known as the **dew point**. When the air reaches its dew point, the water vapor in it condenses around small particles in the atmosphere, such as dust or sea salt, and forms tiny water droplets or ice particles. A **cloud** is a collection of millions of these tiny water droplets or ice particles.

Types of Clouds

Figure 14.4 shows the modern system of cloud classification. Clouds are grouped according to the altitude at which they form and by their different shapes. The typical shapes of nimbus, stratus, cumulus, and cirrus clouds are described below. For example, a cloud might be called a stratocumulus. This is a low-altitude, layered cumulus cloud that spreads out horizontally.

Figure 14.4 Clouds are grouped as being either low, high, or middle. The prefix or suffix indicates a cloud's shape.

Cloud Classification

Height		Shape	
Prefix		**Prefix or Suffix**	
Cirro Describes high clouds with bases starting above 6,000 m.		**Cirrus** Latin meaning: "hair." Describes wispy, stringy clouds.	
Alto Describes middle clouds with bases between 2,000 m to 6,000 m.	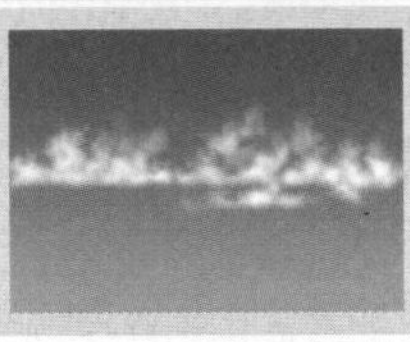	**Cumulus** Latin meaning: "pile or heap." Describes puffy, lumpy-looking clouds.	
Strato Refers to low clouds below 2,000 m.		**Stratus** Latin meaning: "layer." Describes featureless sheets of clouds.	
		Nimbus Latin meaning: "cloud." Describes low, gray rain clouds.	

As shown in **Figure 14.5**, cirrus clouds are thin, feathery, white clouds that form at high altitudes. They are made up of ice crystals and form when the wind is strong. Cumulus clouds are usually puffy and white with flat bottoms. These clouds usually indicate fair weather. If the air that makes up a cumulus cloud is unstable, the cloud can grow through middle altitudes into a towering cumulonimbus cloud. The suffix -*nimbus* or the prefix *nimbo-* in a cloud's name indicates that precipitation might fall from the cloud. Cumulonimbus clouds can produce thunderstorms with heavy rain and strong winds. Stratus clouds are layered clouds that form at lower altitudes as fog lifts away from Earth's surface. They usually cover large areas of the sky, blocking out the Sun. Nimbostratus clouds are dark stratus clouds that usually produce light to heavy continuous rain.

Explore It!

Fill a glass with water and place several ice cubes in it. Observe the glass. In your Science Notebook, explain why water droplets form on the outside of the glass.

Figure 14.5
Clouds form in different shapes and at different heights.

(Labels in figure: (km) scale from 0 to 13; Cirrus; Cirrostratus; Freezing level, above which clouds consist of ice crystals; Cirrocumulus; Cumulonimbus; Altocumulus; Altostratus; Nimbus; Cumulus; Stratocumulus; Stratus; Nimbostratus)

Precipitation

Water vapor that has condensed in the atmosphere might fall as precipitation. Precipitation includes all forms of water that fall from the clouds. The four types of precipitation are rain, snow, sleet, and hail.

Rain is liquid water that forms from clouds. Snow forms when water vapor in clouds changes directly into a solid due to low temperatures. Snow can fall as individual ice crystals or as combined ice crystals that make up snowflakes. Sleet forms as rain falls through a layer of freezing air, producing falling ice. Hail consists of balls of ice. It usually forms in cumulonimbus clouds as warm updrafts of air carry raindrops upward, where they freeze. As the frozen raindrops fall again, they combine with water and the ball of ice grows. Eventually, the hail becomes heavy enough to fall to Earth's surface.

CONNECTION: Language Arts

Clouds have inspired many works of literature and poetry. The English Romantic poet Percy Bysshe Shelley (1792–1822) wrote a poem entitled "The Cloud," using a literary technique called personification. Use library resources or the Internet to learn the meaning of this term. If you wish, write your own cloud poem using personification.

After You Read

1. What term describes rain, sleet, hail, and snow?
2. Describe the relationship between evaporation and condensation.
3. In the morning, the grass might be wet from dew. Use the information in your vocabulary map to write a well-developed paragraph explaining why dew forms.

Learning Goals

- Explain how and where air masses form.
- Describe the major types of air masses that influence weather in North America.
- Describe the four major types of fronts.
- Relate fronts to weather changes.

New Vocabulary

air mass
air mass modification
front

14.2 Weather Patterns

Before You Read

Preview the lesson by looking at the photos and figures and reading the headings and the Learning Goals. In your Science Notebook, write a bulleted list of what you think the lesson will be about.

Changes in weather are caused by the movements and interactions of air masses. An **air mass** is a large body of air that takes on the characteristics of the area over which it forms. Air masses form when air remains over the same area, or source region, for days or weeks. During this period, the temperature and humidity of the air mass become similar to that of the source region. For example, an air mass that develops over the Gulf of Mexico will likely be warm and wet. This is because the Gulf area is warm and has a lot of water evaporating into the air.

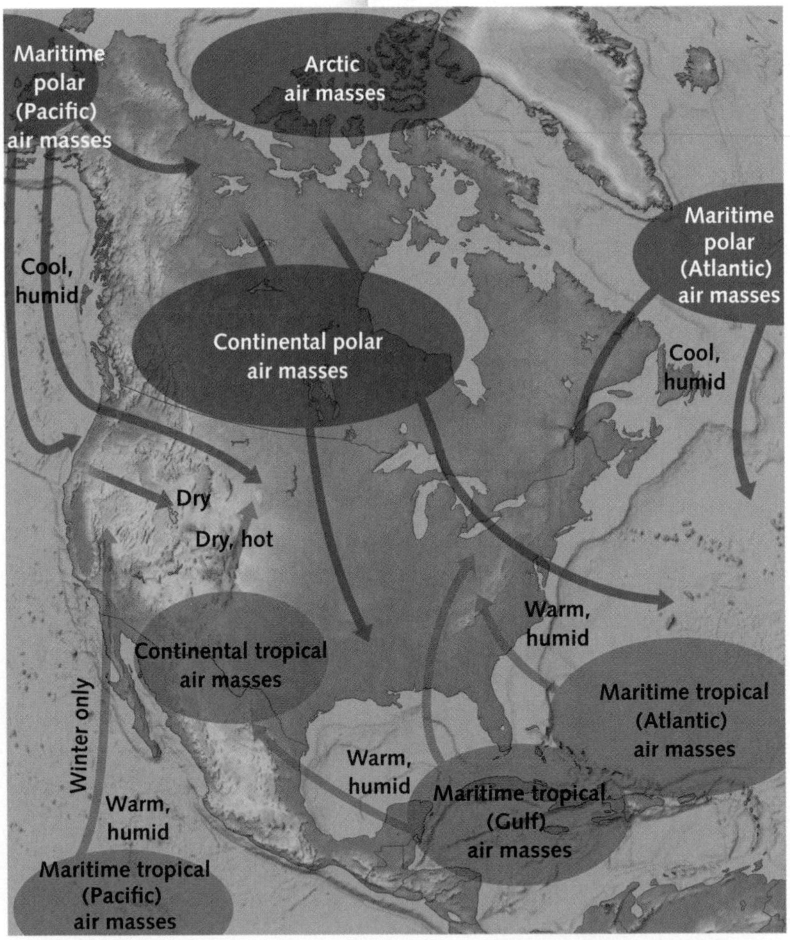

Figure 14.6 These major air masses affect the weather across the United States.

Types of Air Masses

Air masses are classified according to their source regions. **Figure 14.6** shows the main types of air masses. The characteristics of these air masses can be represented on maps with a two-letter symbol. The first letter of each symbol indicates the moisture characteristics of the air mass. Maritime air masses (m) form over water and are wet. Continental air masses (c) form over land and are dry. The second letter of each symbol represents the temperature characteristics of the air mass. Polar air masses (P) form over the polar regions and are cold. Tropical air masses (T) form over the tropics and are warm. The five main types of air masses include the warm and dry continental tropical (cT), the warm and humid maritime tropical (mT), the cold and dry continental polar (cP), the cold and humid maritime polar (mP), and the arctic (A). Arctic air masses are similar to continental polar air masses but are much colder.

Cold Air Masses   The five main types of air masses shown in **Figure 14.6** are all present in North America. The cold winter weather in the United States is influenced by four polar air masses: arctic air masses, continental polar air masses, and two maritime polar air masses—one that forms over the Pacific, and one that forms over the Atlantic. Arctic air masses develop over latitudes above 60°N, in ice- and snow-covered regions including Siberia and the Arctic Basin. These air masses are responsible for the coldest temperatures of winter in North America. A continental polar air mass develops over land in northern Canada and Alaska. It brings cold weather to the United States in winter. During summer, it brings cool, dry, weather.

Figure 14.7 Arctic air masses bring cold weather deep into North America. Ice storms in the south, results of cold arctic air pushing south, can leave a coating of ice everywhere.

There is a maritime polar air mass that forms over the cold waters of the North Pacific Ocean. It is not as cold as the air mass that develops over Canada. It is, however, very wet. In the winter, this air mass brings snow and rain to the Pacific coast of the United States. It brings cool, foggy weather to the Pacific coast in the summer.

New England and eastern Canada are influenced by a maritime polar air mass that forms over the North Atlantic Ocean. It produces cold, cloudy weather with precipitation in the winter. During the summer, it brings cool, foggy weather.

Warm Air Masses   Four warm air masses influence the weather in the United States. They include three maritime tropical air masses and a continental tropical air mass. Maritime tropical air masses develop over tropical and subtropical oceans, such as the Gulf of Mexico and the Caribbean Sea in the Atlantic. These air masses move north, bringing hot and humid summer weather to the eastern two-thirds of the United States and Canada. They bring mild, cloudy weather to these areas in the winter. Another maritime tropical air mass also develops over warm areas in the North Pacific. A continental tropical air mass forms over the desert areas of the Southwest and Mexico. This air mass moves northeastward, bringing clear, dry, hot weather in the summer.

Movement of Air Masses

Air masses eventually move, transferring heat from one area to another. Their movement is part of the larger cycle of distributing Earth's heat energy throughout the atmosphere. As described in Chapter 13, this constant redistribution of heat in the atmosphere is what causes Earth's weather.

 Extend It!

Select one of the air masses from **Figure 14.6** and research how it affects weather in the United States. Record your findings in your Science Notebook. Be sure to describe which region of the United States the air mass affects, what weather it brings, and the time of year during which it typically occurs.

As an air mass moves, it begins to take on the characteristics of the new surface, or source region, that it travels over. This process of exchanging heat and moisture with the new surface is known as **air mass modification**. Eventually, an air mass will change enough to become part of the air over the new source region. **Figure 14.8** summarizes the characteristics of the main types of air masses before they begin to move and change.

Figure It Out

1. What are the characteristics of the air in a maritime polar (mP) air mass that forms over the North Pacific Ocean?

2. Describe how the moisture in a maritime tropical (mT) air mass that forms over the Gulf of Mexico would modify as it moved inland over the western coast of North America.

Air Mass Characteristics

Air Mass Type	Winter	Summer
A	bitter cold, dry	
cP	very cold, dry	cool, dry
cT	warm, dry	hot, dry
mP (Pacific)	mild, humid	mild, humid
mP (Atlantic)	cold, humid	cool, humid
mT (Pacific)	warm, humid	warm, humid
mT (Atlantic)	warm, humid	warm, humid

Figure 14.8 This table shows the characteristics of the main types of air masses before air mass modification.

As You Read

Write a summary in your Science Notebook explaining what this lesson is about. Describe how this lesson relates to the other lessons in the chapter. Was your prediction about the content of the lesson correct? Explain.

What is air mass modification?

Figure 14.9 Conditions that can lead to the development of tornadoes are affected by air masses. When three air masses—maritime tropical, continental tropical, and continental polar—come together, tornadoes are more likely to occur. The Midwest is the region of the United States where these air masses are most likely to meet.

Fronts

At Earth's middle latitudes, air masses with different characteristics sometimes meet. The boundary that forms between them is called a front. A **front** is a narrow region separating two air masses of different densities. Differences in temperature, pressure, and humidity cause these different densities. Fronts are usually associated with weather in the middle latitudes, where there are both warm and cold air masses. Fronts do not occur in the tropics because only warm air masses exist there. There are four different types of fronts: cold fronts, warm fronts, stationary fronts, and occluded fronts. The arrival of a front indicates a change in weather.

Cold Fronts   A cold front forms when a cold air mass meets and displaces, or moves, a warm air mass. Because the cold air is denser than the warm air, it moves under the warm air. This causes the warm air to rise steeply upward. As the warm air rises, it cools and condenses. Cold fronts can produce clouds, thunderstorms, heavy rain, or snow. Cooler weather usually follows a cold front because the warm air is pushed away from Earth's surface. A cold front and its representation on a weather map are shown in **Figure 14.10a**.

Warm Fronts   A warm front forms when a warm air mass meets and overrides a cold air mass. The warm less-dense air moves over the cold, denser air and gradually replaces it. The air ahead of a warm front develops a front boundary that is less steep than the boundary ahead of a cold front. Warm fronts usually bring extensive cloudiness and drizzly rain. After a warm front passes, weather conditions are generally warm and clear. A warm front and its representation on a weather map are shown in **Figure 14.10b**.

Explain It!

It's early spring and the weather in your area has been warm. A cold front is rapidly moving toward your area, however, and is expected to arrive the next day. In your Science Notebook, write a weather forecast for your local television or radio station. Explain what happens as a cold front meets a warm front and what changes in the weather are likely to occur as the cold front moves in.

Figure 14.10 a) On a weather map, a cold front is represented as a solid blue line with blue triangles pointing in the direction of the front's movement. **b)** A warm front is represented on a weather map as a solid red line with red semicircles pointing in the direction of the front's movement.

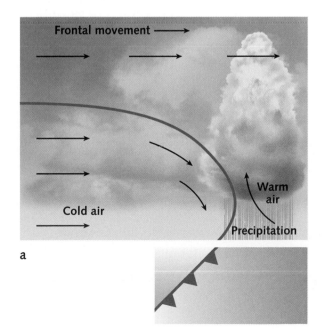

a

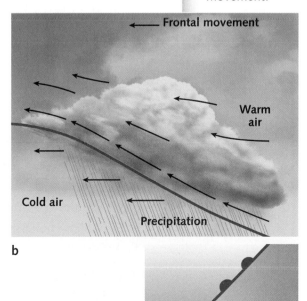

b

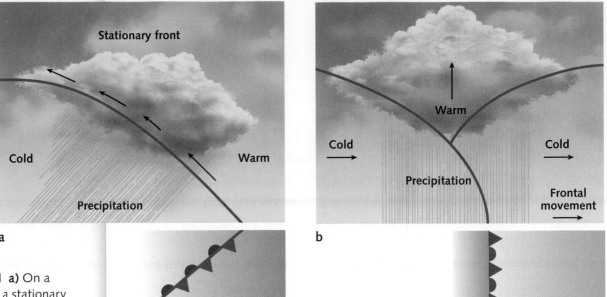

Figure 14.11 a) On a weather map, a stationary front is represented by a combination of short segments of cold- and warm-front symbols.
b) On a weather map, an occluded front is represented by a line with alternating purple triangles and semicircles that point toward the direction of the front's movement. Precipitation is common on both sides of an occluded front.

Stationary Fronts   Stationary fronts form when a cold air mass meets a warm air mass and neither air mass moves into the other's territory. When this occurs, the boundary between the air masses stays still. Stationary fronts usually form when there are only small differences in temperature and pressure between two air masses. The weather associated with a stationary front is similar to that produced by a warm front. A stationary front and its representation on a weather map are shown in **Figure 14.11a**.

Occluded Fronts   An occluded front forms when a faster-moving cold air mass overtakes a slower-moving warm air mass and forces the warm air upward. It is important to remember that a warm front involves warm air gliding over a cold air mass. As the warm air rises, this cold air mass collides with the cold front that is moving in. As a result, the warm air is squeezed upward between the two cold air masses. Occluded fronts produce cool temperatures and large amounts of precipitation. An occluded front and its representation on a weather map are shown in **Figure 14.11b**.

After You Read

1. How does the temperature and humidity of an air mass compare to that of its source region?

2. Review your notes about the figures in this lesson. Fill in any missing information. Then use your notes to explain what fronts are. Create a flowchart that identifies what causes fronts to form.

3. What kind of front forms when a cold air mass displaces a warm air mass?

14.3 Severe Weather

Before You Read
In Your Science Notebook, create a chart with three columns. Label the first *Thunderstorms*, the second *Tornadoes*, and the third *Hurricanes*. As you learn about these three kinds of severe weather, add information to your chart that describes their characteristics.

Learning Goals

- Describe the formation and characteristics of thunderstorms.
- Recognize the dangers of severe thunderstorms.
- Describe how tornadoes form.
- Describe the formation of hurricanes.

New Vocabulary

thunderstorm
lightning
thunder
tornado
hurricane
storm surge

Recall Vocabulary

air pressure, p. 231
Coriolis effect, p. 242

In the middle latitudes, weather changes from day to day as air masses shift and move. Sometimes storms develop along a front and bring severe weather that can result in damage to property and loss of human life. This lesson will discuss three major types of severe weather and how each forms. These types of severe weather are thunderstorms, tornadoes, and hurricanes.

Thunderstorms

Thunderstorms are small, intense, weather systems that produce heavy rain, strong winds, lightning, and thunder. As discussed earlier in this chapter, thunderstorms can occur along cold fronts. They can also develop when the air near Earth's surface is warm and moist at the same time that the atmosphere is unstable. The atmosphere is considered to be unstable when a rising air mass is warmer than the surrounding air. As long as the air in a rising air mass is warmer than the surrounding air, it will continue to rise.

The rapid rising of warm, moist air into an unstable atmosphere is what causes thunderstorms. When the rising warm air cools and reaches its dew point, the water vapor in the air condenses and forms cumulus clouds. In an extremely unstable atmosphere, these clouds may grow into towering cumulonimbus clouds. At the same time, the strengths of the storm's updrafts, or rising winds, and downdrafts, or descending winds, increase. The storm is then considered to be severe. Thunderstorms are capable of producing some of the most violent weather on Earth.

Figure 14.12
Cumulonimbus clouds, characteristic of many severe thunderstorms, can reach heights of more than 15 km.

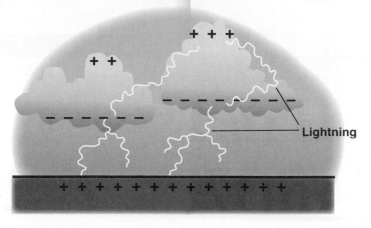

Figure 14.13 A lightning bolt can heat the air surrounding it to about 30,000°C. This temperature is about five times hotter than the surface temperature of the Sun!

As You Read

Review the chart in your Science Notebook. Explain your chart to a group of four students. Then work with a partner to add or correct information in your chart. Use what you have learned so far to describe the characteristics of thunderstorms in your Science Notebook.

What causes lightning?

Lightning Thunderstorms often produce lightning. **Lightning** is electricity caused by the rapid rush of air in a cumulonimbus cloud. The upper parts of clouds carry a positive electrical charge. The lower parts of clouds, however, carry a negative electrical charge. This negative charge at the bottom of a cloud attracts a positive charge on the ground below. As shown in **Figure 14.13**, when enough charge accumulates between these oppositely charged surfaces, lightning occurs. When lightning strikes, a tremendous amount of heat energy is released and transferred to the air. This causes the air to expand quickly and send out sound waves. **Thunder** is a loud rumbling sound that results from the rapid expansion of air along a lightning strike. Because sound waves travel more slowly than light waves, lightning may be visible well before thunder is heard. This is true even though both lightning and thunder are actually generated at the same time.

Severe Thunderstorms Severe thunderstorms may result in strong winds, hail, flooding, and tornadoes—all of which can cause damage to property and loss of human life. Hail associated with thunderstorms can cause great damage to crops, especially in the central United States. When rain from thunderstorms falls faster than the ground can absorb it, flooding may occur. Flooding is the main cause of thunderstorm-related deaths in the United States. Lightning strikes during thunderstorms are the cause of approximately 7,500 forest fires each year in the United States. These fires result in the loss of millions of acres of forest. Lightning strikes are also sometimes responsible for injuries and deaths.

Figure 14.14 Hailstones can grow large enough to cause significant damage. This car was damaged during a hailstorm.

Tornadoes

A **tornado** is a violent, rotating column of air that is in contact with the ground. Tornadoes occur in only one percent of all thunderstorms. The air in a tornado is visible due to the dust and debris it picks up and to the condensing water vapor in its rotating column of air. A tornado forms when the speed and direction of wind change suddenly with height. When the conditions are right, the air near Earth's surface may begin to rotate horizontally, as shown in **Figure 14.15a**. If this rotating cylinder of air is close enough to a thunderstorm's upward-moving winds, or updrafts, it might be tilted from a horizontal to a vertical position. Rising winds then speed up the rotation of the air column. As the rotation of the air column speeds up, air from its center is removed and the pressure in the center of the air column decreases. The difference in pressure between the center and outer portion of the tornado produces violent winds.

The average tornado has wind speeds between 120 and 180 km/h. Rarer, more violent, tornadoes have reached wind speeds up to 500 km/h. Few tornadoes are larger than 200 m in diameter, and most tornadoes last only a few minutes. They can, however, be extremely destructive. Tornadoes can occur at any time and at any location. Their paths are unpredictable. About 75 percent of the world's tornadoes occur in the United States. The majority of these tornadoes form in the spring and early summer when cold, dry air masses from Canada collide with warm, moist air from the Tropics. More than 700 tornadoes form each year in a region of the central United States known as Tornado Alley. This region extends from northern Texas through Oklahoma, Kansas, and Missouri.

Figure 14.15
a) A horizontal rotation in the lower atmosphere is created by a change in wind direction and speed.
b) Strong updrafts from a thunderstorm tilt the rotating air from a horizontal to a vertical position.
c) The rotating winds form a tornado.

a

b

Figure 14.16 A devastating tornado hit the town of Greensburg, Kansas, on May 9, 2007, with an estimated wind speed of 205 mph. **a)** This is an aerial view of Greensburg before the tornado hit. **b)** Damage from the tornado was severe.

Native Americans on the Great Plains lived with tornadoes and severe storms for thousands of years. Their holy men wrote about the spiritual aspects of storms they experienced, including tornadoes. Black Elk (1863–1950) was one such holy man. He was an Oglala Lakota who witnessed the end of traditional Lakota Sioux life on the Great Plains. In his book, *Black Elk Speaks*, he describes a religious vision he received in which he rode upon a tornado.

Tornado Classification The Fujita tornado intensity scale ranks tornadoes according to their path of destruction, wind speed, and duration. The scale ranks tornadoes from the F0 category to the F5 category. An F0 tornado has winds of up to 118 km/h, while an F5 tornado can have winds of more than 500 km/h. Only about one percent of tornadoes reach the violent F4 or F5 categories. These tornadoes can rip trees from the ground, lift buildings, and throw trucks into the air. Most tornadoes do not exceed the F1 category.

Tornado Safety In order to reduce tornado-related deaths each year, the National Weather Service issues tornado warnings before a tornado strikes. The presence of dark, greenish skies, large clouds, or a noise like that of a train during a thunderstorm can be signs of a tornado. Should any of these signs be present, seek shelter in an underground basement or interior room on the lowest floor of a building. Stay away from windows. If you are outdoors, lie flat in a nearby ditch or depression. Do not stay in your car or try to outrun a tornado with your car.

Hurricanes

Hurricanes are the most powerful storms on Earth. A **hurricane** is a large, rotating, low-pressure storm that forms over warm tropical waters. These storms have different names in different parts of the world. For example, hurricanes that form over the western Pacific Ocean are called typhoons, and hurricanes that form over the Indian Ocean are called tropical cyclones. Usually, hurricanes form between 5° and 20° north latitude and between 5° and 20° south latitude over warm, tropical oceans. The water at higher latitudes is too cold for hurricanes to form.

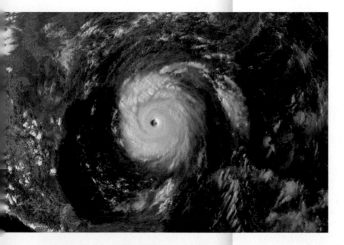

Figure 14.17 Notice the characteristic rotating nature of Hurricane Katrina in this satellite photo taken in August 2005.

Formation of Hurricanes Hurricanes need two conditions to form: a large supply of very warm ocean water and some sort of disturbance to lift warm air up and to keep it rising. Usually, a hurricane begins as a group of thunderstorms moving over tropical ocean waters. Unlike storms at midlatitudes that are caused by warm and cold air masses colliding, a hurricane gets its energy from warm, humid air over the tropical ocean. Winds traveling in different directions collide and cause an area of low pressure to form at the ocean's surface. Warm, humid air from the lower atmosphere is drawn toward this low-pressure center.

As a hurricane intensifies, more warm air moves toward the low-pressure center to replace the air that has risen. Heat energy is released into the atmosphere through the cooling and condensing of water vapor in rising air. This release of heat energy is what produces powerful

1. Would a hurricane originating in the Gulf of Mexico likely hit the west coast of Africa? Why or why not?
2. Explain why hurricanes in the northern hemisphere eventually travel northward, while hurricanes in the southern hemisphere eventually travel southward.

Hurricane Breeding Grounds

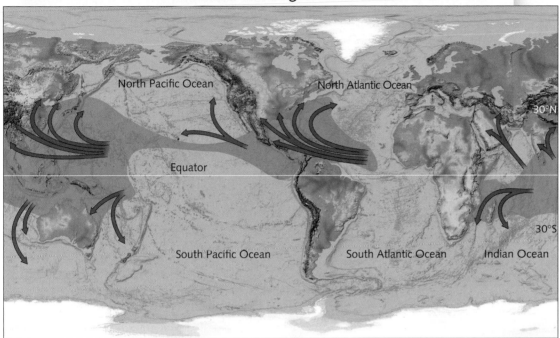

Figure 14.18 Hurricanes form in all of the tropical oceans on Earth except for the cooler waters of the South Atlantic and South Pacific Oceans. Hurricanes move according to the wind currents that steer them. In the deep Tropics, hurricanes often move steadily toward the west. They eventually turn toward the poles as they reach the edges of continents or areas of high-pressure systems. The movement of hurricanes is indicated by red arrows in the diagram.

hurricane winds. As warm air moves toward the low-pressure center of a growing hurricane, the Coriolis effect causes the storm to rotate. The storm rotates faster and increases in speed as more energy is released through condensation. In the northern hemisphere, hurricanes rotate in a counterclockwise direction. In the southern hemisphere, they rotate in a clockwise direction.

Once a hurricane forms, it continues to grow through contact with the warm ocean water. The hurricane will keep on growing as long as there is a source of warm air being fed into the system. When the hurricane moves over land or into colder waters, it loses its source of energy and dies down.

Did You Know?

Hurricane Katrina was classified as a Category 5 hurricane according to the Saffir-Simpson scale. In order to be classified as a Category 5 storm, a hurricane must have wind speeds greater than 250 km/h (155 mph), and cause storm surges, or waves of ocean water over land, greater than 6 m in height. Hurricane Katrina touched land on August 23, 2005 and caused great destruction along much of the north-central Gulf Coast of the United States.

Only a small percentage of tropical storms, also called disturbances, develop into true hurricanes. A tropical depression is a disturbance over a tropical ocean that rotates around a center of low pressure. A tropical depression is classified as a tropical storm when wind speeds around the low-pressure center are greater than 65 km/h. If air pressure continues to fall and winds around the center reach 120 km/h, the storm is classified as a hurricane. Hurricanes are classified using the Saffir-Simpson scale. This scale rates hurricanes from 1 to 5 based on their wind speed and storm surge heights. Hurricanes that are rated Category 3 or higher are most likely to cause property damage and loss of life.

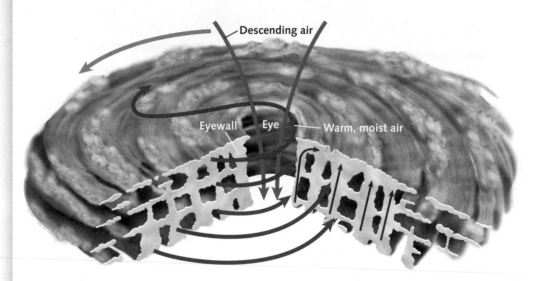

Figure 14.19 The rising moist air in this cross section of a hurricane is indicated by red arrows. It forms clouds in bands around the eye, or calm center, of the hurricane. The strongest hurricane winds occur in the eyewall of the storm.

Hurricane Damage   As hurricanes approach land, they can cause great damage. Most hurricane damage is caused by flooding due to heavy rains and storm surges. A **storm surge** occurs when hurricane winds drive ocean water toward coastal areas, where it washes over the land. Storm surges can reach up to six meters above normal sea level. Storm surges that occur during high tide can cause property damage and loss of life. Violent hurricane winds, reaching speeds as high as 300 km/h, may also cause great damage. They might destroy buildings and homes, and knock down trees and telephone poles. The National Hurricane Center issues warnings about incoming hurricanes. It also provides the public with information about the strength, position, and movement of storms.

After You Read

1. Explain the conditions that lead to severe thunderstorms.
2. What criteria does the Fujita tornado intensity scale use to rank tornadoes?
3. Review the chart in your Science Notebook. Add to the chart to describe the damage caused by hurricanes. Then write a well-developed paragraph that compares and contrasts thunderstorms, tornadoes, and hurricanes.

14.4 Predicting the Weather

Before You Read

In your Science Notebook, create a two-column chart titled *Predicting Weather*. Write *Collecting Data at Earth's Surface* above the left column and *Collecting Data in the Upper Atmosphere* above the right column. Write or draw any information that you predict you will learn about collecting weather data in the appropriate columns.

In order to predict the weather, meteorologists measure conditions both at Earth's surface and in the upper atmosphere. These atmospheric conditions include temperature, air pressure, wind speed and direction, and relative humidity.

Collecting Data at Earth's Surface

The most common weather instrument is the thermometer. A **thermometer** is a device used to measure temperature. Thermometers are usually sealed tubes that contain a liquid, such as alcohol or mercury, that expands when it is heated. The column of liquid in a thermometer rises as the temperature increases and falls as the temperature decreases. An instrument called a barometer is used to measure air pressure. Most barometers are made of a sealed glass tube containing mercury. As air pressure pushes on the mercury inside the tube, the mercury rises. A type of barometer called an aneroid barometer uses a vacuum inside a metal chamber to measure air pressure. The chamber expands or contracts as air pressure changes.

The speed of surface winds is measured with an instrument called an **anemometer**. An anemometer usually has cupped arms that catch the wind and spin as it blows. Instruments used to indicate wind direction include **wind vanes** and **wind socks**. The wind pushes the larger tail end of the wind vane, spinning it so that the narrower end points into the wind. A wind sock is a cone-shaped cloth bag with an opening at each end. The wind enters through the wide end of the bag and leaves through the narrow end. This causes the wide end to point into the wind.

a

c

b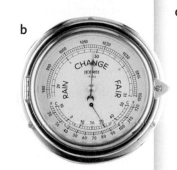

d

Figure 14.20 Instruments commonly used to collect weather data include **a)** the thermometer, **b)** the barometer, **c)** the anemometer, and **d)** the hygrometer.

An instrument called a **hygrometer**, shown in **Figure 14.20d**, uses wet- and dry-bulb thermometers to determine relative humidity. As water evaporates from the wet bulb, it cools and creates a temperature difference between the wet bulb and the dry bulb. The reading of this temperature difference is used along with a relative humidity chart to determine relative humidity.

In order to create an accurate understanding of weather, data from weather instruments must be gathered at the same time from many different locations. The United States National Weather Service operates a surface observation network to collect weather data from across the country. This network of sites collects weather data at intervals of about once per hour. Most of these data are collected by the Automated Surface Observing System (ASOS). The ASOS is made up of stand-alone devices located all over the country. These devices measure a variety of surface data including rainfall and the heights of cloud layers. They also estimate the amount of sky covered by clouds at a given location.

Figure 14.21 This automated weather system device is one of many around the country that measures surface data at regular intervals.

Figure 14.22 Weather balloons carry radiosondes into Earth's upper atmosphere to collect weather data.

Collecting Data in the Upper Atmosphere

In order to make accurate weather forecasts, meteorologists must gather atmospheric data from high in the troposphere. Studying weather at higher altitudes requires the use of more sophisticated technology. Weather balloons carrying a package of sensors called a **radiosonde** are used to gather data from up to 30,000 m above Earth's surface. The sensors on the radiosonde measure temperature, air pressure, and humidity. Radio signals send readings back to a ground station that tracks the location of the radiosonde. By tracking how fast the radiosonde is moving, meteorologists are able to gather data on wind speed and direction as well. The data collected is then plotted on a chart and used to forecast changes in the atmosphere that affect surface weather.

Weather Radar While surface observation sites and radiosondes provide a great deal of weather data, neither can pinpoint the location of falling rain at a given moment. Meteorologists must use radar to locate where rain is falling. A radar system uses a transmitter to generate waves in the form of energy. These waves leave the transmitter through antennae. The waves are programmed to bounce off of large raindrops. The radio waves are scattered as they bounce off the raindrops. The scattered waves are then picked up by other antennae, and data is sent to a computer where it is displayed on a screen. Meteorologists use the data to determine the distance from the raindrops to the location of the antennae that received the signals. The radar system rotates in a circle, allowing meteorologists to tell where rain is falling over an area with a diameter of about 400 km.

Doppler Radar The radar used by meteorologists to track precipitation is called Doppler radar. Doppler radar is based on the Doppler effect. The **Doppler effect** is the change in wave frequency that occurs in energy as it moves away from an observer. Many people experience the Doppler effect when a moving car blows its horn. The horn sounds like one note as the car approaches. When the car passes by, the sound of the horn shifts to a lower note. In reality, it is the same horn making the same sound the whole time. The change in the tone of the sound is caused by the Doppler effect.

The Doppler effect is used by meteorologists to plot the speed at which raindrops move away from or toward a radar station. Wind is what moves raindrops. By providing information about the speed that raindrops are moving, Doppler radar also provides information about the wind speeds moving the raindrops. This makes Doppler radar useful for measuring wind speeds associated with areas experiencing rain and severe weather.

As You Read

Review the information about collecting weather data that you predicted in your Science Notebook. Compare your chart to a partner's. Add information to your two-column chart as you finish reading the lesson.

What types of weather data does a radiosonde gather?

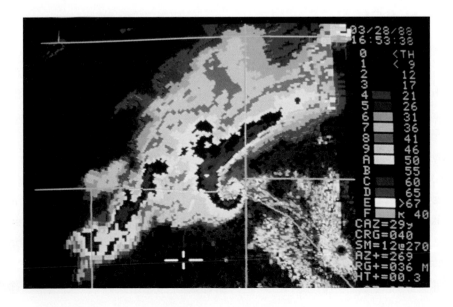

Figure 14.23 Doppler radar is based on the Doppler effect. The hook echo on this Doppler radar image from Norman, Oklahoma, indicates the possible formation of a tornado.

Figure 14.24
Meteorologists use infrared satellite images enhanced with colors to spot features of interest such as this hurricane. Clouds associated with strong storms reach great heights in the atmosphere.

Weather Satellites

Weather satellites orbiting Earth track the movement of clouds. Photos of Earth, taken at regular intervals by the satellites, are transmitted to ground stations. The data received is then plotted on maps. In order to make their forecasts, meteorologists often combine precipitation data obtained from weather radar with cloud data obtained by satellites.

While some satellites need visible light to take photos, others use infrared imagery. Infrared imagery does not require visible light. Instead it detects and uses differences in thermal, or heat, energy to map cloud cover and surface temperatures. Using infrared imagery, meteorologists can determine the temperatures of different clouds. As described earlier, different types of clouds form at different levels in the atmosphere. Information about a cloud's temperature therefore provides meteorologists with information about its height and type. Clouds that reach great heights are associated with strong storms.

Weather Maps

Meteorologists base their forecasts on weather data obtained from many sources. In the United States, the National Weather Service (NWS) produces weather maps based on data gathered from over 1,000 weather stations across the country. On these maps, each station is represented using a station model. A **station model** is a record of weather data for a particular site at a particular time. **Figure 14.25** shows the meteorological symbols used to represent weather in a station model.

To plot data over larger regions, meteorologists use lines called **isopleths** that connect points of equal value. Isopleths can represent

PEOPLE IN SCIENCE Ruth Aiken   1952–

When Ruth Aiken joined the National Weather Service (NWS) in 1975, there were few women in the field of weather forecasting. Today, Aiken is a Lead Forecaster for the NWS in Raleigh, North Carolina. She is also an active member of the National Weather Association. In her spare time, she speaks at schools, and encourages all students to study meteorology, science, and mathematics.

Aiken enjoys the challenge of North Carolina's diverse weather. The state's landscape sometimes allows snow and thunderstorms to occur at the same time! Aiken works with a team and uses Doppler radar to predict the paths of storms. Issuing severe weather warnings to the public is the most important part of her job. Aiken constantly strives to make faster, more accurate predictions about severe weather. She has earned several awards, including the NWS's Best All-Around Forecaster Award and a Technology All-Star Award.

different weather variables, such as pressure or temperature. Lines of equal temperature are called **isotherms**. Lines of equal pressure are called **isobars**. Meteorologists can tell a great deal about weather by looking closely at isobars or isotherms on a map. For example, isobars that appear close together indicate a large change in pressure over a small area. This could result in strong winds. Isobars also indicate the locations of high- and low-pressure systems, as shown in **Figure 14.26**. By using isobars, isotherms, and station model data, meteorologists are able to get a good idea of the weather conditions at a particular time and place.

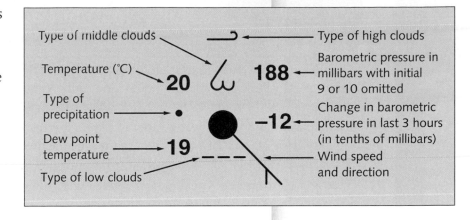

Figure 14.25 Weather data for a specific area at a specific time is shown in a station model such as the one above.

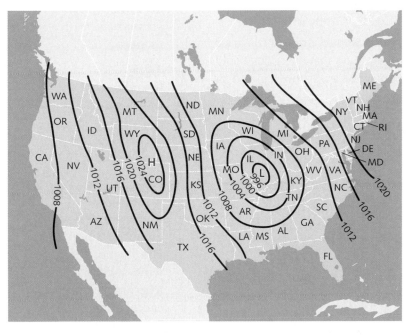

Figure 14.26 Air pressure data at a specific time in the United States is shown on this map. Pressure values are given in millibars (mb).

Figure It Out

1. According to the map, in what state is the air pressure the lowest? What is the air pressure at this location?

2. In which areas of the country would you expect the lightest winds, and why?

After You Read

1. What instrument is used to measure air pressure?

2. How do meteorologists track precipitation?

3. Review the information you included in the two-column chart in your Science Notebook. How do meteorologists use infrared imagery to predict storms?

KEY CONCEPTS

14.1 Water in the Atmosphere

- Water moves from Earth's surface to the atmosphere and back in the water cycle. Evaporation, condensation, and precipitation are processes in the water cycle.

- Humidity is the amount of water vapor in the air. Relative humidity is the amount of water vapor in the air compared to the maximum amount of water vapor that the air can hold.

- There are four basic types of clouds—cirrus clouds; cumulus clouds; nimbus clouds; and stratus clouds.

- Precipitation is liquid or solid water that occurs as rain, snow, sleet, or hail.

14.2 Weather Patterns

- Air masses form as a large area of uniform temperature and moisture. Maritime air masses form over oceans, continental air masses form over continents, polar air masses form over the poles, and tropical air masses form over the Tropics.

- A cold front is a cold air mass that wedges under a warm air mass. A warm front is a warm air mass that overrides a cold air mass. An occluded front occurs when a fast-moving cold air mass overtakes a slow-moving warm air mass. A stationary front occurs when two air masses stop moving.

- The arrival of a front indicates a change in weather.

14.3 Severe Weather

- The rapid rising of warm, moist air into an unstable atmosphere causes thunderstorms.

- Severe thunderstorms may result in strong winds, hail, flooding, and tornadoes.

- Tornadoes form when high-speed winds create a tight, circular rotation of air. A hurricane is a huge, rotating, low-pressure storm and produces high winds and heavy rain.

14.4 Predicting the Weather

- Instruments used to gather weather data include the thermometer, the barometer, the anemometer, and the hygrometer.

- Weather in the upper atmosphere is measured by using a weather balloon carrying an instrument called a radiosonde. A radiosonde measures temperature, humidity, and air pressure. Weather is also tracked using satellites orbiting Earth.

- Doppler radar is used to track precipitation.

- Weather map symbols help meteorologists describe the weather conditions at a particular time and place.

VOCABULARY REVIEW

Write each term in a complete sentence or write a paragraph relating several terms.

14.1
weather, p. 249
meteorology, p. 249
water cycle, p. 250
evaporation, p. 250
condensation, p. 250
precipitation, p. 250
humidity, p. 250
saturated, p. 250
relative humidity, p. 250
dew point, p. 251
cloud, p. 251

14.2
air mass, p. 254
air mass modification, p. 256
front, p. 257

14.3
thunderstorm, p. 259
lightning, p. 260
thunder, p. 260
tornado, p. 261
hurricane, p. 262
storm surge, p. 264

14.4
thermometer, p. 265
anemometer, p. 265
wind vane, p. 265
wind sock, p. 265
hygrometer, p. 266
radiosonde, p. 266
Doppler effect, p. 267
station model, p. 268
isopleth, p. 268
isotherm, p. 269
isobar, p. 269

True or False
If the statement is true, write "true." If it is false, change the underlined word or words to make the statement true.

1. Clouds form by <u>evaporation</u>.
2. <u>Maritime tropical</u> air masses are made up of warm, moist air.
3. <u>Stationary fronts</u> usually bring thunderstorms followed by cooler weather.
4. Hurricanes <u>lose strength</u> as they move slowly over warm water.
5. A wind vane indicates wind <u>direction</u>.
6. Isobars <u>separate</u> areas of uniform pressure.

Short Answer
Answer each of the following in a sentence or brief paragraph.

7. What happens to relative humidity when the temperature reaches the dew point?
8. Describe how clouds form.
9. Which type of front forms when a warm air mass overruns a cold air mass?
10. Describe the conditions needed for a hurricane to form in the Atlantic.
11. Describe how weather in the upper atmosphere is measured.

PREPARE FOR CHAPTER TEST

To prepare for the chapter test, create a question from each Learning Goal. Use the information in your Science Notebook to answer each question. Then use these answers to write a well-developed essay about the chapter. Use the Key Concept on the first page of this chapter as your topic sentence.

Critical Thinking
Use what you have learned in this chapter to answer each of the following.

12. **Predict** How can you predict the weather by looking at the clouds? Give at least one example.
13. **Apply Concepts** If the weather forecast indicated that a continental tropical air mass was moving in your direction, what type of weather would you expect?
14. **Infer** Why does a hurricane lose strength as it moves over land?
15. **Apply Concepts** Why would a weather forecaster look at weather data from the past several days before making a forecast for tomorrow?

Standardized Test Question
Choose the letter of the response that correctly answers the question.

16. What causes the most damage to property and lives during a hurricane?
    A. flooding
    B. lightning
    C. high winds
    D. tornadoes

> **Test-Taking Tip**
>
> Remember that qualifying words such as *only*, *always*, *all*, and *never* mean that the statement has **no** exceptions.

Chapter 15

Climate

KEY CONCEPT Climate describes the long-term weather patterns of an area and is influenced by many different factors.

Imagine that you live in northern Minnesota, and it is a cold, snowy day in January. You and your friends have just come back from ice-skating. You call your cousin who lives in Florida. She is going for a walk on the beach in the warm sunshine. Next, you call your aunt who lives in San Francisco. She tells you it is cold and rainy and that this is typical weather for January in northern California.

Why do places in the same country have such different weather patterns? This chapter explains the factors that determine an area's long-term weather patterns.

Think About Weather Patterns

If you could choose a state to live in based on your favorite weather patterns, where would you live?

- Examine a map of the United States and choose an area that has weather patterns you think you would enjoy.
- In your Science Notebook, describe the weather patterns of this area during each season of the year. Then explain why you would prefer living there.

www.scilinks.org

Climates of the World
Code: WGES15

15.1 What Is Climate?

Before You Read

In your Science Notebook, make a T-chart. Label one side of the chart *Weather* and the other side *Climate.* On the *Weather* side, write today's weather conditions in the area where you live. On the *Climate* side, describe your area's weather patterns during each season of the year.

Learning Goals

- Explain the difference between weather and climate.
- Identify the factors that determine climates.

New Vocabulary

climate
tropics
polar zone
temperate zone
elevation
windward
leeward
surface current
prevailing wind

Recall Vocabulary

weather, p. 249
precipitation, p. 250

What is the difference between weather and climate? Weather is the condition of the atmosphere at a specific time and place. Weather conditions can change from day to day. **Climate** describes the weather patterns of an area over a long period of time.

If you live in Chicago, Illinois, you might have some very hot weather in the summer. Does that mean that Chicago has a hot climate year-round? Definitely not. Winters in Chicago are usually cold and snowy. Climate is determined by factors that include latitude, topography, ocean currents, and prevailing winds.

Minimum Temperatures for January

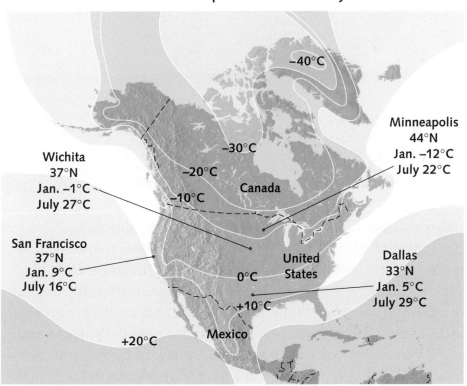

Figure 15.1 This map of North America shows the average minimum temperatures for the month of January. It also shows the average temperatures during January and July for four selected cities. The latitudes of the cities are also shown.

Latitude

Imaginary horizontal lines, called lines of latitude, circle the globe. Latitude is the distance north or south, measured in degrees, from the equator. Latitudes closer to the equator have higher average temperatures. Latitudes farther from the equator and closer to the poles have lower average temperatures.

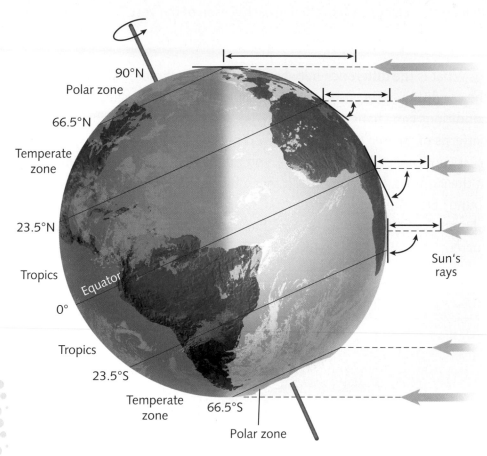

Figure 15.2 Latitude greatly affects climate. The Sun's rays are most intense at latitudes near the equator that receive them directly.

Why do areas at different latitudes on Earth have different temperatures? It is a result of the amount of solar radiation received by any one place on Earth. It varies because our planet is curved and tilted on its axis. As shown in **Figure 15.2**, solar radiation strikes the tropics most directly. The **tropics** is the area between 23.5° south of the equator and 23.5° north of the equator. Solar radiation strikes the **polar zones**, located from 66.5° north and south of the equator to the poles, at a low angle. The direct solar rays result in higher temperatures in the tropics, and the less-direct solar rays result in lower temperatures in the polar zones. The **temperate zones**, which lie between 23.5° and 66.5° north and south of the equator, have more moderate climates.

Topography

The topography, or physical features of a region, such as mountains or lakes, also affects climate. Water cools down and heats up more slowly than land. This is why areas near large bodies of water are generally warmer in winter and cooler in summer than areas farther from large bodies of water. The surface temperature of the water affects the temperature of the air directly above it. When this air blows over the land, it changes the temperature of that area. Temperatures are also affected by **elevation**, which is the distance of a location above sea level. Temperatures generally decrease at higher elevations. For this reason, mountain climates tend to be cooler than climates at sea level.

Climates on opposite sides of a mountain can also differ. As air rises up one side of a mountain, it cools. The water vapor it contains condenses to liquid and falls to the ground as rain or snow. As a result, the climate on this side of the mountain, called the **windward** side, is usually cool and moist. On the opposite side of the mountain, called the **leeward** side, this now dry air warms as it descends. The climate on the leeward side of a mountain is usually dry and desertlike.

Figure It Out

1. Which side of a mountain has a drier climate?
2. Why do most mountains get a lot of rain and snow?

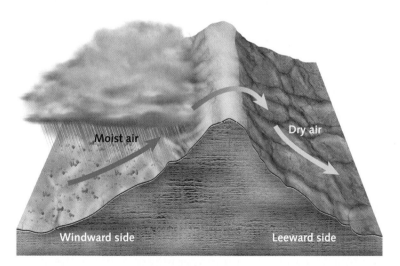

Figure 15.3 Moist air on the windward side of the mountain is forced to rise. Because cool air cannot hold as much moisture as warm air, the water vapor in the air condenses to liquid. The dry air then crosses over the mountain to the leeward side, sinks, and warms.

Ocean Currents

Surface currents are streamlike movements of warm or cold water that occur at or near the surface of the ocean. Because water has the ability to absorb and release heat, the circulation of ocean surface currents greatly affects an area's climate. Warm currents heat the air and cause warmer temperatures in nearby land areas. Cold currents cool the air and cause cooler temperatures on land.

Ocean currents coming from near the equator carry warm water. These warm currents heat the air above them and cause land areas near them to be warmer. For example, the Gulf Stream carries warm water north from the equator. It then passes Iceland, which is located just below the arctic circle. The warm water from the Gulf Stream heats the air above it, creating warmer temperatures in southern Iceland. Greenland, a country neighboring Iceland, is not influenced by the Gulf Stream and experiences much colder temperatures.

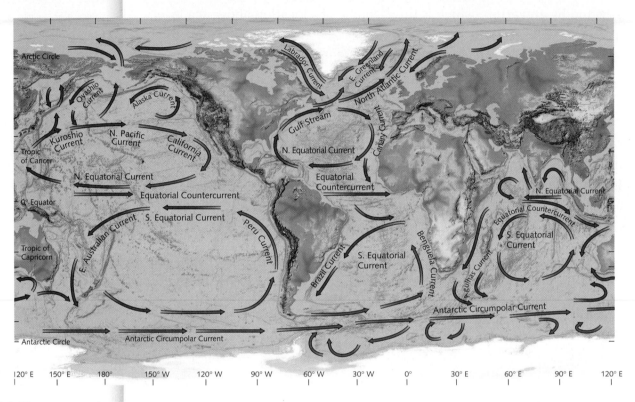

Figure 15.4 The movement of warm surface currents is represented by red arrows. The movement of cold surface currents is represented by blue arrows. This map shows the major ocean currents of the world.

Ocean currents coming from near the poles carry cold water, cool the air above them, and cause land areas near them to be cooler. For example, the California current is a Pacific Ocean current that moves south along the western coast of North America. The movement of cool northern waters southward makes the coastal waters of the western U.S. cooler than coastal areas at similar latitudes on the east coast of the United States.

Prevailing Winds

Prevailing winds are winds that blow primarily from one direction. Prevailing winds affect the temperature of an area and the amount of precipitation it receives. Warm air can hold more water vapor than cold air. If prevailing winds form from warm air, they will carry moisture. If they form from cold air, they will likely be dry. Winds blowing across land will be drier than winds that absorb moisture as they travel over water. As a result, warm winds that have traveled over water will likely bring rain. Similarly, cooler winds that travel over dry land will not.

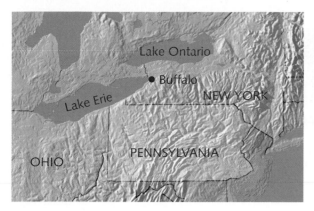

Figure 15.5 Buffalo, New York, is located on the eastern edge of Lake Erie and east of most of the Great Lakes. The city often gets huge winter snowstorms because of the moisture that blows in off the lakes. This is called lake-effect snow.

PHYSICS CONNECTION: Specific Heat

The specific heat of a substance is determined by the amount of heat, measured in calories, that is needed to raise the temperature of one gram of the substance by one degree Celsius. Water's specific heat is 1.00 cal/g C°, while air's specific heat is 0.25 cal/g C°. This means that water needs to absorb four times more heat from the atmosphere than air does in order to reach the same temperature. Knowing the specific heat of a substance has many practical applications. For example, it is important to understand the concept of specific heat when designing motors and large machinery because engine parts expand and contract when they are heated. If two metal parts with different specific heats are joined together, they will expand and contract at different rates. This could cause a metal joint to either fuse together or crack apart. Decreased efficiency, a fire, or even an explosion could result.

Table of Specific Heats	
Substance	Specific Heat (cal/g C°)
air	0.25
aluminum	0.22
copper	0.09
glass	0.20
water	1.00
wood	0.42

After You Read

1. Explain why areas at higher degrees of latitude tend to be colder.

2. How do ocean currents affect the temperatures of nearby land areas?

3. Review the T-chart you created in your Science Notebook. Choose one factor (other than latitude) that affects climate. In a well-developed paragraph, explain how this factor affects the climate where you live.

Figure 15.6 Koeppen's classification system is made up of six main climate divisions and 14 subdivisions.

Before You Read

Create a concept map in your Science Notebook. Write and circle the title *Earth's Climates*. Draw six circles around the title. Then draw lines connecting each circle to the title. Predict some of the types of climates that you will be writing in the circles.

There are many types of climates on Earth, but they can be divided and classified into major groups according to certain characteristics. The **Koeppen classification system** was developed by a German climatologist named Wladimir Koeppen. It uses temperature and precipitation to divide Earth's climates into six major types. These six climate types, along with their subtypes, are shown in **Figure 15.6**.

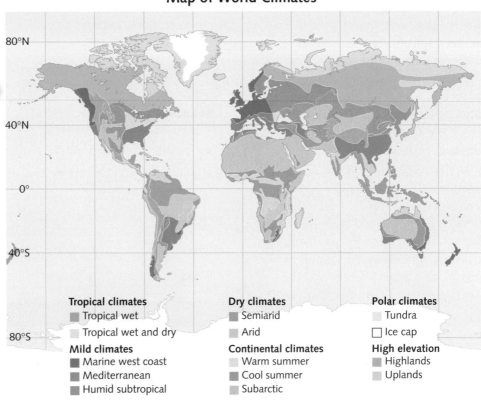

Map of World Climates

Tropical climates
- Tropical wet
- Tropical wet and dry

Mild climates
- Marine west coast
- Mediterranean
- Humid subtropical

Dry climates
- Semiarid
- Arid

Continental climates
- Warm summer
- Cool summer
- Subarctic

Polar climates
- Tundra
- Ice cap

High elevation
- Highlands
- Uplands

Tropical Climates

Tropical climates are characterized by high temperatures year-round. They receive strong sunlight all year because they are located close to the equator. Some tropical areas also receive large amounts of rainfall each year. Tropical rain forests occur in tropical climates with heavy rainfall. These forests are home to the largest variety of animal and plant species on Earth.

Refer to **Figure 15.6**. Areas called tropical wet zones receive rainfall year-round from moist air blowing in from the ocean. Areas that border tropical wet regions north and south of the equator are called tropical wet and dry zones. While these regions are warm year-round, they also have dry winter seasons caused by dry prevailing winds blowing in from large land areas. Tropical wet and dry zones contain large grasslands called savannas. **Savannas** are made up of tall grasses and scattered trees.

Figure 15.7 a) Savannas are home to giraffes, which tend to live in dry, open wooded areas. **b)** The vegetation is lush and dense in this wet tropical rain forest.

a

b

Dry Climates

Most of the world's deserts are classified as dry climates. These areas cover about 30 percent of Earth's land surface. Dry climates include both arid and semiarid regions. Arid regions include the world's driest deserts, such as the Sahara, shown in **Figure 15.8**. Many dry climates are located near the tropics in areas where dry, continental air dominates and there is very low rainfall and almost no vegetation. Semiarid regions, which are sometimes called **steppes**, are slightly more humid than arid regions. They receive a little more precipitation and tend to be located at higher latitudes than deserts.

Mild Climates

The Koeppen classification system divides mild climates into humid subtropical, marine west coast, and Mediterranean climates. The humid

subtropical climate experiences high humidity. Warm and moist maritime tropical air creates hot, humid, summers similar to those in the tropics. Winters are relatively mild. Most of the southeastern United States has this type of climate.

Figure 15.8 Some areas in the Sahara may get no rain for years at a time.

As You Read

Write the names of the six major climate types in each of the six circles on your concept map. Underneath each name, write two characteristics of that type of climate.

Why do tropical wet areas receive precipitation year-round while tropical wet and dry areas do not?

The marine west coast climate gets a constant flow of moist air from the ocean, which causes precipitation throughout the year. Because the ocean moderates these coast climates, they experience mild winters and cool summers. The Mediterranean climate is influenced by the Mediterranean Sea and its warm ocean currents. Areas with this climate experience warm, dry summers and wet, mild winters. Though it is named for the Mediterranean Sea, this climate occurs in other places, including the coast of central and southern California.

Continental Climates

Continental climates are generally located within the interior of most continents at midlatitudes. The types of continental climates are warm summer, cool summer, and subarctic climates. Continental climates are present in much of North America. These climate areas are influenced by polar air masses during the winter and by tropical air masses during the summer. As a result, they experience great swings in seasonal temperatures. The air masses from Earth's poles cause cold temperatures during the winter. Air masses from Earth's tropics cause warm temperatures, and often precipitation, during the summer. Strong storms and rapid changes in the weather occur when the polar and tropical air masses collide.

Figure 15.9 Moist, cool air and frequent precipitation help to sustain this temperate rain forest in the Pacific Northwest. This area has a marine west coast climate.

Polar Climates

The coldest regions on Earth have polar climates. These climates occur at high latitudes in both the northern and southern hemispheres. Temperatures in polar climates stay low year-round. The temperature of the warmest month is less than 10°C. Because cold air holds less moisture than warm air, polar climates have low levels of precipitation. The snow that does fall in these climates often does not melt. Areas at high elevations, where it is very cold, experience climates similar to polar climates.

Figure 15.10 Polar bears have thick fur coats and are well adapted to the polar climate.

Localized Climates

A **microclimate** is a small area with a climate that is different from the climate of the larger region that surrounds it. The top of a mountain is a microclimate because it is colder than the lower-elevation areas surrounding it. This is true even for areas at high elevations in tropical regions. This explains the presence of glaciers in the Andes mountain range in South America.

Cities can also be microclimates, where the temperature is a few degrees warmer than the surrounding rural areas. This difference in temperature occurs because buildings and pavement absorb solar radiation and radiate heat into the surrounding air. Temperatures are also higher in cities because there is less vegetation. Vegetation radiates less heat into the air than does concrete or asphalt. City areas that have warmer climates than surrounding rural areas are called **heat islands**.

Figure 15.11 The desert climate at the foot of the Andes mountain range in Chile contrasts sharply with the polar climate at higher elevations.

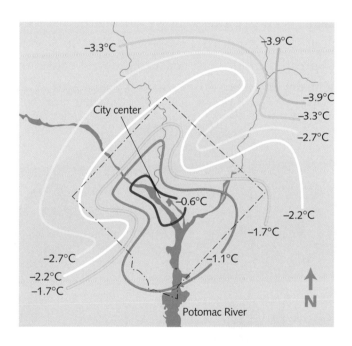

−3.3°C
−3.9°C
−3.9°C
−3.3°C
−2.7°C
City center
−0.6°C
−2.2°C
−1.7°C
−2.7°C
−1.1°C
−2.2°C
−1.7°C
N
Potomac River

Figure 15.12 This diagram shows winter temperatures in Washington, D.C. The buildings and paved surfaces of the city create a microclimate. The temperature in the center of the city is −0.6°C, nearly 3°C warmer than temperatures in some parts of the surrounding area.

Did You Know?

Have you ever seen the roof of a building with plants growing on it? These green roofs are becoming more common. Covering roofs with low-growing plants is one way to lower the average temperatures in cities. Planting trees and other vegetation along city streets is another way. This increased vegetation reduces the heat island effect.

After You Read

1. Explain the difference between arid and semiarid climates.

2. Review your concept map. Describe two characteristics of polar climates.

3. An area is in the midlatitudes, is not near an ocean, and has warm summers and cold winters. To which of the six main climate types does this area belong?

4. Why do cities often have microclimates that are warmer than surrounding rural areas?

Learning Goals

- Describe the different types of climatic changes.
- Identify the causes of climatic changes.

New Vocabulary

ice age
interglacial interval
season
El Niño
elliptical
sunspot

Before You Read

Reword each of the lesson's Learning Goals so that it forms a question. Write the questions in your Science Notebook. As you read, write the answers to the questions.

Long-Term Climatic Changes

Earth's climate generally does not change very much during a human lifetime. Earth's climate has changed many times, however, over the last 4.6 billion years. There have been a number of **ice ages** in Earth's history. During these periods, the average temperature on Earth was about 5°C lower, and large sheets of ice, called glaciers, covered much of our planet's surface.

Ice ages last for thousands of years, and the last one ended about 10,000 years ago. As **Figure 15.13** shows, during the last ice age, glaciers covered much of North America, Europe, and Asia. In North America, the ice sheets spread from the east coast to the west coast, and as far south as present-day Indiana.

Figure It Out

1. The areas of the map that appear in white represent land covered by ice during the last ice age. What do the areas of the map that appear in green, light blue, and darker blue represent?

2. Locate the continent of North America. If glaciers covered Earth today as they did during the last ice age, which country would be completely covered by ice?

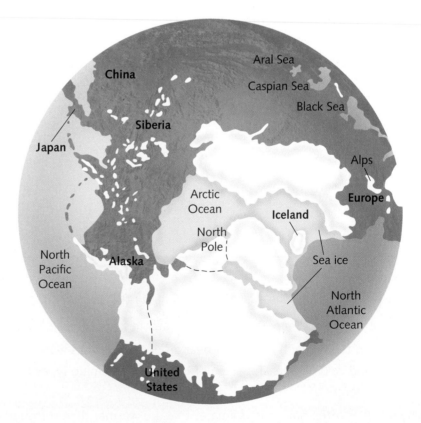

Figure 15.13 The ice sheets that covered much of North America, Europe, and Asia during the last ice age caused great changes in climate worldwide.

Research shows that ice ages have alternated with warmer periods called **interglacial intervals**. We are currently in an interglacial interval. What causes ice ages and other climatic changes? Scientists do not know all the answers. There are, however, a number of hypotheses that will be discussed in this lesson.

Seasons

Unlike ice ages, which last for thousands of years, **seasons** are short-term periods of climatic change. Earth's seasons are caused by regular variations in temperature, daylight, and weather patterns. As **Figure 15.14** shows, Earth is tilted on its axis. The tilt of Earth on its axis as it orbits the Sun causes different areas of our planet to receive different amounts of solar radiation.

When the north pole is tilted toward the Sun, it is summer in the northern hemisphere. This means that the northern part of Earth experiences stronger sunlight, more hours of daylight, and warmer temperatures than the southern part of Earth. Because the south pole is tilted away from the Sun during this period, it is winter in the southern hemisphere. As Earth orbits the Sun, the angle of the axis stays the same. Halfway around the orbit, the northern hemisphere is tilted away from the Sun, and the southern hemisphere is tilted toward the Sun.

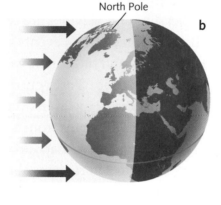

North Pole

Figure 15.14 a) It is summer in the northern hemisphere and winter in the southern hemisphere, when the north pole is pointed toward the Sun. **b)** Neither pole points toward the Sun during the spring and fall.

El Niño

An **El Niño** is a warm ocean current that develops off the western coast of South America, near Peru, every two to seven years. Usually, this warm water travels to the western Pacific Ocean near Australia. It is held there by trade winds traveling west. Normally, the trade winds, which blow from east to west, push ocean water from the South American coast westward toward Indonesia. Sometimes, however, the trade winds slow down or even move in the opposite direction. When this happens, an El Niño begins, and the warm water off Indonesia moves back across the Pacific Ocean toward the South American coast. As the water heats the air above it, the normally cool, dry climate off the northwestern coast of South America becomes warmer and wetter. As a result, large amounts of hot, moist air move into the upper atmosphere and cause dramatic climate changes across the world.

Figure 15.15 El Niños can cause extreme weather events, such as floods **(a)** and droughts **(b)**, that often result in property damage and loss of life.

As You Read

Work with a partner to find the answers to the questions you posed at the beginning of the lesson. Write the answers in your Science Notebook.

It is December 29th, you are in a warm, sunny place, and there are 16 hours of daylight. What hemisphere are you in, and what season is it?

El Niños can bring violent storms to the California coast and droughts to Australia. They can also bring cool, wet winters to Texas and other Gulf coast states. El Niños also cause a decline in the ocean food supply off the Peruvian coast, which causes thousands of birds to die. El Niños do, however, lead to quieter hurricane seasons in the Atlantic Ocean.

Other Natural Events Affecting Climate

Seasons and El Niños are two examples of naturally occurring climate change. Other natural events that can affect climate include changes in Earth's orbit and tilt, Earth's wobble, volcanic eruptions, and solar activity.

Earth's Orbit   Earth currently orbits around the Sun in an **elliptical**, or oval, pattern. However, over the course of a 100,000-year cycle, Earth's orbit alternates from a more elliptical to a more circular pattern. **Figure 15.16** shows that during a circular orbit, the distance between Earth and the Sun remains almost the same throughout the orbit. The amount of solar radiation is constant, resulting in more consistent temperatures on Earth. During an elliptical orbit, however, the distance between Earth and the Sun varies. For most of this orbit, Earth is farther away from the Sun and receives less solar radiation. This results in more variation in temperatures on Earth. These temperature changes should not be confused with Earth's changing seasons. Recall that seasonal changes are caused by the tilt of Earth's axis and its orbit around the Sun.

Figure 15.16 Scientists theorize that changes in the shape of Earth's orbit may trigger changes in climate.

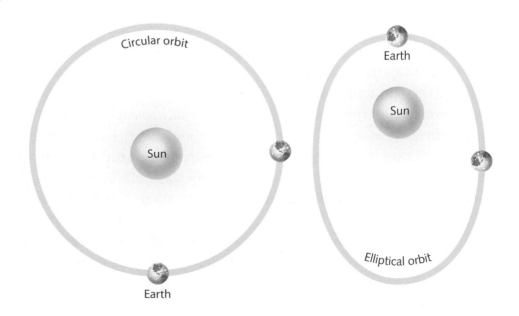

Earth's Tilt Some scientists think that climatic changes might also be triggered by variations in the tilt of Earth's axis. We already know that Earth's tilt is responsible for the seasons. Currently, Earth's axis is tilted at an angle of 23.5 degrees. This measurement can vary by about 2° every 41,000 years, from 22.1° to 24.5°. As the angle of tilt increases, seasonal differences in temperature and precipitation could become more dramatic.

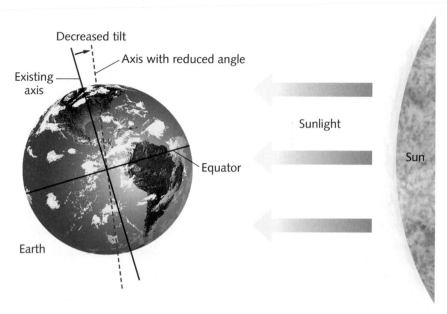

Figure 15.17 If the angle of tilt of Earth's axis decreased, there would likely be less of a temperature difference between winter and summer.

Earth's Wobble Climatic changes could also be caused by a change in the spin of Earth on its axis, called wobble. The Earth's wobble is similar to that of a toy top as it spins and slows down. Earth's poles do not spin in a perfectly straight line. Currently, Earth's axis points toward Polaris, the north star. Scientists think that by about the year 14,000, the wobble will have increased and Earth's axis will point toward Vega, another star. This will lead to colder winters and warmer summers in both the northern and southern hemispheres.

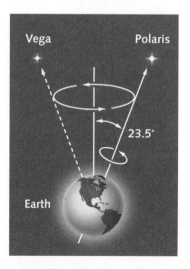

Figure 15.18 Between now and the year 14,000, Earth's axis will point to different points in the sky. During this time, there may be no pole star such as we have now. It will all depend on the position of Earth's axis and the position of the stars.

CONNECTION: History

Nicolaus Copernicus, an astronomer who lived from 1473–1543, formulated the first heliocentric theory. Heliocentrism is the belief that the Sun is at the center of the solar system or universe. Copernicus's theory was accepted by very few people at the time. Why? During Copernicus's time, people did not know that there was a difference between the solar system and the universe. They also believed that Earth, rather than the Sun, was located at the center of the universe. Copernicus's theory was revived and defended by Galileo during the 1600s, causing great controversy with the Catholic Church.

Solar Activity

Some scientists think that solar activity may be linked to changes in Earth's climate. **Sunspots** are areas with strong magnetic fields that appear as dark spots on the Sun. In 1893, an English astronomer named E.W. Maunder discovered that there was very little sunspot activity on the Sun from 1645 to 1716. He also discovered that, during these years, Europe experienced temperatures that were below normal. Later studies showed that increased solar activity coincides with warmer-than-normal climates. The studies also showed that periods of low solar activity coincide with colder climate conditions.

Volcanic Eruptions   Volcanic eruptions influence climate by sending large amounts of dust, ash, and smoke into the atmosphere. The particles block out the Sun's rays and can result in lower temperatures around the world. Usually, volcanic eruptions cause relatively short-term climate changes.

Figure 15.19 Mount St. Helens, in Washington State, continues to send ash and dust into the atmosphere. This eruption took place on October 1, 2004.

After You Read

1. Explain what causes the seasons in the northern and southern hemispheres.
2. Describe the effects of El Niños on worldwide weather patterns.
3. Describe an aspect of either Earth's orbit or its tilt that may cause climatic change.
4. Review the notes in your Science Notebook. Use your notes to explain how volcanic eruptions can affect Earth's climate.

15.4 Human Impacts on Climate

Before You Read

In your Science Notebook, create a K-W-L-S-H chart. In the column labeled *K*, write what you already know about how people impact the climate. In the column labeled *W*, write what you want to learn about how people impact the climate.

Not long ago, a rise in global temperatures, known as global warming, was something only scientists talked about. Now, however, almost everyone has heard about global warming. What exactly is global warming and what can be done about it? To understand how global warming works, it is important to understand how Earth's atmosphere stores heat from the Sun.

The Greenhouse Effect

The greenhouse effect is the natural heating of Earth's surface caused by certain gases in the atmosphere. While some of the Sun's incoming radiation is reflected back into space by Earth's clouds, some is absorbed by Earth's surface. This energy is then released and held as heat by gases in Earth's atmosphere, including water vapor, methane, and carbon dioxide. These atmospheric gases are called greenhouse gases. Without the greenhouse effect to trap heat from the Sun, our planet could not support life as we know it. This is the situation on the planet Mars, which has a very thin atmosphere and temperatures that drop to −90°C. Too much of a greenhouse effect, however, could cause Earth's temperature to rise dangerously. Over the past 200 years, global temperatures have in fact been rising.

Learning Goals

- Explain the greenhouse effect and its role in global warming.
- Describe how humans impact climate.
- Identify possible consequences of global warming.
- Identify things that can be done to combat global warming.

New Vocabulary

fossil fuel
deforestation
carbon sequestration
reforestation

Recall Vocabulary

global warming, p. 239
greenhouse effect, p. 239
atmosphere, p. 230

Figure 15.20 The greenhouse effect is Earth's natural heating process. Gases in the atmosphere trap and release heat in a way that is similar to the way heat is trapped and released in a greenhouse.

Global Warming

There has been much debate among scientists about what is causing global warming. There is, however, increasing evidence that it is occurring largely as a result of rising levels of carbon dioxide (CO_2) in the atmosphere. Carbon dioxide is a major greenhouse gas that traps heat in Earth's atmosphere. An increase in the amount of CO_2 in Earth's atmosphere can result in more heat being trapped on Earth. This, in turn, leads to an increase in global temperatures.

Since 1980, Earth has experienced 19 of its 20 hottest years on record. Based on available evidence, almost all scientists now agree that global warming is occurring. Other factors that might be involved in global warming include the natural cycles of the Sun and Earth. It is clear, however, that humans are altering Earth's climate to some degree and that CO_2 plays a major role. In fact, the level of CO_2 in Earth's atmosphere is higher than it has ever been at any time in Earth's history.

Human Impacts on Global Warming

How have humans caused CO_2 levels to rise? For approximately the last 150 years, since the Industrial Revolution, people have been burning **fossil fuels** such as oil, coal, and natural gas. When they are burned, these fuels release CO_2 into the atmosphere. Automobile emissions from the burning of gasoline are a primary source of atmospheric CO_2. Power plants and factories also release large amounts of CO_2 into the atmosphere.

The cutting down of forests, or **deforestation**, also leads to increased levels of CO_2. In many countries, forests are burned to clear land for agriculture. Burning of all types of materials releases CO_2.

Because plants use carbon dioxide to make food, removing them leads to higher levels of CO_2 in the atmosphere. In many countries, especially those in tropical areas, deforestation is occurring at an alarming rate.

As You Read

In the column labeled *L* in your K-W-L-S-H chart, write three things you have learned about how humans impact the climate. Compare your notes with a partner's. Add or correct information as needed.

How does driving a car contribute to global warming?

Figure 15.21 Running automobile engines and smoke from factories and power plants increase levels of carbon dioxide in Earth's atmosphere.

Figure 15.22 This rain forest in Tarapoto, Peru, has been cut down for the building of a highway.

While the United States contains only about four percent of the world's population, it produces about 25 percent of the world's CO_2 emissions. China comes in second for total emissions, and produces much less CO_2 per person than the United States. That is changing, however, as China's population grows along with its use of fossil fuels.

Carbon Dioxide Emissions (in million metric tons)		
	1980	2004
North America	5,439.17	6,886.88
Central America, South America	623.36	1,041.45
Europe	4,657.92	4,653.43
Eurasia	3,027.53	2,550.75
Middle East	494.75	1,319.70
Africa	534.47	986.55
Asia, Austrialia	3,556.07	9,604.81
Total	18,333.26	27,043.57

Source: U.S. Department of Energy

Figure It Out

1. Which region was the top producer of CO_2 in 1980? In 2004?

2. Which region was the third-largest producer of CO_2 in 2004?

3. What happened to Asia's and Australia's level of CO_2 production from 1980 to 2004? What might account for this change?

Figure 15.23 Countries around the world emit, or release, different amounts of CO_2. The amount of CO_2 each emits depends on the country's population, how much energy it consumes, and the amounts of fossil fuels it burns. This table lists regional worldwide CO_2 emissions from 1980 and 2004. It is important to note that countries that emit the most CO_2 do not necessarily have the largest populations.

Consequences of Global Warming

A slow rise in Earth's average temperatures may not seem like something to worry about, but global warming could have major consequences. Rising temperatures speed up the melting of glaciers and ice caps. This, in turn, causes sea levels to rise and increases flooding of low-lying areas. According to research done by the National Aeronautics and Space Administration (NASA), the polar ice cap is currently melting at a rate of 8.5 percent every ten years. In addition, arctic ice thickness has decreased 40 percent in the last 40 years. Recent scientific studies predict that glaciers in the European Alps will disappear by the year 2050.

Sea Ice Minimum 1979   Sea Ice Minimum 2005

Figure 15.24 Global warming is likely the cause for the decrease in the amount of arctic sea ice that is shown in these photos, taken in the same place at the same time of year in 1979 and in 2005.

Figure 15.25 Grinnell Glacier, in Glacier National Park, is one of many glaciers that have been decreasing in size. The photo on the left was taken in 1981; the photo on the right was taken in 2006.

Changing precipitation patterns caused by global warming might cause severe droughts or floods, both of which could result in the loss of lives and property. Global warming could also alter ecosystems as species unable to survive warmer temperatures either die or migrate to cooler climates. Polar bears, for example, are already having difficulty finding enough food because melting sea ice makes it harder for them to hunt seals.

Combating Global Warming

Conserving energy is one way to combat global warming. Most of the energy we use comes from fossil fuels that release carbon dioxide into the atmosphere when they are burned. Using more efficient appliances and automobiles reduces our need to burn polluting fuels. Other ways to conserve energy include driving less, using more renewable energy resources, and insulating our homes well.

Even small, everyday changes can make a difference. These might include taking the bus or riding a bike instead of driving a car. They might also include using more efficient light bulbs, turning off lights when they are not in use, wearing a sweater and turning down the heat during the winter, and using less air conditioning during the summer.

a

b

Figure 15.26 a) When you ride your bike instead of driving, you get exercise and save energy. **b)** These compact fluorescent bulbs use less energy and last longer than incandescent light bulbs.

Capturing CO$_2$ Scientists are researching ways to reduce CO$_2$ levels in the atmosphere. One possible strategy is called **carbon sequestration**. Carbon sequestration involves capturing and storing carbon gases underground. Carbon dioxide is collected from fossil fuel-burning power plants, and the captured gas is injected into underground storage areas. This is a promising technology, but it is still in the experimental stage. Scientists are also uncertain about what will happen to the stored CO$_2$ over thousands of years.

Reforestation, or planting new trees, is another way to capture CO$_2$ from the atmosphere. Trees not only use CO$_2$ from the atmosphere to make food, they also store carbon in their trunks, stems, leaves, and roots. Reforestation efforts would need to occur along with efforts to slow current deforestation rates around the world.

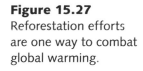
Figure 15.27
Reforestation efforts are one way to combat global warming.

Policy Solutions Policy-makers in many countries are putting into effect and considering different options to reduce CO$_2$ emissions. One solution is to limit the amount of CO$_2$ that industries and individuals can produce. Another option is to tax carbon emissions so that it is costly for industries to produce too much carbon dioxide. All these solutions have costs and benefits that have to be considered.

After You Read

1. Why have CO$_2$ levels risen dramatically over the last 150 years?

2. Explain some possible effects of global warming on agriculture.

3. List three things that you and your family can do to reduce your consumption of fossil fuels.

4. Complete your K-W-L-S-H chart by writing at least two things that you would still like to know about global warming in the S column. Note how you can find this information in the H column. Then conduct research and record the answers in your Science Notebook.

Extend It!

Most schools, especially those in older buildings, are not as energy efficient as they could be. Talk to a custodian and walk around your school. Then develop a list of ways that your school can reduce its energy use. This could include things such as replacing inefficient light bulbs and sealing drafty windows. Recommend these changes to your school principal.

CONNECTION: Economics

The *cap-and-trade* system encourages companies to reduce their CO$_2$ emissions by making it expensive for them to pollute the air. An environmental regulator sets a cap, or highest level allowed, for carbon dioxide emissions. This requires polluting companies to lower their levels of carbon emissions by a specific amount. Some companies will not be able to lower their CO$_2$ emissions to the levels required. These companies are free to buy permits to emit more CO$_2$ from other companies that can meet the emissions requirements. In this way, companies that can more easily reduce their emissions can sell their extra permits to companies that can't.

KEY CONCEPTS

15.1 What Is Climate?

- Weather is the condition of the atmosphere at a specific time and place. Climate describes the weather patterns of an area over a long period of time.
- Climate is determined by factors that include latitude, topography, ocean currents, and prevailing winds.
- Latitude determines the amount of solar radiation an area of Earth receives, which affects temperature. Temperature is also affected by elevation and distance from large bodies of water.
- Ocean currents influence nearby land temperatures. Prevailing winds influence both the temperature of an area and the amount of precipitation it receives.

15.2 Classifying Earth's Climates

- The Koeppen classification system uses temperature and precipitation to divide Earth's climates into six major types: tropical, dry, mild, continental, polar, and high elevation.
- Tropical climates are characterized by high temperatures year-round.
- Dry climates include both arid and semiarid regions.
- Mild climates are greatly influenced by nearby oceans and ocean currents. Continental climates are located within the interior of most continents at midlatitudes.
- Polar climates occur at high latitudes in both the northern and southern hemispheres.

15.3 Climate Change

- Long-term climatic changes include ice ages and interglacial intervals.
- Short-term climatic changes are regularly caused by seasonal changes and a warm ocean current in the Pacific Ocean called an El Niño.
- Other natural events that can affect Earth's climate include changes in Earth's orbit, changes in Earth's tilt, Earth's wobble, solar activity, and volcanic activity.

15.4 Human Impacts on Climate

- The greenhouse effect is the natural heating of Earth's surface caused by gases in the atmosphere. Increased amounts of CO_2 in Earth's atmosphere can lead to global warming.
- Humans contribute to global warming by burning fossil fuels and by cutting down forests.
- Global warming could have severe consequences that include a rise in sea levels, flooding, droughts, stronger storms, and decreases in the populations of Earth's varied life forms.

VOCABULARY REVIEW

Write each term in a complete sentence, or write a paragraph relating several terms.

15.1
climate, p. 273
tropics, p. 274
polar zone, p. 274
temperate zone, p. 274
elevation, p. 275
windward, p. 275
leeward, p. 275
surface current, p. 275
prevailing wind, p. 276

15.2
Koeppen classification system, p. 278
savanna, p. 279
steppe, p. 279
microclimate, p. 281
heat island, p. 281

15.3
ice age, p. 282
interglacial interval, p. 283
season, p. 283
El Niño, p. 283
elliptical, p. 284
sunspot, p. 286

15.4
fossil fuel, p. 288
deforestation, p. 288
carbon sequestration, p. 291
reforestation, p. 291

PREPARE FOR CHAPTER TEST

To prepare for the chapter test, create a question from each Learning Goal. Use the information in your Science Notebook to answer each question. Then use these answers to write a well-developed essay about the chapter. Use the Key Concept on the first page of this chapter as your topic sentence.

True or False

If the statement is true, write "true." If it is false, change the underlined word or words to make the statement true.

1. The <u>leeward</u> side of a mountain tends to be dry.
2. Continental climates occur in much of <u>the arctic</u>.
3. Temperatures in a big city are often slightly <u>cooler</u> than in the surrounding areas.
4. When Earth's orbit is in a more <u>elliptical</u> pattern, it passes closer to the Sun.
5. When a volcano erupts, it usually causes <u>long-term</u> climate change.
6. Fossil fuels release <u>carbon dioxide</u> into the atmosphere when they are burned.

Short Answer

Answer each of the following in a sentence or brief paragraph.

7. Explain how the latitude of an area affects its climate.
8. Describe the type of weather brought on by prevailing winds blowing from the ocean.
9. Describe what winter and summer weather is like in a Mediterranean climate.
10. Explain why large cities form heat islands.
11. When was the most recent interglacial interval?
12. List four possible consequences of global warming.
13. Identify two steps that individuals can take to use less energy and fossil fuels.

Critical Thinking

Use what you have learned in this chapter to answer each of the following.

14. **Evaluate** Consider all of the natural events that affect climate, and evaluate how much these factors are currently influencing the climate.
15. **Relate** How does the possibility of warmer global temperatures relate to rising sea levels?
16. **Analyze** Describe the climate of your area and analyze the factors that influence it.

Standardized Test Question

Choose the letter of the response that correctly answers the question.

17. Which of the following does NOT affect the temperature of a specific location on Earth?
    A. elevation
    B. Earth's orbit
    C. distance from large bodies of water
    D. latitude

Test-Taking Tip

Remember that qualifying words such as *usually*, *sometimes*, and *generally* mean that the statement can be considered both true and false depending on the specific circumstances.

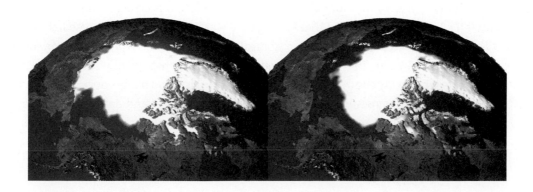

Chasing Storms

TORNADOES ARE NOT the biggest storms on Earth, but they are among the most destructive. Their wind speeds can top 250 miles per hour. They can flatten houses and toss cars as if they were toys.

Most people try to keep clear of a twister. Some people, however, actually look for them and then get as close as possible. Many of these people are storm chasers.

Most storm chasers simply find thunderstorms and tornadoes interesting and exciting. They want to see these powerful storms up close. During tornado season on the Great Plains, from March through July, dozens of storm chasers travel hundreds or even thousands of miles to find these storms.

You may wonder how storm chasers find tornadoes. They start by using weather forecasts, radar, satellite links, and other tools to find strong thunderstorms. These are the storms that are most likely to form tornadoes. When chasers find the right conditions for a huge storm, they head toward it. If they're lucky, they might get to the area just in time to see a tornado touch down. The idea is to get as close as possible, while staying safe. Storm chasers don't do formal research, but they often take pictures and videos that researchers find useful.

Meteorologists also chase tornadoes, but they do it for research purposes rather than as a hobby. Even when using special instruments, some data on twisters can only be acquired by getting up close. For example, some scientists park trucks fitted with Doppler radar near a swirling tornado. The radar penetrates the storm and shows its structure in a way that would not be possible from farther away.

Research and Report

The National Weather Service issues watches and warnings for weather conditions such as thunderstorms and tornadoes. With a partner, research these warnings and watches, and write a short report on them. Explain what they are, contrast them, and then explain what should be done when each is issued. Include information on the types of watches and warnings that are most common where you live.

 CAREER CONNECTION: METEOROLOGIST

WHAT WILL the weather be like tomorrow? You ask that question all the time. If it rains, you know your ball game might be cancelled. If it's hot, you won't need that heavy sweater. You get the scoop on the day's weather from a meteorologist.

Meteorologists are scientists who study the atmosphere. They study its composition, structure, and the way it moves and changes. Then they determine the way these changes affect the environment. Sometimes, this means forecasting the weather—which is what most meteorologists do. However, meteorologists also use computer models to predict future climate trends, such as global warming. They also do research that helps control air pollution. The work of meteorologists affects everything from transportation safety to farming.

Meteorologists use many tools. They use images from weather satellites and data from radar and weather balloons. They also gather data from weather stations all over the world. The data they collect is used to create computer models that help make forecasts.

Predicting El Niño

EL NIÑO EVENTS throw weather into chaos. During an El Niño event, areas that usually get enough rain turn dry. In other areas, unusually stormy weather causes floods. Because El Niños of the past have caused great damage, scientists have worked hard to find ways to predict them.

In order to figure out how to predict an El Niño event, scientists needed to understand the signs of an El Niño. Certain conditions occur in the ocean and atmosphere when an El Niño starts. Water in the eastern Pacific Ocean near the equator gets warmer. As a result, the water expands, causing the ocean surface to rise slightly. Air pressure drops over the eastern Pacific and rainfall increases. Scientists knew that if they could detect these conditions in the ocean, they could predict when an El Niño was underway.

Several countries worked together to set up an El Niño detection system made up of networks of buoys in the Pacific Ocean. Buoys [BOO eez] are floating devices that are attached to the floor of a body of water. In this case, the buoys hold instruments that can detect the changes El Niño causes. For example, dozens of Tropical Atmosphere Ocean (TAO) buoys are attached to the floor of the tropical portion of the Pacific Ocean. They provide data on conditions of the sea surface and lower atmosphere, including humidity and temperature.

Other buoys, called Argo floats, also provide data. They can sink thousands of meters below the ocean surface. They are programmed to travel on currents beneath the ocean surface for periods of ten days. At the end of each period, they pop up to the surface to send data—then dive to begin the cycle again. The floats give scientists data on the speed and direction of currents. They also collect temperature readings on water below the surface. The data from all the buoys are beamed to satellites and then sent back to computers on the ground.

Other parts of the El Niño monitoring system include satellites and tidal gauges. Some satellites carry instruments that can detect sea-surface temperature changes. Tidal gauges register changes in the sea surface as the ocean warms and expands.

The network has already paid off. In 1997, the system showed a mass of warmer-than-normal water moving east across the Pacific. Meteorologists used the data to predict the 1997–1998 El Niño. They then predicted another one four years later. El Niños will keep happening, but from now on the strange weather they cause won't be a surprise.

Most meteorologists have a college degree in meteorology or atmospheric sciences. Meteorologists might work for private businesses, or they might work for the government. All meteorologists do a very important job. During weather emergencies—such as hurricanes, floods, or blizzards—they give people information that can protect property and save lives.

Unit 7

Earth's Waters

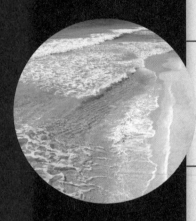

Chapter 16   **Freshwater**

Where does Earth's freshwater collect, and how does it help shape the land?

Chapter 17   **Oceans**

How do ocean currents, marine life, tides, and evaporation of ocean water affect life on Earth?

Chapter 18   **The Marine Environment**

How are living things in the ocean affected by factors such as light, water depth, and distance to shore?

Freshwater

KEY CONCEPT Earth's freshwater, which collects in streams, rivers, lakes, wetlands, and aquifers, helps shape Earth's surface.

Oceans hold about 97 percent of Earth's water. This water is very salty—much too salty to drink. Another 2 percent of the water is frozen in glaciers or polar ice caps. Earth's available freshwater is only 1 percent of its total water supply. Freshwater is present in streams, rivers, ponds, lakes, and wetlands. Unlike seawater, freshwater contains little or no salt.

Even though Earth's freshwater supply is relatively small, its effects are great. Water shapes the land, is crucial to the survival of plants and animals, and affects the weather. Without water, Earth's surface would be hot, rocky, and lifeless.

Think About the Uses of Freshwater

How do you use freshwater during a typical day? Think of ways water is used in your home, at school, and in businesses and industries.

- Are all of the different uses of water equally important? Explain your answer.

- In your Science Notebook, discuss ways that you could reduce your use of freshwater.

NSTA
SCiLINKS.
THE WORLD'S A CLICK AWAY

www.scilinks.org

Freshwater Ecosystems
Code: WGES16

Stream and River Development

Learning Goals

- Explain how streams and rivers form.
- Discuss how Earth's freshwater shapes the land.
- Explain the major factors that affect the rate of stream erosion.
- Describe a watershed.

New Vocabulary

water cycle
runoff
weathering
erosion
channel
gradient
discharge
load
tributary
watershed
divide

Figure It Out

1. How does water enter Earth's atmosphere and then return to Earth's surface?

2. Describe two ways that precipitation falling on land can reach the ocean.

Before You Read

In your Science Notebook, draw a sequence chart with five boxes connected by arrows. At the top of the first box, write *Precipitation*. At the tops of the remaining boxes, write *Runoff*, *Streams*, *Rivers*, and *Oceans*.

The river shown on page 297 carries water in one direction only—downhill, from the mountains toward the ocean. Yet, the river does not dry up. The river's freshwater is constantly renewed by the water cycle. The **water cycle** is the continual movement of water between Earth and the atmosphere.

Effects of the Water Cycle

How does the water cycle renew Earth's freshwater supply? The Sun provides the energy for the water cycle. Heat from the Sun causes water to evaporate, or change to a gas called water vapor. As shown in **Figure 16.1**, water evaporates into the air from oceans and other bodies of water. When water evaporates, any salts or other substances that were mixed into it are left behind. Water also evaporates from the leaves of plants through a process called transpiration. Water vapor eventually cools and changes to a fluid during a process called condensation. It then falls back to Earth's surface as rain, snow, or another form of precipitation. Precipitation is always freshwater.

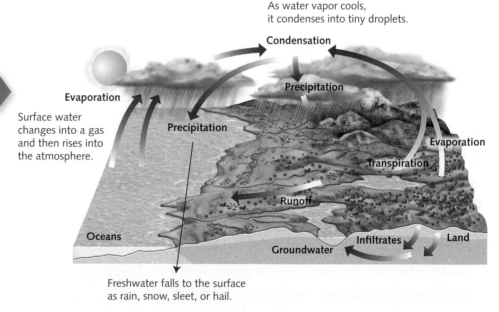

As water vapor cools, it condenses into tiny droplets.

Condensation

Precipitation

Evaporation

Surface water changes into a gas and then rises into the atmosphere.

Precipitation

Evaporation

Transpiration

Runoff

Oceans

Groundwater

Infiltrates

Land

Freshwater falls to the surface as rain, snow, sleet, or hail.

Figure 16.1 Water can move through many different paths of the water cycle. The Sun provides the energy for evaporation.

Once liquid water reaches Earth's surface, the force of gravity pulls it either downhill or into the ground. Water that soaks into the ground is called groundwater. Rainfall that flows downhill along Earth's surface is called **runoff**. Runoff is especially strong after a heavy rain or when banks of snow melt in spring. Runoff often feeds streams or rivers, or it collects in ponds and lakes.

Moving Water and Erosion

What changes can freshwater cause to the land? For a dramatic example, look at the photograph of the Grand Canyon on page 196. About 70 million years ago, this region of Arizona was pushed upward as two tectonic plates crashed into one another. As a result, the Rocky Mountains were uplifted, and the Colorado River began to erode and form the Grand Canyon.

Weathering is a process that breaks down or changes rocks on or near Earth's surface. **Erosion** is the movement of soil or sediment from one location to another by forces such as water, wind, and gravity. About 65 to 70 million years ago, the Colorado River began to deepen. With the help of wind, rain, ice, and gravity, the Grand Canyon was weathered and eroded to its present average width of 16 kilometers.

Rushing water in streams or rivers is not the only water-related cause of weathering and erosion. Precipitation may also shape the land. For example, when rain soaks the soil along a hillside, the waterlogged soil may slide downward, taking plants and buildings with it. This sudden erosion is called a landslide or mudslide. Anyone who wants to build a house near a steep slope should understand how landslides occur.

Underground rocks also can be weathered and eroded by water. These processes help change rock into soil. In addition, when water seeps into a type of rock called limestone, it can chemically change the limestone into a softer substance. The water erodes the weathered limestone, leaving an open space called a cave in the rock.

Ice, too, can be an important agent of erosion. Earth's climate has cooled and warmed several times over the past 4.6 million years. During the cool periods, or ice ages, huge glaciers advanced from both the north and south poles. They acted like giant bulldozers, carving out huge valleys and carrying away rocks in their paths.

Moving air can weather and erode rock, too. A strong wind can blow soil and dust for many kilometers. These particles can act like sandpaper, sculpting rocks into a variety of shapes.

Figure 16.2 a) Water caused the erosion of the riverbank beside this tree. **b)** Water erosion also played a part in the formation of this cave. **c)** This unusual rock formation was formed by wind erosion.

As You Read

Inside the boxes of your sequence chart, write something you have learned about each type of moving water or the erosion it causes. Explain your chart to a partner. Then listen as your partner explains his or her chart to you. Add or correct information as necessary.

Describe what causes a landslide.

a

b

c

Streams and Rivers

How do streams and rivers form? When precipitation gathers on Earth's surface as runoff, it usually flows quickly. Some runoff flows in thin sheets across the land. Typically, however, runoff collects in small channels. A **channel** is a sloping pathway in which water flows. As runoff erodes the ground under it, a channel can form. Once this process begins, the next rainfall or snowmelt might widen and deepen the channel.

If enough water flows through a channel every day, the channel may become a permanent stream. Streams usually join together to form rivers. A river is simply a wider, deeper, and longer version of a stream. Rivers often join together as well. Eventually, they empty their waters into lakes or oceans.

Gravity causes all streams and rivers to flow downhill. Their paths and speeds vary greatly, however. In most cases, water travels straightest and fastest over a steep slope. Along a mountainside, for example, a stream might rush quickly over a path that is almost a straight line. On flatter lands, streams and rivers move much more slowly.

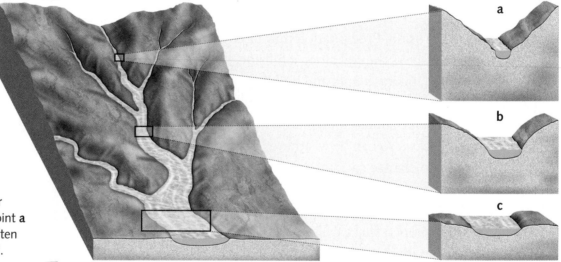

Figure 16.3 Water always flows downhill. The stream channels become wider as water flows downhill from point **a** to point **c**. Channels often become deeper as well.

Streams and rivers are also affected by the type of land surface they flow over. Friction from porous rock beds or loose sediment, for example, can cause water to slow. Smooth, hard rocks offer less friction and allow water to flow over them more quickly.

Plants and animals may also cause a stream or river to slow down or to alter its course. For example, a fallen tree may block a stream and force it into a new path. In many places, beavers cut down trees and drag them into rivers to build their homes. A beaver dam may cause water to back up, spill out of its channel, and create a new path. Dams and other structures built by humans also change rivers.

Factors Affecting Stream Erosion

Why do some streams flow faster than others? To study and compare streams, scientists measure properties including their gradients, discharges, and loads. The gradient, discharge, and load of a single stream or river can vary from one location to another.

Gradient is a measure of the change in elevation over a certain distance. For example, a stream running down a mountainside would have a higher gradient than a stream flowing through a flat meadow. A high gradient gives a stream or river more energy to erode rock and soil. A river or stream with a low gradient has less energy for erosion. Scientists measure the gradient along many sections of a stream or river. A stream often begins with a steep gradient. The stream's gradient usually decreases as it nears the ocean and flows over less steep land.

Discharge is a measure of the volume of stream water that flows over a specific location in a particular amount of time. When a major storm occurs or when snow melts quickly, the discharge of a stream increases. As a stream's discharge increases, its speed and erosive energy also increase.

The materials carried by a stream's water are collectively called the stream's **load**. The size of particles a stream can carry is determined by its speed. A fast-moving stream can carry larger particles in its load. A stream's load affects its rate of erosion. Large particles, such as rocks and pebbles, being carried by a fast-moving stream scrape and bounce along the sides and bottoms of the streambed causing rapid erosion. Streams can also carry small rocks and soil that remain suspended in the water. These materials make the stream look muddy. Other materials that make up a stream's load may be completely dissolved in the water.

Figure 16.4 When the gradient increases, so does a river's speed. Fast-moving, shallow waters called rapids can result.

Figure 16.5 The brown water in this river indicates a heavy load of suspended materials, such as small rocks and soil.

River Systems

Tributaries are smaller streams or rivers that flow into larger ones. Streams and rivers on land make up a network that moves water across the land into the oceans. This network of rivers and streams, which drains a land area of its runoff, is called a river system. Like parts of other systems, the streams and rivers of a river system can affect one another. Eroded soil and pollutants in one stream can be carried downstream and throughout an entire river system.

River systems are divided into regions called watersheds. A **watershed**, or drainage basin, is an area of land that is drained by a river system. A watershed includes the main river and all of its tributaries. You can compare a watershed to a huge sink. Like water in a sink after the drain is opened, all the water in a watershed flows downhill toward one place.

A watershed can cover a small area or a large one. As shown in **Figure 16.6**, much of the United States is part of a very large watershed that drains into the Mississippi River. This watershed includes lands that drain into the Missouri, Ohio, Tennessee, and Arkansas Rivers, as well as other tributaries of the Mississippi River.

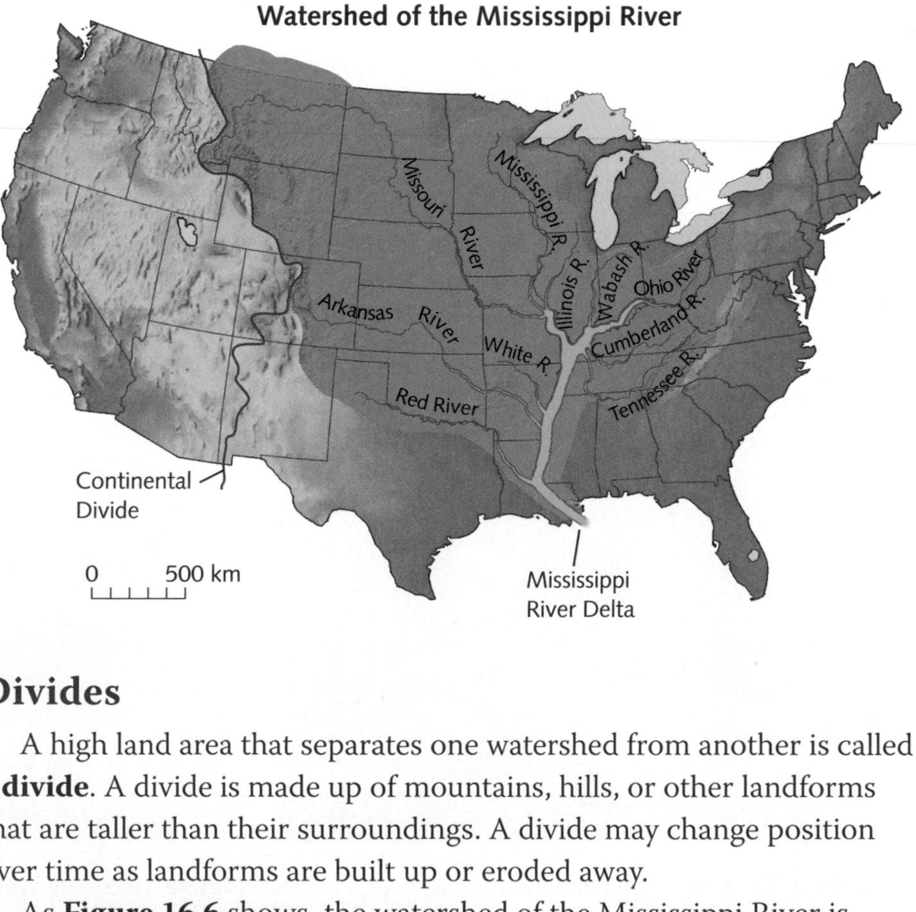

Figure 16.6 Trace the paths of the Mississippi River and its tributaries. If you compared the central United States to a sink, the drain would be located in southeast Louisiana.

Watershed of the Mississippi River

Divides

A high land area that separates one watershed from another is called a **divide**. A divide is made up of mountains, hills, or other landforms that are taller than their surroundings. A divide may change position over time as landforms are built up or eroded away.

As **Figure 16.6** shows, the watershed of the Mississippi River is bordered on the west by the Rocky Mountains. The divide that runs through these mountains is called the Continental Divide. Rivers that form east of the divide flow east toward the Mississippi River and the Atlantic Ocean. Rivers that form west of the divide flow west toward the Pacific Ocean. Other divides form the northern and eastern border of the Mississippi watershed.

In the United States today, highways and railroads easily cross divides. In earlier years, however, rivers were the country's main transportation routes. Cities such as Cincinnati, St. Louis, and New Orleans all grew because of traffic from boats and barges along the Ohio and Mississippi Rivers. Divides limited the paths that a river barge could travel. No river can flow across a divide.

To solve this transportation problem, people built canals to connect natural waterways. By including dams and locks within the canal, as shown in **Figure 16.7**, a boat or barge could cross a divide. The Erie Canal, completed in 1825, connected Lake Erie to the Hudson River, which flowed south to New York City. Other canals connected the Great Lakes to the Mississippi River.

Figure 16.7 A lock and dam act like an elevator. When the Erie Canal opened, a set of 83 locks allowed boats and barges to cross the hilly lands of New York State.

After You Read

1. What are three ways that Earth's freshwater helps shape the land?

2. Describe how a tributary may affect the river it flows into.

3. Review the facts about moving water that you recorded in your sequence chart. In your Science Notebook, write a well-developed paragraph or short essay that describes a raindrop as it enters and travels through a river system. Include facts about the bodies of water it joins and the erosion it causes.

 Explore It!

Watersheds are separated from each other by divides. Build a divide in the middle of a plastic box using modeling clay. Then build a watershed on either side of the divide. Make streams and rivers in each watershed by using your fingers to indent the clay. Then pour water over the top of your divide and describe its path as it flows through the two watersheds.

 **CONNECTION: Math**

A river's gradient is like the mathematical slope of a line. To calculate the gradient, divide the vertical drop by the horizontal distance covered. If a river starts at an elevation of 5,000 m and travels 400 km downstream to a lake that is at an elevation of 1,000 m, what is the river's gradient?

Before You Read

Write and circle the word *Deposition* in the middle of a page in your Science Notebook. Draw five lines out from this word to begin a concept map. As you read, think about words or concepts that are related to deposition.

As described earlier, a river or stream typically carries a load of dirt, small rocks, and other materials. Together, this is called sediment. As the water slows down, the sediment settles from the water to the river bottom. The largest pieces of sediment settle to the bottom of a river first. Smaller and smaller pieces of sediment settle as the water continues to slow down. The sinking of this sediment to the bottom of a body of water is called **deposition**.

Meanders

A river tends to get wider over its course. This occurs when it is joined by tributaries and runoff that add to its water. A river also widens when it slows down as it flows over flatter land.

A **meander** is a bend or curve in a stream channel caused by moving water. A meander forms when the water along one **riverbank**, or land bordering the river, begins flowing faster than the water along the opposite riverbank. The riverbank in contact with the faster-flowing water tends to be eroded away. At the same time, the riverbank in contact with the slower-flowing water tends to become wider with deposited sediment. Together, these actions reshape the river channel so that it turns to the left or to the right, forming a meander. As the process continues, the curves of the meander become wider and more exaggerated. Sometimes, a river erodes a "shortcut" across the neck of a meander. The rest of the meander is walled off in a C-shaped section, forming an oxbow lake. A wider, slower river is more likely to form meanders.

Figure 16.8 The Mississippi River changes shape throughout its course. The last few hundred kilometers of the river are made up of many meanders.

Upper Mississippi River

Lower Mississippi River

Alluvial Fans and Deltas

Sometimes a large amount of sediment is deposited over a fairly small area. This can occur when the gradient of a stream or river abruptly decreases. This happens when the land a river is flowing over flattens very quickly. The result is a fan-shaped deposit called an **alluvial fan**. Alluvial fans usually form at the base of a steep slope and are made mostly of sand and gravel. They are most common in dry, mountainous regions, where rivers have not had the chance to dig out a gentler slope.

Rivers also slow down when they join an ocean or large lake. Where a river meets a large body of water, a triangle-shaped deposit called a **delta** is formed. Delta deposits are usually made up of silt or clay particles. As a delta builds up, a wall of sediment may split the river channel in half, sometimes repeatedly. In this way, a delta may divide the end of a river into many smaller, fingerlike streams that carry water the last few kilometers into the lake or ocean. The delta of the Mississippi River does just that, creating tiny riverbanks that jut into the Gulf of Mexico.

Floodplains

Every stream or river travels through a banked path called a channel. Sometimes, however, an unusually heavy water supply will swell a stream or river. When the water overflows the riverbanks, the event is called a flood.

Floodwater collects on the broad, flat areas on either side of a stream or river. These areas are called **floodplains**. During a flood, a floodplain may look like a wide, shallow lake. When the river returns to its normal size, floodwaters typically flow back to the river and the floodplain dries out.

Floodwaters can ruin houses, cars, roads, and other structures that humans build. People and farm animals have drowned in floodwaters, too. Yet, floods can provide an important benefit to the land. Like other river water, floodwaters carry sediment that was eroded upstream. Sediment deposited on the floodplain can add nutrients to the soil, making it ideal for growing many crops.

As You Read

On each line surrounding the word *Deposition*, write the name of a landform that deposition forms or affects. In each circle, write the definition of the landform.

Where do alluvial fans usually form?

Figure 16.9 The water that created the alluvial fan at the base of this cliff in California's Death Valley is long gone.

Figure 16.10 The delta at the mouth of the Mississippi River formed over millions of years. It divides the river into small streams that extend into the Gulf of Mexico.

Extend It!

Large streams and rivers are likely to flood as a result of heavy, prolonged rainfall or snowmelt. Research a large stream or river that flows in your state. Has it flooded recently? If so, what damage did it cause? Do dams or levees help control it? Record your findings in your Science Notebook.

Managing Floods

A stream or river may flood after a heavy rainstorm or after days of repeated rain. Flooding also results from rapid snowmelt. Remember that runoff, streams, and rivers are all part of a river system. This means that flooding can occur far from the source of the floodwaters.

How much damage can floods cause? One answer came during the summer of 2005. The effect of Hurricane Katrina on New Orleans was catastrophic. As a result of heavy rains, four of the city's protective flood barriers collapsed. In addition, the high winds pushed a dome-shaped mass of seawater, called a storm surge, up on land. The storm surge, along with the collapsed flood barriers, resulted in flooding of more than 80 percent of the city. Some areas were under as much as six meters of water. At least 1,800 human lives were lost.

To manage and prepare for floods, communities along major rivers usually build levees. A **levee** is a high ridge, usually made of soil and other natural materials, built along a riverbank. Its purpose is to keep the river from overflowing. Levees have protected communities from many floods. Should a levee fail, however, the flooding can be much worse than it would have been otherwise. This is because the large amount of water that has built up behind the levee is suddenly released in one large flood.

Some communities have decided to allow their streams and rivers to flood naturally. In 1972, a flood on Rapid Creek and other streams destroyed homes and businesses in Rapid City, South Dakota. In response, the city decided not to build dams or levees, but to move the city away from the floodplain instead. The local government bought and tore down buildings there. Today, the floodplain is used as parkland.

Figure 16.11 The high water level in this New Orleans neighborhood shows the effects of flooding after two levees were breached.

After You Read

1. Why does the rate of deposition change along the length of a river?

2. Discuss two ways that a river community could prepare for a flood.

3. Review the terms and definitions in your concept map. In your Science Notebook, describe the shape of a typical river along its course.

16.3 Lakes and Wetlands

Learning Goals

- Explain how lakes form.
- Describe the process of eutrophication.
- Identify different types of wetlands and explain their importance.

New Vocabulary

lake
reservoir
eutrophication
irrigation
wetland
swamp
marsh
bog
estuary

Before You Read

Draw a T-chart in your Science Notebook. Label one side *Causes* and the other side *Effects*. In your own words, define the terms *cause* and *effect*.

Lakes are found all over the world in many shapes and sizes. Lake Superior, the world's largest freshwater lake, borders three U.S. states and part of Canada. Lake Baikal, in Russia, is the deepest lake on Earth. Drop a weight on its surface, and it will sink more than 1.6 km to the bottom. Other lakes, however, are small and shallow enough to fit inside a school auditorium. These are often called ponds.

A **lake** is a depression in the land that collects and holds water. Most lakes hold freshwater, but there are saltwater lakes, as well. Utah's Great Salt Lake is an example. During prehistoric times, it was a much larger lake—today it has mostly dried up and retreated to lower-lying areas.

How Lakes Form

Some lakes are actually wide, flat regions of rivers. Others, such as oxbow lakes, form from separated sections of rivers. Lakes can also be artificially formed when water collects behind human-built dams along rivers.

Many of the lakes existing today formed from the actions of glaciers. During the ice ages, glaciers advanced across much of Earth's land. They often gouged out deep cavities in the rock. Later, as the glaciers melted, the resulting water filled these cavities. Thousands of small and midsized lakes in Minnesota and Wisconsin were formed in this way. Their larger neighbors, the Great Lakes, were once a vast river basin that was filled with water from melting glaciers.

A **reservoir** is a natural or human-made lake used to store water. Often the water provides drinking water for a community. Although human-made reservoirs do not form naturally, they look and act like natural lakes in most ways.

Figure 16.12 Clean, undisturbed lakes provide drinking water, recreation, and beauty. They also can support a diverse community of fish, birds, and other wildlife.

Explain It!

How do people's actions threaten lakes? How can people help lakes last as long as possible? In your Science Notebook, write a public service announcement for a local television or radio station explaining how people can help keep lakes healthy.

As You Read

This lesson presents some changes that take place in lakes and wetlands. In the T-chart in your Science Notebook, record the causes and effects of these changes.

How does a rapid increase in the growth of algae affect the level of oxygen in a lake?

How Lakes Change

After a lake forms, water from precipitation and runoff can maintain the lake's water supply. Underground water may also maintain a lake's water supply. Without some source of incoming water, however, evaporation will quickly cause a lake to dry up. Despite a steady water supply, over thousands of years most lakes eventually fill in with sediment and become dry landforms.

Eutrophication (yew troh fih KAY shun) is the process by which a lake becomes overly rich in nutrients that are washed in from the surrounding watershed. This causes a great increase in the growth of algae. The algae then use up much of the oxygen in the water. This leaves little oxygen for the plants and animals that also live in the water. The plants and animals suffocate and die. The decay of a large number of plants and animals results in a further decrease in oxygen levels in the lake's water.

This decrease in oxygen levels results in a change in the kinds of organisms in the lake. For example, fish that thrive in a relatively deep lake are not likely to survive in shallow, weedy waters. The bacteria and other organisms that help decompose the plants in shallow, weedy waters use up much of the oxygen in the water. This further reduces the amount of oxygen available for fish.

In some cases, human actions speed up the process of eutrophication. Fertilizers are nitrogen-rich compounds that humans use to help plants grow. Home owners spread fertilizers on their lawns, and farmers spread them on fields of crops. Unfortunately, fertilizers dissolve in rainwater and are carried in runoff. When they collect in a lake, they often lead to eutrophication. Industrial toxins, untreated sewage, and animal wastes may also collect in lakes and cause eutrophication.

Throughout the process of eutrophication, sediment from runoff and the remains of plants and animals collects on the lake bottom. The richer the nutrients on the lake bottom, the greater the mass of plant life it can support. In shallow water, some plants will grow from the lake bottom to the surface. Eventually, perhaps after thousands of years, these plants and their successors will dominate the landscape.

Figure 16.13 Added nutrients may encourage the growth of algae in a lake or river. A heavy mat of algae upsets the delicate balance between the lake's oxygen supply and the living things that depend on this oxygen.

The Demand for Water

Over the past hundred years, the water level in many of the large lakes of California has dropped. The reason for this drop is that these lakes are being tapped for irrigation. **Irrigation** is the application of water by humans to land to assist in the production of crops. In California, a vast irrigation system of pipes and canals carries water across the state. The system brings freshwater to cities and farms from mountain streams, lakes, and reservoirs.

Wherever the human population grows, so does the demand for freshwater. Often, lakes and rivers are tapped to meet that demand. Although the water cycle replenishes these bodies of water, it does so at a limited rate. If communities are not careful, their actions can sometimes cause these bodies of water to dry out. Freshwater supplies are especially limited in the southwestern United States. This region of the country has a hot, dry climate. In cities such as Phoenix, Arizona, many home owners have desert plants rather than grass growing on their property. These plants need little water to grow.

Figure 16.14 California's cities and farms tap water supplies from the mountains. Lakes, such as Mono Lake, have shrunk as a result.

CONNECTION: Ecology

An invasive alien species is a species that is introduced outside of its natural habitat. When invasive alien species arrive in a freshwater ecosystem, they can compete with the native species there and sometimes take over their new environment. Below are three examples of how invasive alien species have affected nonnative ecosystems.

Zebra mussels These small mollusks from Europe appeared in 1988 in a lake near Detroit, Michigan. They have since spread throughout the Great Lakes and into nearby lakes and rivers. Zebra mussels reproduce quickly and use up nutrients that native fishes and mollusks need to survive. In Vermont's Lake Champlain, zebra mussels have clogged pipes used to transport water for human use.

Snakehead fish These fast-growing, fast-moving fish are native to Africa and Asia. Snakeheads can even walk a few steps on land! Exotic species such as snakeheads can disrupt natural aquatic systems by feeding on and competing with native fishes.

Snakehead fish have invaded the Mississippi River near New Orleans. They have been successful competitors and have seriously reduced a number of native species populations.

Eurasian milfoil This water plant may appear ordinary, but it readily takes hold on lake bottoms and grow very quickly in shallow water. It is rapidly increasing the rate of eutrophication in lakes from Wisconsin to Washington State.

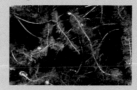

Figure 16.15 Cyprus trees grow well in swamps along the southern coast of Florida. Their roots often poke out of the water, creating tiny islands for insects and other animals.

Figure It Out

1. Based on the photo, describe some of the characteristics of a marsh.

2. Why do you think there are no trees in the marsh?

Figure 16.16 This great white egret is fishing in a freshwater marsh in Louisiana.

Wetlands

A **wetland** is a land area that is covered with water for a large part of the year. Swamps, marshes, and bogs are examples of wetlands.

A **swamp** is a wetland that supports trees, shrubs, or other woody plants. Many swamps form in flat, low-lying areas along streams. Swamps are common throughout the United States, especially along the Atlantic coast. In the Southeast, swamps provide homes for many rare or endangered animals, including the American crocodile.

A **marsh** tends to have more water than a swamp, and it has few or no trees. Grasses grow well in marshes, providing nesting grounds for cranes, herons, and other wading birds. Like swamps, marshes are common along the Atlantic coast. Saltwater marshes form where rivers or streams meet the ocean. In many of these marshes, the saltiness of the water changes from day to day or even from hour to hour. Only certain plants and animals can survive such changes, making saltwater marshes a unique habitat.

A **bog** is an area of soaked, spongy soil that may not be covered in standing water. Bogs get their water from rain and have few nutrients to support the growth of large plants. However, a type of moss called *Sphagnum*, or peat moss, thrives in bogs. It grows in dense mats that act like a soft, green carpet over the ground. Peat moss from bogs is often harvested and used for fuel.

Figure 16.17 The soil in bogs provides few nutrients. Pitcher plants, which use their leaves to trap and digest insects, thrive in bogs.

Bogs were once quite common in the northern half of North America, where glaciers once covered the land. Today, most bogs have been drained for cropland or mined for peat. Unfortunately, while bogs can be destroyed in a short period of time, they take hundreds or thousands of years to form.

Importance of Wetlands

Wetlands play an important role in improving water quality. They act as filters, trapping and removing pollution, sediment, and bacteria from water as it soaks into the ground. Wetlands also act as natural reservoirs that store and hold water after heavy rains. This is especially important in the southeast United States, where hurricanes often strike and bring abundant rainfall in a short amount of time. When wetlands are filled in for development, storm waters flow over them as runoff, sometimes causing flash floods.

Because of their abundant water and rich soil, wetlands provide vital habitats for many types of wildlife. Migratory water birds rely on wetlands for food and shelter. Wetlands connected to the ocean, where freshwater and salt water meet, are called **estuaries**. Estuaries provide the sheltered habitat and food that fish, turtles, and other marine life need to survive and produce young.

Protecting Wetlands

Over half of the original wetlands in the United States have been lost, due in great part to human actions. In Florida, for example, the marshes and swamps of the Everglades depend on a slow, steady supply of water from the north. As towns and cities grow, humans are draining much of this water supply. As a result, the Everglades have been gradually shrinking.

In recent years, people have begun to recognize the value of wetlands in nature as well as in human communities. There are many ways to help protect wetlands. Using docks or boardwalks to cross wetlands, rather than filling them in, is one way. Finding ways to keep the water that feeds wetlands flowing, rather than diverting it, is also important. Leaving a buffer of natural vegetation along the edges of wetlands protects them from erosion and pollution. Federal, state, and local laws also help protect the country's remaining wetlands from development. For example, the Comprehensive Everglades Restoration Plan (CERP) has been set up to help protect and restore the Everglades in Florida. It is funded in part by U.S. and state agencies.

CONNECTION: Anthropology

Humans have recognized the link between birds and wetlands for thousands of years. Prehistoric people drew pictures of birds and wetlands on cave walls, scratched them onto rocks, and used them to design artifacts. For example, ancient drawings on rocks—called petroglyphs—depicting wetland birds have been found in what is now New Mexico's Petroglyph National Monument. Scientists believe that these beautiful petroglyphs were created by a Native American group between 1300 and 1650.

Figure 16.18 Called *the Mother of the Everglades*, Marjorie Stoneman Douglas (1890–1998) worked tirelessly to protect the Everglades and educate people about it.

Did You Know?

Only a few animals eat living spartina grass, the dominant plant in many salt marshes. However, dead, rotting spartina provides food for small fishes, crabs, and other animals. In this way, spartina supports the salt marsh food web.

After You Read

1. Compare how both a river and a glacier may form lakes.
2. Explain the difference between a marsh and a swamp.
3. In your Science Notebook, write one or two paragraphs explaining the importance of wetlands. Refer to your T-chart for supporting facts.

Before You Read

Draw three boxes to create a sequence chart in your Science Notebook. Add arrows to connect the boxes from one to the next. Label the chart *The Flow of Groundwater*.

Rain and melted snow can form runoff. Most of the time, however, these waters soak into the ground instead of staying on the surface. Water that collects underground is called **groundwater**. Groundwater is present to some extent throughout the world, even under deserts. The total volume of groundwater on Earth is about 30 times greater than the volume of freshwater in lakes and rivers. Groundwater slowly moves through the ground, eventually returning to Earth's surface.

Water is able to collect underground in small spaces, called pores, between particles of soil, sand, or rocks within Earth's crust. **Porosity** is the percentage of pore space in a material. Much of Earth's surface is covered in a layer of soil, which is relatively porous. Below this porous surface, however, lies a rock layer that is not as porous. Groundwater collects in this rock layer, creating a water-filled layer called an aquifer.

As shown in **Figure 16.19**, groundwater fills all of the underground pore spaces in an area called the zone of saturation. Above this zone, pore spaces are moist but are filled mostly with air. This area is called the zone of aeration. The upper boundary of the zone of saturation is the **water table**. The depth of the water table may change quite often. Water tables usually rise during rainy weather and fall during dry weather. The water table is usually at or near Earth's surface in a wetland. It may be hundreds of meters below Earth's surface in a desert.

Figure It Out

1. Is the water table lower or higher during a period with little precipitation?

2. How do the zones of saturation and aeration compare?

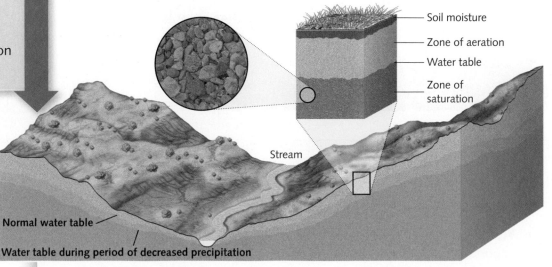

Figure 16.19 The depth of the water table changes with surface features and with seasonal precipitation.

Soil moisture
Zone of aeration
Water table
Zone of saturation
Stream
Normal water table
Water table during period of decreased precipitation

Aquifers

Like water on the surface, groundwater flows downward due to gravity. Its flow, however, is often quite slow. **Permeability** is the ability of a material to let water pass through it. Sand and gravel, which are very porous, have high rates of permeability. So do limestone, sandstone, and many other large-grained rocks. Rocks that contain clay and silt are made of tightly packed grains that contain very small pore spaces. Water flows through these materials very slowly, at rates measured in meters per year. These materials are described as impermeable. They do not allow water to pass through them.

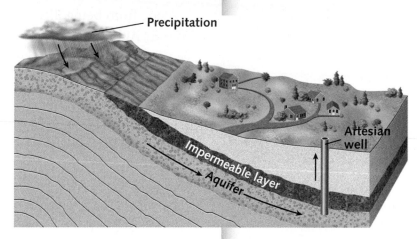

Figure 16.20 Deep aquifers form between layers of impermeable rock. They are usually recharged with water from lands at higher elevations.

Below the surface, layers of permeable and impermeable rock determine where and how groundwater collects. A rock layer that stores and allows the flow of groundwater is called an **aquifer**. **Figure 16.20** shows how an aquifer can form below an impermeable layer.

Wells

How can the water in aquifers be removed? Often, the answer is to dig a well. A **well** is a deep hole dug or drilled to reach the water table. Once it is reached, the hole fills with groundwater. If a well is not dug deep enough, it will dry up when the water table falls below the bottom of the well. This can happen if too much water is pumped out of the well, if too much water is pumped out of other wells nearby, or if there is too little precipitation. Precipitation and runoff can replace the groundwater removed by a well. This replacement water is called **recharge**. For the well to remain useful, recharge must keep pace with the amount of water removed.

Unfortunately, groundwater near Earth's surface is often polluted. Changes in the water table also make shallow wells unreliable. For this reason, many wells are dug into deep aquifers. In some cases, the water pressure in these aquifers is quite high. In fact, it can be so high that water spurts up the well shaft on its own, with no pump necessary. Such a well is called an **artesian well**. The name comes from the French province of Artois, where the first such wells were dug almost a thousand years ago.

As You Read

In the first box of your sequence chart, describe how water enters the ground. In the second box, list the changes that groundwater may cause underground. In the third box, describe how water leaves the ground.

Why might a well that once produced water become dry?

Springs

Aside from being lifted up in wells, does groundwater ever leave the ground? Although groundwater can stay underground for hundreds or even thousands of years, natural processes eventually bring it back to Earth's surface. Some aquifers connect to the ocean or to large rivers. Other aquifers feed springs. A **spring** is a natural opening in the ground through which groundwater flows to Earth's surface.

Springs often form where aquifers are especially shallow. Other springs are natural versions of artesian wells, and are called artesian springs. In these springs, water pressure in a deep aquifer forces water upward through cracks in the rock. The temperature of a spring's water is usually about the same as the average annual temperature of the region where the spring is located. **Hot springs**, however, are springs that produce water with temperatures higher than that of the human body. There are thousands of hot springs in the United States alone. Many more are located throughout the world.

How do hot springs form? Remember that Earth is extremely hot below the crust. Many hot springs form near volcanoes, fault zones, hot spots, and other places where Earth's crust is unusually active or thin. Yellowstone National Park in Wyoming is one such place, as are the volcanoes of the Pacific Northwest. Other hot springs form from aquifers that run unusually deep into Earth's crust. The hot springs of the Appalachian Mountains are examples. In any hot spring, Earth's interior heats the groundwater, which then rises to the surface.

In some cases, hot water builds up underground as steam. A **geyser** is a hot spring that shoots steam and water vapor into the air at regular intervals. Yellowstone National Park is home to the famous Old Faithful geyser, which erupts in a 40-m column of steam about once an hour. Other Yellowstone geysers erupt in even taller columns.

Figure 16.21 A hot spring or geyser, such as Yellowstone's Old Faithful, provides evidence of Earth's hot interior below the crust.

Figure 16.22 Even in the Sahara, a spring can bring groundwater to the surface. A spring may form a pool of water, called an oasis, in the desert.

Groundwater Erosion and Deposition

Moving water on Earth's surface can weather and erode rocks. It can also deposit sediment to form new landforms. These same processes occur underground. When water sinks through soil and decaying plant matter, it combines with the carbon dioxide in these materials to form a compound called carbonic acid (H_2CO_3). This is the same compound that gives soda water its tart, fizzy taste and texture.

When combined with even a small amount of carbonic acid, water becomes a powerful agent for weathering certain types of rocks. Limestone is one example. Over thousands of years, acidic groundwater can weather and erode huge volumes of rock from a limestone bed. When the water table drops, a cave is left behind. A **cave** is a large, naturally hollowed-out space in or above the ground. Some underground caves are more than one kilometer long and 100 m high. Many caves are made up of mazelike passages, wide chambers, and deep shafts.

Deposition also helps form caves. As water seeps down from the cave ceiling, it leaves behind deposits of calcium carbonate, a type of limestone. As the water drips downward and evaporates, the dissolved calcium carbonate forms sharp, icicle-shaped projections called stalactites. At the same time, the calcium carbonate in the water drops that make it to the cave's floor form cone-shaped features called stalagmites.

When the water table is lower than the level of a cave, the top of the cave is no longer supported by water underneath. When this happens, the roof may collapse, leaving a round depression on the surface called a **sinkhole**. In areas where the water table is high, sinkholes often form lakes. Many of the small lakes in Florida formed in this way.

Figure 16.23 Weathering, erosion, and deposition combined to form the beautiful, oddly shaped features of Mammoth Cave in Kentucky.

After You Read

1. Explain how groundwater collects in an aquifer.
2. How do wells and springs compare?
3. Review the paths and actions of groundwater you recorded in your sequence chart. In your Science Notebook, draw a diagram that shows the movement of groundwater. Then write a few sentences explaining the importance of groundwater for life on Earth's surface.

Extend It!

Speleology is the scientific study of caves. One subject of great interest to speleologists is the world's longest cave system, the joint Mammoth Cave and Flint Ridge Cave system in west-central Kentucky. These caves have a combined length of 530 km. Research the history of this cave system and its interesting features. Record your findings in your Science Notebook.

KEY CONCEPTS

16.1 Stream and River Development

- The water cycle renews Earth's supply of freshwater. Precipitation gathers as runoff, which feeds streams and rivers. Evaporation returns water to the atmosphere as water vapor.

- Rushing water erodes and shapes the land, forming channels that carry streams and rivers.

- The gradient, discharge, and load of a stream all affect its rate of erosion.

- A watershed is the region drained by a river system. A river and its tributaries act as a system that moves water and sediment through the watershed.

16.2 Stream and River Deposits

- As rivers slow down, they deposit sediment, creating landforms including oxbow lakes, alluvial fans, and deltas.

- Floods can cause great damage, but are natural events that often add nutrient-rich sediment to floodplains.

- Many communities along major rivers build tall, thick walls called levees to block floodwaters. Some communities prefer to allow their streams and rivers to flood naturally.

16.3 Lakes and Wetlands

- Many lakes were formed by the actions of glaciers. Some lakes form from parts of rivers. Others may be artificially formed behind human-built dams.

- Eutrophication begins when a lake becomes rich in nutrients. This leads to an explosive growth of algae, which results in decreased oxygen levels in a lake.

- Wetlands include swamps, marshes, estuaries, and bogs. All wetlands help filter and store freshwater, and they provide habitats for unique communities of living things.

16.4 Groundwater

- Groundwater soaks through the soil and flows downward due to gravity.

- Groundwater fills all of the underground pore spaces in the zone of saturation. The upper boundary of the zone of saturation is the water table.

- Groundwater collects in aquifers, or layers of permeable rock. Some aquifers connect to the ocean or to large rivers. Others feed springs, which bring groundwater back to the surface.

- A cave forms when groundwater weathers and erodes a large space in a limestone bed.

- A sinkhole forms when the water table is lower than the level of a cave and the roof of the cave collapses.

VOCABULARY REVIEW

Write each term in a complete sentence or write a paragraph relating several terms.

16.1
water cycle, p. 298
runoff, p. 299
weathering, p. 299
erosion, p. 299
channel, p. 300
gradient, p. 301
discharge, p. 301
load, p. 301
tributary, p. 302
watershed, p. 302
divide, p. 302

16.2
deposition, p. 304
meander, p. 304
riverbank, p. 304
alluvial fan, p. 305
delta, p. 305
floodplain, p. 305
levee, p. 306

16.3
lake, p. 307
reservoir, p. 307
eutrophication, p. 308
irrigation, p. 309
wetland, p. 310
swamp, p. 310
marsh, p. 310
bog, p. 310
estuary, p. 311

16.4
groundwater, p. 312
porosity, p. 312
water table, p. 312
permeability, p. 313
aquifer, p. 313
well, p. 313
recharge, p. 313
artesian well, p. 313
spring, p. 314
hot spring, p. 314
geyser, p. 314
cave, p. 315
sinkhole, p. 315

MASTERING CONCEPTS

True or False
If the statement is true, write "true." If it is false, change the underlined word or words to make the statement true.

1. During the spring, snow may melt and flow over Earth's surface as <u>precipitation</u>.

2. Rivers become larger and wider when their <u>tributaries</u> join them.

3. Meanders are most common in the <u>steepest</u> sections of rivers.

4. Melt from <u>glaciers</u> filled the Great Lakes and other lakes.

5. Pitcher plants are common in nutrient-poor wetlands called <u>swamps</u>.

6. Groundwater collects in permeable rock layers called <u>water tables</u>.

Short Answer
Answer each of the following in a sentence or brief paragraph.

7. How does Earth's freshwater supply compare to its total supply of water?

8. Why does a river channel change size and shape over a river's course?

9. What human actions will increase the rate of eutrophication of a lake?

10. Compare an ordinary well to an artesian well.

11. How can floods benefit a floodplain?

12. Explain how caves form.

PREPARE FOR CHAPTER TEST

To prepare for the chapter test, create a question from each Learning Goal. Use the information in your Science Notebook to answer each question. Then use these answers to write a well-developed essay about the chapter. Use the Key Concept on the first page of this chapter as your topic sentence.

Critical Thinking
Use what you have learned in this chapter to answer each of the following.

13. **Apply Concepts** How can heavy rains cause floods on a river hundreds of kilometers away from where they fall?

14. **Cause and Effect** Freshwater is renewed by the water cycle. Why do many communities encourage people to conserve freshwater?

Standardized Test Question
Choose the letter of the response that correctly answers the question.

15. A very dry desert surrounds a small lake. What is the most likely source of the water in the lake?
    A. precipitation
    B. a stream or river
    C. groundwater
    D. a glacier

Test-Taking Tip

Don't get stuck on a difficult question. Instead, make a small mark next to the question. Remember to go back and answer the question later. Other parts of the test may give you a clue that will help you answer the question.

Oceans

KEY CONCEPT Because oceans cover nearly $\frac{3}{4}$ of Earth's surface, their currents, marine life, and tides, as well as the evaporation of ocean water, all affect life on land.

Even if you live far away from the ocean shore, the world's oceans affect your life. Ocean water supplies most of the water vapor in the atmosphere, which in turn supplies water for rain, snow, and other forms of precipitation. Ocean currents help moderate, or control, temperatures, especially in coastal regions. Ocean animals are harvested for food. Algae in the ocean also play an important role. Through the process of photosynthesis, they supply almost 50 percent of the oxygen in Earth's atmosphere.

Think About Oceans

What would you need to explore the deep ocean? What would you hope to find out? In your Science Notebook, describe a one-week research expedition to explore an ocean of your choice. Be sure to list all needed supplies.

- Do you think exploring Earth's oceans is important? Explain why or why not.
- Why do you think humans have explored Earth's oceans much less thoroughly than its lands?

NSTA

SCiLINKS®
THE WORLD'S A CLICK AWAY
▼
www.scilinks.org

Oceans **Code: WGES17**

17.1 The World's Oceans

Before You Read

Write the title of this lesson in the middle of a page of your Science Notebook. It will be the title of a concept map for this lesson. On the left side of the page, list the words and terms you already know about the world's oceans.

Learning Goals

- Identify and locate the world's oceans.
- Describe the work of oceanographers.
- Explain how the world's oceans formed.

New Vocabulary

ocean
sea
iceberg
oceanography
sonar
sea level

An ocean can seem enormous when we fly over it in an airplane or stand looking out at it from the edge of a beach. Oceans are much too large to see all at once. They cover 71 percent of Earth's surface and hold about 97 percent of Earth's water. Oceans truly are huge.

Oceans and Seas

An **ocean** is a vast body of salt water. Typically, three major oceans are identified on Earth: the Pacific Ocean, the Atlantic Ocean, and the Indian Ocean. Two smaller oceans, the Arctic Ocean and the Antarctic Ocean, are located near Earth's poles. The Pacific Ocean is the largest ocean. It contains about half of Earth's water supply and covers an area larger than all of the continents put together.

In many places, the continents serve as a natural boundary between two oceans. Yet, all the oceans are connected. Scientists often refer to a single world ocean rather than several oceans. Water flows freely throughout the world ocean.

A **sea** is smaller than an ocean, and it is usually near land or surrounded by land. Many seas are connected to the world ocean. Other seas, such as the Aral Sea in Asia, are landlocked—that is, surrounded on all sides by land.

Figure It Out

1. Which hemisphere is covered by more water, the northern or the southern?

2. Earth is round. Why does this map of Earth have such an unusual shape?

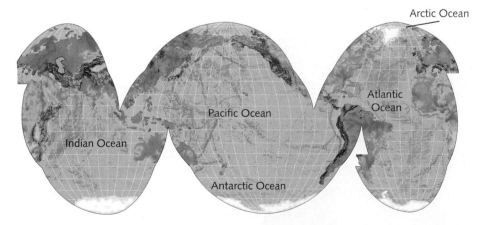

Figure 17.1 This map was divided to show the size of Earth's oceans. Although individual oceans are identified, all ocean water is connected.

Figure 17.2 Like pancakes on a huge griddle, patches of sea ice cover much of the Arctic Ocean.

As You Read

In the space around the lesson title in your Science Notebook, record important facts about oceans.

What are some signs of global warming in the polar regions that scientists have observed?

Earth's oceans have changed in size and shape over time. Some oceans have disappeared, or have shrunk to much smaller sizes. The Great Salt Lake of Utah, for example, was once part of the much larger ancient Lake Bonneville. This lake was large enough to have been considered an inland sea. Today, huge tracts of flat, salt-filled lands cover much of northern Utah. They formed when the lake's salt water evaporated.

Oceans near the Poles

In the Arctic Ocean and Antarctic Ocean, water cycles between the liquid and solid state. Ice that forms on the ocean surface is called sea ice. Vast expanses of sea ice cover the polar oceans, especially during the winter. Ice is less dense than liquid water, so it floats.

Sea ice forms gradually. When the temperature drops, an icy slush begins to cover the ocean's surface. The slush slowly freezes into round pieces called pancake ice. As more water freezes, the ice pieces grow and thicken to cover the surface in a continuous sheet. Such a sheet is called pack ice. In the coldest parts of the polar oceans, pack ice covers the water all year long. In some places, the ice is many meters thick.

In recent years, scientists have been observing unusually high temperatures in the polar regions, as well as a decrease in the total ice pack. For most scientists, this is evidence that Earth's temperatures are gradually increasing, an event called global warming. Global warming could have serious consequences for everyone living on Earth.

Icebergs

When a glacier or an ice pack meets an ocean, a large piece of ice often breaks off. This forms an iceberg. An **iceberg** is a large mass of floating ice. Ocean currents can carry icebergs hundreds of kilometers from their points of origin.

In the North Atlantic Ocean, many icebergs drift into the shipping lanes between Europe and North America. In 1912, the British ship *Titanic* collided with one such iceberg. The ship sank, killing about 1,500 people. Today, the U.S. Coast Guard runs the International Ice Patrol. Its mission is to track icebergs and to alert ships of dangers.

Figure 17.3 Although an iceberg floats, most of its volume and mass is underwater. The visible portion above the water is only "the tip of the iceberg," a phrase used when describing something with a huge, hidden part.

Oceanography

Oceanography is the study of Earth's oceans. It combines many fields within science and mathematics. An oceanographer studies the geology of the ocean floor, the chemistry of ocean water, and the physics that explains ocean currents and tides. Studying the living things of the ocean is also part of oceanography.

Why is studying the oceans important? Oceanographers answer this question in different ways. Some may discuss ocean pollution. In the past, people regularly dumped all sorts of wastes and garbage into ocean waters. Such pollution still continues in many places, with unknown effects. Other oceanographers may investigate global warming, coral reefs, ocean animals, or fossil fuels from the ocean floor.

Figure 17.4 Most scientists prefer to study their subjects as closely as possible. For oceanographers, this means wearing a wet suit and diving into ocean waters.

Technology for Studying the Ocean

For many years, the nature of the ocean floor remained a mystery. Although boats crossed the ocean, the water below was too deep and too dark for sailors to see much below the surface. The early submersibles, which are devices that dive under the water, could safely carry people only to shallow depths.

Today, submarines can travel to nearly every part of the ocean, even below the polar ice caps. Nevertheless, scientists have visited and studied only a small fraction of ocean waters and the ocean floor. Deep-water expeditions are expensive and require special skills.

PEOPLE IN SCIENCE Dr. Amy Bower   1959–

Amy Bower grew up in the ocean-side town of Rockport, Massachusetts. She liked to walk along its beaches and search for interesting living things under the rocks. Today, Dr. Bower works just down the shore from the beaches she once walked. She is an oceanographer at the Woods Hole Oceanographic Institute. One of her interests is the way water travels between seas and oceans. Water in a sea often has different temperatures and salt concentrations than water in a nearby ocean. Dr. Bower researches how these waters mix together and how that mixing forms ocean currents.

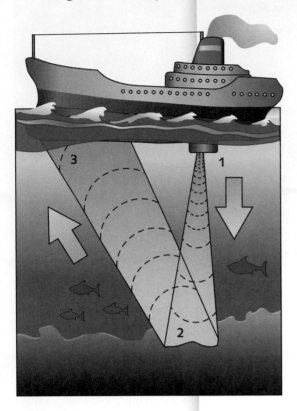

Fortunately, technology has provided other ways to study oceans. **Sonar** uses sound waves to detect and measure objects under water. It is used to measure ocean depth. *Sonar* stands for "sound navigation and ranging." As shown in **Figure 17.5**, a ship on the water surface bounces a sound wave off the ocean floor. The time that the sound wave takes to return is a measure of the ocean depth. In a technique called side-scan sonar, sound waves are bounced at an angle off the floor. This allows sonar to detect the sides of underwater hills or the sloping wall of a trench.

Oceans can also be studied from outer space. Satellites in orbit around Earth monitor oceans using radar and other technology. They provide data on ocean currents, temperatures, tides, and other properties.

Figure 17.5 1. Low frequency sound waves are emitted from the ship. 2. Sound waves bounce off the ocean floor. 3. Detectors on the ship receive the bounced waves.

Figure 17.6 From 1993 to 2006, the *TOPEX/ Poseidon* satellite used radar and other tools to monitor ocean currents, tides, and temperatures. It was joined by the *Jason* satellite in 2002.

Extend It!

Sound waves are not only useful for detecting objects on the ocean floor. Doctors use sound waves to see what is going on inside the human body. Sound waves can also be used to conduct surgery without scalpels or stitches. Research how sound waves are used in medicine. Record your findings in your Science Notebook.

Forming an Ocean

Of all the planets, only Earth has a known vast supply of water in the liquid state. Where did Earth's water supply come from? How did the oceans form? Scientists have hypothesized that Earth's water supply could have had one of two sources.

One source is the material that formed Earth, which scientists consider to be made of the same material as meteorites. Meteorites found on Earth contain up to 0.5 percent water. If early Earth contained the same percentage of water, it would have been more than enough to fill the oceans we have today. The hypothesis is that volcanic activity brought this water from Earth's interior to its surface and atmosphere.

During Earth's early years, volcanoes were much more common and erupted more frequently than they do today. The planet was also much hotter. Scientists propose that Earth's first atmosphere was formed by water vapor and other gases that were released from volcanoes. When the planet cooled, the water vapor condensed and fell to Earth as rain, forming the first oceans.

Another hypothesis involves comets. Comets are mixtures of frozen water and pieces of rock that travel quickly through space. If comets collided with Earth, they would have added water to the planet's supply as they melted.

Changing Oceans

Recall from Chapter 6 that Earth's crust is divided into several large slabs called tectonic plates. Slowly but steadily, these plates move over Earth's surface. Over millions of years, the continents change size, shape, and position. The world ocean changes in these ways, too.

The world ocean also changes in volume. This affects **sea level**, which is the height of the surfaces of the oceans. Sea level has risen and fallen throughout Earth's history. The most significant cause of these changes is climate. When Earth's climate cools, more water becomes frozen near the poles, and sea level drops. When the climate warms and the ice melts, sea level rises.

Carbon dioxide
Hydrogen
Chlorine   Water vapor
Nitrogen

CONNECTION: History

In 1872, the British treasury agreed to fund the first purely scientific ocean expedition ever conducted. Many think that this 111,000-km expedition (which lasted from 1872 to 1876) represents the beginning of modern oceanography. Professor Charles Wyville Thomson directed the scientists on board the ship *Challenger*. Throughout their ocean voyage, *Challenger's* crew recorded observations, performed soundings using sonar, and dredged up samples from the ocean floor from hundreds of locations around the world. Using this data, scientists were able to map the contours of the great ocean basins and gain a better understanding of the patterns of ocean currents and temperatures.

Figure 17.7 The illustration shows how scientists picture Earth's surface soon after it formed. Volcanic eruptions and comet strikes *(inset)* may both have added water to Earth's atmosphere and surface.

After You Read

1. Why do scientists often refer to a single world ocean rather than to separate oceans?

2. List three different subjects that an oceanographer might investigate.

3. Explain why oceans are worth studying. Include facts about oceans from your concept map.

Learning Goals

- Explain what is meant by salinity.
- Describe how temperature relates to the three ocean layers.
- Describe how the absorption of light affects ocean life and water temperatures.
- Explain how the oceans moderate Earth's climate.

New Vocabulary

salinity
temperature profile
thermocline

Before You Read

Think about the oceans. In your Science Notebook, write facts you know or ideas you have about the ocean's salt content, absorption of light, temperature, and effects on nearby land. Leave two empty lines underneath each fact.

Salinity

The **salinity** of ocean water is a measure of its concentration of dissolved salts. The salt comes from the nonstop process of weathering and dissolving of minerals. These minerals are then transported to the sea. Smaller amounts of minerals come from fertilizer and other substances that run off the land. Scientists measure salinity in units called parts per thousand. One part per thousand equals one gram of salt per thousand grams, or 1 kg, of water. On average, ocean water has a salinity of 35 parts per thousand, or 3.5 percent. The remaining 96.5 percent is water.

Some ocean waters are saltier than others. In the subtropics, the rate of evaporation is high and precipitation is low. Here, salinity may reach 37 parts per thousand. In regions where much freshwater is added, such as the mouth of a river or the edge of a melting glacier, salinity may drop to 32 parts per thousand. Remember, however, that all ocean water is connected. As waters mix, salinity stays within a narrow range.

What makes up ocean salt? It is mostly ions of sodium and chloride, the same components that make up ordinary table salt. But other ions are present in small amounts. In fact, most elements that exist somewhere on Earth are also present in ocean water.

Ocean water also contains dissolved gases and nutrients. The gases include oxygen, nitrogen, and carbon dioxide. The nutrients include many of the same compounds present in freshwater and in soil. Both gases and nutrients are essential for the survival of the ocean's living things.

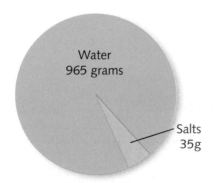

Water
965 grams

Salts
35g

Figure 17.8 Although ocean water is much saltier than freshwater, its salts are dissolved, or thoroughly mixed. Salts actually make up only a small percentage of ocean water.

Absorption of Light

Water transmits much of the light that strikes it. To *transmit* means "to allow to pass through." This explains why it is easy to see through a thin layer of water. It gets harder to see through water that is deeper, however, because water does not transmit light completely. It always absorbs some light. When sunlight travels down from the ocean surface, more and more of that light is absorbed as the depth increases. Little or no light reaches the ocean's deepest parts.

The distribution of light affects both the temperature of ocean waters and the ocean's living things. Ocean surface temperatures range from –2°C near the poles to 30°C near the equator. Yet, throughout the ocean, temperature decreases with depth. Even in the tropics, the deepest ocean water is always cold. Little light reaches these depths to heat the water.

Why do living things need light? Remember that light powers photosynthesis, the process that algae and plants use to make food. In the ocean, the light needed for photosynthesis reaches down only about 100 m. For this reason, most ocean life lives above the 100-meter mark. Algae and plants form the base of the food supply of ocean animals, just as they do for land animals. Algae and plants also produce the oxygen that animals need to live.

Even so, many living things survive in the ocean's darkest, deepest waters. These organisms have adapted to a cold, low-light, low-oxygen environment. Typically, these organisms survive on nutrients and dead plant and animal matter that sink from the water above.

Explore It!

Tape a picture to the bottom of a 1 L clear glass beaker. Wrap the beaker's sides with black construction paper. Add water in 100 mL increments. At what depth of water can you no longer see the picture?

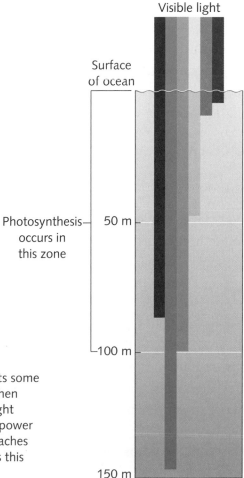

Figure 17.9 a) The ocean surface reflects some of the sunlight that strikes it, especially when that light strikes at an angle. **b)** Enough light reaches the top 100 m of ocean water to power photosynthesis. **c)** Only faint blue light reaches below 100 m. Unusual organisms, such as this viperfish, live at these depths.

Temperature Profile

Figure 17.10 shows a typical **temperature profile**, which is a graph of ocean temperatures at different depths. Such profiles change depending on location and season but usually follow similar patterns. For this reason, scientists divide ocean water into three layers.

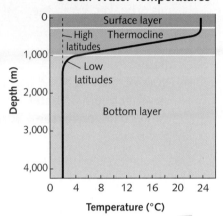

Ocean Water Temperatures

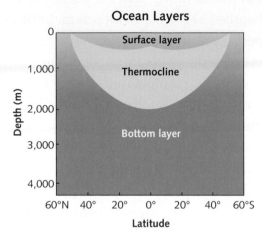

Ocean Layers

The surface layer of ocean water is the brightest and warmest layer. It is usually about 100 m thick. The **thermocline** (THUR muh kline) layer lies below the surface layer and above the colder, dark bottom layer of ocean water. Within the thermocline layer, water temperature decreases rapidly with depth.

In **Figure 17.10**, the rate of decrease in temperature in the thermocline layer is about 4°C for every kilometer. The temperature in the ocean's bottom layer stays just above the freezing point of water.

The depths of these three layers change with latitude, or distance from the equator. The thermocline is deepest near the equator and gradually becomes less deep with increasing latitude. At the highest latitudes near the poles, the three ocean zones do not exist. Because the surface waters are always very cold, the temperature changes only slightly as water depth increases.

Ocean Layers and Density

The density of water varies with differences in temperature. This explains why ocean layers stay more or less separate from one another. Warm water is less dense than cold water so it tends to rise above cold water. It also spreads out and takes up more space than colder water. Lesson 17.3 explains how this tendency helps ocean currents to form.

Oceans and Climate

Oceans play a critical role in keeping Earth's temperature within a range that allows life as we know it to exist. How do they do this? Oceans absorb energy from sunlight more slowly and retain it longer than dry land does. If the oceans absorbed and released the Sun's energy quickly, Earth's average temperature would range from above 100°C during the day to below –100°C at night! With heat being exchanged this quickly between the atmosphere and Earth's surface, violent weather patterns

As You Read

With a partner, discuss what you just read about ocean properties. In your Science Notebook, write any facts that differ from the ideas about oceans you listed earlier.

Why is ocean water colder at greater depths?

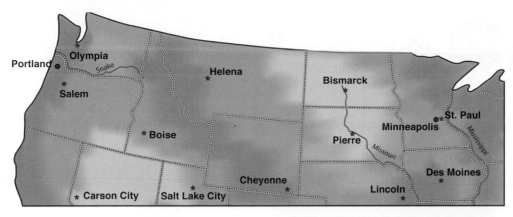

Portland, Oregon
Average July temperature: 24° Celsius
Average January temperature: 1° Celsius

Minneapolis, Minnesota
Average July temperature: 28° Celsius
Average January temperature: –11° Celsius

Figure 17.11 The average July and January temperatures of Portland, Oregon, and Minneapolis, Minnesota, are shown here. Places near the ocean tend to have more moderate climates than those farther inland.

would occur. Most living things on the planet would not survive these extreme conditions.

Because of their ability to absorb and release energy from sunlight slowly, oceans tend to moderate the climate of lands near them. For example, the cities of Portland and Minneapolis, shown in **Figure 17.11**, lie at about the same latitude. This means they receive about equal amounts of sunlight every day. Yet, Portland has a relatively mild climate. Its summers are warm but not very hot, and its winters are cool but not very cold. In comparison, the city of Minneapolis has much greater seasonal extremes. The main reason for this climate difference is Portland's neighbor to the west, the Pacific Ocean.

After You Read

1. Are all ocean waters equally salty? Are all at the same temperature? Explain.
2. Why does most ocean life live within about 100 m of the ocean's surface?
3. Review the list of ocean properties you recorded in your Science Notebook. Use this list to write a well-developed paragraph describing the three layers of ocean waters.

Figure It Out

1. What are the July and January temperature differences between Portland and Minneapolis?

2. Identify another pair of cities on the map that have similar latitudes. Predict how oceans affect the climates of these cities.

Explore It!

Place a cup of soil and a cup of water under a hot lamp. Using a thermometer, check the temperature of each every 30 minutes for several hours. Compare how the temperatures of the soil and water change over time. Record your results in your Science Notebook.

Learning Goals

- Compare surface currents and deep ocean currents.
- Explain how waves and tides form.

New Vocabulary

surface current
Coriolis effect
gyre
upwelling
density current
wave
crest
trough
wavelength
breaker
tsunami
tide
spring tide
neap tide

Recall Vocabulary

trade wind, p. 243

Before You Read

Use the title of this lesson and the headings to create a lesson outline in your Science Notebook. On a separate page, list any questions you have about the topics.

If you ever visit San Francisco, California, be sure to bring a jacket, even in the summer. San Francisco has colder, wetter weather than cities nearby. This weather is partly due to an ocean current in the Pacific Ocean.

Surface Currents

Similar to air that moves as winds in the atmosphere, water moves as currents in the ocean. A current is a mass movement of water in one direction. A **surface current** is a wind-driven movement of ocean water that affects the upper few hundred meters of the ocean. **Figure 17.13** shows many of the surface currents that flow across the world ocean.

Three main factors explain why surface currents form. The first is the pattern of global winds. As you learned in Chapter 13, winds tend to blow in patterns across Earth's surface. The patterns are especially regular across oceans, where no landforms affect them. Surface ocean water moves with the winds, forming surface currents. The second factor is the **Coriolis effect**, which is a result of Earth's rotation on its axis. It causes currents north of the equator to deflect, or bend, to the right and currents south of the equator to deflect to the left. The third factor is Earth's continents. Currents change shape, size, speed, and direction as they approach coastlines.

Gyres Earth's continents deflect surface currents and cause them to flow in closed, circular current systems called **gyres** (JI urs). As **Figure 17.13** shows, there are five major gyres: the North Pacific, the North Atlantic,

Figure 17.12 The cold waters of the California Current bring cold weather and fog to the city of San Francisco.

the South Pacific, the South Atlantic, and the Indian Ocean. Gyres help even out Earth's temperature differences. As water circulates through a gyre, it warms near the equator and cools in higher latitudes.

The Gulf Stream and the North Atlantic Current are shown in **Figure 17.13**. The Gulf Stream carries water from an equatorial region, so it is a warm-water current. The warm water travels all the way to Great Britain and Scandinavia. As a result, northern Europe has a much warmer, gentler climate than its latitude would otherwise suggest.

The California Current, also shown in **Figure 17.13**, is a cold-water current along the western coast of North America. It cools the coastal regions it passes, among them the city of San Francisco.

Currents and Global Warming

Could global warming affect ocean currents? Many scientists are concerned that warmer air temperatures might cause currents to weaken or shift position. If this happens, the changes on land could be quite severe. Today, snow and freezing temperatures are rare in London, Copenhagen, Amsterdam, and other cities of northern Europe because the Gulf Stream warms them. If the Gulf Stream weakened or changed its course, these areas could experience a change in climate.

As You Read

As you read the lesson, add details to the outline in your Science Notebook. Share your outline with a partner and correct or add information as necessary. Include definitions for any unfamiliar terms.

Explain why surface currents do not travel in continuous loops around Earth.

Figure It Out

1. Compare gyres to circumpolar currents.

2. Use the map to predict whether the western or eastern coast of South America is warmer.

Major Ocean Currents

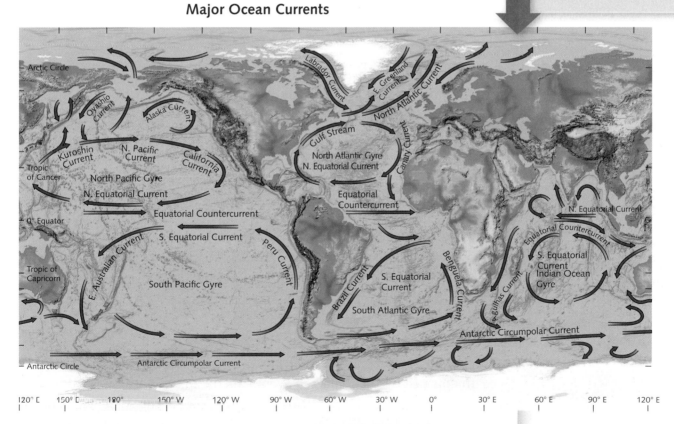

Figure 17.13 Because of the Coriolis effect, currents in gyres circulate clockwise in the northern hemisphere and counterclockwise in the southern hemisphere.

Upwelling

Waters in surface currents travel horizontally across the upper layer of the ocean. However, waters can also move up or down through the ocean. The upward motion of ocean water is called **upwelling**. Remember that deep ocean waters typically are very cold—so, upwelling brings cold water to the surface.

Most upwelling occurs on the western edges of continents in the trade wind belts. The reason for the upwellings is shown in **Figure 17.14**. Winds create surface currents that move water away from shore. An upwelling replaces the water that surface currents carry away.

Upwelling waters are rich in nutrients that collect on the ocean floor. For this reason, these waters support large communities of fish and other marine life. Some of the world's richest fishing grounds are found in upwellings, such as those that occur along the coasts of Peru and northern California.

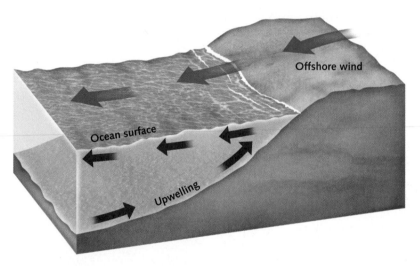

Figure 17.14 As trade winds blow surface waters offshore, deep, colder water rises to the ocean's surface.

El Niño

Every few years, the trade winds blow more weakly than normal across the southern Pacific Ocean. This weakening and its effects are called El Niño. During an El Niño year, a chain of events affects people all over Earth. One effect is the weakening of upwelling along the coast of Peru. The waters become warmer, nutrients drop, and the fish population suffers. Other effects include increased rainfall in parts of North and South America and droughts in Australia.

In contrast with El Niño, an event called La Niña sometimes affects the southern Pacific Ocean. During a La Niña year, the trade winds blow quite strongly. Upwelling increases off the coast of Peru, and the waters there become even colder than normal.

Explain It!

Imagine that you are standing on the edge of the ocean with the wind at your back. In your Science Notebook, use a flowchart to explain an El Niño and the events that occur.

El Niño and La Niña have been occurring for thousands of years. Although much is known about them, many questions remain. Many scientists are concerned that El Niño years could become more frequent due to global warming.

Deep-Ocean Currents

Winds are not the only source of ocean currents. A **density current** forms when ocean waters with different temperatures and salinities meet. A density current moves water along the bottom part of the ocean.

A density current forms in cold waters near the poles. Recall that when ocean water freezes, salts stay dissolved in the liquid water. Thus, waters near the poles are both cold and very salty. This makes them denser than other waters, so they sink. The cold, salty water travels slowly but steadily along the ocean bottom, toward the equator. There, the waters become warmer and less salty, and thus less dense. As a result, they rise.

Evaporation also can contribute to density currents. For example, summers in the Mediterranean Sea are especially warm and dry. As water evaporates, the remaining seawater becomes saltier and thus denser. This forms a density current from the Mediterranean Sea into its neighbor, the Atlantic Ocean. Along the surface, the current flows in the reverse direction, moving the more dilute ocean water into the saltier sea.

For evidence of these currents, consider the photograph shown in **Figure 17.16**. This photograph shows ripples on the ocean floor. Elsewhere on the ocean floor, scientists have found clay mounds that resemble sand dunes. Such features show that deep ocean water moves in currents, much like the air in the atmosphere moves as winds.

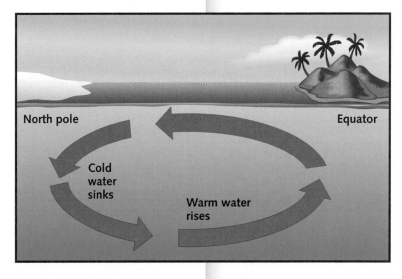

North pole

Equator

Cold water sinks

Warm water rises

Figure 17.15 Cold, salty water sinks at the poles, forming a density current that travels to warm, equatorial waters.

Figure 17.16 Sedimentary structures on the ocean floor, such as the ripple marks shown here, provide evidence of deep water currents.

Waves

The ocean surface is not flat. It bunches into moving crests and troughs called waves. A **wave** is a rhythmic movement that carries energy through space or matter—in this case, ocean water. Winds are the main causes of ocean waves.

Wave Characteristics

Figure 17.17 shows how waves move in the open ocean. The highest point of a wave is called the **crest**. The lowest point of a wave is called the **trough**. The distance between two adjacent crests or two adjacent troughs is the **wavelength**. Typically, the wavelength increases with the speed of the wind.

As **Figure 17.17** also shows, waves do not carry water very far. Instead, they move water in a circular path. The size of the circular path decreases with depth below the surface. Below a depth of about one-half wavelength, waves have very little effect.

Wave height is the vertical distance between a crest and a trough. It typically depends on three factors: wind speed, wind duration, and fetch. In ocean science, fetch is the distance that a wind blows over water. Ocean waves typically are taller than lake waves, because winds over oceans tend to move faster, last a longer amount of time, and have a greater fetch.

b

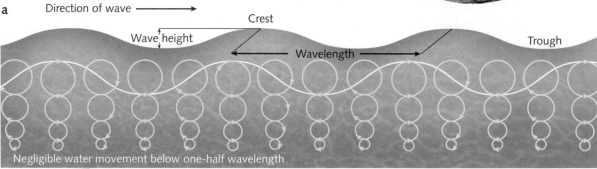

a

Direction of wave ⟶

Crest

Wave height

Wavelength

Trough

Negligible water movement below one-half wavelength

Figure 17.17 **a)** Water is not carried forward by a wave. Instead, it moves through a circular path. **b)** The same is true for floating objects, such as ocean buoys.

Breakers

Ocean waves tend to slow down and lose energy as they approach the shoreline. This happens because of friction between the water and the ocean floor. As the waves slow down, wavelength decreases and the waves bunch together. Incoming waves become taller and steeper. When the water is especially shallow, the crests of the waves move faster than the troughs. This causes the crests to collapse forward in a rush of white water.

The collapsing waves near the shoreline are called **breakers**. Breakers can be very powerful. Over many years, repeated pounding from breakers can weather the rocks along a shoreline into fine pieces.

Figure 17.18 At the crest of a breaker, fast-moving water breaks apart from the rest of the wave. Surfers enjoy riding breakers just below the crest.

Tsunamis

A **tsunami** (soo NAH mee) is a huge ocean wave that is caused by a major disturbance to the ocean floor. Earthquakes are the most common of these disturbances, but volcanic eruptions, landslides, and even meteor strikes can cause tsunamis.

Tsunami waves travel about 800 km per hour across the open ocean. However, they are not especially noticeable until they approach land. When a tsunami reaches shallow water near a shoreline, it can form huge, fast-moving breakers. In December 2004, tsunami waves at least 9 m high struck the coastlines of islands in the Indian Ocean. Other tsunamis have produced waves as tall as 30 m.

The heights of tsunami waves depend on many factors, including the power of the original disturbance and the shape of the ocean bottom. Some very strong earthquakes have caused tsunamis that were quite mild, while weaker earthquakes have caused very destructive tsunamis. Scientists continue to research ways to predict tsunamis and warn people that they are approaching.

Figure 17.19 Fast-moving breakers caused by tsunamis can destroy any structure along the shoreline. The Indian Ocean tsunami of 2004 killed over 200,000 people.

Tides

The two photographs in **Figure 17.20** show the effects of ocean tides. A **tide** is a periodic rise and fall of sea level. Along most ocean shores, the tide rises and falls twice a day. Yet, some places have only one high tide and one low tide a day. The height difference between high tide and low tide can vary greatly. Tides vary from day to day, as well as from place to place.

Tides and Gravity

Tides form because of the pull of gravity from both the Moon and the Sun. Because the Moon is so much closer to Earth than the Sun, its influence on Earth's tides is greater. As the Moon moves through its orbit, its gravity pulls at everything on Earth to bring it closer. Earth's gravity keeps everything in place except the water, which bulges out in the direction of the Moon. Not only does the Moon have an effect on the water closest to it, but its gravitational force pulls Earth toward it, too. The water on the opposite side of Earth from the Moon is not affected as strongly. So, as Earth moves toward the Moon, it moves away from that water. The result is two bulges of water—one being formed by the Moon's gravity and one being formed by Earth's movement away from the water on its side farthest from the Moon. The bulges of water shift position as Earth rotates on its axis, which is why tides repeat in a daily cycle.

The force of gravity from the Sun also causes ocean waters to bulge, but not as strongly as the Moon's gravity. As a result, the Sun acts to strengthen or weaken tides. As shown in **Figure 17.21** on page 335, when the Sun and the Moon are aligned with Earth the tidal bulge is especially large. This causes a very strong tide called a **spring tide**. Spring tides always occur during a new moon or full moon phase.

When the Sun and the Moon form a right angle with Earth, the tidal bulge is much smaller. This causes a weak tide called a **neap tide**. Neap tides always occur during the first-quarter or third-quarter moon phases.

Tidal Variations

The positions of Earth, the Moon, and the Sun are not the only factors that affect the strength of tides. Latitude and the shape of the ocean floor are also factors. In the Gulf of Mexico, for example, the differeence between high tide and low tide, also called the tidal range, is about one meter. Farther north, along the coast of the New England states, the tidal range is about six meters.

The world's highest tides have been measured in the Bay of Fundy, an arm of the Atlantic Ocean between the Canadian provinces of New Brunswick and Nova Scotia. Tides there typically reach 15 m and are sometimes even higher.

Figure 17.20 A shoreline can look very different at high and low tide.

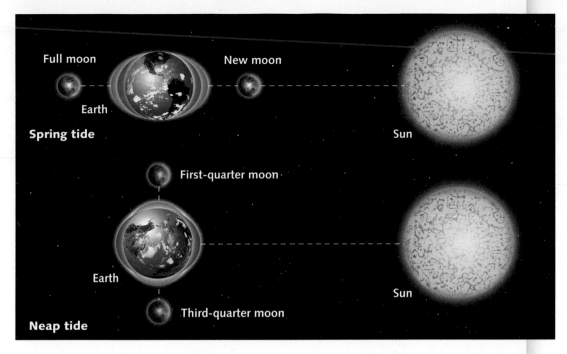

Figure 17.21 When the Sun, the Moon, and Earth are aligned, spring tides occur *(top)*. When the Sun, the Moon, and Earth form a right angle, neap tides occur *(bottom)*.

The Effect of Tides

Daily tide charts are published for shoreline locations all over the world. A tide chart shows the height of tide waters throughout the day. Fishers, boaters, and ship captains consult tide charts to help plan their journeys into the ocean. Some harbors and channels are open only during high tide.

While fish cannot read tide charts, some act as if they do. During the summer months, California grunion swim to beaches to spawn. They always do this a few days after a spring tide. Scientists have not been able to explain how the grunion time these events.

The most important effect of tides may have occurred long ago in Earth's history. As described in Chapter 12, life began in Earth's oceans and thrived there. The continents spent long years as barren slabs of rock. As tides rose and fell, they most likely stranded ancient marine plants and animals along shorelines, just as they do today. According to one theory, this was one way that marine life colonized the land.

After You Read

1. Compare surface currents with deep-ocean currents.

2. Why do tides differ from day to day? Why do they differ from place to place?

3. Review the outline you created in your Science Notebook. Use it to help you write a short essay explaining how ocean water moves vertically, horizontally, and in a circular path.

Summary

KEY CONCEPTS

17.1 The World's Oceans

- Oceans hold 97 percent of Earth's water and cover 71 percent of its surface area. All oceans are connected.

- The Pacific Ocean, the Atlantic Ocean, and the Indian Ocean are Earth's major oceans.

- Two smaller oceans, the Arctic Ocean and the Antarctic Ocean, are near Earth's poles.

- Oceanographers study the ocean using technologies such as sonar from boats, and radar from satellites.

- Earth's oceans might have formed from water that erupted from volcanoes or arrived in comets.

17.2 Properties of Ocean Water

- The salinity of ocean water is a measure of its concentration of dissolved salts.

- The average salinity of ocean water is about 3.5 percent.

- Ocean waters are warmest at the surface and coldest near the bottom. In between is the thermocline, a layer in which temperature decreases rapidly with depth.

- The light needed for photosynthesis reaches to about 100 m deep in the ocean. The ocean bottom is very dark and very cold.

- Oceans tend to moderate the climates of lands near them as well as Earth's climate as a whole.

17.3 Motions of the Oceans

- Winds form surface currents, many of which form large loops called gyres. When waters with different densities and temperatures meet, they form density currents.

- Winds bunch surface waters into waves. Water moves in a circular path as a wave passes.

- Tsunamis are huge ocean waves caused by earthquakes or other major disturbances to the ocean floor.

- The gravitational pull of the Moon and the Sun causes ocean waters to bulge, creating tides.

VOCABULARY REVIEW

Write each term in a complete sentence, or write a paragraph relating several terms.

17.1
ocean, p. 319
sea, p. 319
iceberg, p. 320
oceanography, p. 321
sonar, p. 322
sea level, p. 323

17.2
salinity, p. 324
temperature profile, p. 326
thermocline, p. 326

17.3
surface current, p. 328
Coriolis effect, p. 328
gyre, p. 328
upwelling, p. 330
density current, p. 331
wave, p. 332
crest, p. 332
trough, p. 332
wavelength, p. 332
breaker, p. 333
tsunami, p. 333
tide, p. 334
spring tide, p. 334
neap tide, p. 334

PREPARE FOR CHAPTER TEST

To prepare for the chapter test, create a question from each Learning Goal. Use the information in your Science Notebook to answer each question. Then use these answers to write a well-developed essay about the chapter. Use the Key Concept on the first page of this chapter as your topic sentence.

True or False

If the statement is true, write "true." If it is false, change the underlined word or words to make the statement true.

1. The vast majority of Earth's water is stored in <u>lakes</u>.

2. The average <u>temperature</u> of ocean water is 35 parts per thousand.

3. Cold, salty water is <u>denser</u> than warm, less-salty water.

4. An earthquake can cause a huge ocean wave called a <u>breaker</u>.

5. Lands near the ocean tend to have more <u>moderate</u> climates than those farther inland.

6. The positions of Earth, the Moon, and the Sun cause <u>density currents</u> to form.

Short Answer

Answer each of the following in a sentence or brief paragraph.

7. Explain why scientists often refer to a single world ocean rather than separate oceans.

8. List three factors that affect the height of tides.

9. Are all ocean waters equally salty? Explain.

10. What is the cause of El Niño? Describe some of its effects.

11. Where does photosynthesis take place in the ocean? Why doesn't it take place elsewhere in the ocean?

12. Describe how density currents are formed.

Critical Thinking

Use what you have learned in this chapter to answer each of the following.

13. **Apply Concepts** Why are icebergs made of freshwater and not salt water?

14. **Cause and Effect** How might global warming affect the oceans? How might these changes to the ocean affect land?

Standardized Test Question

Choose the letter of the response that correctly answers the question.

15. Which of these is the coldest?

   A. the ocean surface near the equator

   B. the ocean bottom near the equator

   C. the ocean surface in the Gulf of Mexico

   D. a cold-water surface current

Test-Taking Tip

When answering an essay question, be sure to include main ideas and supporting details in each paragraph.

The Marine Environment

KEY CONCEPT Ocean floor features include mountains, plains, slopes, trenches, and canyons. Ocean habitats are defined by temperature, water depth, and light.

Where can you find Earth's largest animal? In the ocean! A blue whale typically grows as long as 24 m. A blue whale's food, however, is much smaller. The whale strains the water for tiny, shrimplike animals called krill.

The marine environment is a place of many extremes. Earth's tallest mountains rise from the ocean floor and its deepest trenches drop from it. Temperatures of ocean waters range from chilling cold to scalding hot. Certain places along the ocean floor give rise to one of Earth's most unusual food webs—one that is not powered by sunlight.

Think About the Ocean's Living Things

Oceans are home to many plants and animals. In your Science Notebook, list up to 20 organisms that live in ocean waters and list a few characteristics of each one.

- What percent of the ocean's living things do you think you've identified?

- Do you know more about living things on land or in the ocean? Why?

www.scilinks.org

Marine Life **Code: WGES18**

18.1 The Ocean's Edge and Floor

Before You Read
Look at the diagrams and photographs in this lesson. In your Science Notebook, record your ideas about the different features that make up the ocean border and floor.

People once thought that the ocean floor was smooth and gently sloped, much like the bottom of a swimming pool. When scientists began exploring, however, they discovered that the ocean floor is made up of mountains, trenches, canyons, and slopes. Some regions are as flat as any plains on land. Others regions are as steep as the steepest cliffs on land.

Shorelines

There are many forces that can weather and erode rocks. All of these forces can act along shorelines. A **shoreline** is the boundary formed where water, such as that of an ocean, meets land. Winds, waves, tides, and currents all act to shape and change shorelines. Sometimes these changes occur very quickly. For example, a hurricane or other storm might reshape a shoreline in only a few hours.

Ocean waters near the shoreline form into tall waves called breakers. Breakers can crash on the shore with great force. They also carry tiny pieces of rock, shells, and other sediment suspended in the water. This sediment rubs or abrades the solid rock on the shore. As a result, breakers act as powerful agents of weathering and erosion. They wear down rocks and then wash the pieces away.

Figure 18.1 Breakers helped to shape this shoreline located in Scotland. The original landform that met the ocean was once smooth and hill-like. Then breakers acted like a sculptor and carved the cliff, cave, and sea stack shown here.

Beaches

Over time, the actions of waves, tides, and currents might create a beach. A beach is a sloping band of sand, mud, or small rocks along a shoreline. Sandy beaches typically form from sediment that waves wash ashore. Sediment is also transported and deposited on the shore by rivers and streams that empty into the ocean. Other beaches, including most rocky beaches, form as waves weather and erode the shoreline rocks.

Like other shoreline features, beaches are constantly changing. Just off the shore, incoming waves create a current that runs parallel to the shoreline. This is called a longshore current. Waves and longshore currents act together to move beach sand down the shoreline.

Depositional Features

Along many coasts, ocean waters deposit sediment several meters away from mainland beaches. Features such as barrier islands, spits, and baymouth bars all form from sediment deposited near the shoreline. These features can change very suddenly, especially during a severe storm. Many of these depositional features are shown in **Figure 10.9** in Chapter 10. For example, a feature called a spit forms where a shoreline changes direction. When a growing spit crosses a bay, a baymouth bar forms.

Longshore currents can deposit sediments in a strip parallel to the shoreline. These sediments pile into a feature called a sandbar. When the sandbar rises above the ocean surface, it forms a barrier island. The relatively calm section of ocean between a barrier island and the mainland is called a lagoon. All of these depositional features are especially common along the Atlantic coast of the United States.

Figure 18.2 Majuro Island is a barrier island in the Marshall Islands. Most barrier islands form less than a kilometer from the mainland.

From Continent to Ocean

When viewed from above, it might appear that continents end where dry land meets the ocean. In fact, every continent extends at least a few kilometers underneath the ocean.

The submerged parts of continents are called **continental margins**. As shown in **Figure 18.3**, a continental margin includes three distinct regions: the continental shelf, the continental slope, and the continental rise.

Figure It Out

1. What is the steepest part of the continental margin?

2. Describe the boundary between a continent and an ocean.

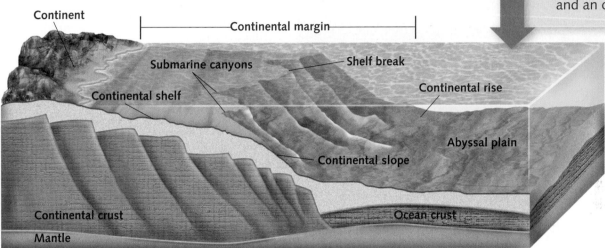

Continent · Continental margin · Submarine canyons · Shelf break · Continental shelf · Continental rise · Abyssal plain · Continental slope · Continental crust · Ocean crust · Mantle

Figure 18.3 This diagram illustrates the major features of the continental margin.

Continental Shelf

The **continental shelf** lies closest to the shoreline. It is the shallowest part of the continental margin. Along the Atlantic coast of the United States, the continental shelf extends hundreds of kilometers into the ocean. On the Pacific coast, the continental shelf is only a few kilometers wide. The average depth of water above the continental shelves is about 130 m.

Earth's oceans have swelled and shrunk many times throughout history. During the last ice age, for example, ocean waters retreated from the continental shelves. The enlarged continents formed a land bridge that connected the northeastern tip of Asia to the northwestern tip of North America—lands that are now Siberia and Alaska, respectively. Early humans might have crossed this land bridge—known as the Bering Land Bridge—and become the Native American peoples.

Today, the continental shelves are covered by nutrient-rich waters. These waters support large numbers of fishes, clams, oysters, shrimps, crabs, and other animals that people harvest for food. Deposits of oil and natural gas have been found beneath the sediment and rocks of the continental shelves.

CONNECTION: Law

In 1953, the United States Congress created the Outer Continental Shelf Lands Act. This act defines the outer continental shelf as all submerged lands lying within three miles (5 km) of shore that are under United States jurisdiction. Amendments to the Act include an oil spill liability fund. This fund encourages companies extracting oil and gas on the outer continental shelf to be environmentally responsible. Another amendment requires companies that are mining the outer continental shelf for mineral resources to give a portion of their profits to coastal states.

Figure 18.4 Much like an avalanche on land, a turbidity current picks up rocks and sediment as it flows down a continental slope. A submarine canyon forms when many such currents cut along the same channel.

Continental Slope

Beyond the continental shelf, the ocean floor becomes very steep. On average, the floor drops 100 m across a distance of 1 km. This steep region is called the **continental slope**. Scientists define the continental slope as a continent's true edge. It is made of the same kind of rock as the rest of the continent.

Look again at **Figure 18.3**. As the diagram shows, the continental slope is not smooth and even, but has varied features. **Submarine canyons** are deep, V-shaped canyons that cut down into the continental slope. Some are about the size of the longest and deepest canyons on land, such as the Grand Canyon in Arizona.

How do submarine canyons form? In a few cases, rivers cut the upper part of a canyon. Off the coast of New York City, for example, the Hudson River carved a submarine canyon that extends 740 km across the continental margin into the deep ocean. This happened during the last ice age, when much of the continental shelf was above water.

Most submarine canyons, however, formed from a type of underwater mudslide called a turbidity current. A **turbidity current** is a rapidly flowing, deep-water current that carries a heavy load of sediment. Some turbidity currents are triggered by earthquakes. Others form when large storm waves stir up sediment along the continental shelf. Regardless of its origin, a turbidity current can cause significant weathering and erosion.

Continental Rise

A turbidity current drops its sediment load along the bottom of the continental slope. This sediment forms the **continental rise**, a gently sloping feature at the foot of the continental margin. A continental rise can be compared to a land formation called an alluvial fan, as discussed in Chapter 16.

In some places, a continental rise may be several kilometers thick. In other places, especially near the edge of the Pacific Ocean, the continental rise is absent. Here, the continental margin ends in very deep depressions called deep-sea trenches.

The Ocean Basin

Most of the ocean does not lie over the continental margins. Instead, it lies over the vast central regions of the ocean floor. These regions are called ocean basins. They cover about 60 percent of Earth's surface.

The smooth, flat regions of the ocean floor that are located 5 or 6 km below sea level are called **abyssal** (uh BIH sul) **plains**. An abyssal plain is covered by hundreds of meters of fine, muddy sediments and sedimentary rock. Most of the sediments are washed into the oceans by rivers, although some form from dead marine organisms. Underneath these layers lies basalt, a type of volcanic rock. This rock forms the crust underneath the entire ocean basin.

Not all of the ocean basin is flat. For example, **deep-sea trenches**, the deepest parts of the ocean basins, cut several kilometers into the surrounding ocean floor. Such trenches are especially common in the Pacific Ocean. They are relatively narrow, but may be thousands of kilometers long. Elsewhere in the ocean basin are chains of tall volcanic mountains called **mid-ocean ridges**. As their name implies, mid-ocean ridges generally run along the middles of oceans. The tallest of these mountains reach above the ocean surface, forming volcanic islands. Iceland and the Azores of the Atlantic Ocean are examples of such islands. Both of these formed as a result of plate tectonics, discussed in Chapter 6.

Figure 18.5 In the Atlantic Ocean, the mid-ocean ridge runs parallel to the coastlines of the surrounding continents. The country of Iceland is actually the top of an especially tall mountain of the ridge. A photo of the landscape in Iceland reveals the island's volcanic nature *(inset)*.

Physiographic Map of the Atlantic Ocean

Seamounts

Along with the volcanic mountains of the mid-ocean ridges, tens of thousands of other mountains dot the ocean basin. Most of them formed from volcanoes that became extinct long ago. A **seamount** is an underwater volcanic mountain at least one km high. Sometimes waves weather and erode the tops of these mountains, creating formations called guyots (GEE ohs).

Seamounts typically form in chains as Earth's crust moves over a hot spot. A hot spot is a region where molten material from the mantle rises up toward the crust. Over time, it breaks through the crust and a volcanic mountain is formed. Hot spots do not move. When plate tectonic activity causes the crust above the hot spot to move, it takes the volcanic mountain with it and the volcano becomes extinct. A new volcano then forms above the hot spot. The Hawaiian Islands formed in this way.

Hydrothermal Vents

Perhaps the most unusual features in the ocean are the hydrothermal vents and the communities they support. A **hydrothermal vent** is a geyser, or hot spring, that erupts on the ocean floor. They are typically located along a mid-ocean ridge. Much like geysers on land, a hydrothermal vent shoots out water that has been heated by magma below. Vents are nicknamed white smokers or black smokers according to the color of the materials that the ejected water carries.

Because little to no light reaches the deep ocean floor, scientists were surprised when they discovered thriving communities of organisms living near hydrothermal vents. These living things include tubeworms, special kinds of clams, mussels, and shrimps.

How does this community survive in darkness? The creatures that live there depend on unusual bacteria that make food using chemicals and thermal energy from the hydrothermal vents. These bacteria form the basis of a unique food chain that does not begin with energy from the Sun. They convert chemical energy into food using a process called chemosynthesis.

Figure 18.6 The Hawaiian Islands formed when Earth's crust moved slowly over a hot spot below the Pacific Ocean. The chain also includes seamounts.

Figure 18.7 This white smoker is a hydrothermal vent. Tubeworms commonly live near hydrothermal vents. For their nourishment, they rely on bacteria that convert chemicals to energy.

After You Read

1. Use the notes in your Science Notebook to help you answer these questions. What are the deepest ocean features? What are the tallest?

2. Compare and contrast submarine canyons and canyons on land.

3. Describe an underwater walk from the shoreline to the ocean's center. Include at least five ocean features.

18.2 Life Zones in the Ocean

Learning Goals

- Identify and describe the three groups of marine organisms.
- Identify and describe the benthic and pelagic environments.
- Classify the zones of the benthic and pelagic environments.

New Vocabulary

habitat
benthic environment
pelagic environment
plankton
nekton
benthos
intertidal zone
sublittoral zone
bathyal zone
abyssal zone
hadal zone
neritic zone
oceanic zone

Before You Read

Predict how life forms are separated into zones throughout the ocean. In your Science Notebook, draw a vertical line. Label the left side with the life zones of the ocean. Add information about each life zone to the right side.

Marine organisms usually live in distinct regions of the ocean's water or floor. The creatures that live in the darkest, deepest waters are very different from those that live closer to the surface or shoreline. Like living things on land, marine organisms are adapted for specific habitats. A **habitat** is the natural conditions and environment in which an organism lives. Ocean habitats are defined by temperature, water depth, and the presence of light. Structures on the ocean floor also help form habitats.

Defining Ocean Life Zones

To organize ocean habitats, scientists separate them into two major marine environments. The **benthic environment** is the ocean floor and all the organisms that live on or in it. The **pelagic environment** includes all of the water in the ocean and the marine organisms that live above the ocean floor. Each of these environments is subdivided into ecological zones based on the different organisms that live there. **Figure 18.8** shows where each of these zones is located.

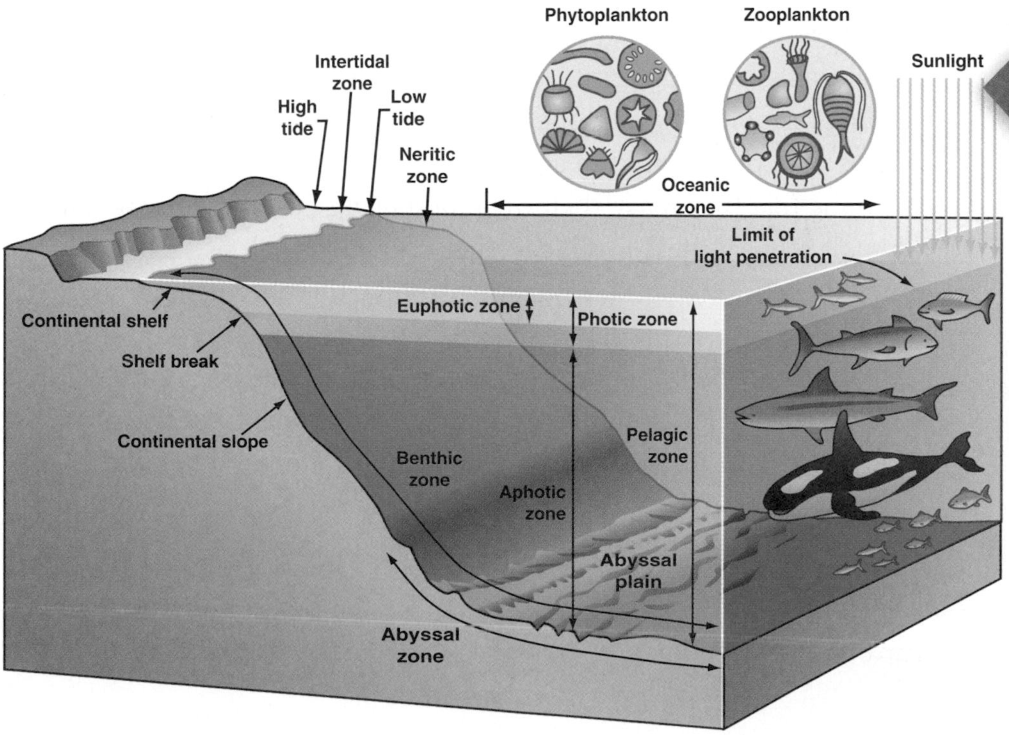

Figure It Out

1. What is the name of the ocean life zone that lies between the high and low tide lines?

2. Anglerfish live in the deepest ocean water. Would you expect an anglerfish to eat seaweed? Why or why not?

Figure 18.8 Ocean habitats are organized into different life zones. Each life zone supports a characteristic community of living things.

Plankton

Nekton

Benthos

Figure 18.9 Plankton, such as these diatoms, support all other marine organisms in the food chain. Nekton, such as these fish, swim freely about the ocean. Benthos, such as this dark-fingered coral crab, live on the ocean floor.

Some marine animals move among different life zones as part of their life cycles. Many fishes and turtles, for example, begin their lives near the shoreline. As adults, they live in the open water, but return to shore to lay eggs. Other marine creatures stay in one life zone throughout their lives.

Three Groups of Marine Life

Scientists divide all marine organisms into three general groups according to how they move and the depth of the water in which they live.

Plankton are organisms that float at or near the ocean's surface. Most plankton are microscopic, or too small to see without the help of a microscope. There are two types of plankton: phytoplankton and zooplankton. Phytoplankton are algae and other tiny, plantlike organisms that perform photosynthesis. They are important globally because they produce a large percentage of the oxygen in Earth's atmosphere. Zooplankton are tiny shrimplike creatures. They are the main source of food for many large sea animals, including whales.

Nekton are organisms that swim freely in ocean waters. They include jellies, starfish, squids, octopuses, all types of fish, and many other animals. Whales, sea lions, and dolphins are examples of air-breathing nekton. They return regularly to the ocean's surface to take in oxygen.

Benthos (BEN thahs) are organisms that live on or in the ocean floor. Among them are clams, starfish, corals, sponges, seaweeds, oysters, crabs, lobsters, and many types of worms. The crab shown in **Figure 18.9** is one example.

Like all other organisms, the living things of the ocean form feeding relationships with one another. An ocean food chain typically begins with phytoplankton and ocean plants. They are producers, meaning that they make their own food using the Sun's energy. The animals that eat these producers include many small fish and other consumers belonging to the nekton group. Still other nekton, such as larger fishes, are predators that feed on their fellow nekton.

Among the benthos are many scavengers, which are animals that feed on dead plant or animal matter. Some scavengers, such as crabs, scurry along the ocean floor, picking at animal remains for food. Other benthos scavengers, such as clams and oysters, are filter feeders. They generally stay in one place, and strain the ocean water for tiny bits of once-living matter.

The Benthic Environment

Scientists divide the benthic environment into five zones based on the depth of the ocean floor and where different types of organisms live. These zones include the intertidal zone, the sublittoral zone, the bathyal zone, the abyssal zone, and the hadal zone.

Intertidal Zone   As discussed in Chapter 17, ocean waters advance and retreat along the shoreline every day. This is the cycle of the tides. The region of the shoreline that is located between the low tide and high tide lines is called the **intertidal zone**. It is the most changeable life zone of the ocean, transforming with the tides twice each day. As the tide flows in, the intertidal zone is covered with ocean water. As the tide flows out, the intertidal zone is exposed to the air and the Sun. Because tides vary from place to place, so does the intertidal zone. The zone is wide and well-defined along some shorelines and is narrow or nearly absent along others.

Intertidal organisms must be able to survive both under water and in the open air. Without some sort of anchor to the ocean floor, these organisms would be washed away with the tides. Clams and mussels burrow into the rocks or sand. Other animals, including starfishes and anemones, attach themselves to rock faces or other hard surfaces. This is also true of certain types of seaweed and lichens.

Scientists divide the intertidal zone into smaller regions according to the distance that the tide advances. The region closest to the ocean is covered in tidewaters almost all of the time. The region farthest from the ocean is merely splashed with water during high tide. Different communities of organisms thrive in these different regions.

Along rocky shorelines, the retreating tide often leaves behind small pools of water called tide pools. A few hardy organisms, such as starfishes and sea urchins, can live in tide pools. Tide pools differ greatly from one another depending on the volume of water they contain.

As You Read

Write the name of each ocean life zone in your Science Notebook. Discuss each zone with a partner. Add information to your chart and define each zone. Then rewrite your definition in your own words, and include examples of its living things.

What is the major difference between the ocean's benthic environment and its pelagic environment?

Figure 18.10 Every tide pool is unique. Shown here is a tide pool from Sooke Harbour, along the coast of British Columbia.

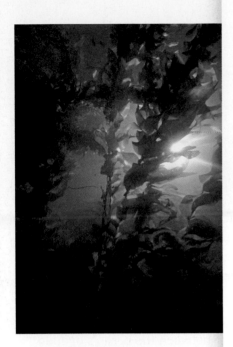

Figure 18.11 Kelp is a type of seaweed that grows in thick masses in the sublittoral zone off many coasts. Producers such as kelp support a high density of animal life by providing a source of food and releasing oxygen into the water.

The Sublittoral Zone   The **sublittoral** (sub LIH tuh rul) **zone**, which extends from the low tide line to the edge of the continental shelf, lies beyond the intertidal zone. The sublittoral zone reaches 200 m below sea level. Plants and most animals, however, stay in the upper 100 m of this zone, where sunlight reaches the ocean floor. This benthic zone is more stable than the intertidal zone, meaning that temperatures, water pressure, and sunlight remain fairly constant. As a result, this ocean floor zone supports thriving communities of plants and animals.

In many places, the sublittoral zone is home to large masses of seaweed and other underwater plants. The great kelp forest off the coast of California is one example. Elsewhere, the sublittoral zone supports coral reefs. Corals are made of tiny, simple organisms called polyps that live inside hard skeletonlike structures. Each animal grows on the skeletal remains of the animals that died before it. In this way, over many years, coral reefs are formed. These reefs are home to the most diverse communities of living things in the ocean.

Deep-Water Benthic Zones   The **bathyal** (BATH ul) **zone** extends from the edge of the continental shelf to the abyssal plain, which means it covers the continental slope. Here, the water depth plunges from 200 m to about 4,000 m. Plant life is scarce because little sunlight reaches this zone. Animals that live in the bathyal zone include sponges, starfishes, and octopuses.

The **abyssal zone** covers the vast abyssal plain. This benthic zone, which can reach 6,000 m in depth, is dark and cold. Because it is so deep and dark, scientists have explored only a fraction of it. Although no plants live in the abyssal zone, some animals do. Crabs, sponges, worms, and sea cucumbers can be found here. In addition, this zone includes the communities that surround hydrothermal vents.

Even colder and darker than the abyssal zone is the **hadal** (HAY dul) **zone**, the deepest benthic zone. This zone consists of the floors of deep-ocean trenches and any organisms that live there. Despite having the greatest water pressure on Earth, living things manage to survive in the hadal zone. Scientists have discovered organisms including sponges, worms, and clams living in this largely unexplored area.

Figure 18.12 Essentially no sunlight reaches the abyssal and hadal zones. These sponges lived in complete darkness before they were brought up to the surface.

The Pelagic Environment

From shoreline to shoreline, the water above the ocean floor holds vast populations of ocean plants, animals, and other types of organisms. This is the pelagic environment. Its habitats are defined mostly by differences in temperature and illumination from sunlight. The two major zones of the pelagic environment are the neritic zone and the oceanic zone.

The **neritic zone** includes the waters over continental shelves. These waters are warm, shallow, and well-lit. Fishes and other nekton live on a plentiful food supply that includes organisms from the ocean floor. Thanks to an abundance of sunlight and food, the neritic zone contains the largest concentration of marine life. Much of the fish and other seafood that we eat is harvested from the neritic zone.

The **oceanic zone** includes all of the water that covers the sea floor except for the continental shelf. As discussed in earlier chapters, water temperature is relatively warm near the surface of these waters. Below 100 m, however, the temperature drops quickly. The waters become darker with depth, as well. Because the Sun penetrates and warms the surface waters, most marine life lives in the upper regions of the oceanic zone. The oceanic zone is home to many of the same species that live in the neritic zone, but in smaller numbers.

Figure 18.13 This anglerfish lurks in waters that are cold, dark, and deep. The lure on its face is bioluminescent, meaning that it glows in the dark.

The deep waters of the oceanic zone are home to some of the ocean's most unusual creatures, such as the anglerfish shown in **Figure 18.13**. In its dark home, its only visible body part is the glow-in-the-dark lure that sticks up from its face. Small prey are attracted to this lure, and the anglerfish uses its wide, powerful mouth to catch and eat them. Other animals that live in the deeper parts of the oceanic zone include some species of crustaceans and mollusks, and even giant squids.

CONNECTION: Literature

In 1841, at the age of 21, Herman Melville embarked on an 18-month-long whaling voyage. During this voyage, Melville met a man named Owen Chase. Chase gave Melville a written account of Chase's father's experiences on the ship *Essex*, which was sunk by a whale. This story, along with Melville's own experiences on the whaling ship, is said to be the inspiration for his most famous novel, *Moby Dick*, published in 1851.

Extend It!

Overfishing has caused a drastic decline in the populations of many species of ocean fish that people enjoy eating. Research a common species of ocean fish. Find out where it lives and how fishing has affected its population. Find out what can be done to protect fish populations from overfishing.

After You Read

1. Explain which ocean life zone changes the most from day to day.
2. What factors differentiate the zones of the benthic environment from one another?
3. Use the list and definitions of ocean life zones in your Science Notebook to explain why different communities thrive in different zones.

Learning Goals

- Explain how human actions have impacted Earth's oceans.

- Describe the changes being observed in Earth's oceans.

- List some ways humans can protect Earth's oceans.

New Vocabulary

overfishing
coral bleaching
dead zone

Before You Read

Preview the headings, Learning Goals, and photographs in this lesson. Write a short paragraph in your Science Notebook to predict the lesson's topics.

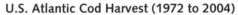

Oceans have changed significantly over the course of Earth's long history. During the last ice age, oceans were much colder and covered less of the continental shelves. Earlier, when dinosaurs roamed Earth, much of the continental lands were covered by shallow, salty seas. The living things that inhabited these oceans differ from those living in the oceans today.

Oceans continue to change today, but for reasons that are different from those of long ago. Human actions, such as overfishing and polluting Earth's atmosphere and waters, have had a negative impact on ocean resources around the world. These impacts on Earth's oceans also have serious consequences for life on land.

Overfishing

For thousands of years, humans have caught ocean animals for food. Today, however, overfishing is causing the populations of many marine species to decline rapidly in number. **Overfishing** occurs when too many fish or other marine animals are harvested. This decreases the overall populations of these species. Over the past 50 years, overfishing in the North Atlantic Ocean has decreased the populations of fishes such as cod, haddock, and flounder by as much as 95 percent. Crustacean populations, including lobsters and crabs, have also declined.

Figure 18.14 Atlantic cod was once used in fish sticks and other popular food products. Today, this fish is more rare and thus more expensive.

Figure It Out

1. What trend does the data show for the United States Atlantic cod harvest?

2. For the years shown, when was the cod harvest greatest? Predict whether the harvest will ever reach such levels again.

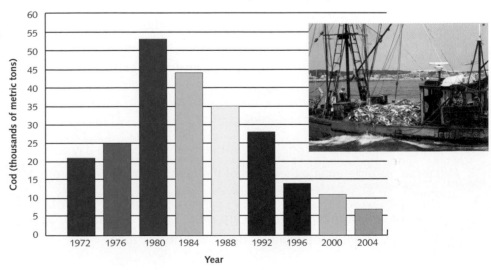

U.S. Atlantic Cod Harvest (1972 to 2004)

If people stopped fishing in ocean waters, struggling species would most likely recover. However, millions of people worldwide rely on fish and other seafood as part of their diet. In addition, many people earn their living by fishing. The problems caused by overfishing do not have simple solutions.

Changing Coral Reefs

Coral reefs thrive in the clear, warm waters of the sublittoral zone. A coral reef is home to a great variety and number of anemones, mollusks, fishes, and other ocean animals. People depend on reef ecosystems for food, especially in many developing countries.

Yet reefs around the world are suffering. **Coral bleaching** is the whitening of coral colonies due to the death of the algae that live within healthy corals. These tiny plants provide the corals with food for growth and give corals their normal healthy color. Without these algae, the coral colony slowly starves to death. Scientists suggest that coral bleaching involves the quality of ocean water. Possible factors include rising water temperatures caused by global warming, water pollution, changes in water pH, and silt runoff from coastal areas.

Bleached coral can recover if conditions are corrected quickly. Otherwise, the corals die. If enough corals are lost, the entire reef ecosystem will die. Scientists continue to study the causes and effects of coral bleaching, as well as ways to help solve this problem.

Dead Zones

For many years, people have harvested fish, shrimp, and crabs off the Pacific coasts of Oregon and Washington State. However, every summer from 2001 to 2006, observers noticed that a huge number of marine organisms died within a particular region of ocean water in this area. Scientists informally call such a region a dead zone. A **dead zone** forms when the oxygen levels in the water become so low that the water can no longer support significant populations of living things.

The number of dead zones in the world's oceans has been increasing since the 1970s. These dead zones threaten fish populations as well as the animal and human populations that depend on fish. One of the world's largest dead zones is in the Gulf of Mexico. It occurs where the Mississippi River dumps fertilizer runoff from the Midwest into the Gulf.

Dead zones are often caused by pollution that began on land. Common sources of pollution include sewage from cities, fertilizer from farms or lawns, and pollution from cars and factories that falls into the oceans as acid rain. Changing ocean currents are the suspected cause of the dead zones off coastal Oregon.

Figure 18.15 The Great Barrier Reef stretches more than 2,000 km off the northeast coast of Australia. In 2002, it suffered a huge bleaching event, from which it has mostly recovered.

As You Read

For each lesson heading, write one or two sentences that summarize the topic presented.

What are some causes of ocean dead zones?

Figure 18.16 The dead zone off the Oregon coast could have serious consequences for the state's fishing industry. These ocean scientists are measuring and comparing water samples to determine the water's oxygen content.

Figure 18.17 Higher storm surges and increased erosion of the coastline forced the relocation of Shishmaref, a fishing village on the shores of the Arctic Ocean. The house in the top photo may soon experience the same fate as the house in the bottom photo.

Advancing Ocean Waters

For 4,000 years, the village of Shishmaref was perched on a barrier island off the northern shoreline of Alaska. By 2004, however, the majority of residents agreed that the village was doomed. Especially during stormy weather, the advancing ocean was eroding the foundations of buildings and damaging the city's water system. After much debate, the residents decided to move farther inland.

Why did the Arctic Ocean advance upon Shishmaref? Many scientists point to global warming as the cause. Higher temperatures have been reducing the amount of sea ice that normally covers much of the Arctic Ocean. Open waters allow more powerful waves and storm surges to reach the shoreline. In addition, the warmer weather has been reducing the layer of permafrost, or ground that is frozen all year, along the coastline. This has allowed more of the ground to wash away.

CONNECTION: **Computer Science**

Oceans are affected by factors such as temperature, sunlight, and salinity. Changes in these factors affect ocean currents, the living things of the ocean, and weather patterns all over Earth.

Today, ocean scientists, or oceanographers, are trying to predict the effects that Earth's rising temperatures will have on its oceans. Computer scientists are helping them achieve this task by using computer programs to create models of the world's ocean system. Computer modeling helps scientists study the effects that changing one variable—such as average temperature—might have on the entire system.

Computer models are useful in many other fields of science, as well. Meteorologists predict the weather using computer models of the atmosphere. Doctors and medical students often study computer models of the human body. Geologists use computers to analyze data about Earth's crust and make models of rock layers.

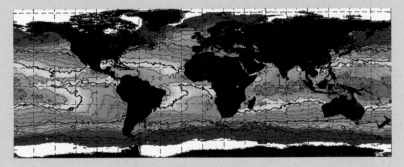

Protecting the Oceans

Although humans have harmed the world's oceans, we are now working to protect them. The United States government runs NOAA, the National Oceanic and Atmospheric Administration. The mission of NOAA is to understand and predict changes in Earth's environment and also to manage ocean resources wisely. NOAA helps pay for scientific research on ocean issues and distributes information worldwide. Scientists at universities, large aquariums, and other organizations also conduct research on oceans.

Ocean pollution remains a serious issue. Yet many scientists agree that global warming is the most serious problem currently facing oceans. Most of the harmful impacts on Earth's oceans discussed in this lesson were caused, at least in part, by a gradual increase in ocean temperatures.

If ocean waters were to warm significantly, corals and other marine life would suffer. If sea levels rose worldwide, more communities would be forced to relocate to higher ground. Most seriously, ocean currents could be affected.

Deep-water currents form because of temperature and salinity differences within ocean waters. If temperatures were to change enough, those currents could change direction or location. Some scientists think that this has already begun to happen. For evidence, they cite increased frequencies of El Niño events, as well as the occurrence of dead zones such as the one off the Oregon coast. As discussed in Chapter 15, changes in ocean currents could seriously affect Earth's climate, or long-term weather patterns.

Staying informed about the problems and issues that affect oceans is one way to help protect them. Information can be shared with classmates, friends, parents, and other adults. People who live near an ocean, or those who visit one, should be sure to treat the ocean and marine life with respect.

Figure 18.18 Staying informed and sharing information about oceans is the first step in protecting them. How can you help oceans and marine life?

Explain It!

Write a newspaper editorial about global warming or another environmental issue you care about. Include facts and statistics to support your claims.

After You Read

1. Complete writing summaries for each heading in this lesson. Describe two ways in which humans might be harming ocean resources.

2. Discuss the types of changes to the ocean that global warming might be causing.

3. Why should we be concerned about changes to the ocean? State your reasons in a well-developed paragraph. Incorporate the topic summaries you wrote in your Science Notebook.

Summary

KEY CONCEPTS

18.1 The Ocean's Edge and Floor

- The ocean's shoreline includes beaches of rocks and sand. Barrier islands and other depositional features form along many shorelines.

- Continental margins are undersea extensions of the continents. They include the continental shelf, continental slope, and continental rise.

- Much of the ocean floor is the flat abyssal plain. Underwater volcanoes form on the ocean floor and make up the mid-ocean ridges.

- A hydrothermal vent is a geyser in the ocean floor, typically located along a mid-ocean ridge. The food web near hydrothermal vents is based on bacteria that convert chemicals to energy.

18.2 Life Zones in the Ocean

- Scientists divide marine organisms into three general groups: plankton, nekton, and benthos.

- The benthic environment is the ocean floor. The pelagic environment is the water. Each is divided into separate life zones.

- Ocean life zones are defined by the water's temperature, depth, and illumination.

- The intertidal zone is the most changeable life zone. The sublittoral and neritic zones have the greatest abundance and diversity of ocean life. The oceanic zone is home to many of the same species as the neritic zone, but in lesser abundance and diversity.

- Deep-water zones, including the bathyal, abyssal, and hadal zones, are home to relatively few living things.

18.3 The Changing Ocean

- Overfishing has reduced populations of marine animals worldwide.

- Coral reefs are in decline worldwide and the number of dead zones in the world's oceans is increasing. Possible factors include rising water temperatures caused by global warming, water pollution, and silt runoff from coastal areas.

- Rising ocean waters due to the melting of ice at Earth's poles may threaten coastal communities around the world.

- Humans can help protect Earth's oceans by staying informed and involved in managing ocean resources wisely.

VOCABULARY REVIEW

Vocabulary Review
Write each term in a complete sentence or write a paragraph relating several terms.

18.1
shoreline, p. 339
continental margin, p. 341
continental shelf, p. 341
continental slope, p. 342
submarine canyon, p. 342
turbidity current, p. 342
continental rise, p. 342
abyssal plain, p. 343
deep-sea trench, p. 343
mid-ocean ridge, p. 343
seamount, p. 344
hydrothermal vent, p. 344

18.2
habitat, p. 345
benthic environment, p. 345
pelagic environment, p. 345
plankton, p. 346
nekton, p. 346
benthos, p. 346
intertidal zone, p. 347
sublittoral zone, p. 348
bathyal zone, p. 348
abyssal zone, p. 348
hadal zone, p. 348
neritic zone, p. 349
oceanic zone, p. 349

18.3
overfishing, p. 350
coral bleaching, p. 351
dead zone, p. 351

True or False

If the statement is true, write "true." If it is false, change the underlined word or words to make the statement true.

1. The water of the ocean makes up the <u>benthic</u> environment.

2. The <u>intertidal zone</u> is the most changeable life zone of the ocean.

3. Ocean food chains not powered by sunlight are found near <u>seamounts</u>.

4. Turbidity currents running down the continental slope may form <u>guyots</u>.

5. Clams, lobsters, and other bottom-dwellers are examples of <u>plankton</u>.

6. <u>Overfishing</u> has reduced populations of Atlantic cod, haddock, and other seafood.

Short Answer

Answer each of the following in a sentence or brief paragraph.

7. Why are there no plants living on the abyssal plain?

8. Explain why the intertidal zone is a stressful place for marine organisms to live.

9. Describe a hydrothermal vent.

10. Describe possible roles for plankton, nekton, and benthos in an ocean food chain.

11. Does all marine life stay in only one ocean life zone? Explain and give at least one example.

12. Why might global warming cause changes to ocean currents?

PREPARE FOR CHAPTER TEST

To prepare for the chapter test, create a question from each Learning Goal. Use the information in your Science Notebook to answer each question. Then use these answers to write a well-developed essay about the chapter. Use the Key Concept on the first page of this chapter as your topic sentence.

Critical Thinking

Use what you have learned in this chapter to answer each of the following.

13. **Apply Concepts** Describe three ways that the oceans or marine life affect your life on land.

14. **Compare and Contrast** Choose two life zones in the ocean. How are they alike? How are they different?

Standardized Test Question

Choose the letter of the response that correctly answers the question.

15. Which two ocean zones are home to whales and dolphins?

    A. intertidal zone and sublittoral zone

    B. neritic zone and abyssal zone

    C. neritic zone and oceanic zone

    D. oceanic zone and hadal zone

Test-Taking Tip

When writing supporting details in an essay, don't stray from the topic. Read through each sentence to make sure it relates in some way to your main idea.

The Everglades: A Wetland in Danger

THE EVERGLADES is a vast wetland at the tip of Florida. It is home to hundreds of species of birds, reptiles, fishes, and mammals. Everglades National Park was created in 1947 to protect this unique environment. The Everglades has a mix of plants and animals so rare that even the United Nations named it an International Biosphere Reserve.

But the Everglades is in trouble. The shallow river of water that has always flowed through it, feeding its plants and wildlife, doesn't flow freely anymore. It now flows to farm fields and houses. As a result, the Everglades is shrinking. Can it be saved?

River of Grass

The Everglades have been nicknamed *The River of Grass* because of its flat, watery landscape and abundant grass and plant life. Until recently, the water of Lake Okeechobee spilled over the southern edge of the lake and flowed across southern Florida to Florida Bay. Within this shallow river, several habitats developed: marsh, swamp, coastal mangrove, and dry pine forest. Millions of wading birds, alligators, crocodiles, deer, bears, bobcats, and panthers lived here.

Up until the late 1800s, Native Americans also lived in the Everglades. Then new settlers arrived. They saw the Everglades as a useless swamp, and began to drain it.

A Disappearing Wetland

Changes continued throughout the 1900s. Marshes were drained for growing farms and towns.

Engineers built a huge system of levees, canals, pipes, and pumps that blocks the natural flow of water through the Everglades. A dam now stops the waters of Lake Okeechobee from freely flowing into the wetland. When the gates close, parts of the park become dry. It becomes harder for animals to get water, and some aquatic creatures

South Florida National Parks

Lake Okeechobee

Big Cypress National Preserve

Biscayne National Park

EVERGLADES NATIONAL PARK

Dry Tortugas National Park

do not survive. When the gates open, too much water often floods into the park, washing away the nests and eggs of many animals.

With its wetlands disappearing, and the seasonal flow of water disrupted, the park's wildlife has suffered. Ninety percent of its wading birds have disappeared in the last 60 years. Deer and turtles populations have declined by at least 75 percent. Several Everglades species are endangered. The Florida panther is now almost extinct.

Fertilizers and pesticides from farms north of the Everglades mix into waters that flow into the wetland. In many places, alien species have crowded out the native sawgrass, disrupting food webs.

Is there a solution?

It was not until 2000 that Congress approved a plan to save this unique wetland. The plan will take more than 30 years to complete, and will cost at least $8 billion.

The plan has three major goals: to restore the natural water flow to the Everglades, to restore areas of wetland that were drained, and to clean up water that flows into the wetland. To do this, engineers will have to remove the canals and levees that stop the natural flow of water. Some of the farmland around the Everglades will be returned to its natural state as wetland. Scientists hope that restoring the natural flow of the river of grass will help rebuild wildlife populations.

Some people think this plan could save the Everglades. Others say that the work is moving too slowly and that too much water will continue to go to towns and farms instead of the wetland. Time is important to the survival of the Everglades.

Research and Report

You just read about the plan to save the Everglades. With a small group, use the library or Internet to research one part of the project. Report what is planned and what progress has been made. Share your findings with your classmates.

Turning Salty Water Fresh

FINDING FRESH, CLEAN drinking water is easy in some places. But in others, there isn't enough to go around, or the existing supply is disappearing fast. Some people say the solution is to use the salty ocean water that covers most of Earth. The problem is that people can't drink salt water. But what if there was a way to take the salt out? There is. It's called desalination.

There are several desalination processes. Two major ones are distillation and reverse osmosis. In distillation, the salt water is heated. When the water evaporates and becomes water vapor, it leaves the salt behind. The water vapor is then cooled, causing it to condense into freshwater. In reverse osmosis, pumps push salt water through a thin membrane. Its tiny holes are large enough to let water molecules pass through, but the membrane traps dissolved salts. Salt water that passes through the membrane becomes freshwater.

Most of the world's desalination plants are in the desert countries of the Middle East and North Africa, but there are also desalination plants in the United States. Florida has the most plants. There are plants in California, Arizona, Texas, and several other states as

This desalination plant is on Lake Mead in Nevada.

well. They provide drinking water and water for industrial processes.

Desalination can provide freshwater in places where it is scarce, but there are problems with the processes. They use a lot of energy, and it is often difficult to get rid of the salty waste that's left behind. Desalination is expensive, too. If it can help provide freshwater where there is none, it could be worth the cost.

CAREER CONNECTION: FISHER

IF YOU ENJOY eating fish, shrimp, or crab, thank a fisher. Fishers work hard to keep homes and restaurants supplied with tasty seafood.

Some fishers work on large boats that stay at sea for days or even weeks at a time. Crews are large and each person has a certain job to do. The captain and first mate plan and oversee the work. Boatswains operate fishing gear and supervise deckhands. Deckhands help with the catch, keep the decks clean, and maintain equipment. Other fishers work on small boats in teams of two or three. On small crews, each person has to pitch in to do every job—from running the boat to placing nets or traps for fish.

Being a fisher is a great job for people who enjoy the sea and love to work outdoors. However, fishers work long hours in conditions that can be difficult and dangerous. They face hazards of fog, storms, and rough seas. Fishers must carefully follow safety rules to make sure they do not become injured or get swept overboard in rough weather.

Fishers don't need a college degree. The best way to become a fisher is to get a job on a fishing boat and learn by experience. Captains of large fishing boats must have a license from the Coast Guard. Some people who want to become fishers take courses in navigation, marine safety, and vessel operation. Because some of the large ships use satellite navigation, depth sounders, and electronic equipment to track schools of fish, courses in fishing gear technology might also be useful.

Earth's Resources and Environment

Chapter 19
Earth's Natural Resources

How can Earth's natural renewable and nonrenewable resources be used in a way that ensures a continuous supply?

Chapter 20
Human Impact on Earth's Resources

How do humans impact Earth's land, air, and water resources?

Earth's Natural Resources

KEY CONCEPT Many of Earth's resources that are essential for life are nonrenewable, but with conservation and the development of alternative resources, a continuous supply could be ensured.

Have you ever tried to grow a plant? How did you keep it healthy? You probably watered it and made sure it had sunlight. Like plants, all living things depend on Earth's resources to grow, develop, maintain life processes, and reproduce.

To survive, people need food, water, and shelter. Water comes from Earth's rivers and lakes. Homes are made with brick and wood, and contain glass and metal. All of these things come from Earth. In fact, all of the material things you use every day—from your toothbrush to your school computer—are made from Earth's resources.

Think About What You Eat

In your Science Notebook, make a list of everything you eat in a typical day.

- How many of your foods came from plants? How many came from animals?

- Look at the package label on one of your food items. In your Science Notebook, describe where you think the food came from and what resources were necessary to get it to your home.

www.scilinks.org

Natural Resources
Code: WGES19

Before You Read

In your Science Notebook, write each of the vocabulary terms in this lesson. Leave some space below each term. In your own words, write a definition for each term as you come across it in the lesson.

What are natural resources?

A **natural resource** is any substance, organism, or form of energy that is used by living things and is not made by humans. Every living thing on Earth needs natural resources to survive. Natural resources provide us with food, water, and the materials and energy we need to build and heat our homes. Natural resources are also used to make products that simplify everyday life. For example, we have machines made of metal and powered by electricity that wash our dishes and our clothes. Natural resources can be divided into two groups: renewable resources and nonrenewable resources.

Renewable Resources

A **renewable resource** is a natural resource that can be used and replaced over a relatively short period of time. Plants are examples of renewable resources. When a tree is cut down, a new seedling can replace it. Though many natural resources are renewable, people often use them more quickly than they can be replaced. For example, people might cut down trees faster than new ones can grow to replace them. Other examples of renewable resources include all living things, fresh air and water, fertile soil, and elements that cycle through Earth's systems such as nitrogen, carbon, and phosphorus. Renewable resources that cannot be used up completely include the energy that comes from the Sun, wind, water, and from Earth's hot interior.

Figure 19.1 Living things, such as these garden plants, are renewable resources. If managed carefully, they can be replaced as fast as they are used.

Living Things Living things are considered renewable resources because they reproduce and can be replaced in a fairly short amount of time. People who manage natural resources may use techniques to ensure that an available renewable resource is not completely used up. A **sustainable yield** is achieved when a renewable resource is replaced at the same rate at which it is used. For example, a lumber company could use up the resources provided by a forest by cutting down all of the available trees at once. However, the same company could achieve a sustainable yield of trees by carefully scheduling the cutting and replanting of trees so that they are always available.

Fresh Air and Freshwater Living things need fresh air and freshwater to survive. Fresh air contains oxygen and carbon dioxide. These are elements that animals and plants need to live. Both oxygen and carbon dioxide move through the environment in the carbon cycle. A simple version of the carbon cycle is shown in **Figure 19.2**. Humans and animals, for example, breathe in oxygen and exhale, or breathe out, carbon dioxide. Carbon dioxide is taken in by plants and used to perform photosynthesis. Oxygen is produced as a waste product and released into the environment.

Freshwater, or water that is not salty, has unique properties that make it ideal for the transport of nutrients throughout the body. Freshwater is also used by people for farming and recreation. As discussed in Chapter 16, although most of Earth is covered by water, only a fraction, or small amount, of that water is freshwater. Freshwater is present on Earth's surface in lakes, rivers and streams, and in the ground as groundwater. It is important to note, however, that while freshwater is a renewable resource, it can be used up if it is removed faster than it can be replaced by precipitation.

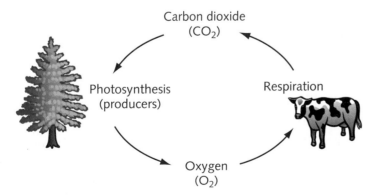

Figure 19.2 Animals breathe in oxygen from the air and breathe out carbon dioxide as waste. Plants take in carbon dioxide from the air and release oxygen as waste.

Figure 19.3 This photo was taken in the 1930s, during the Dust Bowl years. Lack of rain and poor farming practices caused damage to the topsoil across the central United States.

Soil Fertile soil is an important renewable resource. It contains the nutrients plants need to grow. Without fertile soil, people could not grow enough food to survive. As discussed in Chapter 9, soil is formed by the breakdown of rocks and decaying plant and animal matter. Topsoil, the uppermost layer of soil, can be easily damaged. Farm animals can eat plants that anchor soil with their roots. This loose soil can get blown away by wind or washed away by water. Planting trees among farm fields can help prevent soil loss because the roots of the trees hold soil in place, and the trees help block the wind.

The Sun Not all renewable resources come directly from Earth. The Sun provides energy for every process on our planet. All of our food comes indirectly from the Sun. Plants use sunlight to make food, animals eat plants, and people eat both plants and animals. Because energy from the Sun will continue to be available for billions of years, it is considered to be a renewable resource.

Nonrenewable Resources

Many of the resources we use are not renewable. A **nonrenewable resource** is a resource that cannot be replaced or that can only be replaced by natural processes over thousands or millions of years. Most nonrenewable resources are present in limited amounts in Earth's crust. Examples of nonrenewable resources include diamonds and other gemstones; metals such as gold, copper, and silver; and fossil fuels.

Figure 19.4 This ring is made from all nonrenewable resources.

Metals and Gemstones Metals such as copper, gold, and silver are present in small amounts in Earth's crust. Because these metals can be easily shaped into new forms, they are often used in jewelry. Gold and silver are also used for electronics because they are good conductors of electricity. Copper is often used to make pipes and electrical wires.

Diamonds are another example of a nonrenewable resource. They exist in limited amounts in Earth's crust and take hundreds of millions of years to form. Diamonds are gemstones that are often used in jewelry. Because diamonds resist scratches and chipping better than other materials, they are also used for many industrial purposes such as cutting and sanding. Earth's supply of nonrenewable resources such as metals and gemstones could be completely exhausted. This is because they are being extracted, or removed from the ground, and used at a faster rate than the rate at which they form.

Fossil Fuels Fuels that form over millions of years from the remains of once-living things are called **fossil fuels**. Because fossil fuels take such a long time to form, they are considered nonrenewable resources. Coal, oil, and natural gas are all fossil fuels. Fossil fuels are used to heat homes, make electricity, and run cars and other vehicles.

Certain fossil fuels, such as oil, are being used at an extremely fast rate. This is especially true in countries with a high standard of living, such as the United States. **Figure 19.5** shows the amount of oil that is consumed for different uses in the United States each year. If we continue to use oil at such a fast rate, the supply could run out within a few decades.

It is important to find ways to conserve our natural resources so they last for future generations. Using renewable natural resources, such as solar and wind power, to make electricity and to power engines is one way to cut down on our use of fossil fuels. Another way to conserve natural resources is to recycle or, in some cases, to reuse resources to make new products. Being careful not to use more resources than we need is also helpful.

Did You Know?

Many of the diamonds used for industrial purposes are not natural diamonds. They are actually made in a laboratory. In nature, diamonds are formed over millions of years by the exposure of carbon to extreme heat and pressure. By using the same process in a laboratory, diamonds can be made in a few days instead of millions of years! Once this technique is perfected, diamonds may no longer be considered nonrenewable resources.

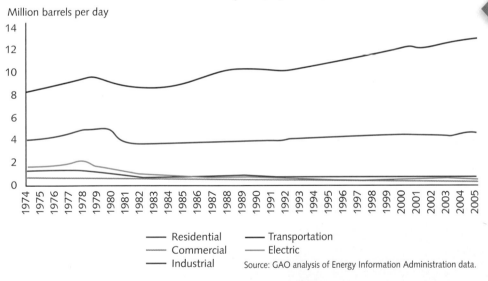

Annual U.S. Oil Consumption, by Sector, 1974–2005

Million barrels per day

— Residential — Transportation
— Commercial — Electric
— Industrial Source: GAO analysis of Energy Information Administration data.

Figure It Out

1. Which sector has experienced the largest increase in oil use?

2. Oil use for the production of electricity has stayed approximately the same since 1982. Explain why this might be so.

Figure 19.5 Oil use in the United States has steadily increased.

After You Read

1. How might a lumber company achieve a sustainable yield of trees?

2. Review the definitions of the vocabulary terms in your Science Notebook. Explain the difference between renewable and nonrenewable resources.

3. Describe how conservation of nonrenewable resources might affect their supply.

Before You Read

Reword the Learning Goals of this lesson so they form questions. Write the questions in your Science Notebook. As you read, write answers to these questions.

What are energy resources?

Every time someone takes a hot shower, watches television, or does research on a computer, they use energy. Energy resources are natural resources that provide the power for these activities. People have been using energy resources for thousands of years to stay warm, cook food, and generate light. Today, energy resources are also used for transportation and electricity. This lesson is about conventional energy resources, or energy resources that humans have depended on for many years. New, or alternative, energy resources are discussed in **Lesson 19.3**.

Biomass

Conventional, or traditionally used, energy resources usually come from living things, most often plants. Plants capture and store the Sun's energy when they use sunlight, carbon dioxide, and water to make sugar. The energy stored in this sugar is transferred to the bodies of living organisms when they eat plants or eat animals that have eaten plants. Plant matter is also used as **fuel**, which is material that is burned to provide power or heat. The total amount of plant or animal matter on Earth that could be converted to fuel is called **biomass**. Fuels that come from living things are called **biomass fuels**. Examples of biomass fuels include wood, field crops, and peat. Solid waste from animals, which often contains bits of plants, can also be used for fuel. Humans have used biomass energy sources for thousands of years. In addition to being burned directly for heat, biomass fuels are now being converted into gas and alcohol fuels.

Figure 19.6 The abundance of buffalo waste on the prairie gave pioneers a seemingly endless supply of fuel for cooking and warmth.

Wood and Field Crops Wood is the largest source of biomass fuel. Before the twentieth century, wood was used to heat more than 90 percent of American homes. Today, most homes in the United States are heated by electricity and natural gas. However, wood is still the main fuel used for heating and cooking in many other parts of the world—especially in developing countries. Wood is fairly inexpensive in areas where there are many trees, but in areas of the world with few trees, solid waste from animals is often used for fuel. This was also the case in the United States during the westward migration of people. As pioneers moved across the country, they collected waste from buffalo and burned it as fuel.

Field crops such as corn, hay, and straw are also used as energy resources in areas where wood is scarce. Even after a crop is harvested, the remains—including stalks, hulls, and shells—can be used for fuel. In the United States, interest in the use of field crops for energy has increased in recent years. Corn and grains can also be made into a liquid fuel called ethanol. Ethanol is added to gasoline to reduce the harmful chemicals produced by running engines.

Peat Another biomass fuel that has been used for centuries in the northern hemisphere is peat. Peat is harvested from bogs, where it forms over thousands of years. Bogs are areas that contain abundant plant material and are continuously wet and spongy. Over time, dead and partially decayed plant materials settled to the bottom of bogs. Here, the plant material is compressed by the weight of the water and sediments above it. Over thousands of years, these compressed materials become the light and spongy material known as **peat**. Peat is harvested from bogs, dried, and ultimately burned as fuel. Peat is still used to heat homes in Ireland, England, parts of northern Europe, and the United States.

Figure 19.7 Peat is cut from bogs, dried in the Sun, and then burned to heat homes.

As You Read

Look at the answers to the questions you wrote in your Science Notebook. Make corrections or additions as you learn more about energy resources and fuels.

How is the energy of the Sun related to biomass fuels?

 **CONNECTION: Archaeology**

Bog water is acidic and has low levels of oxygen. These conditions slow down the growth of bacteria that decompose dead organic matter, including dead bodies. Over the centuries, the remains of hundreds of people have been discovered in peat bogs. The majority of these "bog bodies" have been found in Ireland, Great Britain, the Netherlands, northern Germany, and Denmark. These human remains date as far back as 8000 B.C. Unlike most ancient remains, the skin and internal organs of bog bodies are still intact. These bodies provide scientists with rare, preserved specimens of life from long ago.

Fossil Fuels

Figure 19.8 shows that the largest percentage of energy used by industrialized countries comes from a nonrenewable resource: fossil fuels. **Fossil fuels** form as a result of the compression and partial decay of plants and other once-living matter. All fossil fuels are energy sources that formed over thousands of years. The high concentration of carbon and hydrogen in fossil fuels makes them efficient energy sources. Fossil fuels exist in solid, liquid, and gas forms. They include coal, oil, and natural gas.

Coal The most commonly used and most abundant solid fossil fuel is coal. **Coal** is a solid brownish-black rock that is formed from plants that lived millions of years ago. Peat that is under continuous pressure for thousands of years will eventually turn into a type of coal. Coal was once used to power trains and heat homes. Today, more than 90 percent of the coal used in the United States generates electricity. Coal is also used as a basic energy source in many industries, including the steel, cement, and paper industries.

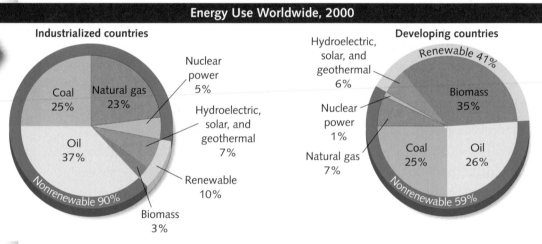

Figure 19.8 These circle graphs shows the relative amounts of energy from different sources that were used by industrialized and developing countries worldwide in 2000.

Oil Like coal, liquid fossil fuels are used for both industrial purposes and to generate electricity. Unlike coal, however, liquid fossil fuels are still commonly used to heat homes and run engines. **Petroleum** is a natural, or crude, oil found underground in certain areas where conditions were right for it to accumulate as it formed. It might also appear on Earth's surface along beaches or in areas where it oozes upward into pits or creeks. Petroleum is refined to make common energy resources that include jet fuel, gasoline for cars, fuel oil for home heaters, and other fuels such as kerosene and propane. The majority of transportation fuels in the United States come from petroleum. Not all petroleum products are fuels, however. Petroleum is also used to make plastics, waxes, and the oil and asphalt used to pave roads.

Natural Gas   The third major type of fossil fuel is natural gas. **Natural gas** is a mixture of gasses that accumulates underground. It often occurs with petroleum and coal deposits. Like the other fossil fuels, natural gas is used to generate electricity and heat buildings. It is also used as a cooking fuel; stoves in many homes burn natural gas. In recent years, some cars and buses have been designed to run on natural gas. Because it is the cleanest burning fossil fuel, natural gas-powered vehicles do not pollute the air as much as those that run on liquid gasoline.

Figure 19.9 Some buses use natural gas for fuel. Natural gas is the cleanest burning fossil fuel.

Impacts of Using Fossil Fuels

Fossil fuels, including coal, oil, and natural gas, are the primary sources of energy in the United States. However, there are costs involved in locating and preparing these fuels for use. Expenses include the costs of labor to mine for coal or drill for oil. They also include the costs of labor and materials needed to build energy-generating plants. Transporting fuel to and from power plants is also costly. These costs are all included in our electricity bills or in our gas prices when we fill up our tanks at the gas station.

Some energy costs are not covered by our gas or electricity bills, however. These include the impacts to the environment caused by burning fossil fuels. The burning of coal and oil causes air pollution that can affect human health. Coal mining that is carried out without care for the land destroys the habitats of many plants and animals. The burning of fossil fuels has led to an increase in the amount of carbon dioxide in Earth's atmosphere. This has resulted in global warming, acid rain, and water pollution. Researchers are looking for ways to develop cleaner burning fossil fuels that will result in less damage to human health and the environment.

 **Extend It!**

Energy resources are used to provide electricity to your home and school. Research the costs of producing and burning these energy resources. Record your findings in your Science Notebook.

After You Read

1. Could paper be considered a fuel? Why or why not?

2. What is the main use of coal in the United States?

3. Use the information in your Science Notebook to describe some of the environmental impacts associated with burning fossil fuels.

Alternative Energy Resources

Before You Read

In your Science Notebook, create a chart with three columns. Label the first column *Alternative Energy Resource*, the second column *Definition*, and the third column *How It Is Used*. As you learn about alternative energy resources, add information to your chart.

What are alternative energy resources?

Today, most people rely on nonrenewable fossil fuels for their energy needs. Earth's petroleum resources are being used at a very fast rate. Some scientists think they might be used up within the next 60 years. Scientists, government agencies, and private companies are looking for ways to continue to meet the world's energy needs into the future. They are researching alternative energy resources that are renewable and do not harm the environment. Some of these alternative energy resources are described below.

Solar Energy

Remember that the Sun is the source of most of the energy on Earth. **Solar energy** is the energy from the Sun that warms Earth and gives us light. Solar energy can be used to heat buildings, make electricity, and charge batteries. Sunlight is free and, unlike the burning of fossil fuels, the use of solar energy does not create any pollution.

Passive Solar Heating Buildings may be heated by solar energy in two ways: by passive solar heating or by active solar heating. Passive solar heating captures sunlight directly and converts it into heat. For example, buildings designed for passive solar heating have large windows that face the Sun. Sunlight shining through the windows warms the building during the day. Materials, such as tile and brick, also collect and store the Sun's heat during the day and slowly release it after the Sun sets. Buildings that rely on passive solar heating must be located in areas that receive consistent sunlight.

Active Solar Heating Unlike passive solar heating, active solar heating requires collectors, such as solar panels, to absorb solar energy. Heat collected by these panels can be used immediately or stored for later use. Fans or pumps distribute the collected energy throughout the house. This energy can be used to heat the house, or to heat water for showers and washing dishes. Because this method stores the Sun's energy, active solar heating can be used even in areas that do not receive steady sunlight.

Figure 19.10 The solar panels on the roof of this house collect heat from the Sun throughout the day.

Photovoltaic Cells Scientists are still working on developing an efficient way to store large amounts of solar energy for long periods of time. If they can, people might someday be able to meet all of their energy needs by using only energy from the Sun. Currently, solar energy is converted into electricity by **photovoltaic cells**. These cells are thin, transparent wafers made up of layers of boron and phosphorus-enriched silicon. These materials absorb the Sun's light and release electrons that can be used as electricity. Single photovoltaic cells produce only a small amount of electricity. Several photovoltaic cells electrically connected to each other, however, can produce greater amounts. Today, many public utility companies in the United States use photovoltaic cells to produce electricity.

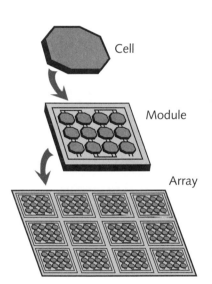

Cell

Module

Array

Figure 19.11 Single photovoltaic cells are wired together into modules. Modules are then wired together to form arrays, such as those that make up these solar panels.

Energy from Water

Hydroelectric power is electricity produced by flowing water. There are several ways to capture the power of flowing water. Water from waterfalls can be redirected into turbines. As the water falls over the turbines, they turn and drive a generator that produces electricity. Dams can also be built across rivers to create reservoirs of stored water. As this water flows through pipes at controlled rates, it causes turbines to spin and produce electricity. The energy of ocean waves can also be used to generate electricity. Today, about 10 percent of the electricity used in the United States is generated by water. While the use of water power does not pollute the environment, the building of dams can have negative impacts. The changes that dams cause to natural patterns of water flow can destroy wildlife habitats and interrupt the migration routes of fish. The large areas that become flooded when dams are built can even force people to move from their homes.

As You Read

Look at the chart in your Science Notebook. Fill it out by listing the alternative energy resources you read about. Define each resource and describe how each is used. Work with a partner to add to or correct the information on your chart.

What is the difference between passive and active solar heating?

 Explore It!

You can observe that sunlight produces heat.

- Inflate a balloon and tie its end.

- Using a magnifying glass, focus sunlight onto one spot on the balloon. Hold the magnifying glass still for several minutes.

- Observe what happens to the balloon. Why do you think this occurs? Record your thoughts in your Science Notebook.

Figure 19.12 These wind turbines use the energy of the wind to generate electricity.

Wind Energy

As shown in **Figure 19.12**, wind energy is captured by wind turbines. Wind turbines look something like traditional windmills. The wind turns the blades of the turbines. The energy of the movement of the blades is then used to produce electricity. There are many benefits to using wind power. Wind is an unlimited resource that does not pollute the environment. The land underneath wind turbines can also continue to be used for other purposes, such as farming. As a result, wind energy is one of the least expensive ways to produce electricity. The major disadvantage of using wind energy is that it is only economical to build wind turbines in areas with steady winds. Most of the wind farms in the United States are located in California and Hawaii.

Figure It Out

1. Which state generates the most electricity from wind power?

2. How many states generate more than 101 MW of electricity from wind power?

Figure 19.13 The map shows the amount of electricity, in megawatts (MW), being produced by wind power for each U.S. state.

Megawatts of Wind Power Generated by Each U.S. State, 2006

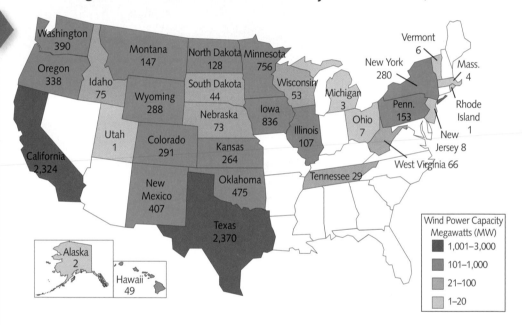

Washington 390
Oregon 338
Idaho 75
Montana 147
Wyoming 288
Utah 1
California 2,324
Colorado 291
New Mexico 407
North Dakota 128
South Dakota 44
Nebraska 73
Kansas 264
Oklahoma 475
Texas 2,370
Minnesota 756
Wisconsin 53
Iowa 836
Illinois 107
Michigan 3
Ohio 7
Tennessee 29
Vermont 6
New York 280
Penn. 153
West Virginia 66
New Jersey 8
Mass. 4
Rhode Island 1
Alaska 2
Hawaii 49

Wind Power Capacity Megawatts (MW)
- 1,001–3,000
- 101–1,000
- 21–100
- 1–20

CONNECTION: Environmental Science

Making Fuel from Trash

On average, every person in the United States produces 4.5 pounds of garbage per day. Most of that trash ends up in landfills where decomposition produces large amounts of methane gas. Although methane is a greenhouse gas that pollutes the air, it can also be a source of energy. The Environmental Protection Agency is currently working with various groups and companies to capture and use methane gas from landfills to make electricity.

First, wells are sunk into a landfill to collect the gas. The gas is then sucked into pipes, compressed, and sent to production plants to be used as fuel. In 2005, there were 395 landfill gas projects in the United States. The electricity generated by these projects is enough to heat 1.2 million homes.

Geothermal Energy

Geothermal energy is energy produced by naturally occurring steam and hot water beneath Earth's crust. Water trapped underground in rock fractures or in porous rock is heated by Earth's internal heat. Some of this water becomes steam. The water and steam usually escape at continental plate boundaries. Sometimes their release takes the form of amazing displays. For example, Old Faithful is a famous U.S. geyser—a tall fountain of steam and hot water—that shoots up regularly in Yellowstone National Park. In Reykjavik (RAYK yuh veek), Iceland, geothermal energy is so plentiful that almost 80 percent of the buildings are heated directly by water from geothermal wells. Many geothermal power plants use steam to generate electricity. One major advantage of geothermal energy is that it is abundant. A disadvantage, however, is that it can only be used near the sites where it is present.

Figure 19.14 The material rising from these nuclear power plant cooling towers is steam.

Nuclear Energy

Nuclear energy is an alternative source of energy associated with changes in the nucleus of an atom. Most nuclear energy is produced by a process called fission. During fission, the nuclei of radioactive atoms are split and a large amount of energy is released. This energy is used to heat water to produce the steam that powers electric generators.

Nuclear power has some advantages. It can produce electricity at relatively low costs and it does not pollute the air. However, nuclear power plants produce dangerous radioactive wastes. These wastes must be stored properly so that radiation cannot escape into the environment. Nuclear accidents, such as the 1979 incident at Three Mile Island in Pennsylvania and the 1986 explosion at Chernobyl in Ukraine, frightened people. Public concern about the safety of nuclear power plants has slowed the increase of their use throughout the world. Some countries, such as France, have developed technologies to recycle radioactive waste and reuse it as nuclear fuel.

CONNECTION: Math

There are several types, or grades, of coal. Grades of coal with a high percentage of carbon, such as anthracite, produce the most usable energy and release the least amount of pollution. Grades of coal with a lower percentage of carbon, such as lignite, produce less usable energy and more pollution. To determine the percentage of carbon in a sample of coal, divide the mass of carbon by the total mass of the coal sample. Then multiply the result by 100.

After You Read

1. Review the chart you created in your Science Notebook. Use the information to answer the following question in a well-developed paragraph. What are some advantages of using alternative energy sources?

2. Describe at least two ways in which solar energy is used.

3. What are some problems associated with using nuclear energy to generate electricity?

Summary

KEY CONCEPTS

19.1 Earth's Natural Resources

- A natural resource is any substance, organism, or form of energy that is used by living things and is not made by humans. Natural resources can be divided into two groups: renewable resources and nonrenewable resources.

- Renewable resources are natural resources that can be replaced over a relatively short period of time. They include all living things, fresh air and water, fertile soil, and elements that cycle through Earth's systems.

- Nonrenewable resources are natural resources that cannot be replaced or that can only be replaced by natural processes over thousands or millions of years. They include gemstones, metals, and fossil fuels.

19.2 Conventional Energy Resources

- Conventional energy resources are those that people have depended on for many years for fuel, heat, and electricity.

- Biomass fuels are conventional energy resources that come from living or once-living things. They include wood, solid animal wastes, field crops, and peat.

- Fossil fuels are conventional energy resources formed from the remains of living things that died millions of years ago. They include coal, petroleum, and natural gas.

- The burning of fossil fuels has led to an increase in the amount of carbon dioxide in Earth's atmosphere. Rising carbon dioxide levels contribute to global warming, acid rain, and water pollution.

19.3 Alternative Energy Resources

- Alternative energy resources are nonconventional energy resources that are being developed to provide electricity and heat. Alternative energy resources usually come from nonliving things.

- Examples of alternative energy resources include solar energy, wind and water energy, geothermal energy, and nuclear energy.

- The advantages of alternative energy resources include the fact that they are renewable, and most do not cause air pollution.

- The disadvantages are that some alternative energy resources, such as geothermal, wind, and water energy, are limited to the geographical areas where they are abundant. Some alternative energy resources can also have negative environmental impacts. For example, nuclear power plants produce dangerous radioactive wastes that must be safely stored.

VOCABULARY REVIEW

Write each term in a complete sentence, or write a paragraph relating several terms.

19.1
natural resource, p. 360
renewable resource, p. 360
sustainable yield, p. 361
nonrenewable resource, p. 362
fossil fuel, p. 363

19.2
fuel, p. 364
biomass, p. 364
biomass fuel, p. 364
peat, p. 365
coal, p. 366
fossil fuel, p. 366
petroleum, p. 366
natural gas, p. 367

19.3
solar energy, p. 368
photovoltaic cell, p. 369
hydroelectric power, p. 369
geothermal energy, p. 371
nuclear energy, p. 371

PREPARE FOR CHAPTER TEST

To prepare for the chapter test, create a question from each Learning Goal. Use the information in your Science Notebook to answer each question. Then use these answers to write a well-developed essay about the chapter. Use the Key Concept on the first page of this chapter as your topic sentence.

MASTERING CONCEPTS

True or False
If the statement is true, write "true." If it is false, change the underlined word or words to make the statement true.

1. A <u>sustainable yield</u> is achieved when a renewable resource is replaced at the same rate at which it is used.

2. Sunlight is a <u>nonrenewable</u> resource because it is always available.

3. Conventional energy resources usually come from <u>nonliving things</u>.

4. In the United States, coal is most often used for <u>heating homes</u>.

5. Alternative energy resources usually come from <u>nonliving things</u>.

6. Geothermal energy can be used for <u>making electricity</u>.

Short Answer
Answer each of the following in a sentence or brief paragraph.

7. How do plants capture and store the energy of the Sun?

8. Describe why diamonds are useful for industrial purposes.

9. Identify two natural resources that are directly necessary for human life.

10. Explain how peat is prepared for use as a fuel.

11. List five products made from petroleum.

12. How are photovoltaic cells used to make electricity?

13. What are some examples of moving water that can be used to generate electricity?

Critical Thinking
Use what you have learned in this chapter to answer each of the following.

14. **Relate** How might the amount of fertile soil on the planet affect the food supply?

15. **Infer** Researchers are continually searching for new energy resources. What properties would an ideal energy resource have?

Standardized Test Question
Choose the letter of the response that correctly answers the question.

16. Which of the following energy resources is a nonrenewable resource?
   A. wind energy
   B. geothermal energy
   C. fossil fuels
   D. solar energy

Test-Taking Tip

If you don't understand the directions, you can usually ask the teacher to explain them better. When the directions are clear enough for you to understand the question completely, you are less likely to pick the wrong answer.

Human Impact on Earth's Resources

KEY CONCEPT Even though the use of natural resources affects Earth's land, air, and water, all organisms, including humans, need natural resources to live.

All living things need natural resources—including air, food, and water—to live. Many organisms live in balance with the natural resources their environment provides. Others change their environments to better meet their needs. Of all living things on Earth, humans have the greatest ability to change their environments. They also have the greatest impact on Earth's natural resources.

Think About Using Natural Resources

The way humans use natural resources affects the environment. Think about a neighborhood park, your school grounds, or another open area. How has the land been shaped by people?

- Describe this area. Have people added or removed plants? Are there ponds or streams? If so, are they human-made or natural? Do any animals live there?

- In your Science Notebook, explain how you think the land, water, and air in this environment might be different if people did not live and work nearby.

NSTA

SCI LINKS
THE WORLD'S A CLICK AWAY

www.scilinks.org

Human Activities/Environmental
Issues **Code: WGES20**

20.1 Human Impact on Land

Before You Read

Make a four-column chart in your Science Notebook. Write the main headings from this lesson at the top of each column. The headings are *Extraction of Mineral and Rock Resources, Agriculture, Deforestation,* and *Urban Development.* Write a few sentences in each column summarizing what you might already know about each of these topics.

- Explain the environmental impact of extracting mineral and rock resources.

- Describe the environmental impacts of agriculture and deforestation.

- Discuss the environmental impact of urban development.

New Vocabulary

mining
reclamation
monoculture
crop rotation
deforestation

Every person uses Earth's natural resources daily for food, building materials, and energy. Humans would not be able to survive without these resources, many of which come from the land. Some natural resources are buried in the ground. These include metals such as gold and copper. Above ground, land is used for farming, building houses, and making roadways. This lesson describes some ways that humans impact the land around them. It also explores ways to reduce the damage to the land caused by humans.

Extraction of Mineral and Rock Resources

Rocks and minerals are resources that form naturally in Earth. Granite and marble, for example, are rock resources used for building. Coal is a rock resource used for fuel. Mineral resources include metals and gemstones. All of these things are natural resources that must be removed, or extracted, from Earth. **Mining** is the process of taking mineral resources from the ground. It is often a difficult procedure and can affect a large area of land. There are two major types of mining: surface mining and underground, or subsurface, mining.

Figure 20.1 In modern underground coal mines, a machine called a shearer does the actual cutting of the coal.

CONNECTION: Biology

The soil at abandoned mining sites often contains toxic metals and other chemicals from mining wastes. Phytoremediation (fi toh rih mee dee AY shun) is a process that uses plants to clean up pollution in the environment. Plants remove harmful chemicals from the ground when their roots take in water and nutrients from polluted soils, streams, and groundwater. The plants and local bacteria can then help break down many of the toxic chemicals. The plants also help prevent wind, rain, and groundwater from carrying pollution to other areas.

Surface Mining   Surface mining is used to remove rock, mineral, and ore deposits located close to Earth's surface. Common deposits located just beneath the surface include iron, bauxite (aluminum ore), copper, coal, and gold. Usually, bulldozers and other pieces of heavy equipment are used to remove the soil and rock above the mineral or ore deposit. This material is called overburden. Because surface mining removes large amounts of surface materials from the land, it always has negative effects on the environment and human settlements.

In 1977, the United States passed the Surface Mining Control and Reclamation Act. This act recognized that mining activities needed to be better balanced with caring for the environment. The act requires that land that has been mined go through the process of reclamation. **Reclamation** is the replanting of vegetation on mined land and the restoration of the land to its original shape. Even with reclamation efforts, however, very few mined land areas ever return to their original condition.

Figure 20.2 The land in the left photo is being strip-mined. The photo on the right shows the same site after reclamation efforts.

Underground Mining   Underground mining is used to remove rock and mineral deposits from deep below Earth's surface. Tunnels are dug to allow workers and equipment to reach the materials. Explosives might be used to break up a deposit. The materials are then transported to the surface by small railroad cars or conveyor belts. Underground mining can be dangerous. Mine workers might inhale dust or toxic gases, or become trapped underground.

Underground mining has less of an impact on the landscape than does surface mining. It can, however, bring harmful materials from underground to Earth's surface. Toxic metals and other compounds might be present in the waste material removed from mines. If these materials are not handled properly, rainwater can carry them into streams and soil.

Agriculture

Most of our food comes from large-scale, industrial farms that practice monoculture. In **monoculture**, only one type of crop is grown in a particular area. The United States grows almost all of its major crops—including corn, wheat, soybeans, and cotton—in monoculture. Growing and harvesting large quantities of a single crop at once reduces the costs of producing crops and their prices in the market. However, growing only one crop removes certain essential nutrients from the soil. Other disadvantages of monoculture relate to the use of pesticides.

As You Read

In your four-column chart, list the effects on the environment of extracting mineral and rock resources, agriculture, deforestation, and urban development. Share and discuss your chart with a partner. Correct any incorrect information.

How does industrial farming lead to a decrease in the fertility of topsoil?

Figure 20.3 This field contains only one type of crop—soybeans.

Pesticides   Pests are attracted to fields, such as those in large-scale farms, that are planted with only one or two types of crops. To control insects and weeds, these farms require large amounts of toxic, or poisonous, chemicals called pesticides. Some pesticides remain in the environment for long periods of time. Pesticides carried by wind and rain can pollute nearby waters. The chemicals might harm wildlife, including fishes and birds, and they often kill helpful organisms such as worms that help keep the soil fertile.

Adding to the problem, growing the same crops year after year reduces the amount of nutrients in the soil. As a result, large amounts of fertilizers are used to replace the nutrients crops need to grow. Like pesticides, excess fertilizers run off into streams and pollute nearby waters.

The loss of topsoil is also an issue, especially for large-scale farms. Clearing large areas of land for farming leaves no vegetation to hold soil in place. As a result, valuable topsoil can be eroded more easily by wind and water.

Figure 20.5 These coffee beans were certified according to the standards of the Sustainable Agriculture Network. This South American conservation group works with thousands of farms to ensure that farmland is managed to conserve natural resources and protect wildlife.

Good farming practices can help protect the environment. Planting trees close to fields prevents topsoil from being blown away by the wind. Leaving the remains of crops on fields during the winter helps to hold topsoil in place. This also reduces runoff of pesticides and fertilizers into streams. Changing the type of crop grown in a field from one year to the next, a practice called **crop rotation**, can replenish nutrients in the soil. Crop rotation is a common practice of many farmers in the United States and in numerous other countries around the world. Some farmers carefully map their fields to monitor plant growth. In this way, they are able to apply fertilizer only to areas where it is absolutely necessary.

Figure 20.4 Rows of trees between farm fields stop the wind from blowing topsoil away.

Deforestation

Thousands of hectares of Earth's forests are cut down every year in order to meet the demand for paper, lumber, charcoal, and firewood. **Deforestation** is the removal of trees from a forested area without replanting enough new trees to replace them. Often, areas harvested for lumber are clear-cut. This means that every tree in the forest is cut down. Clear-cutting is extremely damaging to the environment. It results in loss of habitat for wildlife. In addition, without trees to hold forest soil in place, topsoil erodes and clogs nearby streams with sediment. Deforestation also impacts the world's climate. Trees release oxygen into the atmosphere, and take in and store carbon dioxide. As forests are cut down, there are fewer trees taking in carbon dioxide from the atmosphere. As described in Chapter 15, increased levels of carbon dioxide in the atmosphere contribute to global warming.

There are alternatives to clear-cutting. Selective logging is the removal of only certain trees, while leaving the rest of the forest standing. This practice helps protect wildlife habitat and reduces topsoil erosion. Leaving buffer zones of trees along banks of streams can help prevent eroded sediment from reaching the water. There are also everyday actions people can take to reduce deforestation. These include recycling and reusing paper and wood products whenever possible.

Urban Development

Over six billion people currently live on Earth, and the human population continues to grow. As it grows, the sizes of urban areas, such as cities and towns, also grow. The development of land for the growth of urban areas impacts the environment. Land that was once fields, forests, or wetlands is cleared to build houses, schools, and shopping centers. Both humans and wildlife feel the impact of urban development. For example, natural wetlands filter water, help control flooding, and provide critical habitats for wildlife. When a wetland is filled in for construction, humans become subject to poor water quality and increased flooding, while animals are forced to leave the area or die. In addition, as large areas of land are covered with pavement, rainwater cannot follow the normal process of soaking into the ground and returning to lakes and streams. This often leads to flooding during heavy rains.

Figure 20.6 This woman is replanting trees in the tropics. Reforestation helps to prevent soil erosion in deforested areas.

Another problem associated with large populations is that they generate a lot of garbage, or solid waste, which might pollute the surrounding environment. Most of this solid waste is buried underground in landfills. Often, dangerous chemicals end up in city landfills. These chemicals might leak out into the area's water supply. Industries located in urban areas often use toxic heavy metals, such as mercury, lead, or arsenic, and other dangerous chemicals. Improper disposal or accidental spills of these materials might also pollute soils and groundwater.

Explore It!

Fill a rectangular plastic box about halfway with soil. Pat the soil down gently and cover half of it with waxed paper. This side represents an urban area partially covered with pavement. Try not to crumple the waxed paper. It should lay fairly flat.

Pour a cup of water over the soil on the side of the container without the waxed paper and observe what happens. This side of the container represents unpaved land. Next, pour a cup of water directly over the waxed paper and observe what happens. Record your observations and possible explanations in your Science Notebook.

1. What is the total percentage of solid waste produced by paper, yard trimmings, and food scraps?

2. Explain which sources of solid waste could be reduced by recycling.

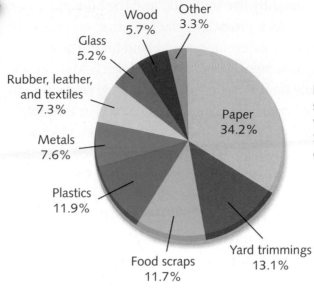

2005 Total Solid Waste Generation
245 Million Tons (Before Recycling)

Other 3.3%
Wood 5.7%
Glass 5.2%
Rubber, leather, and textiles 7.3%
Metals 7.6%
Plastics 11.9%
Food scraps 11.7%
Yard trimmings 13.1%
Paper 34.2%

Figure 20.7 This graph shows the percentage of solid waste generated in the United States by different sources during 2005.

Today, many cities recognize the need to protect the environment as their populations grow. As a result, the governments and citizens of these areas are making efforts to decrease the negative effects of land development and waste disposal. For example, there are now laws that require developers who destroy wetland areas to build new wetlands in other areas. In addition, modern landfills are safer than landfills of the past, as shown in **Figure 20.8**. Trash is now buried over layers of clay or plastic to prevent toxic liquids from leaking into the soil and the water supply. Methane, a gas that is produced as trash breaks down, is released from the ground through pipes to avoid buildup and possible explosions. Methane can also be collected to generate electricity.

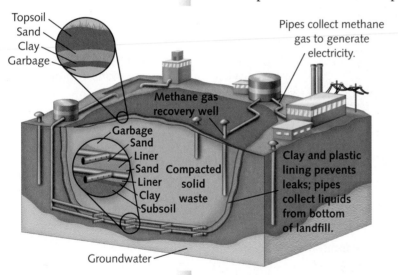

Topsoil
Sand
Clay
Garbage

Pipes collect methane gas to generate electricity.

Methane gas recovery well

Garbage
Sand
Liner
Sand
Liner
Clay
Subsoil

Compacted solid waste

Clay and plastic lining prevents leaks; pipes collect liquids from bottom of landfill.

Groundwater

Figure 20.8 Modern landfills are less harmful to the environment than landfills of the past.

After You Read

1. Which human activities clear trees and other plants from the land?

2. Describe an alternative to clear-cutting.

3. Review the chart in your Science Notebook. Using your notes, write a well-developed paragraph that summarizes the impact to the environment caused by agriculture.

4. How can modern landfill design help protect the environment?

20.2 Human Impact on Air

Learning Goals

- Describe the types and sources of air pollution.
- Identify the impact of air pollution.
- Explain the causes and effects of acid precipitation.

New Vocabulary

smog
ozone
greenhouse effect
global warming
acid precipitation

Before You Read

Reword each Learning Goal for this lesson so that it forms a question. Write the questions in your Science Notebook. As you read, write the answer to each question.

Fresh air is a natural resource that sustains life on Earth. Air is a mixture of gases. It is made up mostly of nitrogen and oxygen, with small amounts of carbon dioxide, water vapor, and other substances. To stay healthy, many living things need clean air to breathe. Unfortunately, human activities regularly release harmful materials into the air, causing air pollution.

Types of Air Pollution

Automobiles are a major source of air pollution. As they burn gasoline, their exhaust systems release harmful substances into the air. When the Sun's rays come in contact with these substances, a type of air pollution called **smog** results. Smog often appears as a yellow-brown haze over large cities. When there is too much smog, the air becomes harmful to breathe. **Ozone** is a gas molecule made up of three oxygen atoms, and is the major chemical in smog. As described in Chapter 13, ozone is present in two layers of the atmosphere. The layer closest to Earth's surface is the troposphere. In the troposphere, ground-level ozone is an air pollutant that is harmful to breathe. It also damages crops, trees, and other vegetation by causing loss of leaves, reduced photosynthesis, and plant tissue damage. Ozone in the stratosphere, which is the second layer of Earth's atmosphere, protects life on Earth from the Sun's harmful ultraviolet (UV) rays.

Air pollution also occurs in the form of solid particles of materials known as particulate matter. Particulate matter is made of numerous materials that include ash, dust, and pollen. These particles can

Figure 20.9 Smog is visible as a haze over Mexico City.

irritate eyes, noses, and throats and can make breathing difficult. They can also damage human lungs. Some air pollution occurs naturally, such as that caused by volcanic eruptions and forest fires.

Worldwide Impact of Air Pollution

Breathing polluted air can be harmful to humans. Air pollution also harms plants and animals. Worldwide impacts of air pollution include global warming; the depletion, or reduction, of *good* ozone from Earth's upper atmosphere; and acid precipitation.

Global Warming As described in Chapter 15, the **greenhouse effect** is the natural heating of Earth's surface caused by certain gases in the atmosphere. While some of the Sun's incoming radiation is reflected back into space by Earth's clouds, some is absorbed by Earth's surface. This energy is then released and held as heat by gases such as water vapor, methane, and carbon dioxide in Earth's atmosphere. These atmospheric gases are called greenhouse gases. Without the greenhouse effect to trap heat from the Sun, our planet could not support life as we know it. Too much of a greenhouse effect, however, could cause Earth's temperature to rise dangerously. Over the past 200 years, global temperatures have, in fact, been rising. The rise in Earth's average surface temperature is known as **global warming**.

As You Read

Fill in any unanswered questions in your Science Notebook. Review your questions and answers with a partner. Discuss what you have written and make any necessary changes.

In which layer of Earth's atmosphere is harmful ozone present?

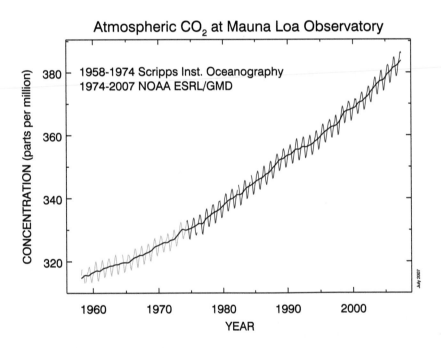

Figure 20.10 The amount of carbon dioxide in the atmosphere has risen dramatically since the 1960s.

Most scientists agree that global warming is occurring largely because of rising levels of carbon dioxide (CO_2) in the atmosphere. Other factors that might be involved in global warming include the natural cycles of the Sun and Earth. It is clear, however, that human activities that involve burning fossil fuels such as oil, coal, and natural gas play a major role in increasing atmospheric CO_2 levels. Automobiles, power plants, and factories all burn fossil fuels. **Figure 20.10** shows how the concentration of carbon dioxide in Earth's atmosphere has increased since the 1960s.

Global warming could have severe consequences. Rising temperatures speed up the melting of glaciers and ice caps. This, in turn, causes sea levels to rise and increases flooding of low-lying areas. Changes in wind and rainfall patterns might affect agriculture worldwide. These changes might also lead to the eventual extinction of plant and animal species that cannot adapt to rapid changes in climate.

Thinning of the Ozone Layer

Air pollution produced by humans affects ozone in the second layer of Earth's atmosphere, the stratosphere. As described earlier, ozone in the stratosphere protects life on Earth from the Sun's harmful ultraviolet (UV) rays. UV radiation has been linked to human skin cancer and eye diseases. It can also be harmful to the health of other animal and plant species. A hole in the ozone layer over the south pole was first detected and measured during the 1980s. At about this time, an increase in ozone-damaging chemicals called chlorofluorocarbons (CFCs) was detected in Earth's atmosphere. This ozone hole has appeared nearly every year since the 1990s. Its size changes from year to year, and continued growth remains a concern.

The CFCs that damage Earth's ozone layer are manufactured by humans. These chemicals were once commonly used in air-conditioning units, as coolants for refrigerators, and in aerosol spray cans. An international treaty called the Montreal Protocol on Substances That Deplete the Ozone Layer went into effect in 1989. This treaty called for the phasing out of the production of CFCs worldwide. As a result, the amount of CFCs in Earth's lower atmosphere has declined. The CFCs already in the atmosphere, however, will remain there for many years.

CONNECTION: Health

Like outdoor air pollution, indoor air pollution can be damaging to human health. Short-term health effects of indoor air pollution on humans include irritation of eyes, nose, and throat; headaches; dizziness; and fatigue. Long-term health effects include some respiratory diseases, heart disease, and cancer. Sources of indoor air pollution include fuels such as oil, gas, kerosene, coal, and wood that release gases and particles into the air when they are burned. Other sources include building materials, mold growing on damp carpets, and household cleaning products. While it is important to decrease the use of air-polluting substances in the home, good indoor ventilation systems can also help prevent health problems. These systems bring in and circulate enough outdoor air to lessen the impact of emissions from indoor pollution sources. They also carry pollutants out of the home.

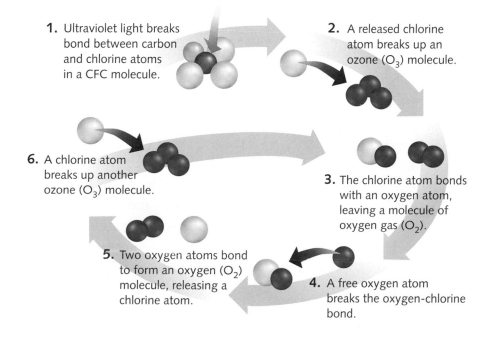

1. Ultraviolet light breaks bond between carbon and chlorine atoms in a CFC molecule.

2. A released chlorine atom breaks up an ozone (O_3) molecule.

3. The chlorine atom bonds with an oxygen atom, leaving a molecule of oxygen gas (O_2).

4. A free oxygen atom breaks the oxygen-chlorine bond.

5. Two oxygen atoms bond to form an oxygen (O_2) molecule, releasing a chlorine atom.

6. A chlorine atom breaks up another ozone (O_3) molecule.

Figure 20.11 It only takes a few chlorine atoms from CFCs to destroy many ozone molecules.

Acid Precipitation

The acidity of any substance is expressed by its pH. The pH scale, shown in **Figure 20.12**, ranges from 0 to 14. Substances with a pH of 7 are considered neutral. Substances with a pH of less than 7 are acidic, and those with a pH of greater than 7 are alkaline, or basic. The pH of water varies, depending on its locations and how it is being used.

Normal precipitation is slightly acidic, at a pH of 5.6. **Acid precipitation** is precipitation with a pH less than 5. Acid precipitation affects the environment in negative ways. Too much acid can kill the plants and animals living in lakes and streams. Acid precipitation damages forest soil by removing some essential nutrients. It weakens trees, especially those at high elevations, and makes them more susceptible to disease and pests. It also speeds up the decay of city buildings, statues, and sculptures.

Explain It!

In your Science Notebook, write a public service announcement for a local television or radio station explaining the benefits of reducing air pollution. Make sure to mention the effects both on human health and on the environment.

Figure It Out

1. What is the pH of milk? What is the pH of vinegar? Which is more acidic?
2. According to this chart, what can you tell about the effects of acid precipitation on fish populations?

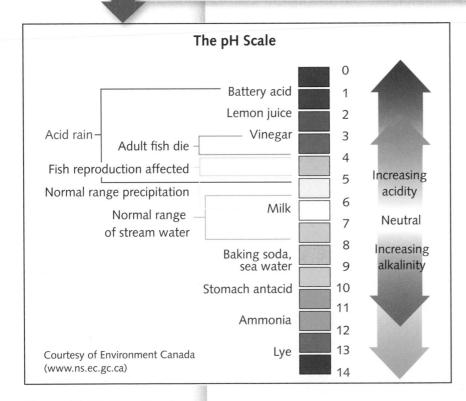

The pH Scale

Courtesy of Environment Canada
(www.ns.ec.gc.ca)

Figure 20.12 The pH scale ranges from 0 to 14, with 7 being neutral. Highly acidic acid precipitation can be harmful to the environment.

Acid precipitation is caused in great part by air pollution. The release of sulfur dioxide and nitrogen oxide combine with moisture in the atmosphere to create acid precipitation. Sulfur dioxide and nitrogen oxides come primarily from automobile exhaust and the smoke from coal-burning power plants. Smoke that rises high into the air might be carried long distances and then become acid precipitation. For example, sulfur dioxide generated by power plants in the midwestern United States is often carried by winds toward the eastern states and Canada. There, it combines with moisture in the air and falls to the ground as acid precipitation.

PEOPLE IN SCIENCE John J. Mooney and Carl D. Keith

John J. Mooney and Carl D. Keith are American chemists who together invented a device called the catalytic converter. This device has helped combat air pollution around the world. A catalytic converter changes most of the harmful gases created by running an automobile engine into gases that are safer for the environment. The 1970 U.S. Clean Air Act placed restrictions on the amounts of pollutants that could come from car exhaust. Catalytic converters allowed cars to meet the new guidelines by reducing the amounts of nitrogen oxides, carbon monoxide, and chemicals called hydrocarbons that are released from car tailpipes. These devices are now used in automobiles and trucks all over the world. Mooney and Keith were not only coinventors of catalytic converters, they also helped market them. They worked closely with the automotive industry to increase acceptance of the new technology.

Combating Air Pollution

Because air pollution can travel with the wind, controlling it requires the cooperation of countries around the world. The Kyoto Protocol is an international agreement committing industrialized nations to reduce their emissions of greenhouse gases to specific levels. This agreement, which went into effect in 2005, was not ratified, or accepted, by the U.S. Senate. The Bush Administration also rejected the Kyoto Protocol. As described below, the U.S. government has developed some policies for decreasing air pollution.

In the United States, the Clean Air Act requires the Environmental Protection Agency to regulate all air pollutants that pose a threat to public health by establishing the National Ambient Air Quality Standards (NAAQS). Six air pollutants are monitored under these standards: ozone, nitrogen dioxide, sulfur dioxide, carbon monoxide, particulate matter, and lead. The Clean Air Act has been especially successful at reducing lead levels in the atmosphere over the last 30 years. Other ways to reduce air pollution include increased use of alternative energy resources, such as solar and wind power. The development of new technologies, such as more efficient engines and devices that reduce harmful emissions, also help combat air pollution.

Did You Know?

Choosing to drive an energy-efficient car, such as a hybrid car that is powered by both gas and electricity, might be the most helpful thing you can do to reduce air pollution. For every gallon of gasoline burned, scientists estimate that 19 pounds of carbon are released into the atmosphere!

After You Read

1. Review the questions and answers in your Science Notebook. What are some ways in which human activities can cause air pollution?

2. How are air pollution and global warming related to one another?

3. How does air pollution lead to the formation of acid precipitation?

Before You Read

Preview the lesson by looking at the pictures and reading the headings and the Learning Goals. In your Science Notebook, write a paragraph describing what you think the lesson will be about.

All living things depend on water for survival. While there is a lot of water on Earth, 97 percent of it is salt water that is located in the oceans. Most of Earth's freshwater—the type of water humans and many other organisms need to survive—is frozen in glaciers and the polar ice caps. Less than one percent of the freshwater on Earth is located in lakes and rivers. People depend on this supply of freshwater for everyday activities such as drinking, washing, cooking, and bathing. Humans also rely on the freshwater supply to grow crops for food. As shown in **Figure 20.13**, industry and power plants put a heavy strain on the water supply also.

In many parts of the world, the demand for freshwater is greater than the available supply. As the world's population continues to grow, many more areas will experience this problem. Access to clean freshwater is critical to the health of humans and many other living organisms. For this reason, it is important to keep Earth's waters clean. Unfortunately, the quality of water around the world is often negatively impacted by human activities.

Figure It Out

1. For which purpose is the largest percentage of water used in the United States?

2. Which three types of usage together account for about one-fifth of the total water usage in the United States?

Use of Water in the United States, 2000

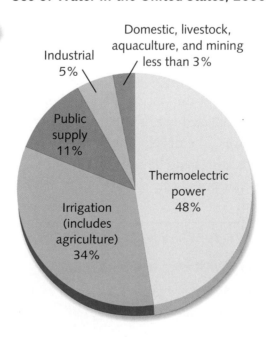

Industrial 5%

Public supply 11%

Domestic, livestock, aquaculture, and mining less than 3%

Thermoelectric power 48%

Irrigation (includes agriculture) 34%

Figure 20.13 This graph shows the percentage of the total water supply used for various purposes in the United States.

Sources of Water Pollution

Sources of water pollution are grouped into two main types: point sources and nonpoint sources. **Point sources** generate pollution from a specific source and location. **Nonpoint sources** generate pollution from more widespread sources and locations. Because point sources of pollution come from a single source and location, they are often easier to identify and control.

Point Sources   One of the most common point sources of pollution is the discharge of untreated sewage into natural waters. This method of getting rid of sewage is common in countries around the world that do not have modern sewage treatment facilities. Modern sewage treatment plants that are not working properly might also release bacteria and viruses into the water supply. Other examples of point sources include toxic wastes from industrial plants or commercial businesses that are illegally dumped into streams or rivers.

Nonpoint Sources   Pollution from nonpoint sources is usually associated with rainfall or melting snow moving over and through the ground. Rainwater absorbs many pollutants in the air. It also dissolves pollutants on the ground and carries them to streams and rivers as runoff as it flows over the land. Examples of nonpoint sources of pollution include automobile emissions, road dirt and grit, and runoff from parking lots. Other nonpoint sources include pesticides and fertilizers from farms and lawns, sediment from construction and logging sites, bacteria and nutrients from livestock, pet wastes, faulty septic systems, and runoff of toxic materials from mining operations.

As You Read

In a group of four, talk about the topics discussed in the lesson. Then work with a partner to write notes based on your discussion. Finally, write a well-developed paragraph in your Science Notebook summarizing what this lesson is about. Describe how this lesson relates to the other lessons in the chapter. Was your prediction about the content of the lesson correct? Explain.

Figure 20.14 The soap used to wash a car outdoors flows into storm drains that carry it to lakes and rivers. Detergents in soaps can harm the animals and plants that live in aquatic environments. Washing cars in commercial car washes decreases nonpoint source pollution. These car washes use water several times before it is sent to the sewer system for treatment.

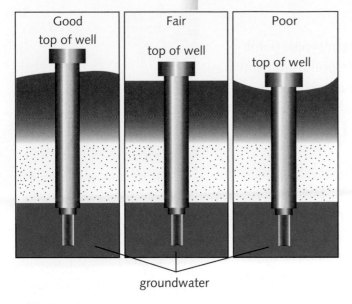

Good
top of well

Fair
top of well

Poor
top of well

groundwater

Figure 20.15 A well should be located at the top of a land area that slopes down on either side. This way, polluted rainwater will not collect near the well and seep into the groundwater.

● ● ● ● ● ● ● ● ● ● ● ●

Extend It!

Use the library or Internet to research oil spills. When and where did the last spill occur? What was done to clean up the spill? Find out how animals that have been covered by oil can be cleaned. Record your findings in your Science Notebook.

Groundwater Pollution   The freshwater contained within the rock layers below Earth's surface is called **groundwater**. In many areas, people drink groundwater from wells. Groundwater is also used to water crops and raise animals on many farms. Chemicals dissolved in rainwater can seep into groundwater and pollute it. Other sources of groundwater pollution include leaking gasoline-storage tanks, chemical-storage barrels, landfills, road salts, and sewage from septic systems.

Ocean Pollution   Earth's oceans provide a habitat for millions of plant and animal species. The oceans also moderate the temperature of our planet and provide humans with essential food and energy resources. Pollution from toxic wastes, plastic debris, and oil spills threatens the health of the oceans. Many of the world's largest cities are located near or along coastlines. Sewage water from these heavily populated areas often ends up in waters near the shoreline. High levels of nitrogen and phosphorus in human wastewater can cause a large and rapid increase in the population of bacteria in coastal waters. These bacteria use up oxygen as they decompose. Eventually, this results in the formation of large areas on the ocean floor where animals and plants cannot survive. These areas are known as dead zones.

Trash and other polluting materials can enter the ocean directly from ships. Marine animals might suffer or die from eating plastics and other garbage. Oil is another major pollutant of ocean waters. Ships transporting crude oil might spill it into the ocean. Oil spills can occur at ocean mining sites, where oil is pumped from beneath the ocean floor. Oil also naturally seeps from rock layers beneath the ocean into ocean waters. Large oil spills can affect areas spanning many kilometers.

Figure 20.16 The IXTOC I oil well in Mexico's Bay of Campeche spilled 140 million gallons of oil when it exploded in 1979. The only oil spill in history larger than the IXTOC I spill was the deliberate release of oil (from a number of sources) during the 1991 Gulf War.

Reducing Pollution and Conserving Water

Preventing the pollution of water is less difficult and less expensive than trying to clean it up after the pollution has occurred. In 1972, the U.S. Congress passed the Clean Water Act. One of the main goals of this act is to stop the release of pollutants into rivers, streams, lakes, and wetlands. Another major goal of the Clean Water Act is to clean up polluted waters so that they can once again be used for recreational purposes. The Clean Water Act is considered a success in many ways. Since it was passed in 1972, many of the nation's waters are once again safe for swimming and fishing. There has also been an increase in the number of communities served by sewage-treatment plants. However, there is still room for improvement. In 1974, Congress passed the Safe Drinking Water Act to ensure access to unpolluted drinking water. More progress has been made over the years through several amendments to the Clean Water Act. Many water supplies, however, still do not meet the safety requirements of this act.

Figure 20.17 This is a garden in Arizona. Some cities in the dry western United States have reward programs for homeowners that landscape using plants that require little water. This type of landscaping is called xeriscaping.

Conserving water and protecting water quality go hand in hand. High demands for water contribute to nonpoint source pollution. Runoff from excess water used for agriculture and landscape maintenance increases water pollution. Finding ways to reuse and recycle water is one way for large-scale industries and businesses to conserve water. For example, treated wastewater might be useful for another purpose, such as watering the lawns around corporate buildings. Individual actions can also play a part in reducing water pollution and conserving water. Installing low-flow showerheads and low-flush toilets in homes conserves water. Disposal of hazardous wastes through city waste collection programs, and keeping trash off the ground, keeps pollutants out of the water supply.

After You Read

1. Describe the difference between point and nonpoint sources of pollution.

2. What types of human activities can cause ocean pollution?

3. Review the preview and summary you wrote in your Science Notebook. Based on your notes, what are some things individuals can do to conserve water and reduce water pollution?

KEY CONCEPTS

20.1 Human Impact on Land

- Surface mining negatively impacts the land by removing large amounts of surface materials. Underground mining can bring toxic materials to Earth's surface, and miners might inhale toxic gases or become trapped underground.

- Large-scale farms use large amounts of pesticides and fertilizers that are harmful to the environment. Monoculture reduces the amount of nutrients in the soil over time.

- Both agriculture and forestry can cause topsoil loss and destroy wildlife habitat.

- Urban development can destroy wildlife habitat and lead to increased runoff of pollutants as well as flooding.

20.2 Human Impact on Air

- Air pollution occurs both as smog and as particulate matter. Burning fuels such as wood, coal, or gasoline causes smog. Ash, dust, and pollen pollute the air as particulate matter.

- Worldwide impacts of air pollution include global warming, the depletion of "good" ozone from Earth's upper atmosphere, and acid precipitation.

- Acid precipitation is created when air pollution, in the form of emissions of sulfur dioxide and nitrogen oxide, combines with moisture in the atmosphere.

- Acid precipitation can kill or damage living organisms. It also damages buildings, statues, and sculptures.

20.3 Human Impact on Water

- Sources of water pollution are grouped into two main types: point sources and nonpoint sources.

- Sources of water pollution include automobile emissions, sediment, pesticides, fertilizers, faulty septic systems, bacteria and nutrients from livestock, and runoff of toxic materials from mining operations.

- The goal of the Clean Water Act is to stop the release of pollutants into rivers, streams, lakes, and wetlands. Legal measures such as this decrease pollution over time. Proper disposal of toxic substances and trash also helps reduce water pollution.

- Reusing and recycling both help conserve water. Installing water-saving devices in homes also helps conserve water.

VOCABULARY REVIEW

Write each term in a complete sentence or write a paragraph relating several terms.

20.1
mining, p. 375
reclamation, p. 376
monoculture, p. 377
crop rotation, p. 378
deforestation, p. 378

20.2
smog, p. 381
ozone, p. 381
greenhouse effect, p. 382
global warming, p. 382
acid precipitation, p. 384

20.3
point source, p. 387
nonpoint source, p. 387
groundwater, p. 388

PREPARE FOR CHAPTER TEST

To prepare for the chapter test, create a question from each Learning Goal. Use the information in your Science Notebook to answer each question. Then use these answers to write a well-developed essay about the chapter. Use the Key Concept on the first page of this chapter as your topic sentence.

MASTERING CONCEPTS

True or False

If the statement is true, write "true." If it is false, change the underlined word or words to make the statement true.

1. The practice of growing only one type of crop at a time is called <u>agriculture</u>.

2. <u>Pesticides</u> replace nutrients lost from the soil.

3. <u>Trees</u> in a forest prevent soil from being eroded and washed away.

4. Sulfur dioxide and <u>carbon dioxide</u> react with water to produce acid precipitation.

5. <u>Particulate matter</u> in the atmosphere traps heat from the Sun to warm Earth's surface.

6. Trash thrown off boats can cause <u>ocean pollution</u>.

7. Sewage treatment plants might be <u>point sources</u> of pollution.

Short Answer

Answer each of the following in a sentence or brief paragraph.

8. How is surface mining different from underground mining?

9. Describe the process of reclamation.

10. Explain how farmers can protect the environment.

11. What steps can cities take to reduce pollution?

12. Where do chlorofluorocarbons (CFCs) come from?

13. How can air pollution in western U.S. states lead to acid precipitation in eastern states?

14. What causes ocean dead zones?

Critical Thinking

Use what you have learned in this chapter to answer each of the following.

15. **Relate** Trees and other plants take carbon dioxide from the air and release oxygen. Could deforestation have an effect on global warming? Why or why not?

16. **Infer** Coal-burning power plants release sulfur dioxide and nitrogen oxides into the air. How might this lead to water pollution?

Standardized Test Question

Choose the letter of the response that correctly answers the question.

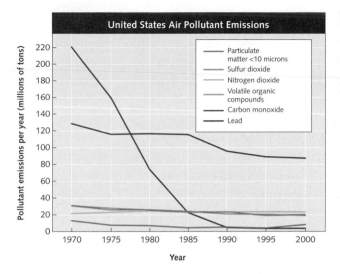

17. The graph above shows the amounts of six different air pollutants released each year in the United States, from 1970 to 2000. Which of the pollutants decreased most sharply between 1975 and 1985?

   A. lead

   B. carbon monoxide

   C. particulate matter

   D. sulfur dioxide

Test-Taking Tip

Make sure you understand what kind of answer you are being asked to provide. A graphic organizer might help you organize your thoughts if you see words such as *illustrate, list, define, compare, explain,* and *predict.*

The Power of Wind

PEOPLE HAVE USED wind power for thousands of years. It has pushed sailing ships around the world. It has turned windmills to grind grain and pump water. Now wind is making electricity.

At the moment, wind power makes up less than one percent of the electricity used by Americans. But, wind power might soon be producing much more. Wind turbines—the machines that turn wind into electric power—appeared about 30 years ago. However, they were limited to just a few areas. Now, companies are building them everywhere—from California to New Jersey. Wind farms are situated on windy plains or in mountain passes. Some have thousands of turbines. All together, the wind turbines in use in the United States in 2007 could provide power for more than two million homes.

State laws are helping the use of wind power grow. About 20 states have laws that require electric companies to generate a certain amount of their electricity from renewable sources within the next few years. These laws are helping to increase the use of energy sources such as wind and solar power. Several electric utilities companies are building wind turbines to add to the electricity they produce. In some places, customers can contribute money to support the building of renewable energy facilities, such as wind farms. As more wind turbines are built, they will reduce the need for power plants that burn polluting fuels such as coal.

Why wind? It's a free energy source. It doesn't produce pollution. It will never run out. Plus, there are many parts of the United States where it's very windy. Still, there are some problems. Wind turbines kill many birds that fly into them. What's more, wind doesn't blow all the time, so scientists must find a reliable way to store the power generated by wind turbines for when it's needed. Scientists are working out these problems, though, and as they do the use of wind power will increase.

 ## CAREER CONNECTION: ENVIRONMENTAL TECHNICIAN

Do you like to solve problems? Is protecting the environment important to you? Would you rather work outdoors than in an office? If the answer is "yes" to each of these questions, you might enjoy a career as an environmental technician.

Environmental technicians work with environmental scientists and engineers. They do research, conduct tests, and collect data. Environmental technicians collect the air,

water, and soil samples that help government agencies keep track of pollution. Some environmental technicians monitor plants and wildlife at national parks. Those who work at water treatment plants test water to make sure it's clean and safe. They might make sure the pollution control equipment at a factory, power plant, or landfill is working properly. Environmental technicians also help develop the tools and procedures used to prevent or stop pollution problems.

Most environmental technicians have a strong background in science and math. They earn a two-year associate degree and get training in the latest technology in their field. They also have to learn environmental regulations.

Environmental technicians work hard, but they have a lot of job satisfaction. What they do protects everyone's health and safety.

Driving into the Future

ENGINEERS ARE WORKING TODAY on the cars people will drive in the future. These cars will look different from the cars of today. They will be made of different materials. They will probably be smaller and lighter in weight. Most importantly, however, they will run on cleaner fuels.

The types of gasoline-fueled cars most people drive have been around for about 100 years. They run on fuels such as gasoline and diesel that are expensive and nonrenewable. They also create a lot of pollution, including gases that increase global warming.

The new fuels will be friendlier to the environment. Some will come from plants such as corn or grasses. Some cars will fill up on hydrogen. There could even be cars that get all their power by plugging into an electric outlet. These fuels will all have a couple of things in common. They will create less pollution than the fuels we use today. They will also be fuels we can make here in the United States.

Hybrids are cars with an engine that runs on a fuel such as gasoline or on ethanol, which is a plant fuel often made of corn. They also have an electric motor. The hybrid can run on electricity and then switch to gasoline when its battery runs down. Hybrids produce much less pollution than most of the cars on the road today. Because they run on electricity some of the time, they also use less fuel, and they go farther on the fuel they use. One hybrid can go more than 80 km on a single gallon of gasoline. That's twice as far as many other cars on the road today.

In the future, cars might also run on hydrogen fuel cells. Fuel cell vehicles get their power from the chemical reaction between hydrogen fuel and oxygen from the air. The by-products of the reaction are the energy that runs the car's motor and the release of harmless water vapor as waste. There are some drawbacks, however. As a gas, hydrogen takes up more space than liquid gasoline. Engineers will have to find a way to store enough of it safely inside a vehicle to drive long distances. Also, a whole new network of hydrogen fueling stations must be built. This will take time.

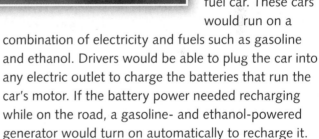

Battery-powered electric cars could also be in our future. Drivers of these cars may be able to power up their cars by plugging them into an electric outlet. The electricity would charge a battery that runs the car's motor. These cars would produce no pollution from their tailpipes. If the source of the electricity they use is renewable, such as wind or solar power, the cars would produce no pollution at all. Car makers are also introducing the plug-in flex fuel car. These cars would run on a combination of electricity and fuels such as gasoline and ethanol. Drivers would be able to plug the car into any electric outlet to charge the batteries that run the car's motor. If the battery power needed recharging while on the road, a gasoline- and ethanol-powered generator would turn on automatically to recharge it.

Hydrogen fuel cells and electric plug-in cars might not be available to the everyday driver for several years, but many people are driving hybrids now. Gradually, we're moving toward cars that are more efficient and better for the environment. In the future, everyone will breathe a little easier.

Investigative Reporting

Research the topic of alternative fuels for cars. Where do these fuels come from? How are they made? What types of technologies are being developed to use these fuels? Work with a partner to write a report that describes an alternative fuel source and how it might one day be used in everyday life.

Unit 9

Exploring Space

Chapter 21 — Earth and Its Moon

What tools do astronomers use to observe the universe and the movements of Earth, the Sun, and the Moon?

Chapter 22 — The Solar System

How does our understanding of the solar system help us to understand the motions and organization of planets and other celestial bodies?

Chapter 23 — Stars

How are all stars alike? What properties are used to differentiate one star from another?

Chapter 24 — Galaxies and the Universe

How does studying the universe and the groupings of stars within it help scientists to better understand the origins of our solar system?

394

Chapter 21

Earth and Its Moon

KEY CONCEPT Astronomers use a variety of tools to study the universe and to explain the movements of Earth, the Sun, and the Moon.

Have you ever seen an Earthrise like the one above? Astronauts on the *Apollo 11* mission took this photograph as their spaceship flew through space toward the Moon. The blue and white object is our own planet Earth. We can't feel it, but Earth is hurtling through space at 105,000 kilometers per hour.

Ancient people looked at the sky and wondered about the stars and other bright objects they saw. Over time, their observations and questions developed into the science of astronomy. Astronomy helps us understand Earth, the Moon, and the other objects we see in the night sky.

Think About Testing Predictions

Scientists propose hypotheses to explain the events of the natural world. They make predictions about their hypotheses and run experiments to test them.

Predict what objects you will see in the sky tonight. Test your predictions by making observations tonight. Tomorrow, ask yourself, "Were my predictions accurate?" How could you improve your predictions for the next night?

www.scilinks.org
Earth's Moon **Code: WGES21**

Before You Read

Read the four main headings and four subheadings in the lesson. Create a chart in your Science Notebook with four columns. Use each heading as a column title. Then write a sentence summarizing what you know about each topic.

Earth's Position in Space

Our understanding of Earth as a moving body in space is a fairly recent development. For most of human history, people believed that Earth was the center of the universe. Stories were created to explain the objects visible in the day and night skies. For example, some Native Americans believed that the points of light in the night sky were holes poked into a blanket that covered the Sun. The Australian Aborigines described the Milky Way as a river with bright stars for fish.

Cosmology is the study of the universe, how it formed, and its future. Questions about cosmology led ancient peoples to make observations and measurements of the positions and movements of objects in the sky. These observations revealed the predictable motions of these objects and the roundness of Earth. Gradually, people began to realize that Earth is one of many planets circling one of many stars in the universe.

Planet Earth   Earth is a planet. A planet is an object in space that orbits around a star. Planets do not create their own light. The brightness of Earth in photos taken from space is caused by sunlight reflecting off Earth's surface. Planet Earth is basically a ball of rock, 12,800 km across with a mass of 6×10^{24} kg. The motion of Earth spinning on its axis and its orbit around the Sun cause day and night, seasons, and many other natural events.

Figure 21.1 Earth rotates on its axis like a ball spins on a fingertip. Each 24-hour rotation makes up one complete day.

Earth's Rotation

Imagine spinning a ball on the end of your finger. The top and bottom of the ball stay in place while every other point on the ball's surface moves in circles. Earth spins, or rotates, on its axis in the same way. One full rotation takes 23 hours and 56 minutes to complete. Earth also moves a little through space each day in its orbit around the Sun. As a result, Earth must rotate a bit more than one full circle in order for the same spot on Earth to face the Sun directly each day. This is why one full solar day is 24 hours.

Day and Night People measure their lives in hours, days, months, and years. For thousands of years, people defined a day as the time it took the Sun to move through the sky and return to its original position. Early astronomers proved through their observations that Earth, rather than the Sun, is moving. As Earth rotates, each place on our planet experiences daylight when it faces the Sun and night when it faces away from the Sun.

Earth's movement also causes the apparent motion of objects in space. The Sun, the Moon, and stars all appear to move from east to west as Earth spins eastward on its axis. This illusion is similar to what a person experiences when sitting in a moving car. When a car passes a large truck, it might appear that the truck is moving backward. Today, we know that it is Earth that is moving.

Time Zones Until the late 1800s, timekeeping around the world varied from town to town. The clocks in each town were set to 12:00 noon when the Sun reached its highest point in the sky each day. Travelers would reset their watches each time they entered a new town. This system worked until the railroads sped up the pace of travel. Train passengers needed to know exactly when trains would arrive and leave the station. A standard system of time zones was established in 1884. The prime meridian, an invisible line that runs through Greenwich, England, was selected as zero degrees longitude. **Figure 21.2** shows how the world is divided into 24 time zones, each separated by one hour. The International Date Line, located at 180° longitude, marks the place where one day ends and the next begins.

As You Read

After you finish each section of the lesson, return to the chart in your Science Notebook. Write a new sentence to summarize what you have learned about each topic. Compare your notes with those of a partner. Make any necessary additions or corrections.

Why do the Sun, the Moon, and stars all appear to move from east to west?

Did You Know?

There are nine time zones in the United States and its territories. They include eastern, central, mountain, Pacific, Alaska, Hawaii-Aleutian, Samoa, Wake Island, and Guam.

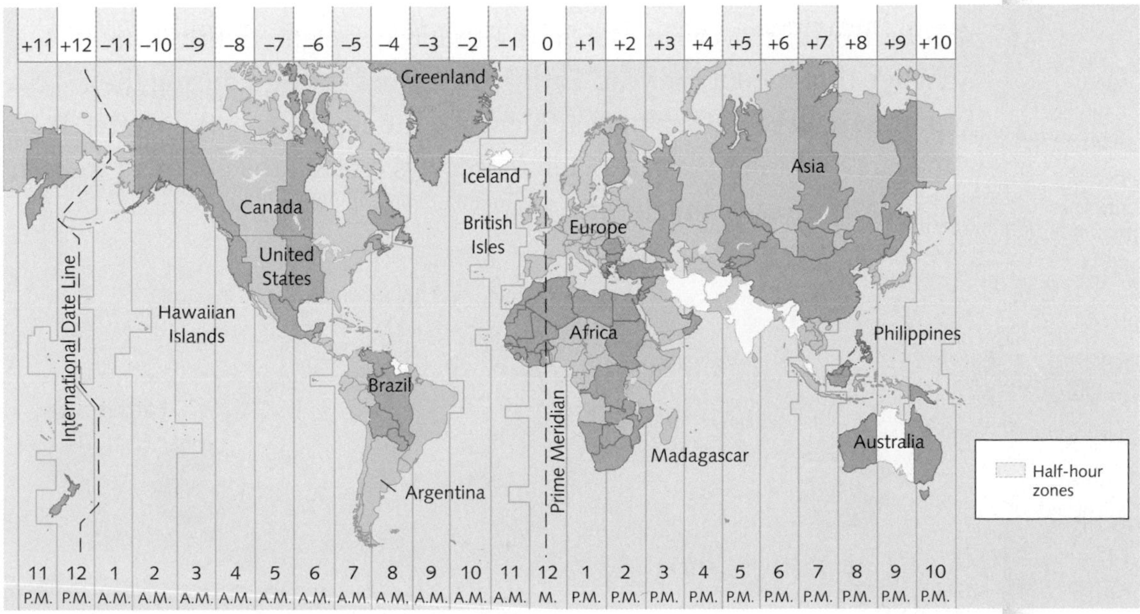

Figure 21.2 Earth is divided into 24 time zones. They are spaced 15° of longitude apart. Because Earth rotates through 360° of longitude every 24 hours, it covers 15° of longitude, or one time zone, every hour.

Figure 21.3 Earth's orbit around the Sun forms a plane called the ecliptic. Earth's axis points in the same direction throughout its year-long orbit.

Figure It Out

1. What does the red line circling Earth represent?

2. Which position number shows summer in the northern hemisphere?

Earth's Orbit

The path that one object in space takes around another is called its **orbit**. An object that orbits another is called a **satellite**. Earth is a satellite of the Sun. The Moon is a satellite of Earth. Earth's orbit around the Sun is in the shape of an ellipse, or a slightly squashed circle. The path that Earth takes around the Sun is called the **ecliptic**. Due to the motion of Earth, the Sun appears to move across the sky. The path that the Sun takes across the sky is also called the ecliptic. When viewed from the side, the ecliptic appears as a flat plane. Earth travels around the Sun at an average distance of 150 million km.

It takes Earth 365.25 days to complete one revolution, or orbit, all the way around the Sun. A year in our calendar is 365 days, roughly the period of one Earth orbit. The extra 0.25 days from each revolution are collected every four years into a leap day. The leap day is added into the calendar every fourth year as February 29.

Earth's Tilt Earth's axis is an imaginary line that travels from the north pole to the south pole. But instead of making a 90° angle with the plane of the ecliptic, the axis is tilted 23.5° toward the plane of the ecliptic. **Figure 21.3** shows this relationship. It also shows how Earth's axis points in the same direction throughout each orbit. As a result, at one point in its orbit, Earth's northern hemisphere tilts toward the Sun. At another point, six months later, the northern hemisphere tilts away from the Sun. Earth's tilt and its orbital motion around the Sun are what cause the seasons. As discussed in Chapter 15, the parts of Earth that are tilted toward the Sun experience summer. The parts of Earth tilted away from the Sun experience winter.

Earth's tilt also causes the Sun's altitude, or height, in the sky to change throughout the year. Earth's tilt toward the Sun during the summer makes the Sun appear higher in the sky. During the winter, it appears lower in the sky. Ancient observers tracked the apparent motion of the Sun to calculate the seasons.

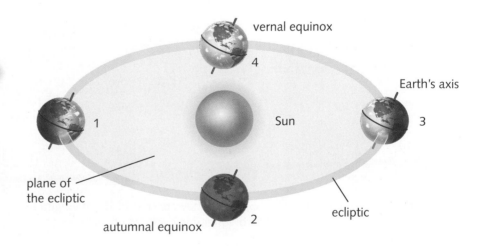

Solstices and Equinoxes

On average, every place on Earth spends half of its time in daylight and half in darkness. The actual number of daylight hours on any particular day of the year, however, varies from place to place. The longest day in either the northern or southern hemisphere is called the **summer solstice**. On this day, the Sun appears highest in the sky. Position 1 in **Figure 21.3** corresponds to the summer solstice in the northern hemisphere. This day is June 21 and is defined as the first day of summer. During the summer solstice, the number of daylight hours is at its maximum in the northern hemisphere and at its minimum in the southern hemisphere. In the southern hemisphere, June 21 is the shortest day of the year. During the summer solstice, the arctic circle region experiences constant daylight, while the antarctic circle region experiences constant darkness.

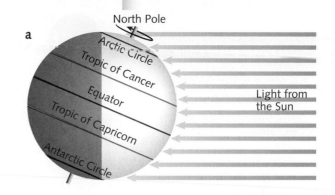

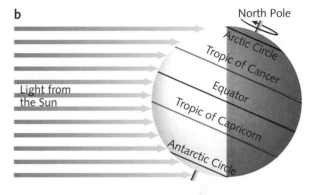

Figure 21.4 a) During the summer solstice, the Sun's rays are vertical at the Tropic of Cancer. **b)** During the winter solstice, they are vertical at the Tropic of Capricorn.

Position 3 in **Figure 21.3** corresponds to the **winter solstice**. On this day in the northern hemisphere, the Sun is at its lowest altitude in the sky. Winter begins on the winter solstice, around December 21. During the winter solstice, the number of daylight hours is at its minimum in the northern hemisphere and at its maximum in the southern hemisphere. This means it is the antarctic circle region that experiences constant daylight, while the arctic circle region experiences constant darkness. The summer solstice in the northern hemisphere is the winter solstice in the southern hemisphere. This is because when one side of Earth is tilted toward the Sun, the other side is tilted away. As a result, the longest day in North America is the shortest day in Australia.

Between solstices, the length of day and night begins to even out. Positions 2 and 4 in **Figure 21.3** correspond to the **autumnal equinox** and the **vernal**, or spring, **equinox**. During the equinoxes, Earth's axis is not pointed at the Sun and both hemispheres receive equal amounts of sunlight. The vernal equinox in the northern hemisphere is equal to the autumnal equinox in the southern hemisphere.

After You Read

1. Describe how hours, days, and years are based on Earth's movements.

2. Why are the lengths of days and nights equal in Earth's northern and southern hemispheres during the equinoxes?

3. Based on the chart in your Science Notebook, explain how life on Earth could be different if our planet's axis were not tilted.

21.2 Earth's Moon

Learning Goals

- Compare the Moon and Earth in terms of their properties and movements.
- Describe the surface features of the Moon and how the Moon formed.
- Explain what causes Earth's tides and the phases of the Moon.
- Explain solar and lunar eclipses.

New Vocabulary

impact crater
synchronous rotation
perigee
apogee
solar eclipse
umbra
penumbra
lunar eclipse

Before You Read

Create a lesson outline. Use the lesson title as the outline title. Label the headings with the Roman numerals *I* through *VI*. Use the letters *A*, *B*, *C*, etc., under each subheading to record information you want to remember.

Look up into the sky on a clear night. The Moon will likely be the brightest object in the sky. The Moon is Earth's only natural satellite. Though Earth and the Moon are similar in age and composition, they differ in many ways. Unlike Earth, the Moon is a barren rock with no atmosphere, no life, and extreme temperature shifts. The average distance of the Moon from Earth is 384,000 km. Yet even from this great distance, the Moon affects Earth's ocean tides and lights up Earth's sky during its monthly cycle of phases.

Moon Characteristics

The Moon has only a little over one percent of Earth's mass and has only one-sixth of Earth's gravity. Its diameter is about one-quarter of Earth's diameter. In fact, fifty Moons could fit inside Earth. The density of the Moon is also less than that of Earth. As shown in **Figure 21.5**, the Moon has a layered structure much like Earth. The light of the Moon is actually sunlight reflected by its surface. Dust on the Moon absorbs sunlight and causes the surface temperature to rise to 130°C. At night, with no atmosphere and no resulting greenhouse effect to keep heat close to the Moon's surface, the temperature can fall to –170°C.

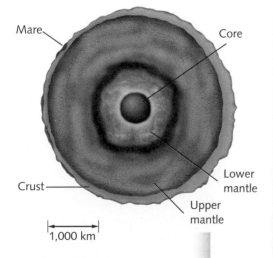

Figure 21.5 The Moon's layered structure is similar to that of Earth.

Earth and Moon Properties

	Moon	Earth
Diameter	3,476 km	12,756 km
Age	4.5 billion years	4.6 billion years
Orbital period (length of year)	27 d, 7 h, 43 m	365.25 d
Rotation (length of day)	27 d, 7 h, 43 m	23 h, 56 m, 04 s
Atmosphere	none	nitrogen, oxygen, argon, carbon dioxide, water
Temperature Range	–170°C to 130°C	–89°C to 56°C

Figure 21.6 This table compares properties of the Moon and Earth.

Surface Features As the Moon cooled billions of years ago, the volcanic and seismic activity of the early Moon slowed. The Moon's surface is made up of regions called *maria* (singular, *mare*) and *highlands*. The Moon's maria are dark, flat plains made by lava flows. The highlands are mountainous, light in color and covered with craters. Scientists think the Moon's craters are **impact craters**, formed when objects from space crashed into its surface.

With no atmosphere to produce weather and no flowing water, there is no erosion on the Moon. The Moon's surface looks just as it did when it first formed. Even the footprints left in the lunar dust by the Apollo astronauts are visible today.

Figure 21.7 This close-up photo of the Moon's surface shows many impact craters. The large impact crater visible in the lower right is called Tycho. It is 85 km wide.

The Moon's Origin

Scientists have proposed several different theories to explain the Moon's origin. The explanation most commonly accepted today is the impact theory. As shown in **Figure 21.8**, this theory states that a Mars-sized object collided with Earth about 4.5 billion years ago. At that time, the Sun and planets were still forming. As the object struck Earth, materials from both the object and Earth's outer layers were thrown into space. These materials were thrown out far enough to avoid falling back to Earth but not far enough to escape Earth's gravity. Eventually, they merged together to form the Moon.

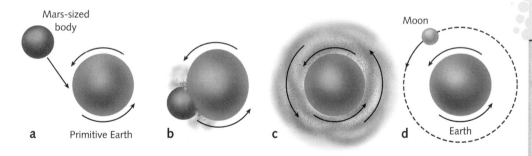

a Primitive Earth   **b**   **c**   **d** Earth   Mars-sized body   Moon

Figure 21.8 It is thought that when a Mars-sized object collided with Earth **(a)** and **(b)**, the materials thrown into space **(c)** merged together to form the Moon **(d)**.

Rotation and Orbit

The Moon's periods of orbit and rotation are both 27 days, 7 hours, and 43 minutes. This means that the Moon experiences **synchronous rotation**, or that it rotates exactly one time each time it travels around Earth. As a result, as the Moon orbits Earth, the same side is always facing our planet.

The Moon's orbit around Earth is shaped like an ellipse. The Moon comes as close as 356,000 km to Earth at **perigee** (PER uh jee), the closest point in its orbit. At the farthest point in its orbit, called **apogee** (A puh jee), it is 407,000 km from Earth. To viewers on Earth, when the Moon is at perigee, it appears 30 percent larger than when it is at apogee.

Phases of the Moon

The changes in the appearance of the Moon throughout each month are called lunar phases. When the Sun, Earth, and the Moon line up so that the bright side of the Moon faces Earth, we see a full moon. At other times, a viewer on Earth sees part or none of the Moon's bright side. **Figure 21.9** shows how the phases of the Moon depend on the positions of Earth, the Moon, and the Sun.

Figure It Out

1. How are the positions of the Sun, the Moon, and Earth related to one another during a new moon?

2. Explain why the Moon's surface isn't visible from Earth during a new moon.

Figure 21.9 The Moon passes through all of its phases every 29.5 days. During the waxing phases of the Moon, the amount of reflected sunlight seen on Earth increases. During the waning phases, it decreases.

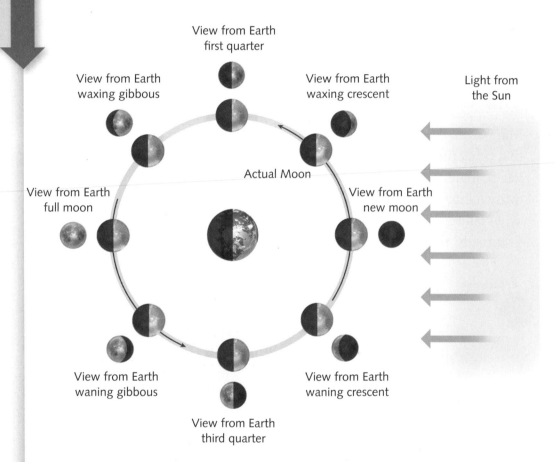

View from Earth
first quarter

View from Earth
waxing gibbous

View from Earth
waxing crescent

Light from
the Sun

Actual Moon

View from Earth
full moon

View from Earth
new moon

View from Earth
waning gibbous

View from Earth
waning crescent

View from Earth
third quarter

Tides

The Moon's gravity pulls at Earth as it moves through its orbit. As a result, Earth's water is pulled, or bulges, toward the Moon on the side closest to it. Earth's water also bulges outward on the side of the planet opposite the Moon. This is because Earth itself is pulled slightly toward the Moon—and away from the water on the side not facing the Moon. These bulges of water, or tides, repeat in a daily cycle as Earth rotates on its axis. Tides are discussed in greater detail in Chapter 17.

Solar and Lunar Eclipses

A **solar eclipse** occurs when the Moon passes directly between Earth and the Sun. Though the Sun is much larger than the Moon, the apparent sizes of the Moon and the Sun as viewed from Earth are similar. For this reason, during a total solar eclipse, the Moon can completely block the Sun. The only light visible during a total solar eclipse comes from the dimly lit outer gaseous layers of the Sun called the corona.

As shown in **Figure 21.10a**, during a solar eclipse, the Moon casts a shadow on Earth that is made up of two regions. The inner portion of the Moon's shadow, where none of the Sun's light reaches, is called the **umbra** (UM bruh). The outer portion of the Moon's shadow, where some of the Sun's light reaches Earth is called the **penumbra** (puh NUM bruh). People who witness an eclipse from within the umbra will see a total solar eclipse. People who witness an eclipse from within the penumbra area of the Moon's shadow will see a partial solar eclipse.

Earth can also line up between the Moon and the Sun. Recall that the Moon does not produce its own light. The Moon appears to glow only because it reflects some of the sunlight that strikes it. When Earth's shadow blocks that sunlight, the Moon experiences a **lunar eclipse** and becomes almost dark. As shown in **Figure 21.10b**, a total lunar eclipse occurs when all of the Moon is inside Earth's umbra.

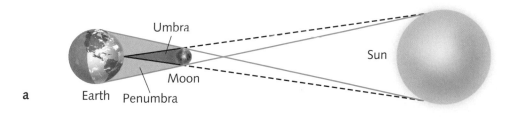

a   Earth   Penumbra   Umbra   Moon   Sun

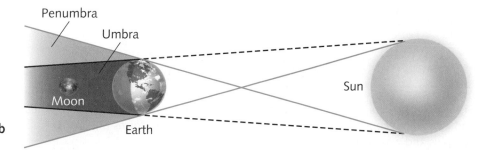

b   Penumbra   Umbra   Moon   Earth   Sun

Figure 21.10 a) A solar eclipse occurs when the Moon passes between the Sun and Earth. **b)** Earth's shadow blocks sunlight from reaching the Moon during a lunar eclipse.

After You Read

1. Explain why erosion does not occur on the Moon.

2. When viewed from Earth, why does the Moon's overall size appear to change?

3. Review the information in your outline. In your Science Notebook, write a well-developed paragraph summarizing the formation of a total lunar eclipse. Include a drawing of the Moon, the Sun, and Earth.

Learning Goals

- Describe electromagnetic radiation.
- Compare and contrast reflective and refractive telescopes.
- Explain how astronomers gather information about objects in space.

New Vocabulary

astronomy
electromagnetic radiation
wavelength
frequency
electromagnetic spectrum
telescope
refracting telescope
reflecting telescope

Did You Know?

Astrology is an ancient practice that predicts people's personalities and life events based on where the Sun was on the day they were born. Ancient astrologers noted that the Sun's path moved through 12 constellations that made up the Zodiac. Many people still practice the art of astrology today, but it has little basis in science.

Before You Read

Draw a five-column table in your Science Notebook. Title the table *Astronomy*. Label the columns *Who*, *When*, *What*, *How*, and *Why*. Use the table to organize the information you learn about astronomy.

Astronomy is the scientific study of the Sun, the Moon, and other celestial bodies, or objects in space. Throughout history, travelers have used the positions of the stars to find their way across vast expanses of ocean or desert. Ancient cultures recognized patterns of stars and drew imaginary pictures around them. The patterns, called constellations, played an important role in the everyday lives of these people. For example, early farmers used the appearance of certain star groups to signal the start of the planting or harvesting seasons. **Appendix C** contains star charts showing the constellations that are visible in the night sky during each of the seasons.

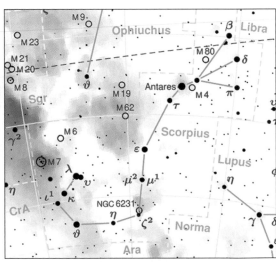

Figure 21.11 The constellation Scorpius, the scorpion, represents death, darkness, and everything considered evil. The bright red star, Antares, forms the heart of Scorpius and was said to give the scorpion its evil nature.

Over time, people began to observe the sky for less practical reasons. They wanted to understand Earth's place in the universe. More than 2,000 years ago, Greek astronomers began to make systematic observations of objects they saw in the night sky. They were able to deduce the shapes and relative positions of many celestial bodies. Astronomy became the first field of science.

Learning About the Universe

Astronomers rely on the light that comes from objects in space to learn more about our universe. This light, or **electromagnetic radiation**, is made up of electric and magnetic disturbances that travel through space as waves. **Wavelength** is the distance between the peaks on a wave of radiation as it travels through space.

People are only able to see some of the wavelengths of electromagnetic radiation. The wavelengths within a range visible to the human eye are called visible light. Types of electromagnetic radiation that the human eye cannot see include infrared and ultraviolet radiation, radio waves, microwaves, X rays, and gamma rays.

The Electromagnetic Spectrum   As shown in **Figure 21.12**, electromagnetic radiation is classified, or described, according to its wavelengths. The symbol for wavelength is the Greek letter lambda, λ. Radiation with long waves, such as radio waves, carries less energy than short-wave radiation, such as gamma rays, which is more intense. Electromagnetic radiation can also be classified by its **frequency**, or the number of waves occurring per second. The symbol for frequency is f. The **electromagnetic spectrum** contains all the types of electromagnetic radiation organized by their wavelengths and frequencies.

As You Read

Fill in the columns in your *Astronomy* table in your Science Notebook as you read the lesson. Explain your chart to a small group. Then work with a partner to ensure that key facts and supporting details are included in your chart.

Explain why the unaided human eye cannot detect most objects in space.

Figure It Out

1. Which type of electromagnetic radiation has the longest wavelength? Which has the shortest wavelength?

2. Which colors of visible light have the highest frequencies?

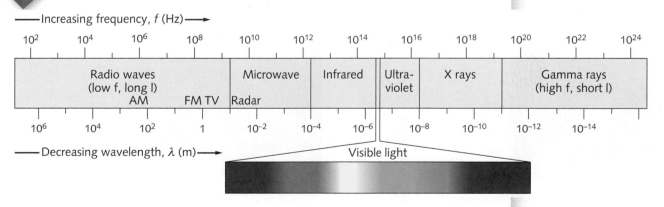

Figure 21.12 The electromagnetic spectrum ranges from low-energy radio waves to high-energy gamma rays. Radiation with a shorter wavelength carries more energy. Notice how small the range of visible light is compared to the rest of the spectrum.

Viewing Objects in Space

A **telescope** is an instrument for collecting and magnifying visible light or other forms of electromagnetic radiation from a distant object. The invention of the first telescopes led to a great increase in human understanding of the universe. These early telescopes provided evidence that the Sun was at the center of the solar system, that other planets have moons, and that celestial bodies are not perfectly spherical.

Refracting Telescopes   The earliest telescopes, invented during the 1570s, were refracting telescopes. As shown in **Figure 21.13a**, **refracting telescopes** use a set of lenses to bring visible light to a focus, or central point. A large, curved lens, called the objective lens, focuses incoming light. Galileo improved upon the original design of these early telescopes and developed more powerful refracting telescopes by 1609. The telescope became famous when Galileo identified and tracked the movement of four of Jupiter's moons as well as surface features on Earth's Moon. Larger telescope lenses are able to gather more light and make faint objects look brighter. A second lens in the eyepiece of the telescope magnifies the image. Binoculars are actually a pair of small refracting telescopes set side by side.

There are practical limits to the size of a refracting telescope. Magnification can only be improved by moving the focus farther behind the objective lens. This results in longer and longer telescopes that require larger lenses. Eventually, large lenses sag under their own weight and produce distorted images.

Refracting telescope

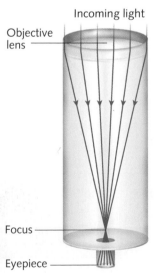

Incoming light

Objective lens

Focus

Eyepiece

a

Reflecting telescope

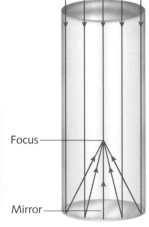

Incoming light

Focus

Mirror

b

Figure 21.13 Telescopes can be reflectors, refractors, or a combination of both. **a)** Refracting telescopes use lenses to gather, bend, and focus light. Small refractors are inexpensive and make a good choice for the beginning stargazer. **b)** Reflecting telescopes use mirrors to form an image. Some of the largest telescopes in the world today are reflectors.

One group of scientists in the United Kingdom uses computer simulations to predict and describe the possible effects and consequences of an asteroid impact on Earth. Their parameters consider an asteroid less than one km in diameter. The computer program, called NEOImpactor, has predicted that an asteroid just 200 m across could cause tsunamis around the world.

NEOImpactor was not designed to frighten people. It is being used as a tool to predict possible scenarios involving collisions of asteroids with Earth. The results of the computer simulations may enable people to prepare for these types of events before they occur. For example, governments might decide to develop programs to detect all the near-Earth objects orbiting the Sun. Based on simulations such as NEOImpactor, governments might also develop systems to deflect or blow up dangerous asteroids before they reach Earth.

Reflecting Telescopes   In 1671, Isaac Newton invented the first reflecting telescope. As shown in **Figure 21.13b**, **reflecting telescopes** use a series of curved and flat mirrors to bring visible light to a focus. Larger mirrors produce brighter images. Reflecting telescopes can be very powerful, because light can be bent and folded several times using mirrors inside a short barrel. Many smaller mirrors can also be laid like tiles to form larger mirrors. By fitting reflecting telescopes with special equipment, they can also be used to study infrared and ultraviolet light.

Professional astronomers typically use reflecting telescopes that are located at observatories far from city lights. The world's best observatories are located at high elevations where there is little light pollution and less atmosphere to interfere with incoming electromagnetic radiation. Telescopes in orbit around Earth can produce the best images of objects in space, because there is no atmosphere to blur images.

Telescopes for Different Wavelengths
Most objects give off several different wavelengths of energy at the same time. To collect data about each of these different wavelengths, astronomers must use different types of telescopes. Like visible light, infrared and ultraviolet radiation can be focused using mirrors. Focusing gamma rays and X rays require specially designed telescopes. The array of radio telescopes, shown in **Figure 21.14**, is arranged in an orderly design, to collect and focus radio waves.

Figure 21.14 This array of 27 radio telescopes in New Mexico is being used by astronomers to map the center of our galaxy.

Figure 21.15 Rocks from space that survive passage through Earth's atmosphere are called meteorites. Scientists analyze meteorites and samples of rock brought back by spacecraft to learn more about our solar system.

Explore It!

Use an online mapping program to see Earth from space. Enter your address and look at your home and your school. Then choose another location outside the United States to explore. Describe your observations in your Science Notebook.

Studying Rocks from Space

Astronomers can learn a lot about celestial bodies by analyzing rocks that have fallen to Earth from space. Tens of thousands of kilograms of space material fall toward Earth each day. Most of this material is dust that burns up in Earth's atmosphere. About ten percent of the rocks, or meteoroids, survive the passage to Earth's surface. Once on Earth, they are called meteorites. Scientists analyze meteorites to learn about the geology and history of the space objects they came from. For example, meteorites from Mars give clues about whether life could survive on Mars. Since the first Moon rocks were brought back to Earth by the Apollo astronauts, scientists have been studying them to gain an understanding of the Moon's composition and history.

Astronomy from Space

There are limits to the knowledge we can gain from Earth-based observatories and investigations. Sending spacecraft into space gives astronomers the ability to take clearer pictures, close-up images, collect samples, and, perhaps one day soon, set foot on neighboring planets.

Artificial Satellites Artificial satellites are launched by rockets into orbit around Earth. Satellites, powered by solar energy, send the information they gather back to Earth. Some satellites collect information about our own planet. Weather satellites, mapping satellites, and military satellites are some examples. Communications satellites receive and transmit signals from TV, radio, or telephones and send them back to Earth. Many satellites are orbiting observatories that collect information about the Sun, the Moon, the stars, and the planets.

Space Probes A vehicle that carries scientific instruments to planets or other bodies in space is called a space probe. Because the distance between stars is so large, probes are limited to our own solar system. Space probes delivered the Mars rovers to photograph and analyze rock samples on Mars. Other probes have explored each of the other planets, the Sun, the Moon, asteroids, and comets.

Figure 21.16 a) The Hubble Space Telescope is a reflecting telescope in orbit around Earth. **b)** This photo of the Mars landscape was taken by the Mars Exploration rover *Spirit.* Space probes carried the Mars Exploration rovers into space.

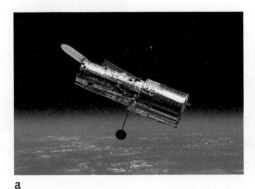

a

b

Human Space Flight   Humans have long dreamed of
flying in a spaceship to another world. Until recent decades,
however, scientists were not sure whether humans could
survive the challenges of space. The first successful human
space flight took place in 1961. Astronaut Yury (YOO ree)
Gagarin (guh GAY run), of the U.S.S.R., returned safely to
Earth. Within ten years, the United States sent astronauts to
walk on the Moon.

The early spacecrafts that carried astronauts had to land on
Earth by falling into the ocean. This was called a splashdown.
As a result, a new spacecraft was needed for each mission.
The space shuttle program, which began building spacecraft
that could be used more than once, began in 1981. To date, five
shuttles have flown more than 100 missions. The shuttles and
their astronauts have carried up and installed many parts of
the *International Space Station* (ISS). Sixteen countries have
contributed to building the ISS. The ISS has orbited Earth for
more than ten years, allowing astronauts to experience life in
space for months at a time. One focus of ISS investigations is
to help prepare for human space flight to Mars.

Human space flight continues to touch the human spirit in
ways that cannot be measured. It also continues to produce a
great deal of valuable scientific information. Critics of sending
humans into space argue that robotic missions are much less
expensive and less dangerous to human life. As of 2007, five
failed U.S. space missions have killed 19 astronauts. Scientific
benefits must be weighed against the costs and risks of sending
humans into space. Currently, both human and robotic space flight will
continue to play integral roles in international space programs. As new
technologies are developed, many different directions are possible for
the future of space flight.

Figure 21.17 a) This mission specialist,
attached to a foot restraint, made a first-
of-its-kind spacewalking repair to the
International Space Station in 2005. **b)** A full
view of the *International Space Station*

After You Read

1. Describe how the invention of the telescope changed astronomy.

2. Use the information from your chart to summarize how astronomers learn
   about conditions on other planets.

3. Explain why the following statement is either true or false: "Humans can
   see all parts of the electromagnetic spectrum."

4. In your Science Notebook, write a well-developed paragraph explaining
   why scientists must use different types of telescopes to study different
   wavelengths of energy.

Did You Know?

Probes launched from
Earth to other planets
must seek a very small
target in a very large
space. Guiding a probe
from Earth to land on
the planet Mars is like
shooting an arrow from
Los Angeles and hitting a
specific building in Iowa.
Fortunately, engineers
on Earth have several
opportunities to adjust
the speed and direction
of a space probe before
it reaches its target.

KEY CONCEPTS

21.1 Planet Earth

- Human curiosity about objects in the sky led to the understanding that Earth is a planet that orbits the Sun.

- Earth's rotation causes day and night. The Sun, the Moon, and stars all appear to move from east to west as Earth spins eastward on its axis.

- At one point in its orbit, Earth's northern hemisphere tilts toward the Sun. At another point, the northern hemisphere tilts away from the Sun. Earth's tilt and its orbital motion around the Sun are what cause the seasons.

21.2 Earth's Moon

- The Moon is Earth's only natural satellite, and is the closest natural object to it in space.

- Unlike Earth, the Moon has no atmosphere; ancient volcanic activity and meteorite impacts shaped most of its features.

- The phases of the Moon depend on the positions of Earth, the Moon, and the Sun. The Moon passes through all of its phases every 29.5 days.

- Gravity exerted by the Moon and the Sun pulls Earth's water in daily cycles called tides as Earth rotates on its axis.

- A solar eclipse occurs when the Moon passes between the Sun and Earth. A lunar eclipse occurs when Earth lines up between the Moon and the Sun.

21.3 Astronomy

- Electromagnetic radiation is made up of electric and magnetic disturbances that travel through space as waves.

- Astronomers rely on the electromagnetic radiation that comes to Earth from objects in space to learn more about our universe.

- Electromagnetic radiation can be detected by several types of telescopes both on Earth and in space.

- Refracting telescopes use a set of lenses to bring visible light to a central point, or focus. Reflecting telescopes use a series of curved and flat mirrors to bring visible light to a focus.

- The development of space missions such as satellites, probes, and human space flight have greatly increased human understanding of the universe.

VOCABULARY REVIEW

Write each term in a complete sentence or write a paragraph relating several terms.

21.1
cosmology, p. 396
orbit, p. 398
satellite, p. 398
ecliptic, p. 398
summer solstice, p. 399
winter solstice, p. 399
autumnal equinox, p. 399
vernal equinox, p. 399

21.2
impact crater, p. 401
synchronous rotation, p. 401
perigee, p. 402
apogee, p. 402
solar eclipse, p. 403
umbra, p. 403
penumbra, p. 403
lunar eclipse, p. 403

21.3
astronomy, p. 404
electromagnetic radiation, p. 405
wavelength, p. 405
frequency, p. 405
electromagnetic spectrum, p. 405
telescope, p. 406
refracting telescope, p. 406
reflecting telescope, p. 407

PREPARE FOR CHAPTER TEST

To prepare for the chapter test, create a question from each Learning Goal. Use the information in your Science Notebook to answer each question. Then use these answers to write a well-developed essay about the chapter. Use the Key Concept on the first page of this chapter as your topic sentence.

True or False

If the statement is true, write "true." If it is false, change the underlined word or words to make the statement true.

1. Earth completes one orbit around the Sun each <u>day</u>.

2. Tides are caused, in great part, by the Moon's <u>gravity</u>.

3. <u>Astrology</u> is the scientific study of celestial bodies.

4. A <u>solar eclipse</u> occurs when the Moon's shadow blocks sunlight from reaching a portion of Earth.

5. <u>Gamma rays</u> have a higher frequency than radio waves.

6. The vernal equinox in the northern hemisphere is the <u>summer solstice</u> in the southern hemisphere.

Short Answer

Answer each of the following in a sentence or brief paragraph.

7. Explain why people's early notion that the stars revolve around Earth is mistaken.

8. What forces shaped the Moon's features in the past? What forces shape them today?

9. Imagine that you want to study the visible light produced by the farthest stars in the universe. What type of telescope would you use and where would you locate it?

10. Explain how it can be 3:00 P.M. in California at the same time it is 6:00 P.M. in New York.

11. Compare and contrast the orbit and rotation of the Moon and Earth.

12. Describe what a person standing on the side of the Moon closest to Earth would experience during a lunar eclipse.

13. Explain why the seasons are more extreme farther away from the equator.

Critical Thinking

Use what you have learned in this chapter to answer each of the following.

14. **Predict** Earth's axis is tilted at a 23.5° angle from vertical. Predict how conditions on Earth would change if that angle increased to 30°.

15. **Evaluate** the following statement: As the Moon moves farther away from Earth, the difference between high and low ocean tides will decrease.

16. **Recommend** In 2004, President George Bush announced the goal of landing a piloted spacecraft on Mars. Do you agree that this is a worthy goal? Write a short letter to a newspaper giving your recommendation about the Mars mission.

Standardized Test Question

Choose the letter of the response that correctly answers the question.

17. What is the name of the inner portion of the Moon's shadow, where none of the Sun's light reaches?

    A. the ecliptic

    B. the umbra

    C. the penumbra

    D. the eclipse

Test-Taking Tip

If "All of the above" is one of the choices in a multiple-choice question, be sure that none of the choices are false.

Chapter 22

The Solar System

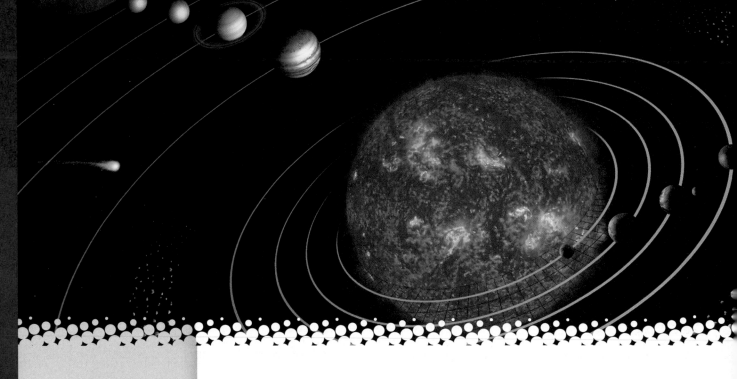

KEY CONCEPT The model of our solar system is based on our understanding of how gravity governs, or influences, the motion and organization of planets and other celestial bodies.

Gravity is the attraction two objects have for one another. Humans experience the pull of Earth's gravity all the time. Without gravity, we would not stick to Earth's surface. Instead, we would fly off into space! Whenever we exercise and move, our muscles and bones work hard against gravity. Astronauts in space work in environments with little to no gravity. To keep their bodies strong in space, they exercise regularly using special weight-lifting machines, stationary bicycles, and treadmills.

Think About Gravity

Gravity affects our lives, our interactions with our surroundings, and the physical processes on Earth in many ways.

Think about the things you do every day and about how the world around you operates. How might things on Earth be different if there were no gravity? How might your body be different? How would you travel from one place to another? What would eating a meal be like? Record your thoughts about an Earth without gravity in your Science Notebook.

www.scilinks.org

Solar System **Code: WGES22**

22.1 The Formation of the Solar System

Before You Read

In your Science Notebook, write the first eight vocabulary terms in this lesson. Leave some space below each term. Then write a definition for each term in your own words as you read about it in the lesson.

The Solar Nebula

The **solar system** is made up of the Sun, which is a star, and the planets and other bodies that travel around it. It is widely accepted among astronomers that our solar system formed from huge clouds of gas and dust called **interstellar clouds**, or **nebulas**. Nebulas exist in vast regions of space between the stars. They are made up mostly of the gases hydrogen and helium. The dust is composed of elements such as carbon and iron.

The gas and dust in a nebula is so spread out that its density is very low. Because the density is so low, there is not a large force of gravity between the particles. However, various events can cause the nebula to condense, or get smaller. For example, an old star exploding or two nearby nebulas colliding can cause material to crash into the nebula and begin this process. When a nebula condenses, its gravitational force becomes stronger. This causes the nebula to collapse inward toward its center and become much denser. If the nebula is rotating, it will spin faster as it collapses and take on the shape of a flattened, rotating disk. The hot, condensed material at the center is called a **protostar**. Eventually, the dense concentration of gas at the center of this rotating disk becomes a star. When nebulas begin to condense and form stars and star systems, they are called planetary nebulas. The nebula that formed into our own solar system is called the **solar nebula**. The formation of Earth's Sun and other stars is discussed in more detail in Chapter 23.

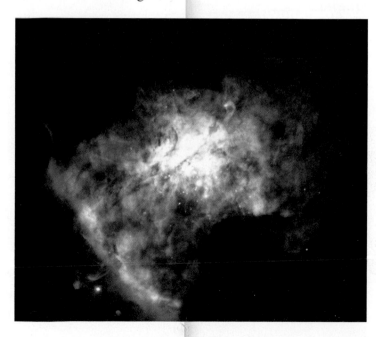

Figure 22.1 Light from stars inside a nebula reflects off dust and lights up the nebula. This photo is of the Orion Nebula, located in the center of the three stars that make up Orion's belt.

Planet Formation

As the solar nebula collapsed, tiny grains of condensed matter began to stick together as they collided. These solid particles, called **planetesimals**, formed the building blocks of planets. These planetesimals continued to grow in size, collide, and join together. The biggest planetesimals continued to grow as they gathered the dust and debris in their paths. Eventually, they formed the planets of the solar system.

The planets that formed in the outer solar system had gravities strong enough to attract the gases, dust, and planetesimals surrounding them. As a result, they grew into large planets called gas giants. The gas giants include the planets Jupiter, Saturn, Uranus (yoo RAY nus), and Neptune. Closer to the Sun, it was too hot for gases to remain. Some astronomers think the Sun's strong gravity may have pulled in the gases surrounding the inner planets as they formed. Heavier elements, such as iron and nickel, were left behind. These elements eventually combined to form rocky and dense planets, rather than gaseous planets. The inner, or terrestrial, planets are Mercury, Venus, Earth, and Mars.

Figure 22.2 The inner planets are made of heavy elements that condensed close to the Sun. The outer planets are farther from the Sun, where it is cooler, and are made up of lighter elements in the form of ice and gases.

Did You Know?

The Perseid meteor shower occurs every year from August 9–13, when Earth passes through the orbit of a comet named Swift-Tuttle. The Swift-Tuttle comet was named for two astronomers, Lewis Swift and Horace Tuttle. They discovered the comet in 1862. It was last seen in 1992 and is expected to return in 2122.

Figure It Out

1. What was Neptune's distance from the Sun when it formed? What was the temperature?
2. Explain how the composition of Neptune compares to that of Jupiter.

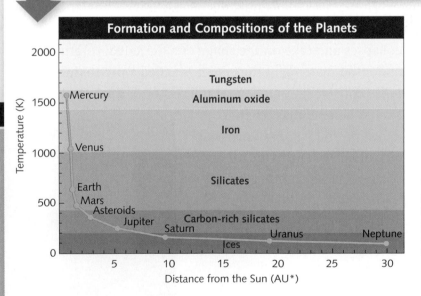

Formation and Compositions of the Planets

*AU stands for astronomical unit and is equal to the average distance between the Sun and Earth.

Asteroids

Asteroids are small, rocky bodies that orbit the Sun. Most asteroids orbit the Sun in a wide area between Jupiter and Mars. This area is called the asteroid belt. It is thought that asteroids are pieces of planetesimals left over from the time that the solar system formed. They range in size from a few kilometers to about 1,000 km in diameter. Sometimes asteroids collide as they orbit and break into smaller pieces.

A fragment of an asteroid or any material that falls from space toward Earth and enters Earth's atmosphere is called a **meteoroid**. When a meteoroid enters Earth's atmosphere, it burns up and produces a streak of light. This light is visible from Earth and is called a **meteor**. If the meteor does not completely burn up, the remaining part hits Earth and is then called a **meteorite**. Although more than 100 meteorites hit Earth every year, most are very small and do not cause any damage.

Comets

Comets are also leftovers from the formation of the solar system. They are small bodies made of ice and rock. Just as the orbits of planets around the Sun are elliptical in shape, most comets' orbits also are elliptical. On average, comets range in size from one to ten km in diameter. Occasionally they are larger.

There are two clusters of comets in space—the Kuiper (KY per) belt and the Oort (ORT) cloud. Both belts are located in the far reaches of the solar system, beyond the orbit of Neptune. When the gravity of a passing star or planet disturbs a comet, it can be pulled in toward the inner solar system. When a comet's elliptical orbit carries it close to the Sun, it begins to evaporate and becomes much brighter. It also forms a head and one or more tails. Halley's comet was a well-known comet that was last visible from Earth in 1985–1986. It is expected to appear again in 2061.

When Earth intersects with a comet's orbit, particles from the comet burn up when they enter Earth's upper atmosphere, producing a **meteor shower**. People often describe these burning particles as falling or shooting stars. While many meteors are caused by dust particles from comets, most meteorites are pieces of asteroids.

Figure 22.3 This crater in Arizona was formed when a large meteorite hit Earth 50,000 years ago. Meteorites this large are very rare.

Figure 22.4 Comet Hale-Bopp was discovered in 1995. It was visible in the night sky for about 18 months. It will not be visible again until the year 4397.

Extend It!

Choose a famous meteorite or comet, and find out more about it. What year did it hit Earth, or what years has it been visible in the sky? What was it made of, and where do astronomers think it originated? If it's a comet, describe its orbit, and how often can it be seen from Earth. Write your findings in your Science Notebook.

After You Read

1. Review the list of vocabulary words you wrote in your Science Notebook. Use the words to write a well-developed paragraph that explains how the planets formed.

2. Describe what causes a nebula to condense and collapse, beginning the process of star formation.

3. Explain the difference between a meteoroid and a meteorite.

Before You Read

Create a table to organize the information presented in this lesson. Use the lesson title as the table title, and create columns labeled *Copernicus*, *Kepler*, and *Newton*. Preview the lesson by looking at the diagrams. As you read, write the important discoveries of each scientist under his name. Include important information along with supporting details.

In the solar system, each planet revolves around the Sun in the same direction. A planet's **orbital period** is the time it takes for the planet to make one complete revolution, or orbit, around the Sun. What holds planets in their orbits around the Sun? Why don't they fly off into space or get pulled toward the Sun by gravity? Scientists asked these questions for many years before they discovered the answers.

Early Models of the Solar System

Up through the end of the Middle Ages, people believed that Earth was the center of the universe. They believed that the Sun, planets, and stars revolved around Earth. This **geocentric**, or Earth-centered, model of the universe was challenged during the early 1500s by Nicolaus Copernicus, a Polish astronomer.

Copernicus suggested a Sun-centered, or **heliocentric**, model of the solar system where Earth and the other planets orbited the Sun. He thought that the planets all revolved around the Sun in the same direction in circular orbits. He also thought that each planet took a different amount of time to revolve around the Sun. Copernicus was correct in most of his assumptions. He was, however, incorrect about the shape of the orbits of the planets. He thought they were perfect circles. During the next hundred years, other astronomers would find evidence that supported the heliocentric model.

Kepler's First Law

During the 1600s, German mathematician Johannes Kepler was able to demonstrate that each planet orbits the Sun in a closed curve called an **ellipse**, rather than in a circle. This discovery is known as Kepler's first law. Unlike a circle, which has a single point at its center, an ellipse is an oval shape that is centered on two points called the foci (singular: focus). As shown in **Figure 22.5**, the line that runs through both foci is called the major axis. It is also the maximum diameter of the ellipse.

Figure 22.5 The paths of the planets that orbit the Sun are elliptical in shape. The major axis of an ellipse passes through its foci. The semimajor axis is half of the major axis.

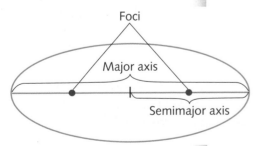

Although every planet's orbit is different in size and shape, the Sun is located at one of the foci in every planet's orbit. The semimajor axis is the average distance between the Sun and a planet in its own orbit.

It is important to note that because planets have elliptical rather than circular orbits, they are not always the same distance from the Sun. As shown in **Figure 22.6**, a planet is at **perihelion** when it is closest to the Sun. It is at **aphelion** when it is farthest away from the Sun.

Kepler's Second and Third Laws

Kepler also discovered that the planets move faster when they are closer to the Sun and slower when they are farther away. He found that an imaginary line between the Sun and a planet will sweep out equal amounts of area in an elliptical orbit in equal amounts of time. This is known as Kepler's second law. For example, as shown in **Figure 22.7**, a planet must move farther around its orbit in the same amount of time to keep the area of *c* in the diagram equal to the areas of either *a* or *b* in the diagram.

Kepler's third law is based on a mathematical relationship between the size of a planet's ellipse and its orbital period. Using this mathematical relationship, Kepler was able to demonstrate that a planet's distance from the Sun can be calculated if the planet's orbital period is known.

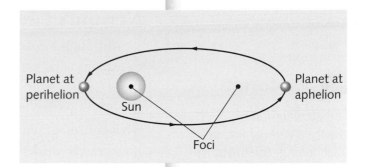

Figure 22.6 Because the orbits of planets are elliptical in shape, during the course of one orbit, the planets experience both perihelion and aphelion.

As You Read

In the table that you created in your Science Notebook, continue to add to the list of discoveries that were made by each scientist. Describe how each relates to the motion of the planets.

Before Copernicus, how did astronomers believe the solar system was organized?

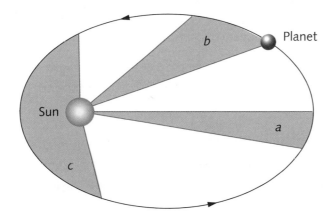

Figure 22.7 This diagram illustrates Kepler's second law, which states that an imaginary line between the Sun and a planet sweeps out equal amounts of area in equal amounts of time. Knowing that the planets speed up at certain points in their orbits enables astronomers to accurately predict the position of a planet at any given time.

Figure 22.8 In this diagram, the arrows represent the force of gravity. **a)** Object that have more mass exert a greater amount of force on other objects. **b)** The force of gravity between two objects increases as the distance between them decreases.

Newton's Law of Universal Gravitation

Although Kepler made many important discoveries, he was not able to explain what caused the planets closest to the Sun to move faster than those farther from the Sun. During the late 1600s, Sir Isaac Newton, an English scientist, came up with an answer. Newton did not understand what caused gravity. He was, however, able to use his understanding of how gravity works to explain the forces of attraction between objects.

Newton developed the theory that small objects fall toward Earth because the objects and Earth are attracted to one another by the force of gravity. Newton realized that the strength of the gravitational force depended on two things: the masses of the objects and the distance between them.

For example, if two objects were moved twice as far apart, the attraction between them caused by gravity will decrease by a factor of 2 × 2 = 4, or be one-fourth as strong. If the objects are moved five times as far apart, the attraction between them caused by gravity will decrease by a factor of 5 × 5 = 25, or be one-twenty-fifth as strong. Similarly, if the distance between two objects remained the same, but the mass of one object doubled and the other tripled, the attraction between them caused by gravity would increase by a factor of 2 × 3 = 6, or be six times as strong.

a

The more mass an object has, the greater amount of force it exerts.

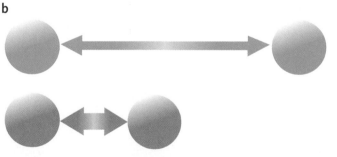

b

The closer two objects are to each other, the greater the force of gravity between them.

Based on the previous discussion of gravity, why do the planets orbit the Sun, rather than crashing into it? Newton explained this through the concept of inertia. **Inertia** is the tendency of an object at rest to remain at rest and of an object in motion to stay in motion.

This does not change unless the object is acted upon by another force. The planets are moving quickly through space. If they were not pulled by gravity toward the Sun, they would fly off into space along a straight path due to their inertia. The Sun's gravity, however, pulls the planets toward it. The resulting paths of the planets are curved orbits. The same is true of the Moon's orbit around Earth.

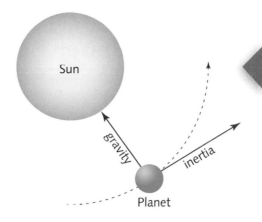

Figure 22.9 Inertia causes a planet to travel along a straight path (red arrow), but gravity pulls the planet toward the Sun (blue arrow). The combination of these two forces keeps the planet in orbit around the Sun.

Figure It Out

1. If there were no force of gravity, in what direction would the planet move in relation to the Sun?

2. How do you think the orbit of the planet might change if the gravity of the Sun increased?

PEOPLE IN SCIENCE Sir Isaac Newton 1642–1727

Sir Isaac Newton was a mathematician and a physicist. He is considered by many to be the father of modern science. Newton was born in 1642 in England. At the age of 19, he entered Cambridge University. It is said that when Newton was in his midtwenties, he observed an apple falling to the ground in his orchard. This observation led to his idea that the force of gravity influenced not only the motion of the apple, but that of the Moon and planets as well. Although this story might be true, it took him many years to formulate his theories of gravity and his laws of motion. Newton based his ideas on the discoveries of other scientists, including Copernicus, Kepler, Galileo, Robert Hooke, and Edmund Halley.

In 1687, Newton published his masterpiece, called the *Principia*, in which he explained his laws of motion: (1) every object continues in a state of rest, or when in motion, in a straight line, unless acted upon by a force; (2) the object's change in motion is proportional to the force acting upon it; and (3) to every action there is an opposite and equal reaction. He also explained how the law of gravity governs the movement of the planets and calculated the masses of the planets from their gravitational forces. This publication is considered to be one of the greatest works in the history of science.

After You Read

1. Explain when a planet is at perihelion.

2. Describe the two factors that affect the strength of the gravitational force on an object.

3. Choose one scientist from the table you created in your Science Notebook. Write a well-developed paragraph describing how his discoveries contributed to our understanding of planetary motion.

Learning Goals

- Describe how scientists measure distances in space.
- Identify the inner planets and describe their properties.

New Vocabulary

terrestrial planet
gas giant planet
light-year
astronomical unit
retrograde rotation
prograde rotation

Before You Read

Think about what you do when you compare and contrast. Then select two planets in our solar system that you know something about. Earth can be one of the planets. In your Science Notebook, compare and contrast them. You may write sentences or draw pictures to show the similarities and differences.

During the early seventeenth century, Italian astronomer and physicist Galileo Galilei first used a telescope to observe the planets and stars. Over the years, advancements in technology led to the development of more powerful telescopes. During the 1950s and 1960s, both the Russians and Americans developed spacecraft to carry people into space. Since then, spacecraft equipped with cameras and other devices continue to collect data about every planet in our solar system.

The inner four planets of our solar system, in order from closest to farthest from the Sun, are Mercury, Venus, Earth, and Mars. These planets are also called **terrestrial planets** because they have solid, rocky surfaces. The next four planets from the Sun are Jupiter, Saturn, Uranus, and Neptune. These **gas giant planets** do not have solid surfaces. They are also much larger and more gaseous than the terrestrial planets. This lesson will discuss each of the terrestrial planets. The basic properties of each are shown in **Figure 22.10.** The gas giants are discussed in the next lesson.

Figure It Out

1. Which terrestrial planet has the highest average temperature? Which has the lowest average temperature?
2. Which of the terrestrial planets have diameters close to that of Earth?
3. Which terrestrial planet has a mass that is most similar to that of Earth?

Figure 22.10 Some basic properties of the terrestrial planets are shown in this table.

Planet	Distance from Sun (AU)	Orbital period (Earth days)	Period of rotation (Earth days)	Mass (kg)	Diameter (km)	Average temperature (°C)
Mercury	0.39	87.96	58.7	3.3×10^{23}	4,878	167
Venus	0.723	224.68	243	4.87×10^{24}	12,104	464
Earth	1	365.26	1	5.98×10^{24}	12,756	15
Mars	1.524	686.98	1.026	6.42×10^{23}	6,787	−65

Measuring Distance in Space

Scientists use **light-years**, or the distance that light travels in one year, to measure long distances in space. The distance of one light-year is equal to 9.5 trillion km. Distances in space can also be measured using light-minutes or light-hours. It takes light 60 minutes, or one hour, to travel 1,080,000,000 km. This distance equals one light-hour. Light from the Sun takes 8.3 minutes to reach Earth, so the distance between Earth and the Sun is 8.3 light-minutes.

Scientists also measure distances in space using astronomical units. One **astronomical unit** (AU) is equal to the average distance between Earth and the Sun. This distance is equal to approximately 150 million km. The distance of Venus from the Sun is 0.723 AU, the distance of Mercury from the Sun is 0.39 AU, and the distance of Mars from the Sun is 1.524 AU.

Mercury

Mercury is the closest planet to the Sun. It has no moons and is only about one-third the size of Earth. Mercury rotates very slowly on its axis. As a result, one day on Mercury, or Mercury's period of rotation, is 59 Earth days long. This gives the side of Mercury that is facing the Sun plenty of time to heat up—with daytime temperatures reaching up to 427°C. The slow spin of Mercury also gives the side of the planet that is not facing the Sun plenty of time to cool down at night. In addition, with almost no atmosphere, heat easily escapes the planet's surface.

CONNECTION: Physics

Gravity is the force that keeps you from floating off Earth into space. It also determines your weight. Your weight is actually different from your body's mass. While the mass of your body stays the same, regardless of gravity, the weight of your body does not. For example, a person that weighs 100 pounds on Earth weighs only 38 pounds on Mars. This is because Mars's surface gravity is lower than that of Earth. However, the same person would weigh 260 pounds on Jupiter, because Jupiter's surface gravity is greater than that of Earth. Surface gravity is determined by a planet's mass and its diameter.

Figure 22.11 This photomosaic of Mercury was put together from different images taken by *Mariner 10* in 1974.

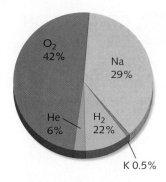

Figure 22.12 Mercury's very thin atmosphere is made up mostly of oxygen, sodium, hydrogen, helium, and potassium.

Night temperatures on Mercury can be as low as –173°C. As a result, Mercury is extremely hot during the day and extremely cold during the night. This is the largest difference between day and night temperatures of any of the planets in our solar system.

Mercury is the smallest of the planets. Because Mercury is smaller than Earth and has less mass, it exerts less of a force of gravity. On Mercury, a person would weigh only 39 percent of what he or she weighs on Earth. *Mariner 10* visited Mercury in 1974 and 1975, and mapped 45 percent of its surface. Images from *Mariner 10* show that the surface of Mercury is similar to that of the Moon. It is covered with craters and plains. Scientists think that Mercury has a dense nickel-iron core and a zone of melted material in its interior. To date, *Mariner 10* is the only spacecraft to have visited Mercury. However, the *Messenger* spacecraft, launched in 2004, is scheduled to visit Mercury in 2008 and then orbit it in 2011.

Venus

The next closest planet to the Sun is Venus. It is sometimes called the Evening Star, because it looks so bright from Earth. Some astronomers have called Venus Earth's twin, because the two planets have similar diameters, masses, and densities. Astronomers think that the interior of Venus is similar to that of Earth, and that it has a liquid metal core.

The surface conditions on Venus, however, are very different from those on Earth. The average surface temperature of Venus is extremely hot, and can reach 464°C. In comparison, Earth's average surface temperature is 15°C. In addition, the atmospheric pressure on Venus is much greater than it is on Earth. Standing on Venus would feel the same as being 915 m under water!

Figure 22.13 The *Magellan* spacecraft used imaging radar to produce this view of the surface of Venus beneath its thick atmosphere.

As shown in **Figure 22.14**, Venus's atmosphere is made up mostly of carbon dioxide and nitrogen. Like Earth, Venus has a greenhouse effect, and its atmosphere traps heat close to the planet's surface. However, the concentration of carbon dioxide in Venus's atmosphere is much higher than that in Earth's atmosphere, and it prevents heat from escaping back into space. As a result, Venus is the hottest planet in the solar system. It is so hot that liquid water cannot exist on its surface. In contrast to Earth's clouds, which are made of water vapor, Venus's thick clouds are made of sulfuric acid. The United States orbiter spacecraft *Magellan* mapped the surface of Venus with radar waves. *Magellan*'s radar penetrated the dense atmosphere. It showed a surface with a few impact craters that have been mostly smoothed out by volcanic lava flows.

One day on Venus is 243 Earth days in length. Radar measurements revealed that Venus rotates in a clockwise direction—the opposite direction from Earth and most other planets in the solar system. The clockwise spin exhibited by Venus is called **retrograde rotation**. Counterclockwise spin is called **prograde rotation**.

Earth

Earth is the third planet from the Sun and the fifth largest in the solar system. It is the only planet known to support life. Why is Earth able to support life? Earth's distance from the Sun and its nearly circular orbit keep its temperatures within a critical range. Earth is warm enough so that most of its water does not freeze, and it is cool enough so that its

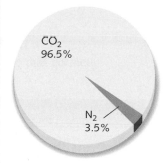

CO_2 96.5%

N_2 3.5%

Figure 22.14 Because Venus's atmosphere is made up mostly of carbon dioxide and nitrogen, heat cannot easily escape. This makes the surface very hot.

As You Read

Extend the chart you created in your Science Notebook for comparing and contrasting two planets so that you can compare and contrast all four terrestrial planets.

Compare the atmospheres of Mercury and Venus. How do the different atmospheres of these planets affect their average surface temperatures?

Figure 22.15 Photographs of Earth from space were first taken during the *Apollo 11* mission to the Moon in 1969.

water does not completely evaporate. Liquid water, which is necessary for life on Earth, covers 71 percent of Earth's surface. The existence of this water was a key factor in the development of life on our planet. Based on what scientists know, Earth is the only planet in the solar system that has liquid water at its surface.

Earth's atmosphere, composed primarily of nitrogen and oxygen, is another factor that has enabled life to exist on the planet. Recall from Chapter 13, the role of Earth's atmosphere in climate and weather. The density of Earth's atmosphere creates a greenhouse effect that keeps the planet warm enough to support life. Without the atmosphere's greenhouse effect, temperatures on Earth would drop too low for life to survive. Too much of a greenhouse effect, however, would lead to the evaporation of all liquid water on Earth. Earth's magnetic field also protects life on the planet by deflecting harmful radiation from the Sun.

Mars

Mars is the fourth planet from the Sun, and it is sometimes called the red planet. This is because its soil has a high iron content that gives it a reddish color. Strong winds are common and cause frequent dust storms. Mars has a longer year than Earth. It takes 687 days to orbit the Sun. Mars is small, with a diameter about half of Earth's. Gravity on Mars, like that on Mercury, is only about 39 percent of Earth's. Mars has two moons named Phobos and Deimos. It is likely that they were both once asteroids that were captured by the planet's gravitational pull.

Figure 22.16 This image of Mars was created from 100 different *Viking* orbiter images.

As shown in **Figure 22.17**, the composition of Mars's atmosphere in similar to that of Venus. Yet, the density and pressure of Mars's atmosphere is much lower than that of Venus. For this reason, the greenhouse effect on Mars is not strong.

Mars has many topographical features, such as mountains, volcanoes, canyons, valleys, and craters. The highest volcano on Mars is called Olympus Mons. It is 26 km high and is extinct. In comparison, Earth's highest volcano, Mauna Loa in Hawaii, is only 9 km high. Mars's thin atmosphere combined with its distance from the Sun, makes it a cold planet. Like Earth, however, it experiences seasons because it is tilted on its axis. On a summer day, the temperature can reach as high as 27°C, but at night the temperature drops to below 0°C. Winter nights on Mars can get as cold as −125°C. While there is frozen water on Mars in the northern ice cap, the planet does not get warm enough for it to melt.

NASA's 2004–2005 Mars Exploration Rover Mission landed two robotic rovers on Mars to collect data. The rovers continue to photograph clouds and land features on Mars today. They also analyze rock and soil samples as they travel over the planet's surface, and send the data back to Earth.

Although there is no liquid water on the surface of Mars today, there is evidence that liquid water was present in the past. Photographs of Mars's surface show dry riverbeds. In addition, the walls of some craters on Mars contain debris that was likely deposited by mudflows. This evidence of the past presence of liquid water indicates that Mars was once warmer with a denser atmosphere. Water that might have existed on Mars's surface is now either frozen in its polar ice caps or present under the soil. If underground water does, in fact, exist on Mars, there is the chance that some form of primitive life may exist there as well.

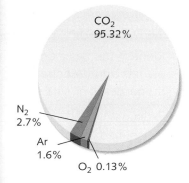

Figure 22.17 Mars's atmosphere is made up mostly of carbon dioxide, nitrogen, argon, and oxygen.

 Explain It!

Choose one of the inner, terrestrial planets. In your Science Notebook, write an imaginary travel brochure for the planet. Describe the planet in your brochure, including features such as temperature, topography, atmosphere, and surface gravity. Using facts from your Science Notebook, include reasons why you might want to visit this planet.

After You Read

1. How many kilometers does light travel in one light-year?

2. Calculate how much a person, who weighs 140 pounds on Earth, would weigh on Mercury.

3. Review the chart in your Science Notebook. Then write a well-developed paragraph explaining why Earth, unlike the other planets in our solar system, has the ability to support life.

4. Explain why scientists think there was once liquid water on Mars.

22.4 The Outer Planets

Before You Read

Create a K-W-L-S-H chart in your Science Notebook. Think about the title of this lesson, "The Outer Planets." In the column labeled *K* on the chart, write a few things you already know about the outer planets Jupiter, Saturn, Uranus, and Neptune. In the column labeled *W*, write what you want to learn about the outer planets.

The outer planets are also called the gas giant planets. These planets do not have solid surfaces and are larger than the terrestrial planets. The interiors of the gas giants are made up of either gas or liquid. They might also have small, solid cores. All of the gas giant planets are very cold at their surfaces. They are made up of elements including hydrogen, helium, carbon, nitrogen, and oxygen.

All of the gas giant planets have rings made up of icy particles. They also have natural **satellites**, or moons that orbit them. The outer planets include Jupiter, Saturn, Uranus, and Neptune. Until recently, they also included Pluto, which is rocky rather than gaseous. Pluto is now considered by astronomers to be a dwarf planet rather than a planet. Dwarf planets will be discussed later in this lesson. The basic properties of each of the gas giant planets are shown in **Figure 22.18**.

Jupiter

Jupiter, the fifth planet from the Sun, is by far the largest of the planets. Gaseous Jupiter is more than 300 times more massive than solid Earth. The diameter of Jupiter is only ten times smaller than the Sun's diameter. Jupiter has a very short period of rotation—its day is only ten Earth hours long. This is the shortest day of all the planets. Jupiter's rapid rotation causes the clouds in its atmosphere to move quickly.

Figure It Out

1. Which gas giant planet spins the fastest on its axis?
2. Describe the relationship between the average temperatures of the gas giant planets and their distances from the Sun.
3. Which gas giant planet has the greatest mass?

Planet	Distance from Sun (AU)	Orbital period (Earth years)	Period of rotation (Earth hours)	Mass (kg)	Diameter (km)	Average temperature (°C)
Jupiter	5.203	11.862	9.84	1.9×10^{27}	142,796	−110
Saturn	9.539	29.456	10.2	5.69×10^{26}	120,660	−140
Uranus	19.18	84.07	17.9	8.68×10^{25}	51,118	−195
Neptune	30.06	164.81	16.1	6.42×10^{26}	48,600	−200

Figure 22.18 Some basic properties of the gas giant planets are shown in this table.

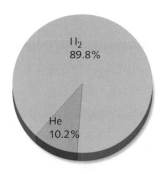

Figure 22.19 Jupiter's atmosphere is made up mostly of hydrogen and helium.

H_2
89.8%

He
10.2%

The clouds in Jupiter's atmosphere separate into dark areas of sinking gases called belts and light areas of rising gases called zones. Slight temperature and chemical differences in these belts and zones give Jupiter a banded, or striped, appearance as shown in **Figure 22.20**. Another striking feature of Jupiter is its Great Red Spot. The spot is a long-lasting storm system that has existed on Jupiter for more than 300 years. The Great Red Spot has a diameter of about one and one-half times that of Earth.

As You Read

In the column labeled *L* in your K-W-L-S-H chart, write three important things that you have learned about the outer planets. Include key facts and supporting details.

What states of matter does hydrogen exist in on Jupiter?

Like the Sun, Jupiter's atmosphere is composed primarily of hydrogen and helium gases. The outer layers of the atmosphere also contain water, methane, and ammonia. The thick clouds in Jupiter's atmosphere create very high pressure. The pressure causes the hydrogen gas to become liquid at 10,000 km below the surface. Below that, the high pressure changes the liquid hydrogen into liquid metallic hydrogen. This form of hydrogen has properties of both a liquid and metal. This liquid metallic layer generates a strong magnetic field.

Beneath this liquid layer, it is possible that Jupiter has a solid core about the size of Earth. At this core, temperatures may be as high as 30,000°C—almost five times higher than the surface temperature of the Sun. Jupiter radiates much more heat into space than it receives from the Sun. This is because heat is constantly being transported from its interior to its outer atmosphere, where it is radiated into space.

Jupiter's Moons and Rings Jupiter has more moons than any other planet—63 have been discovered so far. Four of Jupiter's large moons, the Gallilean satellites, were discovered by Galileo in 1610. These moons are Io, Europa, Gannymede, and Callisto. They are composed of a mixture of ice and rock. Io is made of rocky materials and has active volcanoes. Europa possibly has an ocean beneath its icy surface. In 1979, two *Voyager* spacecraft traveled to Jupiter. They took photographs that showed a thin ring around the planet. Until then, astronomers thought that only Saturn had a ring. We now know that all of the gas giant planets have rings.

Figure 22.20 Jupiter's clouds, belts, and zones can be seen in this digital mosaic of images taken by the *Cassini* spacecraft in 2000.

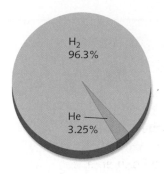

Figure 22.21 Like Jupiter's atmosphere, Saturn's atmosphere is made up mostly of hydrogen and helium.

CONNECTION: Mythology

All of the planets in the solar system except Earth were named for either mythological Roman or Greek gods. Pluto, a dwarf planet, was also named for a Roman god. Mercury was named after a speedy messenger in Roman mythology. Venus was named after the Roman goddess of love and beauty. Mars was named after the Roman god of war. Jupiter was named after the king of gods in Roman mythology. Saturn was named after the Roman god Saturn, who was the father of Jupiter. Uranus was named after the Greek god of the heavens. Neptune was named after the Roman god of the sea.

Saturn

Saturn is the second largest planet in the solar system. It has the largest and most visible ring system. Although Saturn is large, it has a very low density—a density even lower than that of water. Saturn is similar to Jupiter in many ways. As shown in **Figure 22.21**, its atmosphere is composed mainly of hydrogen and helium. Its interior is very hot, like Jupiter's, and gives off more heat than it receives from the Sun. It also has a strong magnetic field. Like Jupiter, Saturn rotates very quickly. Because Saturn spins so rapidly, the winds at its equator are extremely strong, causing violent storms. Saturn's atmosphere also forms light- and dark-colored bands, although they are not as dramatic as those of Jupiter.

Saturn's Rings and Moons   Saturn has seven major rings, which are actually made up of thousands of smaller rings called ringlets. The rings are mainly composed of icy particles that vary in size from microscopic to several meters across. The rings extend out to almost 300,000 km from Saturn, but are less than 200 m thick. Saturn's satellites include seven medium-sized moons, a number of smaller moons, and a large moon called Titan. Titan is larger than Earth's moon.

Three missions have visited Saturn: *Pioneer 11* flew by in 1979 and took images, as did two *Voyager* spacecrafts between 1977 and 1981. The *Cassini* spacecraft arrived at Saturn in 2004. *Cassini* sent a probe to Titan in 2005 to explore the moon's surface conditions. It continues to gather data about Saturn today.

Figure 22.22 This photograph of Saturn was taken by *Voyager 2* in 1979. Note the four moons visible in this photo.

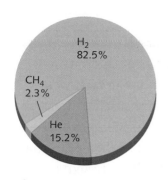

Figure 22.23 Uranus's atmosphere is made up mostly of helium and hydrogen, with a small amount of methane. Methane (CH_4) makes the planet appear blue.

Uranus

Uranus, the seventh planet from the Sun, was discovered in 1781 by an English astronomer, William Herschel. Because it is so far from the Sun, it has a long period of revolution—its year is equivalent to almost 84 Earth years. It is also a cold planet, with temperatures as low as –215°C.

While Uranus is much smaller than Jupiter or Saturn, it is four times larger than Earth and contains almost 15 times more mass. An unusual feature of Uranus is that its rotational axis is tilted almost 90 degrees, so that it appears to be lying on its side. As a result, Uranus spends 22 years of each orbit with its south pole facing the Sun. During the second half of Uranus's orbit, it spends 22 years with its north pole facing the Sun. Astronomers think that Uranus may have been hit by a very large object, such as an asteroid, that tipped the planet onto its side.

As shown in **Figure 22.23**, the atmosphere of Uranus is composed mostly of hydrogen and helium, plus a small amount of methane. The methane in Uranus's atmosphere reflects blue light back into space so that the planet appears blue. It has few clouds or storms in its atmosphere, so there are no visible belts or zones like those observed on Jupiter and Saturn. The interior of Uranus is similar to that of Jupiter and Saturn—it is fluid except for a small, rocky core. Uranus also has a strong magnetic field.

Uranus's Rings and Moons Uranus's two larger moons, Titania and Oberon, were discovered in 1787. In 1977, *Voyager 2* was launched. Its destination was Uranus. Nine years later, in 1986, it flew by Uranus and provided more information about the planet, including the discovery of new moons and rings. Today, we know that Uranus has many moons and ten rings. Uranus's rings are very dark, making them difficult to spot. Astronomers think they might be made of carbon compounds. The rings of Uranus don't encircle the planet horizontally, the way Saturn's do. Instead, as shown in **Figure 22.24**, they stand upright. This makes the planet look like a hanging bull's-eye target when viewed straight on.

Explain It!

Science fiction stories often include aliens or other extraterrestrial life forms. With the right environmental conditions, it is possible that life exists elsewhere in the universe. In your Science Notebook, explain why it is unlikely, however, that complex forms of life such as humans exist on other planets in our solar system.

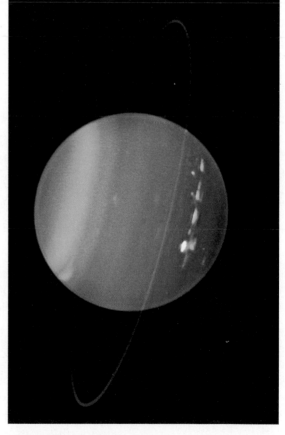

Figure 22.24 This photograph of Uranus shows its rings and how the rotational axis of the planet is tilted so that it is lying on its side.

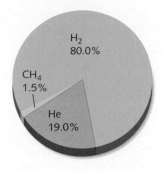

Figure 22.25 Neptune's atmosphere, like that of Uranus, is made up mostly of hydrogen and helium, with a small amount of methane.

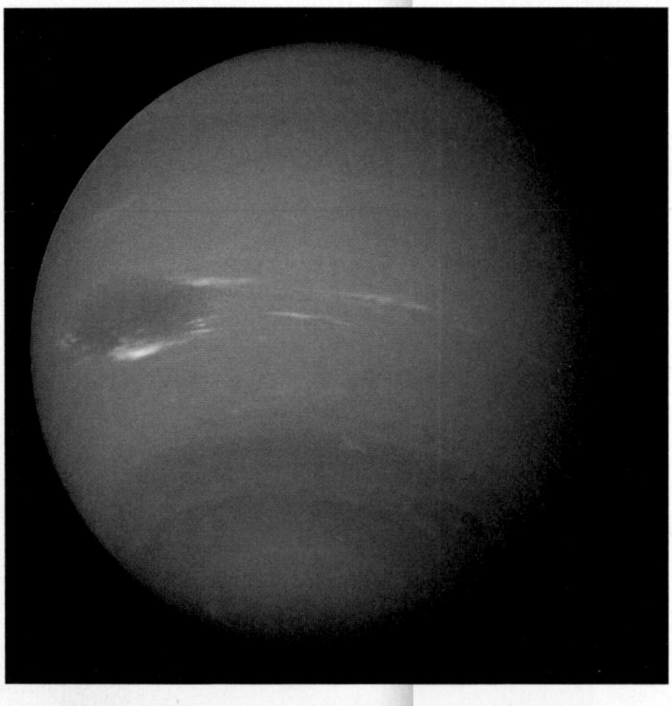

Figure 22.26 This photograph of Neptune was taken before 1994. It shows bands in the planet's atmosphere as well as the Great Dark Spot, which has since disappeared.

Neptune

Irregularities in the orbit of Uranus led astronomers to believe that another planet's gravitational force must be pulling Uranus off its predicted path. Based on these predictions, the planet Neptune was discovered in 1846. Neptune and Uranus are sometimes called the twin giants because of their similar colors, sizes, masses, and temperatures. Like Uranus, Neptune also has a strong magnetic field. While Neptune is too far from our planet to observe its details with Earth-based telescopes, *Voyager 2* flew past the planet in 1989 and sent back new images and information.

Neptune's atmosphere is similar to that of Uranus in its composition. It contains mainly hydrogen and helium, with a small amount of methane that causes it to appear, like Neptune, bluish in color. Unlike Uranus, however, Neptune does have visible clouds and atmospheric belts and zones. It even had a large storm, called the Great Dark Spot, that was visible when the *Voyager 2* probe flew past the planet in 1986. This storm, which was similar to Jupiter's Great Red Spot, disappeared from Neptune in 1994. Neptune's year is equal to 165 Earth years. The planet has a fairly short day length of 16 Earth hours. The temperature on Neptune dips down to about −220°C.

Neptune's Rings and Moons   Neptune has six narrow rings that were directly observed by the *Voyager 2* probe as it flew by the planet. They are made of microscopic-sized particles of dust. Neptune also has many moons. Its largest moon, Triton, is unusual in that it has a retrograde orbit. This means that it orbits Neptune in a clockwise direction.

The Dwarf Planets

Pluto was discovered in 1930. Formerly classified as a planet, Pluto was reclassified as a dwarf planet in 2006. It was originally estimated that Pluto's mass was ten times that of Earth. With improvements in measuring techniques over the 50 years following its discovery, Pluto's size was recalculated several times. Each time, the planet's mass was estimated to be smaller. Its mass is now estimated to be only about two-thousandths that of Earth's.

Before *Voyager 2* passed Neptune in 1989, it was thought that another celestial body, such as Pluto, was needed to explain the slightly irregular orbits of Uranus and Neptune. Data from the *Voyager 2* spacecraft revealed, however, that Neptune and Uranus balance out one another's orbits around the Sun.

Pluto was never classified as a terrestrial planet because of its small size and its low density. Because Pluto is composed of rock and ice, and because it is so small, it could not be classified as a gas giant planet either. In terms of its size and composition, Pluto actually has more in common with Triton, Neptune's largest moon, than it does with the other planets. Some astronomers theorize that Pluto was once a satellite of Neptune, before escaping and moving into its own orbit.

In 1992, another small Pluto-like body was discovered in the far reaches of the solar system. Over the next few years, several hundred more Pluto-like bodies were observed. In August 2006, after years of debate, the International Astronomical Union voted to change the definition of a planet. According to the new definition, an object classified as a planet must: (1) orbit the Sun; (2) be large enough so that its gravity pulls it into a nearly round shape; and (3) be dominant enough in its orbit to clear away other objects.

Pluto did not fit the new definition of a planet because it has not cleared its orbit of other objects. As a result, Pluto is now classified as a **dwarf planet**. To be considered a dwarf planet, an object must meet two of the criteria of a planet. It must (1) orbit the Sun and (2) have a nearly round shape. Moons, however, cannot be counted as dwarf planets.

Ceres, the largest known asteroid in the solar system, and another Pluto-sized body called UB313, or Eris, have also been classified as dwarf planets. As a result of advances in technology, it is expected that over the coming years, hundreds, or even thousands, more dwarf planets will be identified.

Figure 22.27 This image, taken by the *Hubble Space Telescope*, shows a view of Pluto with its moon, Charon.

After You Read

1. Explain two ways that Jupiter and Saturn are similar.

2. Why do Uranus and Neptune appear blue?

3. Why doesn't Pluto fit into the new definition of a planet?

4. Using the completed K-W-L columns, describe what is unusual about the orbit of Triton, Neptune's largest moon. Complete your K-W-L-S-H chart by indicating what you would still like to know about the gas giant planets in the S column and how you can find this information in the H column.

Summary

KEY CONCEPTS

22.1 The Formation of the Solar System

- The Sun formed in an interstellar cloud of gas and dust called a nebula.

- Planets formed from planetesimals, gas and dust particles that clumped together and grew in size, collided, and merged.

- Asteroids are most likely leftover pieces of planetesimals that also orbit the Sun. Meteoroids are fragments of asteroids or any material that falls from space and enters Earth's atmosphere.

- Comets are small bodies made of ice and rock that travel in elliptical orbits around the Sun.

22.2 Planetary Motion

- Earth-centered models of the universe are called geocentric. Coepernicus suggested a heliocentric, or Sun-centered, model of the universe.

- The planets have elliptical orbits, and they move faster when closer to the Sun. A planet's distance from the Sun can be calculated if the planet's orbital period is known.

- Two objects attract each other with a force that depends on their masses and the distance between the two objects. Gravity is the force that keeps the planets in orbit around the Sun. Inertia keeps the planets from being pulled in toward the Sun.

22.3 The Inner Planets

- Distances in space can be measured in light-years, light-hours, or light-minutes, and also in terms of astronomical units, or AU.

- Mercury is the smallest planet and is the closest to the Sun. It has a very long day and great variation in temperature.

- Venus is the hottest planet, partly due to its thick atmosphere and greenhouse effect.

- Earth is the only planet that has conditions enabling it to sustain complex life forms—temperatures that allow for liquid water and a hospitable atmosphere.

- Mars is red from iron in the soil and shows evidence of the former presence of liquid water.

22.4 The Outer Planets

- Jupiter is the largest planet and has the shortest day. It has a thick atmosphere made of rising and sinking gases.

- Saturn rotates rapidly and has a very low density. It has a large ring system made up of icy particles.

- Uranus lies almost on its side, and it is very cold due to its distance from the Sun.

- Neptune is the farthest planet from the Sun.

- Pluto was reclassified as a dwarf planet in 2006.

VOCABULARY REVIEW

Write each term in a complete sentence or write a paragraph relating several terms.

22.1
solar system, p. 413
interstellar cloud, p. 413
nebula, p. 413
protostar, p. 413
solar nebula, p. 413
planetesimal, p. 414
asteroid, p. 414
meteoroid, p. 415
meteor, p. 415
meteorite, p. 415
comet, p. 415
meteor shower, p. 415

22.2
orbital period, p. 416
geocentric, p. 416
heliocentric, p. 416
ellipse, p. 416
perihelion, p. 417
aphelion, p. 417
inertia, p. 418

22.3
terrrestrial planet, p. 420
gas giant planet, p. 420
light-year, p. 421
astronomical unit, p. 421
retrograde rotation, p. 423
prograde rotation, p. 423

22.4
satellite, p. 426
dwarf planet, p. 431

PREPARE FOR CHAPTER TEST

To prepare for the chapter test, create a question from each Learning Goal. Use the information in your Science Notebook to answer each question. Then use these answers to write a well-developed essay about the chapter. Use the Key Concept on the first page of this chapter as your topic sentence.

True or False

If the statement is true, write "true." If it is false, change the underlined word or words to make the statement true.

1. A meteor that does not completely burn up and hits Earth is called a <u>meteorite</u>.

2. The <u>farther</u> two objects are from each other, the stronger the force of gravity between them.

3. <u>Inertia</u> causes objects to move in a straight line unless they are acted upon by an outside force.

4. The topography on Mars indicates that it probably once had liquid <u>water</u>.

5. The outer planets have longer periods of <u>rotation</u> than the inner planets.

6. Spacecraft missions to the outer planets have shown that they all have <u>rings</u>.

Short Answer

Answer each of the following in a sentence or brief paragraph.

7. Explain how a star forms from a nebula.

8. Describe what comets are and how they are related to meteor showers.

9. Use Newton's law of universal gravitation to explain why the planets orbit the Sun.

10. Compare Earth's period of revolution to its period of rotation.

11. Describe some of the topographical features on Mars.

12. Explain what the light- and dark-colored bands on Jupiter and Saturn are.

Critical Thinking

Use what you have learned in this chapter to answer each of the following.

13. **Evaluate** Choose another planet to compare with Earth. Evaluate some of the ways in which the two planets are different and why there is life on Earth but not on the other planet.

14. **Relate** Explain how the orbiting of the planets around the Sun compares to the orbiting of the Moon around Earth.

15. **Analyze** How would the number of planets in our solar system change over the coming years if Pluto had not been reclassified as a dwarf planet?

Standardized Test Question

Choose the letter of the response that correctly answers the question.

16. According to Newton's law of universal gravitation, if two objects are moved three times as far apart, how much will the attraction between them decrease?

    A. by a factor of 3

    B. by a factor of 6

    C. by a factor of 9

    D. by a factor of 30

Test-Taking Tip

Remember that words such as *most likely* and *not* may change the meaning of the question. Be sure to read the question carefully before examining all the answer choices.

Chapter 23

Stars

KEY CONCEPT All stars, including the Sun, produce energy through fusion and are classified by numerous physical properties including mass, brightness, and surface temperature.

Have you ever been outdoors on a cool, clear night, far from the lights of a city or town? If so, you may have seen thousands of twinkling stars in the sky. The star closest to us is the Sun. It is one of billions of stars in the universe. Without the Sun's heat, life on Earth as we know it would not exist.

Every star in the sky, including Earth's Sun, is a hot, glowing ball of gas. Some groups of stars form recognizable patterns in the sky. These patterns are called constellations.

Think About the Night Sky

It is best to observe stars without the bright light that is reflected off a full moon or that shines from streetlights. However, even with lights nearby, it is still possible to see a number of stars in the night sky.

- Go outside on the next clear night, and look up at the sky. How many stars are visible? Are some of the stars brighter than others? Do some appear to be bigger than others?

- In your Science Notebook, list your observations about the stars you see.

www.scilinks.org

Stars **Code:** WGES23

Before You Read

Review the vocabulary for this lesson. Many of the terms describe the layers of the Sun. In your Science Notebook, draw a small circle to represent the interior of the Sun. Draw five circles around the first circle to represent the Sun's layers. Your drawing should look like a target with a bull's-eye in the center. Label the layers of the Sun in your diagram as you read about them.

The Composition and Structure of the Sun

The Sun is very large. It contains more than 99 percent of all the mass in our solar system. It would take 109 Earths lined up side by side to equal the diameter of the Sun. Because the Sun is the largest object in our solar system, its mass and gravity control the motions of the planets. Through observation and the help of technology, astronomers have learned much about the Sun.

The Sun does not have a solid surface. Like the gas giant planets, the Sun is made up entirely of gases held together by gravity. The Sun is composed mostly of hydrogen and helium, along with small amounts of other elements as shown in **Figure 23.1**. At the Sun's core, where its temperatures are highest, its gases are compressed by gravity to a very high density. Moving outward from the core, the density of the Sun's gases decreases.

The Sun's Atmosphere   The Sun's atmosphere is made up of three layers: the photosphere, the chromosphere, and the corona. The **photosphere**, shown in **Figure 23.2**, is the lowest layer of the Sun's atmosphere. It is it approximately 400 km thick and appears as the visible surface of the Sun. The average temperature of the photosphere is about 5,800 K (5,527°C). Most of the light from the Sun comes from this layer. Unlike the photosphere, the chromosphere and the corona that are located above it are transparent to the human eye.

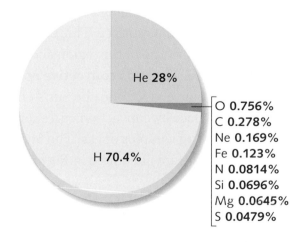

Composition of the Sun by Mass

He 28%

O 0.756%
C 0.278%
Ne 0.169%
Fe 0.123%
N 0.0814%
Si 0.0696%
Mg 0.0645%
S 0.0479%

H 70.4%

Figure 23.1 This graph shows the ten most common elements present in the Sun. The remaining 0.0106% is made of elements that are very rare.

Figure It Out

1. Which layer of the Sun's atmosphere extends farthest into space?
2. What are the three internal regions of the Sun and what are they made up of?

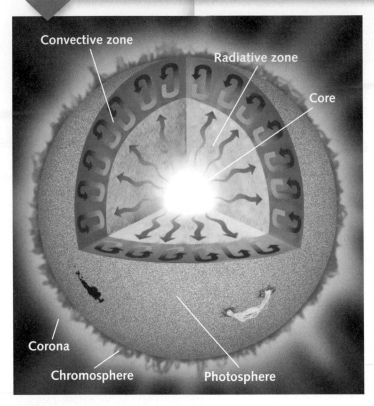

Figure 23.2 The Sun's atmosphere is made up of three layers: the photosphere, the chromosphere, and the corona. The Sun's interior is made up of three zones: the core, the radiative zone, and the convective zone.

As You Read

Write the names of the Sun's six layers in the correct circle in the diagram that you drew in your Science Notebook. Indicate which layers are part of the Sun's atmosphere and which are part of the Sun's interior.

Does the Sun have a solid surface? Explain why or why not.

As shown in **Figure 23.2**, the **chromosphere** is the layer of the Sun's atmosphere located above the photosphere. It is about 2,500 km thick and is hotter than the photosphere. Its temperature is approximately 30,000 K (29,727°C) at its upper limit. The presence of more helium gives this layer its red color.

The outermost layer of the Sun's atmosphere is called the **corona**. It extends several million kilometers from the top of the chromosphere. Its temperature ranges from 1–2 million K (999,726°C–1,999,726°C). The gases that make up both the corona and chromosphere are thin. For this reason, these layers are only visible when the light from the photosphere is blocked. This occurs during a solar eclipse or when special instruments are used to view the Sun.

Interior Regions of the Sun   The energy of the Sun is produced at its **core**, or center. The temperature at the Sun's core is about 15 million K (14,999,727°C). The density of the Sun's core is 160,000 kg/cm³. This is many times higher than the density of the most dense element on Earth, osmium, which is 22.58 g/cm³. Despite this high density, the Sun's interior remains gaseous because of its extreme temperatures. It takes millions of years for energy produced at the Sun's core to reach its surface. This energy is transferred from gas particle to gas particle in the region above the core known as the **radiative zone**. The Sun's **convective zone** lies above the radiative zone. In the convective zone, the Sun's energy is carried the rest of the way to its surface by convection currents. Here, heat is transferred through moving volumes of gas. The Sun's core, radiative zone, and convective zone are illustrated in **Figure 23.2**.

Energy Production in the Sun

Albert Einstein was the first to demonstrate that matter can be converted into energy according to his famous equation: $E = mc^2$, where E is energy, m is mass, and c is the speed of light. Because light travels at an extremely high speed, a small amount of matter can produce a large amount of energy. Einstein's work led to an understanding of a powerful source of energy called nuclear fusion.

Fusion is the combining of lightweight nuclei, such as those of hydrogen, into heavier nuclei. In the Sun's core, helium is the product of the fusion of hydrogen nuclei. The helium that forms has a mass that is less than the mass of the combined hydrogen nuclei. This means that the mass lost during the fusion of hydrogen to helium is converted to energy. This process of producing energy through the fusion of hydrogen to helium is what powers the Sun.

Activity on the Sun's Surface

Although the Sun looks stable in the sky, it actually experiences a lot of activity at its surface. **Sunspots** are dark, cooler patches on the surface of the photosphere. They are located in areas where the Sun's intense magnetic field prevents hot gases from rising to the surface. The number and location of the Sun's sunspots changes in a regular cycle. The maximum number of sunspots occurs every 11.2 years on average.

Figure 23.3 The Sun's corona can be seen during a solar eclipse, such as this one that occurred on October 24, 1995. This image was created by combining eight separate photos taken from Earth's surface.

Did You Know?

The Sun produces about 3.85×10^{26} watts of energy per second. This is an enormous amount of energy. The largest power plants on Earth can produce about 5,000 megawatts of power. Looking at it this way, the Sun produces the same amount of energy every *second*, as over two billion of these power plants could produce every *year!*

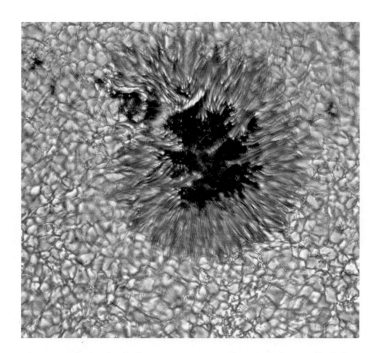

Figure 23.4 The lighter, outer ring of a sunspot is called the penumbra. The darker, inner ring of a sunspot is called the umbra. This sunspot is approximately 100 km in diameter.

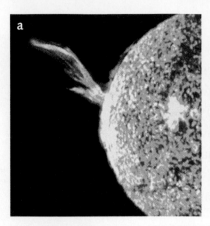
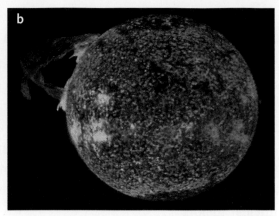

Figure 23.5 a) Solar flares erupt from the surface of the Sun. **b)** Prominences sometimes last for several months and can reach temperatures greater than 50,000 K.

Explain It!

Imagine that you travel in a spaceship that takes you close enough to the Sun to observe its features. Write a postcard to a friend at home describing what the surface of the Sun looks like. Describe solar activity you might see, including sunspots, solar flares, and solar prominences. Complete the postcard by drawing what you have described on the front of the card.

The Sun's magnetic field might also cause solar flares. **Solar flares** are violent eruptions of particles and radiation from the Sun's surface. These eruptions send streams of electrically charged particles into the solar system. **Solar winds**, made up of gas flowing outward from the corona, carry these charged solar particles to all the planets in the solar system. As the charged particles from the Sun collide with gases in Earth's upper atmosphere, spectacular light displays called **auroras** result. These displays, also known as the aurora borealis or northern lights and the aurora australis or southern lights, are most commonly seen near Earth's poles.

Solar flares are also associated with solar features called prominences. A **prominence**, shown in **Figure 23.5b**, is an arc of gas that shoots up from the chromosphere. A prominence might also form in the corona and fall back to the Sun's surface.

Figure 23.6 The most common color for auroras is yellowish-green. This photo of an aurora was taken in Ontario, Canada.

After You Read

1. Next to the diagram of the Sun that you made in your Science Notebook, write at least one feature of each one of the Sun's six layers.

2. Describe how energy is produced in the Sun.

3. What causes the aurora, or the northern and southern lights?

23.2 Classifying Stars

Before You Read

In your Science Notebook, write each of the vocabulary terms in this lesson. Using your own words, write a definition for each term as you read about it.

Learning Goals

- Identify the basic properties of stars.
- Compare the different types of spectra.
- Identify the ways in which stars can be classified.
- Describe how distances to stars are measured.

New Vocabulary

apparent magnitude
absolute magnitude
luminosity
spectrum
parallax

Properties of Stars

Stars differ from one another in their basic properties. These properties include: diameter, mass, brightness, the amount of energy they produce, surface temperature, their age, and their composition. The diameters and masses of stars can range from one-tenth the mass and diameter of the Sun to 50 or 100 times its mass and diameter.

How bright a star looks from Earth is different than its actual brightness. This is because its distance from Earth affects how bright it appears. The apparent brightness of a star to observers on Earth is called its **apparent magnitude**. The actual brightness of a star is its **absolute magnitude**. To calculate the absolute magnitude of a star, its distance from Earth must be known.

Consider two identical flashlights. If one flashlight is nearby and the other flashlight is 6 m away, the one that is closer will look brighter. It is the same with stars. If two stars have the same absolute magnitude, the one closer to Earth will appear brighter and have a greater apparent magnitude.

Figure 23.7 shows how astronomers rate the brightness of each star. The lower the number on the scale, the brighter the star. For example, a star with an absolute magnitude of −5 is brighter than a star with an absolute magnitude of +5. The Sun has an absolute magnitude of +4.8, which is in the middle range of brightness. However, it has an apparent magnitude of −26.8. This is because it is closer to us than any other star, and it is therefore the brightest object in the sky.

Figure It Out

1. Identify an object in the sky that has similar apparent and absolute magnitudes. Explain how this can be.

2. Why does the Moon have a much greater apparent magnitude than absolute magnitude?

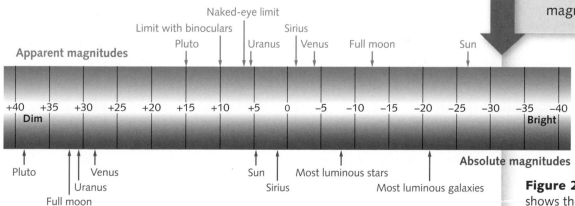

Figure 23.7 This diagram shows the apparent and absolute magnitudes of some familiar objects in the sky.

Scientific notation, which uses powers of 10, can make large numbers shorter and easier to understand. For example, light travels at the speed of 300,000,000 meters per second. In scientific notation, 300,000,000 is written as 3×10^8. It is the same number but written as the product of 3 and 10 to the power of 8 (that means $10 \times 10 \times 10 \times 10 \times 10 \times 10 \times 10 \times 10$). To find the power of 10 for any large number, put a decimal after the first digit and count the number of places from the decimal to the end of the number. How would you write the number 6,000,000 using scientific notation?

Luminosity is the measure of energy output per second from the surface of a star. It is measured in watts. Astronomers must know both the distance of a star from Earth and its apparent magnitude to determine its luminosity. The hotter and larger a star is, the more luminous it is. Measures of luminosity vary greatly from star to star.

Spectra and Classifying Stars

A **spectrum** is visible light arranged according to waves of energy called wavelengths. When white light is shined through a prism, the light is separated into individual wavelengths and the most familiar spectrum, a rainbow, appears. A spectrum with no breaks in it is called a continuous spectrum. A rainbow is an example of a continuous spectrum because every color is seen along it. A continuous spectrum is produced by the glow of light from a heated liquid or solid or by heated gas that is highly compressed and dense.

In general, solids, liquids, or dense gases emit light at all wavelengths when heated. When light passes through a cloud of gas, an absorption spectrum is produced. This is because the gas particles absorb some of the wavelengths. The colors that are seen have wavelengths that were not absorbed by the cloud of gas. If a thin cloud of gas does not have a hot energy source behind it, it will produce an emission spectrum. This simply represents the composition of the cloud of gas itself. As shown in **Figure 23.8b**, Earth's Sun produces an absorption spectrum with dark lines at specific wavelengths.

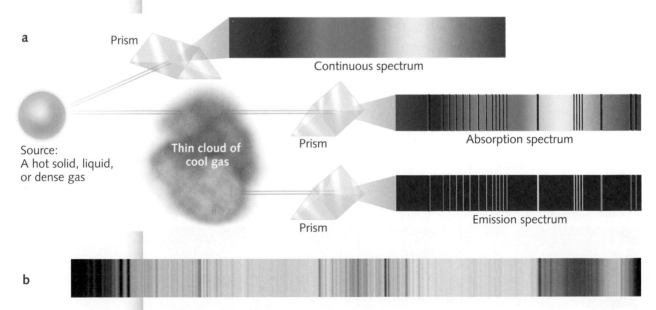

Figure 23.8 a) The three types of spectra—continuous, absorption, and emission—are shown. **b)** The Sun's spectrum is an absorption spectrum.

All stars are made up almost entirely of the same elements. Though it varies with the age of a star, usually about 73 percent of a star's mass is made up of hydrogen. Helium makes up about 25 percent, and the last 2 percent is made up of other elements. Despite their similarities, stars can be classified by the unique patterns of lines in their absorption spectra. The spectra produced by stars vary due to differences in temperature between stars. Cooler stars produce spectra with many lines. Hotter stars produce more simple spectra with fewer lines.

Stars are assigned letters based on the types of spectra they produce. As shown in **Figure 23.9**, these letters also correspond to the surface temperatures of stars. The hottest O stars may have surface temperatures as high as 50,000 K. The coolest M stars may have temperatures as low as 2,000 K. Earth's Sun is a G star, with a temperature in the range of 5,000 K to 6,000 K. The temperature differences of stars appear as different colors. The hottest of all stars, O stars, are blue. M stars, the coolest stars, appear red in color.

Spectral Class	Temperature (K)	Color of Star
O	> 25,000	blue-white
B	10,000–25,000	blue-white
A	7,500–10,000	white
F	6,000–7,500	yellow-white
G	5,000–6,000	yellow
K	3,500–5,000	orange
M	< 3,500	red

Figure 23.9 This table shows how the spectral class of a star is related to its surface temperature and color.

Measuring Distances to Stars

Astronomers use light-years to measure long distances in space. A light-year is the distance that light travels in one year or about 9.5 trillion km. The Sun is only 150 million km from Earth. The next nearest star, Proxima Centauri, is about 40 trillion km, or 4.2 light-years from Earth. Polaris, the North Star, is 431 light-years from Earth.

How do astronomers determine the distance to stars when they are so far away? They take advantage of the fact that the stars appear to move in the sky when observed from Earth. **Parallax** is the apparent change in a star's position in the sky due to the movement of the observer. Stars do not actually move. Their positions in the sky appear to shift because Earth is moving.

Figure 23.10 shows how parallax is used to determine the distance to a star. Scientists photograph a star against background stars from a fixed position on Earth. Six months later, when Earth has traveled halfway around its orbit, a second photograph is taken. Recall that the distance around any circle, including Earth's orbit, is 360°. Any segment along the circle is called an arc. By measuring the distance the object "jumped," scientists can calculate the size of the parallax in units called arc seconds. They use this information to measure the distance to stars.

Figure 23.10 Astronomers can use the shift in position of a star as viewed from opposite sides of Earth's orbit to calculate its distance from Earth.

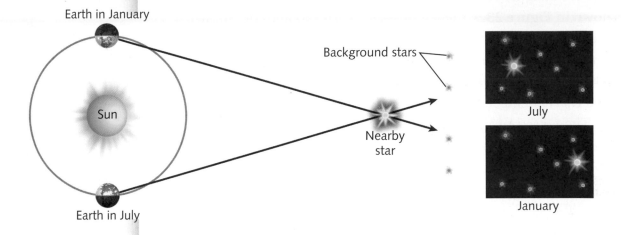

PEOPLE IN SCIENCE Todd Henry   1964–

Earth has existed for billions of years in our solar neighborhood. There are, however, many stars relatively close to our planet that have not yet been identified. Astronomer Todd Henry, at Georgia State University, has been trying to identify these stars. Henry is the head of the Research Consortium on Nearby Stars (RECONS). The group works at the Cerro Tololo Inter-American Observatory in La Serena, Chile. They use the parallax method, among others, to measure the distances to stars in the southern sky.

Henry and his team of researchers focus on the stars that appear to move fastest across the sky. The fast movement of these stars, which he calls "stellar roadrunners," might be a clue that they are closer to Earth than other stars. Of the 400 stellar roadrunners currently being studied, 28 have been determined to be Earth's neighboring stars.

After You Read

1. How does the color of a star relate to its temperature?
2. What is the difference between apparent magnitude and absolute magnitude?
3. How do astronomers estimate the distance of a star from Earth?
4. Using the definitions in your Science Notebook, describe how astronomers measure long distances in space.

Learning Goals

- Explain how stars are organized on the Hertzsprung-Russell diagram.

- Describe how a star is formed.

- Describe the life cycle of a medium-sized star.

- Explain what happens at the end of a massive star's life.

New Vocabulary

Hertzsprung-Russell diagram
main sequence
red giant
supergiant
white dwarf
supernova
neutron star
black hole

Recall Vocabulary

nebula, p. 413
protostar, p. 413

Before You Read

Scientists sometimes use time lines to place events in the sequence in which they occurred. In your Science Notebook, draw a time line as a horizontal line that represents the life of a star. Preview the lesson to look for important stages in the life of a star, and write them in the correct order on the time line.

The Hertzsprung-Russell Diagram

Each class of star has a specific mass, luminosity, temperature, age, and diameter. The **Hertzsprung-Russell diagram** (H-R diagram) is a graph that shows the relationships between different classes of stars. As shown in **Figure 23.11**, luminosity is plotted along the vertical axis of the graph. Recall that the higher the value of apparent magnitude, the lower the luminosity and the dimmer the star. This means that the stars at the bottom of the diagram are dimmer, and the stars at the top are brighter. Temperature and spectral type are plotted on the horizontal axis. Hot (blue) stars are located on the left, and cool (red) stars are located on the right.

There is a diagonal pattern of stars called the **main sequence** that runs from the top-left to the bottom-right of the diagram. Stars spend most of their lifetimes as main sequence stars, and as more hydrogen is converted to helium, they change into one of the other types of stars shown. The Sun is located in the middle of the main sequence. It is an average star in terms of brightness and temperature.

Figure 23.11
Massive stars are plotted at the left end of the H-R diagram. Stars with small masses tend to be located at the lower-right end. As stars on the main sequence age, they move up and to the right, becoming giants or supergiants. Eventually, they become white dwarfs and end up in the lower-left area of the diagram.

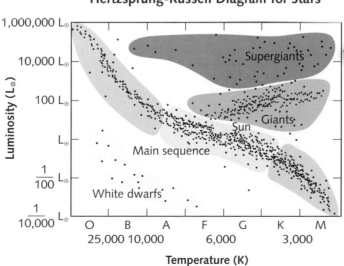

Hertzsprung-Russell Diagram for Stars

Figure It Out

1. Which spectral class of stars on the H-R diagram would you expect to have the hottest temperatures? Explain.

2. Which stars on the H-R diagram would you expect to be the brightest? Explain.

The Birth of a Star

All stars begin as a cloud of gas and dust called a nebula. Due to its own gravity, the cloud of dust and gas contracts and collapses in on itself. At the same time, the rotation of the cloud causes it to take on the shape of a disk. The hot glowing center of condensed dust and gas is called a protostar.

Eventually, the hot protostar becomes dense enough for fusion to take place. Remember that in a fusion reaction, hydrogen is converted into helium, and energy is produced. Once the protostar begins to give off light and heat, it has become a stable star. The star's life cycle from this point on is determined by its mass.

As You Read

Go back to the time line that you drew in your Science Notebook. Review the important events that you wrote on the time line after previewing the chapter. Change or add to them as necessary.

How does a red giant star become a white dwarf star?

a

Infalling material

Protostar

Rotating disk

Figure 23.12
a) A protostar forms from the gas and dust of a nebula such as this portion of the Tarantula Nebula **(b)**.

b

Extend It!

Choose a star other than the Sun to research. Answer the following questions: How did the star get its name? What constellation is it part of? What kind of star is it, how old is it, and how far is it from Earth? How hot is it, and how bright is it? Write a well-developed paragraph in your Science Notebook that answers these questions.

A Medium-Sized Star's Life Cycle

A medium-sized star such as the Sun continues to fuse hydrogen into helium for the first few billion years of its life. However, as it gets older, it starts to use up its supply of hydrogen. The star's core is now mostly helium, and it begins to shrink while its outer shell expands, cools, and turns red. The star is now considered a **red giant**.

Supergiant stars are even bigger and brighter than red giants. Although a red giant is cool on its surface, it keeps getting hotter in its helium core, until the helium atoms fuse into carbon atoms and the star begins to die. The surface gases blow away, and only the hot core is left. This tiny, dense star, with its matter packed tightly together, is called a **white dwarf**. It finally dies when it burns up all its energy. This will probably happen to the Sun in about five billion years.

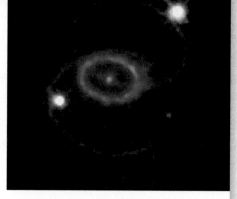

A Massive Star's Life Cycle

At the end of its life, a massive star may not lose enough mass to become a white dwarf. Like a medium-sized star, a massive star becomes a red giant or a supergiant as it ages. However, after it runs out of hydrogen and fuses helium atoms into carbon, its massive core is so hot that the carbon atoms fuse into iron. This iron core absorbs energy until it collapses. Then the entire outer portion of the star is blown off in a huge explosion called a **supernova**. A supernova explosion can light up the sky more brightly than the Sun for a short period of time.

A supernova explosion produces heavy elements such as silver, gold, and lead. These elements and gases from the star blow into space and create a new nebula, out of which another star may eventually form. Astronomers observed and recorded a supernova in 1954 that lit up the sky for 23 days. A supernova that occurred in 1987 is shown in **Figure 23.13**.

When a large star dies during a supernova explosion, what happens to leftover materials from the core? Stars that are 1.5 to 4 times larger than the Sun will become **neutron stars**. A neutron star is only about 20 km in diameter, but it is extremely dense. It is so dense that a teaspoon of its matter would weigh almost a billion tons on Earth!

Stars with masses more than about 20 times that of the Sun are too massive to form neutron stars. Instead, the core of a very massive star that has exploded will collapse on itself forever. This continuous collapsing compacts the core of the star into a smaller and smaller volume. The extremely dense object that remains is called a **black hole**. The interesting thing about a black hole is that it has become so collapsed on itself that it is essentially a single point in space. That is why a black hole is sometimes called a singularity. The gravitational force of a black hole is so strong that not even light can escape it. X rays given off by gas or dust from a nearby star as they are being pulled into a black hole can sometimes be observed by astronomers on Earth. This enables them to detect the existence of black holes.

Figure 23.13 This image taken by the Hubble Space Telescope shows rings that formed in a supernova observed in 1987. It was created by the explosion of a star in a galaxy called the Large Magellanic Cloud.

 **CONNECTION: Cultural**

For centuries, Andean farmers in Bolivia and Peru have looked to the stars in June to forecast the impact of the weather on their potato crops. If the constellation Pleiades looks clear and bright just before sunrise, early rains and a plentiful potato crop are expected. If the stars look dim, however, rains are expected to be lighter and to arrive later in the growing season. Dim stars signal farmers to wait until later in the season to plant potatoes in order to reduce the impact on the crop of too little rain. Modern scientists have found a very real relationship between the occurrence of an El Niño event and an increase in high, almost transparent clouds over the Andes mountain range. These clouds create a haze over the stars, dimming the farmers' view of them. Four to eight months later, the El Niño results in a hot, dry growing season that reduces the potato crop.

After You Read

1. Approximately what temperature and magnitude would a star in the lower-right corner of the Hertzsprung-Russell diagram have?

2. What is a supernova?

3. Review the time line you have created in your Science Notebook. What series of events occurs before and after a massive star dies?

KEY CONCEPTS

23.1 Earth's Sun

- The Sun is made up of six layers. The corona, the chromosphere, and the photosphere form the atmosphere. The core, the radiative zone, and the convective zone form the interior.

- The Sun and all stars produce energy through the process of fusion. During fusion in the Sun, hydrogen nuclei fuse together to form helium, releasing energy in the process.

- Activity on the Sun's surface that is caused by magnetic fields includes sunspots, solar flares, and solar prominences.

- Charged particles from the Sun's corona, called solar wind, sometimes interact with gases in Earth's upper atmosphere, producing auroras.

23.2 Classifying Stars

- Stars differ from one another in their basic properties. These properties include diameter, mass, brightness, luminosity, surface temperature, age, and composition.

- A spectrum with no breaks in it is called a continuous spectrum. When light passes through a cloud of gas, an absorption spectrum is produced. If a thin cloud of gas does not have a hot energy source behind it, it will produce an emission spectrum.

- Stars can be classified by the unique patterns of lines in their absorption spectra. They can also be classified by their temperature, color, age, and brightness.

- The actual brightness of a star is its absolute magnitude. How bright a star appears to observers on Earth is its apparent magnitude.

- One method astronomers use to measure distances to stars is parallax, which is the apparent change in a star's position in the sky.

23.3 The Life Cycle of Stars

- The Hertzsprung-Russell diagram (H-R diagram) is a graph that shows the relationships between different classes of stars.

- A star begins in a cloud of gas and dust called a nebula, and then it becomes a protostar. When fusion takes place and light and heat are emitted, the protostar has become an actual star.

- A medium-sized star becomes either a red giant or a supergiant as it gets older and cooler. As it uses up its supply of hydrogen and the helium fuses into carbon, it becomes a white dwarf.

- A massive star also becomes a red giant or supergiant. When its helium fuses into carbon, the carbon then becomes iron. What is left of the star explodes in a supernova. The material that is left then becomes either a neutron star or pulsar, or if the star is really large, it forms a black hole.

VOCABULARY REVIEW

Write each term in a complete sentence or write a paragraph relating several terms.

23.1
photosphere, p. 435
chromosphere, p. 436
corona, p. 436
core, p. 436
radiative zone, p. 436
convective zone, p. 436
fusion, p. 437
sunspot, p. 437
solar flare, p. 438
solar wind, p. 438
aurora, p. 438
prominence, p. 438

23.2
apparent magnitude, p. 439
absolute magnitude, p. 439
luminosity, p. 440
spectrum, p. 440
parallax, p. 441

23.3
Hertzsprung-Russell diagram, p. 443
main sequence, p. 443
red giant, p. 444
supergiant, p. 444
white dwarf, p. 444
supernova, p. 445
neutron star, p. 445
black hole, p. 445

PREPARE FOR CHAPTER TEST

To prepare for the chapter test, create a question from each Learning Goal. Use the information in your Science Notebook to answer each question. Then use these answers to write a well-developed essay about the chapter. Use the Key Concept on the first page of this chapter as your topic sentence.

MASTERING CONCEPTS

True or False

If the statement is true, write "true." If it is false, change the underlined word or words to make the statement true.

1. The <u>corona</u>, the innermost layer of the Sun's atmosphere, is sometimes called the surface of the Sun.

2. <u>Sunspots</u> are caused by strong magnetic fields in the interior of the Sun.

3. Stars on the left side of the Hertzsprung-Russell diagram are <u>cooler</u> than those on the right.

4. A <u>medium-sized star</u> may explode in a supernova at the end of its life.

5. The actual brightness of a star is called its <u>absolute magnitude</u>.

6. Stars in the sky <u>appear to</u> move as Earth revolves around the Sun.

Short Answer

Answer each of the following in a sentence or brief paragraph.

7. Explain how the Sun produces energy.

8. Describe what solar flares and solar prominences are.

9. Describe how stars are arranged on the Hertzsprung-Russell diagram.

10. Explain what must happen for a protostar to become a star.

11. Explain why two stars with the same absolute magnitude can appear to have different brightness.

12. Identify the color of a star that is in the O class and has a surface temperature of 30,000°C or higher.

Critical Thinking

Use what you have learned in this chapter to answer each of the following.

13. **Evaluate** How can the Sun's apparent magnitude of −26.8 be so much greater than its absolute magnitude of +4.8?

14. **Compare** How does a star's life cycle compare to that of a person?

15. **Analyze** In terms of brightness and temperature, how do stars located in the middle of the H-R diagram main sequence compare to stars located on either end?

Standardized Test Question

Choose the letter of the response that correctly answers the question.

16. What is luminosity?

    A. measure of a star's apparent magnitude

    B. measure of a star's energy output

    C. measure of a star's distance from Earth

    D. measure of star's diameter

> **Test-Taking Tip**
>
> If "None of the above" is one of the choices in a multiple-choice question, be sure that none of the choices is true.

Chapter 24

Galaxies and the Universe

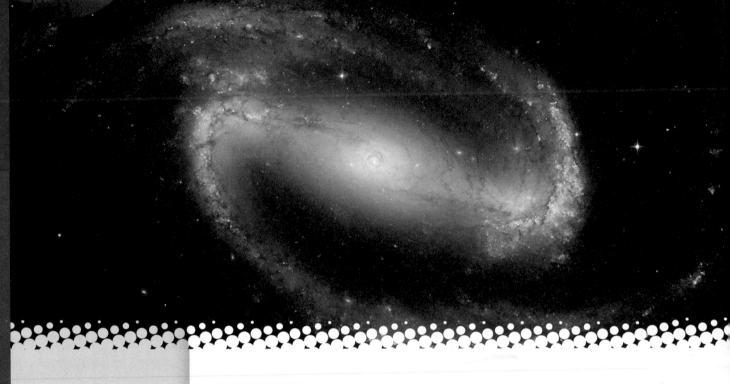

KEY CONCEPT Scientists study the universe, and the groups of stars and galaxies within it, to better understand the origin of our solar system.

Your day most likely begins around the time the Sun rises. Daylight ends hours later, when the Sun sets. Imagine living on a planet in another star system. How many suns might shine in that sky? It is likely to be more than one. Astronomers estimate that most stars exist in groups of two or more. These groups of stars are held closely together by gravity. The study of galaxies and the universe helps scientists to understand the beginnings of our solar system and our own planet, Earth.

Think About Galaxies and the Universe

Earth and our solar system are part of a much larger star group containing more than 100 billion stars. Each star system is capable of supporting life.

- Use what you know about the other planets in the Solar system to explain why it is doubtful that they support life.

- The universe contains several hundred billion other star groups. In your Science Notebook, explain how likely you think it is that life exists somewhere else in the universe.

24.1 Galaxies

Learning Goals

- Identify a galaxy's type based on its shape.

- Compare and contrast various space objects.

- Explain how observing quasars allows astronomers to view early stages of the universe.

New Vocabulary

galaxy
spiral galaxy
elliptical galaxy
irregular galaxy
globular cluster
open cluster
quasar

Recall Vocabulary

nebula, p. 413

Before You Read

In your Science Notebook, create a chart with three columns. Label the columns *Spiral Galaxies*, *Elliptical Galaxies*, and *Irregular Galaxies*. Write anything you already know about each type of galaxy. As you read the lesson, describe each galaxy and draw a simple sketch of its shape.

When gravity holds stars together in a group, the group is called a star system. The size of the system can range from a pair of stars to a larger-sized star cluster to a huge galaxy. A **galaxy** (GA luk see) consists of a large group of stars, planets, and other space objects. Galaxies have different sizes and shapes. A dwarf galaxy might contain a few million stars, whereas a giant galaxy might contain more than a trillion. Earth is part of the Milky Way galaxy, which contains perhaps 100 billion stars.

Groups of Galaxies

Galaxies are not spread out evenly in space. Instead, much like stars, galaxies often occur in groups. For example, the Milky Way galaxy is part of a small group of galaxies called the Local Group. The Local Group contains about 30 galaxies. Another group is the giant Virgo galaxy cluster, shown in **Figure 24.1a**. It is located about 50 million light-years away from the Local Group and contains about 2,000 galaxies.

Strong gravitational forces pull on the galaxies in a galaxy cluster. Over time, these forces can change the cluster. Gravity can even cause galaxies to collide. As shown in **Figure 24.1b**, the nearby Andromeda galaxy appears to show evidence of one galaxy "swallowing" another.

a

b

Figure 24.1 a) The Virgo galaxy cluster is shown in this photo taken by the *Hubble Space Telescope*. About two thousand galaxies make up the cluster. How many galaxies can you count? **b)** The two nuclei, or centers, visible in the Andromeda galaxy suggest that gravitational forces have caused two galaxies to collide.

Figure 24.2 The M100 galaxy, in the constellation Coma Berenices—also known as Berenice's hair— is a spiral galaxy. Notice how the long arms extend from the central bulge.

As You Read

Review the sentences you originally wrote about galaxies to make sure they are correct. Share your sentences with a partner. Make any needed corrections or additions.

Which type of galaxy is shaped like a flattened disk?

Figure 24.4 Strong gravitational forces have caused the two galaxies known as the Antennae galaxies to collide. It is estimated that the collision has been occurring over a one hundred-million-year period.

Galaxy Types

American astronomer Edwin Hubble, for whom the *Hubble Space Telescope* is named, began categorizing galaxies in the 1920s based on shape. It was later discovered that a galaxy's shape is related to its age. This relationship is described later in this lesson.

Spiral Galaxies The Milky Way and most other galaxies are spiral galaxies. **Spiral** (SPI rul) **galaxies** have long arms that extend outward and bend around a large central bulge. The arms form a flattened disklike shape. As shown in **Figure 24.2**, a spiral galaxy looks somewhat like a pinwheel.

A galaxy's central bulge contains mostly older stars. Younger stars, along with dust and gases, are contained in the spiral arms. The bluish color of the arms seen in **Figure 24.2** is due to the bluish light given off by the younger stars.

Elliptical Galaxies Smooth, regularly shaped galaxies without spiral arms are called **elliptical** (ih LIHP tih kul) **galaxies**. These galaxies are tightly packed groups of stars that contain little dust or gas. Elliptical galaxies are more three-dimensional in shape than spiral galaxies. Whereas spiral galaxies have flat, disklike shapes, elliptical galaxies are usually shaped like spheres or footballs.

Elliptical galaxies have bright centers and contain only old stars. Elliptical galaxies and the stars within them are generally older than spiral galaxies. This is why they have very little dust and gas—most of it has been used up in star formation. The sizes of elliptical galaxies vary greatly. **Figure 24.3** shows galaxy M87, also called Virgo A. This giant elliptical galaxy is one of the most identifiable objects in the night sky.

Figure 24.3 The very bright center of M87 is typical of elliptical galaxies. This galaxy produces a jet of gas that emits visible light.

Irregular Galaxies Galaxies that are not spiral or elliptical are called **irregular galaxies**. As the name suggests, irregular galaxies do not have normal, uniform, or symmetrical shapes. They are generally the youngest galaxies. Their shapes are due to the fact that there has not been enough time for gravitational forces to pull the stars into spiral or elliptical galaxies. **Figure 24.4** shows the irregularly shaped Antennae galaxies. The odd shapes are due to gravitational forces that have pulled the two galaxies together.

The Contents of Galaxies

Besides stars, galaxies contain larger features such as nebulas and star clusters. Nebulas (NEB yuh luhz) consist of giant clouds of dust and gases. As **Figure 24.5** shows, the glowing or illuminated gases of a nebula can produce vivid colors. Some nebulas are present in areas where new stars form. Spiral galaxies often contain nebulas, whereas elliptical galaxies do not.

Star clusters are groups of stars that are bound together by gravity. **Globular** (GLOB yuh ler) **clusters** are groups of older stars. There are thousands to millions of stars in a globular cluster, all packed tightly into a roughly spherical shape. Globular clusters are often near spiral and elliptical galaxies. By contrast, **open clusters** are much smaller and are generally made up of young stars. They are located within spiral arms.

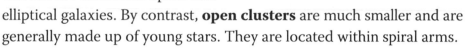

Formation of Galaxies

Light from distant space objects takes a very long time to reach Earth. Thus, observing distant objects allows astronomers to observe early stages of the universe. Astronomers are very interested in faraway star-like objects known as **quasars** (KWAY zharz). Quasars are some of the brightest objects in the universe. Though they look like stars, quasars emit radio waves and light waves that stars do not. Astronomers now think that quasars are associated with young, forming galaxies. Quasars appear to be about the size of an average-sized solar system. **Figure 24.6** shows quasar 3C 273, the brightest quasar visible from Earth.

Figure It Out

1. What evidence is there that the nebula contains gases?
2. Is the Crab Nebula regular or irregular in shape?

Figure 24.5 In 1054 A.D., Chinese astronomers observed the explosion of a star. The result of the explosion was the formation of the Crab Nebula pictured here.

Figure 24.6 It is estimated that quasar 3C 273 is 2 trillion times (2,000,000,000,000 times) brighter than the Sun. It appears much less bright in the night sky because it is so far away, about 2.4 billion light-years from Earth.

Explain It!

Distances on Earth are often measured in meters. In space, astronomical units (AU), light-years, and parsecs are used to measure distance. Research and define each unit of measure and explain how the units are related to one another.

After You Read

1. How does an elliptical galaxy compare to a globular cluster in terms of its size, number of stars, and shape?
2. Imagine that a quasar suddenly increases in brightness. How would astronomers know approximately when the increased brightness occurred?
3. Review the information you have recorded in your Science Notebook. Arrange the following in order of most symmetrical to least symmetrical: an elliptical galaxy, a spiral galaxy, an irregular galaxy.

Before You Read

Reword the Learning Goals of this lesson so that they form questions. Write the questions in your Science Notebook. As you read, record answers to the questions.

Everything that exists throughout space is the **universe** (YEW nuh vurs). In other words, the universe contains everything. It is hard to imagine how tremendously huge the universe actually is. Thinking about the universe leads to many questions. How did the universe begin? How is it changing? Will the universe come to an end? These are the questions of cosmology (kahz MOL uh jee), the study of the origin and the future of the universe.

The Big Bang Theory

Great thinkers throughout history have pondered the origin of the universe. Many of their ideas and beliefs were not scientific and could not be proven. The scientific theory best supported by observations and mathematical models is the big bang theory. The **big bang theory** states that the universe began from a tiny point and has continually increased in size.

According to the big bang theory, the universe was packed into a space smaller than a grain of sand. This dense speck of energy and matter was subjected to extremely high pressures and temperatures. Then the speck began to rapidly expand. This expansion was the beginning of the universe. The universe cooled as the expansion continued. Today, Earth is part of a vast and much cooler cosmos. **Figure 24.7** illustrates the evolution of the universe following the big bang.

Figure 24.7 The big bang theory proposes that the universe originated from a single point. As space expanded, matter and energy formed stars and galaxies. During the *plasma* stage, the universe was dominated by radiation.

Figure It Out

1. Approximately how many years after the big bang did atoms begin to form?

2. What happened between the *plasma* stage of the universe's formation and the period of time when atoms began to form?

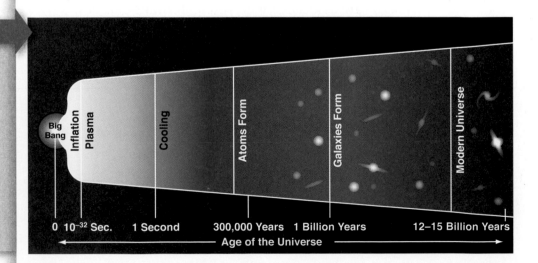

Big Bang | Inflation | Plasma | Cooling | Atoms Form | Galaxies Form | Modern Universe

0 10⁻³² Sec.   1 Second   300,000 Years   1 Billion Years   12–15 Billion Years

Age of the Universe

Supporting Evidence The big bang theory leaves many questions unanswered. It is not known why the universe expanded or how the galaxies formed. No one knows what existed before the big bang. The theory, however, does fit well with scientific observations.

The extremely hot and dense speck of matter and energy that formed the universe would have emitted a lot of radiation. That radiation should still exist, now spread throughout the universe. Scientists discovered such radiation in 1965. They detected weak background noise while using the antenna shown in **Figure 24.8**. The noise was due to **cosmic** (KAHZ mihk) **background radiation**, or low-level radiation from space. The radiation corresponded to a temperature of about 2.7 K (−270°C). This temperature closely matched the temperature of the universe predicted by the big bang theory. Other theories of the universe cannot explain the presence of cosmic background radiation.

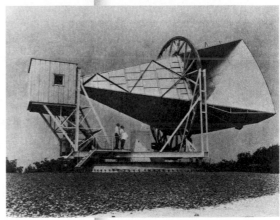

Figure 24.8 Using this large radio antenna at Bell Labs in Holmdel, New Jersey, scientists accidentally discovered cosmic background radiation.

Universal Expansion

In 1929, American astronomer Edwin Hubble concluded that the universe was expanding. His conclusion was based on scientific observations. At the time, it was known that all galaxies were moving away from Earth. Hubble discovered that the farther away a galaxy was, the faster it was moving away. This was proof of an expanding universe. It also suggested that the universe was once squeezed together.

If the universe is expanding, what is it expanding from? What if scientists traced the expanding universe back in time? Doing so pulls the universe back to a single point. The existence of this single point would correspond to the beginning of the universe. This type of thinking led to the big bang theory.

Earth and the Expanding Universe You might think that Earth is at the center of the universe—after all, everything is moving away from it. This is not the case. Imagine blowing up a balloon. The entire surface of the balloon expands outward at the same time. When a medium such as space expands evenly, all points in the medium become farther apart. No matter where you are in the medium, everything is moving farther away from you.

As You Read

Continue to answer the questions you wrote in your Science Notebook. Be sure to include key facts, supporting details, and vocabulary.

Use what you have learned to evaluate the following statement: *The big bang was a big explosion in space.* Explain the accuracy of this statement.

Astronomers noticed that light emitted by distant galaxies was shifted toward the red end of the visible light spectrum. A redshift occurs when the distance between a light-emitting object and the person observing it increases. Something similar happens to sound waves as the source of a sound moves relative to an observer. The redshifts of distant galaxies and quasars are easily measured by astronomers. They provide evidence that the universe is expanding and that most galaxies are moving away from Earth.

Explore It!

Use a felt-tip pen to mark three dots in a line on a balloon before it is inflated. Use a centimeter ruler to measure and record the distance between the dots. Partially inflate the balloon and hold it closed. Measure and record the distance between the dots. Further inflate the balloon and repeat the measurements. How did the distance between dots change as the balloon was inflated? Explain how the balloon models the expanding universe.

Figure 24.9 Just as the raisins in this loaf of bread move apart as the bread rises, the stars and galaxies of the universe move apart as it expands.

The Age of the Universe Astronomers have used different methods to estimate the age of the universe. Based on the mass of the oldest known stars, the universe is estimated to be between 11 and 18 billion years old. However, based on its expansion rate and cosmic radiation levels, the universe is estimated to be about 13.7 billion years old. This estimate might be more accurate than the star mass-based estimate. As a comparison, the human species, *Homo sapiens*, has lived on Earth for less than 50,000 years.

Is the big crunch coming? The universe is expanding. Will the expansion continue, or will the universe start to contract and come back together? Recent measurements of Hubble's original data seem to indicate that universal expansion is actually speeding up. The only thing that could be responsible for this is if there is a force that is in opposition to gravity, sometimes called antigravity. It therefore appears that the big crunch will not be happening at all.

What will happen depends on the momentum, or movement, of the universe and the gravitational forces acting on it. The universe's momentum acts to keep the expansion going. Gravity acts to pull everything back together. Currently, the rate of expansion of the universe is increasing. However, no one knows for sure what will happen billions of years from now.

The Structure of the Universe

The universe is made up of repeating patterns of structures. In our solar system, Earth and the other planets orbit the Sun. Astronomers have discovered similar planetary systems around other stars. Stars tend to occur in groups, such as those in open and closed star clusters and galaxies. Galaxies also often occur in groups as galactic clusters and superclusters. Gravity is responsible for all of these groupings.

As matter was spread throughout the expanding universe, gravity pulled it together into clumps and strands. Areas dense with matter are called filaments. Filaments form thin threadlike structures through space and are the largest structures in the universe. **Figure 24.10** shows a computer model of filament formation in the universe. The filaments seen in the model are similar to those observed in the universe. In some reference sources, these filaments are called superstrings.

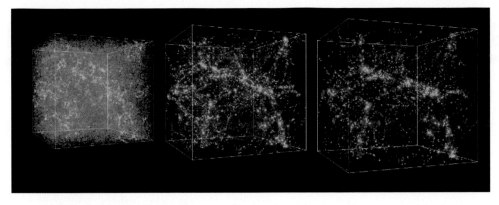

Figure 24.10 These images are from a computer model of an expanding universe. Notice how gravity tends to form thin strands of concentrated matter.

Extend It!

New discoveries about the nature and origin of the universe are constantly being made. Use the Internet to research recent NASA space probe missions. Write a short report describing a recent mission and its scientific findings.

Theory of
CONNECTION: **Special Relativity**

The study of the universe and physics has produced some complex ideas. One such idea is the theory of special relativity. American physicist 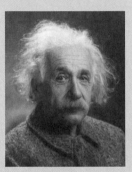 Albert Einstein, shown in the photograph, proposed the theory. It states that motion through space and time are related. That is, the speed at which you move through space changes how fast you move into the future. The theory predicts several outcomes—which have been proven true—that seem to defy common sense. The theory is closely tied to the speed of light.

One unusual result of the theory is called the twin paradox. Imagine you have a twin brother or sister. You travel to a distant planet in a vehicle that travels near the speed of light. When you return to Earth, you are considerably younger than your twin brother or sister. Your near–light-speed travel through space has slowed your travel through time.

Another odd result of the theory is that mass and energy are equivalent. This means that mass can be converted to energy, and vice versa. Mass and energy are related by the following equation: $E = mc^2$ where E = energy, m = mass, and c = the speed of light squared. Because the speed of light is a large value (3×10^8 m/s), a tiny amount of mass can be converted into a huge amount of energy.

After You Read

1. How was the mass and energy of the universe distributed before it expanded?

2. Identify a scientific observation that supports the big bang theory.

3. Review the notes you recorded in your Science Notebook about the expansion of the universe. In a well-developed paragraph, explain how proof of the expansion of the universe led to the big bang theory.

Did You Know?

We can attribute our understanding of the basic laws of the universe to Dr. Stephen Hawking, a mathematician and theoretical physicist at Cambridge University in England. It was Dr. Hawking who interpreted Einstein's general theory of relativity to mean that space and time began with the big bang and should end with black holes. He also determined that black holes are not completely black. They emit radiation and should eventually evaporate and disappear. He also thinks that the universe has no edge or boundary. In other words, it goes on forever. Dr. Hawking has published many popular works, including *A Brief History of Time*, *Black Holes and Baby Universes*, and *The Universe in a Nutshell*.

KEY CONCEPTS

24.1 Galaxies

- Galaxies are large groups of stars ranging in size from a few million stars to more than a trillion stars.

- There are three main types of galaxies: spiral galaxies, elliptical galaxies, and irregular galaxies.

- Spiral galaxies have flat, disklike shapes with arms extending from a central bulge. Elliptical galaxies are spherical or football shaped.

- The odd shapes of irregular galaxies are often due to gravitational forces.

- Galaxies contain star clusters and clouds of dust and gas called nebulas.

- Observing faraway quasars allows astronomers to learn about early stages of the universe.

24.2 The Universe

- The big bang theory states that space expanded and continues to expand from a single point.

- Matter and energy were carried with space as it expanded.

- The existence of cosmic background radiation supports the big bang theory.

- The redshift in light observed from distant galaxies provided proof that the universe is expanding.

- Acceptance of the idea that the universe is expanding led to the development of the big bang theory.

- Based on the observed expansion rate of the universe, the universe is estimated to be about 13.7 billion years old.

VOCABULARY REVIEW

Write each term in a complete sentence or write a paragraph relating several terms.

24.1
galaxy, p. 449
spiral galaxy, p. 450
elliptical galaxy, p. 450
irregular galaxy, p. 450
globular cluster, p. 451
open cluster, p. 451
quasar, p. 451

24.2
universe, p. 452
big bang theory, p. 452
cosmic background radiation, p. 453

PREPARE FOR CHAPTER TEST

To prepare for the chapter test, create a question from each Learning Goal. Use the information in your Science Notebook to answer each question. Then use these answers to write a well-developed essay about the chapter. Use the Key Concept on the first page of this chapter as your topic sentence.

True or False

If the statement is true, write "true." If it is false, change the underlined word or words to make the statement true.

1. Earth is part of the <u>Andromeda</u> galaxy.

2. Like stars, galaxies are often <u>alone in space</u>.

3. An <u>elliptical</u> galaxy has a flat, disklike shape.

4. A <u>quasar</u> is an intensely bright, faraway, starlike object.

5. Everything that exists in space is part of the <u>universe</u>.

6. Cosmic background radiation <u>supports</u> the big bang theory.

7. The farther a galaxy is from Earth, the <u>slower</u> it moves away from Earth.

8. <u>Gravitational forces</u> are responsible for groupings of stars and other space objects.

Short Answer

Answer each of the following in a sentence or brief paragraph.

9. Explain why the shape of a spiral galaxy appears different when viewed from different places in space.

10. Explain what causes galaxies to collide.

11. Identify the ages of stars in the central bulge and in the arms of a spiral galaxy.

12. Contrast a globular star cluster and an open star cluster.

13. Describe the state of the universe before it began to expand.

14. Explain how the existence of cosmic background radiation supports the big bang theory.

Critical Thinking

Use what you have learned in this chapter to answer each of the following.

15. **Explain** Galaxies can be thought of as star *factories*. Identify the materials used in the formation of a star and explain how gravity is involved in the process.

16. **Apply Concepts** Quasars emit more light than most other space objects. Yet, when viewed from Earth, most quasars are fairly dim. Explain why this is the case.

17. **Predict** Explain what will happen if gravitational forces overcome the momentum of the expanding universe.

Standardized Test Question

Choose the letter of the response that correctly answers the question.

18. What is the shape of most galaxies in the universe?

   A. globular

   B. irregular

   C. elliptical

   D. spiral

Test-Taking Tip

Be careful of the word *except*. This word often means that all the answers are correct *except* for one.

Mission to Mars

MARS IS EARTH'S neighbor in space. However, the two planets are very different. While Earth is a watery world that is full of life, Mars is a cold desert that seems lifeless. Many scientists, however, think there are clues that indicate life might be hiding on Mars.

Using robots, NASA's scientists have been working hard to unlock the secrets of Mars. The robotic probe *Mariner 9* reached Mars in November 1971. It orbited the planet and took pictures of most of its surface. Since then, probes in space have mapped the planet and studied its weather and atmosphere. During the early 2000s, several robot rovers rolled around the planet, taking pictures and studying Mars's rocks and soil.

Scientists have learned that Mars has no liquid water on its surface. However, Mars's features show that, in the past, it might have contained water on its surface. Mars has frozen water at its icy poles—and probably under its surface. Where there's water, there could be life now, or there might have been in the past.

The search for life is one reason to continue the exploration of Mars. Two rovers, *Spirit* and *Opportunity*, are now roaming the Martian surface. In August 2007, NASA launched *Phoenix*. After a ten-month journey, it will land on the northern polar area of Mars. *Phoenix*'s robot arm will then dig into the surface, scooping up soil, rock, and ice. The arm will transfer the samples into special chambers on *Phoenix*. There, the samples will be heated and chemically analyzed. Scientists hope that the analyses will show the presence of the organic compounds needed for life.

In 2010, NASA will send *Mars Science Laboratory (MSL)* to Mars. *MSL* will carry a new and improved robot rover. It will have a laser to blast the surface off rocks, letting scientists study what is inside. *MSL* will have tools to grind and crush rocks and soil. It will also test the air to find gases that could have been produced by living things. *MSL* will spend a year studying Mars, looking for signs of life past or present.

Scientists don't expect to find anything on Mars resembling human life. They do hope, however, to find microbes that can live in extreme environments. We already know that such microbes exist on Earth in the coldest, driest, or hottest places.

The robot probes are also helping scientists find the best places for a possible human landing on Mars one day. Astronauts could expand the search for life on the planet, but until people get to Mars, robot explorers will continue to lead the way.

CAREER CONNECTION: ROBOTICS ENGINEER

IN 2004, THE TWIN ROBOT rovers *Spirit* and *Opportunity* rolled from a spacecraft that landed on the surface of Mars. Since then, they have sent back pictures of the planet, conducted tests for water, and searched for life. Robotics engineers working for NASA designed the robot rovers, built them, tested them, and now drive them from a control center on Earth.

NASA's robotics engineers figure out what data NASA scientists need to collect during a mission. Then they figure out what kinds of robots can help the scientists achieve their goals. Sometimes the engineers work in robotics labs. At other times, they go into the desert to test their designs in an environment that resembles that of Mars.

Crossing Paths with a Comet

NASA HAS SENT space probes to study planets, moons, and the Sun. Until the early 2000s, however, no NASA probes had studied comets. Then, in February 1999, *Stardust* lifted off from Cape Canaveral. Its mission? Bring back a piece of Comet Wild 2.

Stardust reached Comet Wild 2 in January 2004. As it passed through the comet's tail, it trapped tiny particles of comet gas and dust. In January 2005, *Stardust* returned to Earth. A small capsule parachuted to Earth, carrying with it pieces of the comet.

NASA's second comet mission was in January 2005, when *Deep Impact* left Earth for Comet Tempel 1. When it reached the comet that July, the main spacecraft released an impactor robot. The impactor guided itself into the comet's path, then smashed into the comet at about 23,000 miles per hour. Cameras on the impactor and the main spacecraft took images of the comet before, during, and after the impact. Instruments in space and on Earth recorded the spray of particles that blasted out of the comet. The particles were then analyzed to determine the comet's composition.

The comets have already taught scientists new things about the solar system. Before *Stardust,* most scientists thought that comets formed at the edge of the solar system from dust and other material left over after the planets formed. Some of the particles from Comet Wild 2 showed that comets might have formed at the same time as the rest of the solar system. They might be made of some of the same material that formed the planets. The robot probes also found that particles from Comet Wild 2 and Comet Tempel 1 are different. So the formation of comets is more complex than anyone thought. Because of the two missions, scientists now know much more about comets, but they also know there is much more to learn.

Deep Impact reached Comet Tempel 1 after a six-month voyage of 83 million miles.

Many robotics engineers work at NASA, but they work in other places, too. Some design assembly line robots that build cars. Others make robots that take the place of people in hazardous environments, where there is strong radiation or toxic chemicals. Robotics engineers also work with airplanes and military weapons that can be controlled remotely.

Most robotics engineers have a background in math, physics, and computers. They are creative, enjoy a challenge, and love to solve puzzles. Robotics engineers generally have a bachelor's degree in a field such as mechanical or electrical engineering. For advanced research, they usually need a master's degree or doctorate.

Research and Report

What are some of the major milestones in the history of space exploration? Research the past 60 years of space exploration. Make a time line showing the highlights. Use sketches or cut pictures from magazines to illustrate your time line, and then share it with your class.

LAB SAFETY
Safety Symbols

These safety symbols are used in laboratory and field investigations in this book to indicate possible hazards. Learn the meaning of each symbol and refer to this page often. *Remember to wash your hands thoroughly after completing laboratory procedures.*

Safety Symbols	Hazard	Examples	Precaution	Remedy
Disposal	Special disposal procedures need to be followed.	certain chemicals, living organisms	Do not dispose of these materials in the sink or trash can.	Dispose of wastes as directed by your teacher.
Biological	Organisms or other biological materials that might be harmful to humans	bacteria, fungi, blood, unpreserved tissues, plant materials	Avoid skin contact with these materials. Wear mask or gloves.	Notify your teacher if you suspect contact with material. Wash hands thoroughly.
Extreme Temperature	Objects that can burn skin by being too cold or too hot	boiling liquids, hot plates, dry ice, liquid nitrogen	Use proper protection when handling.	Go to your teacher for first aid.
Sharp Object	Use of tools or glassware that can easily puncture or slice skin	razor blades, pins, scalpels, pointed tools, dissecting probes, broken glass	Practice common-sense behavior and follow guidelines for use of the tool.	Go to your teacher for first aid.
Fume	Possible danger to respiratory tract from fumes	ammonia, acetone, nail polish remover, heated sulfur, moth balls	Make sure there is good ventilation. Never smell fumes directly. Wear a mask.	Leave foul area and notify your teacher immediately.
Electrical	Possible danger from electrical shock or burn	improper grounding, liquid spills, short circuits, exposed wires	Double-check setup with teacher. Check condition of wires and apparatus.	Do not attempt to fix electrical problems. Notify your teacher immediately.
Irritant	Substances that can irritate the skin or mucous membranes of the respiratory tract	pollen, moth balls, steel wool, fiberglass, potassium permanganate	Wear dust mask and gloves. Practice extra care when handling these materials.	Go to your teacher for first aid.
Chemical	Chemicals that can react with and destroy tissue and other materials	bleaches such as hydrogen peroxide; acids such as sulfuric acid, hydrochloric acid; bases such as ammonia, sodium hydroxide	Wear goggles, gloves, and an apron.	Immediately flush the affected area with water and notify your teacher.
Toxic	Substance may be poisonous if touched, inhaled, or swallowed.	mercury, many metal compounds, iodine, poinsettia plant parts	Follow your teacher's instructions.	Always wash hands thoroughly after use. Go to your teacher for first aid.
Open Flame	Open flame may ignite flammable chemicals, loose clothing, or hair.	alcohol, kerosene, potassium permanganate, hair, clothing	Tie back hair. Avoid wearing loose clothing. Avoid open flames when using flammable chemicals. Be aware of locations of fire safety equipment.	Notify your teacher immediately. Use fire safety equipment if applicable.

Eye Safety	Clothing Protection	Animal Safety	Radioactivity
Proper eye care should be worn at all times by anyone performing or observing science activities.	This symbol appears when substances could stain or burn clothing.	This symbol appears when safety of animals and students must be ensured.	This symbol appears when radioactive materials are used.

METRIC SYSTEM AND SI UNITS

The International System of Measurement, or SI, is accepted as the standard for measurement throughout most of the world. The SI is a modernized version of the metric system, which is a system of measurement based on units of ten. In the United States, both the metric system and the standard system are used.

The SI system contains seven base units. All other units of measurement can be derived from these base units by multiplying or dividing the units by a factor of ten or by combining units.

- When you change from a smaller unit to a larger unit, you divide.
- When you change from a larger unit to a smaller unit, you multiply.

Prefixes are added to the base unit to identify the new unit created by multiplying or dividing by a factor of ten.

SI Base Units

Measurement	Unit	Symbol
length	meter	m
mass	kilogram	kg
time	second	s
electric current	ampere	A
temperature	Kelvin	K
amount of substance	mole	mol
intensity of light	candela	cd

Frequently Used Non-SI Base Units

Measurement	Unit	Symbol
volume	liter, cubic centimeter	L, cm³
density	grams/cubic centimeter, grams/liter	g/cm³, g/L

Common SI Prefixes

Prefix	Symbol	Equivalents
mega-	M	1,000,000
kilo-	k	1000
hecto-	h	100
deka-	da	10
deci-	d	0.1 or 1/10
centi-	c	0.01 or 1/100
milli-	m	0.001 or 1/1000
micro-	μ	0.000001 or 1/1,000,000
nano-	n	0.000000001 or 1/100,000,000,000
pico-	p	0.000000000001 or 1/100,000,000,000,000

STAR CHARTS

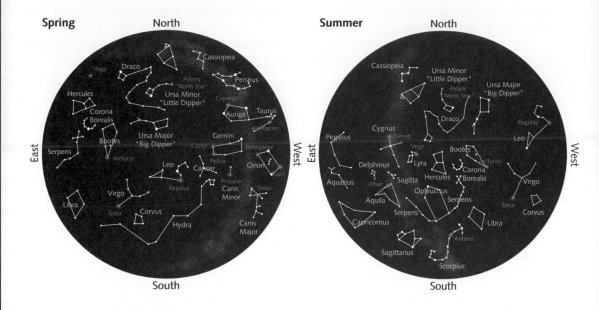

Spring · North · East · West · South

Summer · North · East · West · South

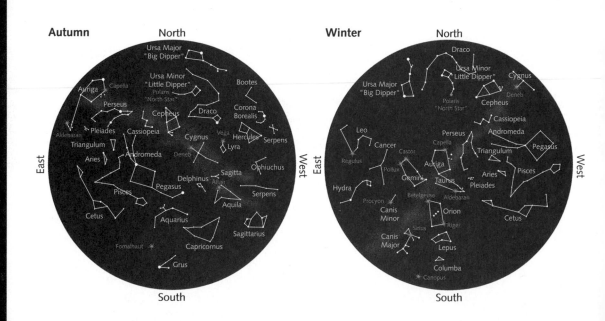

Autumn · North · East · West · South

Winter · North · East · West · South

THE PERIODIC TABLE OF ELEMENTS

PERIODIC TABLE OF THE ELEMENTS

Columns of elements are called groups. Elements in the same group have similar chemical properties.

Element — Hydrogen
Atomic number — 1
Symbol — H
Atomic mass — 1.008

The first three symbols tell you the state of matter of the element at room temperature. The fourth symbol identifies elements that are not present in significant amounts on Earth. Useful amounts are made synthetically.

State of matter
- Gas
- Liquid
- Solid
- Synthetic

Legend (color)
- Metal
- Metalloid
- Nonmetal

The color of an element's block tells you if the element is a metal, nonmetal, or metalloid.

Rows of elements are called periods. Atomic number increases across a period.

The arrow shows where these elements would fit into the periodic table. They are moved to the bottom of the table to save space.

The number in parentheses is the mass number of the longest-lived isotope for that element.

* The names and symbols for elements 111–114 are temporary. Final names will be selected when the elements' discoveries are verified.
** Elements 116 and 118 were thought to have been created. The claim was retracted because the experimental results could not be repeated.

Group	Element	Atomic No.	Symbol	Atomic mass
1	Hydrogen	1	H	1.008
1	Lithium	3	Li	6.941
1	Sodium	11	Na	22.990
1	Potassium	19	K	39.098
1	Rubidium	37	Rb	85.468
1	Cesium	55	Cs	132.905
1	Francium	87	Fr	(223)
2	Beryllium	4	Be	9.012
2	Magnesium	12	Mg	24.305
2	Calcium	20	Ca	40.078
2	Strontium	38	Sr	87.62
2	Barium	56	Ba	137.327
2	Radium	88	Ra	(226)
3	Scandium	21	Sc	44.956
3	Yttrium	39	Y	88.906
3	Lanthanum	57	La	138.906
3	Actinium	89	Ac	(227)
4	Titanium	22	Ti	47.857
4	Zirconium	40	Zr	91.224
4	Hafnium	72	Hf	178.49
4	Rutherfordium	104	Rf	(261)
5	Vanadium	23	V	50.942
5	Niobium	41	Nb	92.906
5	Tantalum	73	Ta	180.948
5	Dubnium	105	Db	(262)
6	Chromium	24	Cr	51.996
6	Molybdenum	42	Mo	95.94
6	Tungsten	74	W	183.84
6	Seaborgium	106	Sg	(266)
7	Manganese	25	Mn	54.938
7	Technetium	43	Tc	(98)
7	Rhenium	75	Re	186.207
7	Bohrium	107	Bh	(264)
8	Iron	26	Fe	55.845
8	Ruthenium	44	Ru	101.07
8	Osmium	76	Os	190.23
8	Hassium	108	Hs	(277)
9	Cobalt	27	Co	58.933
9	Rhodium	45	Rh	102.906
9	Iridium	77	Ir	192.217
9	Meitnerium	109	Mt	(268)
10	Nickel	28	Ni	58.693
10	Palladium	46	Pd	106.42
10	Platinum	78	Pt	195.078
10	Darmstadtium	110	Ds	(281)
11	Copper	29	Cu	63.546
11	Silver	47	Ag	1C7.868
11	Gold	79	Au	196.967
11	Unununium	*111	Juu	(272)
12	Zinc	30	Zn	65.409
12	Cadmium	48	Cd	112.411
12	Mercury	80	Hg	200.59
12	Ununbium	*112	Uub	(285)
13	Boron	5	B	10.811
13	Aluminum	13	Al	26.982
13	Gallium	31	Ga	69.723
13	Indium	49	In	114.818
13	Thallium	81	Tl	204.383
14	Carbon	6	C	12.011
14	Silicon	14	Si	28.086
14	Germanium	32	Ge	72.64
14	Tin	50	Sn	118.710
14	Lead	82	Pb	207.2
14	Ununquadium	*114	Uuq	(289)
15	Nitrogen	7	N	14.007
15	Phosphorus	15	P	30.974
15	Arsenic	33	As	74.922
15	Antimony	51	Sb	121.760
15	Bismuth	83	Bi	208.980
16	Oxygen	8	O	15.999
16	Sulfur	16	S	32.065
16	Selenium	34	Se	78.96
16	Tellurium	52	Te	127.60
16	Polonium	84	Po	(209)
16		**116		
17	Fluorine	9	F	18.998
17	Chlorine	17	Cl	35.453
17	Bromine	35	Br	79.904
17	Iodine	53	I	126.904
17	Astatine	85	At	(210)
18	Helium	2	He	4.003
18	Neon	10	Ne	20.180
18	Argon	18	Ar	39.948
18	Krypton	36	Kr	83.798
18	Xenon	54	Xe	131.293
18	Radon	86	Rn	(222)
18		**118		

Lanthanide series

Element	Atomic No.	Symbol	Atomic mass
Cerium	58	Ce	140.116
Praseodymium	59	Pr	140.908
Neodymium	60	Nd	144.24
Promethium	61	Pm	(145)
Samarium	62	Sm	150.36
Europium	63	Eu	151.964
Gadolinium	64	Gd	157.25
Terbium	65	Tb	158.925
Dysprosium	66	Dy	162.500
Holmium	67	Ho	164.930
Erbium	68	Er	167.259
Thulium	69	Tm	168.934
Ytterbium	70	Yb	173.04
Lutetium	71	Lu	174.967

Actinide series

Element	Atomic No.	Symbol	Atomic mass
Thorium	90	Th	232.038
Protactinium	91	Pa	231.036
Uranium	92	U	238.029
Neptunium	93	Np	(237)
Plutonium	94	Pu	(244)
Americium	95	Am	(243)
Curium	96	Cm	(247)
Berkelium	97	Bk	(247)
Californium	98	Cf	(251)
Einsteinium	99	Es	(252)
Fermium	100	Fm	(257)
Mendelevium	101	Md	(258)
Nobelium	102	No	(259)
Lawrencium	103	Lr	(262)

Glossary/Index

A

Aa lava, 138

Aboriginal Australians, on universe, 396

Abrasion the action of rocks and sediment grinding against each other and wearing away exposed surfaces, 151

    by wind, 179

Absolute dating the process of establishing the age of an object by determining the number of years it has existed, 200–203

    dendrochronology and, 202
    isotopes and, 200
    key beds and, 203
    radiocarbon dating and, 201–202
    radiometric dating and, 201
    varves and, 203

Absolute magnitude the actual brightness of a star, 439

Absorption spectrum, 440

Abyssal plain a smooth, flat region of the ocean floor that is located 5 or 6 km below sea level, 343

Abyssal zone a region that covers the abyssal plain and reaches 6,000 meters in depth, 348

Acid precipitation rain that contains acids due to air pollution, has a pH less than 5, and is harmful to the environment, 152, 384. *See also* Acid rain

    in chemical weathering, 152–153
    pH of, 153

Acid rain, 4, 152, 367, 384

Acids
    from living things, 153
    pH of, 152
    pH scale for, 46

Acoustics, 91

Active solar heating, 368

Active volcano a volcano that has erupted in the last 10,000 years and is likely to erupt in the future, 131, **142**

Adaptation traits that help a species survive and reproduce in their environments, 210

    by fish, 214

Africa
    evolution of hominids in, 223
    Great Rift Valley in, 102

Agriculture, 377–378

Aiken, Ruth, 268

Air
    as gaseous solution, 45
    gases in, 229
    human impact on, 381–385
    motion of, 229
    as natural resource, 361
    saturation of, 250
    weathering from, 299

Air mass a large body of air that takes on the characteristics of the area over which it forms, 254–256

    cold, 255
    map symbols for, 254
    movement of, 255–256
    in tornadoes, 256, 261
    types of, 254–255
    warm, 255

Air mass modification the process of exchanging heat and moisture with the new source region, 256

Airplanes
    in troposphere, 233
    volcanic eruptions and, 286

Air pollution
    acid precipitation and, 384
    catalytic converter and, 385
    chemicals in, 152
    combating, 385
    from fossil fuels, 367
    indoor, 383
    ozone layer and, 383
    worldwide impact of, 382–383

Air pressure weight exerted on a specific area by the column of air above it, 231–232

    data on map, 269
    measurement of, 265
    winds and, 241–245

Alaska, air masses over, 255

Algae, 318, 325, 346
    in coral reefs, 351

Alluvial fan a fan-shaped deposit that forms when the land a river is flowing over flattens very quickly, 305

Alps, formation of, 220

Alternative energy resources, 368–371

Alto clouds, 252

Aluminum, 62
    in Earth's crust, 58

Aluminum ore, bauxite as, 376
Amber, 193
Amphibians, 215
    extinction of, 215
Andesite, 73
Andes mountain range, 105
    climate and, 275, 281
Andromeda galaxy, 449

Anemometer an instrument used to measure the speed of surface winds, 265

Aneroid barometer, 265
Angiosperm, in Cretaceous Period, 219
Anglerfish, 345, 349
Animals
    behavior before earthquakes, 124
    fossils of, 93
    land, 215
    marine, 346
    mechanical weathering caused by, 151
    in Mesozoic Era, 216
    in ocean, 325
    in Precambrian Time, 213
    rock tools made by, 67
    vertebrate, 214
Antarctica
    climate of, 95
    fossil ferns in, 194
    ice sheet in, 174
Antarctic Ocean, 319
Antares (star), 404
Antennae galaxies, 450
Anticlines, 106
Antigravity, 454

Aphelion the position of a planet when it is farthest away from the Sun, 417

Apogee the farthest point the Moon comes from Earth, 402

Apollo 11 mission, 395
    Earth photos from, 423
Appalachian Mountains
    formation and age of, 109
    hot springs of, 314
    in Triassic Period, 216

Apparent magnitude the apparent brightness of a star to observers on Earth, 439

Aquifer a rock layer that stores and allows the flow of groundwater, 313

Aral Sea, 319

Archaeopteryx, 217
Archean Eon, 207, 212
Arctic Ocean, 319, 320
    global warming and, 352
Arctic region
    air masses in, 254, 255
    melting of ice in, 289–290
Arctic soil, 160

Arête a sharp, steep ridge that forms where two cirques on opposite sides of a valley meet, 176

Argon, as elemental matter, 44
Arizona, meteorite crater in, 415
Armero, Colombia, 140

Artesian well a well that is dug into a deep aquifer, 313

Arthropods, ancestors of, 214
Artificial satellites, for gathering information in space, 408
Ash, volcanic, 139, 140–141, 286
Asia, land bridge connecting North America and, 220, 341

Asteroid small, rocky bodies that orbit the Sun, 414–415, 431

    crash into Earth in Cretaceous Period, 203, 206, 219
    environmental changes caused by crash of, 215
    simulations of impacts on Earth, 407

Asthenosphere the part of the upper mantle that can slowly flow, 90

    plate movement and, 100, 101
Astronauts, 409
    on *Apollo 11*, 395
gravity and, 412

Astronomical unit (AU) a unit that is equal to the average distance between Earth and the Sun, 421

Astronomy the study of objects and events beyond Earth's atmosphere; the scientific study of the Sun, the Moon, and other objects in space, 7, 395, 404–409, 439

    computerized simulations for, 407
    Copernicus and, 285
    from space, 408–409
Atacama Desert, Chile, 275

Atlantic Ocean, 319. *See also* Ocean(s)
    after breaking apart of Pangaea, 216
    continental drift and, 92, 93, 94
    overfishing in, 350
    physiographic map of, 343
    tectonic plate boundaries in, 101
    widening of, 96

Atmosphere the layer of mixed gases that surrounds earth, 5, 230

    carbon dioxide in, 288, 382
    collecting weather data in, 266–267
    composition of, 231
    computer models for, 352
    of Earth, 323, 424
    Earth's first, 212
    gases in, 229, 231
    global warming and, 239
    greenhouse effect and, 238–239
    greenhouse gases in, 239
    heat and, 230, 236–240
    heat energy in, 255
    humidity in, 250
    of Jupiter, 427
    layers of, 233–235
    of Mars, 425
    of Mercury, 422
    meteorology as study of, 249
    of Moon, 400
    of Neptune, 430
    ozone and, 381
    ozone layer in, 5
    of Saturn, 428
    solar energy in, 236
    solid particles in, 231
    of Sun, 35, 436
    temperature differences in, 232
    of Uranus, 429
    of Venus, 422, 423
    water in, 249–253
    Atmospheric pressure. *See* Air pressure

Atmospheric science the study of the atmosphere, 6

Atom(s) the smallest unit that makes up matter, 37

    combining of, 41–46
    matter and, 35
    in minerals, 57
    in molecules, 42
    nucleus of, 200
    unstable, 41

Atomic mass the total mass of the protons and neutrons in an atom, 39

of elements, 40

Atomic number the number of protons in an atom, 39

Atomic structure, 38
AU. *See* Astronomical unit (AU)

Aurora a light display that results from charged particles from the Sun colliding with gases in Earth's upper atmosphere, 438

ionosphere and, 235
Aurora australis (southern lights), 235
Aurora borealis (northern lights), 235
Australia
Aboriginal views of universe in, 396
El Niño and, 284
evolution of animals in, 211
Great Barrier Reef of, 351
Australopithecus. See Lucy *(Australopithecus)*, female fossil
Automated Surface Observing System (ASOS), 266
Automobiles
catalytic converter and, 385
energy-efficient, 385
global warming and, 288
nonpoint pollution from, 387

Autumnal equinox a period of time in the southern hemisphere between the winter and summer solstice when the length of day and night begins to even out, 399

Avalanche a landslide that occurs in mountainous areas with thick accumulations of snow, 184

Axis
of Earth, 285, 396, 398
of Uranus, 429

Azimuthal projection a way to accurately show the shortest path between two points by transferring the points and lines on a globe onto a flat piece of paper that touches the globe at only one point, 19

Azores, formation of, 343

B

Bacteria, in deep ocean food chain, 344
Badlands National Park, South Dakota, rills at, 167
Bakker, Robert, 218
Balance, for measuring mass, 12
Bangor, Maine, lumber shipping in, 306

Barometer an instrument used to measure air pressure, 231, 265

Barrier island an island formed from long ridges of sand that are separated from the mainland and deposited or shaped by the longshore current, 171, 340

Basalt, 72, 73
in Earth's crust, 212
in sculptures, 156
Bases
pH of, 152
pH scale for, 46
Basins, ocean, 343

Bathyal zone a region that covers the continental slope and extends from the edge of the continental shelf to the abyssal plain, 348

Bauxite, 376

Baymouth bar a spit that grows and crosses a bay, 171, 340

Bay of Campeche, Mexico, oil spill in, 388
Bay of Fundy, tides in, 334

Beach any area of a shoreline made up of material deposited by waves, 169, 340

efforts to prevent erosion of, 172
sand of, 169
wave action and, 170
Beagle (ship), 210

Bedding the distinct horizontal layers often contained in sedimentary rocks, 76

Bedrock the layer of rock found underneath soil, 158

soil formation and, 159
Bees, coevolution with flowering plants, 219

Bell Labs, 453
Belts, around Jupiter, 427

Benthic environment the ocean floor and all the organisms that live on or in it, 345, 347–348

Benthos organisms that live on or in the ocean floor, 346

Bering Land Bridge, 341

Big bang theory the theory that the universe began from a tiny point and has continually increased in size, 452, 453, 455

Binoculars, 406
Bioluminescence, 349

Biomass the total amount of plant or animal matter on Earth that could be converted to fuel, 364

Biomass fuel fuel that comes from living things, 364, 365

Biosphere all of the living things on Earth and their environments, 6

geographers and, 7

Bipedal having two feet and walking upright, 222, 223

Birds
in Cenozoic Era, 220
in Jurassic Period, 217
wetlands and, 311
Bivalve, cast of, 192
Black and white smokers, in ocean floor, 97
Black Elk (Oglala Lakota tribe), on tornadoes, 262

Black hole the extremely dense remains of the gravitational collapse of a star, 445, 455

Bog an area of soaked, spongy soil that may not be covered in standing water, 310, 365

acidic water in, 365
Bonds. *See* Chemical bonds
Bones
fossil, 194
in mammal's necks, 221
Bonneville, Lake, 320

Glossary/Index

Boundaries
    convergent, 101, 102–103
    divergent, 102
    transform, 104
Bower, Amy, 321
Brain (human), development of, 222, 223

Breaker a collapsing wave near the shoreline, 333, 339

Breakwaters, beach erosion and, 172
Breathing, oxygen and carbon dioxide in, 361
Breezes
    mountain and valley, 245
    sea and land, 244–245
Bridalveil Falls (Yosemite National Park), 176
Brightness, of stars, 439
Buffalo, New York, snow in, 277
Buffalo waste, as fuel, 364
Buildings, earthquake-resistant, 126
Bush Administration, Kyoto Protocol and, 385

C

Calcite, 58
    luster of, 60
Calcium carbonate, 152
    deposits in caves, 315

Caldera a large depression in the ground resulting from the explosion or collapse of a volcano, 135

California
    El Niño and, 284
    water supplies in, 309
California Current, 276, 328, 329
California grunion, tides and, 335
Calories, specific heat measured in, 277

Cambrian explosion the sudden appearance of a large number of new species in the oceans, 214

Canada
    acid precipitation and, 384
    air masses over, 255
Canals, 303
Cancer, radiation used to treat, 202
Canyons, submarine, 342
Cap-and-trade system, 291

Carbon
    atoms in diamonds, 37
    from gasoline burning, 385
    isotopes of, 200
    in oceans, 6
Carbon-12, 200
Carbon-14, 200
    half-life of, 201
    used to date fossils, 201

Carbonaceous film a film made of carbon or carbon-containing compounds that takes the shape of the original organism, 193

Carbon dioxide (CO_2), 361
    in atmosphere, 231, 288
    in chemical weathering, 152
    emission reduction policies, 291
    emissions of, 288–289
    in fire extinguishers, 50
    global warming and, 382
    as greenhouse gas, 239
    increase in emissions of, 240
    mass extinction and decrease in, 215
    in ocean water, 324
    released by decaying plants, 156
    U.S. production of, 289
    from volcanic eruptions, 212
Carbonic acid, 152, 315
    stalagmite and stalactite formations and, 152
    weathering of rocks and, 156
Carbon monoxide, from cars, 385

Carbon sequestration a technology where carbon gases are captured and stored underground, 291

Cardinal directions, 18
Cars. *See* Automobiles
Cascade Range, 103, 109
Cassini (spacecraft)
    Jupiter views by, 427
    Saturn views by, 428

Cast sediment that hardens into rock and takes the shape of its mold, 192

    of organism, 192
Catalytic converter, 385
Category 5 hurricane, Katrina as, 263

Cave a large, naturally hollowed-out space in or above the ground, 315

    formation of, 152
    formations in, 58
Celsius temperature scale, 13

Cementation a process that occurs when dissolved minerals in water form crystals and cement sediment together to form solid rock, 74

    in sedimentary rock formation, 74

Cenozoic era the present era where mammals, including modern humans, evolved, 209

    human origins in, 222–223
    ice ages during, 220–221
    mammals rise in, 221
    Neogene Period of, 220
    Paleogen Period of, 220
    Quaternary Period of, 220
Centimeters, 12
Ceratopsians, 219
Ceres (asteroid), 431
Cerro Tolo Inter-American Observatory, Chile, 442
CFCs. *See* Chlorofluorocarbons (CFCs)
Challenger (ship), ocean expedition by, 323

Channel a sloping pathway in which water flows, 300

Charon (moon), 431
Chase, Owen, 349

Chemical bond a force that holds two atoms together, 41–43

    covalent, 42
    ionic, 42–43
    metallic, 43
Chemical changes, in matter, 47
Chemical equations, 51
Chemical formulas, 45
    list of common substances, 45

Chemical reaction a process during which one or more substances are turned into one or more new substances, 50

    temperature increases and, 155

Chemical sedimentary rock rock formed when water evaporates from oceans and lakes, leaving behind dissolved minerals, 75

Glossary/Index

Chemical symbols, 36

Chemical weathering the breakdown of rocks and minerals due to changes in their chemical composition, 152–153

climate and, 155
surface area of rocks and, 157
Chemistry
acids and bases in, 46
of minerals, 56
Chemosynthesis, 344
Chernobyl, Ukraine, nuclear accident in, 371
Chile
Atacama Desert in, 275
desert climate in, 281
largest earthquake in, 121
China, CO_2 emissions from, 289
Chloride, in ocean salt, 324
Chlorine
atoms from CFCs, 383
sodium and, 43
Chlorofluorocarbons (CFCs), 5, 383
Chloroplasts, 213

Chromosphere the layer of the Sun's atmosphere located above the photosphere, 436

Cinder cone volcano a small volcano with steep sides that forms on the sides of shield and composite volcanoes, 134

of Sun, 435

Cirque a bowl shaped depression that is carved out by glaciers, 176

Cirro clouds, 252
Cirrus clouds, 252
Cities and towns
development of, 379
as microclimates, 281
Classification
of Earth's climates, 278
of hurricanes, 263, 264
of matter, 44–45
of tornadoes, 262

Clastic sedimentary rock rock made of fragments of previously existing rocks, 75

Clasts, 76
Clean Air Act (1970), 385
Clean Water Act (1972), 389
Clear-cutting, 378

Cleavage the result when a mineral breaks smoothly and evenly along one or more planes of weakly bonded atoms, 61

of minerals, 61
Cliffs, wave-cut, 170

Climate the weather patterns of an area over a long period of time, 272, 273

during Cenozoic Era, 220–221
changes in, 210, 282–286
classification of Earth's, 278–281
continental, 280
cooling of, 219
dendrochronology used to determine changes in, 202
for dinosaurs, 219
dry, 279
Earth's orbit and, 284
El Niño and, 283–284
as evidence of continental drift, 95
global warming and, 288–291
human impacts on, 287–291
information from fossils about, 194, 195
localized, 281
map of, 278
mild, 279–280
oceans and, 326–327
Pangaea formation and, 215
polar, 280
seasons and, 283
soil formation and, 160–161
sunspots and, 286
topography and, 275–276
tropical, 278–279
varves used to determine temperature changes in, 203
volcanic effect on, 140
weathering and, 155–157
Climate zones, 274
"Cloud, The" (Shelley), 253

Cloud a collection of millions of tiny water droplets or ice particles, 241, 251

Earth's radiation balance and, 239
formation of, 251
interstellar, 413
in Jupiter's atmosphere, 426, 427
in literature, 253
shapes of, 253
in thunderstorms, 259
types of, 252
water vapor and, 231

weather information about, 268
Clusters, of stars, 451

Coal a solid brownish-black rock that is formed from plants, 76, **366**

continental drift and, 95
mining of, 376
as nonrenewable resource, 363
Coastal deltas, 169
Coastal erosion, and deposition, 169
Coastlines, depositional features of, 171
Coast redwoods (*Sequoia sempervirens*), 216
Cod, overfishing of, 350
Coevolution, 219
Cold air masses, 255
Cold front, 257
Color, of minerals, 60
Colorado River
Grand Canyon and, 299
sedimentary rock deposited by, 197
Columbia Plateau, as lava plateau, 135
Coma Berenices constellation, 450

Comet small bodies made of ice and rock, 415, 431

Earth's surface and, 323
Halley's, 415
oceans and, 212
Swift-Tuttle, 414
Communicating, of scientific results, 11
Communication satellites, 408
Compaction, in sedimentary rock formation, 74
Compass rose, 21

Composite volcano a volcano that forms from alternating layers of lava and volcanic rocks and ash, 134

Composition the minerals in a rock, 69

of rocks, 69

Compound materials that contain two or more chemically combined elements, 44

ionic, 45
minerals as, 56
Comprehensive Everglades Restoration Plan (CERP), 311

Compression the stress that occurs when something is squeezed, 105

    in earthquakes, 115

Computer models, in oceanography, 352

Computer science, for astronomy predictions, 407

Conchoidal fracture, 61

Conclusions, drawing, 11

Condensation the process of water changing from a gas to a liquid, 250, 298

Conduction the transfer of energy between objects that come into direct contact with one another, 237

Cone-bearing trees. *See* Conifers

Conic projection a way to map small areas by transferring the points and lines from a globe onto a cone, 18–19

Conifers, evolution of, 216

Conservation

    of natural resources, 363

    of soil, 162–163

    of water, 389

Conservation of mass, law of, 51

Constellations, 404, 434

Contact metamorphism magma comes in contact with solid rock and causes the texture and mineral composition of the rock to change, 79

Continental climates, 280

Continental-continental convergent boundaries, 103

Continental crust, 88, 102

Continental Divide, 302

Continental drift Alfred Wegener's hypothesis that proposed that all of Earth's continents were once joined together as a single landmass, 92, **93**–95, 199

    climatic evidence of, 95

    fossil evidence of, 94

    rock formation evidence of, 94

    seafloor spreading and, 95–98

Continental glacier ice sheets that cover broad continent-sized areas, 173, **174**, 175

Continental margin the submerged part of a continent, 341

Continental plates, collision by, 103

Continental polar air masses, 254, 255

Continental rise a gently sloping feature at the foot of the continental margin, 342

Continental shelf the shallowest region of the continental margin that lies closest to the shoreline, 341

Continental slope the region of the continental margin where the ocean floor becomes very steep, 342

Continental tropical air masses, 254, 255

Continents

    Earth's crust in, 212

    motion of, 92–98

    movement of, 220

Contour interval the difference in elevation between one contour line and the next, 23

Contour line a line on a topographic map that connects points that all have the same elevation, 22

    index contours and, 24

    as peaks and depressions, 25

Contour plowing, 163

Control group the group in an experiment in which you change only one variable at a time, 10

Controlled experiment an experiment in which you change only one variable at a time, 9

Convection the transfer of energy by the flow of a heated substance, 100, 237

Convection cell the circular patterns caused by the rising and sinking of air, 241

Convection current, 237

Convective zone the region of the Sun where the Sun's energy is carried the rest of the way to its surface by convection currents and heat is transferred, 436

Conventional energy resources, 364–367

Convergent boundary a boundary where two tectonic plates push into one another and meet, 102

    of tectonic plates, 102–103, 104

    volcanoes at, 132, 136

Convergent motion, in earthquakes, 115

Copernicus, Nicolaus, 285, 416

Copper

    chemical composition of, 56

    mining of, 376

    as nonrenewable resource, 362

Coral(s), 213, 214, 217

    fossils of, 76

Coral bleaching the whitening of coral colonies due the death of the algae that live within healthy corals, 351

Coral reefs, 351

Core the layer of Earth that extends from the mantle to the center of Earth; the region of the Sun where energy is produced, 89, 436

    of Earth, 5, 89

    magnetic field created by, 209

    of Sun, 436

Coriolis effect the deflection of the wind's direction due to Earth's rotation, 242, **328**, 329

    global winds and, 243

Corona the outermost layer of the Sun's atmosphere, 436, 437, 438

    of Sun, 435

Correlation the matching of rock layers from one geographic region to another, 199

    of rock layers, 199

Corundum, hardness of, 63

Cosmic background radiation low-level radiation from space, 453

Cosmology the study of the universe, how it formed, and its future, 396

Covalent bond the bond that forms between two atoms that share electrons, 42

Cover crop, 162

Crabs, 346

Crater the bowl-shaped depression formed by a volcanic explosion, 135

    impact, 401

    on Moon, 401

    volcanic, 135

Crater Lake, as caldera, 135

Creep the slow, steady downhill flow of loose, weathered soil, 185

Crest he highest point of a wave, 332

    of wave, 333

Cretaceous Period the final period of the Mesozoic Era where mass extinction made dinosaurs extinct and ended the era, 219

    angiosperms in, 219

    dinosaurs in, 219

    mass extinction in, 219

Cro-Magnons, 223

Crop(s)

    as biomass fuel, 365

    monoculture and, 377

Crop rotation the practice of changing the type of crop grown in a field from one year to the next, 163, 378

Cross-cutting relationship a principle that states that a band of rock that intrudes across rock layers must be younger than those layers, 198

Crustaceans, 349

    overfishing of, 350

Crust the outer layer of Earth, 88

    of Earth, 5, 67, 88–89, 212

    continental, 102

    faults and, 108

    formation of ocean, 96

    hot spots beneath, 133

    movement of, 87

    oceanic, 101, 102

    rock cycle and, 81

    rocks in, 97

    tectonic plates in, 99

    at transform boundaries, 104

    volcanoes and, 140

Cryptogamic soil, 162

Crystal a solid substance whose atoms are arranged in a specific repeating pattern, 57

    in igneous rocks, 73

    in lava, 72

Cumulonimbus clouds, 252, 259

Cumulus clouds, 252

Curie, Marie, 202

Currents, 275–276, 328–331

    dead zones and, 351

    deep-ocean, 331

    global warming and, 329

    longshore, 340

    temperature changes in, 353

    turbidity, 342

Cyanobacteria single-celled, ocean-dwelling organisms, 213

Cycads, 214

Cycles

life cycles of stars, 443–445

    of resources, 66

    of rock, 80–81

    of tides, 347

    of water, 250, 298

Cyclones, 262

Cyprus trees, 310

D

Dams, 303

    for hydroelectric power, 369

Dante II robotic volcano explorer, 143

Darwin, Charles, 210

Data

    analyzing, 10

    collecting, 10

Dating. *See* Absolute dating; Relative dating

David (Michelangelo statue), 81

Days

    Earth's rotation and, 397

    on Jupiter, 426

    length of, 13, 399

    on Neptune, 430

Dead Sea, water in, 331

Dead zone a region that forms when the oxygen levels in the water become so low that the water can no longer support significant populations of living things, 351, 353, 388

Death Valley, 161

    alluvial fan in, 305

    desert pavement in, 179

Decay, eutrophication of lakes and, 308

Decaying plants

    chemical weathering by, 153

    weathering and, 156

Decomposers, 161

Decomposition, of organic material, 161

Deep-focus earthquakes, 122

Deep-ocean currents, 331

Deep-sea trench the deepest part of the ocean basin, 96, 342, **343**

    maps of, 96

    in subduction zone, 103

Deflation the lowering of the land surface resulting from the wind's removal of surface particles, 179

Deforestation the cutting down of forests, which leads to increased levels of CO_2 in the atmosphere, 288, 378

Deformation the changing of a rock's shape due to stress, 105

    rock, 114

Deimos (moon), 424

Delta a triangular deposit of silt and clay that forms when a stream enters a large body of water, 169, 305

Dendrochronology the science of comparing yearly growth rings in trees to date events and changes in past environments, 202

Density a measure of the mass per unit volume of a material or object, 13, 61

    formula for, 13

    of minerals, 61

of ocean water, 326
of Saturn, 428
of Sun's core, 436

Density current a current that forms when ocean waters with different temperatures and salinities meet, 331

Dependent variable the variable that is observed to find out if it changes as a result of the independent variable, 10

Deposition a process that occurs when layers of sediment sink to the bottom of bodies of water and build up, 74, 167, 304

    erosion and, 166–185
    by groundwater, 315
    in sedimentary rock formation, 74
    in streams and rivers, 304–306
    water erosion and, 167–172
    by wind, 180
Depositional ocean features, 340
Depressions, on contour maps, 25
Deserts
    Atacama, 275
    climate of, 281
    Sahara, 279
Desert soil, 161
Detergents, water damage from, 387
Deuterium, as hydrogen isotope, 39
Devonian Period
    mass extinction in, 215
    seed plants in, 214
    vertebrates in, 214

Dew point the temperature at which air is completely saturated, 251

Diamonds
    in Canada, 73
    carbon atoms in, 37
    chemical composition of, 56
    density of, 61
    as elemental matter, 44
    hardness of, 62, 63
    laboratory-made, 363
    luster of, 60
    as nonrenewable resources, 362
Diatoms, 346

Differential weathering the process by which some rocks weather faster than others, 154

Dinosaur a four-legged reptile that lived in nearly every land habitat, 217

    in Cretaceous Period, 219
    discovery of, 218
    fossils of, 77, 191
    in Jurassic Period, 217
Diorite, 73
Directions, on maps, 18, 21

Discharge a measure of the volume of stream water that flows over a specific location in a particular amount of time, 301

    by stream, 301
Disturbances, tropical storms as, 264

Divergent boundary a boundary between two tectonic plates that are moving away from each other, 102

    of tectonic plates, 101, 102, 104
    volcanoes at, 132
Divergent motion, in earthquakes, 115

Divide a high land area that separates one watershed from another, 302–303

Doldrums the belt of low pressure circling the globe around the equator, 244

Dome mountain a mountain that is formed when Earth's crust heaves upward without folding or faulting occurring, 109

Doppler effect the change in wave frequency that occurs in energy as it moves away from an observer, 267

Dormant a state of inactivity, 142

    volcanoes, 142
Drawing conclusions, 11
Drumlins, 177
Dry climate, in deserts, 275, 279, 281
Ductile deformation, 114

Dune piles of sand formed from the blowing of wind in the same general direction, 180

Dust Bowl, 362
Dwarf galaxy, 449

Dwarf planet an object that orbits the Sun and has a nearly round shape, 426, 430–**431**

Ears, pressure and, 231
Earth, 395, 423–424. *See also* Atmosphere; Geologic time; specific subjects
    age of, 192
    ancient surface of, 323
    asteroid crash into, 203, 206
    climate information from fossils, 194, 195
    climate of, 283, 284
    climates on, 278–281, 282–286
    composition of, 88
    crust of, 212
    development of living things on, 209
    effect of clouds on, 239
    elements on, 36–40
    energy from atmosphere, 239
    energy from Sun, 239
    expansion of universe and, 453
    features of, 7
    first atmosphere of, 212
    human-caused changes to, 221
    iron core of, 209
    layers of, 88–89, 90
    length of day on, 13
    locating places on, 19–20
    magnetic field of, 209
    mapping of, 16–29
    in Milky Way galaxy, 449
    natural resources of, 359–371
    orbit of, 283, 284, 396, 398
    in Paleozoic Era, 214–215
    photo of, 4
    as planet, 396–399
    position in solar system, 209
    position in space, 396
    in Precambrian Time, 212–213
    properties of, 400
    radiation balance of, 239, 240
    reasons for living things on, 209
    rock types on, 67–69
    rotation of, 328, 396–397
    star's distance from, 442
    structure of, 90
    studying history of, 191–203
    Sun of, 435–438
    systems on, 3, 4–6

tectonic plates and changes in species on, 209
tides and, 334, 335, 403
tilt of, 285, 398
volcanic eruptions and atmosphere of, 209
water cycle on, 298–299
wobble of, 285
Earth-centered model. *See* Geocentric model

Earthquake the shaking of the ground caused by sudden movement of matter within Earth, 91, 112–127, **113**

animal behavior before, 124
buildings resistant to, 126
causes of, 114
damage from, 125–126
data for, 10
along faults, 104, 198
focus of, 113, 122
GIS for, 29
measuring and locating, 118–122
predicting, 123, 124–125
safety preparation for, 126–127
society and, 123–127
strength and depth of, 115, 122
tsunamis and, 117
worldwide frequency of, 124
Earth science
branches of, 6–7
defined, 4
East Africa, Great Rift Valley in, 102
Eastern hemisphere, 20
Eclipses, solar and lunar, 403

Ecliptic the path that Earth takes around the Sun, 398

path, 398
Ecology, 309
maps for, 29
Ecosystems
of coral reef, 351
invasive alien species in, 309
maps of, 29
Egret, 310
Einstein, Albert, 437
special relativity theory and, 455
Elastic deformation, 114

Elastic rebound the return of elastically deformed rock to its original shape after the rock has experienced enough stress to cause it to break, 114, **115**

Electric charges, of atoms, 37

Electricity
generated by wind, 229
hydroelectric power for, 369
from methane, 380
from natural gas, 366

Electromagnetic radiation a light that is made up of electric and magnetic disturbances that travel through space as waves, 405

Electromagnetic spectrum a spectrum that contains all of the types of electromagnetic radiation organized by their wavelengths and frequencies, 405

Electromagnetic waves, 117

Electron a tiny particle that has a negative electric charge, 37

atomic structure and, 38
in metallic bonds, 43
Electronic balances, 12

Elemental matter a material that is made up of a single kind of element, 44

Element a substance that cannot be broken down into simpler substances by normal physical or chemical means, 36–40

atomic numbers of, 39
organizing, 40
periodic table of, 40
in planets, 414
in Sun, 435
symbols of, 36
Elephants, loss of habitat, 221

Elevation the distance of a location or object above sea level, 22, 275

index contours and, 24
on maps, 22

Ellipse a closed curve with an oval shape, 416

Elliptical galaxy a smooth, regularly shaped galaxy that does not have a spiral arm, 450

nebulas in, 451

Elliptical a pattern of rotation that describes the Earth's rotation around the Sun, 284

orbit, 284

of Earth, 284
of Moon around Earth, 402
of planets, 415, 416–417

El Niño a warm ocean current that develops off the western coast of South America every two to seven years, 283–284, **330–331**, 353

Emissions
carbon dioxide, 288–289, 290–291
nonpoint pollution from, 387
Emperor Seamount Islands, 133
Endangered species, sand dune lizards as, 181
Energy
adding to matter, 49
conservation of, 290–291
conversion of matter into, 437
from earthquakes, 114, 115
from fossil fuels, 367
geothermal, 371
of moving water, 168
nuclear, 371
from nuclear fission, 202
remote sensing of, 26
removing from matter, 49
solar, 368–369
from stars, 434
from Sun, 236, 250, 362, 437
theory of special relativity and, 455
from water, 369
wind, 370
worldwide use of (2000), 366
Energy efficiency, 290
Energy resources, 364
alternative, 368–371
conventional, 364–367
Environment. *See also* Global warming
acid precipitation and, 384
agriculture and, 377–378
air quality and, 381–385
ecosystems and, 309
greenhouse effect and, 287, 382
human impact on resources and, 374–389
making fuel from trash, 370
marine, 338–353
in ocean life zones, 345
in ocean's deep waters, 325
urban development and, 379
water pollution and, 386–389
Environmental Protection Agency (EPA), 385
methane gas and, 370

Eon a unit of time that is measured in billions of years, 207

in Precambrian Time, 207

Epicenter the point on Earth's surface directly above the focus of an earthquake, 113

    of earthquakes, 114
    locating, 119

Epoch the division of periods, 209

Equations, chemical, 51
Equator, latitudes and, 19, 20, 274
Equinoxes, 398, 399

Era a unit of time that is measured in hundreds of millions to billions of years, 207

    in Phanerozoic Eon, 209
Erie Canal, 303
Eris (Pluto-sized body), 431

Erosion the movement of soil or sediment from one location to another by forces such as water, wind, and gravity, 162, 299

    beach, 172
    deforestation and, 378
    deposition and, 166–185
    in farming, 377
    by glaciers, 173–177
    of Grand Canyon, 166
    by groundwater, 315
    and meanders, 304
    moving water and, 299
    reduction of, 162, 163
    reforestation and, 379
    in sedimentary rock formation, 74
    of shoreline, 339
    by streams, 301
    water erosion and deposition, 167–172
    wave, 170
    wind erosion and deposition, 178–181
Eruptions, 132, 136–139, 286
    Earth's atmosphere and, 209
    inclusion formed after, 198
    key beds formed after, 203
    of Mount St. Helens, 185
    predicting, 142–143
    strengths of, 137

Eskers long, winding ridges of sediment, 177

Essex (ship), 349

Estuary a wetland connected to the ocean where freshwater and salt water meet, 311

Ethanol, 365
Eurasian milfoil, 309
Eurasian Plate, 132
Europe, split from Greenland, 220
Eusthenopteron, 215

Eutrophication the process by which a lake becomes overly rich in nutrients that are washed in from the surrounding watershed, 308

    Eurasian milfoil and, 309

Evaporation the process of water changing from a liquid to a gas, 48, 49, 50, **250**

    density currents and, 331
    mineral formation through, 58
    of water, 298
    water salinity and, 324
Evening Star, Venus as, 422
Everglades, restoration of, 311
Evidence, from fossils, 194

Evolution a change in the characteristics that are passed on from one generation to another in a population as a result of environmental change, 210

geography of, 211

Exfoliation the process during which outer rock layers are stripped away, **151**

    of rocks, 151
Exit Glacier (Kenai Fjords National Park), 177

Exosphere the outermost layer of Earth's atmosphere, 235

Experiment
    controlled, 9
    safety for, 11

Experimental group the group in an experiment in which the independent variable is changed, 10

Extinctions
    in Cretaceous Period, 219
    in Paleozoic Era, 214, 215

Extinct no longer living or in existence, 211

    species, 211

Extinct volcano a volcano that has not erupted for tens of thousands of years, 142

Extrusive igneous rock rock that forms from molten material that has cooled and crystallized close to or on Earth's surface, 71

Eye of hurricane, 264

 F

Fahrenheit temperature scale, 13
Fall (of earth material), 182
Farming
    practices of, 377–378
    in temperate climates, 161

Fault-block mountain a mountain that is formed when land on one side of a normal fault drops down relative to the land on the other side, **108**

Fault the surface along which rocks break and slide past each other, **106**–107

    cross-cutting relationships applied to, 198
    as transform boundaries, 104

Fault zone an area where complex patterns of faults exist due to tectonic plate movement, 113

Feldspar, in granite, 154
Ferns
    fossils of, 194, 195
    of Paleozoic Era, 214
    in Triassic Period, 216
Fertile soil, 362
Fertilizers
    eutrophication and, 308
    in farming, 377
    as nonpoint pollution, 387
Field crops, as biomass fuel, 365
fig trees, 221
Filaments, in universe, 454
Filter feeders, 346
Fire extinguishers, carbon dioxide in, 50
First Law, of Kepler, 416–417
Fish
    in Cenozoic Era, 220
    dead zones and, 351
    in Devonian Period, 214

fossils of, 194
in Jurassic Period, 217
as marine life, 346
overfishing in oceans and, 349, 350
tides and, 335
Fishing, in upwellings, 330
Fissures, on Earth's surface, 135
Flies, 217
Flooding, 305
managing, 306
urban development and, 379

Floodplain an area where floodwater collects on the broad, flat areas near streams and rivers, 305

Florida
cyprus trees in, 310
Everglades in, 311
humidity in, 251
lake formation from sinkholes, 315
weathering in, 155
Flounder, overfishing of, 350

Flow mass movement that occurs when Earth materials flow like thick syrup, 182, **184**

Flowering plants
bees coevolution with, 219
in Cenozoic Era, 220
evolution of, 219

Focus the underground location where an earthquake occurs, **113**

of earthquake, 122
Fog, 249

Folded mountain a mountain that is formed when rock layers are pushed together and fold upwards, 108

Folding occurs when stress from tectonic forces causes rock layers to bend, 106

Foliated metamorphic rock rock that contains wavy layers and sometimes bands of minerals, 80

Food chain, in deep ocean, 344
Food supply, of ocean animals, 325
Food webs, in oceans, 338
"Fool's gold," pyrite as, 59
Footprints, fossil, 193
Footwall, 106
Forecasts, weather, 248, 249, 265–269
Forest fires, from lightning strikes, 260

Forests
reforestation and, 291
tropical rainforests, 278
Formulas
chemical, 45
for minerals, 57
Fossil footprints, 193

Fossil fuel a nonrenewable resource that forms over millions of years from the compression and partial decay of plants and other once-living matter; fuel such as oil, coal, and natural gas that release CO_2 into the atmosphere when burned, 288, 363, 366–367

coal as, 366
global warming and, 382
impacts of, 367
large scale burning of, 240
natural gas as, 367
petroleum as, 366

Fossil the preserved remains or traces of a once-living organism, 67, 76, 192

absolute dating of, 200–203
in amber, 193
buying and selling of, 195
carbonaceous film and, 193
of dinosaurs, 191, 218
as evidence of continental drift, 93
formed by freezing, 193
index fossil, 199
information about Earth's climate from, 194, 195
lessons from, 194
Lucy (*Australopithecus*), 222
molds and casts, 192
oldest, 213
paleontology and, 77
permineralization and, 193
petrification and, 192, 193
radiocarbon dating of, 201–202
relative dating and, 196–199
trace fossil, 193

Fracture the result when a mineral breaks in random places, 61

Freezing, 48
fossil formation by, 193
mechanical weathering by, 150

Frequency the number of waves per second, **405**

of earthquakes, 124
of electromagnetic radiation, 405

Fresh air, as natural resource, 361
Freshwater, 297–314
frozen, 249
groundwater as, 312–315
as resource, 361
supplies of, 309
Friction, water movement speed and, 300

Front a narrow region separating two air masses of different densities, 257

cold, 257
occluded, 258
stationary, 258
warm, 257

Frost wedging a physical action that causes a rock to split apart, 150

in high mountains, 155

Fuel material that is burned to provide power or heat, 364

biomass, 364
fossil, 288, 363, 366–367
from trash, 370
Fujita tornado intensity scale, 262

Fusion the combining of lightweight nuclei into heavier nuclei, 437

in stars, 444

 G

Gabbro, 69, 73
Gagarin, Yury, 409

Galaxy a star system that consists of a large group of stars, planets, and other space objects, 448–455, 449

collisions of, 449, 450
expansion of universe and, 453
features of, 451
groups of, 449
redshifts of, 454
types of, 450
Galilean satellites, Jupiter's moons as, 427
Galilei, Galileo, 285
telescope and, 406
Gap Analysis Program, 29
Garbage, environment and, 379
Gaseous solution, 45

Gases, 49
　In air, 230
　in atmosphere, 5, 229, 231
　atmospheric water as, 249
　in Earth's first atmosphere, 212
　greenhouse, 287
　as matter, 36
　measurement in liters, 12
　in ocean water, 324
　physical changes in state of, 49
　plasmas as, 48
　Sun composed of, 435
　volcanic, 138–139
　water vapor as, 231

Gas giant planet a large planet that does not have a solid surface, 414, **420**, 426

Gasoline. *See also* Air pollution; Petroleum
　air pollution from burning, 385

Gemstone minerals that are valued for their beauty, durability, and rarity, **63**, 362–363

General theory of relativity, 455

Geocentric the older model of the universe that stated that the Sun, planets, and stars revolved around Earth, **416**

Geographic information system (GIS) a computer-based tool for representing information on maps, **29**

Geographic north pole, 21

Geography the study of Earth's features, such as mountains, rivers, and oceans, and the distribution of life on Earth, **7**

　of evolution, 211
Geologic time, 206–223
　beginning of life in, 213
　Cenozoic Era in, 220–223
　circle graph of, 207
　divisions of, 207–209
　eons of, 207
　epochs of, 209
　eras of, 207
　evolution in, 210
　humans in, 223
　mass extinctions in, 211
　measurement of, 211
　Mesozoic Era in, 216–219
　Paleozoic Era in, 214–215

periods of, 209

Geologic time scale a time line that divides Earth's history into specific time periods, **207**, 208

Geology the study of anything having to do with the solid Earth, 7. *See also* Rock(s)
　computer models for, 352
　of ocean floor, 321

Geothermal energy energy produced by naturally occurring steam and hot water beneath Earth's crust, **371**

Geyser a hot spring that shoots steam and water vapor into the air at regular intervals, **314**
　geothermal energy and, 371
　hydrothermal vents as, 344
Giant sequoia tree, 221
Giant stars, 443
Ginkgo trees, 217
Giraffes, 221
GIS. *See* Geographic information system (GIS)
Glacier National Park, 290

Glacier large mass of ice, **173**
　continental, 173, 174
　continental drift and, 95
　creation of landscapes by, 175
　deposits of, 177
　erosion by, 173–177
　evidence left by, 221
　formation of, 173
　lake formation from, 307
　landscape features carved by, 176
　in last ice age, 220
　melting of, 289, 290
　movement of, 174
　valley, 173, 174
　world distribution of, 173

Global Positioning System (GPS) a tool that allows people to find their exact locations on Earth, **28**, 104

Global warming a gradual rise in global temperatures caused by greenhouse gases; the rise in Earth's average surface temperature, 195, **239**, 287, 288–291, **382**
　advancing ocean waters from, 352

combating of, 290–291
consequences of, 289 290, 383
from fossil fuels, 367
human impact on, 288–289
melting of ice caps and, 289
ocean currents and, 329
ocean protection and, 353
polar ice cap and, 320
Global winds, 243
　polar easterlies, 243
　pressure belts and Coriolis effect and, 243
　prevailing westerlies, 243
　trade winds, 243

Globular cluster a group of older stars that is found near spiral and elliptical galaxies, **451**

Glossopteris fossil, 93, 95
Gneiss, 68, 80
Gods, planets named for, 428
Gold
　chemical composition of, 56
　discoveries of, 59, 73
　mining of, 376
　as nonrenewable resource, 362
　pyrite and, 59
　specific gravity of, 61
　streak of, 60
Gold Rush (1849), 59
GPS. *See* Global Positioning System (GPS)

Gradient a measure of the change in elevation over a certain distance, **301**, 302, 303, 305
　of stream or river, 301
Grams, 12
Grand Canyon
　creation of, 299
　dating fossils in rock layers of, 196, 197
　rock layers of, 197
　weathering and erosion of, 166
Granite, 68, 81, 150, 151
　composition of, 69
　in Earth's crust, 212
　formation of, 71
　minerals in, 154
　polishing of, 156
　in sculptures, 156
　sedimentary rock from, 76
Granitic rocks, 72
Graphite, density of, 61
Grasses, cold weather and, 221
Grasshoppers, 217
Grasslands, 221

Gravitation, Newton's Law of, 418
Gravity, 412, 421
    abrasion caused by, 151
    acceleration of, 418
    Antennae galaxies and, 450
    antigravity and, 454
    of black hole, 445
    erosion and deposition and,
        182–185
    in galaxies, 449
    on Mars, 424
    of Moon, 400, 403
    movement of glaciers and, 173
    of planets, 414
    stream and river flows and, 300
    of Sun, 403, 414
    tides and, 334
    weathering and, 156
Great Barrier Reef, 351
Great Dark Spot, on Neptune, 430
Great Lakes
    creation of, 221
    formation of, 307
    snow and, 277
Great Red Spot, on Jupiter, 427, 430
Great Rift Valley, 102
Great Salt Lake, 320
Great white egret, 310
Greek gods, planets named for, 428
Greensburg, Kansas, tornado in, 261

Greenhouse effect the natural
heating of Earth's surface caused
by certain gases in the atmosphere,
238–239, 287, **382**

    on Earth, 424
    on Mars, 425
    on Venus, 423

Greenhouse gases gases in the
atmosphere that absorb heat to
prevent it from escaping into space,
239, 287

    carbon dioxide as, 212, 215
    increase in, 240
    methane as, 370
    reducing, 385
Greenland, split from Europe, 220
Green River Formation (Wyoming),
    freshwater fish fossils in, 194
Green roofs, 281
Greenwich meridian, 20, 397
Grinnell Glacier, 290

Groundwater freshwater that is
contained within the rock layers
below Earth's surface, 4, **312–315**,
388

    erosion and deposition by, 315
    pollution of, 388
Gulf of Mexico, Mississippi River and,
    305
Gulf Stream, 276, 329

Gully a wide, deep channel, **167**

Gypsum, 58

Gyre a closed, circular current
system that helps even out Earth's
temperature differences, **328**

H

Habitat the natural conditions
and environment in which an
organism lives, **345**. *See also* Marine
environment; specific habitats

    clear-cutting and, 378
    destruction by dams, 369

Hadal zone the deepest benthic
zone that consists of the deep-ocean
trenches, **348**

Haddock, overfishing of, 350
Hadean Eon, 207, 212
Hail, 250, 253, 260

Half-life the time it takes for
one-half of a radioactive sample to
decay, **201**

    of carbon-14, 201
Halite, 152
Hance Rapids (Grand Canyon), cross-
    cutting relationship in rocks at, 198

Hanging valley a valley that forms
when a smaller valley from higher
up on a mountainside meets a larger
U-shaped valley, **176**

Hanging wall, 106

Hardness a measure of how well a
mineral resists to being scratched,
62

Hawaiian Islands
    formation of, 344
    lava flows in, 136
    mongooses on, 211
    Pacific hot spot and, 133
    volcanoes in, 130, 132, 133, 134,
      136
Hawaiian nene, 211
Hawking, Stephen, 455
Hazardous wastes, disposal of, 389
Headlands, wave erosion and, 170
Health, indoor air pollution and, 383
Heat
    compared to temperature, 232
    convection and, 100
    and Earth's atmosphere, 236–240
    in metamorphic rock formation,
      80
    specific, 277
    transfer by conduction, 237
    transfer by convection, 237
    in volcanoes, 132
    Zeroth Law of Thermodynamics
      and, 238
Heat energy
    distribution in atmosphere, 255
    in hurricanes, 262–263
Heating (solar), active and passive, 368

Heat island a city area that has a
warmer climate than its surrounding
rural areas, **281**

Heliocentric the model of the
universe that states that Earth and
the other planets orbited the Sun,
285, **416**

Helium, 48
    in Earth's first atmosphere, 212
    as element, 38
    in exosphere, 235
    in stars, 441
Hematite
    chemical composition of, 56
    luster of, 60
Hemispheres, on Earth, 20, 283, 285
Henry, Todd, 442
Herschel, William, 429

Hertzsprung-Russell diagram a
graph that shows the relationship
between different classes of stars,
443

Heterogeneous mixtures, 44
Himalayas, 103
    formation of, 220
History of Earth. *See also* Geologic
    time
    study of, 191–203
Holocene (Recent) Epoch, 220

Hominid a term that applies to humans and human ancestors, 222

Australopithecus, 222
evolution in Africa, 223
Homo erectus, 222
Homo habilis, 222
Homo sapiens, 223
skulls of, 222
success of, 223
Homo erectus, 222
Homogeneous mixtures, 45
Homo habilis, 222
Homo sapiens, 223
age of, 454

Horn a steep peak in the shape of a pyramid, 176

Horse latitudes the belt of high pressure that circles the globe, 244

Horses, evolution of, 210, 221

Hot spot a break in Earth's crust through which magma erupts, 133

Hot spring a spring that produces water with temperatures higher than that of the human body, 314

hydrothermal vents as, 344
Hubble, Edwin, 450, 453
Hubble Space Telescope, 7, 408, 445, 450
Virgo galaxy cluster photo by, 449
Hudson River, submarine canyon and, 342
Hudson River School of painting, 108
Human remains, in bogs, 365
Humans
climate and, 287–289
demand for water by, 309
earth's resources and, 374–389
eutrophication and, 308
global warming and, 288–289
origins of, 222–223
space exploration by, 409

Humidity the amount of water vapor present in the air, 250

measuring, 266
relative, 250–251
in subtropical climates, 279
temperature and, 251

Humus bits of decayed plant and animal matter that is found in soil, 158

arctic soils and, 160

Hurricane a large, rotating, low-pressure storm that forms over warm tropical waters, 262

classification of, 263, 264
damage from, 264
formation of, 262–264
Katrina, 262, 306
Hybrid cars, 385
Hydrocarbons, 385

Hydroelectric power electricity produced by flowing water, 369

Hydrogen
deuterium isotope of, 39
in Earth's first atmosphere, 212
as element, 38
in exosphere, 235
in stars, 441
in water, 50
Hydrogen atoms, in hydrogen molecule, 42

Hydrology the study of water and how it moves on Earth, 7

Hydrosphere all of the water on Earth, 4

Hydrothermal metamorphism water heated by volcanic activity dissolves minerals, breaks them down, and deposits new minerals, 80

Hydrothermal vent a geyser, or hot spring, that erupts on the ocean floor, 97, **344**

Hygrometer an instrument that uses wet- and dry-bulb thermometers to determine relative humidity, 266

Hypothesis a proposed explanation for an observation, 9

Ice, 231
erosion from, 299
mechanical weathering by, 150
in oceans, 320
in snow, 253

Ice age a period where large sheets of ice covered much of our planet's surface, 176, **221, 282–283**

during Cenozoic Era, 220–221
erosion during, 299
ice sheets during, 282
information from fossils about, 195
lake formation during, 307
oceans during, 341
volcanic effects on, 140

Iceberg a large mass of floating ice, 320

freshwater composition of, 321
Ice caps, 249
melting of, 289, 320
Ice cores, measuring greenhouse gases in, 239
Iceland
formation of, 343
in mid-ocean ridge, 132
Ice pack, near poles, 320
Ice sheets. *See* Continental glaciers
Ichthyosaurs, 216

Igneous rock a rock that forms when magma cools and crystallizes, **68**, 70–73

classifying, 71–73
formation of, 70, 71, 198
intermediate, 73
mineral composition of, 72
in rock cycle, 81
texture of, 71
transformation to metamorphic rock, 78

Impact crater a crater that is formed when objects from space crash into the moon's surface, 401

Inca, terracing by, 163

Inclusion a piece of one type of rock that is surrounded by another type, 198

Glossary/Index

Independent variable a variable that is changed, 9, **10**

Index contour every fifth contour line on a topographic map, 24

Index fossil a fossil that is used to date rock layers, **199**

Indian Ocean, 319
    tropical cyclones and, 262
    tsunami in, 117, 333
Indoor air pollution, 383
Industrial Revolution
    carbon dioxide emissions of steam
        engines in, 240
    coal dust during, 239

Inertia the tendency of an object at rest to remain at rest and of an object in motion to stay in motion, **418**, 419

Information, from artificial satellites, 408
Infrared radiation
    electromagnetic waves as, 117
    telescopes for, 407
Infrared satellite images, for weather tracking, 268

Inner core the solid center of Earth, **91**

Inner planets, 414, 420–425

Inorganic substances that are not made of plant or animal matter, **56**

    minerals as, 55
Insects
    in Cenozoic Era, 220
    in Cretaceous Period, 219
    as first land animals, 215
    in Jurassic Period, 217
Integrated Ocean Drilling Program (IODP), 89

Intensity a measurement of how much damage the earthquake causes to structures in a particular location, **121**

Interglacial interval the alternation of ice ages and warmer periods, **283**

Intermediate igneous rocks, 73
International Astronomical Union,
    planet defined by, 431
International Date Line, 397

International Ice Patrol, 320
International Space Station, 230, 409

International System of Units (SI system) a system of measurement that is used by most countries throughout the world and in almost all scientific activities, **13**

Internet, fossils sold on, 195

Interstellar cloud a huge cloud made up of gas and dust, **413**

Intertidal zone the region of the shoreline that is located between the low tide and high tide lines, **347**

Intrusion, in sedimentary rocks, 198

Intrusive igneous rock rock that forms when magma that pushes into surrounding rocks and crystallizes underground, **71**, 72

Ion an atom with an electric charge, **39**, 235

    in ocean water, 324

Ionic bond the result of two atoms with equal and opposite charges combining to form a bond, **42–43**

Ionic compounds, chemical formulas for, 45

Ionosphere a layer of the atmosphere that lies within the thermosphere where potentially harmful solar energy is absorbed, **235**

Iridium, in key beds, 203
Iron Age, 62
Iron ore, 62
    mining of, 376

Irregular galaxy a galaxy that does not have a normal, uniform, or symmetrical shape, **450**

Irrigation the application of water by humans to land to assist in the production of crops, **309**

Island arcs, 103
Islands
    barrier, 171
    in Pacific Ocean, 133

Isobar lines of equal pressure on a weather map, **269**

Isopleth lines that connect points of equal value on a weather map, **268–269**

Isotherm lines of equal temperature on a weather map, **269**

Isotope atoms of the same element that have different numbers of neutrons, **39**, 200

    of carbon, 200
IXTOC I oil spill, 388

Japan, volcanic eruptions in, 142
Jason (satellite), 322
Jellyfish, 213

Jet stream narrow band of fast, high-altitude, westerly winds that blow in the upper troposphere and in the lower stratosphere, **244**

Jetties, beach erosion and, 172
Johanson, Donald, 222
Journey to the Center of the Earth (Verne), 89
Jupiter, 414, 426
    belts around, 427
    naming of, 428
    volcanoes on moon of, 133
Jurassic Park movies, 218

Jurassic Period the middle period of the Mesozoic Era when oceans began to form and dinosaurs lived, **217**

    dinosaurs in, 217

Katrina (hurricane), 262, 263, 306
Keith, Carl D., 385
Kepler, Johannes, 416
    First Law of, 416–417
    Second Law of, 417
    Third Law of, 417
Kettles, 177

Key bed a layer of sedimentary rock that acts as a time marker to compare rock layers in regions located far from one another, **203**

Kilauea, 133

Kilograms, 12
Kilometers, 12
Kinetic energy, in atoms, 155
Kinichilite, 63
Kobe, Japan, earthquake in, 121
Koeppen, Wladimir, 278

Koeppen classification system
a system that uses temperature
and precipitation to divide Earth's
climates into six major types, 278,
279

Korea, earthquake safety drill in, 127
Krakatau, 140
Kuiper belt, 415
Kyoto Protocol, 385

 L

Lagoons, 171

Lahar a mudflow that occurs as a
result of a volcanic eruption, 184

  after Mount St. Helens eruption,
  185

Lake a depression in the land that
collects and holds water, 307–309.
See also specific lakes

  changes in, 308
  eutrophication of, 308
  evaporation from, 250
  formation of, 307
  from melted glaciers, 221
  runoff in, 299
Lake Baikal, 307
Lake Bonneville, 320
Lake Champlain, zebra mussels in, 309
Lake-effect snow, 277
Lake Placid, topographic map of, 24
Land
  change in geologic time, 210
  human impact on, 375–380
Land animals, in Paleozoic Era, 215
Land breezes, 244–245
Land bridge, 220, 341
Landfills, 380
  in cities, 379
  methane gas from, 370
Landforms
  carved by valley glaciers, 176
  carved by waves, 170
  coastal, 171
  divides and, 302
  erosion, deposition, and, 166–185
  glacier formation of, 173

Land plants, development during
  Ordovician Period, 214
Landsat 7 (satellite), 26
Landscapes
  carved by glaciers, 176
  creation by glaciers, 175
  Hudson River School of painting
  of, 108
  volcanic influence on, 140
Landscaping, water for, 389

Landslide the sudden and rapid
movement downhill of a block of
soil, rock, and debris, **184**, 299

  forecasting of, 184
Land surface temperatures, differences
  in (2000–2005), 240
Languages, development of, 223
La Niña, 330–331
Lapilli, magma as, 139

Lapse rate the rate at which the
temperature within the troposphere
decreases; temperature decreases
about 6.5°C for every kilometer of
altitude, **233**

Large Magellanic Cloud, 445

Latitude lines that are used to
measure distance north or south of
the equator, **19**–20, 21, 274

Lava magma that flows out onto
Earth's surface, 70, **131**

  as erupted material, 138
  formation of igneous rocks by, 198
  pumice and, 72
  types of, 138
  volcanic eruption strength and,
  137
Lava plateau, 135
Lavoisier, Antoine, law of conservation
  of mass of, 9, 51

Law of conservation of mass
the idea that mass cannot be created
or destroyed during a chemical
reaction, 9, **51**

Laws (scientific)
  of conservation of mass, 51
  of Kepler, 416–417
  Newton's Law of Universal
  Gravitation, 417–418
  Newton's laws of motion, 419
Layers, ocean, 326

Leaching the downward transport
of nutrients and minerals from the
topsoil to the lower horizons, **159**

Leeward the side of the mountain
where dry air warms as it descends,
275

Legend, on map, 25
Lehman, Inge, 120
Length, meter as measure of, 12

Levee a high ridge built along a
riverbank, **306**

Libby, Willard, 200, 201
Lichens, 214
  chemical weathering by, 153
Liebig, Justus von, 159
Life. *See also* Ocean(s); specific forms
  beginning of, 213, 335
  Earth's systems and, 6
  in marine environment, 6,
  338–353
Life cycles, of stars, 443–445
Life spans, of organisms, 211
Life zones, in oceans, 345–349
Light
  on deep ocean floor, 344
  from distant galaxies, 454
  electromagnetic radiation as, 405
  ocean absorption of, 325
  spectrum of visible, 440
  from stars inside nebula, 413
  telescopes and, 406
  theory of special relativity and,
  455
Light Detection and Ranging (LIDAR),
  to forecast landslides, 184

Lightning electricity caused by the
rapid rush of air in a cumulonimbus
cloud, **260**

Light waves, 117
  from quasars, 451

Light-year a unit that equals the
distance that light travels in one
year and is used to measure long
distances in space, **421**

Limestone, 75, 76, 152
  caves in, 315
  in sculptures, 156
Liquids
  atmospheric water as, 249
  density of, 13
  as matter, 36
  measuring, 12

physical changes in state of, 48
water as, 231
Liquid solution, 45
Liquid water, on Mars, 425
Liter, 12
Literature, clouds in, 253

Lithosphere the hard, outer shell of Earth; the layer of Earth made up of the crust and the solid portion of the upper mantle, 5, 90

creation of, 91
plates in, 99
Living things
chemical weathering by, 153
eutrophication and, 308
natural resources for, 374
in ocean waters, 325, 345–349
as renewable resources, 360, 361
Lizards, sand dune, 181

Load the materials carried by a stream's water, 301

Local Group, of galaxies, 449
Local winds, 243
Locations
GPS for, 28
naming of, 21
Locks, on canals, 303

Loess fine, wind-blown silt deposits, **181**, 221

Loess Hills, 181
Logging, 378
-logy (word part), 194
Loihi (volcano), 133
Loma Prieta earthquake, 112, 113

Longitude lines that are used to measure distance east or west of the equator, **20**, 21, 397

Longshore bar a sandbar that is formed when waves slow down and lose energy, thereby depositing sand on the beach, 170

Longshore current a current produced when water from incoming waves flows over the longshore bar, 170

Longshore trough, 170
Long Valley Caldera, Red Cones on, 134

Lower mantle the hot, solid part of the mantle that lies between the asthenosphere and the outer core, 91

Lucy *(Australopithecus)*, female fossil, 222
Lumber shipping, on rivers, 306

Luminosity the measure of energy output per second from the surface of a star, 440

Lunar eclipse an eclipse that occurs when Earth's shadow blocks sunlight and the Moon becomes dark, 403

Luster the shininess of a mineral, 60

M87 galaxy, 450
M100 galaxy, 450
Magellan (spacecraft), views of Venus by, 422, 423

Magma melted rock found beneath the Earth's surface, 58, 70, **131**

chemical composition of, 71
formation of igneous rock by, 198
in hot spots, 133
intrusive igneous rocks and, 72
lava compared with, 138
on ocean floor, 96
tides in, 403
volcanic eruptions and, 136, 137
Magma intrusions, 198
Magnesium, 57

Magnetic declination the angle of correction at a particular location between magnetic north and true north, 21

Magnetic field
of Earth, 96, 209
of Jupiter, 427
of Neptune, 430
reversal of, 98
of Saturn, 428
of Sun, 438
of Uranus, 429
Magnetic north pole, 21
magnetic reversal in, 98

Magnetic reversal the change in position of Earth's magnetic poles, 98

Magnetometer, 96

Magnitude a measurement that describes the amount of energy released during an earthquake, 121

of earthquakes, 121, 124
of stars, 439

Main sequence a diagonal pattern of stars that runs from the top-left to the bottom-right of a Hertzsprung-Russell diagram, 443

Majuro Island, 340
Mammals
in Cenozoic Era, 209
in Jurassic Period, 217
neck bones of, 221
primate order of, 222
rise of, 221–222
warm-blooded, 219
Mammoth Cave, 152
Mantle convection, 100

Mantle the layer of Earth between the core and the crust, 5, **89**, 91

tides in, 403

Map a representation of a certain area or part of an area, 17

air pressure on, 269
climate, 278
compass rose on, 21
defined, 17
directions on, 21
of Earth's oceans, 319
of Earth's time zones, 397
ecology and, 29
GIS for, 29
of ice age, 282
latitudes on, 19
locating places on, 19–20
longitude on, 20
mapmaking technology and, 26–29
of ocean floor, 96
as projections, 18–19
of rainfall and climate patterns, 17
topographic, 22–25
understanding of, 17–21
weather, 268
of windpower in U.S. states, 370

Map legend a part of a map that explains what the symbols used on the map represent, 25

Map scale a scale that tells how big or small a map is in comparison to the area it represents, 21

Mapping
    of Earth, 16–29
    satellites for, 408
Marble
    composition of, 69
    as nonfoliated rock, 80
    for sculpture, 81, 156
Marine environment, 338–355. *See also* Ocean(s)
    groups of organisms in, 346
    life zones in, 345–349
    protection of, 353
Mariner 10, Mercury photos by, 421, 422
Marine west coast climate, 280
Maritime air masses, 254
    polar, 254, 255
    tropical, 254, 255
Mars, 424–425
    distance from Sun, 421
    naming of, 428
    photo of, 408
    space probes of, 408
    volcanoes on, 133
    water on, 7
Mars Exploration Rover Mission, 408, 425

Marsh a treeless wetland characterized by grassy vegetation, 310

Mass the amount of matter in an object, 12

    atomic, 39
    gravity and, 421
    law of conservation of, 51
    of Moon, 400
    of outer planets, 426
    of Pluto, 430
    of protons, neutrons, and electrons, 37
    of stars, 441, 443, 444
    of terrestrial planets, 420
    theory of special relativity and, 455

Mass extinction the extinction of a large number of species due to a severe environmental change, 211

in Paleozoic Era, 215

Mass movement the downslope movement of loose sediment and weathered rock resulting from the force of gravity, 182

    factors affecting, 182
    fall, 182
    flow, 182
    slide, 182
    types of, 183–185
    water and, 183
Massive star, life cycle of, 445

Matter anything that has mass and takes up space, 36

    atoms and, 35
    changes in, 47–51
    chemical equations for, 51
    classifying, 44–45
    conservation of mass and, 51
    conversion into energy, 437
    elemental, 44
Matterhorn, 176
Mauna Kea, height of, 135
Mauna Loa, as cinder cone volcano, 134
Maunder, E. W., 286

Meander a bend or curve in a stream channel caused by moving water, 304

Measurement
    of earthquakes, 121
    scientific, 12–13
Mechanical waves, 117

Mechanical weathering the breakdown of rocks into smaller pieces by some physical action, 150–151

    climate and, 155
    surface area of rocks and, 157
Medicine
    computer models for, 352
    sound waves in, 322
Mediterranean climate, 280
Medium star, life cycle of, 444
Megalosaurus, 218
Melting, 48, 50
    of rocks, 70
Meltwater, 177
Melville, Herman, 349
Mendeleev, Dmitri, 40
Mercalli scale, for earthquakes, 121, 122

Mercator projection a way to show all of Earth on one continuous piece of paper by transferring the points and lines of a globe onto a cylinder of paper, 18

Mercury, 421–422
    distance from Sun, 421
    length of day on, 13
    naming of, 428
Meridians, 20
Mesosaurus, 93
    fossils of, 199

Mesosphere the third and coldest layer of the atmosphere, 235

Mesozoic era a period of time when dinosaurs inhabited Earth, 207

    Cretaceous Period in, 219
    dinosaurs in, 217, 218
    Jurassic Period in, 217
    Triassic Period of, 216
Messenger (spacecraft), 422

Metallic bond a bond where all of the electrons are shared by all of the atoms, 43

Metals, 362

Metamorphic rock a rock that forms from extreme heat, pressure, or chemical reactions, 68, 78–81, 198

    formation of, 78
    in rock cycle, 81
    textures of, 80

Metamorphism the process of change from one form to another, 78

    types of, 79–80

Meteor the light that results from a meteoroid entering Earth and burning up, 415

    metamorphism from, 79
Meteors, in mesosphere, 235

Meteor shower particles from a comet that burn up and fall from the sky, 415

    Perseid, 414

Meteorite the remaining part of a meteor that does not burn up and consequently hits Earth, 408, 415

    water in, 322

Meteoroid a fragment of an asteroid or any material that falls from space toward Earth and enters Earth's atmosphere, 415

Meteorology the study of weather patterns in the atmosphere; the study of atmospheric objects, such as clouds, raindrops, snowflakes, and fog, 6, 249

    computer models for, 352
Meter, as measure of length, 12
Methane, 370
    as greenhouse gas, 239
    in landfills, 380
Metric system, 12
Miami Beach, beach cliff erosion and, 172
Mica, cleavage of, 61
Michelangelo, marble statue by, 81

Microclimate a small area with a climate that is different from the climate of the larger region that surrounds it, 281

Mid-ocean ridge a chain of tall volcanic mountains in the ocean basin, 135, **343**

Mild climates, 279–280
Military satellites, 408
Milky Way galaxy, 449
    as spiral galaxy, 450
Milligrams, 12
Milliliters, 12
Mineraloids, 57

Mineral a naturally formed, inorganic, solid substance that has definite chemical composition and a crystal structure, 54–63, **55**

    characteristics of, 55–57
    as compounds, 56
    on continental shelf, 341
    crystal structure of, 57
    definite chemical composition of, 56–57
    dissolving of, 58
    Earth's magnetic field and, 98
    formation of, 58
    formulas for, 57
    as gemstones, 63
    identifying, 59–63
    in igneous rocks, 72, 73
    inorganic nature of, 56
    in magma, 70

    in metamorphic rocks, 80
    mining of, 375–376
    natural formation of, 56
    in ocean water, 324
    from rocks, 153
    in rocks, 69
    as solids, 56
    surface mining of, 376
    uses of, 62–63
    weathering of, 151
Mineral salts, in desert soils, 161

Mining the process of taking mineral resources from the ground, 375–376

    runoff pollution from, 387
    surface, 376
    underground, 376
Minneapolis, Minnesota, temperatures in, 327
Minutes, of latitude, 20
Mississippi River
    delta at mouth of, 305
    drainage into, 302–303
    meanders in, 304
    snakehead fish in, 309

Mixture the result of two or more materials that are combined in a nonchemical way, 44

    hetergeneous, 44
    homogeneous, 45
Moby Dick (Melville), 349

Modified Mercalli intensity scale a scale that rates the types of damage and other effects of an earthquake based on observation, 122

Mohs, Friedrich, 62
Mohs hardness scale, 62, 63
Moisture, weathering and, 155

Mold a hollow space in rock that has the shape of an organism or its parts, 192

Molecule two or more atoms that are held together by covalent bonds, 42

    chemical formula for, 45
    temperature and air molecules, 232
Mollusks, 214, 217, 349

Moment magnitude scale a scale that measures the strength of earthquakes, 121

Mongooses, 211
Monoclines, 106

Monoculture the cultivation of one type of crop in a particular area, 377

Montreal Protocol on Substances That Deplete the Ozone Layer (1983), 383
Moon (of Earth), 395, 400–401
    apparent motion of, 397
    astronauts on, 409
    characteristics of, 400–401
    gravity of, 403
    origin of, 401
    phases of, 402
    properties of, 400
    surface features of, 401
    temperatures on, 238
    tides and, 334, 335, 400, 402
Moon(s), 431
    of Jupiter, 427
    of Mars, 424
    of Neptune, 430
    of Saturn, 428
    of Uranus, 429
Mooney, John J., 385
Moon rocks, 408

Moraines ridges that form on a glacier when till is deposited on its edge, 177

Mosasurs, 216
Motion
    in earthquakes, 115
    Newton's laws of, 419
    planetary, 416–419

Mountain breeze cool air that is drawn in from the slopes of a mountain, 245

Mountains. *See also* specific mountains and ranges
    building of, 105–109
    climate and, 275
    creation of, 102–103
    dome, 109
    fault-block, 108
    folded, 108
    formation of, 79
    frost wedging in, 155
    in lithosphere, 5
    in Triassic Period, 216
    types of, 107–109

valley glaciers in, 174
volcanic, 109
weathering and, 149
Mount Etna, 130
Mount Everest, height of, 135
Mount Fuji, as composite volcano, 134
Mount Mazama, 132
Mount Pelée, 140
Mount Pinatubo, 143
Mount St. Helens, 109, 132, 140
as composite volcano, 134
erupted material from, 135
eruption of, 185, 203, 286
volcanic eruption on, 137
Mount Tambora, 140
Mount Unzen, 140

Mudflow fast-moving mixture of mud and water, 184

Mudslide, 299
Mudstone, 76, 77
Myths, about volcanoes, 132

Naming
of locations on Earth, 21
of planets, 428
Nantucket Island, remote sensing image of, 27
National Aeronautics and Space Administration (NASA)
Mars Exploration Rover Mission and, 425
on polar ice cap, 289
National Ambient Air Quality Standards (NAAQS), 385
National Hurricane Center, 264
National Oceanic and Atmospheric Administration (NOAA), 353
National Weather Service
forecaster at, 268
tornado warnings from, 262
Native Americans
Bering Land Bridge crossed by, 341
petroglyphs of wetland birds by, 311
tornadoes and, 262
on universe, 396
volcano myths of, 132

Natural gas a mixture of gases that accumulates underground, 367

electricity generation from, 366
as nonrenewable resource, 363

Natural resource any substance, organism, or form of energy that is used by living things and is not made by humans, 359–371, **360**

conservation of, 363
off continental shelves, 341
conventional energy resources, 364–367
cycles of, 66
human impact on, 374–389
nonrenewable, 362–363
renewable, 360–362
soil as, 162

Natural selection the theory that environmental factors affect the way adaptations develop, 210

Nature, wetlands in, 311
Navigation
GPS for, 28
wind rose and, 245
Neandertals, 223

Neap tide a weak tide that occurs when the Sun and the Moon form a right angle with the Earth, 334

Nebula interstellar cloud that is made up of hydrogen, helium, carbon, and iron, **413**, 444, 451

Necks, of mammals, 221

Nekton organisms that swim freely in ocean waters, 346

Neogene Period the second period of the Cenozoic Era, 220

NEOImpactor, 407
Neptune, 414, 426, 430
naming of, 428

Neritic zone a region that includes the warm and shallow waters over continental shelves, 349

Neutron a neutral particle that does not have any electric charge, 37

in isotopes, 39, 200

Neutron star a large star that is extremely dense, **445**

Nevado del Ruiz, 140
eruption by, 140, 143
New Mexico
sand dune lizards in, 181
weathering in, 155

New Orleans, flooding in, 306
New River Gorge (valley), 168
Newton, Isaac, 419
Law of Universal Gravitation, 418–419
laws of motion, 419
Niche, for mammals, 221
Nickel coin, as solid solution, 45
Nights
Earth's rotation and, 397
length of, 399
Nile River, delta of, 169
Nimbo- (prefix), 252
Nimbostratus clouds, 252
-nimbus (suffix), 252
Nimbus clouds, 252
Nitrogen
in atmosphere, 231
cycle of, 66
in human wastewater, 388
in ionosphere, 235
in ocean water, 324
from volcanoes, 212
Nitrogen oxide, 152, 385
Nitrous oxide, as greenhouse gas, 239
NOAA. See National Oceanic and Atmospheric Administration (NOAA)

Nonfoliated metamorphic rock rock that does not appear to have any regular pattern, 80

Nonpoint source a source of water pollution that generates pollution from more widespread sources and locations, 387

Nonrenewable resource a resource that cannot be replaced or that can only be replaced by natural processes over thousands or millions of years, 362–363

Normal fault a fault that occurs when the hanging wall of a fault moves down relative to the footwall, **107**, 115

North America. See also specific locations
continental climates in, 280
during last ice age, 220
split from Greenland, 220
tectonic plate boundaries of, 101
temperatures in January, 273
in Triassic Period, 216
North American Plate, 132

North Anatolian Fault Zone, 113
North Atlantic Current, 329
Northern hemisphere
    circulation of current in gyres in, 329
    solstices in, 399
    summer and winter in, 283
Northern lights, 209
North pole
    geographic, 21
    latitude of, 19
    magnetic, 21
    magnetic reversal in, 98
Notation, scientific, 440
Nuclear accidents, 371

Nuclear energy an alternative source of energy associated with changes in the nucleus of an atom, 371

Nuclear fission, 202
Nuclear power plants, 202

Nucleus the center of an atom where all of the protons and neutrons are contained, 38

    differences in, 200
Nutrients
    off continental shelves, 341
    eutrophication and, 308
    in monoculture, 377
    in oceans, 324, 325
    replacing in soil, 163
    in soil, 362, 378
    in upwelling ocean waters, 330

Oasis, 314
Observations, data collection with, 10
Obsidian, 72
Occluded front, 258

Ocean a vast body of saltwater, 318, 319. *See also* Global warming

    advancing waters of, 352
    changes in, 320, 323, 350–353
    climate and, 275–276, 326–327
    continental margins and, 341
    continental shelf and, 341
    depositional features of, 340
    edge and floor of, 339–344
    and erosion and deposition, 169
    evaporation from, 250
    formation of, 212, 322–323
    freshwater and, 297

    habitats in, 345
    layers of, 326
    life zones in, 345–349
    light absorption in, 325
    longshore currents in, 170
    marine environment and, 338–353
    motions of, 328–329
    near poles, 320
    nutrients in, 324, 325, 330
    pollution of, 321, 388
    Precambrian plants and animals in, 213
    predators in Mesozoic, 216
    properties of water in, 324–327
    protection of, 353
    technology for studying, 321–322
    temperature profile of, 326
    tides in, 334
    tsunamis in, 117, 333
    wave erosion and, 170
    waves in, 332
Ocean basin, 343
Ocean currents, 275–276
Ocean floor. *See also* Seafloor spreading
    divergent boundaries on, 102
    hydrothermal vents in, 97, 344
    images of, 96, 97
    organisms living on or near, 346
    rock samples from, 97
    spreading of, 95–98
    studying, 321–322
Oceanic-continental convergent boundaries, 102, 103
Oceanic crust, 88, 89, 102
Oceanic-oceanic convergent boundaries, 102–103

Oceanic zone a region that includes all of the water that covers the sea floor except for the continental shelf, 349

Oceanographers, global warming and, 352

Oceanography the study of Earth's oceans, 6, 321

Ocean trenches, 103
Ocean water, upwelling of, 330
Oil. *See* Petroleum
Oil spills, 388
    liability fund for, 341
Old Faithful geyser, 314, 371
Olivine, 57
Olympus Mons, 425
Onomatopoeia, 223

On the Origin of the Species (Darwin), 210
Oort cloud, 415
Opal, as mineraloid, 57

Open cluster a small group of young stars that is found in spiral arms, 451

Orbit the path that one object in space takes around another, 398

    of Earth, 283, 284, 396, 398
    elliptical, 416
    of Mars, 424
    of Moon, 401–402
    of outer planets, 426
    of planets, 415, 416–417
    of terrestrial planets, 420
    of Uranus, 429

Orbital period the time it takes for the planet to make one complete revolution around the Sun, 416

Ordovician Period
    life on land during, 214–215
    mass extinction in, 215

Ore a material that can be removed from the ground for a profit, 62

    mining of, 376
Oregon, dead zone off coast of, 351
Organic materials, decomposition of, 161
Organic matter, in bogs, 365

Organic sedimentary rock rock formed from the remains of once-living organisms, 76

Organism, life span of, 211
Organisms. *See also* Plants
    beginning of first, 213
    fossils of, 192, 193
    growth after volcanic eruptions, 141
    marine, 345–349
    weathering and, 156

Original horizontality a principle that states that the sediment that forms sedimentary rocks is deposited in flat or nearly flat layers, 197

Orion Nebula, 413
Ortelius, Abraham, 92
Outer Continental Shelf Lands Act (1953), 341

Outer core the outer, liquid layer of the core, 91

Outer planets, 414, 426–431
    properties of, 426
Outer space, ocean study from, 322

Outwash particles that have been eroded, carried, and deposited by meltwater streams, 177

Overburden, 376

Overfishing to fish a body of water extensively and decrease the overall population of certain species of fish, 349, **350–351**

Owen, Richard, 218
Oxbow lake, 304

Oxidation the chemical reaction of oxygen with other substances, **153**

Oxygen, 230, 361
    in air, 229
    in atmosphere, 231
    chemical weathering by, 153
    from cyanobacteria
        photosynthesis, 213
    in Earth's crust, 58
    in eutrophication, 308
    in ionosphere, 235
    ocean dead zones and, 351
    in ocean water, 324
    production in oceans, 325
    in water, 50

Ozone a gas formed by the addition of a third oxygen atom to an oxygen molecule that is present in two layers of the atmosphere, **234**, 381

    in air, 229
    in troposphere, 234
Ozone layer
    hole in, 5
    thinning of, 383

P

Pachycephalosaurus, 219
Pacific Ocean, 319. *See also* Ocean(s)
    California Current in, 276
    climate and, 327
    deep-sea trenches in, 343
    hot spots in, 133
    island arcs in, 103
    Ring of Fire in, 132

Pacific Plate, 133
Pack ice, 320
Pahoehoe lava, 138
Paint, as mixture, 44
Painting, of American landscapes, 108
Paleo- (prefix), 194

Paleogene Period the first period in the Cenozoic era, 220

Paleontologist a scientist who studies fossils, **194**

Paleontology, 77
    meaning of, 194

Paleozoic era a period of time when the first fish, land plants, and air-breathing animals evolved, **207**

    Cambrian Explosion in, 214
    end of, 215
    land animals in, 215
    land plants in, 214
    mass extinctions in, 215
    vertebrates in, 214
Palm trees, 221
Pangaea, 93, 94, 96
    Atlantic Ocean as ridge on, 102
    breaking apart of, 216
    mass extinctions and formation
        of, 215
    mountain formation and, 109
Parallax, 441–442

Parent material the type of material that is the source of soil, **158**

Particulate pollution, 381
Passive solar heating, 368
Peaks, on contour maps, 25

Peat a light and spongy material made from dead and decaying plant materials, **365**

Peat moss, 310

Pelagic environment all of the water in the ocean and the marine organisms that live above the ocean floor, **345**

Pele (Hawaiian volcano goddess), 132
Penobscot River, 306

Penumbra the outer portion of the Moon's shadow, where some of the Sun's light reaches Earth, **403**

    of Sun, 437
Peridotite, 73

Perigee the closest point the Moon comes to Earth, **402**

Perihelion the position of a planet when it is closest to the Sun, **417**

Periodic table of the elements, 40

Period a small time span that is distinguished by plant and animal life, **209**

Permafrost, global warming and, 352

Permeability the ability of a material to let water pass through it, **313**

Permineralization a process where mineral-rich water seeps into pore spaces of an organism's bone or shell and forms a fossil, **193**

Perseid meteor shower, 414
Pesticides
    farming practices and, 378
    in monoculture, 377
    as nonpoint pollution, 387

Petrification a process where mineral-rich water seeps into both the organism's soft parts and the pore spaces of the shell or bone, 192, **193**

Petroglyph National Monument, 311
Petroglyphs, of wetland birds, 311

Petroleum a natural or crude oil found in certain areas where conditions were right for it to accumulate as it formed, **366**

    as nonrenewable resource, 363
    as ocean pollutant, 388
    U.S. consumption of, 363
PH
    of acid precipitation, 153
    of acids, 152
    of rainwater, 153
Phanerozoic Eon, 207
Phases of Moon, 402
Philippine Islands, as island arc, 103
Phobos (moon), 424
Phoenix, Arizona, landscaping in, 309
Phosphorus, in human wastewater, 388

Photosphere the lowest layer of the Sun's atmosphere, **435**

Photosynthesis, 361
  by algae, 318
  by cyanobacteria, 213
  for ocean animals and plants, 325
  in plankton, 346

Photovoltaic cell cell that converts solar energy into electricity, 369

pH scale, 46
  acid precipitation and, 384
Phuket, Thailand, tsunami in, 117, 333
Physical changes in matter, 47
Physics, expansion of universe, 454
Phytoplankton, 346
Pigment, in paint, 44
Pillow lava, 138
Pioneer II (spacecraft), Saturn photos by, 428

Pixel a small square, or basic unit, of the Earth's surface that is being observed, 27

Planet(s)
  definition of, 431
  distance from Sun, 417
  dwarf, 430–431
  Earth as, 396
  formation of, 414–415
  inner, 414, 420–425
  motion of, 416–419
  naming of, 428
  orbits of, 416–417
  around other stars, 454
  outer, 414, 426–431
  water on, 7
Planetary motion, 416–419

Planetesimals solid particles that formed the building blocks of planets, 414

Plankton organisms that float at or near the ocean's surface, 346

Plant roots, weathering by, 156
Plants
  in beginning of Cenozoic Era, 221
  chemical weathering by, 153
  in Cretaceous Period, 219
  cycads, 214
  development on land, 214
  for dinosaurs, 217
  eutrophication and, 308
  evolution of conifers, 216
  marine, 325, 346
  mechanical weathering caused by, 151

in Precambrian Time, 213
  as renewable resources, 360
  seed, 214
  theories of development of, 213
Plasma stage, of universe, 452
Plasma state of matter, 48, 50
Plate tectonics, 87–109. *See also* Tectonic plates
  mountain building and, 105–109
  volcanic islands and, 343
Plesiosaurs, 216
Plucking, 175
Pluto
  as dwarf planet, 426
  naming of, 428
Pluto-sized astronomical bodies, 431

Point source a source of water pollution that generates pollution from a specific source and location, 387

Polar air masses, 254, 280
Polar bears, climate and, 280
Polar climates, 280

Polar easterlies global wind belts that blow from the high-pressure areas over the poles and are deflected westward by the Coriolis effect, 243

Polar ice caps
  on Mars, 425
  melting of, 289
Polaris (north star), Earth's axis and, 285

Polar zone the area located from 66.5° north and south of the equator to the poles where temperatures are lower, 274

Poles
  convection cells and, 241
  ice caps at, 249
  latitudes of, 19
  magnetic reversal of, 98
  ocean currents from, 276
  oceans near, 320
Pollution. *See also* Environment
  acid rain and, 4
  air, 381–385
  CFCs and, 5
  in cities, 379
  dead zones from, 351
  expenses of, 291
  of groundwater, 388
  in oceans, 321, 353, 388

Ponds, runoff in, 299
Pores, underground, 312

Porosity the percentage of pore space in a material, 312

Portland, Oregon, temperatures in, 327
Potassium-40, used to date fossils and rocks, 202
Power plants, sulfur dioxide from, 384

Precambrian time the longest and oldest segment of geologic time, 212–216
  beginning of life in, 213
  eons in, 207

Precipitation any solid or liquid form of water that falls from clouds, 250, 253
  acid, 152–153, 384
  as freshwater, 298
  global warming and, 290
  mineral formation through, 58
Predators, in Mesozoic oceans, 216
Predictions
  of tsunamis, 333
  of volcanic activity, 130
  weather, 265–269
Pressure
  air, 231–232
  changes of state from, 49, 50
  increase in altitude and, 233
  mechanical weathering caused by, 151
  in metamorphic rock formation, 78
  in volcanoes, 132
Pressure belts, 242
  global winds and, 243

Prevailing westerlies global wind belts that blow toward the poles in a circulation pattern opposite that of the trade winds, 243

Prevailing wind wind that blows primarily from one direction and affects the temperature of an area and the amount of precipitation it receives, 276–277

Primary wave (P-wave) the wave that travels fastest from the focus of an earthquake, 116, 119

Primate an order of mammals that had developed body parts and complex behavior, 222

    characteristics of, 222

Prime meridian the meridian that passes through Greenwich, England that is used as a reference line for longitude measurements, 20

Prince William Sound, earthquake in, 121

Principia (Newton), 419

Prints, as trace fossils, 193

Product the new substance formed from a chemical reaction, 50

Prograde rotation a counterclockwise spin, 423

Projection a way to represent a view of a round object on a flat surface, 18

    azimuthal, 19
    conic, 18–19
    Mercator, 18–19

Prominence an arc of gas that shoots up from the chromosphere, 438

Parallax the apparent change in a star's position in the sky due to the movement of the observer, 441

Properties of minerals, 59–62
    cleavage and fracture as, 61
    color as, 60
    density as, 61
    hardness as, 62
    luster as, 60
    specific gravity as, 61
    streak as, 60
Proterozoic Eon, 207, 212

Proton a tiny particle with a positive electric charge, 37, 200

    in metallic bonds, 43

Protostar hot, condensed material found in the center of a nebula, 413, 444

Pumice, 72

P-waves. *See* Primary waves (P-waves)

Pyrite, 59
    specific gravity of, 61
    streak of, 60

Pyroclastic material material made up of ash, rock fragments, and gases that results from an explosive volcanic eruption, 138, 139

    effects of, 140–141

Quartz
    fracture of, 61
    in granite, 154
Quartzite, 78, 80, 81

Quasar a faraway star-like object, 451

    redshifts of, 454

Quaternary Period the third period of the Cenozoic Era, 220, 221

Questions, scientific, 8

Radar
    Doppler, 267
    weather, 267

Radiation energy that is transferred as rays called electromagnetic waves, 236

    electromagnetic, 405
    from Sun, 250, 438
    in universe, 453
Radiation balance, 240
    effect of clouds on Earth's, 239
Radiation poisoning, 202

Radiative zone the region of the Sun above the core where energy is transferred from gas particle to gas particle, 436

Radioactive waste, recycling of, 371
Radioactivity, 202
Radio antenna, cosmic background radiation and, 453

Radiocarbon dating a type of radiometric dating used to determine a fossil's age, 201

    limits on, 202

Radioisotope an isotope that decays through radiation, 200, 201, 202

    used in cancer treatment, 202

Radiometric dating any method of determining the absolute age of a sample by using radioisotopes, 201

Radio signals, in ionosphere, 235

Radiosonde sensors found in weather balloons that gather data about temperature, air pressure, and humidity, 266

Radio telescopes, 407
Radio waves
    from quasars, 451
    telescopes for, 407
Rain, 231, 250, 253. *See also* Precipitation
    acid, 4, 152, 367, 384
Rainbows, 440
Raindrops, 249
Rainforests
    destruction of, 288
    temperate, 280
    tropical, 278
Rainstorms, soil washed away in, 162
Rainwater
    pH of, 152, 153
    pollutants in, 387
    in soil, 162
Rapid City, South Dakota, flooding in, 306
Rapids, 301

Reactant the original substance in a chemical reaction, 50

Recharge water that comes from precipitation and runoff that replaces the groundwater removed by a well, 313

Reclamation the replanting of vegetation on mined land and the restoration of the land to its original shape, 376

Recycling, 380
    of radioactive waste, 371
Red Cones, as cinder cones, 134

Red giant a large bright star that has a low surface temperature, 444

Reforestation the planting of new trees to capture CO_2 from the atmosphere, 291

Refracting telescope an early telescope that used a set of lenses to bring visible light to a central point, 406

Red planet, Mars as, 424
Redshifts, 454
Reefs, coral, 351

Reflecting telescope a telescope that uses a series of curved or flat mirrors to bring visible light to a focus, 406, 407

    Hubble Space Telescope as, 408

Reforestation planting new trees, 291

erosion and, 379

Regional metamorphism large areas of Earth's crust are affected by high pressure and temperature, 79

Relative dating dating of rocks and fossils by comparison of two objects, 197

    correlation and, 199
    cross-cutting relationships principle and, 198
    of fossils, 196–199
    inclusions and, 198
    original horizontality principle and, 197
    superposition and, 197
    unconformity and, 198–199

Relative humidity the ratio of the amount of water vapor in a specific amount of air compared to the maximum amount of water vapor that amount of air can hold, 250–251

    measuring, 266
Relativity, theories of, 455

Remote sensing the process of collecting information about an object or area from far above the surface being studied, 26–27

Renewable energy sources, wind as, 229

Renewable resource a natural resource that can be used and replaced over a relatively short period of time, 360–362

Reptiles
    cold-blooded, 219
    as Earth's dominant animals, 215
    in Triassic Period, 216
Research, on oceans, 353
Research Consortium on Nearby Stars (RECONS), 442

Reservoir a natural or human-made lake used to store water, 307

Residual soil soil that forms directly above parent bedrock, 158

Resources. *See* Natural resources
Results, communicating, 11

Retrograde rotation a clockwise spin, 423

Reverse fault a fault that occurs when the hanging wall moves up relative to the footwall, 107, 115

Revolution, of Uranus, 429
Reykjavik, Iceland, geothermal energy in, 371
Rhinoceroses, 221
Rhyolite, 71
Richter, Charles, 121

Richter scale a magnitude scale that measures the size of seismic waves, 121

Ridge push the process by which an ocean plate is pushed away from the mid-ocean ridge and toward a trench, 100, 101

Rift valley a long narrow valley that is formed when continental crust separates, 102

Rill a small channel that forms on a slope where gravity causes water to flow downhill, 167

Ring of Fire, 132
Rings
    of gas giant planets, 427
    of Jupiter, 427
    of Neptune, 430
    of Saturn, 428
    of Uranus, 429

Ripple marks, in sedimentary rocks, 76
River(s)
    deposits in, 304–306
    erosion and, 299
    evaporation from, 250
    formation of, 168, 300
    lumber shipping on, 306
    suspended materials in, 301
    tributaries of, 302
    in United States, 301

Riverbank land that borders a river, 304

River systems, 302–303
Robotic volcano observers, 143

Rock a naturally occurring solid mixture of one or more minerals, 66–81, 67. *See also* Bedrock; specific types

    abrasion of, 151
    absolute dating of, 200–203
    ages of, 97
    as animal tools, 67
    chemical weathering of, 152–153
    composition and texture of, 69
    continental drift evidence from, 94
    cycles of, 66
    deformation of, 105–106
    in Earth's mantle, 89
    folding of, 106
    igneous, 70–73
    mechanical weathering of, 150–151
    melting of, 70
    metamorphic, 78–81
    from oceans, 97
    permeability of, 313
    rate of weathering, 154–157
    relative dating of, 196–199
    sedimentary, 75–76
    stress on layers of, 106
    studying from space, 408
    surface area and weathering of, 157
    types of, 67–69, 68
    underground mining of, 376
    volcanic, 91, 139
    weathering of, 150–153, 299

Rock cycle the continuous changing and remaking of rock over time, 66, 80–81, 198

Rockfall mass movement that occurs when loose rock falls down a steep slope, 183

Rock layers
    absolute dating of, 200–203
    correlation of, 199
    of Grand Canyon, 197
    relative dating of, 196–199
    unconformity of, 198–199
Rocky Mountains
    in Canada, 79
    Continental Divide in, 302
    formation and age of, 109
Romans
    myths about volcanoes, 132
    planets named for gods of, 428
Roots
    tropical soils and, 160
    weathering and, 156
Rotation. *See also* Rotation of Earth
    of Moon, 401
    of outer planets, 426
    of Saturn, 428
    of terrestrial planets, 420
    of Venus, 423
Rotation of Earth, 396–397
    Coriolis effect and, 242
    currents and, 328
    pressure belts created by, 242
    tides and, 334
Rugose corals, 214

Runoff rainfall that flows downhill along Earth's surface, 298, **299**, 378

    in channels, 300
    eutrophication and, 308
    as nonpoint pollution, 387
    wetland destruction and, 310
Rust, 153

 S

Safe Drinking Water Act (1974), 389
Safety
    during earthquakes, 126–127
    hurricane, 264
    of nuclear power plants, 371
    with scientific experiments, 11
    in tornadoes, 262
Saffir-Simpson scale, of hurricanes, 263, 264
Sago palms, 214
Sahara Desert, 279
    oases in, 314
Sakurai, Kinichi, 63

Sakuraiite, 63

Salinity a measure of water's concentration of dissolved salts, 324

Salt
    as compound, 44
    table salt, 43

Saltation a skipping or bouncing motion, 178

Salt marshes, 310
    spartina grass in, 311
Salt water
    in Dead Sea, 331
    freshwater and, 386
    as liquid solution, 45
    in oceans, 319, 324
Saltwater marshes, 310
San Andreas Fault, 113, 124
    seismic gap along, 125
    as transform boundary, 104
Sand
    colors of, 340
    water and mass movement of, 183
Sandbars, 340
Sand dune lizards, 181
Sand dunes, 180
Sands, on beaches, 169
Sandstone, 68, 78, 81
    composition of, 69

Satellite an object that orbits around another object; a moon that orbits an outer planet, 398, 426

    artificial, 408
    in exosphere, 235
    for information gathering in space, 408
    natural, 426
    for ocean study, 322
    remote sensing by, 26–27
    for volcanic data, 142–143
    weather, 268–269

Saturated a quality of air when it contains the maximum amount of water vapor it can hold, 250

Saturn, 414, 426, 428
    naming of, 428

Savannah a large grassland made up of tall grasses and scattered trees, 279

Scales, for earthquake measurement, 121
Scavengers, on ocean floor, 346

Science experiments, safety rules for, 11
Scientific method, 8–11
Scientific notation, 440
Scientific ocean expeditions, British, 323
Scientific questions, 8
Scorpius (constellation), 404
Sculptures
    marble for, 81
    weathering and, 156

Sea a body of water that is near land or surrounded by land, 319

    water in, 321
Sea arches, 170
Sea breezes, 244–245
Sea caves, 170

Seafloor spreading a theory that states that new ocean crust is formed at mid-ocean ridges and destroyed at deep-sea trenches, 96. *See also* Ocean floor

    continental drift and, 95–98
    along divergent boundaries, 102
    evidence of, 96
Sea ice, 320
    global warming and, 352

Sea level the height of the surfaces of the oceans, 323

elevation of, 22

Seamount an underwater volcanic mountain, 344

Seascapes, volcanic influence on, 140
Seashores, features created by deposition at, 171

Season short-term periods of climatic change, **283**, 398

Sea stacks, 170
Sea walls, beach erosion and, 172

Secondary wave (S-wave) the second-fastest seismic wave, **116**, 119

Second Law, of Kepler, 417
Sediment
    in coastal deltas, 169
    deposition of, 168
    moved by longshore current, 170
    windblown loess, 181
    wind transport of, 178

Sediment rock particles that have been transported away from their source and deposited by wind and water, 68

    in bodies of water, 304, 305
    eutrophication and, 308
    on floodplain, 305
    from ocean waters, 340
    from turbidity current, 342

Sedimentary rock layers of sediment that build up and cement together, **68**, 75–76

    chemical, 75
    clastic, 75
    dinosaur fossils in, 77
    features of, 76
    formation of, 74
    fossils in, 192, 197
    organic, 76
    original horizontality and, 197
    in rock cycle, 81
    transformation to metamorphic
      rock, 78
    types of, 75–76
Seed plants, 214
Seeds, from flowering plants, 219
Seismic belts, 114

Seismic gap a section along an active fault that has not experienced an earthquake for a long period of time, **125**

Seismic risk, 123
    U.S. areas with highest risk, 123

Seismic wave the energy that is released when rocks break at the focus of an earthquake, 91, **116**

Seismogram the record from a seismometer that shows the size and direction of seismic waves, **118**

    reading during earthquake, 119

Seismologist Earth scientists who study earthquakes, 91, **118**, 120

Seismometer a scientific instrument used to record seismic waves (also called a seismograph), **118**, 120

    locating earthquake epicenter
      with, 120
Selective logging, 378
Sensors, remote sensing by, 26–27

Sewage, treatment and discharge of, 387
Shallow-focus earthquakes, 122
Sharks, 217

Shear stress when a material stretches and becomes distorted, **105**

Shelley, Percy Bysshe, 253

Shield volcano a broad, gently sloped mountain with a base in the shape of a circle, **134**

    Mauna Kea as, 135
Ships, ocean pollution from, 388
Shishmaref, Alaska, relocation of, 352
Shooting stars, 235

Shoreline the boundary formed where a body of water meets land, **169**, 339. See also Seashores

    advancing ocean waters and, 352
    erosion at, 169
Shuttles, in space program, 409
Silicon, in Earth's crust, 58
Silt sediment, loess as, 181
Silver, as nonrenewable resource, 362
Singularity, black hole as, 445

Sinkhole a round depression where water collects, **315**

SI system, 12. See also International
    System of Units
Skulls, hominid, 222

Slab pull the process by which an ocean plate being pulled into the asthenosphere pulls the rest of the plate with it, **101**

    as tectonic process, 100

Slip-strike fault a fault that occurs when the hanging wall moves horizontally relative to the footwall when opposing forces cause rock to break, **107**

Sleet, 231, 250
Slide, 182

Slump a cup-shaped depression that results from a landslide, **184**

Smith, Robert A., 4

Smog air pollution that results when the Sun's rays come in contact with harmful substances in the air, **381**

Snakehead fish, 309
Snow, 231, 250, 253. See also
    Precipitation
    lake-effect, 277
Snowflakes, 249, 253
Society, earthquakes and, 123–127
Sodium
    chlorine and, 43
    in ocean salt, 324
Sodium chloride, 43

Soil a mixture of rock and mineral particles, organic material, water, and air, **158**, 362

    arctic, 160
    bedrock and, 158
    composition of, 158
    conservation of, 162–163
    cover crops and, 162
    creation of, 299
    crop rotation and, 163
    cryptogamic, 162
    desert, 161
    erosion of, 162
    fertile, 362
    horizons of, 159
    humus in, 158
    leaching in, 159
    as mixture, 44
    in moving streams, 168
    parent material of, 158
    preventing loss of, 362
    residual, 158
    as resource, 162
    temperate, 161
    terracing and, 163
    transported, 158
    tropical, 160
    washed away in rainstorms, 162
Soil formation
    climate and, 160–161
    weathering and, 149–163
Soil horizons, 159

Soil profile a vertical representation of soil horizons, **159**

Solar activity, 286
Solar day, 396

Solar eclipse an eclipse that occurs when the Moon passes between the Sun and Earth, **403**

Solar energy the energy from the sun that warms the Earth and gives us light, 368–369

in Earth's atmosphere, 236
photovoltaic cells for, 369

Solar flare violent eruptions of particles and radiation from the Sun's surface, 438

Solar nebula the nebula that formed into our own solar system, 413

Solar system a system that is made up of the Sun and the planets and other bodies that travel around it, 412–431, 413. *See also* Universe; specific planets

Earth's position in, 209
formation of, 413–415
geocentric model of, 416
heliocentric model of, 416
Solar system bodies, 431

Solar wind wind that carries charged solar particles to all the planets in the solar system, 438

Solids
atmospheric water as, 249
as matter, 36
minerals as, 56
physical changes in state of, 48
water as, 231
Solid solution, 45
Solid waste, 380
environment and, 379
Solstices, 399
Solution, homogeneous mixture as, 45

Sonar a system that uses sound waves to detect and measure objects underwater and on the ocean floor, 28, 91, **322**

for mapping ocean floor, 96, 97
Sooke Harbour, tide pool from, 347
Sound waves, 454
acoustics and, 91
sonar as, 28, 322
for surgery, 322
Southern hemisphere
circulation of current in gyres in, 329
solstices in, 399
summer and winter in, 283
South pole, 174

latitude of, 19
magnetic reversal of, 98
Southwestern United States, freshwater for, 309
Space
astronomy from, 408–409
Earth's position in, 396
exploration of, 395, 409
measuring distance in, 421
ocean study from, 322
rocks studied from, 408
Space probes, 408, 409
Spacewalks, 409
Spartina grass, in salt marshes, 311
Special relativity, theory of, 455
Species
evolution of, 210
extinction of, 211
invasive alien, 309

Specific gravity the ratio of a material's density to the density of water, 61

Specific heat, 277

Spectrum visible light arranged according to wavelength, 440

electromagnetic, 405
light from distant galaxies and, 454
Sphagnum moss, 310

Spiral galaxy a galaxy that has a long arm that extends outwards and bends around a large central bulge, 450

nebulas in, 451
Spirit (Mars exploration rover), 408

Spit a narrow band of sand that projects into the water from a bend in the coastline, **171**, 340

Splashdowns, 409
Sponges, 213, 217
Spores, compared to seeds, 214

Spring a natural opening in the ground through which groundwater flows to Earth's surface, 314

Spring tide a very strong tide that occurs when the Sun and the Moon are aligned with Earth, 334

Squids, 349
Stalactites, 152
Stalagmites, 152, 315
Star clusters, 451

Starfish, 214
Stars, 404, 434–445
birth of, 444
classification of, 439–442
clusters of, 451
composition of, 441
as constellations, 434
distances to, 441–442
Hertzsprung-Russell diagram for, 443
life cycle of, 443–445
neutron, 445
planets around, 454
plasmas in, 48
State (condition), physical changes in, 48–50
States (of U.S.), humidity in, 251
States of matter, three forms of water as, 231

Station model a record of weather data for a particular site at a particular time, 268, 269

Steam, in volcanic eruptions, 137
Steam engine, 240

Steppe a semiarid region that is slightly more humid than an arid region, 279

Storms
as disturbances and hurricanes, 264
on Neptune, 430
thunderstorms, 259–260

Storm surge the result when hurricane winds drive ocean water toward coastal areas, where it washes over the land, 264

Strain accumulation, in earthquake prediction, 125
Strato clouds, 252

Stratosphere the layer of the atmosphere directly above the troposphere, 234

ozone and, 381
Stratus clouds, 252

Streak the color or a mineral when it is ground into a fine powder, 60

Streams
deposits in, 304–306
erosion and, 299
erosion by, 301
formation of, 168, 300
tributaries of, 302

Stress the amount of force per unit area that is applied to a given material, 105

rock deformation and, 105, 107
on rocks, 115

Strike-slip fault a fault that occurs at a right angle to a transform boundary, 107, 115

Strip cropping, 162
Subatomic particle, 37

Subduction the process by which one tectonic plate slips beneath another tectonic plate, 103

volcanoes and, 132

Sublittoral zone a region that extends from the low tide line to the edge of the continental shelf, 348

Submarine(s), for ocean study, 321

Submarine canyon a deep, v-shaped canyon that cuts down into the continental slope, 342

Subsoil the layer of soil below the topsoil; the B horizon, 159

Subtropics, water salinity in, 324
Sulfur dioxide, from power plants, 384
Sulfur oxide, 152
Summer, 283

Summer solstice the longest day in either the northern or southern hemisphere, 399

Sun (of Earth), 435–438
air temperatures and, 232
apparent motion of, 397
classes of objects orbiting, 431
composition and structure of, 435–436
Earth's orbit around, 284, 396
energy from, 236, 237, 250, 362, 437
fusion in, 437
gravity of, 403
greenhouse effect and, 287
interior of, 436
in main sequence of stars, 443
ozone formation and, 234
planetary distances from, 421
planetary orbits around, 415
planet formation and, 414
radiation from, 229
solar activity and, 286

solar energy from, 368–369
as star, 434
tides and, 334, 335
transfer of energy from, 237
Sun-centered model. *See* Heliocentric model
Sun-centered universe, 285
Sunlight
earth's climate and, 326–327
in oceans, 325, 348

Sunspot an area with strong magnetic fields that appear as dark spots on the Sun; dark, cooler patches on the surface of the photosphere, 286, 437

Supercontinent, 93

Supergiant an extremely bright and large star that has a low density, 443, **444**

Supernova an explosion that causes the outer portion of a star to blow up and light up the sky, 445

Superstrings, in universe, 454

Superposition a principle that states that in an undisturbed sequence of sedimentary rock, each rock layer lies just above the layer on which it formed, 197

Surface area the sum of all the areas of the object's surfaces, 157

weathering and, 157

Surface current stream-like movement of warm or cold water that occurs at or near the surface of the ocean; a wind-driven movement of ocean water that affects the upper few hundred meters of the ocean, 275, 328

Surface gravity, 421
Surface mining, 376
Surface Mining Control and Reclamation Act (1977), 376

Surface wave a wave that travels along Earth's surface and moves in two directions as it passes through rock, 116

Surf zone, 170

Suspension a method of wind transport, 178

Sustainable yield renewable resources are replaced at the same rate they are used, 361

Swamp a wetland that supports trees, shrubs, or other woody plants, 310

S-waves. *See* Secondary waves (S-waves)
Swift, Lewis, 414
Swift-Tuttle comet, 414
Symbols
for air masses, 254
of elements and chemicals, 36
on maps, 25

Synchronous rotation the Moon's full rotation each time it travels around Earth, 401

Synclines, 106

 T

Table salt, 43
chemical formula for, 45
Taiwan, earthquake in, 125
Talc, luster of, 60
Tarantula Nebula, 444
Taxation, of carbon emissions, 291
Technology
for combating air pollution, 385
mapmaking and, 26–29
for ocean study, 321–322
for space exploration, 409
Tectonic plates
boundaries of, 101–104
causes of movement of, 100–101
speed of movement, 104
theory of, 99–104
tracking movement of, 104
volcano formation along, 132

Telescope an instrument for collecting and magnifying visible light or other forms of electromagnetic radiation from a distant object, 406

for different wavelengths, 407
reflecting, 406, 407
refracting, 406
Temperate rainforest, 280
Temperate soil, 161

Temperate zone the area between 23.5° and 66.5° north and south of the equator where moderate climates exist, 274

Temperature
    air and, 229
    atmospheric, 232
    of Earth, 423
    global warming and rise in, 239
    greenhouse effect and, 287
    gyres and, 328–329
    heat compared with, 232
    humidity and, 251
    for January, 273
    on Jupiter, 427
    land surface, 240
    by latitude, 274
    on Mars, 425
    as measure, 13
    in mesosphere, 235
    in metamorphic rock formation, 78
    on Neptune, 430
    of ocean waters, 325, 326
    of outer planets, 426
    in polar regions, 320
    and rise in kinetic energy, 155
    of stars, 441
    in stratosphere, 234
    of Sun, 435, 436
    of terrestrial planets, 420
    in thermosphere, 235
    in troposphere, 233
    of universe, 453
    on Uranus, 429
    variations with altitude, 232
    on Venus, 422
    volcanic effects on, 140
    weathering and, 155

Temperature profile a graph of ocean temperatures at different depths, 326

Tension the stress that stretches an object, 105

    in earthquakes, 115

Tephra rock fragments that are thrown into the air and fall to the ground during a volcanic eruption, 139

Terminal moraine, 177
Terracing, 163

Terrestrial planet a planet that has a solid, rocky surface, 420

    Pluto and, 431
    properties of, 420

Texture the size, shape, and positions of the grains that make up a rock, 69

    igneous, 71–72
    metamorphic, 80
Thailand, tsunami in, 117, 333

Theory an explanation for a broad range of observations that is supported by a body of scientific evidence, 11

Theory of plate tectonics theory that states that Earth's lithosphere is divided into enormous slabs called tectonic plates, 99–104

    of special relativity, 455
Thermal equilibrium, 238

Thermocline a layer of the ocean that lies below the surface layer and above the colder, dark bottom layer, 326

Thermodynamics, 238

Thermometer a device used to measure temperature, 265

Thermosphere the layer of the atmosphere located above the mesosphere, 235

Third Law, of Kepler, 417
Thomson, Charles Wyville, 323
Three Mile Island, nuclear accident at, 371

Thunder a loud rumbling sound that results from the rapid expansion of air along a lightning strike, 249, 260

Thunderstorm small, intense, weather systems that produce heavy rain, strong winds, lightning, and thunder, 259–260

    hurricanes and, 262
    severe, 260
    tornadoes in, 261
Tidal range, 334
Tide pools, 347

Tide a periodic rise and fall of sea level, 334

    chart of, 335
    cycle of, 347
    effects of, 335

    gravity and, 334
    Moon and, 400, 402
    variations in, 334
    in volcano magma and Earth's mantle, 403
Tidewaters, 347

Till material deposited by glacial ice, 177, 221

Tilt, of Earth, 398
Time, defined, 13
Time zones, 397
Titan (moon), 428
Titanic (ship), iceberg collision and, 320
Tombolos, 171
Tools, from rocks, 67
TOPEX/Poseidon (satellite), 322

Topographic map two-dimensional representation of Earth's surface, 22–25

Topography
    climate and, 275–276
    of Mars, 425

Topsoil they layer of soil on the surface; the A horizon, 159

    damage to, 362
    in farming, 377
    in temperate areas, 161
    in tropical areas, 160
"Tornado Alley," 261

Tornado a violent, rotating column of air that is in contact with the ground, 5, 249, 261–262

    air masses and, 256
    classification of, 262
    safety in, 262
    suspended sediment in, 178
Toxic wastes, 387
ocean pollution from, 388

Trace fossil any naturally preserved sign of a living thing's presence, 193

Trade wind a steady global wind that blows from the high pressure belts at 30° north latitude and 30° south latitude toward the low pressure belt located near the equator, 243

    ocean currents and, 330–331
Traits, adaptations, 210
Transantarctic Mountains, 103

Transform boundary a boundary where two tectonic plates slide horizontally past each other, 101, 104, **104**

Transform motion, in earthquakes, 115

Transmission, of light in water, 325

Transpiration, 298

Transportation, across divides, 303

Transported soil soil that forms from material that has been carried in from another location, **158**

Trash
  burial of, 380
  fuels from, 370
  pollution from, 388

Travel-time curves, for P- and S-curves, 119

Tree rings, to determine growth and climate changes, 202

Trees
  deforestation and, 288, 378
  reforestation and, 291
  soil loss and, 362
  topsoil and, 378

Tree sap, hardening into amber, 193

Trenches
  deep-sea, 96, 97, 342, 343
  ridge push and, 101

Triassic Period a period of transition, or change, that took place in the first 42 million years of the Mesozoic Era, **216**

Tributary a smaller stream or river that flows into a larger stream or river, **302**

Triceratops, 219

Trilobites, 214
  fossil of, 197

Triple beam balances, 12

Triton (moon), 430

Tropical air masses, 254, 280

Tropical climates, 278–279

Tropical cyclones, 262

Tropical depression, 264

Tropical oceans, hurricanes in, 263

Tropical plants, at beginning of Cenozoic Era, 221

Tropical rainforests, 278

Tropical soils, 160

Tropical storms, as disturbances and hurricanes, 264

Tropical wet zones, 279

Tropics the area between 23.5° south of the equator and 23.5° north of the equator where temperatures are higher, **274**

  convection cells and, 241

Tropopause the temperature at the upper limit of the troposphere (about -80°C), **233**

Troposphere the layer of the atmosphere closest to Earth's surface, **233**

  ozone in, 234, 381

Trough the lowest point of a wave, **332**

True north the geographic North Pole around which Earth rotates, **21**

Tsunami a large, powerful ocean wave that is caused by a major disturbance to the ocean floor, **117, 333**

Tubeworms, 344

Tuff, 72

Turbidity current a rapidly flowing, deep-water current that carries a heavy load of sediment, **342**

Turbines, wind, 370

Turquoise, luster of, 60

Tuttle, Horace, 414

Twin paradox, 455

Tycho crater, on Moon, 401

Typhoons, 262

Tyrannosaurus rex, 191, 219
  fossil of, 194

Ultrabasic rocks, 73

Ultraviolet (UV) radiation, 381, 383
  electromagnetic waves as, 117
  ozone and, 234
  telescopes for, 407

Umbra the inner portion of the Moon's shadow, where none of the Sun's light reaches Earth, **403**

Unconformity a gap in the rock layer sequence caused by a missing rock layer, **198–199**

Underground mining, 376

United States
  cold winter weather in, 255
  mild climates in, 279
  Outer Continental Shelf Lands Act (1953) in, 341
  rivers in, 301
  seismic risk in, 123
  tornadoes in, 261
  water use in (2000), 386
  wind erosion in, 180
  wind power in, 370

United States Geological Service (USGS), 23

United States Weather Service, 266

Universe everything that exists throughout space, **405, 448–455, 452.** *See also* Solar system

  age of, 454
  Earth in, 7, 396
  expansion of, 453, 454, 455
  heliocentric theory of, 285
  origins of, 452
  structure of, 454

Upwelling the upward motion of ocean water, **330**

Uranium, 202

Uranus, 414, 426, 429
  naming of, 428
  Neptune and, 430

Urban development
  counteracting damage from, 380
  environment and, 379

U-shaped valleys, 175, 176

V

Valley
  formed by erosion, 168
  hanging, 176
  U-shaped, 175, 176

Valley breeze air that is drawn in from a cooler valley, **245**

Valley glacier a glacier that forms in high mountainous areas, **173, 174, 175**

Vapor. *See* Water vapor

Variable a factor that can be changed, **9**

Varves bands of sediment that have accumulated on lake bottoms, 203

Vascular tissue tissues that carry water and nutrients between plant parts, 214

Vega (star), Earth's axis and, 285
Vegetation, replanting on mined land, 376
Ventifacts, 179
Vents, hydrothermal, 344
Venus, 422–423
    distance from Sun, 421
    naming of, 428

Vernal (spring) equinox a period of time in the northern hemisphere between the winter and summer solstice when the length of day and night begins to even out, 398, **399**

Verne, Jules, 89

Vertebrate an animal with a backbone, 214

    in Devonian Period, 214
    as land animals, 215
Vesicular texture, 72
Vesuvius, 140
Viking orbiter, Mars image from, 424
Vinegar, pH of, 152
Viperfish, 325
Virgo galaxy cluster, 449, 450
Visible light
    electromagnetic waves as, 117
    spectrum of, 440
Volcanic islands, 343
    chains as island arcs, 103

Volcanic mountain a mountain that is formed when magma erupts onto Earth's surface, 109

Volcanic rocks, 91

Volcano an opening in Earth's crust, 130–143, **131**

    active, 131, 142
    ash from, 139
    biological communities after eruptions of, 141
    under continental plate, 103
    at convergent boundaries, 132
    deadly, of last 400 years, 140
    defined, 131
    at divergent boundaries, 132
    effects on Earth, 140–141

    eruptions of, 136–139, 203, 209, 286
    formation of, 132–133
    gases from, 138–139, 212
    heights of, 135
    hot springs near, 314
    inclusions formed after eruptions, 198
    in Japan, 142
    lithosphere and, 91
    living with, 143
    on Mars, 425
    myths and legends about, 132
    ocean formation and, 322–323
    in Precambrian Time, 212
    predicting eruptions of, 142–143
    tides in magma of, 403
    tsunamis and, 117
    types of, 134–135
    variables in events of, 10
Volcano Explosivity Index (VEI), 136

Volcanologist a scientist who studies volcanoes, 7, **136**

Volcanology, 142–143

Volume the amount of space an object takes up, 12

    formula for, 12
    of liquids, 48
measurement in liters, 12
Voyager (spacecraft)
    Jupiter photos by, 427
    Neptune images by, 430
    Saturn photos by, 428
    Uranus images by, 429
    volcano images by, 133
Vulcan (Roman god), 132

Waning phases of Moon, 402
Warm air masses, 255
Warm front, 257
Wastes
    eutrophication and, 308
    from mines, 376
    radioactive, 371
    solid, 379, 380
    treatment of, 387
Water. *See also* Freshwater; Lake(s); River(s); Water pollution
    abrasion caused by, 151
    in atmosphere, 249–253
    chemical formula for, 45
    chemical reaction in creating, 50

    in chemical weathering, 152
    conserving, 389
    cycle of, 66
    demand for, 309
    on Earth, 424
    energy from, 369
    energy of moving water, 168
    erosion and, 299
    freshwater, 297–315
    as gas, liquid, and solid, 231
    gravity and weathering by, 156
    heating and cooling of, 236
    human impact on, 386–389
    hydrology and, 7
    in hydrosphere, 4
    on Mars, 7, 425
    mass movement and, 183
    mechanical weathering by, 150–151
    mineral changes from, 80
    obstructions to movement of, 300
    ocean formation and, 322–323
    in oceans, 324–327
    pH of, 152
    as resource, 361
    sediment deposition by, 168
    specific gravity of, 61
    vaporization of, 49
    wave motion and, 332

Water cycle the continuous movement of water between Earth's surface and the atmosphere, 250, 298

Water erosion, deposition and, 167–172
Waterfalls, 176
Water molecule, formation of, 42
Water pollution
    from fossil fuels, 367
    reducing, 389
    sources of, 387–388

Watershed an area of land that is drained by a river system, 302

Water table the upper boundary of the zone of saturation, 312

Water temperature, climate and, 275
Water vapor, 49, 249, 250, 298
    in atmosphere, 231
    as greenhouse gas, 239
    ocean formation and, 323
    as precipitation, 253
    from volcanic eruptions, 212

Wave a rhythmic movement that carries energy through space or matter, 332

in earthquakes, 116
as erosive forces, 169
light, 117
longshore current and, 170
mechanical and electromagnetic, 117
in oceans, 332
tsunamis as, 117, 333
Wave-cut cliffs, 170
Wave-cut platform, 170
Wave erosion, 170

Wavelength the distance between two adjacent crests or two adjacent troughs; the distance between the peaks on a wave of radiation as it travels though space, 332, 405

of colors, 440
of ocean waves, 332
of radiation, 405
telescopes designed for, 407
Waxing phases of Moon, 402

Weather the condition of the atmosphere at a particular place and time, 249. *See also* Climate

air masses and, 254
climate compared with, 273
data collection at Earth's surface, 265
data collection in upper atmosphere, 266–267
El Niño and, 283, 284
forecasts of, 248
fronts and, 257–258
instruments used for measuring, 265
mountains and, 5
observing, 5
patterns of, 254–258
predictions of, 265–269
radar for, 267
satellite tracking of, 268–269
severe, 259–264
water in atmosphere and, 249–253
Weather balloons, 266

Weathering the breakdown of rocks into smaller pieces, 74, 150, 299

in arctic climates, 160
chemical, 152–153
climate and, 155
in desert climates, 161
differential, 154
of Grand Canyon, 166
gravity and, 156
mechanical, 150–151
organisms and, 156
polishing granite and, 156
rate of, 154–157
soil formation and, 149–163
surface area of rocks and, 157
in temperate climates, 161
in tropical climates, 160
Weather maps, 268
fronts on, 257
Weather satellites, 408
Wegener, Alfred, 93, 94, 199
Weight, gravity and, 421

Well a deep hole dug or drilled to reach the water table, 313

water pollution and, 388
Western hemisphere, 20
West Virginia, chemical weathering in, 155

Wetland a land area that is covered with water for a large part of the year, 310–311

Wet zones, tropical, 279
Whale, ancestors of, 221
Whirlpool Galaxy, 7

White dwarf a tiny, dense star that dies after burning all of its energy, 443, **444**

Wildlife, wetlands and, 311

Wind the horizontal movement of air, 230

abrasion caused by, 151
air pressure and, 241–245
causes of, 241–242
Coriolis effect and, 242
in doldrums, 244
Doppler radar for, 267
dune formation and, 180
erosion from, 299
finding direction of, 265
global, 243
in horse latitudes, 244
in hurricanes, 262–264
jet streams, 244
local, 243, 244–245
loess deposition by, 181
measuring speed of, 265
mechanical weathering by, 151
mountain and valley breezes, 245

ocean currents and, 328, 330
polar easterlies, 243
pressure belts and, 242
prevailing, 276–277
prevailing westerlies, 243
as renewable energy source, 229
sea and land breezes, 244–245
in thunderstorms, 260
in tornadoes, 261
trade, 243
types of, 243
Wind energy, 370
Wind erosion, 178–179
in United States, 180
Wind farms, 370
Wind roses, 245

Wind sock a cone-shaped cloth bag used to indicate wind direction, 265

Wind turbines, 370

Wind vane an instrument used to indicate wind direction, 265

Windward the side of a mountain where moist air rises and temperatures are usually cool, 275

Winter, 283

Winter solstice the day when the Sun is at its lowest in the sky and winter begins, 399

Wood, as biomass fuel, 365
Woodrow Wilson bridge, earthquake resistance of, 126
Woods Hole Oceanographic Institute, 321
Woolly mammoth, 221
fossil of, 193, 195
World climates, map of, 278
Worms, 213, 214

Xeriscaping, 389

Art Credits

McGraw-Hill/Garry Nichols

Photo Credits

(t) top, (b) bottom, (l) left, (r) right, (m) middle, (i) inset

Credits